MOON

VIRGINIA & MARYLAND

MICHAELA RIVA GAASERUD

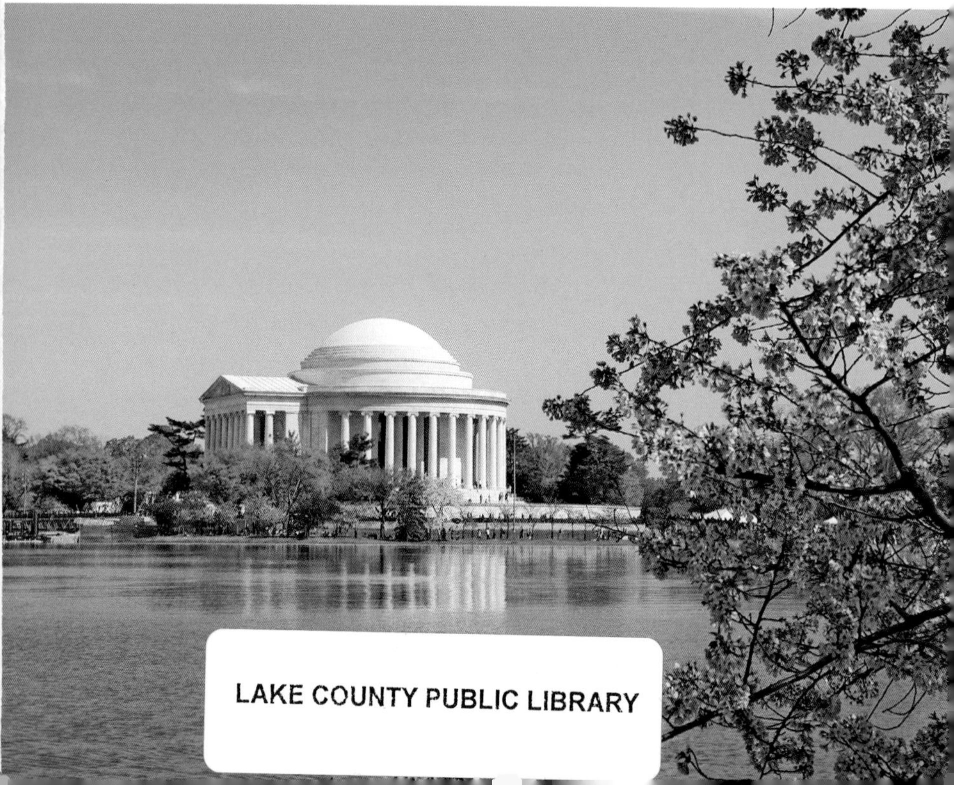

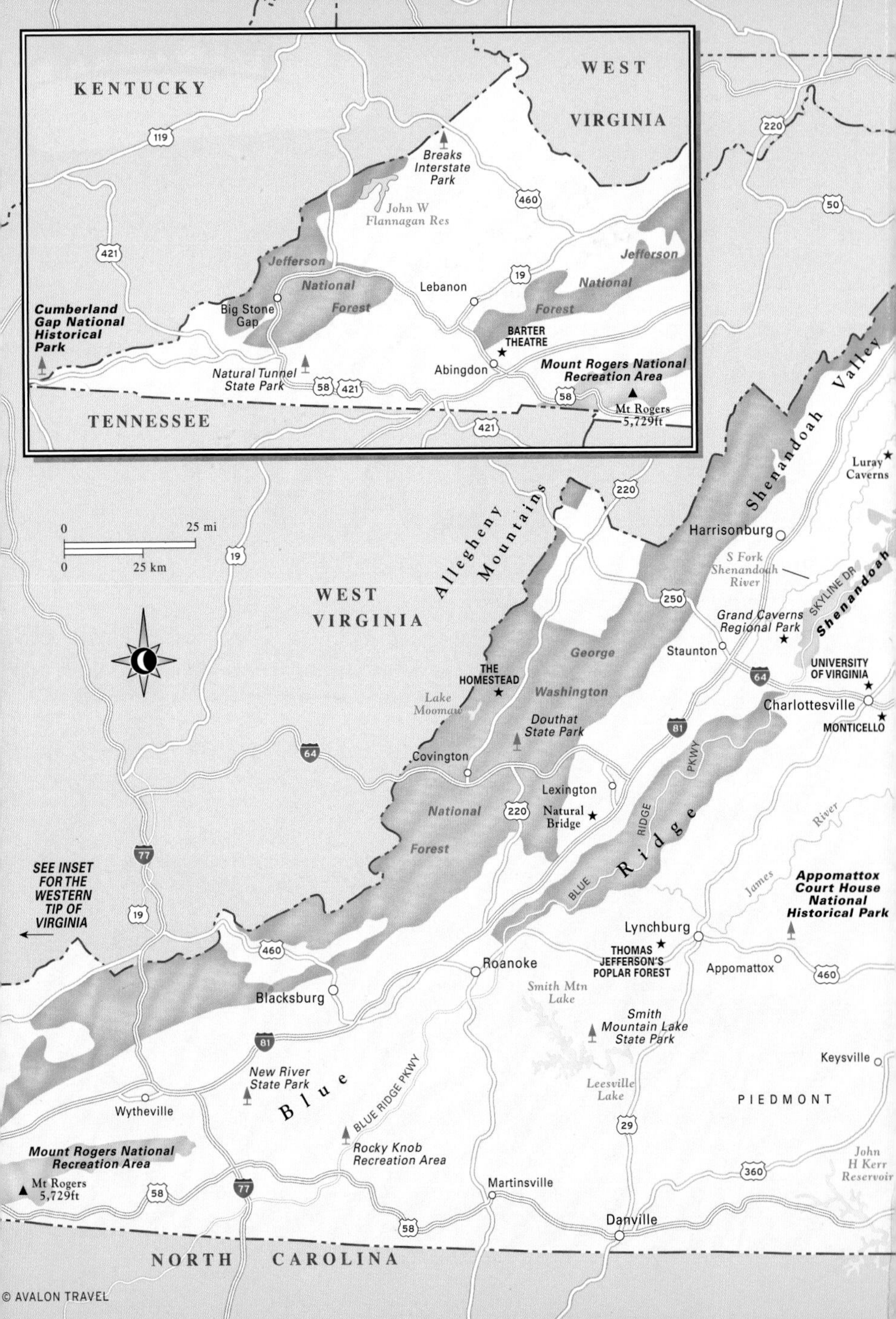
KENTUCKY
WEST
VIRGINIA
119
Breaks
Interstate
Park
460
John W
Flannagan Res
421
Jefferson
National
Forest
Lebanon
19
Cumberland
Gap National
Historical
Park
Big Stone
Gap
BARTER
THEATRE
Natural Tunnel
State Park
58
Abingdon
Mount Rogers National
Recreation Area
Mt Rogers
5,729ft
TENNESSEE
220
50
Shenandoah Valley
Luray
Caverns
Allegheny Mountains
0
25 mi
25 km
WEST
VIRGINIA
Harrisonburg
S Fork
Shenandoah
River
250
SKYLINE DR
Shenandoah
Grand Caverns
Regional Park
Staunton
George
Washington
THE
HOMESTEAD
64
UNIVERSITY
OF VIRGINIA
Charlottesville
MONTICELLO
Lake
Moomaw
Douthat
State Park
81
Covington
PKWY
Lexington
Natural
Bridge
River
National
Forest
77
SEE INSET
FOR THE
WESTERN
TIP OF
VIRGINIA
BLUE
RIDGE
Ridge
James
Appomattox
Court House
National
Historical Park
Lynchburg
THOMAS
JEFFERSON'S
POPLAR FOREST
Roanoke
Appomattox
Blacksburg
Smith Mtn
Lake
Smith
Mountain Lake
State Park
Keysville
New River
State Park
BLUE RIDGE PKWY
Blue
Leesville
Lake
PIEDMONT
Wytheville
29
Rocky Knob
Recreation Area
John
H Kerr
Reservoir
360
Martinsville
Danville
NORTH CAROLINA
© AVALON TRAVEL

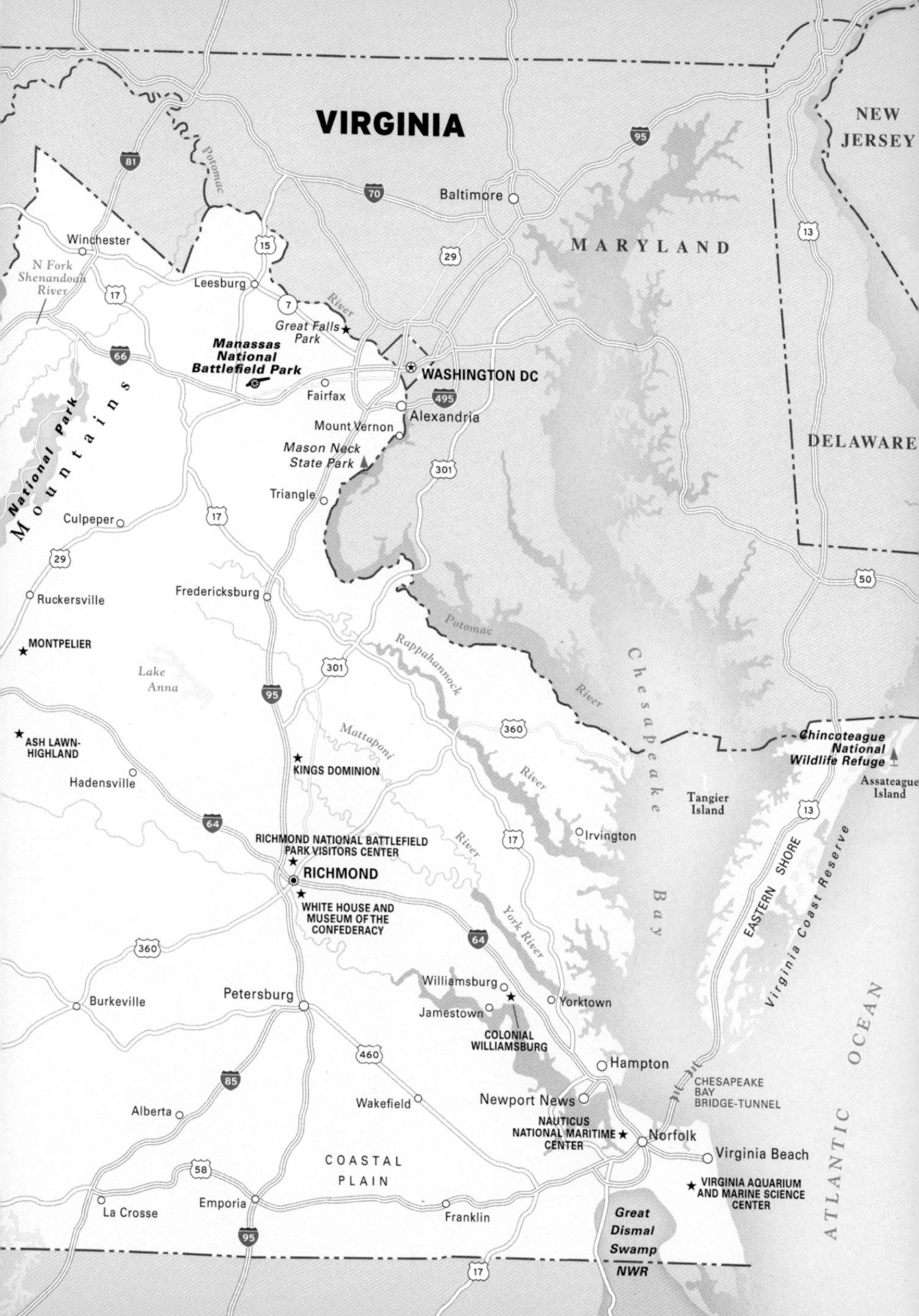

VIRGINIA
MARYLAND
NEW JERSEY
DELAWARE
Baltimore
Winchester
N Fork Shenandoah River
Potomac
Leesburg
River
Great Falls Park
Manassas National Battlefield Park
WASHINGTON DC
Fairfax
Alexandria
Mount Vernon
Mason Neck State Park
Triangle
Culpeper
National Park
Mountains
Ruckersville
Fredericksburg
MONTPELIER
Lake Anna
Potomac River
Rappahannock River
Chesapeake Bay
Mattaponi River
ASH LAWN-HIGHLAND
KINGS DOMINION
Hadensville
Chincoteague National Wildlife Refuge
Assateague Island
Tangier Island
Irvington
RICHMOND NATIONAL BATTLEFIELD PARK VISITORS CENTER
RICHMOND
WHITE HOUSE AND MUSEUM OF THE CONFEDERACY
York River
EASTERN SHORE
Virginia Coast Reserve
Williamsburg
Yorktown
Jamestown
COLONIAL WILLIAMSBURG
Burkeville
Petersburg
Hampton
CHESAPEAKE BAY BRIDGE-TUNNEL
Newport News
Alberta
Wakefield
NAUTICUS NATIONAL MARITIME CENTER
Norfolk
Virginia Beach
COASTAL PLAIN
VIRGINIA AQUARIUM AND MARINE SCIENCE CENTER
La Crosse
Emporia
Franklin
Great Dismal Swamp NWR
ATLANTIC OCEAN
95
81
70
15
29
7
17
66
495
301
360
64
13
50
460
85
58

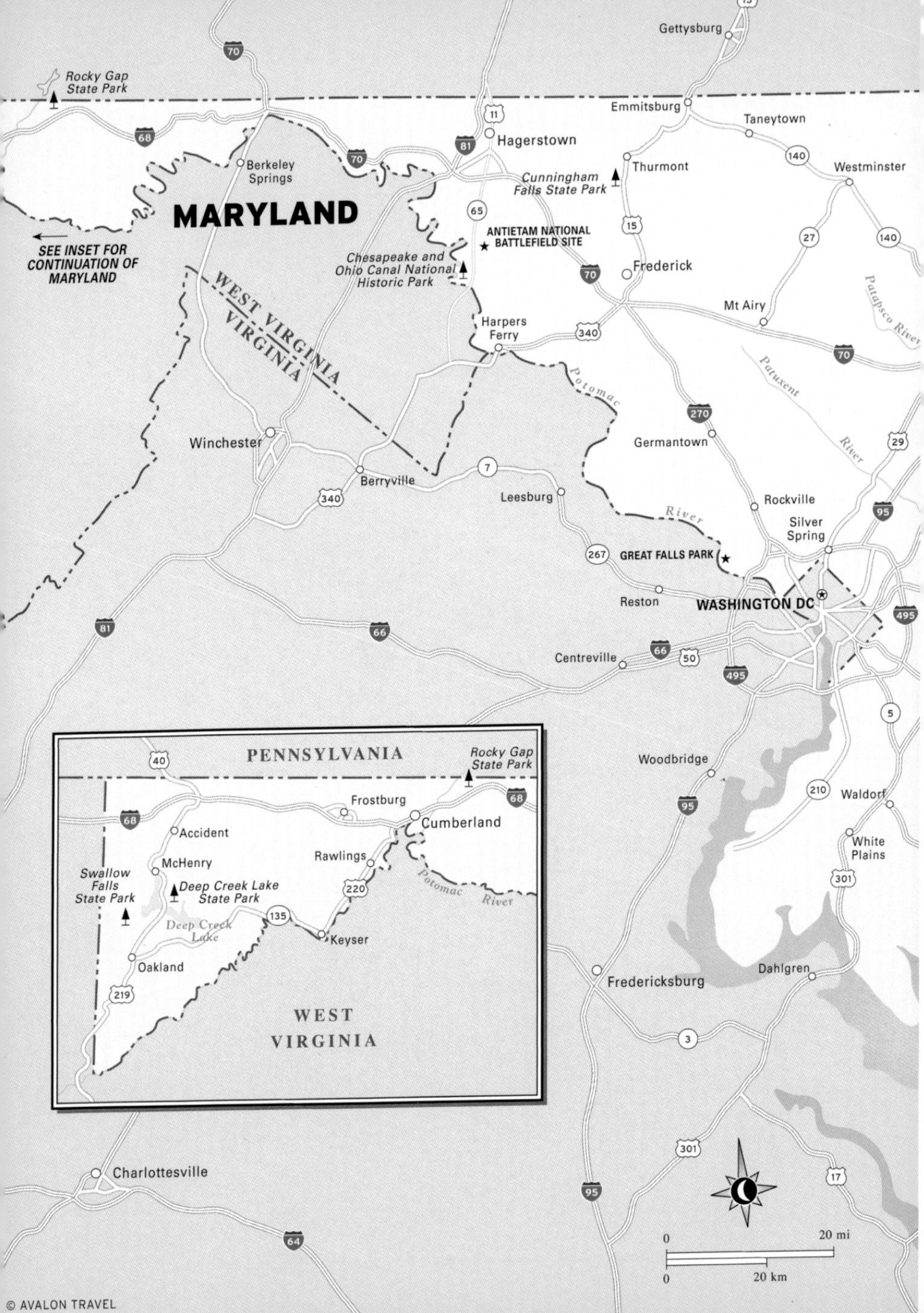

MARYLAND
SEE INSET FOR CONTINUATION OF MARYLAND
Rocky Gap State Park
Gettysburg
Emmitsburg
Taneytown
Hagerstown
Berkeley Springs
Thurmont
Westminster
Cunningham Falls State Park
ANTIETAM NATIONAL BATTLEFIELD SITE
Chesapeake and Ohio Canal National Historic Park
Frederick
WEST VIRGINIA
VIRGINIA
Harpers Ferry
Mt Airy
Patapsco River
Patuxent River
Potomac River
Winchester
Germantown
Berryville
Leesburg
Rockville
Silver Spring
GREAT FALLS PARK
Reston
WASHINGTON DC
Centreville
Woodbridge
Waldorf
White Plains
Fredericksburg
Dahlgren
Charlottesville
PENNSYLVANIA
Rocky Gap State Park
Frostburg
Cumberland
Accident
McHenry
Rawlings
Swallow Falls State Park
Deep Creek Lake State Park
Deep Creek Lake
Keyser
Oakland
WEST VIRGINIA
0
20 mi
0
20 km
© AVALON TRAVEL

PENNSYLVANIA
MARYLAND
West Grove
Oxford
Shrewsbury
Wilmington
Delaware River
Susquehanna River
Bear
Havre de Grace
Bel Air
Fallston
Cockeysville
Elk River
NEW JERSEY
Millville
Middletown
BALTIMORE
Smyrna
DOVER
Chester River
Sudersville
BWI AIRPORT
Camden
Delaware Bay
DELAWARE
MARYLAND
ANNAPOLIS
Wye River
Harrington
Denton
Milford
Choptank River
Easton
Chesapeake Bay
Ellendale
Lewes
Rehoboth Beach
Federalsburg
Georgetown
Huntingtown
Cambridge
Nanticoke River
Laurel
Fenwick Island
ATLANTIC OCEAN
BLACKWATER NATIONAL WILDLIFE REFUGE
Salisbury
Solomons
Fruitland
Berlin
Ocean City
Lexington Park
Wicomico River
Assateague State Park
Potomac River
Dameron
Pocomoke City
Assateague Island National Seashore
MARYLAND
VIRGINIA

Contents

M. DUBOIS

DISCOVER

Virginia & Maryland

Separated by Washington DC and the Potomac River, Virginia and Maryland are often mentioned in daily news of political maneuverings at the nation's capital. Although the news networks paint vivid pictures of power and scandal, there is far more to this region than can be summed up in a sound bite.

In Virginia and Maryland, history comes alive. Follow in the footsteps of Thomas Jefferson at stately Monticello. Raise a glass at George Washington's favorite tavern in Colonial Williamsburg. Tread hallowed ground at Civil War battlefields such as Manassas and Antietam.

Alongside monuments, historic sites, and museums, Washington DC offers urban pursuits like fine dining and buzzing nightlife. And

Clockwise from top left: Mabry Mill; Smithsonian Castle; the weather vane at the Mariners' Museum in Newport News; a shop in Colonial Williamsburg; grape vines at Jefferson Vineyards; Antietam National Battlefield.

don't overlook Baltimore, which refracts big-city charms through its own quirky lens.

Not far from these thriving metropolitan areas you'll find sleepy mountain towns, quaint fishing villages, and an abundance of natural beauty. Wander through glowing fall foliage along the Blue Ridge Parkway. Summit the peak of Old Rag Mountain in Shenandoah National Park. Sail on the Chesapeake Bay before cracking a claw at a waterfront crab house in Annapolis. Stroll the bustling Ocean City Boardwalk. Relax on the quiet beaches of Assateague and Chincoteague Islands, where wild ponies roam free.

Welcome to Virginia and Maryland, where there's always something new to discover.

Clockwise from top left: the Steven F. Udvar-Hazy Center; the Shenandoah River; the schooner *Sultana*; the National World War II Memorial.

ATLANTIC

Planning Your Trip

Where to Go

Washington DC

Washington DC is nestled between Virginia and Maryland on the banks of the Potomac River. Best known for politics, government, and **monuments and museums,** the city is also home to universities, nightlife, art, theater, and sports. One of the largest (and cleanest) cities in the country, Washington DC offers trendy neighborhoods, **upscale shopping,** the **National Cathedral,** the **National Zoo,** and professional sports arenas. The nation's capital is easy to navigate, especially with the help of landmarks like the **Washington Monument** and the **U.S. Capitol.**

Northern Virginia

From the busy halls of the **Pentagon** in **Arlington** and the trendy streets of historic **Old Town Alexandria** to the quaint alleyways of **Middleburg,** Northern Virginia is a cornucopia of culture, history, business, outdoor recreation, culinary delights, and shopping. It is a central corridor for the technology industry, yet houses key attractions such as **Mount Vernon,** the plantation home of **George Washington.** Northern Virginia's residents make up roughly one-third of the entire state population.

Coastal Virginia

Visiting Coastal Virginia is a great way to take a break from everyday stresses and learn about history or relax on the beach. **Colonial Williamsburg,** a living museum that vividly displays what life in colonial times was like, is one of the most popular historical attractions in the country. Just a short drive away is the resort area of **Virginia Beach** and the sleepy seaside communities on **Virginia's Eastern Shore.** The region offers port towns, battleships, and

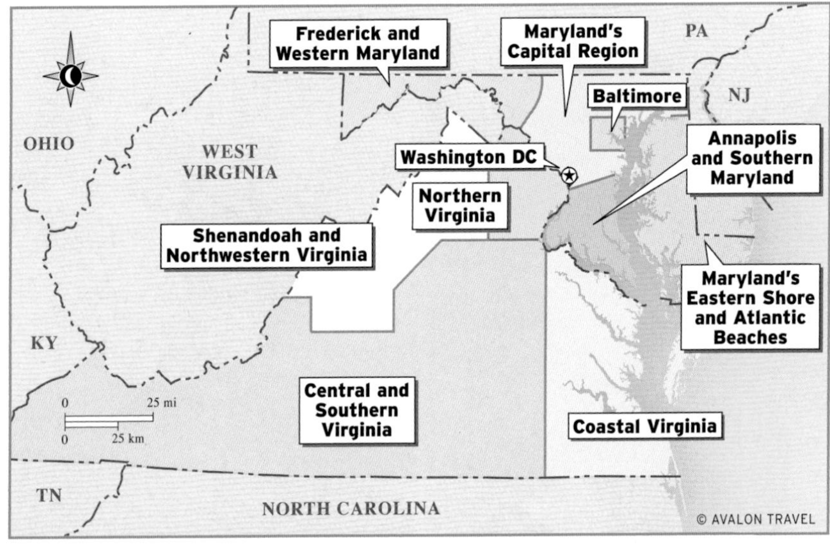

watercraft rentals in Coastal Virginia

beautiful, clean beaches all within a short drive of one another.

Shenandoah and Northwestern Virginia

Shenandoah National Park and Northwestern Virginia form a very special part of the Blue Ridge Mountains. The area is known for its stunning vistas, and picturesque rivers and streams crisscross the region and loosely connect the towns that sit on the park's doorstep. Take a scenic drive along **Skyline Drive,** white-water raft down the **Shenandoah River,** spend an afternoon underground in mysterious **Luray Caverns,** or take a hike on the famous **Appalachian Trail.** Choose adventure or opt to relax—there is no wrong answer.

Central and Southern Virginia

Sprawling Central and Southern Virginia offer some of the most beautiful countryside in America. Awesome mountain vistas, rolling foothills, and enchanting fall foliage can be found in this region, especially along the **Blue Ridge Parkway.** The site of many colleges and universities including the **University of Virginia,** the region was also home to famous Americans such as **Thomas Jefferson** and **James Monroe.** The state capital, **Richmond,** and historic **Fredericksburg, Charlottesville,** and **Roanoke** are key destinations in this vast region.

Maryland's Capital Region

Trendy, sporty, and historic, Maryland's Capital Region is a main suburban area of Washington DC and, as such, is densely populated. **Montgomery County** is sophisticated, urban, and professional with a variety of restaurants, shopping areas, hotels, and upscale neighborhoods. **Prince George's County** is a hub for government agencies including NASA and the Department of Agriculture and is home to the **Washington Redskins.** In addition to offering visitors many interesting attractions, Maryland's Capital Region also serves as a convenient home base for exploring Washington DC.

Baltimore

The city of Baltimore, once a rough industrial

historic Fredericksburg

port, has undergone a series of urban renewal plans over the past few decades. As a result, it has blossomed into a major tourist destination that offers many **fascinating museums, entertainment venues,** professional sporting events such as the **Preakness Stakes,** and the famous **Inner Harbor.** Side trips include **Westminster,** which hosted both Union and Confederate troops during the Civil War, and lovely **Havre de Grace,** sitting at the head of the Chesapeake Bay.

Annapolis and Southern Maryland

The nation's sailing capital, **Annapolis,** is the top destination on the mainland banks of the Chesapeake Bay due to its waterfront location, charming historic district, and trendy boutiques and taverns. A busy recreational harbor, the city features an endless supply of blue crabs, oysters, and other delectable seafood. It is also home to the **U.S. Naval Academy.** Scenic Southern Maryland offers a slower, relaxed pace in its idyllic seaside towns such as **Solomons Island** and **Chesapeake Beach** and historic cities such as **St. Mary's City.**

Maryland's Eastern Shore and Atlantic Beaches

Picturesque fishing towns, blue crabs, and sunsets—these are all traits of Maryland's Eastern Shore. **Chestertown, St. Michaels,** and **Tilghman Island** offer alluring charm and a window into life along the Chesapeake Bay. Maryland's Atlantic beaches are a symphony of contrasts. **Assateague Island** calms your

Drum Point Lighthouse on Solomons Island

Ocean City Boardwalk

spirits as you share the beaches with wild ponies. **Ocean City** offers an exciting boardwalk and active nightlife. Three neighboring beach communities on the Delaware shore—**Bethany Beach, Rehoboth Beach,** and **Lewes**—are popular vacation spots.

Frederick and Western Maryland

Frederick offers old-town charm, antiques shopping, and terrific food. Some of the region's finest restaurants are tucked into the appealing historic downtown. Western Maryland is the **"mountain side"** of the state, where the railroad used to rule and the scenery is tranquil and pretty. **Deep Creek Lake,** with its 65 miles of shoreline, is a popular getaway spot for Washingtonians. Whether your idea of vacation is visiting **Civil War sites,** boating, or riding a steam engine through the mountains, you can find it all in Western Maryland.

When to Go

If you have the luxury of choosing your time to visit, **late spring** (May and June) and **fall** (September and October) are usually the **best times** to explore Virginia and Maryland. The weather is most pleasant, and there are fewer tourists to compete with. Although **summer** is the **prime tourist season,** unless your plans involve some beach time or a stay in a mountain retreat, the humidity can be a bit overwhelming. The fall foliage in the region is some of the most spectacular in the country. A drive through the Blue Ridge Mountains in October can lead to some of the most stunning scenery in the East. If your focus is on historical sites and museums, the **winter** months (with the exception of the holiday season) can mean **short or no wait times** for popular attractions. Just be prepared for some sites to be closed or to have shorter hours.

The Best of Virginia and Maryland

Virginia and Maryland encompass a large amount of land. It can take six hours to drive from Washington DC to the southern end of Virginia and nearly four hours to drive from Western Maryland to the Eastern Shore. A 12-day trip provides the opportunity to hit most of the highlights of the region and get a good feel for both states.

Washington DC makes a good starting point for exploration of Virginia and Maryland. It is centrally located and convenient for air, train, bus, and car travel. Spend a couple of days at the beginning of your trip exploring this marvelous city.

Frederick and Western Maryland

DAY 1

From Washington DC, drive three hours northwest to the far reaches of Maryland to enjoy the mountain air at **Deep Creek Lake.** On your way, stop in **Frederick** for lunch in the historic downtown area. Overnight in one of the lovely cabins at **The Lodges at Sunset Village** at Deep Creek Lake.

DAY 2

Spend the day at **Deep Creek Lake State Park,** enjoying the outdoors. Swim, fish, or canoe on the beautiful lake or take a hike on one of the many trails on Meadow Mountain. Spend the night in another local inn or pitch a tent at the **Meadow Mountain Campground.**

Shenandoah and Northwestern Virginia

DAY 3

Drive 2.25 hours southeast into Virginia and have lunch in charming **Winchester** at **Union Jack**

Shenandoah National Park

Colonial Williamsburg

Pub and Restaurant. Then spend a little time touring this lovely town and visit the **Museum of the Shenandoah Valley** before continuing 30 minutes south to **Front Royal,** the gateway to Shenandoah National Park. Visit a stunning subterranean world at **Skyline Caverns,** then spend the night in Front Royal.

DAY 4

Make this day all about **Shenandoah National Park.** Drive **Skyline Drive** and stop along the way to take in breathtaking vistas or to do a short hike. End your day by driving to Lexington and spending the night in this historic town.

Central Virginia

DAY 5

Spend the morning in **Lexington** seeing the sights. Take a carriage tour or visit the **Virginia Military Institute** and the **George C. Marshall Museum.** Then make the scenic one-hour drive east to **Charlottesville** and visit a vineyard before treating yourself to a night at either the **Clifton Inn** or **Keswick Hall.**

DAY 6

Visit Thomas Jefferson's **Monticello** in the morning and then have lunch on the hip downtown mall in Charlottesville. After lunch, drive southeast about an hour to the state capital of **Richmond.** Orient yourself in this busy city and if time allows, take in the **Science Museum of Virginia.** Overnight in Richmond. For a splurge, spend the night in the historic **Jefferson Hotel.**

Coastal Virginia

DAY 7

Visit **Capitol Square** in Richmond before heading southeast for a one-hour drive to **Colonial Williamsburg.** Dine in **Merchants Square** and spend the night in one of several hotels run by the **Colonial Williamsburg Foundation.**

DAY 8

Lose yourself in U.S. history by dedicating the day to exploring Colonial Williamsburg. Visit the **museums,** shop in the authentic **colonial shops,** grab a sweet potato muffin at the **Raleigh Tavern Bakery,** talk to the costumed interpreters, and drink and dine in the local **taverns.** Spend another night in Williamsburg.

DAY 9

Make the 1.25-hour drive to **Virginia Beach** early so you can enjoy a day on the Atlantic. Visit the **Virginia Aquarium & Marine Science Center** and walk the famous boardwalk. Enjoy fresh seafood at one of the local restaurants and spend the night in a hotel right on the ocean.

Maryland's Eastern Shore and Atlantic Beaches

DAY 10

Drive northeast three hours through the famous **Chesapeake Bay Bridge-Tunnel** and continue up the scenic Eastern Shore to **Ocean City.** Soak in the activity on the busy boardwalk and be sure to eat some **Thrasher's French Fries.** Spend the rest of your day at the beach.

DAY 11

Drive two hours northwest to the charming Eastern Shore town of **St. Michaels.** The sharp contrast to Ocean City will be readily noticeable as you stroll through the historic downtown area full of restaurants and boutiques or perhaps take a cruise from the waterfront. Spend the night in St. Michaels in one of the waterfront inns.

Annapolis

DAY 12

On your last day, drive about an hour northwest over the **Chesapeake Bay Bridge** to Maryland's capital city, **Annapolis.** This beautiful and historic waterfront city on the Chesapeake Bay is the perfect place to end your trip. Visit the **Annapolis City Dock,** the **U.S. Naval Academy,** and the **Maryland State House.** Be sure to dine on local blue crabs if you're a seafood lover.

Annapolis

Best Scenic Drives

scenic fall foliage on Skyline Drive

FALL FOLIAGE

Skyline Drive (page 237)

Starting point: Front Royal, VA
Ending point: Waynesboro, VA
105 miles; 3 hours
Virginia is known for having one of the most spectacular leaf displays in the country, and Skyline Drive in Shenandoah National Park showcases the best of the best.

Blue Ridge Parkway (page 300)

Starting point: Waynesboro, VA
Ending point: Cherokee, NC
469 total, 217 in Virginia; 6 hours in Virginia
The Blue Ridge Parkway begins where Skyline Drive ends. The most scenic portion is the 114 miles between Waynesboro and Roanoke.

HISTORICAL ROOTS

Antietam Campaign Scenic Byway (page 531)

Starting point: White's Ferry, MD
Ending point: Sharpsburg, MD
126 miles; 4 hours
This route begins where Robert E. Lee and his army crossed the Potomac River into Maryland and ends at Antietam National Battlefield, where Lee's forces retreated back into West Virginia.

Colonial Parkway (page 170)

Starting point: Yorktown, VA
Ending point: Jamestown, VA
23 miles; 35 minutes
This parkway was designed to unify the "Historic Triangle" of Williamsburg, Jamestown, and Yorktown, while preserving the area's scenery and wildlife.

SALTY AIR

Chesapeake Bay Bridge-Tunnel (page 215)

Starting point: South Hampton Roads, VA
Ending point: Eastern Shore, VA
20 miles; 30 minutes
This engineering masterpiece, which spans the mouth of the Chesapeake Bay, takes vehicles over a series of bridges and through two-mile-long tunnels.

MOUNTAIN TOWNS

Virginia's Western Highlands (page 258)

Starting point: Monterey, VA
Ending point: Covington, VA
55 miles; 1.25 hours
Take scenic Route 220 through iconic mountain towns such as Warm Springs and Hot Springs, where the famed Omni Homestead Resort is located.

Battles and Brews

Virginia and Maryland have a colorful history. More Civil War battles were fought in Virginia than in any other state, but the region is also known for its Revolutionary War past, colonial history, and, of course, the development of our nation's government and capital. This six-day itinerary starts in Yorktown, Virginia, and ends in Gettysburg, Pennsylvania. The 400-mile trip covers some of the most significant historical cities in the region and includes refreshing stops in some of the best local pubs.

the Philadelphia Tavern

Day 1

Start in Yorktown, Virginia, and take in the **Yorktown National Battlefield,** where the last major battle of the Revolutionary War was fought. The battlefield is part of the **Colonial National Historical Park.** Stop in the **Yorktown Pub** for a beer, oysters, and hush puppies. Spend the night in Yorktown at the **Hornsby House Inn.**

Day 2

Drive two hours north to Fredericksburg and spend the day touring the **Fredericksburg & Spotsylvania National Military Park.** Spend a relaxing evening at the **Kenmore Inn** and have a drink in its historic pub.

Day 3

Drive one hour north to **Manassas National Battlefield Park** and explore the site of two major Civil War battles. Continue on to the old town area of Manassas and have a beer and a

Yorktown National Battlefield

History Comes Alive

Virginia and Maryland offer several unique opportunities to become part of history.

VIRGINA

- **Colonial Williamsburg** (page 171) in Williamsburg, Virginia, is the largest living-history museum in the country at 301 acres. It revives a real colonial American city and draws visitors into the action as part of the town. Costumed interpreters work and dress as those from colonial times did and provide genuine goods and services to tourists. Visitors can sleep in restored inns, dine in authentic taverns, and have conversations with actors portraying 18th-century Americans.
- A few miles from Williamsburg is another living-history museum called the **Jamestown Settlement** (page 181). This museum includes three sections: a Powhatan Village, a settlers' fortress, and the ships the town's inhabitants arrived on. The interpretive guides are very well informed, interesting, and good-humored.

MARYLAND

- Civil War buffs will enjoy the many annual battle reenactments that take place throughout the region. One of the most popular is the **Gettysburg National Civil War Battle Reenactment** (page 523) that is held each July. It includes three exciting battles, field demonstrations, live mortar fire demonstrations, living-history programs, and all-day activities.
- Visitors can step even further back in time and completely away from U.S. history by attending the **Maryland Renaissance Festival** (page 441) near Annapolis. This outstanding annual event spans 19 weekend days in August, September, and October and draws thousands of costumed and plainclothes patrons. Step through the front gate into a 16th-century English village and instantly become part of the show.

Maryland Renaissance Festival

cheesesteak at the **Philadelphia Tavern.** Spend the night in Manassas.

Day 4

Drive 1.5 hours southwest to the **New Market Battlefield,** where Union troops were forced out of the Shenandoah Valley. Then head to scenic Luray for a casual dinner and a beer at **55 East Main Brew House and Grill.** Spend the night in Luray.

Day 5

Drive 1.75 hours north to **Antietam National Battlefield** in Sharpsburg, Maryland, to visit the site of the bloodiest single-day battle during the Civil War. Continue on to historic Frederick and stop in **Flying Dog Brewery** for a tour and tasting. Spend the night in Frederick.

Day 6

Drive 45 minutes north to downtown Gettysburg, Pennsylvania, where the famous **Battle of Gettysburg** spilled onto the streets, and then tour the **Gettysburg National Military Park.** End your day at **Garryowen Irish Pub** for some Guinness and a Reuben sandwich. Spend the night in Gettysburg.

Best Places to Eat Crab

The slogan *Maryland is for Crabs* is meant to be taken literally. The blue crab is the designated Maryland state crustacean, and people in this region know how and where to crack a claw.

VIRGINIA

- **Tim's Rivershore Restaurant & Crabhouse** (page 138) in Dumfries offers a beachy atmosphere and waterfront dining on the Potomac River. This supercasual crab house is a party spot in the summer with live music and a boating crowd.
- **The Crazy Crab Restaurant** (page 168) in the Reedville Marina is a small family-owned restaurant on the waterfront. The seafood can't get any fresher, as you can literally see the owner walk outside and harvest it.
- The **Crab Shack** (page 196) sits on the James River in Newport News and has great views throughout its window-lined dining room and deck. It offers fresh seafood and a casual atmosphere.
- The folks at **A. W. Schuck's** (page 204) in Norfolk believe that any meal can include seafood. They are famous for burgers topped with lump crab, and the portions are huge.
- **Four Brothers Crab House & Ice Cream Deck** (page 221) is out on Tangier Island, the "Soft Crab Capital of the World." A trip to this isolated island in the middle of the Chesapeake Bay requires a 12-mile ferry ride.

Tim's Rivershore Restaurant & Crabhouse

MARYLAND

- The original "Crab Bomb," with 10 ounces of jumbo lump crabmeat, can be found at **Jerry's Seafood** (page 371) in Bowie.
- Quarter-pound crab cakes with no filler, seasoned to perfection, are the calling card of a local Annapolis favorite called **Chick & Ruth's Delly** (page 443). Just a block from the State House, this sandwich shop opened in 1965 under owners Chick and Ruth Levitt, and it has been growing ever since.
- A traditional crab house with huge notoriety in the Annapolis area is **Cantler's Riverside Inn** (page 443). It is situated on a cove right on the water and sells local steamed crabs by the dozen (in all sizes).
- **Buddy's Crabs and Ribs** (page 443) is a lively icon on Main Street in Annapolis. Steamed crabs is the entrée of choice at Buddy's, but the homemade crab cakes are also famous.
- For more suggestions on where to crack a claw in Maryland, see page 444.

Adrenaline Rush

Virginia and Maryland offer more than history, culture, and a beautiful landscape. There are outdoor activities galore for the active traveler. You could spend a lifetime here and still not experience all the recreation available in the region, but in five days, you can get a good taste. This itinerary begins in Harpers Ferry, West Virginia, and ends in Annapolis, Maryland. The total distance is 147 miles.

Day 1: Rafting and Hiking

Begin in historic **Harpers Ferry,** West Virginia, and take an organized rafting trip on the **Shenandoah River,** then hike some of the legendary **Appalachian Trail.** Outdoor enthusiasts could easily spend a week in Harpers Ferry, but two days will allow for the highlights. Overnight in a bed-and-breakfast right in town.

Day 2: Biking and Zip-Lining

Get an early start and bike some of the scenic **C&O Canal Towpath,** then take a thrilling **Harpers Ferry Zip Line Canopy Tour.** A less strenuous alternative is to learn about the town's role in the Civil War era by touring the historic district. Drive one hour to Front Royal, Virginia, in the afternoon and spend the night in town.

Day 3: Hiking

Drive into **Shenandoah National Park** and hike the famous **Old Rag Mountain.** This tough nine-mile hike offers rewarding views and a sense of accomplishment. Spend the night in lovely Luray, Virginia.

Day 4: Kayaking

Give your tired feet a rest by driving two hours to Georgetown in Washington DC and rent a kayak on the waterfront. Paddle on the **Potomac River,** where you'll get a unique perspective on the monuments and bridges. If you're feeling exhausted, a quieter alternative is to window-shop on M Street (although your wallet might get the workout instead). Spend the night in Georgetown.

Day 5: Sailing

Get an early start and drive one hour to **Annapolis,** Maryland, and take a two-hour sailing cruise on a stunning 74-foot wooden schooner. Then stroll along the City Dock and indulge in a local seafood feast at one of the many restaurants near the waterfront.

on top of Old Rag Mountain

Seven Days on the Eastern Shore

Virginia and Maryland share a rare commodity in the Eastern Shore. This coastal area is a 180-mile-long peninsula that sits east of the Chesapeake Bay and west of the Atlantic Ocean. It is sparsely populated in both states and contains one-third of Maryland's land area but only 8 percent of its population. A trip to the Eastern Shore is like stepping back in time. Historic towns, charming fishing villages, vast natural areas, and abundant seafood make this a prime recreation destination.

Day 1

Begin your trip in the northern part of the region in **Chestertown,** Maryland. This historic colonial waterfront town sits on the banks of the Chester River and is a wonderful place to stroll, eat, and just relax. You can also take an educational course on the schooner ***Sultana.*** Stay the night in a local inn.

Day 2

Drive south for an hour to the charming waterfront town of **St. Michaels** in Maryland. This is one of the loveliest spots on the Eastern Shore and where many Washingtonians have second homes. The town has fine restaurants, shopping, a good museum, and a lot of character. Spend the night in St. Michaels in one of the fine inns or a local bed-and-breakfast.

Day 3

Step back in time by taking a ferry from Crisfield, Maryland, to **Tangier Island** in Virginia. Crisfield is a two-hour drive south of St. Michaels, and the ferry is a 1.25-hour ride. The isolated island sits in the middle of the Chesapeake Bay and is rapidly sinking into the bay (it should hang on while you visit). There are no cars on the island, but you can rent a golf cart. The people are friendly, the seafood is fantastic, and there is a nice quiet beach that will make you feel miles away from civilization (which you actually are). If you don't mind the solitude, stay the night on the island, or else head back to the Eastern Shore the same day on the ferry.

Day 4

Continue south from Crisfield (1.25 hours) to the charming village of **Onancock,** Virginia. Rent a kayak, have lunch, and take a leisure day exploring the town. Spend the night in Onancock.

Day 5

Drive about an hour northeast to the Atlantic side of the Eastern Shore to **Chincoteague Island** in Virginia. Explore the **Chincoteague National Wildlife Refuge** and look for signs of the wild ponies that live there. Take a short hike to the **Assateague Island Lighthouse** and spend the night on the island.

Day 6

Leave the calm of nature behind and drive 1.25 hours north to bustling **Ocean City,** Maryland. This beach town is crazy-busy in the summer and offers a wide, active boardwalk, nightlife, and many amusements. Eat some french fries on the boardwalk, ride a Ferris wheel, and then rent a beach umbrella for some downtime on the sand.

Day 7

End your trip with a drive one hour north to the harborfront community of **Lewes,** Delaware. Enjoy a sightseeing cruise from the harbor, spend the afternoon at **Cape Henlopen State Park,** or stroll the enchanting streets of the historic town.

Washington DC

Look for ★ to find recommended sights, activities, dining, and lodging.

Highlights

★ **Washington Monument:** One of the most easily recognized landmarks in the country, this 555-foot-tall monument is a tribute to America's first president and a focal point of the National Mall (page 35).

★ **Lincoln Memorial:** This stunning Doric-style monument sitting on the banks of the Potomac River is a grand memorial to President Abraham Lincoln (page 36).

★ **Vietnam Veterans Memorial:** This moving memorial honors those who fought and died or went missing in action during the Vietnam War (page 37).

★ **National Museum of Natural History:** The most visited natural history museum in the world, this treasure features more than 126 million specimens in 325,000 square feet of exhibit space (page 41).

★ **National Air and Space Museum:** This impressive museum features the largest collection of air- and spacecraft in the world (page 42).

★ **White House:** Tour the home and workplace of the president of the United States (page 44).

★ **Jefferson Memorial:** Sitting on the shore of the famous Tidal Basin is this stunning memorial to the author of the Declaration of Independence (page 45).

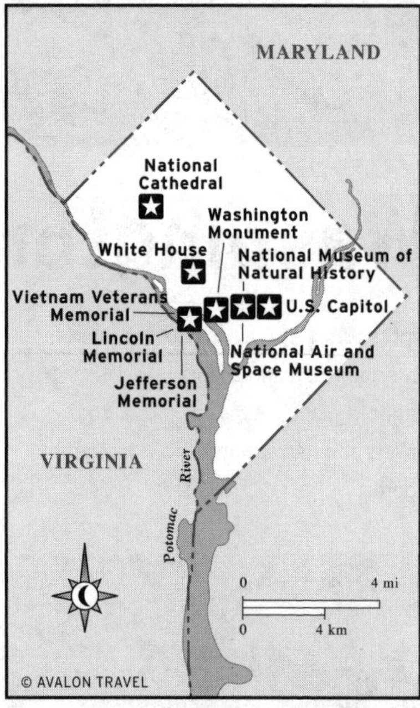

★ **U.S. Capitol:** Perhaps the biggest symbol of the free world, the grand neoclassical-style Capitol Building is the official meeting site for the U.S. Congress (page 47).

★ **National Cathedral:** This massive Gothic cathedral in Upper Northwest DC is the sixth-largest cathedral in the world (page 57).

Awe-inspiring Washington DC, nestled between Virginia and Maryland on the banks of the Potomac River, is best known for government, politics, and museums. Stunning marble monuments dominate the landscape and are a constant reminder of our country's powerful beginnings, while stately government buildings act as the working engine guiding our nation.

One of the largest cities in the nation, Washington is also home to several universities, trendy neighborhoods, professional sports arenas, and attractions like the National Zoo. The city boasts tremendous nightlife, art, theater, and upscale shopping. On average, around 24 million visitors come to DC annually.

Although much of the city is historic and upscale, there are also parts of Washington DC that are impoverished, comprising mostly minority demographics. Many of these residents face homelessness and unemployment. These areas exist side by side with the affluent and wealthy. In a strange way, Washington DC does truly represent the country, even if its residents don't have voting representation in Congress.

ORIENTATION

The city is divided into four quadrants, with the U.S. Capitol sitting in all four. The Capitol Building, however, doesn't sit in the center of the city, which means that the quadrants are not equal in terms of square mileage. The majority of the city, and the lion's share of the attractions, are in the northwest quadrant of Washington. The city is laid out in a grid pattern of lettered and numbered streets, so it is relatively easy to navigate, especially with the help of large landmarks like the Washington Monument and the Capitol Building.

If you asked 10 people how they would divide up the city to explain it to a visitor, you would get 10 different answers. Some would do it simply by quadrants, others by key neighborhoods, and still others by the sights themselves. For the sake of this guide, we are going to divide the city by popular tourist areas so that we can include key areas where many of the popular sights are located, as well as

Previous: architectural detail of the U.S. Capitol; cherry blossoms along the Tidal Basin. **Above:** National World War II Memorial.

Washington DC

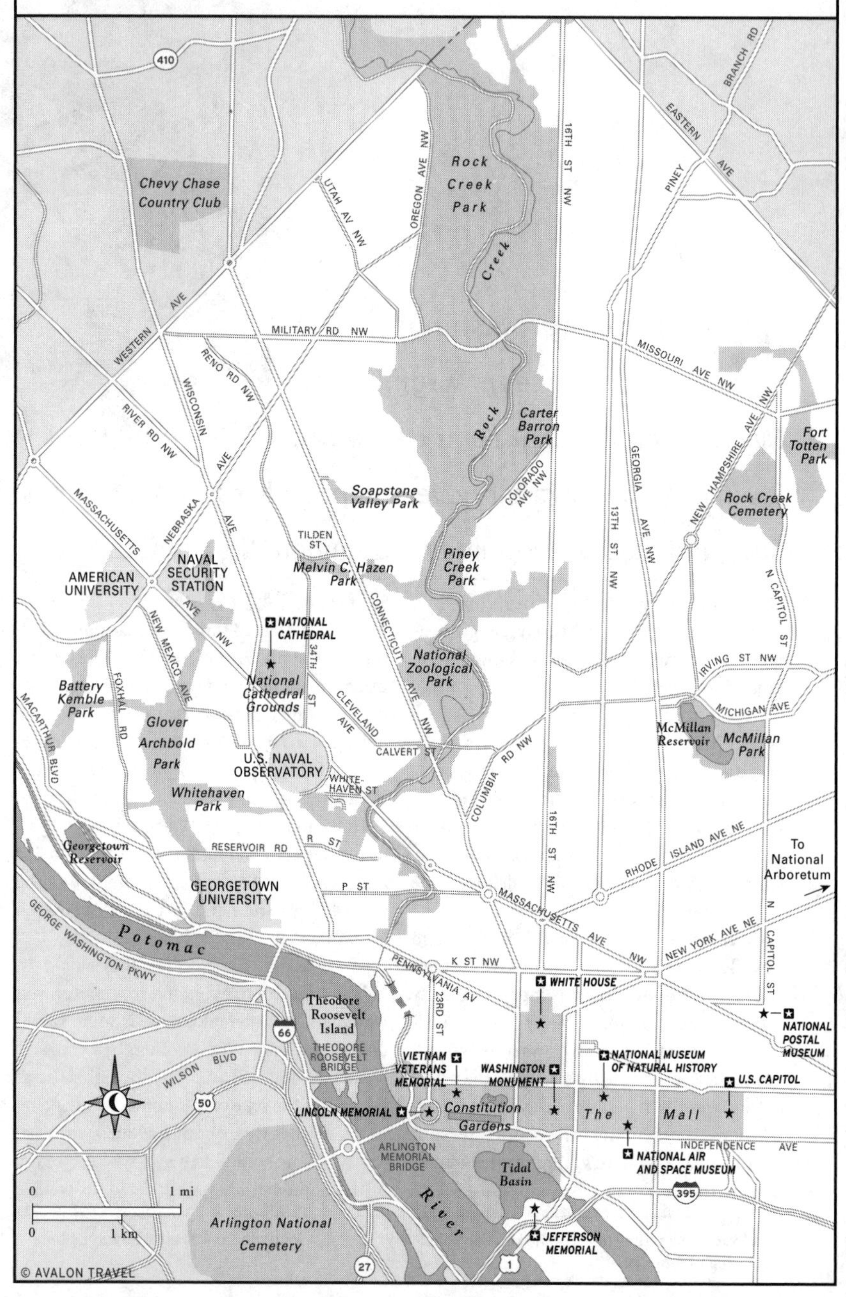

popular neighborhoods where you can find a tremendous selection of food, nightlife, and festivals.

The National Mall

Many people are surprised to learn that the National Mall is a national park and administered by the National Park Service. It is part of an area known as the National Mall and Memorial Parks unit. The exact boundaries of the mall have always been difficult to define, but according to the National Park Service, it is "the area encompassed by Constitution and Pennsylvania Avenues NW on the north, 1st Street on the east, Independence and Maryland Avenues on the south, and 14th Street on the west." It may be easier to visualize by saying that the Mall is basically the entire three-mile stretch between the Lincoln Memorial at the west end and the U.S. Capitol at the east end. The Washington Monument is a focal point of the Mall and sits just to the west of its center. Often, many areas just outside the Mall's official boundaries are still considered to be "on the Mall."

A plan for the National Mall originally designed in 1791 by Pierre L'Enfant laid out a "Grand Avenue," but it was never carried out. The Mall served several other purposes prior to reaching its current state. During the Civil War, the land was utilized primarily for military purposes—drilling troops, the production of arms, and even slaughtering cattle. Permission was even given to the railroad in the late 1800s to lay tracks across part of the Mall.

The National Mall is the primary tourist area in Washington DC, and visitors should plan on spending a significant amount of time here. Simply put, it is packed with monuments and lined with museums. (Some are even underground.) The Department of Agriculture is also on the Mall. When you set out to explore, wear comfortable walking shoes and bring extra camera batteries.

Capitol Hill

Capitol Hill is the political center of the country. It is home to the U.S. Congress and also the largest historical residential neighborhood in the city. It packs in approximately 35,000 residents in less than two square miles. Geographically, Capitol Hill is literally a hill that rises as you approach the Capitol from the west. The U.S. Capitol is on the crest of the hill.

U.S. Capitol

Capitol Hill sits in both the southeast and northeast quadrants of the city. To the north is the H Street Corridor, to the south is the Washington Navy Yard, to the east is the Anacostia River, and to the west is the National Mall.

Many politicians, their staff, journalists, and lobbyists live on Capitol Hill. Residential streets are lined with homes from different periods, many of which are historic.

Pennsylvania Avenue is the hub of the commercial district on Capitol Hill and offers restaurants, bars, and shops. The oldest continually running fresh food market in the city, called **Eastern Market,** is just east of the Capitol Building. This popular shopping spot is housed in a 19th-century brick building.

Who was Pierre L'Enfant?

Washington DC owes a great portion of its inspiring design to Pierre Charles L'Enfant (1754-1825), a French-born American architect and civil engineer. L'Enfant came to America to fight in the Revolutionary War and later became George Washington's number one city planner. L'Enfant designed Washington DC from scratch. He dreamed up a city that was to rise out of a mix of hills, forests, marshes, and plantation land into an extravagant capital city with wide avenues, beautiful buildings, and public squares.

L'Enfant's city included a grand "public walk," which is seen today in the National Mall. His city plan was based on European models, but incorporated American ideals. The design was created from the idea that every citizen is equally important. This is shown in the Mall design, since it is open in all corners.

Downtown

"Downtown" may sound a bit broad, but the term actually refers to the central business district in northwest Washington DC. Geographically, the area is difficult to clearly define, but it is generally accepted as being bordered by P Street NW to the north, Constitution Avenue NW to the south, 4th Street NW to the east, and 15th Street NW to the west.

Some notable areas included in the downtown district are the **K Street Corridor,** which used to be known as the Power Lobbying Corridor and still houses many law firms and businesses (although most of the lobbying firms have relocated to other parts of the city); **Federal Triangle** (bordered by 15th Street NW, Constitution Avenue NW, Pennsylvania Avenue NW, and E Street NW), a triangular area that is home to 10 large federal and city buildings; and **Judiciary Square** (bounded by H Street NW to the north, Pennsylvania Avenue to the south, the I-395 access tunnel to the east, and 6th Street NW to the west), a small neighborhood housing federal and municipal courthouses and offices.

The area also includes the **Penn Quarter** neighborhood, which extends roughly between F and H Streets NW and between 5th and 10th Streets. The name "Penn Quarter" is relatively new. This once sketchy area had new life breathed into it with the opening of the **Verizon Center** (7th and F Streets) in 1997, which was originally called the MCI Center and is home to the **Washington Capitals** professional hockey team and the **Washington Wizards** and **Washington Mystics** professional basketball teams. Now the area is a bustling arts and entertainment district with galleries, museums, restaurants, hotels, and shopping.

At its northern boundaries, Penn Quarter overlaps with the small historic neighborhood of **Chinatown.** Chinatown runs along H and I Streets NW between 5th and 8th Streets NW. It has roughly 20 authentic Asian restaurants and small businesses and is known for its annual Chinese New Year celebration as well as its signature Friendship Arch built over H Street at 7th Street.

Dupont Circle

Dupont Circle is a historic district in Northwest Washington DC. It is technically also the traffic circle at the intersection of Massachusetts Avenue NW, Connecticut Avenue NW, New Hampshire Avenue NW, P Street NW, and 19th Street NW, as well as a park and a neighborhood.

The neighborhood of Dupont Circle lies roughly between Florida Avenue NW to the north, M Street NW to the south, 16th Street NW to the east, and 22nd Street NW to the west.

Dupont Circle is often considered the center of Washington DC's nightlife. It is home to many people in their 20s and also a popular neighborhood among the gay and lesbian community. There are many multilevel apartment buildings and row houses that have been split into apartments here.

Northwest of Dupont Circle along Massachusetts Avenue is an area of the city where many foreign embassies are located. This is commonly referred to as **Embassy Row.** Although less than half of the more than 175 embassies in DC are in this area, it has one of the largest concentrations (most are between Scott Circle and Wisconsin Avenue). Many of the embassies were formerly the homes of wealthy families who made their fortunes from the railroad, mining, banking, publishing, and even politics in the late 1800s. You'll recognize the embassies by the country flags flying out front.

Georgetown

Georgetown has long been known as a trendy yet historic neighborhood with excellent shopping, food, and nightlife. It sits on the Potomac River in Northwest DC, west of downtown and upriver from the National Mall. The area can be loosely defined as being bordered by the Potomac River to the south, Glover Park to the north, Rock Creek to the east, and Georgetown University to the west.

The intersection of M Street and Wisconsin Avenue is the hub of the commercial area, where high-end stores, top-notch restaurants, bars, and The Shops at Georgetown Park are located. Washington Harbor is also a popular area of Georgetown and offers waterfront dining on K Street, between 30th and 31st Streets. The historic Chesapeake & Ohio Canal (C&O Canal) runs between M and K Streets.

Georgetown is home to many politicians and lobbyists and traditionally one of the most affluent neighborhoods in Washington. Famous people who have lived here include

M Street in Georgetown

Choosing the Location of the Nation's Capital

Prior to 1800, the newly formed Congress met in several locations in the mid-Atlantic region. Where to establish the permanent federal government became a highly contested topic that went unresolved for many years. Finally, on July 16, 1790, President George Washington was officially put in charge of selecting a location for the permanent capital and appointing three commissioners to oversee its birth. Washington chose a 10-square-mile piece of land from property in both Virginia and Maryland sitting on both sides of the Potomac River.

The old myth is that DC was built on a swamp. This isn't exactly true. The area was a tidal plain but encompassed tobacco fields, cornfields, woods, waterside bluffs, and wetlands along the river. Washington DC is rich with waterways (the Potomac River, Anacostia River, Rock Creek, and others), but most of the land designated for the city was not marshy.

Congress met in the new location for the first time on November 17, 1800, and the move was completed in 1801. In 1846, land that formerly belonged to Virginia (on what is now the Virginia side of the Potomac River) was returned to Virginia. It is said that George Washington never felt comfortable calling the capital Washington, so instead he referred to it as "The Federal City."

Thomas Jefferson, Francis Scott Key, Alexander Graham Bell, John F. Kennedy, John Kerry, Bob Woodward, and Madeleine Albright.

Many movies have also been filmed in the neighborhood. One of the most notable was the 1973 horror flick *The Exorcist,* which was set here and filmed here in part. Other films include *St. Elmo's Fire* (1985), *No Way Out* (1987), *True Lies* (1994), *Enemy of the State* (1998), *Minority Report* (2002), *The Girl Next Door* (2004), *Wedding Crashers* (2005), and *Transformers* (2007).

Georgetown is not directly accessible by the Metrorail, Washington DC's subway system, but the local DC Circulator bus runs from 19th Street and N Street at the Dupont Metrorail station (on the Dupont-Georgetown-Rosslyn route) to the Rosslyn Metrorail station in Arlington, and it stops along M Street in Georgetown. The Union Station-Georgetown route also stops in Georgetown as it runs from Union Station to Georgetown along K Street. It also has stops on M Street.

Adams Morgan

Adams Morgan is a lively neighborhood in Northwest DC centered on the intersection of 18th Street and Columbia Road. This culturally diverse neighborhood is north of Dupont Circle, south of Mt. Pleasant, east of Kalorama, and west of Columbia Heights. It is considered to be the center of the city's Hispanic community.

Adams Morgan is known for its thriving nightlife. It has more than 40 bars, a great selection of restaurants, nightclubs, coffeehouses, galleries, and shops (most are located along 18th Street). Cuisine from all parts of the globe can be found, from Ethiopian to Caribbean.

Adams Morgan is a popular neighborhood for young professionals and has many 19th- and early 20th-century apartment buildings and row houses.

Upper Northwest

Some of the country's wealthiest people live in the Upper Northwest section of Washington DC. It is a very pretty part of the city that is largely residential with many suburban-looking tree-lined streets. Although the sights are somewhat spread out, many are accessible from the Metrorail.

Just a half mile north of Georgetown is **Glover Park,** a neighborhood of apartment buildings and row houses that were built in the 1920s and '30s. Much of the area's nightlife is found in Glover Park, although compared to neighboring Georgetown, it caters to a slightly older clientele and is less crowded. Glover Park is also slightly west of the **U.S. Naval Observatory** (home to the nation's **Master Clock**) and the vice president's mansion (Number One Observatory Circle).

Northeast of Glover Park is **Woodley Park,** which has some key attractions such as the **National Cathedral** and the **National Zoo.** Farther north are **Cleveland Park, Van Ness,** and **Tenleytown,** along Wisconsin and Connecticut Avenues. Each has their own local restaurants, bars, and shopping. To the west is **American University.**

Southwest of American University is a lesser-known neighborhood called the **Palisades** on the western border of the city along the Potomac River and C&O Canal. This is an elite neighborhood with a few good, high-end restaurants.

Farther north and right on the Maryland state line is **Friendship Heights,** which is technically part of **Chevy Chase.** Friendship Heights has notable wealth and is known for its upscale stores along Wisconsin Avenue and a mall called the **Chevy Chase Pavilion.**

Metrorail's Red Line operates throughout Upper Northwest. The stops are easy to navigate because the stations are named after neighborhoods and sights. The National Cathedral, Glover Park, and the Palisades do not have Metrorail service.

U Street Corridor

The U Street Corridor is a residential and commercial neighborhood in Northwest Washington DC that extends for nine blocks along U Street between 9th and 18th Streets. In the 1920s, this part of the city was known as "Black Broadway," and was one of the largest African American communities in the country. Several famous jazz musicians lived in the neighborhood, including Duke Ellington and Jelly Roll Morton. Others frequented the area's jazz clubs.

Today the U Street Corridor is home to restaurants, nightclubs, music venues, and shops. The intersection of 9th and U Streets is known as "Little Ethiopia" for its concentration of Ethiopian businesses and restaurants.

PLANNING YOUR TIME

Washington DC encompasses approximately 68 square miles, so it is easy to get from one attraction to the next. The truth is, Washington DC has so much to offer, it could take weeks to feel that you've exhausted your opportunities

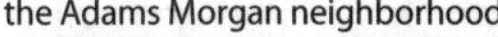

the Adams Morgan neighborhood

Best of Washington DC

DAY 1

Begin your trip with a day dedicated to the **National Mall.** Put on your walking shoes and start with a bird's-eye view of the city from the top of the **Washington Monument,** then walk through the **National World War II Memorial** on your way to the **Lincoln Memorial.** Choose several of the many beautiful **war memorials** to visit, such as the **Korean War Memorial** and the **Vietnam Veterans Memorial.** Pick up lunch at a local food truck and find a nice bench in **West Potomac Park** to rest your feet. Ride Metrorail up to Capitol Hill and spend the afternoon on a tour of the **U.S. Capitol.** When your feet can take no more, catch a cab to **Vidalia** near Dupont Circle for dinner, and then walk east on M Street to enjoy some of the city's nightlife at the rooftop bar at **Ozio Restaurant and Lounge.** Spend the night in the nearby **Hotel Tabard Inn** or, if you feel like splurging, at the **Hay-Adams Hotel,** overlooking the White House.

DAY 2

On your second day in DC, plan to visit some of the **Smithsonian Institution** museums. After breakfast at the inn, if you're feeling spry, walk the 10 or so blocks down to the National Mall or else take a cab. Pick and choose your favorites such as the **National Air and Space Museum** and the **National Museum of Natural History.** Grab lunch inside one of the museums when you need a break, or sample another one of DC's great food trucks outside. When you've overloaded on museums, walk to the **P.O.V. Roof Terrace and Lounge** at the W Washington D.C. Hotel and have a cocktail, then go for a late dinner at the **Old Ebbitt Grill.**

WITH MORE TIME

Take Metrorail into **Old Town Alexandria** for a day in one of the country's oldest port cities. Stroll the historic streets to window-shop in the many **boutiques** and then take a tour of the **Gadsby's Tavern Museum.** Have lunch at **Gadsby's Tavern** and then visit the **Torpedo Factory Art Center,** with three floors of galleries and studios. If you still have energy, take a walking tour of Old Town and then get off your feet for a relaxing dinner at **The Majestic.** After dinner, take Metrorail or a cab back to DC and take a **nighttime tour of the National Mall** (or a cab ride) to see the monuments lit up. Spend one last night in the nation's capital.

for exploration. That's why it is best to focus on a few key areas when familiarizing yourself with the city and to come prepared with a plan of action or at least a list of the top sights you'd like to see.

The National Mall and Memorial Parks are where most of the key monuments and museums are located. This is an area most first-time visitors focus on to see known landmarks such as the Washington Monument, Lincoln and Jefferson Memorials, and several Smithsonian museums. This area can be explored in a long weekend, but allow more time if you want to visit each of the museums.

Most people spend their first trip to Washington DC exploring the National Mall and visiting the government buildings on Capitol Hill. Repeat visitors, or those with ample time, then branch out to explore some of the wonderful neighborhoods in Northwest DC, spending time in Georgetown, Dupont Circle, Adams Morgan, and other key locations to get more of the flavor of the city and to take in the zoo or National Cathedral.

Above all, be realistic about what you and any travel companions can take in during a day. Three or four top sights a day can be more than enough if they include walking through museums and taking tours.

If you are planning to stay in Washington

DC and not stray far from the city limits, there is no need to have a car during your visit. Many of the sights, restaurants, and hotels are accessible by public transportation or a short cab ride, and parking can be expensive and sometimes difficult to find.

Sights

THE NATIONAL MALL

The National Mall (www.nps.gov/nacc) is open 24 hours a day. National Park Service rangers are available to answer questions at most of the sights daily 9am-10pm.

★ Washington Monument

The **Washington Monument** (2 15th St. NW, 202/426-6841, www.nps.gov/wamo, daily except July 4 and Dec. 25, 9am-5pm with longer summer hours, free but ticket required) is one of the most easily recognized landmarks in the country. This slender, 555-foot-tall stone structure is centrally located on the Mall (east of the Reflecting Pool and the Lincoln Memorial) and is a great landmark with which to orient yourself when touring the Mall.

Washington Monument

The Washington Monument is a tribute to the first U.S. president and also the world's tallest true obelisk. Made of marble, granite, and bluestone gneiss, its construction spanned 36 years. Work started in 1848 but was interrupted by several events between 1854 and 1877, including the Civil War. If you look closely at the monument, you can tell that about 150 feet up (a little more than a quarter of the way) the shading of the marble differs slightly. This was due to the long break in construction. The capstone was finally set in 1884, and the monument was dedicated in early 1885. It opened to the public in 1888.

The Washington Monument, upon its completion, was the world's tallest structure. It only held this distinction for one year, however: The Eiffel Tower took over the honor after it was completed in Paris, France.

Visitors can take an elevator to the top of the monument to enjoy stunning views of the city. From the viewing windows, the White House can be seen to the north, the Jefferson Memorial to the south, the Capitol Building to the east, and the Lincoln Memorial to the west.

Although admission is free, tickets must be obtained either in person at the Washington Monument Lodge or over the phone. Located along 15th Street, the Lodge opens at 8:30am and distributes same-day tickets on a first-come, first-served basis. Up to six tickets can be obtained per person. Tickets have specific times, but it is possible to request a preferred ticket time. Be aware that lines form long before the ticket window opens. To order tickets in advance by phone, call 877/444-6777 for individual tickets and 877/559-6777 for

The National Mall

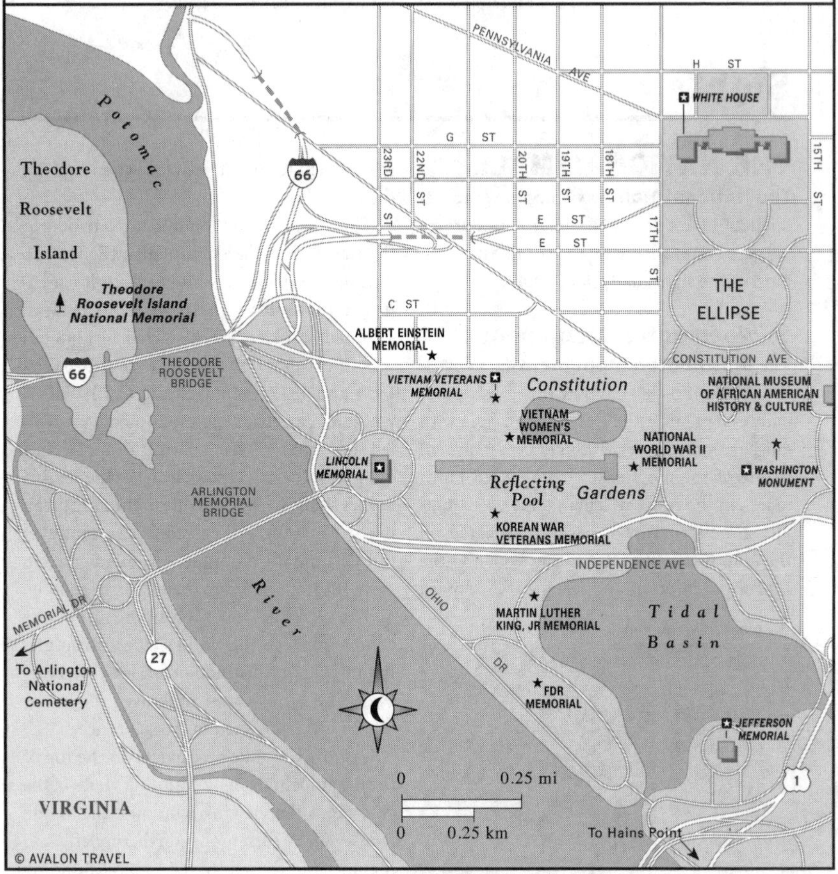

group tickets. Although tickets are free, there is a $1.50 service charge per ticket. Tickets can be ordered up to three months in advance and picked up at the will-call window of the Washington Monument Lodge.

★ Lincoln Memorial

A stunning tribute to America's 16th president is the **Lincoln Memorial** (off 23rd Street NW, 202/426-6841, www.nps.gov/linc, 24 hours, free). This grand limestone and marble monument was built in the Greek Doric style on the western end of the National Mall across from the Washington Monument. It has 36 exterior columns, which represent the number of states that existed at the time of Lincoln's death. The monument was dedicated in 1922.

Inside the memorial is a huge sculpture of Abraham Lincoln and inscriptions from two of his best-known speeches (the Gettysburg Address and his second inaugural address). The sculpture was created by Daniel Chester French, an acclaimed American sculptor of the late 19th and early 20th centuries, and carved by the Piccirilli brothers, who were well-known marble carvers at the time. The

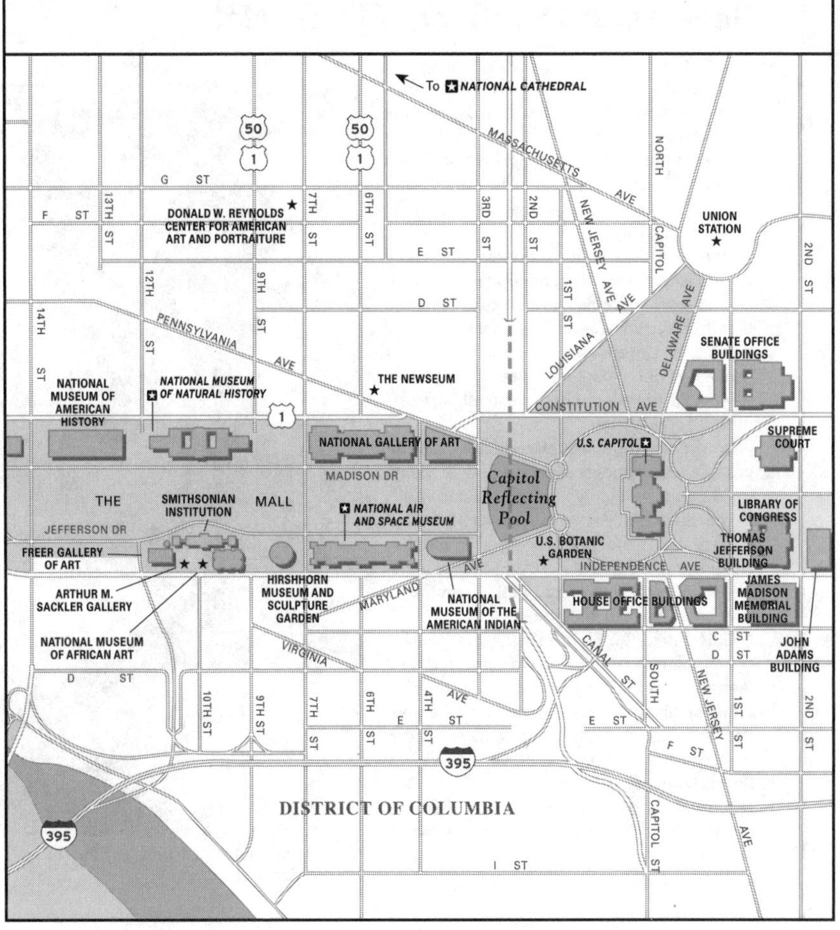

memorial is one of the most recognized landmarks in Washington DC and has been the site of many famous speeches, including Martin Luther King Jr.'s "I Have a Dream" speech.

Albert Einstein Memorial

Where else but on the National Mall can you sit with one of the greatest scientific minds of all time? Just north of the Lincoln Memorial is the bronze **Albert Einstein Memorial** statue sculpted by Robert Berks. It is set in a group of trees on the southwest side of the grounds of the **National Academy of Sciences** (2101 Constitution Ave. NW). Einstein is seated and has papers with mathematical equations in his lap symbolizing his scientific achievements.

War Memorials

★ VIETNAM VETERANS MEMORIAL

One of the most visited war memorials is the **Vietnam Veterans Memorial** (Constitution Avenue between 21st and 23rd Streets, 202/426-6841, www.nps.gov/vive, www.thewall-usa.com, 24 hours, free). This moving memorial

Secrets of the Lincoln Memorial

Many myths surround the Lincoln Memorial. Some say Abraham Lincoln is buried under the monument or entombed inside it, but this is false (Lincoln is buried in Springfield, Illinois). Others think the 57 steps leading up to the statue chamber represent Lincoln's age when he died, but in reality, he was only 56.

One question that is repeatedly asked throughout the local community is what, if anything, lies underneath the memorial? Given that the structure was built on tidal marsh from the Potomac River that was once actually under water, it might make sense that nothing could be under it, but the rumor that something exists there is actually true.

Underneath the Lincoln Memorial is a cavernous area with dirt floors and concrete walls. Hanging from the ceiling beneath where Lincoln sits are hundreds of stalactite formations. The stalactites are long, slender, and pale in color, and they are growing in this artificial cave as the result of water slowly dripping through the monument, which started when it was built.

Other interesting features in the underbelly of the monument are cartoon drawings that were sketched on several support columns by the workers who built the monument. One of the drawings depicts characters from the old *Mutt and Jeff* cartoon, which started running in 1907 and was the first daily newspaper comic strip.

Tours of the cavernous area ceased after 9/11, but this author can vouch for its existence, since in the 1970s and '80s, local children were treated to a tour on elementary school field trips.

the sculpture of Abraham Lincoln in the Lincoln Memorial

honors U.S. service members who fought and died in the Vietnam War and also those who are missing in action. There are three parts to the memorial: the **Three Soldiers Statue,** the **Vietnam Women's Memorial,** and the **Vietnam Veterans Memorial Wall.**

The focal point of the memorial is the Vietnam Veterans Memorial Wall. Completed in 1982, it is actually two 246-foot walls that are sunken into the ground and have the names of more than 58,000 service members who died in the war etched into them in chronological order. (The exact number changes each year as names are added.) When visitors look at the wall, they can see their reflections next to the etched names, symbolically linking the past and present. There is a path along the base of the wall so visitors can walk along it, read names, and if desired, make pencil rubbings of a particular name.

The memorial is at the west end of the National Mall, adjacent to the Lincoln Memorial in West Potomac Park. It is open to the public 24 hours a day, and park staff conduct free daily interpretive tours on the hour 10am-11pm.

NATIONAL WORLD WAR II MEMORIAL

The **National World War II Memorial** (17th Street between Constitution and Independence Avenues, 202/426-6841, www.wwiimemorial.com, www.nps.gov/nwwm, 24 hours, free) honors the more than 400,000 people who died in World War II, the 16 million people who served the United States during the war in the armed forces, and the millions of people who provided support from home. The memorial contains 56 pillars and two triumphal arches arranged in a semicircle around a fountain and plaza. A Freedom Wall sits on the west side of the memorial bearing more than 4,000 gold stars on it, each representing 100 Americans who lost their lives in the war. An inscription in front of the wall reads, "Here we mark the price of freedom." The memorial opened to the public in 2004 and is administered by the National Park Service. It is on the east end of the Reflecting Pool, between the Washington Monument and the Lincoln Memorial.

KOREAN WAR VETERANS MEMORIAL

The beautiful and haunting **Korean War Veterans Memorial** (17th Street SW, 202/426-6841, www.nps.gov/kwvm, 24 hours, free) is also in West Potomac Park, southeast of the Lincoln Memorial. Erected in 1995, it is dedicated to service members who served in the Korean War. The memorial was designed in the shape of a triangle intersecting a circle with walls depicting images of land, sea, and air troops who supported the war. The focal point, however, is 19 larger than life-size stainless steel statues designed by Frank Gaylord within the walled triangle. The seven-foot-tall figures represent a patrol squad with members from each branch of the armed forces making their way through the harsh Korean terrain, represented by strips of granite and bushes. The figures are dressed in full combat gear and look incredibly lifelike. The memorial is lit up at night, and when the figures are reflected on the surrounding wall, there appear to be 38 soldiers, which represents the 38th parallel dividing the two Koreas.

National Gallery of Art

The **National Gallery of Art** (4th St. and Constitution Ave. NW, 202/737-4215, www.nga.gov, Mon.-Sat. 10am-5pm, Sun. 11am-6pm, free), opened in 1937, was conceived by Andrew W. Mellon, who donated funding and a large art collection. The gallery traces the development of Western art from the Middle Ages to current times through paintings,

the National World War II Memorial

the Korean War Veterans Memorial

prints, drawings, sculpture, photographs, and other media. The only portrait in the Western Hemisphere painted by Leonardo da Vinci is housed in this museum. The gallery is a campus that includes the original museum building (the West Building), which features sculpture galleries with over 900 works or art; the newer East Building, which contains a collection of modern paintings, drawings, prints, offices, and research centers; and a 6.1-acre outdoor sculpture garden (open year-round) that offers an ice-skating rink from mid-November through mid-March.

Smithsonian Institution Museums

The **Smithsonian Institution** (www.si.edu) is the largest museum and research complex in the world. It was founded in 1846 and is administered by the U.S. government.

Oddly, the founding donor of the institution was British chemist and mineralogist James Smithson, who had never even been to the United States. Smithson inherited a large estate but had no heirs to leave it to. His will stipulated that his estate would be donated to the founding of an educational institute in Washington DC.

The Smithsonian Institution was established as a trust and functions as a body of the U.S. government, separate from the legislative, executive, and judicial branches. Funding for the museums comes from contributions, the institution's own endowment, memberships, government support, and retail and concession revenues. The Smithsonian employs approximately 6,300 people.

The majority of the Smithsonian museums, 19 in fact, are in DC, and many of them are architectural and historical landmarks. Nine research centers and the National Zoological Park are also part of the Smithsonian collection in DC.

First-timers to Washington DC will want to visit at least one of the major Smithsonian museums. Most of the Smithsonian facilities are open to the public daily except for December 25, with free admission. Visitors should be aware that most of the museums on the National Mall do not offer dedicated parking facilities and require visitors to pass through security screenings upon entry.

SMITHSONIAN CASTLE

Information on the Smithsonian can be found on the south side of the Mall at its headquarters, called the **Smithsonian Castle** (1000 Jefferson Dr. SW, 202/633-1000, daily 8:30am-5:30pm, free). This sandstone building, which opened in 1855, looks like something out of a fairy tale and houses an exhibit hall, administration offices, and Smithson's remains (which were laid to rest in a crypt under the castle).

NATIONAL MUSEUM OF AFRICAN AMERICAN HISTORY & CULTURE

The **National Museum of African American History & Culture** (1400 Constitution Ave. NW, 202/633-1000, www.nmaahc.si.edu, daily 10am-5:30pm, free), which opened in September 2016, powerfully and poignantly explores all facets of the African American experience. Exhibits draw on some 37,000 artifacts to illustrate the nation's journey from slavery through segregation and the Civil Rights movement, right up to the Black Lives Matter activism of today.

You must have a timed entry pass to enter the museum. Passes are sold out several months in advance, but a limited number of same day passes are available daily at 9:15am. Passes can be reserved on the website or by calling 866/297-4020.

NATIONAL MUSEUM OF AMERICAN HISTORY

The **National Museum of American History** (1400 Constitution Ave. NW, 202/633-1000, www.americanhistory.si.edu, daily 10am-5:30pm, free) is devoted to exhibits explaining the cultural, social, scientific, technological, military, and political development of the United States. The museum has three floors housing more than three million artifacts. Wings on each floor represent a different theme, each of which is represented by a large, landmark object. For example, the 1865 Vassar Telescope is in the west wing of the first floor, which is focused on science and innovation.

Some museum highlights include the Star-Spangled Banner, George Washington's uniform, Dorothy's ruby slippers from the *Wizard of Oz,* and the inaugural dresses worn by all the first ladies.

The one-hour guided tours offered are a good way to see the highlights quickly if you have a full docket of sights to get to on the same day. There is no public parking at the museum. Visitors riding Metrorail can use either the Smithsonian Mall stop or Federal Triangle.

★ NATIONAL MUSEUM OF NATURAL HISTORY

Another favorite Smithsonian creation is the **National Museum of Natural History** (10th St. and Constitution Ave. NW, 202/633-1000,

"Henry" at the National Museum of Natural History

www.mnh.si.edu, daily 10am-5:30pm, free). It first opened its doors in 1910 and is said to be the most visited natural history museum worldwide. The main building encloses 325,000 square feet of exhibit space and is overall the size of 18 football fields. The museum collections include more than 126 million specimens.

Visitors can expect to see plants, animals, fossils, rocks, meteorites, and cultural artifacts including "Henry," the iconic 13-plus-foot-tall African elephant (the largest ever killed by humans), the jaws of a giant prehistoric shark, and the stunning Hope Diamond (which is 45.52 carats). There's also a live butterfly pavilion ($6) and an IMAX theater ($7.50-12.50). The museum is also home to the largest group of scientists (approximately 185) dedicated to studying the history of the world. Visitor concierges are available to answer questions throughout the museum and can be identified by their green vests. There is no public parking at the museum. Visitors riding Metrorail should exit at the Smithsonian station (Mall exit) on the Blue and Orange Lines.

NATIONAL MUSEUM OF THE AMERICAN INDIAN

The **National Museum of the American Indian** (4th St. and Independence Ave. SW, 202/633-1000, www.nmai.si.edu, daily 10am-5:30pm, free) opened in 2004 and is the first national museum focused exclusively on Native Americans. The five-story, 250,000-square-foot limestone building sits on more than four acres of what is made to look like wetlands. The museum features approximately 825,000 items that represent more than 12,000 years of history and 1,200 indigenous American cultures. It also offers exhibits, film screenings, public programs, cultural presentations, and school programs.

★ NATIONAL AIR AND SPACE MUSEUM

An overwhelming favorite in the Smithsonian family of museums is the **National Air and Space Museum** (Independence Ave. at 6th St. SW, 202/633-2214, IMAX 866/868-7774, www.airandspace.si.edu, daily 10am-5:30pm, free, IMAX and planetarium entry extra). This incredible museum features the largest collection of air- and spacecraft in the world and is also a center for research on historic aviation, spaceflight, planetary science, geophysics, and terrestrial geology. The current exhibit space of 21 galleries and more than 160,000 square feet of floor space opened in 1976. Most of the hundreds of aircraft,

National Air and Space Museum

spacecraft, rockets, missiles, and other aviation artifacts on display are originals.

Some highlights you can expect to see include the *Spirit of St. Louis*, the Apollo Lunar Module, a DC-3 airplane, a real lunar rock, and the *Star Trek* starship *Enterprise* studio model.

Another great attraction located inside the National Air and Space Museum is the **Albert Einstein Planetarium** ($9). Several shows are offered daily and take visitors through the night sky with a first-of-its-kind SkyVision dual digital projection system and digital surround sound.

Other favorite attractions in the museum include the **Lockheed Martin IMAX Theater** (IMAX shows $9, feature films $15) and flight simulators. One of the best museum shops is also here, and dining facilities are offered on-site.

Museum tours are offered daily at 10:30am and 1pm. There is no public parking at the museum, but several public pay lots are nearby. Metrorail riders should use the L'Enfant Plaza stop and exit at Maryland Avenue.

HIRSHHORN MUSEUM

Many people think the **Hirshhorn Museum and Sculpture Garden** (700 Independence Ave. SW, 202/633-4674, www.hirshhorn.si.edu, daily 10am-5:30pm, free) looks like a giant spaceship parked near the Mall. The design is an open concrete cylinder (231 feet in diameter) standing on four large supports. The idea behind this structure was for it to provide a sharp contrast to everything else around it. It succeeded. This modern art museum, which opened in the 1960s, houses one of the premier collections of contemporary paintings and sculptures in the country focusing on the post-World War II era. A sculpture garden is located outside the museum.

NATIONAL MUSEUM OF AFRICAN ART

The **National Museum of African Art** (950 Independence Ave. SW, 202/633-4600, www.africa.si.edu, daily 10am-5:30pm, free) is part of a quadrangle complex behind the Smithsonian Castle. The building is mostly underground and contains the largest public collection of African art in the nation with approximately 9,000 artifacts. Pieces include sculpture, jewelry, musical instruments, maps, films, and photographs.

FREER GALLERY OF ART AND ARTHUR M. SACKLER GALLERY

The **Freer Gallery of Art** and the subterranean **Arthur M. Sackler Gallery** (1050 Independence Ave. SW, 202/633-1000, www.asia.si.edu, daily 10am-5:30pm, free) together form the national collections of Asian art. They contain the largest Asian art research library in the country (inside the Sackler Gallery) as well as art from all parts of Asia. Their collection of American art includes pieces by well-known artists such as Winslow Homer, Augustus Saint-Gaudens, and John Singer Sargent.

The Freer Gallery features Asian collections spanning 6,000 years that date back to the Neolithic era. Specific collections include stone sculptures from ancient Egypt, Chinese paintings, Persian manuscripts, and Korean pottery.

The Freer's most famous exhibit is the **Peacock Room** painted by American artist James McNeill Whistler. The room has been restored to how it appeared in 1908 when the founder of the museum, Charles Lan Freer, used it to display over 250 ceramic art pieces he had collected from Asia. Freer was a railroad car manufacturer in Detroit who was a self-taught connoisseur.

The Sackler Gallery contains a founding collection of approximately 1,000 items that were donated by American psychiatrist, entrepreneur, and philanthropist Arthur M. Sackler. The collection has both ancient and contemporary items including South and Southeast Asian sculpture, Chinese jade, and Middle Eastern ceramics. The museums are on the south side of the Mall.

MALL CAROUSEL

It may come as a surprise that the Smithsonian operates the **Mall Carousel** (12th St. and

Jefferson Dr. SW, 202/633-1000, www.nationalcarousel.com, daily 10am-5:30pm, $3.50). This favorite children's thrill ride with the blue and yellow awning is in front of the Smithsonian Castle. It offers three minutes of fun on faded painted ponies that were built in the 1940s. The carousel was originally at the Gwynn Oak Amusement Park in Maryland prior to coming to the Mall.

WHITE HOUSE AREA

★ White House

Not technically part of the National Mall, the **White House** (1600 Pennsylvania Ave., 202/456-1111, www.whitehouse.gov, free) sits nearby on Pennsylvania Avenue and can be seen from Constitution Avenue. The White House is easily the most recognized residence in the country as the home and workplace of the president of the United States.

The site for the White House was chosen by George Washington in 1791, but John Adams was the first president to live there in 1800. (Mrs. Adams is said to have hung their wash in the East Room.) The house suffered a fire set by the British during the War of 1812, but it was rebuilt and has undergone several renovations since then. The White House currently has 6 levels, 132 rooms, and 35 bathrooms.

It is possible to take a self-guided tour of the White House (the only presidential home in the world that is open to the public), but requests must be made through your member of Congress. Tours are available Tuesday-Thursday 7:30am-11am and Friday-Saturday 7:30am-1:30pm. Requests can be made up to six months in advance but must be made at least three weeks in advance. There is no charge for the tour, but it is advised to make a reservation early since space is limited. Citizens of a foreign country may request a tour through their individual embassies in Washington DC. All visitors are required to present current government-issued photo identification or a passport.

The **White House Visitor Center** (1450 Pennsylvania Ave. NW, daily 7:30am-4pm, free) is in the Commerce Building. It offers an information booth, exhibits, restrooms, telephones, drinking fountains, and a first-aid area.

Lafayette Square

Lafayette Square (H St. between 15th and 17th Sts. NW, www.nps.gov/nr, 24 hours, free) is a seven-acre park across Pennsylvania Avenue from the White House (it is also known as **Lafayette Park**). The park was designed as part of the White House grounds—and was originally named President's Park—

Presidential Firsts

- Andrew Jackson was the first president to ride in a train.
- James Polk was the first president to have his photograph taken.
- Millard Fillmore was the first president to have a bathtub with running water.
- Rutherford B. Hayes was the first president to have a telephone in the White House.
- Benjamin Harrison was the first president to have a Christmas tree in the White House.
- Theodore Roosevelt was the first president to ride in a car. He was also the first to travel outside the country while in office.
- Calvin Coolidge was the first president to be heard over radio.
- Franklin D. Roosevelt was the first president to fly in an airplane and the first to appear on television.

the White House

but was separated when Pennsylvania Avenue was built in 1804. Lafayette Square has a checkered past. It has been home to a racetrack, a slave market, a graveyard, and a soldier encampment during the War of 1812. It's no wonder the park is said to be the most haunted location in the city. Today, the park offers green grass and five large statues: an equestrian statue of President Andrew Jackson and four of Revolutionary War heroes. The closest Metrorail stop is McPherson Square. The park is maintained by the National Park Service.

President's Park South

President's Park South, which is more commonly referred to as **The Ellipse,** is a 52-acre park that sits just south of the White House. Technically, the Ellipse is the name of the street that runs the circumference of the park. The park is a large grassy circle that is open to the public and is the site of various events. If you hear locals say they are at or on the Ellipse, they mean they are in the park bordered by Ellipse Road.

TIDAL BASIN AREA

The Tidal Basin

The Tidal Basin is a 107-acre reservoir in **West Potomac Park** that sits between the Potomac River and the Washington Channel (a two-mile-long channel that empties into the Anacostia River). Several major memorials are adjacent to the Tidal Basin, including the Jefferson Memorial, the Martin Luther King, Jr. Memorial, and the Franklin Delano Roosevelt Memorial. The Tidal Basin is best known as the center of the National Cherry Blossom Festival; it is lined with many Japanese cherry trees.

★ Jefferson Memorial

Although it was only built in 1942, the **Jefferson Memorial** (701 W. Basin Dr., 202/426-6841, www.nps.gov/thje, 24 hours, free), which sits on the south shore of the Tidal Basin in West Potomac Park, is one of the most recognized memorials in DC. This neoclassical building dedicated to our third president is built on land that once served as a popular bathing beach along the Potomac River.

The memorial building is made up of circular marble steps, a portico, a circular colonnade, and a shallow dome open to the elements. Inside stands a 19-foot-high bronze statue of Thomas Jefferson designed by Rudulph Evans, looking north toward his former residence, the White House. The statue was added to the memorial four years after its

Jefferson Memorial

dedication. Many of Jefferson's writings are inscribed on the memorial.

The site of the Jefferson Memorial is adorned with many Japanese cherry trees, which were a gift from Japan in 1912. The trees are world famous for their beautiful spring blossoms and are the centerpiece for the annual Cherry Blossom Festival.

Martin Luther King, Jr. Memorial

One of the newest memorials is the **Martin Luther King, Jr. Memorial** (1964 Independence Ave. SW, 202/426-6841, www.nps.gov/mlkm, 24 hours, free) in West Potomac Park southwest of the National Mall. The memorial sits on four acres and was unveiled in 2011.

The design of the memorial is based on a line from King's "I Have a Dream" speech: "Out of a mountain of despair, a stone of hope." A 30-foot-high relief of the civil rights leader is called the *Stone of Hope*, sculpted by Lei Yixin, and stands just past two pieces of granite symbolizing the "mountain of despair." Additionally, a 450-foot-long wall includes inscriptions of excerpts from many of King's speeches. Martin Luther King Jr. is the first African American to be honored with a memorial near the National Mall. He is also only the fourth person to be memorialized who was not a U.S. president.

Franklin Delano Roosevelt Memorial

The **Franklin Delano Roosevelt Memorial** (near the intersection of Independence Ave., W. Basin Dr., and Ohio Dr. SW, 202/485-9880, www.nps.gov/frde, 24 hours, free) sits on more than seven acres and consists of four outdoor rooms, one for each of FDR's office terms. Running water is an important component of the memorial, as are sculptures depicting scenes with FDR. Each of the rooms contains a waterfall, and the sculptures become larger and more detailed in consecutive rooms. The intention was to show the increasing complexities faced by FDR during his presidency as related to the depression and war. This is the only memorial to include a depiction of a first lady: Eleanor Roosevelt is depicted in a bronze statue standing before the United Nations emblem.

There is, in fact, another FDR Memorial. FDR was said to have told his trusted friend and Supreme Court justice Felix Frankfurter, "If they are to put up any memorial to me, I should like it to be placed in the center of that green plot in front of the Archives Building. I should like it to consist of a block about the

Who is Featured on U.S. Paper Currency?

- $1 Bill: George Washington (1st U.S. president)
- $2 Bill: Thomas Jefferson (3rd U.S. president)
- $5 Bill: Abraham Lincoln (16th U.S. president)
- $10 Bill: Alexander Hamilton (1st secretary of the treasury)
- $20 Bill: Currently Andrew Jackson (7th U.S. president), but he will eventually be replaced by Harriet Tubman (abolitionist and civil rights activist)
- $50 Bill: Ulysses S. Grant (18th U.S. president)
- $100 Bill: Ben Franklin (statesman)

size [of this desk]." Because of this, the first FDR memorial was erected in the 1960s on the corner of 9th Street and Pennsylvania Avenue. It is a simple memorial that met his wishes and consists of a small block of stone that reads, "In Memory of Franklin Delano Roosevelt 1882-1945."

U.S. Holocaust Memorial Museum

The **U.S. Holocaust Memorial Museum** (100 Raoul Wallenberg Pl. SW, 202/488-0400, www.ushmm.org, daily 10am-5:20pm, free) is dedicated to the interpretation of Holocaust history. Its goal is to help leaders and citizens "confront hatred, prevent genocide, and promote human dignity." This museum, perhaps more than most, is of international interest: Visitors from more than 132 countries have walked through its doors since it first opened in 1993. The museum houses more than 12,750 artifacts including prisoner uniforms, a casting of a gas chamber door, and religious articles. Its collections include 1,000 hours of archival footage and 80,000 photographs. It also has information on 200,000 registered survivors, a library, and archives.

Permanent exhibits that show a chronological history of the Holocaust can be accessed on the first floor. A free pass must be obtained for the permanent exhibits March-August but not during the rest of the year. The passes are available at the museum on the day of your visit or can be reserved online. Entrance to other exhibits and memorial spaces is from the first, second, and concourse levels. There is a café on the 15th Street side of the building. This museum can be overwhelming for young children and is best for teenagers and adults.

Bureau of Engraving and Printing

As its web address indicates, the **Bureau of Engraving and Printing** (14th and C Sts. SW, 202/874-4000, www.moneyfactory.gov, Mon.-Fri. 8:30am-3pm, free) is a huge money factory. It produces U.S. currency notes and literally prints billions of dollars each year. Fresh money is delivered to the Federal Reserve System (the nation's central bank). Visitors can take guided tours or walk along the gallery to view the production floor where millions of dollars are being printed. The free 40-minute tour includes a film and explanation of the production process. No ticket is required for tours September-February. Tours run every 15 minutes between 9am and 10:45am and between 12:30pm and 2pm. During peak season (Mar.-Aug., 8:30am-6pm), free tickets are required for tours. Tickets can be obtained at the ticket booth on-site (which opens at 8am) and are for the same day only. Plan to be in line between 6:30am and 7am for the best chance of getting tickets. One person may get up to four tickets.

CAPITOL HILL

★ U.S. Capitol

The centerpiece of Capitol Hill is none other than the grand neoclassical-style **U.S.**

Capitol Hill

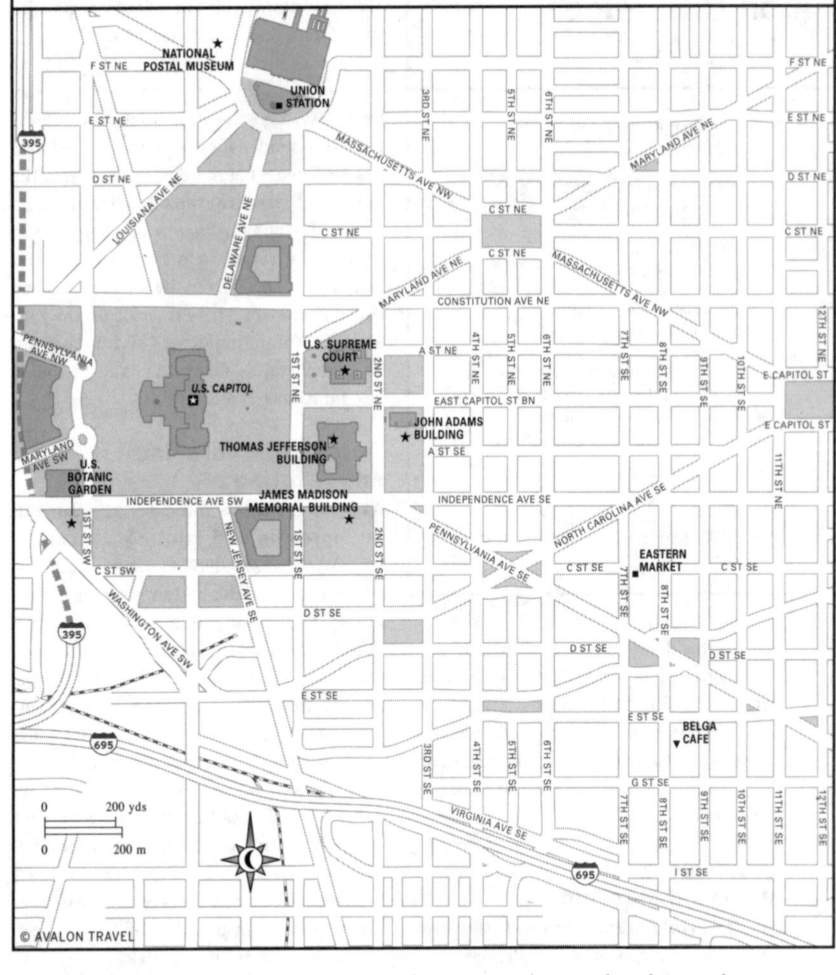

Capitol (1st St. and E. Capitol St., 202/226-8000, www.visitthecapitol.gov, free) itself, which sits on 274 acres at the east end of the National Mall. The Capitol Building is the official meeting location of the U.S. Congress. First-time visitors to the city should take the time to tour this national icon and view our elected officials hard at work.

The Capitol Building comprises a central dome towering above a rotunda, flanked by two wings. The building technically has two fronts, one on the east side and one on the west side. The north wing houses the U.S. Senate chamber and the south wing is for the U.S. House of Representatives chamber. Public galleries sit above each so visitors can watch the proceedings. Each of the many rooms in the Capitol are designated with either an "S" for those on the Senate side of the rotunda or "H" for those on the House side.

George Washington laid the cornerstone of the Capitol in 1793. The Senate wing was

the U.S. Capitol

which opened in 2008. This entry had been planned for many years but wasn't constructed until after two U.S. Capitol Police officers were killed by a visitor in 1998. The center is a security checkpoint, and visitors should be prepared to wait in line for screening before entering. The center also offers educational exhibits, restrooms, and a food court. The visitors center is open Monday-Saturday 8:30am-4:30pm but the Capitol Building itself can only be visited on an official tour. Tours are free but must be arranged in advance through the Advance Reservation System (www.visitthecapitol.gov) or through the office of a senator or representative. Tours are given Monday-Saturday 8:50am-10:50am and last one hour. Those wishing to watch the House or Senate in session must obtain a pass from their senator or representative's office. International visitors can obtain a ticket at the Capitol with valid photo identification. Plan to arrive 45 minutes before a scheduled tour to allow enough time to get through security.

completed in 1800 (Congress held its first session there in 1800) and the House wing was completed in 1811. Since its original construction, the building has undergone many expansions, renovations, and even a rebuilding after it was partially burned by the British during the War of 1812. The Capitol, in its early days, was used for other purposes in addition to government functions. In fact, church services were held there on Sundays until after the Civil War.

Underground tunnels and a private subway connect the Capitol Building with the Congressional office buildings. The Senate office buildings are located to the north on Constitution Avenue, and the House office buildings are located to the south on Independence Avenue. The public may only ride the subway when escorted by a staff member with appropriate identification.

Visitors to the Capitol enter through the three-level underground **U.S. Capitol Visitor Center** (beneath the east front plaza at 1st St. and E. Capitol St., 202/226-8000),

Summerhouse

The **Summerhouse** (on the west front lawn of the U.S. Capitol Building on the Senate side, www.aoc.gov, 24 hours, free), is a little oasis hidden in a group of trees. This small, decorative, hexagonal brick building offers a cool place for visitors to rest. It was constructed around 1880 and is anchored by a fountain that once offered springwater. There are nice benches here with seating for 22 that are covered by a tile roof.

U.S. Supreme Court

Behind the U.S. Capitol Building on 1st Street (between E. Capitol St. and Maryland Ave.) is the **Supreme Court of the United States** (1 First St. NE, 202/479-3000, www.supremecourt.gov, Mon.-Fri. 9am-4:30pm, free). The Supreme Court is the highest court in the nation, and the current building was completed in 1935 (court was previously held in the Capitol Building). The main entrance faces the Capitol Building and welcomes visitors with a 252-foot-wide oval plaza. Fountains,

the U.S. Supreme Court

benches, and flagpoles are on either side of the plaza. Marble columns support the pediment on the Corinthian-style building.

The court building is open to the public during the week, and visitors are encouraged to listen to a variety of courtroom lectures when the Supreme Court is not sitting. Lectures are scheduled every hour on the half hour and begin at 9:30am. The final lecture of the day starts at 3:30pm. A calendar is online with the daily lecture schedule. Visitors can also take in exhibits focused on the work of the Supreme Court, the justices' lives, and the architecture of the Supreme Court building. When the court is sitting, visitors are welcome to see our justice system in action by attending oral arguments. Seating is limited and granted on a first-come, first-served basis and is available for an entire argument or for a three-minute viewing. Prior to the beginning of a session, two lines form in front of the courthouse outside on the plaza. One line is for those wishing to sit in on the entire argument, and the other is for those wishing to witness a three-minute sample.

All visitors are required to pass through a security screening that includes X-raying personal items and walking through metal detectors.

Library of Congress

It's hard to imagine that the original collection of books held by the **Library of Congress** (www.loc.gov) went up in flames during the War of 1812 when the British set fire to the Capitol Building where the collection was kept. Fortunately, Thomas Jefferson had a rather substantial collection of personal books with more than 6,500 volumes that he agreed to sell to Congress to rebuild the collection.

Today the Library of Congress, which is a research library and the country's oldest federal cultural institution, is contained in three government buildings on Capitol Hill and one building in Virginia. It is also the largest library in the world. Its collections include upward of 32 million cataloged books, 61 million manuscripts, more than one million U.S. government publications, one million newspapers from all over the world, and more than 120,000 comic books. Its publications are printed in 470 languages.

The main library building is the beautiful **Thomas Jefferson Building** (1st St. SE between Independence Ave. and E. Capitol St., 202/707-9779). This is the oldest building in the complex, having opened in 1897. This building is a feast for the eyes with its

DC's Skyline: Onward and Upward?

Unlike most large cities in the country, Washington DC has a low skyline. When the first skyscrapers were going up in the late 1800s elsewhere in the world, DC residents became concerned that if tall buildings were constructed in the city, Washington would lose its European feel. So in 1899, Congress passed the Heights of Buildings Act, which limited the vertical reach of buildings in the nation's capital to no more than 130 feet. This act was later amended (in 1910) to allow buildings to be 20 feet higher than the width of the adjacent street. The only exception is on Pennsylvania Avenue between 1st and 15th Streets. More than 100 years later, the act is now being reviewed for possible revision because the inability to expand the skyline upward has limited the city's tax base and potential for growth.

murals, mosaics, sculptures, and impressive main reading room containing 236 desks sitting under a 160-foot dome. A visitors center is located at the west front entrance (Mon.-Sat. 8:30am-4:30pm). Free one-hour guided tours are available, during which visitors can learn about the building's architecture and symbolic art. Tours are given Monday-Friday 10:30am-3:30pm and Saturday 10:30am-2:30pm.

The other two library buildings on Capitol Hill are the nearby **John Adams Building** (2nd St. SE between Independence Ave. and E. Capitol St.) and the **James Madison Memorial Building** (between 1st and 2nd Sts. on Independence Ave. SE). The latter is home to the **Mary Pickford Theater,** which is the "motion picture and television reading room" of the library.

The library primarily exists as a research tool for answering inquiries from members of Congress through the Congressional Research Service. The library is open to the public, but only library employees, members of Congress, and other top-level government officials can actually check books out.

U.S. Botanic Garden

A lovely contrast to memorials, office buildings, and monuments, the **U.S. Botanic Garden** (100 Maryland Ave. SW, 202/225-8333, www.usbg.gov, daily 10am-5pm, free) is the oldest continually operating garden of its type in the country. Just southwest of the Capitol, this national greenhouse opened in 1850 and has been in its current location since 1933. Major attractions at the garden include a rose garden, butterfly garden, the First Ladies' Water Garden, the Lawn Terrace, and an outdoor amphitheater. The garden houses nearly 10,000 living specimens; the oldest are more than 165 years old.

Smithsonian National Postal Museum

A lesser-known Smithsonian Institution museum is the **National Postal Museum** (2 Massachusetts Ave. NE, 202/633-5555, daily 10am-5:30pm, free). Located near Union Station, the museum contains exhibits of stamps and philatelic items, mail delivery vehicles, and historical artifacts from America's postal system.

DOWNTOWN

National Archives

Only in Washington DC can you see the original Declaration of Independence, the Constitution, and the Bill of Rights. These powerful documents live in the Rotunda for the Charters of Freedom at the **National Archives Building** (700 Pennsylvania Ave. NW, visitors entrance on Constitution Ave. between 7th and 9th Sts. NW, 866/272-6272, www.archives.gov, daily 10am-5:30pm, extended summer hours, free). They can be viewed by the public daily, but are then lowered into the vault for safekeeping after hours.

Also known as Archives I, the National Archives Building is the headquarters for the National Archives and Records

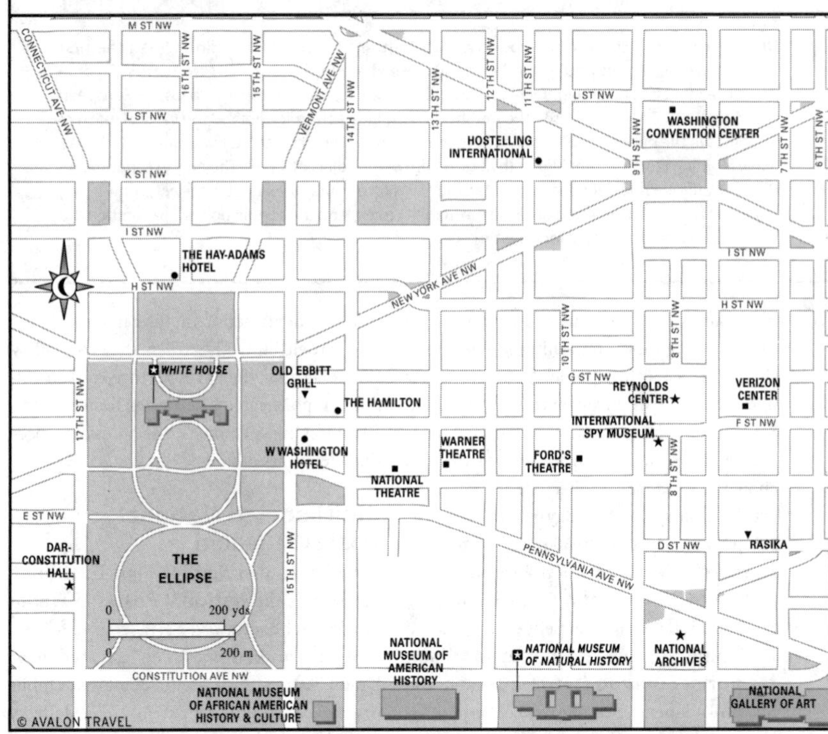

Administration, an independent agency of the U.S. government that is responsible for preserving historical records. Countless additional documents are on permanent exhibit in the public vaults, including treaties, photographs, telegrams, maps, and films. Interactive exhibits allow visitors to get close to some of the most interesting documents.

The Newseum

The Newseum (555 Pennsylvania Ave. NW, 202/292-6100, www.newseum.org, daily 9am-5pm, $22.95 plus tax) is a 250,000-square-foot museum dedicated to 500 years of news history. It stands at Pennsylvania Avenue and 6th Street NW, adjacent to the Smithsonian museums. The exterior is easy to identify: It features a wall of glass and a 74-foot-tall marble engraving of the First Amendment.

The Newseum has seven levels and includes 15 galleries, theaters, visitor services, and retail space. Topics such as news history, photojournalism, news coverage related to historical events, and electronic news are explored in the galleries. The largest features a collection of more than 30,000 historic newspapers. Some exhibits in the museum contain strong images involving topics such as death and hate and can therefore be upsetting to children.

Reynolds Center

The revitalized Penn Quarter area of downtown gets more and more hip each year as space is renovated and new attractions move in. A prime example is the Smithsonian's **Reynolds Center** (8th and F Sts. NW, 202/633-1000, www.americanart.si.edu, daily 11:30am-7pm, free) that covers an entire block in the Chinatown neighborhood in what was one of the first patent office buildings. The Reynolds Center is officially named the **Donald W. Reynolds Center for American Art and Portraiture,** and it consists of two recently renovated Smithsonian museums, the **Smithsonian American Art Museum** and the **National Portrait Gallery.** The massive Greek Revival building dates back to 1836 and originally took 31 years to construct. The Smithsonian American Art Museum features a wide variety of American art and houses works by significant artists such Georgia O'Keeffe, Albert Bierstadt, and Nam June Paik. The National Portrait Gallery contains images of many famous Americans. The museums are above the Gallery Place-Chinatown Metrorail station on the Red, Yellow, and Green Lines.

International Spy Museum

Enter the world of espionage at the only public museum in the country dedicated to professional spies. The **International Spy Museum** (800 F St. NW, 202/393-7798, www.spymuseum.org, hours vary by season but open most days 10am-6pm, $21.95) is another great museum in Penn Quarter. Privately owned, this interesting museum houses the largest collection of international artifacts geared toward the secret world of spies. Exhibits focus on some of the most secretive missions across the globe and strive to educate the public about their role in historic events.

The museum features artifacts created specifically for intelligence services (think lipstick pistols, disguises, and Enigma cipher machines) and brings them to life in state-of-the-art exhibits, interactive computer programs, audiovisual programs, and hands-on learning. Their ever-evolving collections keep this an exciting place to visit and include everything from an Exquisitely Evil exhibit on James Bond villains to an Argo Exposed exhibit with details about the real man behind the true story of *Argo.* Plan on spending a minimum of two hours here.

National Building Museum

If architecture, building, and design intrigue you, the **National Building Museum** (401 F St. NW, 202/272-2448, www.nbm.org, Mon.-Sat. 10am-5pm, Sun. 11am-5pm, $10) is a must see. As the country's leading cultural institution committed to interpreting the impact and history of the "built environment," this family-friendly museum

the Newseum

offers exhibits, public programs, and festivals. The museum itself is a spectacular building with an impressive Great Hall that contains 75-foot Corinthian columns, and a 1,200-foot terra-cotta frieze. Exhibits include *House & Home,* which provides a tour of familiar and surprising homes and *Play Work Build,* an exploration exhibit that allows children and adults to fill an exhibition wall with virtual blocks and then knock them down.

Ford's Theatre National Historic Site and Center for Education and Leadership

Still a thriving theatrical venue, the famous **Ford's Theatre** (511 10th St. NW, 202/347-4833, www.fordstheatre.org, daily 9am-4pm, $3) is the site where President Lincoln was assassinated on April 14, 1865. It also houses a museum focusing on Abraham Lincoln's presidency, assassination, and legacy as well as an education center. Artifacts featured in the museum include the contents of Lincoln's pockets on the day he died, the single-shot .44-caliber derringer that John Wilkes Booth used to kill Lincoln, and two life masks. The education center has a 34-foot tower full of books on Lincoln, accessible by a winding staircase. The books in the tower are made from aluminum and represent 205 real titles on Lincoln. This unusual work of art symbolizes that the last word about Lincoln will never be written.

There are two suggested itineraries for visiting the theater. If you have limited time, the Museum and Ranger Talk, lasting approximately one hour and 15 minutes, includes a self-guided tour of the museum and a 30-minute presentation, given by a National Park Service ranger, inside the theater itself. The presentation covers key facts regarding President Lincoln's assassination. If you have two hours and 15 minutes to devote to the theater, you can take in the Full Ford's Theatre Experience. This includes a theatrical audio tour of the theater (for an additional $5), a self-guided museum tour, a 30-minute presentation by a ranger, a self-guided tour of the Petersen House across the street (15 minutes), where Lincoln was tended to after the shooting and died, and exploration of the **Center for Education and Leadership** (514 10th St., adjacent to the Petersen House, allow 45 minutes), where exhibits explain the aftermath of the assassination including the hunt for John Wilkes Booth and the funeral route. Ford's Theatre is located in the Penn Quarter area.

I Got You Babe

Just southwest of Dupont Circle on New Hampshire Avenue is a small, triangular wedge of land that memorializes pop star and politician **Sonny Bono.** Officially called Sonny Bono Park, the patch of grass has benches and a plaque (that draws a striking resemblance to a manhole cover) honoring the late statesman who died in a ski accident in 1998.

DUPONT CIRCLE

Dupont Circle Park

Maintained by the National Park Service, the **Dupont Circle Park** has been the location of many political rallies, and it is also a gathering place for chess players to challenge one another on permanent stone chessboards (one of the top players there is a formerly homeless man who became a renowned national chess player). The central double-tiered white marble fountain, installed in 1920, offers seating; it replaced a memorial statue of Samuel Francis Du Pont, a rear admiral during the Civil War that was placed there in 1884. The fountain was designed by the cocreators of the Lincoln Memorial and represents the sea, stars, and wind.

The Phillips Collection

The Dupont Circle neighborhood is home to the original late 19th-century Renoir painting *Luncheon of the Boating Party.* It lives at **The Phillips Collection** (1600 21st St. NW, 202/387-2151, www.phillipscollection.org, Tues.-Sat. 10am-5pm, Sun. 12pm-7pm, $12), an intimate impressionist and modern art

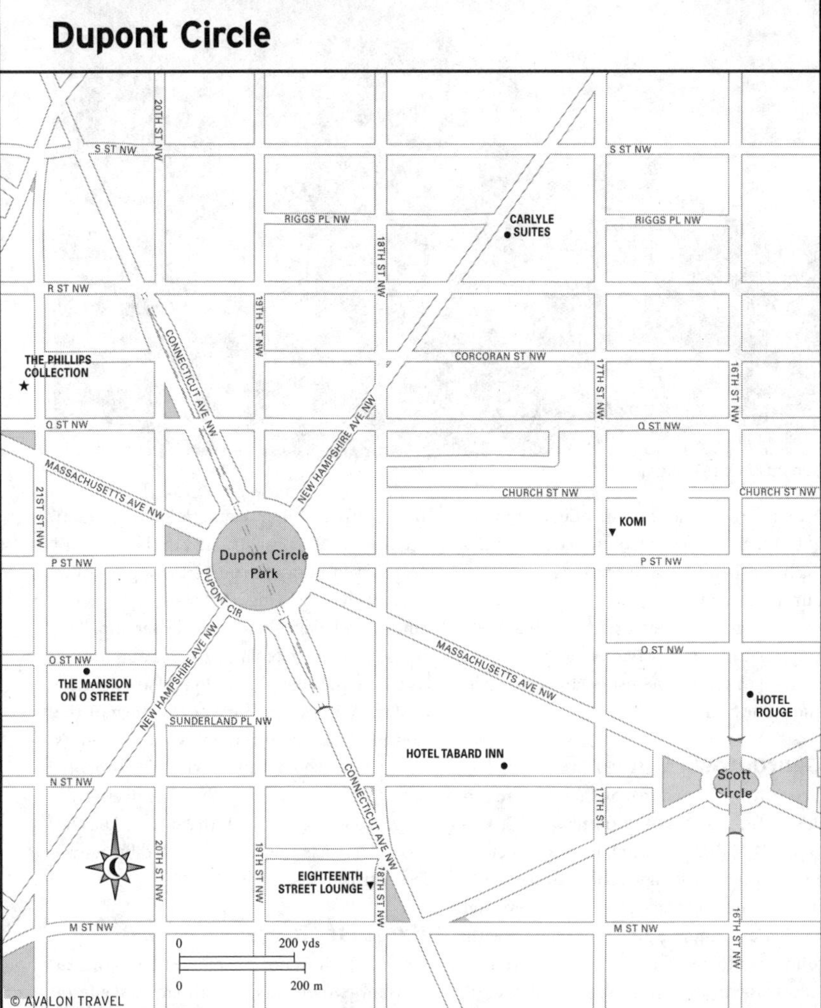

museum founded in 1921 by Duncan Phillips. The museum includes the founder's former home and extensive new galleries. Other featured works (there are more than 3,000) include pieces by Vincent Van Gogh, Claude Monet, Pablo Picasso, Georgia O'Keeffe, and Winslow Homer.

GEORGETOWN

Dumbarton Oaks

The **Dumbarton Oaks Research Library and Collection** (1703 32nd St. NW, 202/339-6401, www.doaks.org, museum Tues.-Sun. 11:30am-5:30pm, free, gardens Tues.-Sun. Nov. 1-Mar. 14 2pm-5pm, free, Mar. 15-Oct. 31 2pm-6pm, $10) is a gorgeous, historic, and romantic estate museum and garden. It was a private estate for many years before being donated to Harvard University in 1940. The estate was the site of a series of important diplomatic meetings in 1944 that laid the foundation for the development of the United

Dupont Circle neighborhood

Nations. Today the museum offers exhibitions of Byzantine and pre-Columbian art (including more than 12,000 Byzantine coins); Asian, European, and American art; and European furnishings. The 10-acre park boasts a fine example of a European-style formal garden, with more than 1,000 rosebushes, an herb garden, and stone fountains.

Georgetown University

Georgetown is anchored by the 104-acre campus of **Georgetown University** (37th and O Sts. NW, 202/687-0100, www.georgetown.edu). Noted for its law school in particular, this private research university offers eight graduate and undergraduate schools with a total enrollment of around 15,000 students. Georgetown was established in 1789 and is the oldest Catholic and Jesuit university in the country. Notable alumni include President Bill Clinton and the late U.S. Supreme Court justice Antonin Scalia.

Old Stone House

The oldest standing building in DC, and also the city's last pre-Revolutionary colonial building still on its original foundation, was built in 1765 and is simply called the **Old Stone House** (3051 M St. NW, 202/426-6851, www.nps.gov/olst, Wed.-Sun. noon-5pm, free). This excellent example of vernacular architecture was constructed in three phases and served many purposes throughout the years including being a hat shop, tailor, locksmith, and even a used car dealership. The house was renovated in the 1950s and turned into a museum by the National Park Service. Today, visitors can learn the history of the house from park rangers and view the home's kitchen, bedrooms, and parlor, all authentically furnished to reflect the daily lives of average Americans in the 18th century. The Old Stone House is said to be haunted by countless spirits.

Exorcist Stairs

One of the most notable movie scenes filmed in Georgetown was the climactic scene in *The Exorcist,* where the priest hurls himself out the window of a house and down a steep staircase to his death to rid himself of the devil. The famed staircase is still part of the Georgetown landscape and has 75 steps that connect Prospect Street with M Street. There are three landings on the staircase and the entire length of the stairs is equal to the height of a five-story building. For filming purposes, a fake front was constructed on the house located at the top of the steps to make it appear that the bedroom in the movie overlooked the

Georgetown

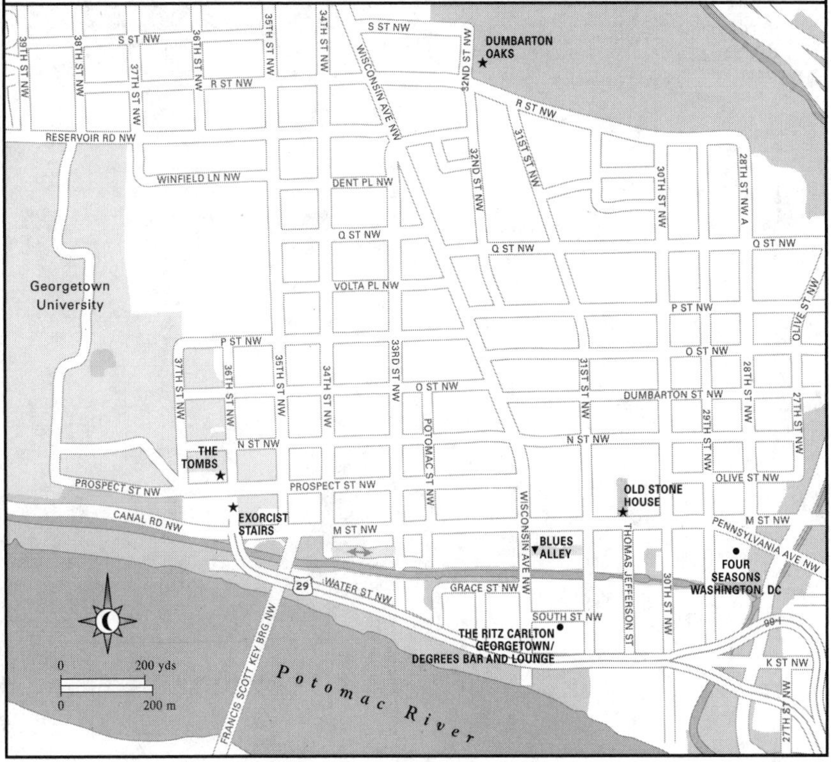

staircase. In real life, the home is set back a healthy distance from the top of the stairs. It is not uncommon to see Georgetown students running the stairs. Hoya athletes are known to run it 10 or more times. The steps are located at the end of 36th Street.

ADAMS MORGAN

Meridian Hill Park

Meridian Hill Park (15th, 16th, W, and Euclid Sts. NW, free) is a 12-acre urban park maintained by the National Park Service. It is near Adams Morgan in the Columbia Heights neighborhood. The park was built in the early 1900s and sits on a hillside. It is well landscaped and includes dramatic staircases, benches, and concrete walkways. The focal point of the park is a 13-basin cascading waterfall fountain in a formal garden. There are also a number of statues in the park. This is a popular place to steal some relaxation in the summer, and many people take advantage of this secret little garden in the city. Drummers form circles on Sunday afternoons in the summertime, but people come to spread a blanket and play catch nearly all year.

UPPER NORTHWEST

★ National Cathedral

Many visitors are filled with awe when they see the beautiful gothic **National Cathedral** (3101 Wisconsin Ave. NW, 202/537-6200, www.nationalcathedral.org, Mon.-Fri. 10am-5:30pm, Sat. 10am-4:30pm, Sun. 1pm-4pm,

Adams Morgan and Upper Northwest

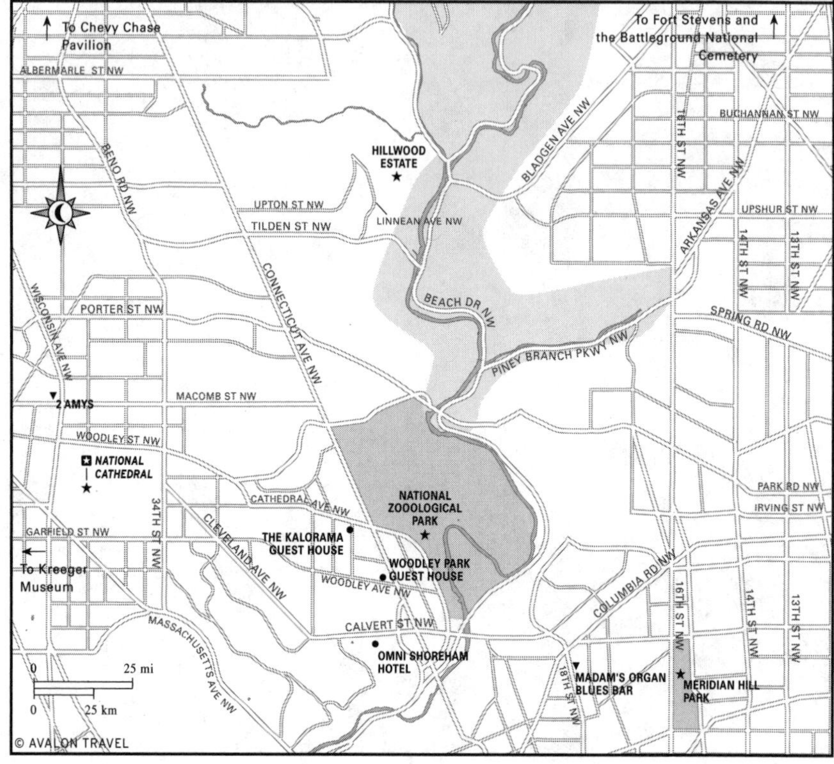

$11). This imposing edifice, which is the sixth-largest cathedral in the world, is hard to miss. It took 83 years (1907 to 1990) to carve the 150,000 tons of stone, and this impressive building has a few tricks up its sleeve. A tour is a must (they offer 16 different ones), since the great docents will provide you access to the towers and crypt that are off limits should you try to go there on your own. Although the regular tours are impressive, the behind-the-scenes tour ($26) is the best. You'll walk through hidden hallways, get a close look at the stunning stained glass windows, and learn the cathedral's secrets (like how Darth Vader lives high on the northwest tower in the form of a grotesque that was sculpted after a public competition was held to suggest designs for grotesques and gargoyles). You'll also get a grand view from the cathedral's roof. Be ready for stair climbing, heights, and close quarters. Participants must be at least 11 years old. Reservations can be made online.

Organ demonstrations are given on most Mondays and Wednesdays at 12:30pm. They are impressive and loud. Regular Episcopal worship services are held at the cathedral; a schedule is posted on the website. A café (Mon.-Fri. 7am-6pm, Sat.-Sun. 8am-6pm) is located in the Old Baptistry building next to the cathedral where the public can purchase light fare such as sandwiches, coffee, and pastries. Parking is available under the cathedral.

Rock Creek Park

It's hard to believe that with all DC has to offer in such a small area, there's room for a

the National Cathedral

1,754-acre park. **Rock Creek Park** (202/895-6070, www.nps.gov/rocr, open during daylight hours, free) is a prime recreation area in the city that offers running, walking, equestrian, and cycling trails, a golf course, a professional tennis stadium, a nature center and planetarium, an outdoor concert venue, playground facilities, wildlife, and cultural exhibits. The park is administered by the National Park Service.

Visitors can enjoy a real sense of outdoors in this urban park, which consists of woods, fields, and creeks and is home to wildflowers and wildlife such as coyotes, beavers, and fox. The park borders Upper Northwest DC to the east and has long stretches of roads (including Rock Creek Parkway and Beach Drive) that are closed to cars on weekends. Fifteen miles of hiking trails, a bike path that runs the entire length of the park and connects the Lincoln Memorial to the Maryland border, and horseback riding from **Rock Creek Park Horse Center** (5100 Glover Rd., 202/362-0117, www.rockcreekhorsecenter.com, Mon.-Fri. 10am-6pm, Sat.-Sun. 9am-5pm, lessons $50-90 per hour, one-hour trail rides $40) are just some of the activities available to visitors. The park's **Nature Center** (5200 Glover Rd., 202/895-6070, Wed.-Sun. 9am-5pm) is a good place to start your exploration. Another attraction is the **Peirce Mill** (2401 Tilden St. NW at Beach Dr., 202/895-6070, Apr.-Oct. Wed.-Sun. 10am-4pm, Nov.-Mar. Sat.-Sun. 12pm-4pm). It is the only existing water-powered gristmill in DC.

The park is relatively safe for a city park, but it is still advisable to enjoy it with a friend. Leashed dogs are allowed in the park. It is good to keep in mind that on weekdays Rock Creek Parkway is one-way going south between 6:45am and 9:30am and one-way going north 3:45pm-6:30pm.

National Zoological Park

The Smithsonian's **National Zoological Park** (3001 Connecticut Ave., 202/633-2614, www.nationalzoo.si.edu, daily Oct. 1-Mar. 14, grounds 8am-5pm, visitor center and exhibit buildings 9am-4pm, Mar. 15-Sept. 30 grounds 8am-7pm, visitor center and exhibit buildings 9am-6pm, free), commonly called the National Zoo, is one of the oldest zoos in the country. The 163-acre park is near the Woodley Park Metrorail station on the edge of Rock Creek Park. The zoo, founded in 1889, is constantly undergoing updates and renovations. Hundreds of animals are tucked into habitats along hillsides, in the woods, and in specially built temperature-controlled animal houses. Since entrance to the park is free, many local residents use the several miles of nicely paved pathways on their regular walking or running routes.

Well-known residents include giant pandas from China, great apes, elephants, Komodo dragons, and much more. Many of the species at the zoo are endangered. Unique exhibits include the Elephant Walk, where Asian elephants can take daily treks for exercise, and a skywalk for orangutans where a series of high cables and towers allow them to move between two buildings and over spectators below. Another favorite is the newly completed American Trail, which features sea lions, wolves, eagles, and other animals native to North America. The zoo also features a Think Tank, where visitors can learn how animals think through a series of interactive displays that are available to the zoo's orangutans at their leisure. The best time to visit the zoo is on weekday mornings when there are fewer crowds and the animals are more active. Although it is free to enter the zoo, there is a parking fee.

Hillwood Estate, Museum & Gardens

Those in the know are fans of the wonderful **Hillwood Estate, Museum & Gardens** (4155 Linnean Ave. NW, 202/686-5807, www.hillwoodmuseum.org, Tues.-Sun. 10am-5pm, $18), the former home of prominent businesswoman, philanthropist, and heiress to the Post Cereal fortune, Marjorie Merriweather Post. This stately and luxurious home with a Georgian-style facade was purchased by Post in 1955 and used for entertaining and to house her abundant collections of French and Russian art, including an extraordinary collection of Fabergé eggs. The artwork is rivaled by the exquisite French and Japanese-style gardens where visitors can relax after taking a tour. One-hour guided tours (11:30am and 1:30pm) and self-guided tours are available with the price of admission. A café and gift shop are on-site.

Kreeger Museum

The **Kreeger Museum** (2401 Foxhall Rd. NW, 202/338-3552, www.kreegermuseum.org, Fri. and Sat. 10am-4pm, Tues. and Thurs. tours by reservation, $10, sculpture garden Tues.-Sat. 10am-4pm, free) is a private museum that often passes under the radar of tourists due to its Foxhall neighborhood location and small size. This little gem of an attraction features 19th- and 20th-century sculptures and paintings by many world-renowned artists such as Monet, Picasso, Rodin, and Van Gogh. It also offers works by local artists and traditional African art. The building is the former home of David and Carmen Kreeger and sits on more than five acres of sculpture gardens and woods.

Battleground National Cemetery

One of the smallest national cemeteries in the nation is the **Battleground National Cemetery** (6600 block of Georgia Ave., 202/895-6000, www.nps.gov, daily dawn-dusk, free). It is the burial ground for 41 Union soldiers who died in the 1864 Battle of Fort Stevens, the sole Civil War battle to take place in DC. The engagement marked the end of a Confederate effort to act offensively against the national capital. The battle is the only one in Civil War history during which the U.S. president (Abraham Lincoln) came under direct fire. Lincoln rode out to observe the fight and was fired on briefly by sharpshooters (he was then ordered to take cover). After the battle, a one-acre plot of farmland was seized and used to bury the dead. That night, Lincoln came to the site and dedicated it as a national cemetery. Visitors can see grave markers, four monuments to the units that fought in the battle, and a marble rostrum that has eight Doric columns. The rostrum is the site of the annual Memorial Day services at the cemetery. The National Park Service manages the cemetery.

Nearby **Fort Stevens** (1339 Fort Stevens Dr., 202/290-1048, www.nps.gov, daily dawn-dusk, free), the actual site of the battle, is partially restored and is also maintained by the National Park Service. It was part of a series of fortifications constructed around Washington

DC during the Civil War. Visitors can see much of the fort still intact, including the cannons (now facing urban streets). You can even stand in the spot where then future Supreme Court justice Oliver Wendell Holmes is said to have shouted at President Lincoln, "Get down, you fool!" when he was shot at.

NORTHEAST DC

National Arboretum

Northeast of Capitol Hill (2.2 miles from the Capitol Building) is a little-recognized attraction that first opened in 1927: the **National Arboretum** (3501 New York Ave. NE, 202/245-2726, www.usna.usda.gov, daily 8am-5pm, free). This lovely 446-acre campus has more than nine miles of roads that connect many gardens and plant collections where there is always something in bloom. Seventy-six staff members and more than 140 volunteers oversee the arboretum, which was created to "serve the public need for scientific research, education, and gardens that conserve and showcase plants to enhance the environment." Parking areas are available near many of the major collections and bike racks are also on hand. The original 22 columns from the east side of the Capitol Building found a home here when the Capitol was enlarged in the 1950s; they now sit on display in a field. The **National Bonsai & Penjing Museum** (daily 10am-4pm, free) is also located on the arboretum grounds, as is a gift shop. Leashed pets are welcome, and there are public restrooms in the administrative building.

TOURS

A great way to see the city is to take an organized tour. There are a wide variety available to choose from including trolley tours, boat tours, and walking tours.

Trolley, Bus, and Boat Tours

One of the most popular motorized tours in the city is given by **Old Town Trolley** (202/832-9800, www.trolleytours.com, daily 9am-5pm, $39). This lively narrated tour covers more than 100 points of interest and offers a "hop on-hop off" format where guests can get off at 20 stops and pick up another trolley (which stops at each location every 30 minutes) at their leisure. Sights include the Lincoln Memorial, Georgetown, the White House, Smithsonian Institution museums, and many more. No reservations are required, and visitors can board and reboard all day. Tickets can be purchased online or at the sales desk in **Union Station** (50 Massachusetts Ave. NE, stop #4) and at the **Washington Welcome Center** (1005 E St. NW, stop #1).

Old Town Trolley also offers a 2.5-hour **Monuments by Moonlight** ($39) tour that allows visitors to see the illuminated monuments and memorials. Stops include the FDR Memorial, Iwo Jima Memorial (in Arlington, Virginia), the Lincoln Memorial, and Vietnam Veterans Memorial. This narrated tour includes some fun ghost stories as well. The tour leaves nightly from Union Station.

Old Town Trolley tours cover more than 100 points of interest.

A third tour through Old Town Trolley that is also popular is their **DC Ducks Tour** (daily 10am-4pm, $39). Guests explore the city on both land and water in a fully restored 1942 "Duck," a unique vehicle that is part bus, part boat. Ninety-minute trips start at Union Station (50 Massachusetts Ave. NE), drive to the National Mall, and end with a cruise along the Potomac River. The tours are narrated by "wise-quacking" captains who offer a wealth of historical facts and corny jokes.

Another "hop on-hop off" tour is the **Open Top Big Bus Tour** (877/332-8689, www.bigbustours.com, daily 9am-4pm, 24 hours $36, 48 hours $44). Guests can take in four routes around the city from a double-decker bus with an open-air top deck. Tickets are available for 24 and 48 hours. Tickets can be purchased online and on any of their buses.

For a view from the water, take an hour-long **DC Cruise** (301/765-0750, www.dccruises.com, $22-25) along the Potomac River. Riders will see the Kennedy Center and many monuments along the way. Cruises leave from Washington Harbor at the foot of 31st Street.

Walking Tours

Free guided walking tours of DC's monuments are available through **DC By Foot** (202/370-1830, www.freetoursbyfoot.com/dc, free but tips appreciated). These unique tours feature animated, energetic tour guides who work purely on tips. Because of this, they do their best to entertain you while providing unique stories about Washington's most famous residents. Private tours are also available.

Ghost tours are a good way to get in touch with the spirits of the city. Several tour operators offer walking tours around some of the most haunted sites in the city. **Washington Walks** (1799 New York Ave. NW, 202/484-1565, www.washingtonwalks.com, $20) offers **Most Haunted Houses** tours (Apr.-Oct. Thurs.-Sat. at 7:30pm). Two-hour walking tours begin at the corner of New York Avenue and 18th Street NW. No reservations are necessary.

Entertainment and Events

THEATER

The premier theater in Washington DC is the **John F. Kennedy Center for the Performing Arts** (2700 F St. NW, 202/467-4600, www.kennedy-center.org). This incredible venue is a landmark on the banks of the Potomac River and first opened in 1971. It hosts more annual performances than any other facility in the country, with approximately 2,000 theater, dance, musical, and multimedia performances each year. There are three primary theaters within the center. The **Concert Hall** seats approximately 2,400 guests and is the largest performance space in the center. It features seven Hadeland crystal chandeliers (courtesy of Norway) and a 4,144-pipe organ (a gift from the Filene Foundation of Boston). The Concert Hall is also home to the **National Symphony Orchestra** (202/467-4600, www.kennedy-center.org). The **Opera House,** with its unique red and gold silk curtain (a gift from Japan), seats approximately 2,300 guests and features a Lobmeyr crystal chandelier (courtesy of Austria). It is the primary venue for opera, ballet, and large-scale musical performances and home to the **Washington National Opera** (202/467-4600, www.kennedy-center.org), the **Suzanne Farrell Ballet** (202/467-4600, www.kennedy-center.org), and the yearly **Kennedy Center Honors.** The **Eisenhower Theater** seats approximately 1,163 guests and hosts smaller-scale operas, plays, and musicals. Public parking is available under the center.

The historic **National Theatre** (1321 Pennsylvania Ave. NW, 202/628-6161, www.nationaltheatre.org) playhouse is the oldest

the National Theatre

theater venue in DC. It is three blocks from the White House and has entertained many presidents since its founding in 1835. In fact, Abraham Lincoln's son Tad was attending a production of *Aladdin and the Wonderful Lamp* at the National Theatre at the time his father was assassinated in Ford's Theatre. Today the theater is known for hosting mostly Broadway musicals.

Originally built as a movie palace in 1924, the **Warner Theatre** (513 13th St. NW, 202/783-4000, www.warnertheatredc.com) was then called the Earle Theatre and hosted live vaudeville and silent movies. During the 1940s the theater showed movies exclusively and was renamed for its owner, Harry Warner of Warner Brothers fame. The theater suffered in the 1970s, but was revived shortly after as a concert venue. After major renovations between 1989 and 1992, the theater reopened with theatrical, dance, and musical productions and has since hosted great performers such as Frank Sinatra. It is a landmark in the Penn Quarter neighborhood.

Nearby, **Ford's Theatre** (511 10th St. NW, 202/347-4833, www.fordstheatre.org) is most famous as the location of the assassination of President Lincoln in 1865. Following his death, the theater closed. After a long stint as a warehouse and an office building, it finally reopened more than 100 years later in 1968 and again began to host performances. Today it is an active venue with a full schedule of plays and musicals.

A well-known regional theater company in DC is the **Shakespeare Theatre Company** (202/547-1122, www.shakespearetheatre.org). This highly regarded company presents primarily Shakespearian productions but also offers works by other classic playwrights. The company manages the **Harman Center for the Arts,** which consists of two venues in Penn Quarter, the **Landsburgh Theatre** (450 7th St. NW) and **Sidney Harman Hall** (610 F St. NW).

For more experimental, cutting-edge performances, catch a production by the **Woolly Mammoth Theatre Company** (641 D St. NW, 202/393-3939, www.woollymammoth.net). They develop and produce new plays and pride themselves on being "Washington's most daring theatre company."

In Southwest DC, **Arena Stage at the Mead Center for American Theater** (1101 6th St. SW, 202/488-3300, www.arenastage.org) takes the title of being the largest not-for-profit theater in the city. It features a broad range of performances including the classics and new play premiers as well as educational programs.

A unique performance venue is the **Carter Barron Amphitheatre** (4850 Colorado Ave. NW, 202/426-0486, www.nps.gov/rocr) in Rock Creek Park. The beautiful 4,200-seat outdoor amphitheater is operated by the National Park Service and offers a range of performances including concerts, theater, and dance. Many are provided at no charge.

The historic **Uptown Theatre** (3426 Connecticut Ave. NW, 202/966-8805, www.amctheatres.com) is a single-screen movie theater in the Cleveland Park neighborhood run by AMC Loews. The theater first opened in 1936 and has been the site for many Hollywood movie premieres. The curved, 70-foot-long and 40-foot-high screen is considered to be the best in the DC area, and the theater can seat 850 people.

ARENAS AND HALLS

There are several large performance arenas in the city. The **Verizon Center** (601 F St. NW, 202/628-3200, www.verizoncenter.com), which anchors the Penn Quarter neighborhood, is home to several professional sports teams (Washington Capitals, Washington Wizards, and Washington Mystics), but also hosts numerous concerts and other large-scale performances. The **Robert F. Kennedy Memorial Stadium (RFK)** (2400 E. Capitol St. SE, 202/587-5000, www.dcunited.com) is the former home of the Washington Redskins and now hosts rock concerts, conventions, and other events. It is also the home field for the D.C. United professional soccer team. RFK Stadium is just east of Capitol Hill.

The historic **DAR Constitution Hall** (1776 D St. NW, 202/628-1776, www.dar.org), near the White House, was built in 1929 by the Daughters of the American Revolution as a venue for their annual convention. This 3,200-seat hall, which formerly only hosted classical shows and opera, is now a concert venue for rock, pop, hip-hop, and soul.

The 2.3 million-square-foot **Walter E. Washington Convention Center** (801 Mt. Vernon Place NW, 202/249-3000, www.dcconvention.com) offers 703,000 square feet of event space, 77 meeting rooms, and the largest ballroom in the city. It hosts countless events throughout the year in the Downtown area.

MUSIC VENUES

The **U Street Corridor** can be called the center of the music scene in Washington DC. Once the haunt of legends such as Duke Ellington, the area carries on his legacy through venues such as **Bohemian Caverns** (2001 11th St. NW, 202/299-0800, www.bohemiancaverns.com), which is known as DC's premier jazz club and one of the oldest jazz clubs in the nation, having opened in 1926. It is at the same address today as it was back then, but was originally in the basement under a pharmacy (it is still downstairs but there's a traditional club upstairs). Although the club has not operated continuously over its long history, it has seen many notable performers including Miles Davis and Bill Evans. Today the club anchors Washington's jazz community. It hosts many headline national performers and local performers, and it has its own jazz orchestra. It is also an integral part of the city's annual jazz festival.

Twins Jazz (1344 U St. NW, top floor, 202/234-0072, www.twinsjazz.com) is another good choice for live jazz, which is offered 5-6 nights a week. This unassuming club with red interior walls looks like someone's home on the outside. It also features Ethiopian, Caribbean, and American food.

For a broader range of music options, the popular **9:30 Club** (815 V St. NW, 202/265-0930, www.930.com) hosts everyone from Echo and the Bunnymen to Corey Smith. This unassuming-looking venue is on the corner of 9th and V Streets. Shows are general admission and standing room only. They have four full bars and a coffee bar, and also serve food.

The **Black Cat** (1811 14th St. NW, 202/667-4490, www.blackcatdc.com) hosts a variety of local, national, and international independent and alternative bands. They offer two stages and are a cash-only establishment.

Two small venues that highlight primarily local bands are the **Velvet Lounge** (915 U St. NW, 202/462-3213, www.velvetloungedc.com) and **DC9** (1940 9th St. NW, 202/483-5000, www.dcnine.com).

Other areas of the city entertain great musical artists as well. An intimate venue for hearing live jazz is **Blues Alley** (1073 Wisconsin Ave. NW, 202/337-4141, www.bluesalley.com) in Georgetown. This local landmark consistently delivers quality jazz and a fun atmosphere. They serve food, but the main attraction is the music.

U Street Corridor

W ST NW
V ST NW
U ST NW
WALLACH PL NW
NW 14TH ST
13TH ST NW
12TH ST NW
11TH ST NW
10TH ST NW
9TH ST NW
8TH ST NW
NW FLORIDA AVE
VERMONT AVE NW
FLORIDA AVE NW
BUSBOYS AND POETS
TWINS JAZZ
BEN'S CHILI BOWL
BOHEMIAN CAVERNS
9:30 CLUB
0 200 yds
0 200 m
© AVALON TRAVEL

Two blocks from the White House, **The Hamilton** (600 14th St. NW, 202/787-1000, www.thehamiltondc.com) hosts visionary musical performers in an intimate setting.

NIGHTLIFE

Downtown

For the chance to rub elbows with celebrities, professional athletes, and young, hip Washingtonians, grab a drink at the downtown **P.O.V. Roof Terrace and Lounge** at the **W Washington D.C. Hotel** (515 15th St. NW, 202/661-2400, www.starwoodhotels.com, Sun.-Thurs. 11am-midnight, Fri.-Sat. 11am-2am). This rooftop bar and terrace is one of the top hot spots in DC and has phenomenal views of the city through 12-foot-tall windows. They serve premium-brand liquor and a tapas menu. No sneakers or athletic wear are permitted; collared shirts are preferred. Expect a wait to get in on weekends.

Perfect martinis and a more relaxed atmosphere can be found across from the White House at the **Off the Record Bar** (800 16th

W Washington D.C. Hotel

Best Rooftop Bars

There may be no better way to soak up the vibe of the city than by grabbing a cool drink on a summer evening at a rooftop bar. Following are some of the most popular DC bars and lounges with a bird's-eye view:

- The **DNV Rooftop Bar** (1155 14th St. NW, 202/379-4366, www.zentanrestaurant.com) is in The Donovan hotel in Thomas Circle at the intersection of Massachusetts Avenue, Vermont Avenue, 14th Street, and M Street NW. This lively poolside lounge offers chaise lounges, a full-service bar, Asian food, panoramic views, and great martinis.
- Take in views of Embassy Row and the Dupont Circle neighborhood from the **Sky Bar** at the **Beacon Bar and Grill** (1615 Rhode Island Ave. NW, 202/872-1126, www.bbgwdc.com). They offer full bar service and light fare.
- A lively rooftop bar located in a Mexican restaurant in the U Street Corridor is **El Centro D.F.** (1819 14th St., 202/328-3131, www.richardsandoval.com). Their two-level rooftop has two bars and 200 types of tequila.
- Another U Street neighborhood favorite is **Marvin** (2007 14th St. NW, 202/797-7171, www.marvindc.com). Their rooftop beer garden offers more than 30 Belgian ales and blondes.
- The largest open-air seating area in Adams Morgan is at **Perry's Restaurant** (1811 Columbia Rd. NW, 202/234-6218, www.perrysadamsmorgan.com). They have good happy hour specials, views of the city, and a fun rooftop atmosphere.
- One of "the" places to go in DC is the **P.O.V. Roof Terrace and Lounge** at the **W Washington D.C. Hotel** (515 15th St. NW, 202/661-2400, www.povrooftop.com). This rooftop bar and terrace is one of the top hot spots in DC and has phenomenal views of the city through 12-foot-tall windows.

St. NW, 202/695-1761, www.hayadams.com, Sun.-Thurs. 11:30am-midnight, Fri.-Sat. 11:30am-12:30am) at the Hay-Adams Hotel.

Just a little west of Downtown and a little south of Dupont Circle on M Street is **Ozio Restaurant and Lounge** (1813 M St. NW, 202/822-6000, www.oziodc.com, Tues.-Thurs. 5pm-2am, Fri. 5pm-3am, Sat. 6pm-3am, Sun. 12pm-2am). This huge, multilevel club is somewhat upscale and often has a business crowd. They have great martinis, cigars, and a lively rooftop lounge.

Dupont Circle

One of the most exclusive nightlife spots in the city is the **Eighteenth Street Lounge** (1212 18th St. NW, 202/696-0210, www.eighteenthstreetlounge.com, Tues.-Thurs. 5:30pm-2am, Fri. 5:30pm-3am, Sat. 9:30pm-3am, Sun. 9pm-2am) in the former home of Teddy Roosevelt. This restored row house mansion is classy, and you must be dressed appropriately to enter. There are high ceilings, a dance floor, retro decor, and multiple rooms, each with its own theme and bar.

The **Bar Rouge** (1315 16th St. NW, 202/232-8000, www.rougehotel.com, daily 5pm-10:30pm) in the Hotel Rouge is a popular choice for happy hour and evening cocktails. This sleek, modern lounge has good happy hour specials on weekdays. They also serve food.

A lively Latin American scene can be found at **Café Citron** (1343 Connecticut Ave. NW, 202/530-8844, www.cafecitrondc.com, Mon.-Thurs. 4pm-2am, Fri.-Sat. 4pm-3am), a two-level lounge that features salsa and other international music. This place can get rowdy on weekends, and they are known for having outstanding mojitos.

Georgetown

A sophisticated place to grab a drink at pretty much any time is the **Degrees Bar and Lounge** (3100 S St. NW, 202/912-4100, www.ritzcarlton.com, Sun.-Thurs. 2:30pm-11:30pm, Fri.-Sat. 2:30pm-1am) in the Ritz-Carlton Georgetown. This relaxing lounge brings a bit of New York City to the nation's capital with its chic decor, dependable drinks, and great potential for people watching. They have a bar and a few small tables for groups.

A Georgetown favorite since 1962, **The Tombs** (1226 36th Street. NW, 202/337-6668, www.tombs.com, Mon.-Thurs. 11:30am-1:30am, Fri. 11:30am-2:30am, Sat. 11am-2:30am, Sun. 9:30am-1:30am) is a casual bar and local hangout for students at Georgetown University. This place served as the inspiration for the setting of *St. Elmo's Fire*. Owned by the Clyde's family of restaurants, it is located in the basement of upscale restaurant 1789. If you're in the mood for good burgers, beer, and a college crowd, or if you're just a fan of *St. Elmo's Fire*, this is the place for you.

If you're looking for live music and an inviting bar scene, check out **Gypsy Sally's** (3401 K St. NW, 202/333-7700, Vinyl Lounge, Tues. 6pm-12am, Wed.-Sat. 6pm-2am., Sun.-Mon. if there is a show in the Music Room; Music Room is open on show nights only). Not quite your typical nightlife spot, it's located in a renovated old building below the Whitehurst Freeway where K Street gives way to a recreation trail. Folk bands draw a casual, down-to-earth crowd that isn't afraid to have a few drinks and dance. When a show is going on, you must have tickets to visit the Music Room, but the Vinyl Lounge upstairs (with views of the Potomac River) is open for dinner and drinks.

A trendy, upscale bar with expert mixologists and a view of the C&O Canal, **Rye Bar** (1050 31st St. NW, 202/617-2400, www.capellahotels.com, daily 11am-2am) is located in the Capella Hotel. This is a quiet, tasteful spot to bring a date and enjoy serious (translation: expensive) drinks. They specialize in fine American rye whiskeys. Leather armchairs, marble tables, dark wood, and large windows accent a sophisticated yet modern ambience.

Adams Morgan

Adams Morgan is known as one of the city's top nightlife area. It has the largest concentration of bars, restaurants, and nightclubs of any neighborhood in the city. Be aware that on weekend nights the streets can be so packed with people that it is hard to move around.

One of the best-known bars is **Madam's Organ Blues Bar** (2461 18th St. NW, 202/667-5370, www.madamsorgan.com, Sun.-Thurs. 5pm-2am, Fri.-Sat. 5pm-3am), which offers a diverse crowd, nightly live music, and dancing. This is a dive-type bar with a slightly older crowd than the frequent college or just-out-of-college patrons that inhabit many of the establishments in Adams Morgan.

Club Heaven and Hell (2327 18th St., 202/667-4355, www.clubheavenandhelldc.com, Wed.-Sun 3pm-2am, closed Mon.-Tues.) has the largest dance floor in Adams Morgan. They have three floors—Heaven, Purgatory, and Hell—with DJs spinning top 40, hip-hop, and retro music.

Bossa Bistro and Lounge (2463 18th St. NW, 202/667-0088, www.bossaproject.com, Tues.-Thurs. 5:30pm-2am, Fri.-Sat. 5:30pm-3am, Sun. 5:30pm-2am, closed Monday) is a cozy neighborhood restaurant that serves Brazilian food and offers live music (such as jazz and international) four nights a week and DJs on other nights. In contrast to many options in Adams Morgan, this is an intimate place to relax in a low-key, dimly lit interior with food and atmosphere.

Habana Village (1834 Columbia Rd. NW, 202/462-6310, www.habanavillage.com, Sun. 5pm-9pm, Mon. 6pm-10pm, Wed. 5:30pm-11pm, Thurs. 5:30pm-2am, Fri.-Sat. 5:30pm-3pm, closed Tues.) is a Cuban restaurant and dance club offering live music and dance lessons.

Bourbon (2321 18th St. NW, 202/332-0800, www.bourbondc.com, Tues.-Fri. 5pm-11pm, Sat. 2pm-11pm, Sun. 4pm-9pm) serves bourbon—several hundred types to be exact. This comfy bar has a neighborhood feel but draws patrons from all over the city because of its unique specialty.

Upper Northwest

Although Upper Northwest is not the most happening nightlife spot in the city, it does offer some friendly, comfortable options for those not looking to see or be seen.

Atomic Billiards (3427 Connecticut Ave. NW, 202/363-7665, www.atomicbilliards.com, Sun.-Thurs. 4pm-2am, Fri.-Sat. 4pm-3am), in the Cleveland Park neighborhood, is a funky, futuristic-looking pool hall. They also have shuffleboard and darts. They serve good beer on tap but don't have a kitchen.

If a basement dive bar with pool, table tennis, shuffleboard, beer, and sandwiches is more your style, try **Breadsoda** (2233 Wisconsin Ave. NW 202/333-7445, www.breadsoda.com, Sun.-Thurs. noon-2am, Fri.-Sat. noon-3am). Tuesdays are tacos-and-table tennis night in this cozy 1970s-style subterranean bar.

For live blues Thursday-Saturday and live jazz on Sunday, grab a beer in the neighborhoody **Zoo Bar** (3000 Connecticut Ave. NW, 202/232-4225, www.zoobardc.com, Sun.-Thurs. 11am-2am, Fri.-Sat. 11am-3am). Across the street from the National Zoo, this is an authentic dive bar surrounded by a touristy neighborhood.

U Street Corridor

Made-to-order drinks are created at **The Gibson** (2009 14th St. NW, 202/232-2156, www.thegibsondc.com, daily from 6pm), just off U Street. This interesting establishment could be called a modern-day speakeasy. Call ahead and make a reservation at the bar or at one of their booths or tables, then ring the bell when you arrive at the nondescript tenement-style building. A professional mixologist will concoct something special for you, or you can order a drink off the small menu. Don't expect to eat (they don't serve food), and above all, don't stay longer than your allotted two hours; there's sure to be someone waiting to take your spot.

EVENTS

The nation's capital hosts countless events year-round. Whether it's a festival, athletic event, or holiday celebration, there is something going on nearly every day of the year.

Restaurant Week (www.ramw.org/restaurantweek, lunch $22, dinner $35) happens twice a year in January and August. Two hundred of the most popular restaurants in DC offer prix fixe lunch and dinner menus. The event is sponsored by the Restaurant Association of Metropolitan Washington. Reservations are recommended.

Chinese dragon dances, live music, and a parade are just some of the festivities during the 15-day annual **Chinese New Year Celebration** (H St. NW between 5th and 9th Sts.) in the Chinatown area of Downtown DC. Beginning with the new moon on the first day of the Chinese New Year and ending with the full moon, this late January or early February celebration brings the area's culture to life with a bang of fireworks. The Gallery Place-Chinatown Metrorail stop will put you in the right place for this free event.

The yearly **Washington Auto Show** (www.washingtonautoshow.com, $12) is a large event that brings more than 700 new vehicles from both domestic and overseas automakers to the Washington Convention Center. The show is held for 10 days at the end of January or beginning of February and draws hundreds of thousands of visitors.

The coming of the Easter Bunny brings the annual **White House Easter Egg Roll** (www.whitehouse.gov), a tradition that started back in 1878 when President Rutherford B. Hayes opened the White House grounds to local children for egg rolling on the Monday after Easter. Successive presidents have continued this long-standing event, which takes place on the South Lawn.

Washington's signature event is the annual **National Cherry Blossom Festival** (www.nationalcherryblossomfestival.org). This three-week event coincides (ideally) with the blooming of the hundreds of Japanese cherry trees that were given to the United States in 1912 by Japan. The trees are planted all around the Tidal Basin and, when blooming, are a spectacular sight to see. Unfortunately, this huge event means gridlock on the highways and congestion on the sidewalks, but it is a great time to photograph the city. There's a parade, a kite festival, concerts, a 10-mile footrace, and much more. The festival is held late March-mid-April.

Memorial Day is big in Washington DC as thousands descend on the city for a day of remembrance. Many family-friendly events are held throughout the city and the free **National Memorial Day Concert** (www.pbs.org) is held on the West Lawn of the U.S. Capitol. The concert features patriotic themes to honor Americans who have served our country during times of conflict. Other events include the **National Memorial Day Parade** (www.americanveteranscenter.org/avc-events/parade) and the **Rolling Thunder Motorcycle Rally** (www.rollingthunderrun.com).

June brings the annual **Capital Pride** (www.capitalpride.org) event celebrating the gay, lesbian, bisexual, and transgender communities. There are more than 50 educational and entertainment events including a street festival and parade.

The **DC Jazz Festival** (www.dcjazzfest.org) is also held in June and features more than 100 jazz performances throughout the city. Major jazz artists from around the globe participate in this 12-day celebration. Venues include clubs, museums, hotels, and restaurants.

The **Smithsonian Folklife Festival** (www.festival.si.edu) takes place annually during the last week in June and the first week in July. It is held outdoors on the National Mall. The festival is a living heritage exposition with music, crafts, and artistry. The festival is free to attend.

There's no better place to celebrate the Fourth of July than the National Mall. **America's Independence Day Celebrations** include a parade along Constitution Avenue (www.july4thparade.com), concerts, and a spectacular fireworks display over the Washington Monument.

The premier running event in DC is the annual **Marine Corps Marathon** (www.marinemarathon.com). Known as "The People's Marathon," this 26.2-mile race was first held in 1975 and now has 30,000 participants each October.

Another completely different type of race is the annual **High Heel Race** in Dupont Circle. Each Tuesday before Halloween at 9pm, dozens of drag queens sporting elaborate outfits sprint down 17th Street NW over the three blocks between R Street and Church Street. The event has been held for more than 25 years and draws thousands of spectators.

During the first week in December, the **National Christmas Tree Lighting** (www.thenationaltree.org) is a special event that takes place on the Ellipse. The president attends the lighting, which is surrounded by additional highlights such as military band concerts and performances by celebrities. A separate event is held annually for the lighting of the national menorah (www.afldc.org).

Shopping

Washington DC has great neighborhood shopping with unique stores and boutiques. Some of the stores are geared toward high-end consumers, but there are also many "finds" if you know where to look.

CAPITOL HILL

Traditional retail shopping can be found on Capitol Hill at **Union Station** (50 Massachusetts Ave. NE, 202/289-1908, www.unionstationdc.com), which has more than 65 stores including national retailers such as Ann Taylor, The Body Shop, Jos. A. Bank Clothiers, and Victoria's Secret. A handful of specialty boutiques are also represented, such as **Lost City Art** (202/289-6977), which offers Indonesian statues, masks, murals, jewelry, and household items; and **Appalachian Spring** (202/682-0505), which offers jewelry, handbags, pottery, and household items.

Eastern Market (225 7th St. SE, 202/698-5253, www.easternmarket-dc.org) is a prime destination in DC for fresh food and handmade arts and crafts. For more than 135 years, the market has been a community hub on Capitol Hill. It offers several shopping spaces: The **South Hall Market** (Tues.-Fri. 7am-7pm, Sat. 7am-6pm, Sun. 9am-5pm) is an indoor space featuring 13 merchants offering a large variety of food such as produce, baked goods, meat, and dairy products. The **Weekend Farmers' Line** is an open-air space that is open on weekends and offers fresh local produce and snacks. Those searching for local crafts and antiques can find them at the **Weekend Outdoor Market.** Vendors in this area carry ethno-specific handcrafts, vintage goods, and arts and crafts.

DOWNTOWN

The revitalized Penn Quarter area features more than just museums, the Verizon Center, and cool new restaurants. The neighborhood has plenty of shopping and features some of the best-known national retailers such as Pottery Barn and Urban Outfitters. A selection of trendy individual shops is also here, such as **Fahrney's Pens** (1317 F St. NW, 202/628-9525, www.fahrneyspens.com), a pen store with a long DC tradition, and **Pua Naturally** (701 Pennsylvania Ave. NW, 202/347-4543), a retail studio that works with a cooperative of master tailors, block printers, and seamstresses in Nepal and India.

DUPONT CIRCLE

Lively Dupont Circle features an eclectic choice of gift shops, clothing stores, bookstores, and art galleries. If you're looking for a quirky gift, one-of-a-kind handcrafts, greeting cards, or chocolate, stop in **The Chocolate Moose** (1743 L St. NW, 202/463-0992, www.chocolatemoosedc.com). Serious antiques lovers will be intrigued by the offerings at **Geoffrey Diner Gallery** (1730 21st St. NW, 202/904-5005, www.dinergallery.com). They have items from the 19th and 20th centuries, contemporary fine art, European and American crafts, and Tiffany lamps.

GEORGETOWN

Everyone from first ladies to celebrities have made their way down M Street looking for a special find. Georgetown offers great antiques, cool clothing, and one-of-a-kind local boutiques. Most of the stores can be found along M Street and Wisconsin Avenues. The famous mall, **The Shops at Georgetown Park** (3222 M St., 202/342-8190, www.shopsatgeorgetownpark.com, Mon.-Sat. 10am-9pm, Sun. noon-6pm) underwent major renovations and was sold to new owners in 2014. Since then it's been steadily adding a mix of major bargain and luxury brands as well as restaurants.

UPPER NORTHWEST

The best shopping in Upper Northwest is in the Friendship Heights neighborhood, along the Maryland state border. The **Chevy Chase Pavilion** (5335 Wisconsin Ave., 202/686-5335, www.ccpavilion.com, Mon.-Sat. 7am-11pm, Sun. 7am-9pm) is an upscale shopping mall that underwent a $32 million renovation in 2012. It features national chains such as J. Crew, World Market, and Old Navy. It is across Wisconsin Avenue from another small, upscale mall, **Mazza Gallerie** (5300 Wisconsin Ave., 202/966-6114, www.mazzagallerie.com, Mon.-Fri. 10am-8pm, Sat. 10am-7pm, Sun. noon-6pm). Mazza Gallerie features stores such as Neiman Marcus, Heritage, and TW Luggage and Leather. There is also a movie theater at the mall and a parking garage. The shopping district is accessible by Metrorail on the Red Line at the Friendship Heights stop.

Sports and Recreation

SPECTATOR SPORTS

The nation's capital is home to many professional sports teams and hosts countless sporting events throughout the year.

The city is in a frenzy over the **Washington Nationals** baseball team, which came to DC in 2005 and moved into their current home, **Nationals Park** (1500 S. Capitol St. SE, 202/675-6287, www.washington.nationals.mlb.com), in 2008. The stadium sits on the banks of the Anacostia River in the Navy Yard neighborhood and seats approximately 41,500 people. The Washington Monument and Capitol Building can be seen from the upper stands.

The **Verizon Center** (601 F St. NW, 202/628-3200, www.verizoncenter.com) in Penn Quarter is home to the city's professional hockey team (the NHL's **Washington Capitals**), two pro basketball teams: (the NBA's **Washington Wizards** and the WNBA's **Washington Mystics**) and Georgetown University's men's basketball team (the Georgetown Hoyas).

Making good use of the former Washington Redskins stadium, DC's professional soccer team, **D.C. United,** plays at **Robert F. Kennedy Memorial Stadium (RFK)** (2400 E. Capitol St. SE, 202/587-5000, www.dcunited.com). At the time of publication, the team was scheduled to move to a brand-new stadium in 2018 at Buzzard Point, two miles south of the U.S. Capitol. The **Washington Redskins** (www.redskins.com) now play at **FedEx Field** in Landover, Maryland.

Other professional sporting events make their way annually to DC. The **Citi Open** (www.citiopentennis.com), formerly the Legg Mason Tennis Classic, is part of the U.S. Open Series. Professional tennis players from around the globe compete for more than $1.8 million in this world-class tennis event. The nine-day tournament is held at the tennis center in Rock Creek Park at the end of July and beginning of August.

The **Washington International Horse Show** (www.wihs.org) is a yearly championship event held at the Verizon Center at the end of October. Approximately 600 horses and riders compete for more than $400,000 in prize money and titles. The event includes show jumping, dressage, equitation, hunters, barrel racing, and terrier races.

CANOEING AND KAYAKING

Those interested in paddling a canoe or kayak on the Potomac River are in for a treat. Viewing the city from the calm of the river puts it in a whole new perspective. Rent a kayak from **Key Bridge Boathouse** (3500 Water St. NW, 202/337-9642, www.boatingindc.com, $15 per hour for a single, $20 for a tandem) in Georgetown and paddle under the Key Bridge and within easy sight of the Washington Monument and Lincoln

Run DC

Runners and triathletes make their way to Washington DC regularly to partake in many annual races. These are just a few of the numerous events scheduled throughout the year.

- **Rock 'n' Roll DC Marathon & Half Marathon** (Mar., www.runrocknroll.competitor.com)
- **Credit Union Cherry Blossom Ten Mile Run** (Apr., www.cherryblossom.org)
- **Capitol Hill Classic 10K** (May, www.capitolhillclassic.com)
- **Komen Global Race for the Cure 5K** (June, www.komendcrace.info-komen.org)
- **Nation's Triathlon** (Sept., www.nationstri.com)
- **Army 10-Miler** (Oct., www.armytenmiler.com)
- **Marine Corps Marathon** (Oct., www.marinemarathon.com)

Memorial. **Thompson Boat Center** (2900 Virginia Ave. NW, 202/333-9543, www.thompsonboatcenter.com, $16.50-55) is another good option for rentals.

BIKING

Those who prefer pedals over paddles can take a relaxing ride along the **C&O Canal Towpath** (a scenic 184.5-mile-long trail connecting Georgetown with Cumberland, Maryland) on the north bank of the Potomac River; rent a bike in Georgetown from **Big Wheel Bikes** (202/337-0254, www.bigwheelbikes.com, $7 per hour or $35 per day). **Bike and Roll Washington DC** (202/842-2453, www.bikeandrolldc.com, $40 per day) offers bike rentals for touring the city's sights from a convenient National Mall location. Their helpful staff can share tips on where to ride.

Another great option for getting around the city on two wheels is joining **Capital Bikeshare** (www.capitalbikeshare.com) for a day, three days, a month, or a year. Members gain access to more than 1,800 bikes in 350 locations throughout the city (including Arlington and Alexandria in Virginia). Twenty-four-hour memberships are $8 and include the first half hour of each ride. Additional time is then charged by the half hour. Passes can be purchased at kiosks at each bike station.

An 11-mile Rail-to-Trail route called the **Capital Crescent Trail** starts in Georgetown on K Street. The trail runs parallel to the C&O Canal Towpath for the first three miles but then goes through upscale neighborhoods in Northwest DC. The initial seven miles between Georgetown and Bethesda, Maryland, are paved, but an additional four miles of unpaved trail (mostly crushed stone) can be ridden to Silver Spring, Maryland. The two trails are connected by a tunnel under downtown Bethesda.

Bike Tours

Year-round daily bike tours around Washington DC are offered by **Capital City Bike Tours** (502 23rd St. NW, 202/626-0017, www.dc.capitalcitybiketours.com, $39). Comfortable beach cruisers are used in the tours and riders can expect to see sights such as the Lincoln Memorial, White House, Vietnam Veterans Memorial, and the Capitol Building. Tours are three hours and leave from the Capital City Bike Tours office.

Another popular bike tour company is **Bike and Roll Washington DC** (202/842-2453, www.bikethesites.com). They offer seasonal guided bike (three hours, $40) and

Segway (2.5 hours, $64) tours from their National Mall location (955 L'Enfant Plaza SW) and year-round tours from their Union Station location (50 Massachusetts Ave., 202/962-0206).

GOLF

Golfers might be surprised to learn that there are three golf courses right in the city (www.golfdc.com). **Langston Golf Course** (2600 Benning Rd. NE, 202/397-8638, $18-32), an 18-hole course, is five minutes from Capitol Hill. **East Potomac Golf Course** (972 Ohio Dr. SW, 202/554-7660, $10-28), which has one 18-hole course and two 9-hole courses, is at Haines Point near the National Mall. **Rock Creek Golf Course** (16th and Rittenhouse Streets NW, 202/882-7332, $15-25) is an 18-hole course at the northern end of Rock Creek Park.

HORSEBACK RIDING

Horse enthusiasts don't need to leave the city to find great riding. **Rock Creek Park Horse Center** (5100 Glover Rd. NW, 202/362-0117) in Rock Creek Park offers trail rides and lessons.

ICE-SKATING

A great way to impress a date on a cold winter night is by going ice-skating at the **National Gallery of Art Sculpture Garden and Ice Skating Rink** (700 Constitution Ave. NW, 202/216-9397). Skate in the shadows of some of the city's most well-known buildings and in view of many of the garden's wonderful sculptures. This enchanting rink is especially romantic at night.

PLAYGROUND

For the coolest playground in town, visit **Turtle Park** (Friendship Park, 4500 Van Ness St. NW, 202/282-2198) in Upper Northwest. The focal point is a huge sandbox with turtle sculptures for climbing on and a "sprayground" for cleaning off the sand and cooling off. There are also ball fields in the park and a recreation center.

Food

THE NATIONAL MALL

Asian Fusion

For a trendy night out, dine at **The Source** (575 Pennsylvania Ave. NW, 202/637-6100, www.wolfgangpuck.com, brunch Sat. 11:30am-3pm, lunch Mon.-Fri. 11:30am-2pm, dinner Mon.-Thurs. 5:30pm-10pm and Fri.-Sat. 5:30pm-11pm, $31-50). This popular Wolfgang Puck restaurant is adjacent to the Newseum and was a date night choice for Michelle and Barack Obama. The Source offers a three-course prix fixe lunch for $45 (and a discount on Newseum admission), and the lower-level lounge offers small plates and a Dim Sum Brunch on Saturday. The modern dining room on the second floor offers a contemporary Asian menu. Floor-to-ceiling windows and a polished tile floor give the space an inviting atmosphere, and there is plush leather seating. There is also a four-person hot pot table and a two-person chef's tasting menu counter. A beautiful wine wall with more than 2,000 bottles is a focal point. A seasonal patio is available for outdoor dining.

CAPITOL HILL

American

On the north side of Capitol Hill in the Atlas District is an authentic cheesesteak place owned by two Philadelphia natives. **Taylor Charles Steak & Ice** (1320 H St. NE, 202/388-6880, www.steakandice.com, Sun.-Thurs. 11am-9pm, Fri.-Sat. 11am-3:30am, under $10) offers flavorful made-to-order cheesesteak sandwiches (they also offer chicken and portobello sandwiches). There are several options for toppings and, of course, house-made cheese whiz. A nice treat is their soda fountain, stocked with birch beer, creamy sodas, and Kool-Aid.

A Capitol Hill classic is the **Tune Inn** (331 Pennsylvania Ave. SE, 202/543-2725, Sun.-Thur. 8am-2am, Fri.-Sat 8am-3am, $5-17). This historic burger-and-beer bar suffered a fire in 2011 but bounced right back to its quirky self (the regulars are even still sitting at the bar). The decor is a symphony in taxidermy (complete with a deer rump and a beer-drinking black bear), but the beer is cheap (by DC standards) and the burgers are tasty. They are open daily for breakfast, lunch, and dinner.

Bakery

A charming little bakery in Northeast, and a relative newcomer to the restaurant scene is the **Batter Bowl Bakery** (403 H St. NE, 202/675-2011, www.the-bbb.com, daily 8am-8pm, under $10). They serve delicious boules, baguettes, and bakery items, plus a scant selection of breakfast and lunch sandwiches (each named after local streets) served on their homemade bread. All sandwiches are made to order, so be prepared to wait a few minutes. They will be packed in a hefty take-out container with a small side salad. The bakery also offers wonderful cookies, macaroons, and Danishes.

Belgian

The intimate **Belga Café** (514 8th St. SE, 202/544-0100, www.belgacafe.com, lunch Mon.-Fri. 11am-4pm, brunch Sat.-Sun. 9am-4pm, dinner Mon.-Thurs. 4pm-10pm, Fri.-Sat. 4pm-11pm, and Sun.4pm-9:30pm, $15-30) serves weekend brunch, weekday lunch, and dinner daily. Their waffles are knee weakening (with savory or sweet toppings), and their dinner entrées are delicious renditions of items such as mussels (flecked with bacon and steamed in red ale), truffle macaroni and cheese, and grilled sea bass. They also have a nice beer list. The place is small (the first floor of a row house), and there is exposed brick inside with an open kitchen (read: the noise level is high). There is usually a wait, but the staff is friendly (even to children) and on nice days there is added seating outside.

DOWNTOWN

American

It's hard to pass on an opportunity to dine at **Old Ebbitt Grill** (675 15th St., 202/347-4800, www.ebbitt.com, Mon.-Fri. 7:30am-1am, Sat.-Sun. 8:30am-1am, $14-28). This historic restaurant is near the White House and was frequented by presidents such as Grant, Cleveland, and Theodore Roosevelt. Currently part of the Clyde's restaurant group, this old favorite is always bustling with political personalities, journalists, and theater patrons. It's a casual, fun place but shows its long history through marble bars and mahogany booths outfitted in velvet. They have an oyster bar and a menu of burgers, pasta, steak, and seafood. They also serve breakfast during the week and brunch on weekends.

Wine lovers will feel at home eating at ★ **Proof** (775 G St. NW, 202/737-7663, www.proofdc.com, lunch Tues.-Fri. 11:30am-2pm, dinner Mon.-Thurs. 5:30pm-10pm, Fri.-Sat. 5:30pm-11pm, and Sun. 5pm-9:30pm, $25-35, four-course tasting menu $75) in Penn Quarter. This "wine-centric" Wolfgang Puck restaurant offers a well-designed modern American menu topped off with friendly, knowledgeable service. There is a tasting menu with wine pairings, first course (small plates), and second course (entrée) selections. The restaurant focuses on local, organic, sustainable ingredients and does so in an elegant yet casual environment with leather seating, European lighting, and wine on the wall. Although the restaurant is known for its international cheese and charcuterie, many of the menu items are worth noting, such as the pillowy gnocchi and the duck breast. End the meal with sticky toffee pudding. This is a great place for a date or to bring out-of-town guests. It is also a convenient choice after visiting the Reynolds Center next door.

Indian

Upscale Indian cuisine can be found at

Food Truck Culture

Food trucks line up to serve lunch.

Food trucks have always been part of the lunch scene in Washington DC, but in the past several years their quality and diversity have elevated them to noteworthy status.

Dangerously Delicious Pies (www.dangerouspiesdc.com) was the first truck to spawn off a brick-and-mortar eatery (at 1339 H St.), although the majority of the trucks are stand-alone businesses. Dangerously Delicious Pies serves both sweet and savory pie slices out of its bright red truck. **Tokyo in the City** rolls fresh sushi with nontraditional names like "Gangnam Style" and "Las Vegas," while the **BBQ Bus** (www.bbqbusdc.com) serves up tender ribs and pulled pork. Even more specialized is **Ball or Nothing,** which serves meatballs. This local favorite offers traditional meatballs, veggie meatballs, wild boar meatballs, and interesting sides such as mascarpone polenta and roasted peach and spinach salad.

So how do you find these rolling treasures? These meals on wheels can be found on many major roads in the business and tourist areas of the city. Some have their own websites that give their location schedule and others use Twitter to provide their up-to-the-minute whereabouts. Many can also be found on **Food Truck Fiesta** (www.foodtruckfiesta.com), a website geared toward tracking the trucks. When in doubt, try the truck with the longest line. It doesn't take long for word to spread about a great food truck find.

★ **Rasika** (633 D St. NW, 202/637-1222, www.rasikarestaurant.com, lunch Mon.-Fri. 11:30am-2:30pm, dinner Mon.-Thurs. 5:30pm-10:30pm and Fri.-Sat. 5pm-11pm, $17-36) in Penn Quarter. This fabulous restaurant is one of the best in the area for modern Indian cuisine. The Palak Chaat or Shrimp Uttapam is a must for an appetizer, and a personal favorite for an entrée is the lamb Roganjosh (although the black cod is also spectacular). The butternut squash makes a good side dish, and what Indian meal is complete without naan? They also offer a pre-theater three-course menu before 6:30pm for $35. This restaurant is red-hot on the popularity list, and a reservation is highly recommended. They have a second location at 1190 New Hampshire Avenue NW.

Italian

The vintage-style pizzeria bistro **Matchbox** (713 H St. NW, 202/289-4441, www.

matchboxchinatown.com, Mon.-Thurs. 11am-10:30pm, Fri. 11am-11:30pm, Sat. 10am-11:30pm, Sun. 10am-10:30pm, $10-31) is a favorite in the Chinatown neighborhood for pregaming before an event at the Verizon Center. They are known for their incredible pizza and also for their mini-burger appetizers topped with onion straws, but they also offer a full menu of sandwiches and entrées. The atmosphere in this multilevel hot spot is fun, lively, and slightly funky. There are also locations on Capitol Hill (521 8th St. SE) and in the U Street Corridor (1901 14th St. NW).

Spanish/Portuguese

The toughest reservation in town and one that will blow you away (first when you taste the food and again when you see the bill) is ★ **Minibar by José Andrés** (855 E St. NW, 202/393-0812, www.minibarbyjoseandres.com, Tues.-Sat., seatings at 6pm, 6:30pm, 8:30pm, and 9pm, $275 per person). This "culinary journey" of molecular gastronomy comprises a preset 25-plus-course tasting menu (1-2 bites each) that is a combination of art and science. There is no menu; you simply eat what is served that evening (examples include beech mushroom risotto with truffle, pillow of PB&J, grilled lobster with peanut butter and honey, and apple meringue shaped pigs with bacon ice cream).

Seatings are small, just six guests at each of four seatings a night. Guests move through different rooms during the meal. The serving team walks guests through each course (plan on staying about 2-3 hours) and shares the beauty of the ingredients that were selected for each and the technique behind their creation. The $275 price tag does not include drinks, tax, or gratuity. Optional drink pairings are available for an additional $85, $115, and $200. Reservations are taken in three-month periods (starting one month prior), but it can take several months to actually get one. This is truly a unique, once-in-a-lifetime dining experience. Reservations are by email only (reserve@minibarbyjoseandres.com).

Turkish/Greek

Another creation of chef José Andrés is the very popular **Zaytinya** (701 9th St. NW, 202/638-0800, www.zaytinya.com, Sun.-Mon. 11am-10pm, Tues.-Thurs. 11am-11pm, Fri.-Sat. 11am-midnight, small plates $7-20). They serve a large and delicious menu of tapas in a casual setting. This is a good choice for both vegetarians and meat eaters. Menu examples include pan-roasted dorado, Turkish-style pastirma, and knisa lamb chops. They also offer a chef's experience for $55. There is a bar overlooking the dining room for people-watching. This is a good place to try some of the creations of one of DC's most famous chefs.

DUPONT CIRCLE

American

Nage (1600 Rhode Island Ave. NW, 202/448-8005, www.nagedc.com, breakfast daily 7am-10:30am, brunch Sat.-Sun. 11am-2:30pm, lunch Mon.-Fri. 11:30am-2:30pm, dinner Mon.-Thurs. 5pm-10pm, Fri.-Sat. 5pm-10:30pm, Sun. 5pm-9pm, $18-31) has undergone many changes in recent years. The result is a fresh-feeling place overseen by a popular local chef. Located in the Courtyard Washington Embassy Row hotel, the restaurant provides an American menu full of favorites such as crab cakes, lobster macaroni and cheese, rockfish, lamb shank, and delightful "bottomless" Bloody Marys and mimosas during weekend brunch ($15).

Just south of the Dupont Circle neighborhood is the famed **Vidalia** (1990 M St. NW, 202/659-1990, www.vidaliadc.com, dinner Mon-Sat starting at 5pm, closed Sunday, $30-40). As the Georgian onion name implies, they serve American food inspired by the South, but with a Chesapeake Bay regional influence. The menu revolves around terrific seasonal vegetables, fruit, and local seafood. The result is selections such as mouthwatering shrimp and grits, tenderloin with corn pudding and broccoli, and duck breast. They also have a five-course tasting menu for $78. Vidalia is below ground, but the sleek modern decor is so nice you won't miss the windows. They also have a well-selected wine bar with more than 30 wines by the glass.

If you're looking for a casual, contemporary little bistro, **CIRCA at Dupont** (1601 Connecticut Ave. NW, 202/667-1601, www.circaatdupont.com, Mon.-Fri. 11am-close, Sat.-Sun. 10am-close, $8-26) is a friendly choice. They have communal tables indoors for those who like to make new friends, along with some regular tables and bar high-tops. They offer a large wine list, good bartenders, a heated patio, and a variety of menu options including small plates, salads, flatbread, sandwiches, steak, and seafood. They are known for their chicken lettuce wraps.

Greek

Tucked inside a seemingly normal-looking row house (next door to a CVS) is one of the best culinary outposts in the city. ★ **Komi** (1509 17th St. NW, 202/332-9200, www.komirestaurant.com, Tues.-Sat. 5:30pm-9:30pm, $150) serves a preset multicourse dinner for $150 per person. The experience starts with several light dishes and progresses to hearty fare and finally dessert. Wine pairing is offered as an option for an additional $75. They do not even have a printed menu. This intimate eatery is steered by a young chef named Johnny Monis, who prepares incredible Greek dishes inspired by family recipes. The menu is different every night, making this the perfect find for foodies—foodies with deep pockets, that is.

Thai

Authentic Thai food can be found at **Little Serow** (1511 17th St. NW, www.littleserow.com, Tues.-Thurs. 5:30pm-10pm, Fri.-Sat. 5:30pm-10:30pm, $49). The food is primarily inspired by northern Thailand, so many of the dishes are not typical of the Thai food at other area restaurants; this is definitely part of the appeal. They do not take reservations. They open at 5:30pm, and people line up at the door as early as 4:30pm. If you don't make it inside for the first seating, they will text you with a time to come back. It's a little hard to find because there is no sign outside (if you see their sister restaurant, Komi, you're close). There is very limited seating, and they cannot accommodate parties larger than four. They offer one fixed-price family-style menu for $49; everyone there eats the same thing (so no ogling the meal next to you). The menu changes weekly and is posted on their website each Tuesday. The dining room is very dark, but the food is absolutely delicious and worth the quirkiness of getting a table. Another plus is the great staff. They're very friendly and attentive.

GEORGETOWN

American

Timeless quality can be found at **1789** (1226 36th St. NW, 202/965-1789, www.1789restaurant.com, Mon.-Thurs. 6pm-10pm, Fri. 6pm-11pm, Sat. 5:30pm-11pm, Sun. 5:30pm-10pm, $28-46), which has been around more than 50 years. Part of the Clyde's family of restaurants, 1789 is tried-and-true with starched linen tablecloths and candlelight. The restaurant has three floors and six rooms for dining, each with a unique name, ambience, and a common theme of antiques and equestrian decor. Jackets used to be required but are now preferred. The restaurant serves a diverse menu broken down into "Sustainable Seafood," "Humanely Farmed Animals," and "Eggs and Flour" (French-inspired crepes, and pasta). The food is high quality and consistent, and the service is impeccable. This is a lovely spot for a date or a business dinner.

Just east of Georgetown on M Street is a traditional American restaurant that is known for hosting power players from DC's political scene. It also prides itself in using simple flavor-enhancing cooking methods like smoking, braising, and roasting. The **Blue Duck Tavern** (24th and M Sts. NW, 202/419-6755, www.blueducktavern.com, breakfast daily 6:30am-10:30am, lunch Mon.-Fri. 11:30am-2:30pm, dinner Sun.-Thurs. 5:30pm-10:30pm, Fri.-Sat. 5:30pm-11pm, brunch Sat.-Sun.

11am-2:30pm, $15-38) is known for both its food and its lovely atmosphere. Handmade wood furnishings and an open kitchen help give it a warm, gathering place-type feel, although with a contemporary flair. The food sounds simple, with selections such as beef ribs, organic chicken, and halibut, but the dishes are elegantly prepared and beautifully served.

Farmers Fishers Bakers (3000 K St. NW, Washington Harbor, 202/298-8783, www.farmersfishersbakers.com, breakfast Mon.-Fri- 7:30am-10am, brunch Sat.-Sun. 9am-2pm, lunch/dinner Mon.-Wed. 11am-10pm, Thurs. 11am-11pm, Fri. 11am-midnight, Sat. 2pm-midnight, Sun. 2pm-10pm, $10-28) is part of the Farmers Restaurant Group and is a modern, upscale, casual option in Washington Harbor. The restaurant group supports American family farmers and sources regionally and seasonally when possible. Farmers Fishers Bakers offer an in-house bakery, full bar with 24 beer taps, a sushi counter, and a patio with views of the water. Guests are greeted outside in winter with a fire pit and the inside decor features several different themes for varying dining experiences. The menu is large and includes pizza, sandwiches, salads, and seafood. Their burger with blue cheese and a side of potato salad is a good choice on any day.

Bakery

The cupcake fad has taken DC by storm. Many people have heard of **Georgetown Cupcake** (3301 M St. NW, 202/333-8448, www.georgetowncupcake.com, Mon.-Sat. 10am-9pm, Sun. 10am-8pm), made famous by the reality television series *DC Cupcakes,* but they may not know about a nearby gem called **Baked & Wired** (1052 Thomas Jefferson St. NW, 703/663-8727, www.bakedandwired.com, Mon.-Thurs. 7am-8pm, Fri. 7am-9pm, Sat. 8am-9pm, Sun. 9am-8pm, under $10), south of the C&O Canal between 30th and 31st Streets. This little independent bakery sells great coffee and a large variety of freshly made bakery items including more than 20 types of cupcakes with names like Chocolate Cupcake of Doom and Pretty Bitchin'. They turn out amazing baked goods amid a fun, inviting atmosphere. Look for the pink bicycle outside and don't forget to take home some Hippie Crack (homemade granola) for later.

Italian

The place to celebrity-spot in Georgetown is **Café Milano** (3251 Prospect St. NW, 202/333-6183, www.cafemilano.com, Wed.-Sat. 11:30am-midnight, Sun.-Tues. 11:30am-11pm, $17-65). Political VIPs and visiting Hollywood stars frequent this upscale Italian restaurant, as do local Georgetown socialites. The southern coastal Italian cuisine is consistently good, but diners come more to people-watch and enjoy the pleasant atmosphere afforded by the floor-to-ceiling windows and open sidewalk patio. There is normally a sophisticated crowd, and good wine is flowing.

Another great choice for Italian is **Filomena Ristorante** (1063 Wisconsin Ave. NW, 202/338-8800, www.filomena.com, daily 11:30am-11pm, $13-46). This well-known restaurant opened in 1983 and serves authentic, delicious Italian cuisine. You can even see the pasta being made on the way in. Many celebrities and dignitaries have dined here, including Bono from U2 and President Clinton. Seating is a little close together but the excellent food will make you overlook this. Portions are large and the service is friendly and attentive. Personal favorites include the Linguini Cardinale and Gnocchi Della Mamma.

ADAMS MORGAN

American

If you're up for pushing your comfort zone on trying new food, consider going to **Mintwood Place** (1813 Columbia Rd. NW, 202/234-6732, www.mintwoodplace.com, brunch Sat.-Sun. 10:30am-2:30pm, dinner Tues.-Thurs. 5:30pm-10pm, Fri.-Sat. 5:30pm-10:30pm, Sun. 5:30pm-9pm, $18-29). They have a truly unique menu with interesting combinations like duck breast with sauerkraut and wood-grilled shrimp and mackerel with goat and espelette curd. This is a great place to try something new and maybe impress a date. The restaurant is small and some of the tables are close together, but it has a casual neighborhood feel despite its chunky price tag.

Good burgers and an excellent beer selection help make the **Black Squirrel** (2427 18th St. NW, 202/232-1011, www.blacksquirreldc.com, Mon.-Fri. 5pm-close, Sat.-Sun. 11am-close, $10-15) a popular choice in Adams Morgan. With nearly 20 burger toppings and more than 50 draft beers (they also do 4-ounce pours), this is a relaxing place with a serious crowd of well-informed beer fanatics and those looking to explore new brew styles.

Cashion's Eat Place (1819 Columbia Rd. NW, 202/797-1819, www.cashionseatplace.com, Sat.-Sun. brunch 10:30am-2:30pm, dinner Tues. and Sun. 5:30pm-10pm, Wed.-Sat. 5:30pm-11pm, $13-26) has been described as "funky elegant," and this seems like an accurate analysis of this low-key Adams Morgan restaurant. They serve American food with a Mediterranean influence. The menu changes daily, making this a wonderful place to return to again and again. They also have a terrific wine list. The interior is spacious and airy and offers sidewalk seating when it is nice outside.

Vegetarian

A vegetarian hot spot that the rest of us can also enjoy, the **Amsterdam Falafelshop** (2425 18th St. NW, 202/234-1969, www.falafelshop.com, Sun.-Mon. 11am-midnight, Tues.-Wed. 11am-2:30am, Thurs. 11am-3am, Fri.-Sat. 11am-4am, under $10) is known for its perfectly crisp, yet soft, balls of fried chickpeas placed inside pita bread or in a bowl. The concept is simple: You order your falafel, they make it for you in under five minutes, and then you decide which of the 21 toppings and sauces you want from the garnish bar. The shop is open late and also offers sides and desserts.

UPPER NORTHWEST

American

One of the sister restaurants to the popular Volt in Frederick, Maryland, is ★ **Range** (5335 Wisconsin Ave. NW, 202/803-8020, www.voltrange.com, lunch and dinner, $5-120). At first glance, the price range may seem like a misprint, but the latest creation by revered chef Bryan Voltaggio is what he terms a shared-plate environment of main courses and side dishes, each ordered separately. The restaurant, located in the Chevy Chase Pavilion, seats 300 patrons. Food is prepared at numerous food stations, where more than two dozen chefs are hard at work. Dishes are served as they are ready and consist of a large variety of choices such as oysters from the raw bar, beef, grilled pork loin, lamb breast, and even pizza. The sides are culinary delights, beginning with the famed bread basket, which offers a cornucopia of fresh-baked delights. The restaurant itself has floor-to-ceiling windows and a curved design. The focus is the food, which is presented beautifully and tastes equally as delightful. Save room for dessert: a tantalizing cart of sinfully delicious options will appear at your table when your main courses are cleared.

In the Palisades neighborhood is **BlackSalt** (4883 MacArthur Blvd. NW, 202/342-9101, www.blacksaltrestaurant.com, lunch Mon.-Sat. 11:30am-2:30pm, brunch Sun. 11am-2pm, dinner Mon.-Thurs. 5:30pm-9:30pm, Fri. 5:30pm-11pm, Sat. 5pm-11pm, Sun. 5pm-9pm, $15-38), a well-known spot serving New American seafood. The seafood is extremely fresh, and they offer innovative combinations like jumbo prawn in pepper stew and Atlantic bigeye tuna with caramelized pork belly. They also offer a five-course tasting menu for $80 and a seven-course tasting menu for $98. Wine pairings are $46 and $60. There's an adjoining seafood market that sells some of the best fish in the city.

A traditional greasy-spoon breakfast joint is **Osman & Joe's Steak 'n Egg Kitchen** (4700 Wisconsin Ave. NW, 202/686-1201, www.osmanandjoes.com, 24 hours, $3-18). It offers all the wonderful eggs, sausages, hash browns, and biscuits you could ask for, with ultracasual 24-hour diner charm. As the name implies, they also have steak, as well as burgers, sandwiches, shakes, and good coffee.

German

Take it from a German girl who has eaten her way through the Old Country: Some of the best traditional German fare in the entire DC area is served at **Old Europe** (2434 Wisconsin Ave. NW, 202/333-7600, www.old-europe.com, lunch Wed.-Sat. 11:30am-2:30pm, Sun. 12pm-3:30pm, dinner Sun. 4pm-9pm, Wed.-Thurs. 5pm-9pm, Fri.-Sat. 5pm-10pm, $8-25). They have all the favorites including schnitzel, sauerbraten, and brats, all served in a lively homeland atmosphere. The menu is wide ranging and includes a good selection of traditional side dishes (potato pancakes, red cabbage, potato dumplings). They also have German wine, beer, and spirits (have you ever seen Jägermeister on a printed menu?).

Greek

A Mediterranean gem that serves wonderful tapas is **Café Olé** (4000 Wisconsin Ave. NW, 202/244-1330, www.cafeoledc.com, brunch Sat.-Sun. 11am-3:30pm, dinner Mon.-Thurs. 11am-9pm, Fri.-Sat. 11am-10pm, Sun. 11am-9pm, $8-16). This popular lunch, brunch, and dinner spot puts a refreshing spin on Greek fare. Their large-size tapas menu (with more than 30 choices) allows diners to taste multiple creations without the usual heaviness of some Greek food. The fare here is flavorful and interesting. This is a good place for vegetarians, meat lovers, and seafood enthusiasts. If you like lamb, they have a special hummus with lamb in it; the spices in the lamb make this a wonderful choice. They also have more than 25 wines by the glass, microbrews, and a martini happy hour on weekdays. The decor is modern, and they have an attractive bar. There is a lot of seating, but the tables are close together. They also have a nice patio. Another plus to this restaurant is that they have validated underground parking. They also do takeout.

Italian

DC's most popular pizzeria is easily ★ **2 Amys** (3715 Macomb St. NW, 202/885-5700, www.2amysdc.com, Mon. 5pm-10pm, Tues.-Thurs. 11am-10pm, Fri.-Sat. 11am-11pm, Sun. noon-10pm, $7-14). This gourmet Italian restaurant specializes in authentic Neapolitan pizza. The incredible smell alone will make your mouth water when you walk into this hopping, noisy establishment. The cute bar area is a great place to wait for your table. You can even make good use of the time by studying the menu. Although they make other menu items just as well, the focus here is really on the pizza, which lives up to the hype. It is actually one of the few restaurants in the country certified by the D.O.C. (Denominazione di Origine Controllata), an Italian entity that specifies the legally permitted ingredients and preparation methods required to make authentic Neapolitan pizza.

Japanese

It's hard to imagine that good sushi can be found in DC at a decent price, but **Kotobuki** (4822 MacArthur Blvd. NW, 202/625-9080, www.kotobukidc.com, lunch Mon.-Sat. noon-2:30pm, dinner Mon.-Thurs. 5pm-9:30pm, Fri.-Sat. 5pm-10:30pm, Sun. 5pm-9:30pm, $8-28) is that needle in a haystack. It is a tiny restaurant (above another one owned by the same people), and there is usually a line for a table, but the prices are good, the fish is fresh, and the sushi is authentic.

U STREET CORRIDOR

American

A long-standing tradition on U Street is ★ **Ben's Chili Bowl** (1213 U St. NW, 202/667-0909, www.benschilibowl.com, breakfast Mon.-Fri. 6am-10:45am, Sat. 7am-10:45am, main menu Mon.-Thurs. 10:45am-2am, Fri.-Sat. 10:45am-4am, Sun. 11am-12am, under $10). This historic eatery opened in 1958 and has seen a lot of history. It has weathered the rise, fall, and rebirth of the U Street Corridor and could well be the only business on this stretch of street that survived both the

Ben's Chili Bowl, in operation since 1958

riots of 1968 following the assassination of Martin Luther King Jr. and the construction of the Metrorail Green Line. Ben's is "Home of the Famous Chili Dog," which is what has drawn people (including Barack Obama and the Travel Channel's Anthony Bourdain) through its doors and to its red barstools for decades. They serve breakfast and a "main menu" the rest of the day, but chili dogs are available anytime they're open. The staff is smiling and friendly, and celebrities and regular folks are all treated equally.

Busboys and Poets (2021 14th St. NW, 202/387-7638, www.busboysandpoets.com, Mon.-Thurs. 8am-midnight, Fri. 8am-1am, Sat. 9am-1am, Sun. 9am-midnight, $9-24) is a local gathering place and restaurant that opened in the DC area more than a decade ago and quickly gained a loyal following. It now has six locations. It is known as a progressive establishment and also as a community resource for artists, activists, and writers. The 14th Street location is large and serves breakfast daily until 11am. The rest of the day they offer soup, sandwiches, panini, pizza, and entrées (after 5pm) with a Southern flair (think catfish, shrimp and grits, and pasta). They offer vegetarian, vegan, and gluten-free selections as well, and there is a progressive bookstore on-site.

Greek

Fantastic gyros are what all the hype is about at **The Greek Spot** (2017 11th St. NW, 202/265-3118, www.greekspotdc.com, Mon.-Fri. 11am-10:30pm, Sat. noon-10:30pm, $4-14). This is a very casual "fast-food" restaurant that makes tasty Greek meals in a hurry. They serve lamb gyros, vegetarian gyros (made with soy steak strips), chicken souvlaki, and other sandwiches and burgers. The food is tender and inexpensive and has developed quite the local following. They also prepare and deliver takeout orders.

Accommodations

Accommodations in Washington DC run the gamut in price range. However, choice hotels near the popular attractions are pricey year-round and some are downright outrageous. An alternative choice for booking a room is to stay across the Potomac River in nearby Arlington or Alexandria, Virginia. It can be less expensive, yet still convenient to the city's major attractions by car, bus, or Metrorail.

UNDER $100

Reservations for a hostel stay can be made months in advance with **Hostelling International-Washington DC** (1009 11th St. NW, 202/737-2333, www.hiwashingtondc.org, $29-119). Accommodations are close to the National Mall, Metrorail, and many of the popular DC attractions. This former hotel has 250 beds and offers shared dorm-style lodging and some semiprivate rooms. Bathrooms are shared, and there is a kitchen and laundry facility on-site. There is also high-speed Internet.

$100-200

One of the best values in the city is the ★ **Hotel Tabard Inn** (1739 N St. NW, 202/785-1277, www.tabardinn.com, $155-250), five blocks from the White House on a pretty, tree-lined street. The hotel has 40 uniquely designed rooms in three town houses. The houses were built between 1880 and 1890. Rates vary depending on the size of the room and whether they have a shared or private bathroom. Reservations are taken for specific price categories, not for specific rooms.

All rates include a guest pass to the local YMCA, and an included continental breakfast is served in the restaurant. Free wireless Internet is also available throughout the inn. The inn is known for having live jazz.

The **Kalorama Guest House** (2700 Cathedral Ave. NW, 202/588-8188, www.kaloramaguesthouse.com, $89-249) is actually two Victorian town houses—the main house and a nice brick town house—in Upper Northwest with 10 guest rooms total. Located in a cute neighborhood less than a block from the National Zoo, it is a good bargain for the area. Don't expect many amenities in the rooms (no telephone and no television). Some of the rooms have shared bathrooms, but you can fall asleep listening to the sound of monkeys howling in the distance at the zoo and wake to a freshly made continental breakfast in the main house.

The **Days Inn Connecticut Avenue** (4400 Connecticut Ave. NW, 202/244-5600, www.daysinn.com, $120-160) is a standard chain hotel in the Forest Hills area of Upper Northwest DC. The hotel is about three miles from the National Mall. It offers free wireless Internet and 37-inch HD TVs. Parking is available for an additional fee.

★ **Woodley Park Guest House** (2647 Woodley Rd. NW, 202/667-0218, www.dcinns.com, $140-240) is one of the nicest bed-and-breakfasts in DC. In a historic neighborhood in Upper Northwest, they offer 15 comfortable and quiet guest rooms and exceptional service. The owners are truly service-oriented, and they help make the city feel personal and accessible. This is a wonderful choice in a quiet location for both business and leisure travel. The rooms have free wireless Internet and a delicious, fresh continental breakfast is served daily.

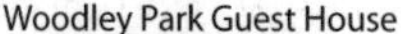

Woodley Park Guest House

The Ghost Suite

It's no secret that the **Omni Shoreham Hotel** (2500 Calvert St. NW, 202/234-0700, www.omnihotels.com, $245-389) in Upper Northwest DC has some pretty peculiar things going on in Suite 870. The grand and historic hotel, which was built in 1930, originally had an extravagant apartment on the eighth floor where a minor shareholder in the property lived with his family and housekeeper. Shortly after they moved into the apartment, the housekeeper was found dead in her bed in the apartment. Not long after, the family's adopted daughter (the only child in the family) also died mysteriously in the apartment amid rumors of suicide or a possible drug overdose.

The family remained in the apartment for 40 years and finally moved out in 1973. The once extravagant apartment was in shambles when they left and was closed off to the rest of the hotel and abandoned. Once the apartment was empty, guests in neighboring rooms began reporting disturbances. Televisions and lights would go on and off, doors would slam shut, people would feel breezes as if someone had walked by, and many reports of loud noises (including someone playing the piano) were reported coming from the apartment. Many of the strange sounds were reported to be coming from Room 864, which was the housekeeper's bedroom.

In 1997 the hotel decided to renovate the apartment and turn it into a presidential suite. During construction, a worker fell from the balcony to his death. Upon completion of the suite's restoration, the hotel appropriately named it "The Ghost Suite."

It is reported that to this day many guests claim seeing a little girl running through the halls and an older woman in a long dress roaming around alone.

$200-300

A wonderful Kimpton hotel in the Dupont Circle neighborhood is the ★ **Carlyle Suites Hotel** (1731 New Hampshire Ave. NW, 202/234-3200, www.carlylesuites.com, $139-339). This art deco hotel has 170 rooms with ample space, sitting areas, fully equipped kitchens, and Tempur-Pedic beds. The eight-story offering is on a residential street, three blocks from the Dupont Circle fountain. There is a restaurant on-site, a fitness center, free bike use, and valet parking ($42). The hotel is pet friendly.

The **Embassy Suites Washington, D.C. at the Chevy Chase Pavilion** (4300 Military Rd. NW, 202/362-9300, www.embassysuites-dcmetro.com, $209-538) has an upscale feel and is located in a high-end shopping area in Upper Northwest. The hotel is conveniently right off the Metrorail at the Friendship Heights stop and caters to business travelers. They offer 198 suites, each with a separate bedroom and sitting room. This is a nice option if you like your space. They also have large bathrooms. The hotel is good for extended stays.

The **Omni Shoreham Hotel** (2500 Calvert St. NW, 202/234-0700, www.omnihotels.com, $245-389) is a luxurious landmark built in 1930 in Upper Northwest DC. It has 836 guest rooms, some of which have wonderful views of Rock Creek Park. This historic hotel hosted its first inaugural ball in 1933 (for Franklin D. Roosevelt) and has hosted inaugural balls for each president that followed during the 20th century (Bill Clinton even played his saxophone there during his ball in 1993). At one time, it was the number one choice for accommodations for dignitaries and the rich and famous and has housed such notables as the Beatles and emperors. The hotel offers rooms and suites of varying sizes and prices, with the lower-end rooms being quite affordable and the upper-end suites being very expensive. An elegant restaurant is located in the hotel. The rooms have free wireless Internet, and there is an outdoor heated pool, a fitness center, and more than 100,000 square feet of meeting space.

OVER $300

For a presidential stay in DC, book a room at the ★ **Hay-Adams Hotel** (800 16th St. NW, 202/638-6600, www.hayadams.com, $379-1,879) at 16th and H Streets NW. This beautiful Downtown hotel has 145 guest rooms and 21 luxury suites. Some of the rooms offer stunning views of local landmarks such as the White House and Lafayette Square. The Hay-Adams was built in 1928 in the Italian Renaissance style and has the appearance of a large private mansion. It sits on the land where the homes of Secretary of State John Hay and historian Henry Adams (author and relative of John Adams and John Quincy Adams) once stood.

The hotel has hosted many important political figures and was the choice for President Obama and his family in the weeks leading up to his first inauguration in 2008.

Visitors taking in the National Mall sights will enjoy the convenient location of this hotel, situated near the White House, Downtown attractions, and the Metrorail. The hotel features beautiful, traditionally decorated rooms with molded ceilings, quality furnishings, ample space, comfortable beds, and wonderful amenities such as fluffy bathrobes. The food at the hotel is also excellent.

The service at the Hay-Adams is outstanding, and from the moment you walk through the front door, it is obvious you will be well taken care of. The hotel's slogan is, "Where nothing is overlooked but the White House," and they mean it.

If you're traveling to DC for the full historical experience and you'd like to indulge in famous accommodations, then the ★ **Willard InterContinental Hotel** (1401 Pennsylvania Ave. NW, 202/628-9100, www.washington.intercontinental.com, $249-3,500) is a good choice. The Willard is more than 150 years old and is considered to be one of the most prestigious hotels in the city. It is one block from the White House and has been called the "Residence of Presidents" because it has hosted nearly every U.S. president since Franklin Pierce stayed there in 1853. Other famous guests include Martin Luther King Jr. (who stayed there during the time he delivered his famous "I Have a Dream" speech), Charles Dickens, Mark Twain, and Buffalo Bill. The hotel even has its own little museum.

The Willard is beautifully restored and has a grand lobby, comfortable rooms, and outstanding service. The hotel has 12 floors, 335 guest rooms, and 41 suites. It also has a wonderful on-site restaurant.

Another beautifully restored historic hotel is **The Jefferson** (1200 16th St. NW, 202/448-2300, www.jeffersondc.com, $375-675), located roughly halfway between the White House and Dupont Circle. Built as a luxury apartment building in 1923, the beaux arts building was converted to a hotel in 1955 and underwent major renovations in 2009, which included incorporating modern-day features (such as a chef's kitchen and spa) into the original framework. The hotel maintains a large collection of antiques, artwork, and original signed documents. It has 95 guest rooms and suites and three on-site restaurants. They also have an Executive Canine Officer (ECO) named Lord Monticello (Monti)—a rescue dog that lives at the hotel. The hotel is dog friendly ($50 fee) and provides dog beds, bowls, treats, and a map of nearby dog-friendly establishments and walking routes.

Off Lafayette Park near the White House is the lovely **Sofitel Washington DC Lafayette Square** (806 15th St. NW, 202/730-8800, www.sofitel.com, $220-600). This sophisticated hotel is art deco with a modern flair. The rooms are beautifully appointed and feature soft lighting and fluffy linens. There is also a comfortable lounge area for guests and an on-site restaurant. The location is perfect for touring the city since it is near the National Mall, Downtown attractions, and the Metrorail. Ask for a room facing south or east (or simply ask to face the White House).

For a five-star stay in Georgetown, make a reservation at the **Four Seasons Washington, DC** (2800 Pennsylvania Ave., 202/342-0444, www.fourseasons.com, $575-2,025). This high-end hotel is known for its spacious rooms and suites. It is also the only five-star, five-diamond luxury hotel in the city. The Four Seasons is a contemporary hotel with a warm and welcoming ambience. The professional staff is truly exceptional and tends to every guest personally. There is a fitness center, a pool, steam rooms, a sauna, and an aerobics studio on-site. Babysitting is also available. This is a very busy hotel when special events are going on in the city, yet even when the hotel is full, it never feels crowded and the service is spot on. The hotel is in a romantic Georgetown neighborhood, yet is convenient to the National Mall and all the city attractions.

A trendy boutique hotel in the Dupont Circle neighborhood is the 137-room **Hotel Rouge** (1315 16th St. NW, 202/232-8000, www.rougehotel.com, $159-599). This popular Kimpton hotel has a modern design, a fitness room, good amenities, and is pet friendly. Red is their signature color, which seems to be worked in everywhere. Their rooms are well outfitted with stocked minibars, high-speed Internet, 37-inch plasma televisions, Aveda bath products, and voice mail. Ten rooms feature kitchenettes and entertainment areas. There is a great bar on-site, and approximately 75 restaurants are within walking distance. They also have a state-of-the-art fitness center. The staff is exceptional. Pets are welcome.

The most imaginative hotel in the city is **The Mansion on O Street** (2020 O St. NW, 202/496-2000, www.omansion.com, $350-25,000), just southwest of Dupont Circle. This one-of-a-kind boutique hotel consists of four 1892 townhomes linked to form a luxury inn complex containing guest rooms, a ballroom, multiple dining rooms, conference rooms, and many surprises. Each accommodation has its specialty: It could be a rainforest shower, pirate's tub, tanning room, a shower made from an English telephone booth, extensive gardens with fountains and a barbecue, an aquarium, or a bathroom that's so incredible that legendary jazz musician Miles Davis decided to have dinner in it. That's just the tip of the iceberg at this ultracreative mansion. There's a museum on-site that is equally creative and changes displays daily; there are also 32 secret doors to explore, and hidden passageways. Everything in the mansion is for sale, so if you really like something, for a price, it can be yours. Many famous people have stayed in this eclectic world of fantasy, including Kim Basinger, Hillary Clinton, and Sylvester Stallone. Reservations are only taken online.

Information and Services

VISITORS INFORMATION

Additional information on Washington DC can be found at www.washington.org and www.visitingdc.com or by stopping by the **Washington Welcome Center** (1005 E St. NW, 202/347-6609, Mon.-Sat. 8am-5pm).

MEDIA

The most widely circulated daily newspaper in Washington DC is the ***Washington Post*** (www.washingtonpost.com), featuring world and local news and with an emphasis on national politics. The ***Washington Times*** (www.washingtontimes.com) is another daily newspaper that has a wide following.

Weekly and specialty newspapers include the ***Washington City Paper*** (www.washingtoncitypaper.com), an alternative weekly newspaper, and the ***Washington Informer*** (www.washingtoninformer.com), a weekly newspaper serving the DC area's African American population.

EMERGENCY SERVICES

In the event of an emergency, call 911.

The **Metropolitan Police Department of the District of Columbia** (202/727-9099, anonymous tip line 202/727-9099, www.mpdc.dc.gov) is the municipal law-enforcement agency in Washington DC. It is one of the 10 largest police forces in the country.

There are no fewer than 10 hospitals in the city. Some of the ones ranked highest nationally include **MedStar Washington Hospital Center** (110 Irving St. NW, 202/877-7000, www.whcenter.org), **MedStar Georgetown University Hospital** (3800 Reservoir Rd. NW, 202/444-2000, www.medstargeorgetown.org), and **George Washington University Hospital** (900 23rd St. NW, 202/715-4000, www.gwhospital.com).

Getting There

AIR

Three major airports serve Washington DC. **Ronald Reagan Washington National Airport (DCA)** (703/417-8000, www.metwashairports.com), just outside the city in Arlington, Virginia, is serviced by the Blue and Yellow Lines of the Metrorail. Taxi service is available at the arrivals curb outside the baggage claim area of each terminal. Rental cars are also available on the first floor in parking garage A. A shuttle operates outside each baggage claim area to the rental car counter. It is a 15-minute drive to downtown Washington DC from the airport.

Washington Dulles International Airport (IAD) (703/572-2700, www.metwashairports.com), 27 miles west of the city in Dulles, Virginia, is a 35-minute drive from downtown Washington DC. Bus service between Dulles Airport and the Metrorail at the Wiehle Avenue Station in Reston (Silver Line) is available through **Washington Flyer** (888/927-4359, www.washfly.com/coach.html, $10 one-way, $18 round-trip). Tickets can be purchased at the ticket counter in the main terminal at arrivals door #4 or at the Metrorail station at Wiehle Avenue. Buses depart approximately every 30 minutes. Passengers going from the Wiehle Avenue Metrorail station should follow signs for the Washington Flyer bus stop. Tickets can be purchased from the bus driver. **Metrobus** (202/637-7000, www.wmata.com) operates an express bus (Route 5A) between Dulles Airport and the L'Enfant Plaza Metrorail station in Washington DC. Passengers can board the bus at the airport at the Ground Transportation Curb (on the Arrivals level) at curb location 2E. An extension of Metrorail's Silver Line is planned and will provide a one-seat ride to downtown Washington DC from Dulles Airport in 2018.

Baltimore/Washington International Thurgood Marshall Airport (BWI) (410/859-7040, www.bwiairport.com), 32 miles from Washington DC near Baltimore, Maryland, is approximately 50 minutes by car to Washington DC. It is serviced on weekdays by MARC commuter trains at the BWI Marshall rail station. Free shuttles are available from the station to the airport terminal. Shuttle stops can be found on the lower level terminal road. Metrobus service is available between BWI and the Greenbelt Metrorail station (Green Line) on the **BWI Express Metro.** Bus service is available seven days a week with buses running every 40 minutes.

Washington Dulles Transportation (703/729-4977, www.sedan4dulles.com) provides chauffeur service for passengers at all three airports. Shuttle service is also available from all three airports by **Super Shuttle** (800/258-3826, www.supershuttle.com).

CAR

Arriving in Washington DC by car is fairly common. Several major highways lead into the city such as I-395 from the south in Virginia, I-66 from the southwest in Virginia, and I-295 from the northeast in Maryland. U.S. 50 is the only primary road that runs through the city (on the eastern side) and connects Virginia and Maryland. Most hotels have some provision for parking although it may come at a significant cost. There is also public parking on some streets and many public garages throughout the city.

TRAIN

Amtrak (800/872-7245, www.amtrak.com) provides service to Washington DC through beautiful **Union Station** (40 Massachusetts Ave., www.unionstationdc.com) on Capitol Hill. Amtrak connects with the **Maryland Area Rail Commuter (MARC)** system (410/539-5000, http://mta.maryland.gov), a service that runs Monday-Friday and connects Union Station with the Baltimore area, southern Maryland, and northeastern West Virginia; and with **Virginia Railway Express** (703/684-1001, www.vre.org), a service that runs weekdays only between Fredericksburg, Virginia, and Union Station and Manassas, Virginia, and Union Station.

BUS

The **Greyhound** (1005 1st St. NE, www.greyhound.com) bus station in Washington DC is about a 10-minute walk (north) from Union Station; however, it is a good idea to take a taxi to and from the bus station, as the area can be a little rough, especially at night.

Getting Around

METRORAIL

Washington DC and the surrounding area has a clean, reliable, and generally safe subway system called the **Metrorail** (202/637-7000, www.wmata.com) that is run by the **Washington Metropolitan Area Transit Authority (WMATA).** The Metrorail system is commonly known as "The Metro" and provides service to more than 700,000 customers a day. The system is number two in the country in terms of ticket sales and serves more than 80 stations throughout DC, Virginia, and Maryland. Visit the WMATA website for current delays and alerts.

There are six color-coded rail lines: Red, Orange, Blue, Yellow, Green, and Silver. The system layout is easy to understand (most stations are named for the neighborhood they serve) and getting from one station to another normally requires no more than a single transfer. Metrorail stations are marked with large "M" signs at the entrance that have colored stripes around them to show which line they serve. A complete list of fares and a map of each train line can be found on the website (fares range $3.15-6.90 during peak hours). Metrorail opens at 5am on weekdays and 7am on weekends. It closes at midnight every day. Bicycles are permitted during non-peak hours. It is important to note that doors on each train do not operate like an elevator door and will not reopen if you stick your arm or hand in them as they close. Never stand in the way of a closing door.

Permanent, rechargeable farecards called **SmarTrip** cards can be purchased online and at Metrorail stations. Riders can recharge their cards online. SmarTrip holders receive a discount on Metrorail and Metrobus service (the cards can be used for both).

METROBUS

WMATA also runs **Metrobus** (202/637-7000, www.wmata.com, $1.75-4) service from Metrorail stops and throughout the city. They operate 325 routes to 11,500 bus stops in Washington DC, Virginia, and Maryland. For a complete listing, visit the website. Bicycle racks are provided on Metrobuses and can accommodate two bikes. Permanent, rechargeable farecards called **SmarTrip** cards can be purchased online and at Metrorail stations. Riders can recharge their cards online. Metrobus accepts SmarTrip or cash.

The **DC Circulator** (202/567-3040, www.dccirculator.com, hours vary by route, $1) is another local bus service with six bus routes to key areas in the city. Some of the areas it serves include Georgetown, Dupont Circle, Rosslyn (in Arlington, Virginia), Union Station, the Navy Yard Metrorail stop, Adams Morgan, and the Potomac Avenue Metrorail stop. SmarTrip cards are accepted.

TAXIS AND PRIVATE TRANSPORT

Some neighborhoods in the city, such as Georgetown and Adams Morgan, are not serviced by Metrorail, so traveling by taxi can be an easy way to reach these areas and is also a good alternative for direct transport between two locations. Fares are charged on a meter on a distance-traveled basis. There are many taxi services throughout the city. Sixteen companies can be booked through **DC Taxi Online** (www.dctaxionline.com). Standard taxi fares in Washington DC are $3.25 for the first eighth of a mile, with each additional eighth of a mile costing $0.27. Hourly wait rates are $25.

Uber (www.uber.com) quickly gained popularity throughout Washington DC. The rideshare service provides on-demand taxi, "black car," and SUV service and can be hailed over the Internet. Charges for the services are made directly to your credit card and a 20 percent driver tip is included. This is a fast, easy way to travel around the city and doesn't require the added time of paying your driver. Rates are quoted on the website.

Northern Virginia

Look for ★ to find recommended sights, activities, dining, and lodging.

Highlights

★ **Arlington National Cemetery:** More than 300,000 plain white headstones stand in neat rows as a somber tribute to those who have served our nation. This active military cemetery is also the site of the Tomb of the Unknowns, the eternal flame at John F. Kennedy's grave site, and Robert E. Lee's house (page 94).

★ **Torpedo Factory Art Center:** This 82-studio art center in Old Town Alexandria hosts three floors of galleries in a former torpedo factory (page 107).

★ **Great Falls Park:** A 77-foot waterfall drops into Mather Gorge on the Potomac River, acting as an impressive backdrop to a park full of outdoor activities (page 120).

★ **National Air and Space Museum Steven F. Udvar-Hazy Center:** This Smithsonian Institution museum features an awe-inspiring aviation hangar that displays historic aircraft on three levels (page 120).

★ **Mount Vernon Estate, Museum, and Gardens:** George Washington's home on the Potomac River gives visitors a window into his private life and the world of an 18th-century plantation (page 121).

★ **Wolf Trap National Park for the Performing Arts:** This unique venue is the nation's only national park created for the performing arts (page 123).

★ **Manassas National Battlefield Park:** This site of two major American Civil War battles is a great place for die-hard historians and tourists. The park encompasses more than 5,000 acres of fields, woods, and streams (page 134).

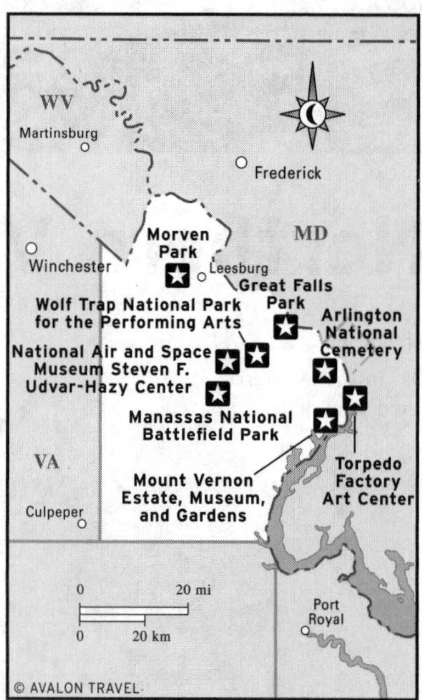

★ **Morven Park:** Once home to governor Westmoreland Davis, this historic estate features the original mansion, two museums, an equestrian center, gardens, and hiking trails (page 144).

Just across the Potomac River from the nation's capital, Northern Virginia is a cornucopia of culture, history, outdoor recreation, culinary delights, and shopping. While most of Northern Virginia is shaped by its proximity to Washington DC, the region also includes rolling hunt country, vineyards, and palatial estates in its western reaches, as well as beautiful views of the Blue Ridge Mountains.

Northern Virginia includes four counties (Arlington, Fairfax, Loudoun, and Prince William) as well as the city of Alexandria. The regional population comprises roughly one-third of the entire population of Virginia. As a central corridor for government contractors and the technology industry, the area tends to be upscale.

The densely populated cities of Arlington and Alexandria abut Washington DC and border the Potomac River. Arlington is known for its national landmarks, military memorials, and trendy restaurants and shopping areas, while Alexandria is best known for its historic Old Town area, which supports a diversity of shops, excellent restaurants, and perhaps the ghosts of our country's founding fathers, who once walked the city's streets and gathered in its taverns.

Loudoun and Fairfax Counties have the highest and second-highest median household income in the country, respectively. Fairfax is the most populous jurisdiction in Virginia, but Loudoun has been growing steadily over the past few decades as new neighborhoods and business parks slowly take over what used to be mostly rolling hills and horse farms.

The second-largest county in Virginia, Prince William, is 35 miles from Washington DC and 20 miles from Washington Dulles International Airport. Its proximity to both has spurred a surge in business and residential growth in recent years. Bordering the Potomac River to the south of Alexandria, the county is rich in Civil War history and is home to Marine Corps Base Quantico.

Northern Virginia attracts entrepreneurs,

Previous: the dog-friendly Alexandria Visitors Center at Ramsay House; Mount Vernon. **Above:** the War Horse statue at the National Sporting Library & Museum in Middleburg.

politicians, advocates, artists, environmentalists, immigrants, and nomads from all corners of the earth. A variety of languages can be heard while walking through nearly any public area, and neighborhoods are as diverse as the people who live in and visit the area. Northern Virginia combines cosmopolitan and countryside, and continues to grow while preserving its deep historic roots.

PLANNING YOUR TIME

Any part of Northern Virginia can be visited in a day trip from Washington DC. The entire area can be covered in a busy few days, but four or five days will give you time to get a real feel for all it offers.

If you plan to stay in Virginia, where you sleep will depend on your priorities. Sights are spread throughout Northern Virginia, so it's best to pick your accommodations based on the atmosphere you like. If you want to stay where restaurants and shopping are within walking distance, consider Old Town Alexandria. If a cozy bed-and-breakfast is more your style, make a reservation in hunt country in Middleburg. Whatever you choose, the biggest consideration for your schedule will be traffic. The Washington DC area is notorious for highway congestion, and this is true year-round.

To avoid the heaviest traffic, don't travel during rush hour, which unfortunately can span many hours each weekday. The best time to travel on weekdays, especially if you are driving I-495 (the Beltway) or I-66, is between 10am and 3pm. Also, if you plan on arriving in the area or leaving the area on a Friday, avoid major arteries (I-495, I-66, and I-95) after 3pm. Friday-afternoon traffic will taint your view of the area. Another thing to be mindful of is High-Occupancy Vehicle (HOV) restrictions (which means a minimum of two or three people must be in the car to use the roadway or specific lanes). Several major arteries such as I-66, I-395, I-95, and the Dulles Toll Road have HOV restrictions during prime commuting hours; for a listing of restrictions, visit www.commuterpage.com. The good news is that drivers around Northern Virginia are generally courteous.

Some public transportation is available in Northern Virginia through the **Washington Metropolitan Area Transit Authority (WMATA)** (www.wmata.com), which operates **Metrobus** and **Metrorail** service, although coverage isn't extensive in all parts of Northern Virginia. It is often more convenient to move around by car if that is an option.

Limited county bus transportation is also available in Arlington County, Alexandria, Fairfax County, and Loudoun County, through the Arlington Transit (ART), Alexandria Transit Company (DASH), Fairfax Connector, and Loudoun County Transit, respectively. These services are geared toward commuters, so again, driving is usually the quickest and easiest way to see the sights.

Two major airports service the Northern Virginia area. The first is **Ronald Reagan Washington National Airport** (703/417-8000, www.metwashairports.com) in Arlington. The Blue and Yellow Metrorail lines connect to this airport. The second is **Washington Dulles International Airport** (703/572-2700, www.metwashairports.com) in Dulles, Virginia.

The **Leesburg Executive Airport (JYO)** (1001 Sycolin Rd., Leesburg, 703/737-7125, www.leesburgva.gov), owned and operated by the city of Leesburg, is one of the two busiest general aviation (GA) airports in Virginia. This airport is 35 miles from Washington DC and is a reliever airport for Washington Dulles International Airport.

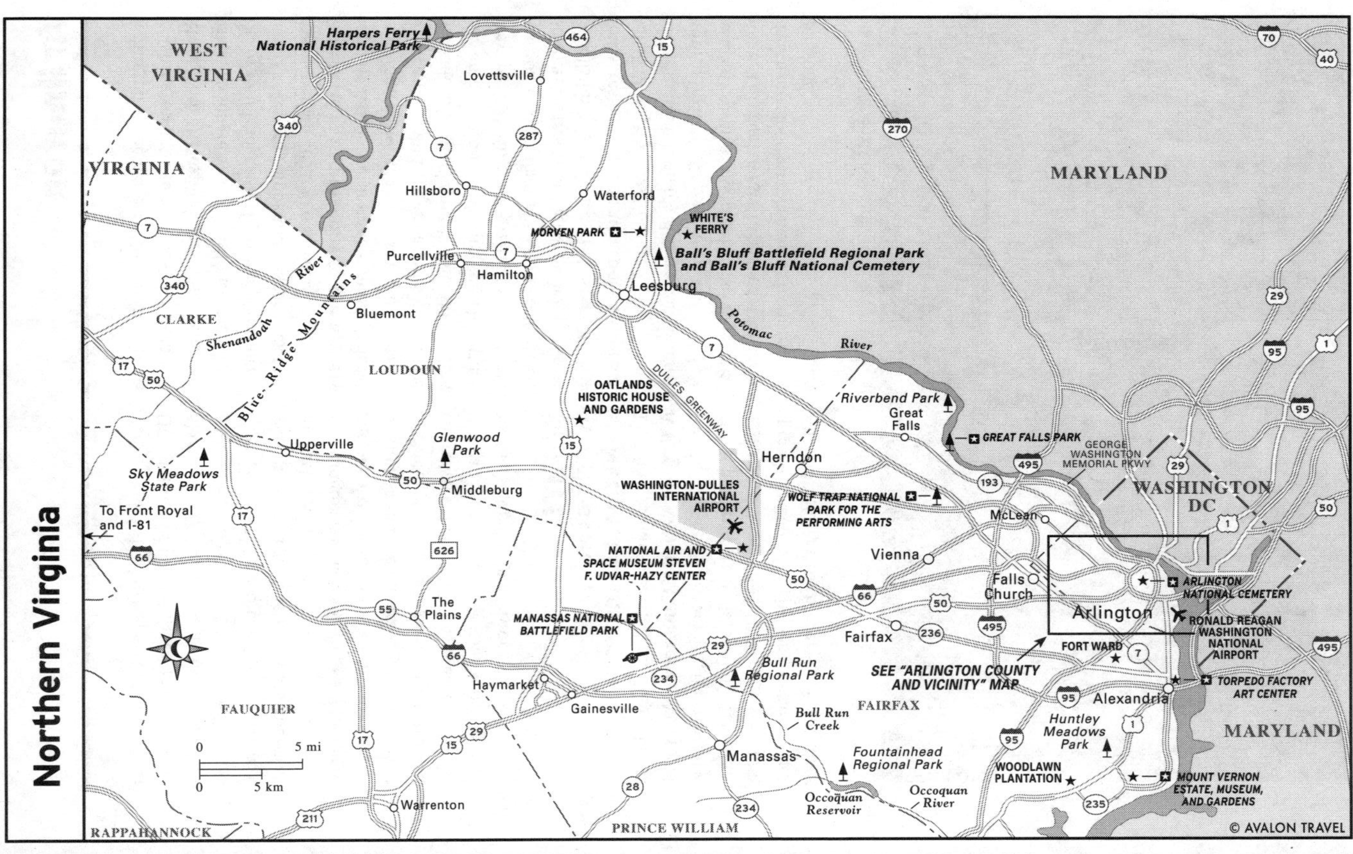
Northern Virginia
WEST VIRGINIA
Harpers Ferry National Historical Park
Lovettsville
VIRGINIA
MARYLAND
Hillsboro
Waterford
WHITE'S FERRY
MORVEN PARK
Ball's Bluff Battlefield Regional Park and Ball's Bluff National Cemetery
Purcellville
Hamilton
River
Leesburg
Blue Ridge Mountains
Bluemont
CLARKE
Shenandoah
Potomac
River
LOUDOUN
OATLANDS HISTORIC HOUSE AND GARDENS
DULLES GREENWAY
Riverbend Park
Great Falls
GREAT FALLS PARK
GEORGE WASHINGTON MEMORIAL PKWY
Upperville
Glenwood Park
Herndon
Sky Meadows State Park
Middleburg
WASHINGTON-DULLES INTERNATIONAL AIRPORT
WOLF TRAP NATIONAL PARK FOR THE PERFORMING ARTS
WASHINGTON DC
To Front Royal and I-81
McLean
NATIONAL AIR AND SPACE MUSEUM STEVEN F. UDVAR-HAZY CENTER
Vienna
Falls Church
ARLINGTON NATIONAL CEMETERY
The Plains
Arlington
RONALD REAGAN WASHINGTON NATIONAL AIRPORT
MANASSAS NATIONAL BATTLEFIELD PARK
Fairfax
FORT WARD
Bull Run Regional Park
SEE "ARLINGTON COUNTY AND VICINITY" MAP
TORPEDO FACTORY ART CENTER
Haymarket
Alexandria
FAUQUIER
Gainesville
FAIRFAX
Bull Run Creek
MARYLAND
Huntley Meadows Park
0
5 mi
Manassas
Fountainhead Regional Park
0
5 km
WOODLAWN PLANTATION
MOUNT VERNON ESTATE, MUSEUM, AND GARDENS
Occoquan Reservoir
Occoquan River
Warrenton
RAPPAHANNOCK
PRINCE WILLIAM
© AVALON TRAVEL

Arlington

Arlington is the closest Virginia suburb to Washington DC. Just across the Potomac River from the capital, Arlington encompasses 26 square miles, is easily accessed from DC by four bridges and by public transportation (11 Metrorail stops and bus service), and has more than 200,000 residents.

Because of its proximity to the nation's capital, Arlington supports many federal buildings, national agencies, and memorials. Between this and the numerous businesses that call Arlington home, it sometimes seems like an extension of Washington DC rather than part of Virginia. Arlington contains more office space than downtown Los Angeles. Business centers in Arlington include the areas of Ballston, Clarendon, and Crystal City, but hotels, restaurants, and attractions are spread out all over Arlington County.

Arlington is a highly diverse community. Approximately 27 percent of the county's residents speak a language besides English at home. This contributes to a wonderful array of authentic food establishments from around the globe.

Originally slated to be part of Washington DC, Arlington was trimmed from the city plan in 1847 when it was established as Alexandria County. In 1920, the name was changed to Arlington, after the George Washington Parke Custis's estate honoring the earl of Arlington.

Arlington is a place you will want to step in and out of during a visit to the nation's capital, but unless you are attending a specific event or coming for work, you don't need to plan an entire week there. It is so easily accessible that you can pick and choose your activities and see the highlights in a day or two.

SIGHTS

★ Arlington National Cemetery

The most famous cemetery in the nation is **Arlington National Cemetery** (1 Memorial Dr., 877/907-8585, www.arlingtoncemetery.mil, Apr.-Sept. daily 8am-7pm, Oct.-Mar. daily 8am-5pm, free). The cemetery is a sprawling 200-acre site where more than 300,000 soldiers from every U.S. military

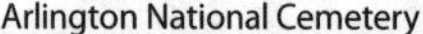
Arlington National Cemetery

Arlington County and Vicinity

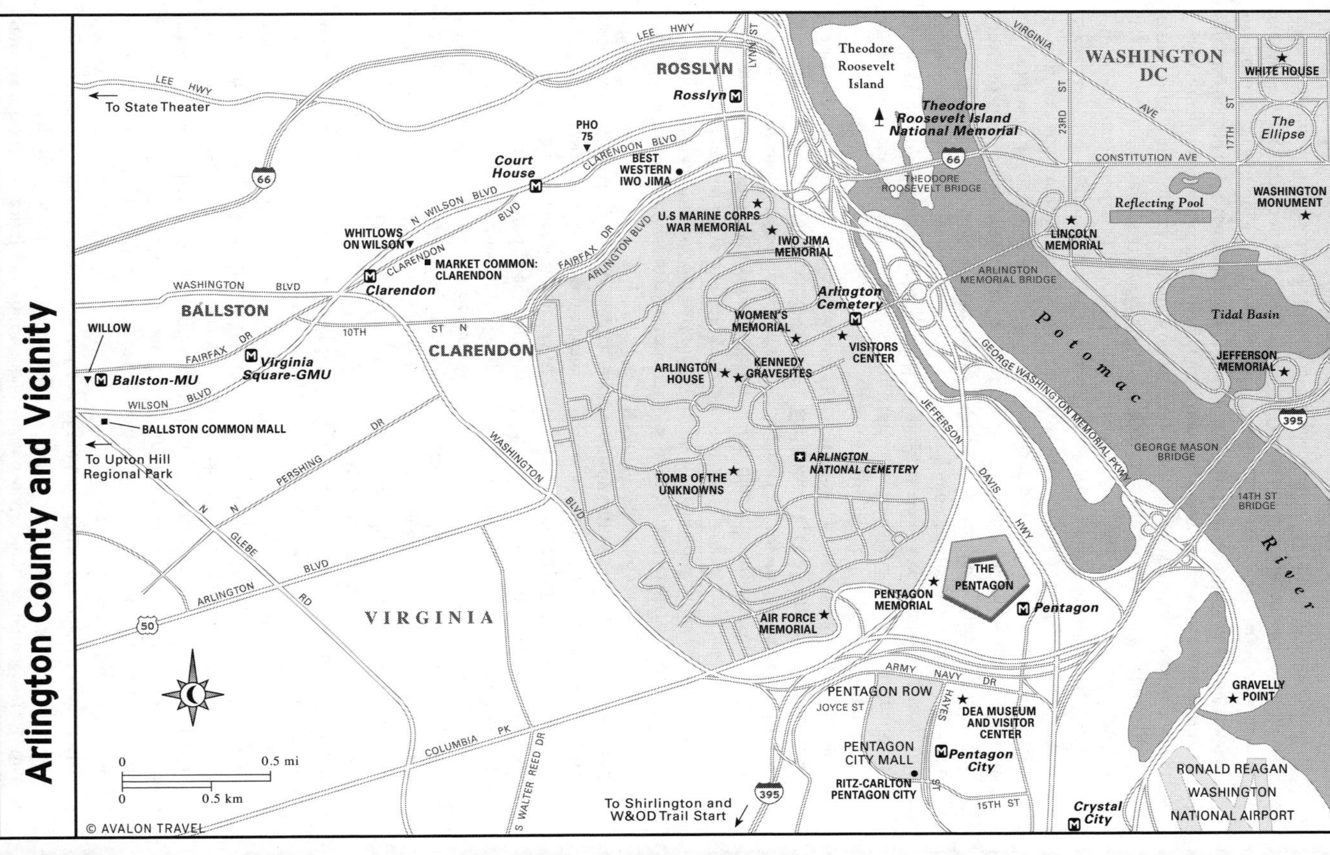

conflict are buried. The uniform white tombstones form an orderly quilt across the rolling green fields of the cemetery and are meticulously maintained. Called "Our Nation's Most Sacred Shrine," as the resting place for many generations of our nation's heroes, the cemetery grows daily: On average, more than two dozen funerals are held each weekday. In 1948, a group of women formed the Arlington Ladies, a volunteer group whose members attend services for all veterans and ensure that no member of the armed forces is ever buried alone.

A welcome center marks the entrance to Arlington National Cemetery and is always open when the cemetery is. Maps, grave locations, guidebooks, and other information on the cemetery can be obtained at the center, and there are restrooms and a bookstore.

Interpretive bus tours of the cemetery depart continuously from the welcome center. Tickets can be purchased at the center for $8.75.

Private cars are not allowed in the cemetery except by special permission, but parking is available off Memorial Drive in a paid parking garage ($1.75 for the first three hours, then $2.50 per hour) and there is a dedicated stop for the cemetery on the Metrorail Blue Line. Please remember that this is not a park but an active cemetery.

There are several key sights within Arlington National Cemetery that are well worth a visit.

The first and the best known is the **Tomb of the Unknowns.** The Tomb of the Unknowns is located in the middle of the cemetery and has a flat-faced form with relieved corners. The sides are also relieved with neoclassical pilasters. The tomb houses the remains of unidentified American soldiers from World Wars I and II and the Korean Conflict. Remains of a Vietnam War soldier were also housed in the tomb until they were identified in 1998 through DNA testing and relocated. That crypt remains empty but serves as a symbol. The Medal of Honor was presented to each of the interred soldiers and these medals, along with the U.S. flags that draped their caskets, are displayed to the rear of the tomb in the Memorial Amphitheater. The tomb is guarded around the clock by the 3rd U.S. Infantry, and the changing of the guard is a popular tourist attraction. Guard changes occur every 30 minutes during the summer and every hour during winter.

Another popular sight at Arlington National Cemetery is the **Women's Memorial** (www.womensmemorial.org), an elegant semicircular retaining wall built of stone at the main entrance to the cemetery. This is the only national memorial honoring American servicewomen. The memorial is open to the public every day except Christmas Day.

A short walk uphill from the Women's Memorial is the eternal flame and burial site of **John F. Kennedy.** This is one of the most-visited graves in the cemetery. **Jacqueline Kennedy Onassis** is buried next to him, and **Robert F. Kennedy** was laid to rest nearby in a grave marked (at his request) with only a single white wooden cross and excerpts from two of his civil rights speeches.

Another sight to visit while in Arlington National Cemetery is the **Arlington House, The Robert E. Lee Memorial** (321 Sherman Dr., Fort Myer, 703/235-1530, www.nps.gov/arho, daily Oct.-Feb. 9:30am-4:30pm, Mar.-May 9am-5pm, Jun.-Aug. 9am-5:30pm, Sept. 9am-5pm, closed Dec. 25 and Jan. 1, free). This former home of George Washington Parke Custis, whose daughter married Robert E. Lee, is actually a national park and maintained by the National Park Service. The Greek revival-style mansion sits on land that was once part of a 1,100-acre plantation where the Lee family lived for three decades before the Civil War. Expect to see period furnishings inside the home and to learn the interesting story of how the home was lost by the family during the Civil War. The site is the highest in Arlington National Cemetery and offers terrific views of Washington DC. The house is open for self-guided tours and is a 10-minute walk from the cemetery welcome center.

Iwo Jima Memorial

The **Iwo Jima Memorial,** also called the **U.S. Marine Corps War Memorial** (1400 N. Meade St., 703/289-2500, open 24 hours, free) stands to honor those Marines who died in defense of the United States. This awe-inspiring memorial is a 32-foot-tall granite and bronze sculpture created in the likeness of a Pulitzer Prize-winning photograph depicting the raising of the American flag on Iwo Jima (a small island off the coast of Japan) in March 1945, near the end of World War II. The sculpture illustrates the U.S. flag being raised by five Marines and a Navy hospital corpsman. The detail in the memorial is stunning, and its enormous size adds to its inspirational appeal. This off-the-beaten-path memorial is definitely worth seeking out. It's a half-mile walk from the Rosslyn Metrorail station and slightly farther from the Arlington Cemetery Metrorail Station.

Pentagon Memorial

The **Pentagon Memorial** (1 Rotary Rd., Pentagon, 703/697-7351, www.pentagonmemorial.net, open 24 hours, free) is a haunting, thought-provoking memorial dedicated to the 184 people who lost their lives at the Pentagon in the terrorist attacks of September 11, 2001. This two-acre memorial is just outside the Pentagon and is made up of 184 benches, one for each of the men and women who died both on the plane that hit the building and inside the building. Illuminated fountains run beneath each bench. If you look at the side of the Pentagon building, it is easy to tell where the plane crashed: The stone replaced in the repair is slightly different in color from the rest of the building. The memorial is open all the time and can be accessed from the Pentagon stop on the Yellow or Blue Lines on the Metrorail.

Air Force Memorial

The **Air Force Memorial** (1 Air Force Memorial Dr., 703/979-0674, www.airforcememorial.org, Apr.-Sept. daily 8am-11pm, Oct.-Mar. daily 8am-9pm, free) is a sight that's visible from a considerable distance. Its three elegant stainless steel and concrete spires

the Iwo Jima Memorial

stretch 270 feet toward the sky, honoring the service and lives of the men and women of the U.S. Air Force.

Drug Enforcement Administration Museum and Visitors Center

The **Drug Enforcement Administration Museum and Visitors Center** (700 Army Navy Dr., 202/307-3463, www.deamuseum.org, Tues.-Fri. 10am-4pm, free) is a learning center dedicated to educating the public about drugs, addiction, law enforcement, and the history of drugs in the United States. It does so through a series of displays that discuss the impact of federal law enforcement on the evolving nature of licit and illicit drug use in the country.

Gravelly Point Park

Gravelly Point Park (George Washington Parkway, daily dawn to dusk, free) is a very popular spot for plane-watching. Its proximity to the runways at Ronald Reagan Washington National Airport offers spectacular close-up views of planes as they approach and depart from the airport. The park sits directly on the Potomac River and offers a boat launch, picnic tables, and plenty of open spaces on which to throw down a blanket. A bike path also runs around the park. There's a three-hour limit on parking (which is enforced), so set your cell phone alarm if you plan to nap. This is also a great spot for watching the fireworks on the National Mall on the Fourth of July, but you'll have to get here early to find parking. The entrance to the park is only available from the northbound lanes of the parkway.

ENTERTAINMENT AND EVENTS

Theater

The **Signature Theatre** (4200 Campbell Ave., 703/820-9771, www.signature-theatre.org), in the trendy shopping area of Shirlington, is a professional nonprofit theater company that features contemporary performances. Although it runs many traditional productions, it is widely known for its musical theater and inventive twists on lesser-known works. A top regional theater with an interesting design, set among a great selection of restaurants and shopping, the Signature Theatre has become a popular destination for the entire metropolitan area. Tickets are reasonably priced but can be difficult to obtain at the last minute.

After seeing a performance at the **Synetic Theater** (1800 S. Bell St., 703/824-8060, www.synetictheater.org) you may reevaluate the whole theater experience. The goal of this award-winning company is to be the premier American physical theater—in short, this means they perform without speaking. Known for their Shakespeare productions, the theater uses movement, acrobatics, dance, music, and a number of other communication forms to create a very distinct form of theater, telling classic stories in an untraditional way.

Nightlife

The **Arlington Cinema & Draft House** (2903 Columbia Pike, 703/486-2345, www.arlingtondrafthouse.com) is a tradition in Northern Virginia. It opened its doors in 1985 and has served up dinner and a movie (with a full bar) ever since. The theater also offers live entertainment and broadcasts sporting events. This is a 21-and-over venue, and it is also available for rent for private parties.

An intimate Clarendon icon, **Iota Club and Café** (2832 Wilson Blvd., 703/522-8340, www.iotaclubandcafe.com, Mon.-Fri. 5pm, Sat.-Sun. 10am, closing varies by performance schedule) is a small venue with live music, poetry readings, good food ($11-30), and a friendly atmosphere. Shows include everything from rock, folk, and alternative to open mic nights. Both shows and food are reasonably priced. Tickets for shows are only available at the door and range $10-17.

Another local institution on Wilson Boulevard is **Whitlows on Wilson** (2854 Wilson Blvd., 703/276-9693, www.whitlows.com, Mon.-Fri. 11am-2am, Sat.-Sun.

9am-2am). This historic venue, which was originally located in Washington DC, features rock, reggae, hip-hop, dance, and blues shows Thursday through Saturday. They have food and drink specials throughout the week. Be sure to look around for reclaimed items such as the bowling lane bar top, booths from St. Patrick's Catholic Church, and chairs from the old Arlington County courthouse.

The State Theatre in nearby Falls Church (220 N. Washington St., Falls Church, 703/237-0300, www.thestatetheatre.com) used to be an old-time movie theater, complete with balcony seating. In recent years, the theater has been renovated as a prime venue for concerts and comedy. There are several levels of seating and standing areas (including the balcony). Food and beverages are served, and table seating can be reserved. This is a fun venue with first-rate entertainment. Parking can be difficult, so plan to arrive early.

Festivals

There are a number of annual festivals held in Arlington. One of the most popular is **The Taste of Arlington** (www.tasteofarlington.com) held each May in Ballston Common (4238 Wilson Blvd.). This lively street festival with entertainment, children's activities, and participation by more than 35 restaurants began in 1987. The **Feel the Heritage** event in February at the **Charles Drew Community Center** (3500 23rd St. S, www.parks.arlingtonva.us) celebrates African American culture with live music, vendors, children's activities, food, and a hall of history.

The **Arlington County Fair** (www.arlingtoncountyfair.us) is also popular. It is one of the largest free annual events on the East Coast and draws over 50,000 people each August. The fair is held at the **Thomas Jefferson Community Center** (3501 S. 2nd St.). Shuttle service is available from nearby Metro stations.

SHOPPING

There are six primary shopping areas in Arlington. **Ballston Common Mall** (4238 Wilson Blvd., 703/243-8088, www.ballston-common.com, Mon.-Sat. 10am-9pm, Sun. noon-6pm) is a four-level enclosed mall at the corner of Glebe Road and Wilson Boulevard. The mall includes national stores such as Macy's, a movie theater, a health club, and many smaller shops. The **Market Common: Clarendon** (2800 Clarendon Blvd., 703/807-2922, www.marketcommonclarendon.net, Mon.-Sat. 10am-9pm, Sun. 11am-6pm) is at the Clarendon Orange Line Metrorail stop. It is primarily an outdoor shopping mall (with garage parking) that has national name-brand retailers such as Crate & Barrel, Barnes & Noble, and Ann Taylor and local boutiques. There is also a Whole Foods Market in the shopping center.

Pentagon Centre at Pentagon City (1100 S. Hayes St., 703/415-2401, www.simon.com, Mon.-Sat. 10am-9:30pm, Sun. 11am-6pm) is a large mall with many national retailers such as Macy's, Nordstrom, and Banana Republic. **Pentagon Row** (1201 S. Joyce Street, www.pentagonrow.com, Mon.-Sat. 10am-9pm, Sun. noon-6pm) also offers shopping and restaurants in a central plaza with outdoor cafés and ice-skating in winter. It is off I-395 (a parking garage is available) near the Pentagon City Metro station on the Yellow and Blue Lines.

The **Village at Shirlington** (2700 S. Quincy St., www.villageatshirlington.com) has become a popular gathering place because of its great choices of restaurants and small shops. It is an outdoor mall, but garage parking is available. If you are in the Crystal City area, there are plenty of restaurants and shops between 12th and 23rd Streets near the Crystal City Metro stop in an area formally known as the **Crystal City Shops** (23rd St. and Crystal Dr., 703/922-4636, www.thecrystalcityshops.com and www.crystalcity.org). Many retailers and restaurants are located below ground along a unique network of walkways.

Washington & Old Dominion Railroad Regional Park (W&OD)

The **Washington & Old Dominion Trail** (www.wodfriends.org) is known as Virginia's skinniest park. It's hard to believe that a regional park can be 45 miles long and just 100 feet wide, but this popular trail is exactly that. It begins at the intersection of Shirlington Road and Four Mile Run Drive in Arlington (just two blocks north of I-395) and follows an old rail route west through Falls Church (crossing over Route 7) and into Vienna. A bridle path parallels the trail starting in Vienna, and the two paths continue through Reston, Herndon, Ashburn, and Leesburg before ending in the cute town of Purcellville on 21st Street.

Trains followed this route for more than 100 years (1859-1968), but today it is widely used for biking, running, walking, and inline skating. The asphalt trail is predominantly rolling although there are many nice flat sections. There are few true hills, but the trail does gain in overall elevation heading west.

Proper trail etiquette includes staying to the right side of the path as you travel and making yourself known to slower traffic as you pass on the left. A simple "Passing left" callout is enough to warn people when you are going around them on the trail.

There are several rest areas. The largest is the Smiths Switch Station in Ashburn. This stop offers two portable toilets, a covered rest area, and vending machines. Another unofficial but extremely popular stop is at the Ashburn Road crossing at the **Carolina Brothers Pit Barbeque restaurant and shop** (20702 Ashburn Rd., 703/729-7070, www.carolinabrothers.com, Sun.-Thurs. 10:30am-7pm, Fri.-Sat. 10:30am-8pm, under $10). It's hard to ignore the smell of their barbecue cooking, and they have a wonderful outdoor area with tables and umbrellas and numerous bike racks. They also sell drinks and snacks. There are several more porta-potty stops along the trail including in Reston and Leesburg. As the trail passes through Vienna, it borders a Whole Foods Market where many people like to stop as well. There's also a community center in Vienna with public bathrooms.

SPORTS AND RECREATION

Trails

There are many paved bike trails throughout Northern Virginia and several go through Arlington. The 18-mile **Mount Vernon Trail** runs between Theodore Roosevelt Island (an 88-acre island and national park that sits in the Potomac River near the Roosevelt Bridge) and Mount Vernon Estate. The trail runs along the George Washington Memorial Parkway and passes by Gravelly Point Park and Ronald Reagan Washington National Airport and goes into Old Town Alexandria.

The **Four Mile Run Trail** is a 6.2-mile paved path that begins at **Bluemont Junction Park** (744 N. Emerson St.) and runs toward the Mount Vernon Trail and Ronald Reagan Washington National Airport. The **Washington & Old Dominion Trail** also begins in Arlington in the Shirlington area and runs west 45 miles to Purcellville, Virginia. One offshoot of the trail is the **Martha Custis Trail,** which intersects the Washington & Old Dominion Trail at mile marker 4. The Martha Custis Trail heads directly into Washington DC through Arlington on a four-mile paved path parallel to Route 66. There are a handful of climbs and some winding turns, but nothing too difficult. For a detailed map visit www.bikewashington.org.

Trail runners will enjoy the **Potomac Heritage Trail.** It begins on the west side of Theodore Roosevelt Island at the parking lot and runs 10 miles to the west end of the I-495 bridge. It passes through woods along the river, crosses small cliff tops, and spans a few streams. It is blazed in blue.

For additional information and trail maps, contact the **Northern Virginia Regional Park Authority** (703/352-5900, www.nvrpa.

org) or the **Arlington County Department of Parks and Recreation** (703/228-4747).

Parks

Upton Hill Regional Park (6060 Wilson Blvd., 703/534-3437, www.nvrpa.org) is a popular family recreation area with a large outdoor water park, a playground, a miniature golf course, and batting cages for both baseball and softball. There is a basic snack bar with reasonable prices. Each activity in the park has its own hours of operation, so it's best to consult the website.

Theodore Roosevelt Island (703/289-2500, www.nps.gov/this) is a beautiful island in the Potomac River accessed off the northbound lanes of the George Washington Memorial Parkway. There are wooded trails and a 47-foot-tall monument to Roosevelt. Ranger tours are available to learn about the local wildlife. The views are beautiful if you can ignore the noise from the planes taking off and landing at Ronald Reagan Washington National Airport.

Another family recreation area is **Bluemont Park** (601 N. Manchester St., 703/228-6525, www.arlingtonva.us). This 70-acre park offers many family activities including picnicking, horseshoes, fishing, a playground, a basketball court, a baseball field, tennis, volleyball, a playground, and Frisbee golf.

For a complete list of Arlington County parks, visit www.arlingtonva.us.

Tennis

There are dozens of public tennis courts in Arlington. To view locations and reserve a court, visit www.arlingtonva.us.

Canoeing and Kayaking

There are two good launch areas on the Potomac River in Arlington. The first is **Columbia Island Marina** (202/347-0173, www.columbiaisland.com) off the George Washington Parkway, and the second is **Gravelly Point Park** (George Washington Parkway).

Four-hour guided "D.C. Monument Tour" kayak trips on the Potomac River are available through **Potomac Paddlesports** (301/881-2628, www.potomacpaddlesports.com, $95). Trips leave from Columbia Island Marina in Arlington.

FOOD

Arlington is known for its diversity of wonderful food. Many eateries serve authentic fare from around the globe and do so at a reasonable price.

American

★ **The Lost Dog Café** (5876 Washington Blvd., 703/237-1552, www.lostdogcafe.com, Mon.-Sat. 11am-11pm, Sun. 11am-10pm, $7-26) is a local favorite for three reasons: great food, great beer, and its ties to the Lost Dog & Cat Rescue Foundation (founded by the restaurant owners). The restaurant is a lively, friendly, and casual café and gourmet pizza deli that serves a creative and delicious assortment of specialty pizzas, sandwiches, salads, and pasta. Menu items are made in house with fresh ingredients and many follow a canine naming convention such as the "Kujo Pie" (tomato sauce with pesto, artichoke hearts, grilled chicken, fresh tomatoes, mozzarella, and basil), the "Big Red Pie" (marinara sauce topped with mozzarella and basil on a whole-wheat pizza crust), and "dog collars" (onion rings). They also offer a good selection of vegetarian options. The bar stocks more than 200 types of beer (with many on tap), and the staff is very knowledgeable and helpful when it comes to choosing the right one. The decor is completely done in "dog"—although due to health regulations, no dogs are allowed inside. There are dog paintings and murals throughout the café and many small portraits of dogs saved through the foundation. A portion of the proceeds from the restaurant goes to the foundation, but even if you aren't a canine enthusiast, the food alone is reason to come. Consult the website for additional locations.

For some classic diner food, try **Metro 29 Diner** (4711 Lee Hwy., 703/528-2464, www.

metro29diner.com, daily 6am-12am, $5-27). This local institution was featured on the TV show *Diners, Drive-ins and Dives.* They provide a monster menu of delicious homemade food and serve it up fresh in their 12,000-square-foot restaurant. All food is made from scratch; they even make their gravy in house and fresh challah bread for their French toast. They serve breakfast, lunch, and dinner, and they're open late. The service is friendly, and the place has a true diner feel.

A very popular choice for steak in Arlington is **Ray's the Steaks** (2300 Wilson Blvd., 703/841-7297, www.raysthesteaks.com, daily 5pm-10pm, $15-45) in the Navy League Building (for GPS directions, use 2301 Clarendon Blvd.). Ray's offers scrumptious steaks at reasonable prices. They also offer a scant selection of salads and seafood.

Asian

The **Bangkok Bistro at Ballston** (715 N. Glebe Rd., 703/243-9669, www.bangkokbistrova.com, Sun.-Thurs. 11am-10:15pm, Fri.-Sat. 11am-10:45pm, $11-25) is a great place to have lunch or dinner after a busy day of shopping. It serves delicious contemporary Thai food in a casual atmosphere and can accommodate large groups. The food is fresh and flavorful, and the presentation carefully planned. The Bistro Sampler is a good way to begin a meal. For first-time Thai diners, the traditional pad thai is a solid choice. The prices are reasonable, and they offer appetizer and drinks specials in the evening on weekdays.

Another good Thai option is **Thai Square** (3217 Columbia Pike, 703/685-7040, www.thaisquarerestaurant.com, Mon.-Thurs. 11:30am-10pm, Fri. 11:30am-11pm, Sat. noon-11pm, Sun. noon-10:30pm, $8.50-17.50). This plain, no-frills restaurant built a reputation on its food. Street parking can be tough, but the service is good and the specials delicious. If you like spicy Thai food, this is an especially good choice.

Some of the most flavorful and creative Chinese food in the area is made at ★ **Peking Gourmet** (6029 Leesburg Pike, Falls Church, 703/671-8088, www.pekinggourmet.com, Sun.-Thurs. 11am-10:30pm, Fri.-Sat. 11am-11pm, $12-43) in nearby Falls Church. The gallery of celebrity photos hanging on the wall speaks volumes regarding the clientele at the restaurant, and it's not unusual to have VIPs in house. The signature dish is the Peking duck, which is nothing short of amazing. It arrives whole and is expertly carved tableside. Other must-try dishes include the chicken and garlic shoots (when available) and the crispy beef. Hands down, this is *the* best Chinese restaurant in Northern Virginia, and as such, it is crowded—so be sure to make a reservation.

If you're craving pho and only pho, stop by **Pho 75** (1721 Wilson Blvd., 703/525-7355, daily 10am-9pm, under $10). It is one of the original pho restaurants in the area, and they know pho. The soup is hot, delicious, and reasonably priced.

French

If you're feeling the itch for French food, try **La Cote D'or Café** (6876 Lee Hwy., 703/538-3033, www.lacotedorcafe.com, lunch daily 11:30am-3pm, dinner daily 5pm-10pm, $15-39), a family-owned restaurant that is named after the Burgundy region in France. They serve delicious bistro-style French food—crepes, filet, and seafood—and a carefully selected wine list. The service is friendly and attentive, and you can expect an overall pleasant dining experience in a comfortable French country atmosphere.

Italian

As the name suggests, **The Italian Store** (3123 Lee Hwy., 703/528-6266, www.italianstore.com, Mon.-Fri. 10am-9pm, Sat. 10am-8pm, Sun. 11am-6pm, $7-23) is a casual authentic takeout pizzeria and sandwich store combined with an Italian market. Simply put, this place is fabulous. Fresh ingredients, homemade pasta, and Italian wines are just part of the recipe for success. This is a very popular carryout restaurant and is geared toward that, so if you come during peak lunch hours, be prepared to wait.

Middle Eastern

For a quick meal or to curb a late-night appetite, stop in **Kabob Palace** (2315 S. Eads St., 703/486-3535, www.kabobpalaceusa.com, open 24 hours, $8-19) in Crystal City. The kabobs are tender and flavorful (the lamb is especially juicy), and the sides are authentic and delicious. Their rice is tasty and fluffy, and their mango lassi is refreshing. The clientele is diverse and lively, and the service is usually good.

Treats and Coffee

After trying the **Best Buns Bread Company** (4010 Campbell Ave. 703/578-1500, www.greatamericanrestaurants.com, Mon. 6am-7pm, Tues.-Fri. 6am-8pm, Fri. Sat. 7am-8pm, Sun. 7am-7pm, under $15) in Shirlington, you will look for an excuse to come back, maybe even the same day. Whether you're craving sweets, bread, or a sandwich, this is the place to go. They are part of the Great American Restaurants group, which includes **Carlyle Grand Café** (4000 Campbell Ave., 703/931-0777, www.greatamericanrestaurants.com, Mon.-Thurs. 11:30am-10:30pm, Fri. 11:30am-11:30pm, Sat. 10:30am-11:30pm, Sun. 9:30am-10:30pm, $15-28) next door. Carlyle Grand serves flavorful American food such as salads, sandwiches, and seafood in a lively environment. They also have a wonderful brunch menu on weekends.

For a good cup of joe, try the **Java Shack** (2507 N. Franklin Rd., 703/527-9556, www.javashack.com, Mon.-Sat. 7am-7pm, Sun. 8am-7pm) just off of Wilson Boulevard. It's pet friendly, people friendly, casual, a little quirky, and best of all, it serves good coffee and tea. The atmosphere is very relaxing, which is rare to find in the hubbub of Northern Virginia. The porch is especially pleasant for catching up with friends on a nice day.

Farmers Markets

Arlington has several good farmers markets: the **Arlington County Farmers Market** (2100 Clarendon Blvd., www.arlingtonfarmersmarket.com, Sat. Apr.-Dec. 8am-noon, Jan.-Mar. 9am-noon), the **Clarendon Farmers Market** (Clarendon's Metro Station Central Park, 703/812-8881, year-round Wed. 2pm-7pm), the **Columbia Pike Farmers Market** (corner of S. Walter Reed Dr. and Columbia Pike, www.columbia-pike.org/fm/, year-round Sun. 9am-1pm), the **Crystal City Farmers Market** (Crystal City Dr. between 18th and 20th Sts., www.crystalcity.org, Apr-Nov. Tues. 3pm-7pm), and the **Rosslyn Farmers Market** (Wilson Blvd. and N. Oak St., 703/522-6628, www.rosslynva.org, May-Oct. Thurs. 11am-2pm).

ACCOMMODATIONS

Spending the night in Arlington can often be a less expensive alternative to staying in Washington DC. There are mostly large chain hotels in Arlington, but there are a few lesser-known alternatives that shouldn't be overlooked.

$100-200

There are few reliable hotels priced under $200 a night in peak tourist season in Arlington. The **Best Western Iwo Jima** (1501 Arlington Blvd., 703/524-5000, www.bestwesternvirginia.com, $169-199) is a consistent option. The hotel is reasonably priced for its location: It's minutes from the Iwo Jima Memorial, a short drive to Ronald Reagan Washington National Airport, and walking distance to the Rosslyn Metro stop. It is also convenient to many Washington DC attractions. There are 141 rooms. The rooms are older and aren't fancy, but they are comfortable and have free wireless Internet. There is also on-site parking.

$200-300

The ★ **Hilton Garden Inn Arlington/Shirlington** (4271 Campbell Ave., 703/820-0440, www.hiltongardeninn.hilton.com, $169-247) is nicely located in a neighborhood of shops, restaurants, and theater. It is also convenient to Washington DC. The rooms are amply sized and have comfortable beds. The service is friendly and professional. There are 142 rooms, and standard amenities come with each, including free high-speed Internet, a fitness center, a business center, and a swimming pool. The hotel also offers complimentary shuttle service to Ronald Reagan Washington National Airport and the Pentagon City Metrorail stop.

If you need to stay near Ronald Reagan Washington National Airport, the 161-room **Hampton Inn & Suites Reagan National Airport** (2000 Jefferson Davis Hwy., 703/418-8181, www.hamptoninn.com, $249-290) is a good option. They offer quick shuttle service to the airport and are close to the Metro. Rooms are spacious and include amenities such as free wireless Internet, flat-screen televisions, microwaves, and refrigerators. The beds are comfortable and the bathrooms are modern.

Over $300

The **Residence Inn Arlington Courthouse** (1401 N. Adams St., 703/312-2100, www.marriott.com, $359-379) is a modern, eco-friendly, 176-room hotel in Courthouse Village by the Courthouse Metrorail stop on the Orange Line. Many shops and restaurants are within easy walking distance, and pizza delivery is available to your room. Suites are pleasantly decorated and include wireless Internet and full kitchens. There is also a beautiful indoor pool with a lifeguard and a fitness center. Breakfast is included. There is on-site parking for an additional fee. The hotel allows pets for an additional fee.

Le Meridien (1121 19th St. N., 703/351-9170, www.lemeridienva.com, $424-599) is a boutique hotel in the Rosslyn area of Arlington. It has 154 guest rooms and is nicely appointed with comfortable modern furniture. The staff is friendly, and the hotel is convenient to the Rosslyn Metrorail stop and a short walk to Georgetown. The on-site gym is above normal hotel standards, and there is a parking garage available. Book a room with a view of Georgetown across the Potomac River and take advantage of happy hour on the large patio. The lobby is located on the fourth floor of the building, which can be a little confusing when checking in. There is also a charge for in-room wireless Internet. Le Meridien is a Starwood hotel.

The **Ritz-Carlton, Pentagon City** (1250 S. Hayes St., 703/415-5000, www.ritzcarlton.com, $339-499) is minutes from the Pentagon City Metrorail station. This hotel is consistent in offering a comfortable stay with great beds and attentive service, and they are top-notch for hosting conferences. The location itself is a draw, just minutes from downtown Washington DC and steps from shopping and restaurants. There are 366 guest rooms, and the hotel is pet friendly (for an additional fee).

Bed-and-Breakfasts

There are six bed-and-breakfasts in Arlington included in the **Alexandria and Arlington Bed and Breakfast Network** (703/549-3415, www.aabbn.com). Most are small, private homes with 1-4 available rooms. Full descriptions and contact information for each are listed on the website. Oddly, not all serve breakfast.

INFORMATION AND SERVICES

For additional information on Arlington, contact the **Arlington Convention and Visitors Service** (1100 N. Glebe Rd., 703/228-0808, www.stayarlington.com, daily 8am-5pm).

GETTING THERE AND AROUND

Arlington is just southwest of Washington DC on the other side of the Potomac River. It is a short drive across the Potomac River via the Memorial, Roosevelt, Francis Scott Key, and 14th Street Bridges or a short ride on **Metrorail** (202/637-7000, www.wmata.com). If you plan to stay in Arlington and tour DC, Metrorail is a great way to get there. Service between Washington DC and Arlington is provided via the Orange, Blue, and Yellow Lines. Key stops in Arlington include Ronald Reagan Washington National Airport (Blue and Yellow), Pentagon City (Blue and Yellow), and Clarendon (Orange).

Regional **Metrobus** (202/637-7000, www.wmata.com) service is available in Arlington and also connects Arlington with DC. A list of the routes serving Arlington can be found at www.arlingtontransit.com. **Arlington Transit (ART)** (703/228-7433, www.arlingtontransit.com, $1.75) provides supplemental bus service to the regional Metrobus system by covering neighborhoods within Arlington County not served by Metrobus.

Ronald Reagan Washington National Airport (703/417-8000, www.metwashairports.com) is in Arlington and is the primary arrival and departure point for air travel to Washington DC.

Old Town Alexandria and Vicinity

One of the country's oldest port cities, Old Town Alexandria has a long and vibrant history. Founded in 1749, the town sits on the banks of the Potomac River and offers scenic views of Washington DC and National Harbor.

Old Town Alexandria was an important shipping port because it was the last good anchorage on the river before the falls upstream. Homes, taverns, shipyards, and public warehouses quickly sprang up along the waterfront, and many of our country's founding fathers walked its streets, frequented its taverns, and worshipped in its churches. Teams of horses and oxen rolled hogsheads (large wooden barrels) of tobacco, the primary export at the time, down the streets of Old Town to the waterfront. Soon hemp and wheat joined it in the export trade to England.

The town is well preserved through meticulous restoration efforts and looks much the same as it did when George Washington and Robert E. Lee once walked its cobblestone

Alexandria's City Hall

Old Town Alexandria

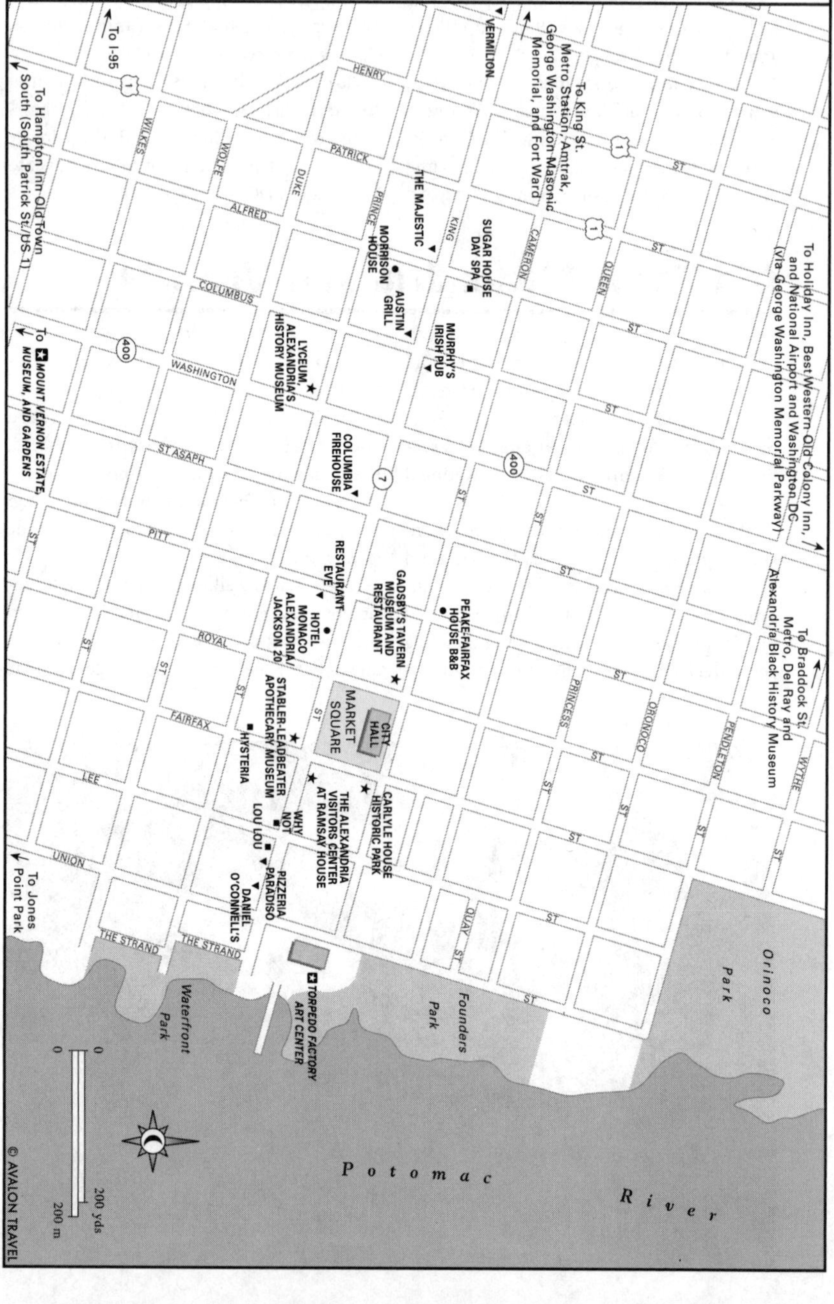

To I-95
To King St. Metro Station, Amtrak, George Washington Masonic Memorial, and Fort Ward
To Holiday Inn, Best Western Old Colony Inn, and National Airport and Washington DC (via George Washington Memorial Parkway)
To Braddock St. Metro, Del Ray and Alexandria Black History Museum
To Hampton Inn Old Town South (South Patrick St./US 1)
To MOUNT VERNON ESTATE, MUSEUM, AND GARDENS
To Jones Point Park

VERMILION
HENRY
PATRICK
WILKES
WOLFE
DUKE
PRINCE
KING
CAMERON
QUEEN
ALFRED
COLUMBUS
WASHINGTON
ST ASAPH
PITT
ROYAL
FAIRFAX
LEE
UNION
THE STRAND
PRINCESS
ORONOCO
PENDLETON
WYTHE
QUAY ST

THE MAJESTIC
SUGAR HOUSE DAY SPA
MORRISON HOUSE
AUSTIN GRILL
MURPHY'S IRISH PUB
LYCEUM, ALEXANDRIA'S HISTORY MUSEUM
COLUMBIA FIREHOUSE
RESTAURANT EVE
HOTEL MONACO ALEXANDRIA/ JACKSON 20
GADSBY'S TAVERN MUSEUM AND RESTAURANT
PEAKE-FAIRFAX HOUSE B&B
CITY HALL
MARKET SQUARE
STABLER-LEADBEATER APOTHECARY MUSEUM
HYSTERIA
THE ALEXANDRIA VISITORS CENTER AT RAMSAY HOUSE
CARLYLE HOUSE HISTORIC PARK
WHY NOT
LOU LOU
PIZZERIA PARADISO
DANIEL O'CONNELL'S
TORPEDO FACTORY ART CENTER

Waterfront Park
Founders Park
Orinoco Park
Potomac River

0 200 yds
0 200 m

streets. More than 4,000 buildings from the 18th and 19th centuries still stand today, giving the city an authentic colonial feel. Other famous residents have included Jim Morrison and Mama Cass. Stroll along the waterfront on a summer evening and enjoy live music or dine in one of the many unique restaurants. This is an area you can see in one day, but may choose to return again and again.

SIGHTS

★ Torpedo Factory Art Center

The **Torpedo Factory Art Center** (105 N. Union St., 703/838-4565, www.torpedofactory.org, daily 10am-6pm and Thurs. until 9pm, free) contains three floors of galleries and studios where visitors can see artists at work and purchase original artwork. The center has 82 studios, six galleries, an art school, and a museum that provides a unique window into Alexandria's history called the **Alexandria Archaeology Museum** (703/746-4399, www.alexandriaarchaeology.org, Tues.-Fri. 10am-3pm, Sat. 10am-5pm, Sun. 1pm-5pm, free). The art center is on the Old Town waterfront, in a former factory that actually produced torpedoes (U.S. Naval Torpedo Station) after World War I. A torpedo that was made in the factory is displayed in the main hall of the building. Today, more than 165 visual artists practice their trade here and encourage visitors to observe them at work. Two workshops are also located inside the Torpedo Factory.

Carlyle House

The beautiful **Carlyle House Historic Park** (121 N. Fairfax St., 703/549-2997, www.nvrpa.org, Tues.-Sat. 10am-4pm, Sun. noon-4pm, $5) is the historic home of British merchant John Carlyle. It was built in 1753 and quickly became the focal point of the political and social circles in Alexandria. One of the first private homes built in Old Town, it is the only 18th-century palladian home built of stone. Tours of the house provide a good window into life in Alexandria prior to the Revolutionary War. Many special events are held at the house throughout the year, including a haunting reenactment of Carlyle's funeral in October and on Halloween.

Gadsby's Tavern Museum

The **Gadsby's Tavern Museum** (134 N. Royal St., 703/746-4242, www.alexandriava.gov, Nov.-Mar. Wed.-Sat. 11am-4pm, Sun. 1pm-4pm, Apr.-Oct. Tues.-Sat. 10am-5pm, Sun.-Mon. 1pm-5pm, $5) includes two 18th-century brick buildings named after John Gadsby: a tavern (circa 1785) and a hotel (built in 1792). Just after the development of Alexandria in the late 1700s, the Gadsby buildings became the center of life and business in Alexandria. Prominent people who visited the establishment included George Washington, Thomas Jefferson, John Adams, James Madison, James Monroe, and the Marquis de Lafayette. The tavern and hotel were restored as a museum that now serves to educate visitors on the history, architecture, and social customs of the colonial period. The short, informative tours are truly fascinating and really give visitors a sense of the history of the period and the people who walked the tavern's halls.

Stabler-Leadbeater Apothecary Museum

An easily overlooked gem is the **Stabler-Leadbeater Apothecary Museum** (105-107 S. Fairfax St., 703/746-3852, www.apothecarymuseum.org, Nov.-Mar. Wed.-Sat. 11am-4pm, Sun. 1pm-4pm, Apr.-Oct. Tues.-Sat. 10am-5pm, Sun.-Mon. 1pm-5pm, $5). Founded in 1792, the apothecary business operated for nearly 150 years; famous customers included Martha Washington and Robert E. Lee (who purchased paint for his home). A short video tour explains an interesting collection of medicine bottles, pill machines, and containers of native-grown cures, but take the guided tour. The guides take their time telling interesting stories of this family business and its customers. Globes filled with colored water stand in the window as some of the first "open" and "closed" signs. The museum is small and plain on the outside, but it's very authentic. Tours are approximately 30 minutes.

Lyceum, Alexandria's History Museum

Lyceum, Alexandria's History Museum (201 S. Washington St., 703/746-4994, www.alexandriava.gov, Mon.-Sat. 10am-5pm, Sun. 1pm-5pm, $2) is, just as its name suggests, a museum dedicated to Alexandria's history. It is housed in an attractive building on South Washington Street fronted by four tall columns; the structure has served as a Civil War hospital, private home, and the nation's first Bicentennial Visitor's Center. The museum is simple but has exhibits on the history of Alexandria, especially during the Civil War, and offers lectures, concerts, school programs, and rental space. There is a gift shop that sells items related to Alexandria including books, maps, and note cards. Several self-guided walking tours of Alexandria begin at the Lyceum. For more information on these, visit www.visitalexandriava.com.

Alexandria Black History Museum

The **Alexandria Black History Museum** (902 Wythe St., 703/746-4356, www.alexandriava.gov, Tues.-Sat. 10am-4pm, $2) is a museum devoted to Alexandria's African American heritage. There are two exhibit galleries in the museum, one of which houses the Robert H. Robinson Library, which opened in 1940 after a sit-in at the segregated Alexandria Library in 1939; it was the first African American library in the area. The other gallery features local history exhibits. A 1797 Free Black Register is one of the most interesting items in the museum and is part of an exhibit that teaches about an area that had both a free black community and enslaved community that existed at the same time. There is also a reading room, art exhibits, and concerts at the museum. The nearby **African American Heritage Park** (Duke Street) is also part of the museum and contains the first African American burial ground in Alexandria, which dates back to the 19th century.

Washington Masonic National Memorial

A hard-to-miss memorial is the **Washington Masonic National Memorial** (101 Callahan Dr., 703/683-2007, www.gwmemorial.org, daily 9am-5pm, extended summer hours, $15), which sits on top of a hill overlooking Alexandria. The memorial was constructed by American Freemasons and is perhaps the most recognized landmark in Alexandria, with its multi-floor tower and observation deck sitting on top of a temple. The entire structure is slightly more than 330 feet tall and was designed as a memorial "lighthouse" to George Washington, who was a Mason. The building was started in 1922, but the interior was not finished until 1970. It also serves as a research and community center and meeting site for Masonic organizations. Tours are offered daily at 9:30am, 11am, 1pm, 2:30pm, and 4pm and last one hour. The tours include access to the tower (by elevator) or access to the observation area (where there is a panoramic view of Alexandria), so a tour is recommended. The museum is a bit dark inside but displays some of George Washington's personal belongings. The memorial is approximately four blocks from the King Street Metrorail station.

Fort Ward Museum and Park

A great place to relax on a nice day and learn a little history is the **Fort Ward Museum and Park** (4301 W. Braddock Rd., 703/746-4848, www.alexandriava.gov, museum Tues.-Sat. 10am-5pm, Sun. noon-5pm, park daily 9am-sunset, free). This fort was constructed during the Civil War by Union troops to protect Washington DC from Confederate forces. It is the best-preserved fort of the system of Union forts and batteries built for that purpose. Since approximately 90 percent of the fort's original walls are intact and much of the fort was restored to its original form, it is easy to see the design. There is a small museum with Civil War collectibles and exhibits and a nice open park with picnic spots and walking paths.

Tours

There are many guided tours available in Old Town. Some of the most popular tours are walking nighttime ghost tours, such as those hosted by **Footsteps to the Past** (703/683-3451, www.footstepstothepast.com, $10-20) and **Alexandria Colonial Tours** (703/519-1749, www.alexcolonialtours.com, $7-13), where tour guides are dressed in period costumes and tell chilling historical stories and legends. There are also self-guided bike tours from **Bike and Roll DC** (3 Cameron St., 202/842-2453, www.bikethesites.com, $16-40) and seasonal sightseeing cruises with **The Potomac Riverboat Company** (205 The Strand., 703/684-0580, www.potomacriverboatco.com, $12). If a meal on the water sounds more relaxing, go aboard one of the **Dandy Restaurant Cruise Ships** (Zero Prince St., 703/683-6076, www.dandydinnerboat.com, $50-108). They offer lunch and dinner cruises, and they are also available for private parties. For a list of tour operators, please visit www.visitalexandriava.com.

ENTERTAINMENT AND EVENTS

Music and Theater

The Birchmere (3701 Mount Vernon Ave., 703/549-7500, www.birchmere.com, $20-75) is a legendary concert hall seating approximately 500 people that hosts nationally known bands in many genres including folk, jazz, bluegrass, country, and rock. There is table seating at the main stage with food service. The bandstand includes a dance area. The theater offers a casual, intimate atmosphere with decent food. Parking is a little tricky, so consult the website for directions.

Other good choices for an evening of live music are **Basin Street Lounge** (219 King St., 703/549-1141, www.219restaurant.com), a sophisticated and intimate establishment above the 219 Restaurant that hosts live jazz Tuesday-Saturday, and **Murphy's A Grand Irish Pub** (713 King St., 703/548-1717, www.murphyspub.com). Murphy's serves traditional Irish food, has a good selection of beers on tap, and has live music most nights. It has a lively pub atmosphere and friendly patrons and servers.

For something completely different, spend an evening at **Medieval Madness at Renaissance Hall** (703/329-3075, www.medievalmadness.org, starting at $65). Bring your appetite, a few close friends, a sense of humor, and an open mind, and you'll have a memorable night eating, drinking, and participating in a political satire set in 15th-century England. Audience participation is key with this show so don't be shy. With new shows premiering every four months, there are many repeat patrons. Shows are presented every Friday at 7pm and Saturday at 6pm.

The Little Theatre of Alexandria (600 Wolfe St., 703/683-0496, www.thelittletheatre.com) was founded in 1934 and is one of just a handful of community theaters in the United States with its own building. Many famous people have sat in its audience including President Harry S. Truman, Lady Bird Johnson, and President George W. Bush. The theater hosts a seven-show season.

Festivals and Events

Old Town hosts numerous festivals and events throughout the year. Following are just some of the fun experiences visitors can participate in. Please visit www.visitalexandriava.com for a full list of events.

The **Alexandria Film Festival** (www.alexfilmfest.com) is an annual tradition in November that celebrates the work of both established and emerging filmmakers from around the world. Dozens of films including independents, shorts, documentaries, animation, and features are shown in multiple locations around Alexandria.

Those fortunate enough to be in Old Town Alexandria during **Alexandria Restaurant Week** (www.visitalexandriava.com) are in for a treat. For one week at the end of January and the beginning of February, more than 60 area restaurants offer special menus at discounted prices. It's a great time for visitors to sample the variety of cuisine available in Old Town and for residents to try new establishments.

The **Alexandria Festival of the Arts** (www.artfestival.com) is an annual street festival that takes place on King Street in September. Voted one of the top 100 art festivals in the United States by *Sunshine Artist Magazine,* the juried festival features pieces from artists selected for the quality and originality of their work. Paintings, sculpture, jewelry, photography, and ceramics are just some of the types of art visitors can expect to see. The show stretches down several blocks of King Street to the waterfront.

SHOPPING

Old Town Alexandria is a shopaholic's dream. Block after block of award-winning boutiques, national-brand stores, and specialty shops can exhaust even the most fit shopper. Whether you're looking for clothes, souvenirs, antiques, artwork, or something unusual and funky, you can participate in a tradition of buying and sharing bounty that started back in colonial times. The primary shopping area stretches 11 blocks from the Potomac River up King Street.

Hysteria (123 S. Fairfax St., 703/548-1615, www.shophysteria.com) offers stylish, up-to-date designer women's clothes and accessories. This store is a local favorite, as is **Lou Lou** (132 King St., 703/299-9505, www.loulouboutiques.com). Lou Lou sells jewelry and accessories at reasonable prices. They offer a wide variety of colors and designs.

For the little ones on your shopping list, try **Why Not** (200 King St., 703/548-4420). They offer unique, high-quality toys at reasonable prices.

To search for a particular type of store, visit www.visitalexandriava.com.

SPORTS AND RECREATION

TopGolf

If you're looking for something different to do, try **TopGolf Alexandria** (6625 S. Van Dorn St., 703/924-2600, www.topgolf.com, Mon.-Sat. 9am-11pm, Sun. 9am-9pm, games start at $7 not including food). TopGolf is a golf entertainment complex where guests can play different point-scoring golf games using personalized microchipped golf balls. The games are similar to bowling and darts, but use golf balls and clubs. No golf experience is necessary.

Parks

CAMERON RUN REGIONAL PARK

Cameron Run Regional Park (4001 Eisenhower Ave., 703/960-0767, www.nvrpa.org, summer daily 11am-7pm, $15.75) may be showing its age, but it's still a fun place to take the kids for a day of water fun (wave pool and waterslides), mini-golf, and batting cages.

HUNTLEY MEADOWS PARK

Wildlife-watching is possible in the middle of suburban Northern Virginia at **Huntley Meadows Park** (3701 Lockheed Blvd., 703/768-2525, www.fairfaxcounty.gov, open daily dawn to dark, free). This 1,425-acre park offers great wetland wildlife-viewing from its half-mile boardwalk trail and observation tower. The park is a noted birding area, with more than 200 species, and also supports beaver, frogs, and dragonflies. A visitors center has exhibits, and there are two miles of hiking trails.

RIVER FARM

The headquarters of the American Horticultural Society (AHS) is at **River Farm** (7931 E. Boulevard Dr., 703/768-5700, www.ahs.org, Mon.-Fri. year-round 9am-5pm, Sat. Apr.-Sept. 9am-1pm, free). River Farm was one of George Washington's five farms. The 25-acre site is beautifully landscaped and includes a circa 1757 home that now houses the AHS. The largest specimen of an Osage orange tree in the country is at River Farm; it is said to have been a gift to the Washington family from Thomas Jefferson (Jefferson received Osage orange seedlings from the Lewis and Clark expedition of 1804-1806). There is no charge for admission to the farm and the house, but donations are appreciated.

Boating

You can launch a boat or kayak from **Belle Haven Marina** (1201 Belle Haven Rd., 703/768-0018, www.saildc.com) or learn to sail at their sailing school. Located on the Potomac River, their sailing school was founded in 1975, and they run the largest full-time sailing program on the Potomac. Boats are available for rent.

Biking

Old Town Alexandria is a very bike-friendly area. There are many bike-friendly businesses that encourage employees and guests to ride bikes to their facilities. The 18-mile **Mount Vernon Trail** runs between Theodore Roosevelt Island (an 88-acre island and national park that sits in the Potomac River near the Roosevelt Bridge) and Mount Vernon Estate. The trail passes right through Old Town Alexandria, but can be a little tricky since it runs along the street. For a map of the trail, visit www.bikewashington.org. Bikes can be rented from **Big Wheel Bikes** (2 Prince St., 703/739-2300, www.bigwheelbikes.com, Mon.-Fri. 11am-7pm, Sat.-Sun. 10am-6pm, $7 per hour or $35 per day).

Golf

The **Greendale Golf Course** (6700 Telegraph Rd., 703/971-6170, www.fairfaxcounty.gov, open year-round $30-39) is an 18-hole regulation golf course covering 148 acres. The terrain is rolling with asphalt cart paths. The course was designed to be challenging with water hazards and tight fairways. The facility includes a putting green, clubhouse with food service, club rentals, power cart rentals, and golfing supplies. Golf lessons are also available.

The nine-hole, par 35 **Pinecrest Golf Course** (6600 Little River Tpke., 703/941-1061, www.fairfaxcounty.gov, open year-round, $19-23) is a challenging executive golf course. The course is narrow and includes hills and ponds. It is geared toward both novice golfers and serious players.

Day Spas

Old Town has many salons and day spas. If you are looking for a massage or any number of professional hair services, visit **The Sugar House** (111 N. Alfred St., 703/549-9940, www.sugarhousedayspa.com). They are in a cute row house on North Alfred Street and offer a warm, professional atmosphere with high-quality (female only) massage therapists. Another good option is **Fountains Day Spa** (422 S. Washington St., 703/549-1990, www.fountainsdayspa.com), in a yellow house on Washington Street and offering high-quality massages and a large variety of other spa services. For waxing and other specialty salon services, **Aida Spa** (1309 King Street, 2nd Fl., 703/535-7875, www.aidaspaoldtown.com) is the place to go. The owner specializes in skin care, face-and-body treatments, and makeup.

FOOD

American

★ **The Majestic** (911 King St., 703/837-9117, www.majesticcafe.net, Mon.-Thurs. 11:30am-10pm, Fri. 11:30am-11pm, Sat. 11am-11pm, Sun. 11am-10pm, $19-27) is a small gem of a restaurant right in the heart of Old Town. It serves American comfort food and has a history dating back to 1932. The decor is modern and inviting and makes for a fun place to gather with friends, family, or business associates. Step off the street right into the bar and grab a drink while you wait for a table. It is obvious that great care goes into designing each menu item, so don't hesitate to ask your server for more details. Seafood is a specialty here, but you may find it prepared with a new twist such as with an unusual spice or paired with a nontraditional side. The Chesapeake Bay Stew is a personal favorite, or the Majestic

Bring Fido

Old Town Alexandria is extremely dog friendly. Specialty shops cater specifically to our canine friends, and many others put out water bowls and treats in front of their doorways.

HOTELS

Many hotels in Old Town allow dogs in their rooms. The Kimpton hotels, in particular, have a history of being pet friendly and include added amenities for dogs such as honor bars stocked with pet treats, pet bedding, and pet bowls. Some dog-friendly hotels include:

- **Morrison House—A Kimpton Hotel** (116 S. Alfred St., 703/838-8000, www.morrisonhouse.com)
- **Residence Inn by Marriott Alexandria Old Town South at Carlyle** (2345 Mill Rd., 703/549-1155, www.marriott.com)
- **Westin Alexandria** (400 Courthouse Sq., 703/253-8600, www.westinalexandria.com)
- **Hotel Monaco Alexandria—A Kimpton Hotel** (480 King St., 703/549-6080, www.monaco-alexandria.com)
- **Holiday Inn & Suites Alexandria-Historic District** (625 1st St., 703/548-6300, www.ihg.com)
- **Lorien Hotel & Spa—A Kimpton Hotel** (1600 King St., 703/894-3434, www.lorienhotelandspa.com)
- **Sheraton Suites Alexandria** (801 N. Saint Asaph St., 703/836-4700, www.sheratonsuitesalexandria.com)

DINING

Dog-friendly dining is also fairly common in Old Town Alexandria. By law, pets are not permitted inside restaurants, but many dining spots have seasonal seating outdoors where well-behaved dogs are permitted to join their owners. Following are examples of dog-friendly restaurants, but others can be found by looking for outdoor cafés where other dogs are sitting or establishments that have water bowls outside their doors. If you are uncertain, be sure to ask the host or hostess about the restaurant's policy.

Burger with its delightful bacon jam. No matter what you choose save room for dessert. If you're lucky to see their coconut cake on the menu, be sure to order it. It is fresh, moist, and just plain out of this world.

Virtue Feed and Grain (106 South Union St., 571/970-3669, www.virtuefeedgrain.com, daily 11:30am-1am, $7-34), is housed in a historic brick building on South Union Street that was used as a feed house on the waterfront in the 1800s. They serve a casual menu of burgers, tacos, and entrees such as salmon, shrimp and grits, and steak. The interior is a symphony in reclaimed materials such as wood, brick, and the original concrete floors with large newly added windows. The two-level space is lively and includes a unique porch with wraparound windows on the second level for private parties. Save room for dessert—they have a scrumptious peanut butter pie.

Gadsby's Tavern (138 N. Royal St., 703/548-1288, www.gadsbystavernrestaurant.com, brunch Sun. 11am-3pm, lunch Mon.-Sat. 11:30am-3pm, dinner daily 5:30pm-10pm, $22-30) offers a rare historical dining experience and one that's unique to Old Town Alexandria. Situated next door to Gadsby's Museum, the tavern has served patrons since the late 1700s. Dine in a space once

Doggie Happy Hour is a regular event at the **Hotel Monaco** (480 King St.), held seasonally on Tuesday and a popular Old Town tradition. Another dog-friendly spot is **Blackwall Hitch** (5 Cameron St., 703/739-6090, www.theblackwallhitch.com). They allow furry friends on their outdoor patio.

Other restaurants with dog-friendly patios include **The Burger Joint** (106 N. Washington St., 703/299-9791, www.bgrtheburgerjoint.com) and **The Dairy Godmother** (2310 Mount Vernon Ave., 703/683-7767, www.thedairygodmother.com), where they offer puppy pops.

PET-SUPPLY STORES

There are several specialty pet-supply stores in Old Town Alexandria and the vicinity where you can purchase gourmet treats, toys, food, and other supplies:

- **The Dog Park** (705 King St., 703/888-2818, www.thedogparkva.biz)
- **The Olde Towne School for Dogs** (529 Oronoco St., 703/836-7643, www.otsfd.com)
- **Barkley Square Gourmet Dog Bakery and Boutique** (211 N. Union St., 703/329-1043, www.barkleysquare.com)
- **Nature's Nibbles** (2601 Mount Vernon Ave., 703/931-5241, www.naturesnibbles.com)

OLD TOWN ATTRACTIONS

Several Old Town Alexandria attractions allow dogs to accompany their owners:

- **Potomac Riverboat Company** (1 Cameron St., 703/684-0580, www.potomacriverboatco.com) offers 40-minute canine harbor cruises on Thursday from June to mid-September. Tickets are $16 for adults and $10 for children. Dogs ride free.
- The **Torpedo Factory Art Center** (105 N. Union St., 703/838-4565, www.torpedofactory.org) allows well-behaved dogs on leashes.
- **Footsteps to the Past** (703/683-3451, www.footstepstothepast.com) offers dog-friendly guided walking tours of Alexandria.
- The **Alexandria Visitors Center at Ramsay House** (221 King St., 703/746-3301) allows dogs to visit with their owners.

frequented by George Washington, Thomas Jefferson, John Adams, James Madison, and James Monroe. The attentive staff is dressed in period attire, and the cozy, candlelit decor depicts the colonial period, but this is not a theater. Great attention is given to both the menu and the dining experience. There is a nice selection of steaks, chops, and seafood, including George Washington's Favorite, which is grilled breast of duck with scalloped potatoes, corn pudding, *rhotekraut* (red cabbage), and a port wine orange glaze.

Another one-of-a-kind dining experience can be had at the **Columbia Firehouse** (109 S. Saint Asaph St., 703/683-1776, www.columbiafirehouse.com, brunch Sat.-Sun. 11am-3pm, lunch Tues.-Fri. 11:30am-3pm, dinner Mon. 5:30pm-9pm, Tues.-Thurs. 5:30pm-10pm, Fri.-Sat. 5:30pm-11pm, Sun. 4:30pm-9pm, $19-31). The restaurant was once a firehouse (built in 1883) and is now a historic, well-preserved eatery in the heart of Old Town. This modern American brasserie and bar still shows its firehouse roots with original exposed brickwork. Other interior details that add to the classic atmosphere include brass rails, stained glass, and dark wood. There is a varied menu of pub food and more intricate dishes that includes a raw bar, salads, sandwiches, steak, and daily specials. If you're a fan of mussels, the Firehouse serves them three delicious ways. Perfect for foodies, families, and friends, this is an upbeat establishment with a comfortable feel.

It would be difficult to suggest restaurants in Old Town without including **Vermilion Restaurant** (1120 King St., 703/684-9669, www.vermilionrestaurant.com, brunch Sat.-Sun. 10:30am-2:30pm, lunch Mon. and Wed.-Fri. 11:30am-3pm, dinner Mon.-Thurs. 5:30pm-10pm, Fri.-Sat. 5:30pm-11pm, Sun. 5pm-9pm, $14-34). They serve contemporary American food at its finest for lunch and dinner with entrées such as trout, crusted lamb, and mushroom risotto. The menu is small but done well. They also offer a four-course tasting menu for $65. The restaurant is committed to locally grown goods.

For a special occasion or important business dinner, spend the evening at one of Northern Virginia's most highly acclaimed restaurants, ★ **Restaurant Eve** (110 Pitt St., 703/706-0450, www.restauranteve.com, lunch Mon.-Fri. 11:30am-2pm, dinner Mon.-Fri. 5:30pm-10pm, Sat. 5:30pm-10pm). Owned by the same people as The Majestic, Eve showcases organically grown, farm-raised food from farms in Virginia and the surrounding area. The Chef's Tasting Room features a prix fixe five- to nine-course menu ($105-165 per person) created daily from locally sourced ingredients, including produce from the chef's own garden and sustainable meat entrées. Vegetarian selections are also available. The elegant Bistro is more casual and serves an upscale menu that changes often. A sample of items includes rib eye, rockfish, and sea scallops ($33-44).

A newcomer to the Alexandria food scene is **Blackwall Hitch** (5 Cameron St., 703/739-6090, www.theblackwallhitch.com, Sun. 10am-10pm, Mon.-Wed. 11am-midnight, Thurs.-Sat. 11am-2am, $8-38), located on the waterfront behind the Torpedo Factory (in the former food pavilion). The restaurant has a great location with a modern coastal atmosphere and menu (seafood, flatbread, sandwiches, steak, and more). The name harkens back to the mid-1800s when ships set sail from London's Blackwall port bound for the Eastern seaboard. Strong hooks kept the ships connected to the docks and the unique blackwall hitch knot allowed for a quick connection. They have live music Wednesday through Sunday.

Belgian

BRABO, adjacent to the Lorien Hotel & Spa (1600 King St., 703/894-3440, www.braborestaurant.com, brunch Sunday 11am-2pm, dinner Mon.-Thurs. 5:30pm-10pm, Fri.-Sat. 5:30pm-11pm, Sun. 5:30pm-9pm, $28-37), initially attracts guests with its warm but elegant atmosphere, but keeps them coming back for the exquisite Belgian cuisine. Icelandic cod fillet, ale-braised pork shank, and red wine-braised beef chuck short rib are just some of the entrées created by the award-winning chef. The service is impeccable, and there's even a communal table for those wishing to mingle. There's also a tasting room and market.

French

Le Refuge Restaurant (127 N. Washington St., 703/548-4661, www.lerefugealexandria.com, lunch Mon.-Sat. 11:30am-2:30pm, dinner Mon.-Sat. 5:30pm-10pm, $25-36) is one of the best-kept secrets in Alexandria. This small family-owned French country bistro feels more like Paris than Virginia. The menu includes favorites like beef Wellington, bouillabaisse, and rack of lamb as well as daily specials. The setting is cozy and even a bit snug, but the food and service are excellent. They also offer a three-course prix fixe lunch for $22 and a three-course prix fixe dinner for $35.

Irish

What could be more Irish than a restaurant called **Daniel O'Connell's** (112 King St., 703/739-1124, www.danieloconnells.com, daily 11am-1am, $11-26)? This lively spot on King Street serves up traditional Irish fare with a few interesting modifications. Try an

A Taste for Del Ray

Just northwest of Old Town Alexandria, along Mount Vernon Avenue, is Del Ray, a hip little neighborhood full of coffee shops, art galleries, specialty food stores, and cafés. This trendy little pocket of Northern Virginia has a population of mostly young families, working couples, and singles who can be seen walking the streets with their dogs or strollers or working on their laptops behind café windows.

This pleasant neighborhood didn't always have a laid-back vibe; in fact, not long ago (10-20 years), it was a place you may have only heard about on the nightly news. In recent years, Del Ray has blossomed into a friendly, funky place to live where eateries now dominate the main thoroughfare and real estate prices have skyrocketed. Also a great place to visit, Del Ray has many good options to satisfy the palate.

One of the most well-known eateries in Del Ray is **The Evening Star Café** (2000 Mount Vernon Ave., 703/549-5051, www.eveningstarcafe.net, brunch Sat.-Sun. 11:30am-2:30pm, lunch Fri. 11:30am-2:30pm, dinner daily from 5:30pm, $15-28). They offer a modern twist on classic southern cooking. Try their buttermilk fried chicken, caramelized skate wing, or loaded tots.

Just off Mount Vernon Avenue, **Del Ray Café** (205 E Howell Ave, 703/717-9151, www.delraycafe.com, Sun.-Thurs. 8am-2:30pm and 5pm-9pm, Fri.-Sat 8am-2:30pm and 5pm-10pm, $17-39) is a farm-to-table French-American café serving breakfast, lunch, and dinner in a cute house with a red-roofed porch. This is an especially good choice for breakfast—try the crab eggs Benedict or one of the organic omelets.

If you're craving food from south of the border, **Los Tios Grill** (2615 Mount Vernon Ave., 703/299-9290, www.lostiosgrill.com, Sun.-Thurs. 11am-10pm, Fri. and Sat.11am-11pm, $7-20), a Tex-Mex and Salvadoran restaurant, and **Taqueria Poblano** (2400-B Mount Vernon Ave., 703/548-8226, www.taqueriapoblano.com, Mon. and Wed.-Fri. lunch 11am-3pm, dinner 5pm-10pm, Sat. 11am-10pm, Sun. 10am-9pm, $4-16), a Mexican restaurant, are both known for their good food and margaritas.

For a good Philly cheesesteak, try **Al's Steakhouse** (1504 Mount Vernon Ave., 703/836-9443, www.alssteak.com, Mon.-Fri. 10am-8pm, Sat. 10am-7pm, $3-17). The plain brick exterior is easy to miss, but locals know this is the best place for a Philly fix.

Cheese lovers won't want to miss **Cheesetique** (2411 Mount Vernon Ave., 703/706-5300, www.cheesetique.com, Mon.-Fri. 11am-10pm, Sat. and Sun. 10am-10pm, $6-11), an artisan cheese shop with a wine and cheese bar. Sample cheese, take home cheese, or order from a menu of cheese-influenced selections.

For dessert try the **Dairy Godmother** (2310 Mount Vernon Ave., 703/683-7767, www.thedairygodmother.com, Sun.-Mon. noon-9pm, Wed.-Sat. noon-10pm, under $10). This funky frozen custard shop was made famous when the Obama family stopped in for dessert back in 2009.

Irish Egg Roll to start your meal or the Dublin Nachos. Follow with some classic fish-and-chips, a Guinness burger, or a fresh fish selection. The menu changes regularly, which is refreshing for an Irish pub, and everything is served with a wide Irish smile. The old brick building gives the restaurant an authentic Old Town feel, and after one too many Guinness stouts, it can be difficult to find your way through the maze of rooms and staircases to the restroom. If you're lucky enough to score a rooftop patio seat overlooking King Street on a nice evening, plan to stay for a while—you won't want to give up your table.

Another fun Irish pub is **Murphy's Irish Pub** (713 King St., 703/548-1717, www.murphyspub.com, daily 11am-2am, $10-15). They offer warm pub fare and entertainment nightly.

Italian

If you're in the mood for pizza, try **Pizzeria**

Paradiso (124 King St., 703/837-1245, www.eatyourpizza.com, Mon.-Thurs. 11:30am-10pm, Fri.-Sat. 11:30am-11pm, Sun. noon-10pm, $12-21), the King Street outlet of a small local chain. The pizza is some of the best in the area and is made with fresh ingredients. The beer list is impressive, and the staff is very friendly and attentive. There is a long list of available toppings including some less traditional options such as roast lamb, potatoes, hot cherry peppers, and capers.

Tex-Mex

Austin Grill and Tequila Bar (801 King St., 703/684-8969, www.austingrill.com, Mon.-Thurs. 11am-11pm, Fri. 11am-1am, Sat. 10am-1am, Sun. 10am-10pm, $7-20) is a casual Tex-Mex restaurant on the corner of King Street and North Columbus Street. But don't let the laid-back atmosphere fool you: This popular restaurant does a great job with its menu and even offers an unexpected burger and sandwich section (which is done every bit as well as their traditional Mexican fare). The restaurant can be lively and it's crowded on the weekends, but the food is reasonably priced and you'll feel satisfied when you're through eating. Be sure to ask for a dessert menu, even if you're not hungry—there is always room for their signature margarita bites.

Treats

Cupcake bakeries have sprung up all over Northern Virginia in recent years. One that does a particularly good job is **Lavender Moon Cupcakery** (116 S. Royal St., 703/683-0588, Sun.-Thurs. 11am-8pm, Fri. and Sat. 11am-9pm, under $10). The selections vary daily, but some sample flavors include s'mores, flourless chocolate, lemon, passion fruit, and blood orange Dreamsicle.

Farmers Markets

There are several farmers markets in Old Town Alexandria and the vicinity. Some are seasonal and some are held year-round: **Old Town Farmers' Market** (301 King St., Sat. 7am-noon, year-round); **Del Ray Farmers' Market** (corner of East Oxford and Mount Vernon Aves., Sat. 8am-noon, year-round); **Four Mile Run Farmer's & Artisans Market** (4109 Mount Vernon Ave., Sun. 9am-1pm, Apr. 1-Oct. 31); and **West End Farmers' Market** (Ben Brenman Park, 4800 Brenman Park Dr., Sun. 8:30am-1pm, May-Nov.).

ACCOMMODATIONS

Hotels

As with most of Northern Virginia, accommodations in Old Town Alexandria consist mostly of chain hotels. However, there are a few good boutique hotels that offer unique lodgings right in Old Town.

$100-200

The **Best Western Old Colony Inn** (1101 N. Washington St., 703/739-2222, www.hotel-alexandria.com, $159-169) is an older hotel with 49 guest rooms conveniently located on North Washington Street in Old Town. The rooms are reasonably priced, and the staff offers consistently good service. A unique amenity is a free snack kitchen for guests. This open room is fully stocked with snacks such as fruit, yogurt, cookies, coffee, ice cream, sodas, and more, and is completely free. It's a nice unexpected perk. Flat-screen televisions and high-speed Internet are also included in each room, and there is free on-site parking.

Reasonably priced accommodations near Old Town Alexandria can be found at the **Holiday Inn Express & Suites Alexandria-Fort Belvoir** (6055 Richmond Hwy., 571/257-9555, www.hiexpress.com, $145-171). This hotel offers 86 spacious rooms and friendly service. Rooms have large flat-screen televisions and comfortable beds. There is a small indoor pool and fitness center. Breakfast is included, as is high-speed Internet, and there is free shuttle service to the Huntington Metrorail station as well as free on-site parking.

$200-300

The stunning ★ **Hotel Monaco Alexandria** (480 King St., 703/549-6080, www.monaco-alexandria.com, $179-309), part of the Kimpton chain, is a luxury boutique hotel in a fantastic location on King Street. It offers 241 guest rooms. The staff is exceptional, and the hotel welcomes children and even provides a family-friendly welcome room with free snacks. Rooms are spacious and very comfortable with many little extras (like animal-print bathrobes). A wine reception is held nightly, and there is an indoor pool and fitness center on the third floor. Saturday nights are "Dive-in Movie Nights," when they dim the lights in the pool area, fill the pool with inflatable furniture, and show family movies. The hotel is dog friendly. Self-parking and valet-parking are both available for $29 per night. They also deliver goldfish to your room upon request (real goldfish, in a bowl).

The **Morrison House** (116 S. Alfred St., 703/838-8000, www.morrisonhouse.com, $219-309) is another boutique Kimpton hotel in Old Town Alexandria. Unlike the other two Kimpton properties in Old Town, this hotel is decorated with federal-style reproduction furnishings such as four-poster beds and is housed in a stately brick building near King Street. The hotel underwent a multimillion-dollar facelift in 2016. The 42 guest rooms and three suites are comfortable and the common areas have a nice open feel. The hotel offers personal service and wine tasting each evening. The staff is very friendly and accommodating, and guests are made to feel welcome. Guests have access to the pool and fitness center at the Hotel Monaco. The Morrison House offers federal government discounts, and the hotel is pet friendly.

The **Residence Inn Alexandria Old Town** (1456 Duke St., 703/548-5474, www.marriott.com, $199-259) delivers consistently high-quality service and 240 comfortable guest suites. The hotel is geared toward extended stays: All suites offer a full kitchen and separate living and dining areas. It is approximately two blocks to the King Street Metrorail station and within walking distance to many Old Town attractions. Shuttle service is available to the Metro and waterfront. A plentiful breakfast is included with your stay and there is an indoor pool and fitness center. Two-bedroom suites are available and parking is available for a fee. Last-minute weekend deals are sometimes available on the website. The hotel is pet friendly.

If you don't have a car and you want to be convenient to the Metrorail and have easy access to shops and restaurants, try the **Hampton Inn Alexandria-Old Town/King Street Metro** (1616 King St., 703/299-9900, www.hamptoninn3.hilton.com, $179-225). This 80-room hotel one block from the King Street Metrorail station offers comfortable rooms, free Internet, complimentary breakfast, a fitness center, and an outdoor pool. The local trolley stops right outside the door, so guests can easily go shopping and dine at local restaurants. Parking is available for a fee, but it is not the most convenient.

OVER $300

Another Kimpton hotel, the **Lorien Hotel & Spa** (1600 King St., 703/894-3434, www.lorienhotelandspa.com, $199-399) is less than two blocks from the Metrorail. This modern, well-appointed boutique hotel offers a friendly atmosphere and 107 very comfortable guest rooms. This award-winning establishment offers many extras, such as a welcome glass of wine and first-class service. As the name implies, there's a full-service spa on-site (the only hotel spa in Old Town). Book a corner room if you like a lot of windows. This is a quiet hotel within walking distance of the waterfront. It is also pet friendly.

Bed-and-Breakfasts

Those looking for a quiet bed-and-breakfast should try the **Peake-Fairfax House Bed & Breakfast** (501 Cameron St., 703/684-3337, www.peakefairfaxhouse.com, $175-195), a nicely restored 1816 house offering two guest rooms with private baths in a convenient location near King Street in Old Town. The rooms are elegantly decorated, and each has a private fireplace. The hosts are very friendly, interesting, and excellent at making recommendations for things to do in town. Walk to shopping and restaurants or relax in the beautiful setting in this home away from home. There is a two-night minimum stay.

INFORMATION AND SERVICES

A good place to begin your exploration of Old Town Alexandria is at **The Alexandria Visitors Center at Ramsay House** (221 King St., 703/746-3301, www.visitalexandriava.com). They offer maps and brochures and sell tickets to some local attractions and tours. If you plan to visit multiple sights, consider purchasing the **Alexandria Key to the City** ($10). This visitor pass provides admission to nine historic sites and includes dozens of discounts at area shops, restaurants, and attractions.

GETTING THERE

Old Town Alexandria is approximately seven miles south of Washington DC on the opposite side of the Potomac River. It is accessible by the George Washington Memorial Parkway and I-495 (Beltway).

Old Town is accessible by **Metrorail** (202/637-7000, www.wmata.com). The Yellow and Blue Lines both stop at the **King Street Metro station,** which is on King Street near the George Washington Masonic Memorial.

Amtrak (800/872-7245, www.amtrak.com) has a train station in Alexandria at 110 Callahan Drive.

GETTING AROUND

The Alexandria Transit Company's **DASH** (703/746-3274, www.dashbus.com, Mon.-Fri. 5am-10:30pm, Sat. 7am-10:30pm, Sun. 7:45am-8:30pm, $1.60) bus system provides reliable bus service in Alexandria and offers service between Metrobus stops, Metrorail, and the Virginia Railway Express. There is service from the King Street Metro stop down King Street to Market Square every 15 minutes or so. The fare is $1.60, and exact change is required. A detailed schedule and route map are available on the website.

The free **King Street Trolley** (www.visitalexandriava.com) is another good way to get around Old Town. This fleet of hybrid trolleys runs every 15 minutes between North Union Street and the King Street Metro station (daily 10am-10:15pm) with 20 stops along Old Town's main shopping and restaurant district.

Round-trip water taxis are also available through **The Potomac Riverboat Company** (205 The Strand., 703/684-0580, www.potomacriverboatco.com, $16) between Old Town Alexandria, the Gaylord National Hotel in National Harbor, Maryland, and directly to Washington Nationals baseball games in DC.

Fairfax County

Fairfax County encompasses 395 square miles and is the largest county in Virginia by population, with more than one million residents. Nearly a quarter of the jobs in the county are technology related, giving it the largest concentration of technology jobs in the country. It is also a very diverse county, with almost one-third of the residents speaking a language other than English at home. Fairfax County is a suburban area of Washington DC with a heavy population of commuters. As the popularity of telecommuting grows, more and more people are able to work from home, but don't let that fool you into thinking the phenomenon has lessened highway congestion during rush hour.

Fairfax County contains half of the DC area's Fortune 500 companies and is also home to many government intelligence agencies including the Central Intelligence Agency, National Reconnaissance Office, and the National Counterterrorism Center.

Visitors will find a densely populated area with pleasant neighborhoods, parks, and many strip malls. There are many good restaurants, excellent shopping, and a diversity of outdoor recreation opportunities in Fairfax County. Depending on your focus, Fairfax County can be explored in a day or two and is easily accessible from Washington DC for dining and events.

SIGHTS

Near the Beltway

I-495 is a 64-mile highway that runs around Washington DC and through Virginia and Maryland; it is commonly known as the **Capital Beltway** or just the **Beltway.** It runs through much of the eastern portion of Fairfax County.

OLD TOWN FAIRFAX

Although the city of Fairfax formally includes just a six-square-mile area, much of the surrounding neighborhoods share a Fairfax address and are within Fairfax County. Established in 1742, the city of Fairfax was the site of several Civil War events and then remained mostly a residential community of farms and homes until the 1950s and '60s. At that time it experienced a rapid population growth that leveled off some in the 1970s but has since resumed. **Old Town Fairfax** is a good starting point for exploration, with its quaint shops and restaurants. The **Civil War Interpretive Center at Historic Blenheim** (3610 Old Lee Hwy., 703/591-0560, www.fairfaxva.gov, Tues.-Sat. 10am-3pm, free) is a 12-acre attraction with an interpretive center and several historic buildings, including the Blenheim farmhouse built in 1859. The house contains the largest and best-preserved Civil War inscription examples in the country, which were left on a wall by more than 100 Union soldiers while they occupied the Fairfax Courthouse in 1862-1863. The inscriptions include art and poetry and provide good insight into the lives of the soldiers during the war. The interpretive center features an illustrated timeline of events that took place during the Civil War in Fairfax. There is also a lecture hall and gift shop. Guided tours are offered at 1pm Tuesday through Saturday.

The **Fairfax Station Railroad Museum** (11200 Fairfax Station Rd., Fairfax Station, 703/425-9225, www.fairfax-station.org, Sun. 1pm-4pm, $4), in nearby Fairfax Station, is a rebuilt train depot and museum that preserves a time in Civil War history when wounded soldiers were transported from the depot to hospitals in Washington DC and Alexandria. It later became a hub for commerce in the county and a center for social activity. The station remained open until 1973. Numerous items were donated to the museum, including a refurbished caboose and a railroad-crossing gate from Norfolk Southern.

The **National Firearms Museum** (11250 Waples Mill Rd., Fairfax, 703/267-1600, www.nramuseum.org, daily 9:30am-5pm, free) contains a diverse collection of civilian and military firearms and accessories.

MEADOWLARK BOTANICAL GARDENS

Meadowlark Botanical Gardens (9750 Meadowlark Gardens Ct., Vienna, 703/255-3631, www.nvrpa.org, June-Aug. daily 10am-8pm, Apr. and Sept. daily 10am-7pm, Mar. and Oct. daily 10am-6pm, May daily 10am-7:30pm, Nov.-Dec. daily 10am-4:30pm, Jan.-Feb. daily 10am-5pm, $5) is a 95-acre property with large ornamental garden displays and unusual native plant collections. A network of walking trails provides access. There are three gazebos at the gardens that can be reserved for private use. A beautiful glass atrium looks out over the park and can be rented for weddings and receptions. During the holidays, they offer a brilliant light display that can be enjoyed along the walking trails.

Western Fairfax County

Western Fairfax borders Loudoun County to the west and Prince William County to the south.

★ GREAT FALLS PARK

Great Falls Park (9200 Old Dominion Dr., Great Falls, www.nps.gov/grfa, daily 7am-dark, individual fee for entering on foot, horse, or bicycle $5, vehicle fee for one vehicle and all passengers $10) is one of Northern Virginia's prime outdoor destinations. In this 800-acre national park, the Potomac River plunges 77 feet into Mather Gorge over a series of jagged rocks. The falls are impressive to say the least and especially so after heavy rain. Three well-placed and maintained overlooks provide spectacular views of the falls. There is a visitors center, plenty of picnic areas, and wooded trails for hiking, mountain biking, and horseback riding. Great Falls Park is also a popular area for rock climbing and white-water kayaking.

COLVIN RUN MILL

A leisurely afternoon can be spent at **Colvin Run Mill** (10017 Colvin Run Rd., Great Falls, 703/759-2771, www.fairfaxcounty.gov, Wed.-Mon. 11am-4pm, parking and grounds are free, tours $7). This historic mill and general store harkens back to a time when things were a bit simpler. Take a tour of the restored mill that was built in 1811 and learn about the large waterwheel and how grain was ground. Visit the general store and purchase stone-ground cornmeal, grits, penny candy, and books. This is a lovely park with plenty of picnic space and interesting seasonal activities.

★ NATIONAL AIR AND SPACE MUSEUM STEVEN F. UDVAR-HAZY CENTER

The **National Air and Space Museum Steven F. Udvar-Hazy Center** (14390 Air and Space Museum Pkwy., Chantilly, 703/572-4118, www.nasm.si.edu, daily 10am-5:30pm, free, $15 parking) is owned by the Smithsonian Institution and is the companion museum to the Air and Space Museum on the National Mall. The two sites together are the crown jewel of the Smithsonian and display the largest collection of space and aviation artifacts in the world. The awe-inspiring aviation hangar building allows for the display of aircraft on three levels. Thousands of artifacts may be viewed on the hangar floor and from elevated skywalks and include helicopters, experimental aircraft, and retired spacecraft and airplanes. The soaring ceilings and open design of the hangar allow visitors to fully appreciate the size and significance of the items. Exhibits include the Lockheed SR-71 Blackbird (the fastest jet in

Great Falls Park

the world), the *Enola Gay*, the de Havilland Chipmunk aerobatic airplane, and the space shuttle *Enterprise*. Visitors can also watch planes take off and land at Washington Dulles International Airport from the Donald D. Engen Tower, which provides a 360-degree view of the airport. The Udvar-Hazy Center is less crowded than the Air and Space Museum in DC, but can still pack in the people on summer weekends. Other features in the museum include an IMAX theater and gift shop. The only dining option inside the center is a McDonalds and McCafe, so if this doesn't suit your palate, make plans to eat at a local restaurant. All visitors must go through security screening when entering.

SULLY HISTORIC SITE

Also in Chantilly is the **Sully Historic Site** (3650 Historic Sully Way, Chantilly, 703/437-1794, www.fairfaxcounty.gov, Wed.-Mon. 11am-4pm, $7), which is in the National Register of Historic Places. The main house was built in 1799 by Robert E. Lee's uncle Richard Bland Lee, who was a politician who served in the Virginia House of Delegates and was the first Northern Virginia representative in the U.S. House of Representatives. The home is a combination of Georgian and federal architecture, and the historic grounds also include original outbuildings. Guided tours are given on the hour and focus on the early life of the Richard Bland Lee family. On-site programs reflect Fairfax County history through the 20th century. There is a gift shop.

Southern Fairfax County

★ MOUNT VERNON ESTATE, MUSEUM, AND GARDENS

Mount Vernon Estate, Museum, and Gardens (3200 Mount Vernon Memorial Hwy., Alexandria, 703/780-2000, www.mountvernon.org, Apr.-Oct. daily 9am-5pm, Nov.-Mar, daily 9am-4pm, $17) is one of the premier attractions in Northern Virginia and is the most popular historic estate in the country. Sitting on the banks of the Potomac River eight miles south of Old Town Alexandria, this picturesque manor was George Washington's plantation house.

The land surrounding Mount Vernon became the property of the Washington family in 1674. George Washington built his mansion in stages between 1757 and 1778. Prior to its construction, a smaller house built for Washington's half-brother Lawrence, who died in 1752, occupied the site. George Washington became the sole owner of the estate in 1761 and intended to be primarily a tobacco farmer (although his military career ended up substantially interfering with this plan). The plantation started out with tobacco as the staple crop, but later grew wheat, grain, and corn.

Visiting Mount Vernon: Once you purchase your ticket to Mount Vernon, you enter through the Orientation Center where a bronze statue of George, Martha, and two of George's step-grandchildren immediately greets you. Be sure to pick up a brochure and map of the estate and then watch the orientation movie in one of the two adjacent theaters. From the orientation center, you will take a walkway that continues to the idyllic Bowling Green, the expansive lawn that surrounds the mansion and outbuildings. Plan on a minimum of three hours for your visit.

The home is constructed of wood and underwent several renovations during Washington's lifetime. The style is loosely considered to be part Georgian and British Palladian, although with classical influences. The house is somewhat modest as far as historic estates go. It has a five-part Palladian design that features a central mansion connected by two curved colonnades to the servants' hall and kitchen. The riverfront facade has a commanding view of the Potomac and its exterior pine boards were beveled and then coated with layers of white paint and sand to make the house appear to be made of brick. The stunning red roof and its large cupola are distinguishing features.

Mount Vernon's interior has been meticulously restored to appear as it did in 1799, during the final year of George Washington's life. As such, the rooms are painted in their original vibrant colors including some in bright shades of blue and green. The interior, as with the exterior, is rather modest but is adorned with original pieces.

The estate is a great place to learn about George Washington's life and times. Tours are self-guided, but spirited costumed interpreters are on hand to reveal stories behind every room in the mansion including how and where George Washington died and who his houseguests were (such as the famous French nobleman, the Marquis de Lafayette).

In addition to the mansion with original furnishings, the nearly 50-acre estate (which at one time was over 8,000 acres) includes a dozen original structures and Washington's tomb (where he and Martha Washington are buried).

George Washington designed the outbuildings, gardens, and lanes running through the estate to be both practical and aesthetically pleasing. The outbuildings supported the work of the plantation and more than a dozen are open to the public including the kitchen, smokehouse, slave quarters, stable, outhouses, and a blacksmith shop. The estate is still a working farm, much as it was when Washington lived here. Costumed interpreters are featured in many of the buildings and give live demonstrations of the work performed in them. Three miles south of Mount Vernon on Route 235 is George Washington's **whiskey distillery and gristmill** (Apr.-Oct. daily 10am-5pm, included with general admission). They are still functioning today as they did in the 18th century and produce authentic products.

Four gardens on six enclosed acres can be visited at Mount Vernon. Staff test new plant varieties and provide beautiful flowers for display. **Gardens and groves** walking tours ($4) are offered daily at 11am and last approximately 60 minutes.

If you are in town in May, partake in the **Mount Vernon Wine Festival & Sunset Tour.** This yearly event celebrates wine history in Virginia with exclusive evening tours of the mansion and cellar. Live jazz is played on the east lawn, and don't be surprised if George and Martha make a special appearance. Tickets sell out quickly and are $36-48.

Getting There: Mount Vernon is accessible by Metrorail and bus. Those arriving by **Metrorail** (202/637-7000, www.wmata.com) can take the Yellow Line to the Huntington Station and then exit onto Huntington Avenue on the lower level. From there, take the **Fairfax Connector** (703/339-7200, www.fairfaxcounty.gov) Bus #101 on the Fort Hunt Line to Mount Vernon.

If arriving by **car,** take the George Washington Memorial Parkway all the way to its southern terminus. **Bicycle** is another great way to arrive. Cyclists can take the scenic Mount Vernon Trail, which runs near the western bank of the Potomac River and offers great views of the water, to the estate.

Another fun option is to arrive by boat through **The Potomac Riverboat Company** (703/548-7655, www.potomacriverboatco.com, $42 including admission to Mount Vernon). Boat trips depart from Old Town Alexandria, Virginia, and National Harbor, Maryland.

WOODLAWN ESTATE

Woodlawn Estate (9000 Richmond Hwy., Alexandria, 703/780-4000, www.woodlawn1805.org, Fri.-Mon. noon-4pm, $10) is a historic plantation home that was originally part of George Washington's Mount Vernon Estate. It is located three miles west of Mount Vernon. The home was built between 1800 and 1805 for George Washington's nephew, Lawrence Lewis, and his bride, Martha Washington's granddaughter, Nelly Parke Custis, as a wedding gift. The main mansion is made of brick and has sandstone trim. It has 86 windows (many that are larger than four feet wide by eight feet tall) and looks imposing with its formal facade. The 126-acre estate originally contained 2,000 acres. The home has since had several owners, including playwright Paul Kester, who moved in with his 60 cats. Take a tour of this beautiful residence and be sure to ask your docent a lot of questions. Guides are very knowledgeable about the estate and participant interaction can really enhance the experience.

The **Pope-Leighey House,** a modest house with an exterior made of cypress, is a Frank Lloyd Wright home that was originally built in Falls Church, Virginia in 1939. When a highway expansion threatened the home, it was given to the National Trust for Historic Preservation and moved to the Woodlawn grounds. The home now resides permanently on the grounds and can be toured. The two homes are a bit of an odd combination, but both are beautiful. A combination admission ticket to both houses is available for $15. Areas of the estate can be rented for special events and the site also houses the Arcadia Center for Sustainable Food & Agriculture.

GUNSTON HALL

Another popular historic plantation is **Gunston Hall** (10709 Gunston Rd., Mason Neck, 703/550-9220, www.gunstonhall.org, daily 9:30am-5pm, grounds open until 6pm, $10), former home of George Mason. The statesman authored the Virginia Declaration of Rights and was one of his era's most influential figures. He was one of the first people to call for American liberties such as religious toleration and freedom of the press. Although Mason helped frame the U.S. Constitution, he declined to sign the document because it did not abolish slavery and lacked a bill of rights. Mason's home was built between 1755 and 1759 and originally sat on 5,500 acres. It was a tobacco and corn plantation. It is famous for its intricate Georgian architecture and extraordinary interior that represents gothic, French modern, Chinese, Palladian, and classical styles. Many details such as the carvings in its Palladian Room were created by an indentured servant named William Bernard Sears, whom Mason brought from London to work on Gunston Hall. The estate now includes 550 acres of surrounding land on the Potomac River, and has reconstructed outbuildings, a 250-year-old boxwood-lined walkway, and hiking trails down to the water. Guided tours are offered daily every half hour.

ENTERTAINMENT AND EVENTS

Music and Theater

★ WOLF TRAP NATIONAL PARK FOR THE PERFORMING ARTS

There are few performance venues in the country that compare to the **Filene Center** at **Wolf Trap National Park for the Performing Arts** (1635 Trap Rd., Vienna, 703/255-1900, www.wolftrap.org). This beautiful indoor/outdoor amphitheater is set on 130 acres of rolling hills and woods, just 20 miles from Washington DC and three miles from the Beltway. It is the country's only national park dedicated to the performing arts. It offers a full lineup of concerts, musicals, dance, and other types of performances through the summer from well-known artists and performance companies. Bring a picnic and eat on the lawn before or during the show (many lawn seats are available), or enjoy one of the on-site eateries (reservations are required). October-May, **The Barns at Wolf Trap,** two 18th-century barns that were relocated from upstate New York, offer indoor performances, making this an interesting and inspiring year-round venue. Free parking is available at the park for performances, and the **Wolf Trap Express Shuttle** offers round-trip service ($5) from the West Falls Church Metrorail station to the Filene Center for most performances. Shuttle service begins two hours prior to showtime and runs every 20 minutes. Return shuttle service leaves 20 minutes after the end of each show but no later than 11pm.

EAGLEBANK ARENA

The **EagleBank Arena** (4500 Patriot Circle, Fairfax, 703/993-3000, www.eaglebankarena.com) is on the campus of George Mason University in Fairfax. In addition to hosting campus events, the center features sporting events, concerts, and family performances.

Filene Center at Wolf Trap National Park for the Performing Arts

Legends such as Bruce Springsteen, Bob Dylan, and the Harlem Globetrotters have performed there.

JAMMIN JAVA

Approximately 15 miles west of Washington DC, in Vienna, Virginia, is **Jammin Java** (227 Maple Ave., 703/255-1566, ext. 8, www.jamminjava.com), a small but important venue in the metropolitan music community. They have live music every night and also hold children's concerts on many mornings. They feature well-known artists such as Ingrid Michaelson, Citizen Cope, and Bon Iver as well as Washington DC favorites such as Bill Kirchen and Eddie from Ohio. All concerts are general admission. Tickets can be purchased online.

Festivals and Events

There are many festivals and events that fill the calendar in Fairfax County. One popular venue is the **Reston Town Center** (11900 Market St., www.restontowncenter.com), which hosts festivals throughout the year including the **Northern Virginia Fine Arts Festival, Pet Fiesta, Taste of Reston,** and **Concerts on the Town** music series held on Saturday nights in the summer. Visit the website for a full schedule and details.

One of the premier festivals in Northern Virginia is the annual **Vintage Virginia Wine Festival** (Bull Run Regional Park, Chantilly, www.vintagevirginia.com, one day $30, two days $45) that is held in early June in Centreville. A 20-minute drive from Washington DC, the festival offers wine-tasting, local winemakers, more than 100 vendors, food, and entertainment.

Beer fans from all over the region participate in the annual **Northern Virginia Fall Brewfest** (7700 Bull Run Dr., Centreville, www.novabrewfest.com, $35), also held at Bull Run Regional Park in Centreville. This "Celebration of American Beer" is held over a weekend in mid-October. The festival features over 50 American breweries. Adult admission (over 21) includes a sampling glass and six beer-sampling tickets. Additional sampling tickets can be purchased. Food, entertainment, and kids' activities are also available.

Celebrate Fairfax (12000 Government Center Pkwy., Fairfax, 703/324-3247, www.celebratefairfax.com, $15) is another popular annual event. It began as the Fairfax Fair and is now the county's largest annual community celebration, entertaining tens of thousands of people during three days in mid-June. The celebration is held on 25 acres and has more than 300 exhibitors sharing food, crafts, and activities. There are also carnival rides, nightly fireworks, and seven stages of live concerts including several big-name bands. Entertainment in the past has included well-known artists such as Third Eye Blind, The Bangles, Rusted Root, and Pat Benatar.

Civil War buffs won't want to miss the **Civil War Encampment Weekend** (3650 Historic Sully Way, 703/437-1794, www.fairfaxcounty.gov, $9) at the Sully Historic Site. For two days in August, visitors can watch Civil War re-enactors re-create daily life during that era. Daily skirmishes include infantry, artillery, and cavalry. Live music and a fashion show are also part of the festivities.

For more than a decade, the **Bull Run Festival of Lights** (Bull Run Regional Park, Chantilly, 703/631-0550, www.bullrunfestivaloflights.com, Mon.-Thurs. $15 per car, Fri.-Sun. $20 per car) has been a highlight of the holiday season for thousands of visitors. This six-week festival is a winter wonderland of light displays that can be explored from the comfort of your car. More than 130,000 spectators drive through this holiday wonderland each season.

SHOPPING

You don't have to look far to find shopping in Fairfax County. Strip malls are everywhere and just about every national chain store imaginable can be found. There are several large malls that are very popular with both visitors and residents.

Tysons Corner Center

The most well-known shopping mall in Northern Virginia is **Tysons Corner Center** (1961 Chain Bridge Rd., Tysons Corner, 703/847-7300, www.tysonscornercenter.com, Mon.-Sat. 10am-9:30pm, Sun. 11am-7pm). With more than 300 stores and restaurants and anchor stores such as Bloomingdale's, Nordstrom, Lord & Taylor, and Macy's, this is a premier destination for serious shoppers. The mall is 13 miles from Washington DC.

Tysons Galleria

The upscale sister mall to Tysons Corner Center is **Tysons Galleria** (2001 International Dr., McLean, 703/827-7730, www.tysonsgalleria.com, Mon.-Sat. 10am-9pm, Sun. noon-6pm). This high-end mall includes stores such as Neiman Marcus and Saks 5th Avenue.

Reston Town Center

The **Reston Town Center** (11900 Market St., Reston, 703/709-9131, www.restontowncenter.com) is a mini city in itself. It's home to many office buildings and a beautiful outdoor shopping and dining area. Many national-brand shops line its streets, and festivals and concerts are scheduled in its center throughout much of the year. The Town Center's focal point is a large fountain in the square. In the winter there is an outdoor ice-skating rink and the center becomes a festive winter wonderland around the holidays.

Old Town Fairfax

If you are looking for something unique, start in **Old Town Fairfax.** You'll find specialty shops such as **The Quilt Patch** (10381 Main St., 703/273-6937, www.quiltpatchva.com), **Paint Your Own Pottery** (10417 Main St., 703/218-2881, www.ciao-susanna.com), and the **Fairfax Surf Shop** (3936 Old Lee Hwy., 703/273-0015, www.fairfaxsurfshop.com).

SPORTS AND RECREATION

Parks

MASON NECK STATE PARK

Mason Neck State Park (Gunston Road, Mount Vernon, 703/339-2385, www.dcr.virginia.gov, daily 8am to dusk, $5) is in southern Fairfax County approximately 20 miles from Washington DC. This 1,825-acre park sits on a peninsula and is bordered by Pohick Bay to the north, Belmont Bay to the south, and the Potomac River to the east. The park offers endless opportunities for outdoor recreation, including more than four miles of unpaved hiking and biking trails and three miles of paved trails and elevated walkways above marsh areas for wildlife-watching. Fresh- and brackish-water fishing is accessible in the park (with a valid Virginia or Maryland fishing license) and cartop boat launch facilities are available. Kayaks and canoes can be rented on-site. The park is also a bird-watcher's paradise. It has resident bald eagles and migratory tundra swans and ducks. A visitor center offers exhibits, a gift shop, and a meeting room. The entrance to the park is off Gunston Road and is shared by the 2,277-acre **Elizabeth Hartwell Mason Neck National Wildlife Refuge** (703/490-4979, www.fws.gov, Oct.-Mar. daily 7am-5pm, Apr.-Sept. daily 7am-7pm, free), which was the first national wildlife refuge specifically established for the protection of bald eagles and also features one of the East Coast's largest heronries.

ALGONKIAN REGIONAL PARK

Algonkian Regional Park (47001 Fairway Dr., Sterling, 703/450-4655, www.nvrpa.org, daily dawn to dusk, free) sits on the banks of the Potomac River and offers trails, a boat launch, picnic facilities, cabin rentals, an 18-hole, par 72 golf course, miniature golf, fishing, ball fields, and a large water park complex. Kayak tours and other scheduled events take place during the summer months.

BULL RUN REGIONAL PARK

Bull Run Regional Park (7700 Bull Run Dr., Centreville, 703/631-0550, www.nvrpa.org, daily dawn to dusk, $7) is a spacious, scenic park with open fields, woodland trails, a water park, and a public shooting center. The park hosts festivals and special events throughout the year and can accommodate thousands of people at a time.

FAIRFAX CITY PARKS

There are 23 parks in the City of Fairfax. Most are local parks with playground equipment, pavilions, picnic areas, fields, and trails. For a list of local parks, visit www.fairfaxva.gov.

LAKE FAIRFAX

Lake Fairfax (1400 Lake Fairfax Dr., Reston, 703/471-5415, www.fairfaxcounty.gov, daily dawn to dusk, free) is a 476-acre park featuring an 18-acre lake, a water park (The Water Mine), campgrounds, ball fields, mountain biking trails, picnic areas, seasonal fishing, boating, a carousel, and a playground. Nominal fees are charged for the water park, carousel, boating, and camping.

FRYING PAN FARM PARK

Frying Pan Farm Park (2709 W. Ox Rd., Herndon, 703/437-9101, www.fryingpanpark.org, daily dawn to dusk, free) is a living-history farm (Kidwell Farm) with animals, wagon rides, horse show facilities, and a country store. Visitors can view farm animals such as cows, goats, pigs, rabbits, and horses and learn about what Virginia farm life was like 80 years ago. Beginner horseback riding lessons are also offered.

Mountain Biking

Wakefield Park (8100 Braddock Rd., 703/321-7080, www.fairfaxcounty.gov, daily dawn to dusk, free) has some of the best mountain biking trails in Northern Virginia. They are great for beginner and intermediate riders with some more challenging sections. The trails are part of a larger network of county trails including the **Cross County Trail** system. There's also a skate park at Wakefield where they hold skateboarding and BMX classes. Wakefield Park offers night riding from dusk to 10:30pm year-round on Monday, Tuesday, and Thursday nights. Otherwise the park is open dawn to dusk.

Another premier mountain biking park is **Fountainhead Regional Park** (Hampton Road, Fairfax Station, 703/250-9124, www.nvrpa.org, daily dawn to dusk, free). Miles of trails were developed in this park along the Occoquan Reservoir by mountain bikers for mountain bikers. These are technical trails, full of tight turns, steep climbs, stream crossings, and log hops. It's one of the best mountain biking areas in the Washington DC region. Call ahead for trail conditions.

Great Falls Park (9200 Old Dominion Dr., Great Falls, www.nps.gov/grfa, daily 7am-dark, $5) also offers nice nontechnical mountain biking with great views of the Potomac River. Nature lovers looking for a moderate ride can pedal to the right (when looking at the river) to pick up a few miles of dirt carriage roads and trails. There are some steep climbs, loose gravel, and rocks but nothing too technical. There are also single-track trails in the park if you head to the left of the parking lot. These trails lead to Riverbend Park and offer some hills. Obtain a trail map from the visitors center before you head out.

Many Fairfax County parks allow mountain biking on their trails. Additional information on the following trails can be obtained from the **Fairfax County Park Authority** (www.fairfaxcounty.gov). **Clarks Crossing** (9850 Clarks Crossing Rd., Vienna) offers 3.2 miles of natural trails connecting to the W&OD Trail. The **Colvin Run Stream Valley** trail (Hunter Mill Rd. and Rte. 7, Reston) is a lovely 3-mile natural trail that runs between Hunter Mill Road and Route 7. The **Fred Crabtree** park trail (2801 Fox Mill Rd., Herndon) offers 2 miles of wooded trails. **Lake Fairfax Park** offers a challenging network of wooded trails in Reston.

Trails

There are many hiking, running, and walking trails in Fairfax County. Most parks in the area offer some kind of recreational trails. To download trail maps in Fairfax County, visit www.fairfaxcounty.gov.

Golf

The premier public golf course in Fairfax County is **Westfields Golf Club** (13940 Balmoral Greens Ave., Clifton, 703/631-3300, www.westfieldsgolf.com, $54-109). This award-winning, nationally recognized course was designed by Fred Couples and is considered enjoyable for novices yet challenging for experienced players. The course incorporates natural wetlands, beech and oak trees, and rolling hills. The atmosphere is inviting and professional, and the service is outstanding. There complex includes a clubhouse, pro shop, driving range, putting green, fitting studio, and restaurant.

Another great course is the **Laurel Hill Golf Club** (8701 Laurel Crest Dr., Lorton, 703/493-8849, www.fairfaxcounty.gov, $34-99). This is an exciting 18-hole course that

Westfields Golf Club

was built on land that once housed the DC Department of Corrections facility at Lorton. This course, run by the Fairfax County Park Authority, was ranked in the top 10 municipal courses nationwide and has hosted several notable tournaments.

Pleasant Valley Golfers' Club (4715 Pleasant Valley Rd., Chantilly, 703/222-7900, www.pleasantvalleygc.com, $40-98) is another Fairfax County Park Authority course, but it is managed independently and is considered higher-end. The well-respected 18-hole course also offers a driving range.

The **Reston National Golf Course** (11875 Sunrise Valley Dr., 703/620-9333, www.restonnationalgc.com, $65-95) is one of Northern Virginia's classic golf courses. It was designed by Ed Ault and is home to the Nike Golf Learning Center, a leading golf instruction program. Reston National offers a driving range and putting and chipping greens. Unsubstantiated legend says that the land the course was built on was once owned by Hugh Hefner. Whether or not this is true, an aerial view of the course does strike a stunning resemblance to the Playboy bunny symbol.

An older course with a lot of character is the **Algonkian Regional Park Golf Course** (47001 Fairway Dr., Sterling, 703/450-4655, www.nvrpa.org, $33.50-47). This 18-hole, par 72 course offers long, straight, flat, tree-lined fairways on the front nine and hills and water holes on the back nine. Electric and pull carts are available. No metal spikes are allowed.

Rock Climbing

Great Falls Park (9200 Old Dominion Dr., Great Falls, www.nps.gov/grfa) is a rock climber's paradise with more than 200 climbing routes on the Virginia side of the river. Most climbs are around 50 feet and overhanging. Trad climbing is not recommended, so bring plenty of rope for toprope anchors. The fall is the best time to climb; the water is low and the climbs offer sun until late in the day.

Canoeing and Kayaking

There are several good launch sites for private canoes and kayaks in Fairfax County. **Algonkian Regional Park** (47001 Fairway Dr., Sterling, 703/450-4655, www.nvrpa.org, $5) has a nice boat ramp on the Potomac River. Paddlers should paddle upstream. **Mason Neck State Park** (Gunston Road, Mount Vernon, 703/339-2385, www.dcr.virginia.gov, $5 admission, $3 launch) is another good spot to launch and offers paddlers several places to paddle including Pohick Bay, Belmont Bay, and the Potomac River. Canoe and kayak rentals are available on-site and a cartop launch is provided. **Fountainhead Regional Park** (10875 Hampton Rd., Fairfax Station, 703/250-9124, www.nvrpa.org, free) offers a launch site on the Occoquan Reservoir ($4), kayak rentals ($12), and a learn-to-kayak program.

Fishing

Burke Lake Park (7315 Ox Rd., Fairfax Station, 703/323-6600, www.fairfaxcounty.gov) has a 218-acre lake with wonderful largemouth bass fishing, making it a popular spot. The park offers bait and tackle sales, rowboat rentals, and a boat launch.

Lake Fairfax Park (1400 Lake Fairfax Dr., Reston, 703/471-5415, www.fairfaxcountry.gov) offers spring trout fishing in its 18-acre lake. Other good fishing spots include **Fountainhead Regional Park** (703/250-9124, www.nvrpa.org) and **Riverbend Park** (8700 Potomac Hills St., Great Falls, 703/759-9018, www.fairfaxcounty.gov).

FOOD

Like much of Northern Virginia, Fairfax County has nearly every chain restaurant you can imagine. For those looking for something unique, there are some special gems if you know where to look.

Near the Beltway

INDIAN

Some of the best Indian food in the region is at ★ **Haandi** (1222 W. Broad St., Falls Church, 703/533-3501, www.haandi.com, lunch daily 11:30am-2:30pm, dinner Sun.-Thurs.

5pm-10pm, Fri.-Sat. 5pm-10:30pm, $11-22). This award-winning restaurant perfects the art of authentic Indian cooking. Although the names of the dishes may sound familiar, the range of flavors, the kitchen's skill with using spices, and the attention to detail are unrivaled. The restaurant is small, but worth the wait for a table. Start with an order of samosa and tantalize your taste buds as you look through the extensive menu of entrées. There are no wrong choices. When in doubt, ask your server for help; they are knowledgeable and eager to help. A daily lunch buffet is offered.

ITALIAN

Some of the best Italian food in Fairfax is at **Dolce Vita** (10824 Fairfax Blvd., Fairfax, 703/385-1530, www.dolcevitaitaliankitchenandwinebar.com, lunch Mon.-Sat. 11:30am-2:30pm, dinner Sun.-Thurs. 5pm-9:30pm, Fri.-Sat. 5pm-10:30pm, $6-26). This cozy little restaurant pairs delicious Italian cuisine with a comfortable, friendly atmosphere. The large wood-burning brick oven is a focal point in the small dining area, which is decorated with scenes from the Tuscan countryside. The food is mostly traditional Italian fare with an emphasis on fresh ingredients. They also prepare slightly lighter sauces and manage to do so without sacrificing any taste. The restaurant has a huge following with locals and those "in the know" and can be crowded during peak hours. They also have a wine bar next door with a daily happy hour, wine tastings, and dinner pairings.

In Old Town Fairfax, a good choice for Italian food is **Villa Mozart** (4009 Chain Bridge Rd., Fairfax, 703/691-4747, www.villamozartrestaurant.com, lunch Tues.-Fri. 11:30am-2:30pm, dinner Mon.-Sat. 5:30pm-10pm, $18-35). This intimate little restaurant offers delicious authentic Italian food and first-rate service. The food is presented beautifully and is equally as pleasing to the palate. The chef/owner goes out of his way with attention to detail, and guests feel welcome and special. Villa Mozart also offers a three-course dinner Monday-Thursday for $39. The restaurant is small and popular, so make a reservation. Parking is behind the building through the alley.

MEXICAN

If you're in the mood for Mexican food, try the **Coyote Grille and Cantina** (10266 Main St., Fairfax, 703/591-0006, www.coyotegrille.com, Mon.-Thurs. 11am-9:30pm, Fri.-Sat. 11am-10pm, Sun. 11am-9pm, $7-16) in Fairfax. They offer authentic recipes and a menu refreshingly different from the usual chain fare. The atmosphere is lively, and they have a loyal local client base. Their Southwestern-style entrées include traditional items such as burritos and fajitas and some unexpected twists such as the addition of sweet potatoes in their Fiesta Salad and their Coyote Burger with chipotle dressing. Their heated year-round patio has a margarita bar where they make more than a dozen varieties of scrumptious margaritas. They also have delicious desserts that go beyond fried ice cream and flan (such as a brownie sundae) and full brunch on Sunday. There is a second location in Chantilly.

PERSIAN

Outstanding Persian food is served at **Shamshiry** (8607 Westwood Center Dr., Vienna, 703/448-8883, www.shamshiry.com, Sun.-Thurs. 11:30am-11pm, Fri.-Sat. 11:30am-1am, $6-18) in the Tysons Corner area. If you're not sure which succulent kabob dish to order, try their specialty Chelo Kabob Shamshiry, a combination of kubideh (ground beef) and barg (steak). The portions are large and the restaurant is very popular, so go early or plan to wait for a table. They also offer carryout.

VIETNAMESE

Four Sisters Vietnamese Restaurant (8190 Strawberry Ln., Falls Church, 703/539-8566, www.foursistersrestaurant.com, daily 11am-10pm, $8.50-35) is all about delicious food, beautiful ambience, and reasonable prices. This award-winning restaurant offers

Local Brew

Even self-proclaimed beer snobs will find something to rave about in Northern Virginia's local beer scene. In recent years, a growing number of new brewers have come onto the radar to compete with the more established breweries. The result is a good selection of locally made beer spread out across much of Northern Virginia.

Lost Rhino Retreat

The English-style gastro brewpub **Mad Fox Brewing Company** (444 W. Broad St., Falls Church, 703/942-6840, www.madfoxbrewing.com, Mon.-Wed. 11am-11pm, Thurs.-Sat. 11am-midnight, Sun. 10am-11pm) was a welcome addition to the Falls Church restaurant scene when it opened. The 63-foot bar is a great place to meet with friends and sample the beers on tap. They normally offer a selection of 7-10 house beers and a varying array of seasonal brews, cask-conditioned proper red ales, and English-, Belgian-, and German-style beers. They also have a second location in Glover Park in Washington, DC (2218 Wisconsin Ave).

Founded by former employees of local craft beer pioneer Old Dominion Brewing, the **Lost Rhino Brewing Company** (21730 Red Rum Dr., #142, Ashburn, 571/291-2083, www.lostrhino.com, Tues. 4pm-9pm, Wed.-Thurs. 11:30am-9pm, Fri.-Sat.11:30am-10pm, Sun. noon-5pm) is a leader in the local brew scene. Named after a surfing term "rhino chaser," that means "someone out to find the best waves, biggest waves, an adventurer," they offer a fantastic selection of artfully crafted beers that just plain taste great. The brewery and tasting room is tucked away in a warehouse in Ashburn, but it's a fun place for a tasting and draws quite a crowd on the weekends. They also have a larger restaurant with space for events in nearby Brambleton called **Lost Rhino Retreat** (22885 Brambleton Plaza, Ashburn, 703/327-0311, www.lostrhinoretreat.com). Try their Rhinoel, Belgian-style dubbel, or Face Plant IPA, and order a giant Bavarian-style pretzel on the side.

Another brewery with Old Dominion ties is **Old Ox Brewery** (44652 Guilford Drive, Ashburn, 703/729-8375, www.oldoxbrewery.com, Wed.-Thurs. 4pm-9pm, Fri. 2:30pm-9pm, Sat. 11am-9pm, Sun. 11am-6pm), which has a 30-barrel brewhouse. They partner with a local food truck or food vendor to provide a varying menu. The brewery is easily accessible from the Washington & Old Dominion Trail between mile markers 25 and 25.5.

Sweetwater Tavern (3066 Gatehouse Plaza, Merrifield, 703/645-8100, www.greatamericanrestaurants.com, Sun.-Mon. 11am-10pm, Tues.-Thurs. 11am-10:30pm, Fri.-Sat. 11am-11:30pm) is part of the Great American Restaurants group, a wildly successful local chain. Sweetwater Tavern brews its own beer and offers many wonderful selections on tap. A fun atmosphere, lively crowd, and tasty selections are standard at Sweetwater. They rotate their beers regularly, but some favorites are the Flying Armadillo Porter, the Jackalope Canyon Ale, and, for something lighter, the Naked River Light. They also have locations in Sterling and Centreville.

The almost-local **Dogfish Head** (www.dogfishalehouse.com) has two Northern Virginia locations of their **Dogfish Head Alehouse** (6220 Leesburg Pike, Falls Church, 703/534-3342, Mon.-Thurs. 11:30am-11pm, Fri.-Sat. 11:30am-midnight, Sun. 11:30am-10pm; 13041 Lee-Jackson Memorial Hwy., Fairfax, 703/961-1140, Mon.-Wed. 11:30am-11pm, Thurs.-Sat. 11:30am-midnight, Sun. 11:30am-10pm). The brewery began in Rehoboth Beach, Delaware, and was the state's first brewpub. Its popularity quickly spread, and they now have 20 styles of beer. The draft choices at the alehouses change frequently, but a few perennial favorites include the 60 Minute IPA, Indian Brown Ale, and the Raison D'Etre.

an extensive and well-planned menu of light and flavorful Vietnamese food. If you aren't sure what to order, they offer dinners for 2, 4, 6, and 10 diners. The selections are wonderful and offer a good sampling of the chef's talents. They also offer a gluten-free menu. Reservations are highly recommended on weekends. Be sure to take note of the flower arrangements in the restaurant—they are made from real, fresh flowers, and they are spectacular.

Western Fairfax County

AMERICAN

One of the Reston Town Center's most noted restaurants is **Passion Fish** (11960 Democracy Dr., Reston, 703/230-3474, www.passionfishreston.com, lunch Mon.-Fri. 11:30am-2:30pm, dinner Mon.-Thurs. 5:30pm-10pm, Fri.-Sat. 5:30pm-11pm., Sun. 5pm-9pm, $19-45). Elegant, open, and airy, the atmosphere alone (which mimics a classic ocean liner) draws diners looking to enjoy seafood. The menu is primarily seafood, with some interesting twists. Selections from the raw bar, sushi, salads, and succulent entrées sit alongside sweet potato fries, mac and cheese, and jasmine rice with red Thai curry. Steak is also available. A favorite venue for business lunches and dinners, the restaurant also has a sophisticated bar menu and seasonal outdoor seating.

For something leisurely or romantic, try the **Vinifera Wine Bar Bistro** (11750 Sunrise Valley Dr., Reston, 703/234-3550, www.viniferabistro.com, daily 6:30am-12am, $19-32) in the Westin Hotel in Reston. It is a great place to bring a date or relax while traveling on business. The trendy spot offers great wine and equally tasty cuisine. Order multiple small plates to accompany wine by the glass or order a full-size entrée for a bigger commitment. Weather permitting, sit on the patio by a fire pit. There is little noise or street activity, making this = a delightful rare find in the area. Even if you aren't on vacation, it will feel like it. They serve breakfast, lunch, and dinner.

Bazin's on Church (111 Church St., Vienna, 703/255-7212, www.bazinsonchurch.com, brunch Sun. 11am-2pm, lunch Tues.-Fri. 11:30am-2pm, dinner Tues.-Thurs. 5pm-10pm, Fri.-Sat. 5pm-10:30pm, Sun. 5pm-9pm, $25-34) in Vienna is a contemporary American restaurant specializing in items made from organic and seasonal ingredients. There is also a wine bar with more than 500 selections from around the world. Wine-tasting is available. Dinner entrées include seafood, pasta, and steak, all prepared with unique and delicious recipes. The brunch offers mouthwatering options such as bananas foster French toast and filet sliders. The atmosphere is inviting with large windows, low lighting, and exposed brick walls. This small section of Vienna has a great contemporary feel to it, yet is easy to get to and has free parking.

If you're looking for a great sandwich or a slice of New York-style pizza, **Santini's** (11804 Baron Cameron Ave., Reston, 703/481-3333, www.mysantinis.com, Mon.-Sat. 9am-10pm, Sun. 9am-9pm, $6-15) in Reston is the place to go. This family-owned New York-style deli is the best sandwich joint in the area. The food is fresh, made to order, and simply delicious. A great place for families and team gatherings, it's also a comfortable spot to grab a beer and watch the game, Santini's offers reasonable prices, fresh food, and friendly, personal service. They also have locations in Sterling, Oakton, McLean, Fairfax, and Chantilly.

Chase the Submarine (132 Church Street NW, Vienna, 703/865-7829, www.chasethe-submarine.com, daily 10:30am-8pm, $8-11) is a 30-seat gourmet sandwich shop with refreshing alternatives to cold cuts and mayo. They feature classics like steak and cheese but with choice rib-eye, peppers, mushrooms, Provolone, and truffle-infused aioli. They also offer unique creations such as the Royale With Cheese, a home-ground blend of rib-eye and beef hearts, with creamy pimento cheese and hot fries. They sell wine and beer and have a specialty food market.

Mookie's BBQ (1141Walker Road, Great Falls, 703/759-2386, www.mookiesbbq.com,

Tues.-Thurs. 11am-9pm, Fri.-Sat. 11am-10pm, Sun. 9am-9pm, $9-30) grew out of a competition barbecue and catering company. They serve outstanding barbecue pork, chicken, ribs, and salads.

FRENCH

For a special celebration or a romantic dinner, it is hard to top ★ **L'Auberge Chez Francois** (332 Springvale Rd., Great Falls, 703/759-3800, www.laubergechezfrancois.com, lunch Tues.-Sat. 11:30am-1:30pm, Sun. noon-7:30pm, dinner Tues.-Thurs. 5pm-9pm, Fri., 5pm-9:30pm, Sat. 4:30pm-9:30pm, Sun. noon-7:30pm, $75-85). This family-owned restaurant began back in 1954 in Washington DC when the original Chez Francois opened in the Claridge Hotel. When the building was sold in 1975, the owner (originally from the Alsatian countryside) relocated the restaurant to Great Falls, at the time a remote area of Northern Virginia. The six-acre parcel was the perfect location for the new *auberge*, and the restaurant has been a destination in itself ever since. The food and service are simply first-rate, with exceptional attention paid to every detail. But what makes this place special is that regardless of who the famous person may be at the next table, or how many couples are getting engaged that night, the atmosphere is always relaxed and comfortable, and the servers are highly professional yet personable. Dinner is a six-course prix fixe menu with entrée selections that include seafood, filet, lamb, and their signature chateaubriand for two. Many little surprises accompany the meal, and every aspect is executed to perfection. Lunch is a four-course prix fixe menu for $42. Reservations are a must, and usually are required weeks in advance for prime times, but walk-ins are accepted on the beautiful terrace when the weather is nice. A scaled-down version of the menu is offered on the lower level of the restaurant in the **Jacques' Brasserie and Jacques' Bar Rouge** (Tues.-Fri. 5pm-9pm, Sat. 4:30pm-9:30pm, Sun. 3pm-7:30pm).

IRISH

The Old Brogue (760C Walker Rd., Great Falls, 703/759-3309, www.oldbrogue.com, Sun. 10am-10pm, Mon.-Thurs. 11am-midnight, Fri.-Sat. 11am-1am, $11-22) is *the* place to go in Great Falls. It's a family-owned institution that began on St. Patrick's Day in 1981. This cozy pub welcomes everyone with an international bar menu, fresh-made food, traditional Irish fare, and live entertainment. Start with Gaelic Bites (breaded potato and corned beef fitters) or some fried brie. Follow that up with traditional beef stew or the savory blackened salmon salad. They also serve Sunday brunch. Everyone is family at the Old Brogue, and it's one of the few places in this fast-paced area where people relax and chat with strangers at the next table.

VEGETARIAN

You don't have to be a vegetarian to enjoy **Sunflower Vegetarian Restaurant** (2531 Chain Bridge Rd., Vienna, 703/319-3888, www.crystalsunflower.com, Mon.-Sat. 11:30am-10pm, Sun. noon-10pm, $9-13). In fact, chances are you would never know it was vegetarian just by tasting the food: The tasty Asian-influenced entrées at Sunflower actually mimic meat in texture and taste. The flavors are delicious. First-timers can't go wrong with the local favorite, General Tso's Surprise. The surprise is that there really isn't meat in it, which you'd never guess.

Southern Fairfax County

AMERICAN

★ **Trummer's on Main** (7134 Main St., Clifton, 703/266-1623, www.trummerson-main.com, brunch Sun. 11am-2pm, dinner Tues.-Thurs. 5:30pm-9pm, Fri. 5:30pm-10pm, Sat. noon-10pm, Sun. 5pm-8pm, $14-42) is the hot spot in Clifton. The chef and owner was named one of *Food & Wine Magazine*'s Best New Chefs shortly after Trummer's opened back in 2010, and happy patrons have been coming ever since. Trummer's offers creative American cuisine and handcrafted cocktails (including their signature drink, the Titanic, which is too good to be missed). The ever-changing main plates include seafood, beef, chicken, pork, and vegetarian selections. The chef also offers a daily tasting menu that can be ordered when making your reservation, and a three-course prix fixe dinner on Sunday. It's imperative to save room for dessert: The pastry chef is nothing short of amazing. The atmosphere is hip and relaxing with high ceilings and many windows. The food presentation is exquisite. The cozy bar with its interesting stone pillars is a great place to meet friends, sample drinks, and try the bar menu.

ACCOMMODATIONS

$100-200

The majority of accommodations in Fairfax County are in national chain hotels. One exception is the **Stafford House** (3746 Chain Bridge Rd., 703/385-9024, www.staffordhouse.net, $119-199) bed-and-breakfast. This comfortable, friendly establishment is a nice change of pace in a convenient location. Each of its two rooms has a private entrance and parking. Breakfast is delivered to your room each morning, and rooms are equipped with many amenities including a fireplace. The owners are very friendly and helpful and contribute to an enjoyable stay.

$200-300

The **Residence Inn Tysons Corner Mall** (8400 Old Courthouse Rd., Vienna, 703/917-0800, www.marriott.com, $177-309) is a six-floor, 121-room hotel near Tysons Corner. They offer a free American breakfast and a beer and wine manager's reception Monday-Thursday. This is an older hotel, but it is kept up well and the staff is friendly and attentive. It is also pet friendly ($75 fee).

The **Hilton McLean Tysons Corner** (7920 Jones Branch Dr., McLean, 703/847-5000, www.hilton.com, $99-344) is another good option in Tysons Corner. It is convenient to shopping and has a modern, attractive decor. There are 458 guest rooms.

Over $300

One hotel that stands out from the crowd in Fairfax County is the **Westin Reston Heights** (11750 Sunrise Valley Dr., Reston, 703/391-9000, www.westinreston.com, $195-389). It is a modern hotel with 191 guest rooms and a quiet location. There is also a wonderful wine bar on-site.

Another good option is the **Hyatt Regency Reston** (1800 Presidents St., Reston, 703/709-1234, www.reston.hyatt.com, $249-649) in the beautiful Reston Town Center. It has 518 rooms and anchors the upscale outdoor mall. The interior has a modern decor, and free shuttle service is available to and from Washington Dulles International Airport.

The **Ritz-Carlton, Tysons Corner** (1700 Tysons Blvd., McLean, 703/506-4300, www.ritzcarlton.com, $369-5,000) is a high-end option in Tysons Corner with 398 guest rooms, direct access to shopping, and a better-than-average fitness room.

Camping

Camping is limited in Fairfax County but there are a few parks with nice campgrounds. The first is **Lake Fairfax Park** (1400 Lake Fairfax Dr., Reston, 703/471-5414, www.fairfaxcounty.gov, $28-50) in Reston. Tent and RV camping are available. There are 136 campsites (54 with electrical hookups), a bathhouse, a dump station, picnic tables, grills, and public telephones. Reservations are required, and the campground is open year-round.

The second is the campground at **Burke Lake Park** (7315 Ox Rd., Fairfax Station, 703/323-6600, www.fairfaxcounty.gov, $28-31). There are 100 wooded campsites (no electric or water hookups), a bathhouse, a dump station, camp store, ice, picnic tables, grills, fire rings, and public telephones. The campground is open mid-April through late October.

Another is **Bull Run Regional Park** (7700 Bull Run Dr., Centreville, 703/631-0550, www.nvrpa.org, $29-47), which offers RV sites with electric-only service, full-service RV sites, tent sites, group camping areas, and rustic cabins. There are two bathhouses and a camp store. All sites include charcoal grills, picnic tables, and fire rings.

INFORMATION AND SERVICES

The **Fairfax Museum & Visitors Center** (10209 Main St., 703/385-8414, www.fairfaxva.gov, daily 9am-5pm) is in the historic former Fairfax Elementary School built in 1873. Visitors can pick up information on special events, transportation, restaurants, and lodging. The museum offers exhibits on the history of Fairfax City and walking tours of Old Town Fairfax in the spring and fall. Additional information on the entire county can be found at www.fxva.com.

GETTING THERE AND AROUND

Fairfax County is accessible in some areas by **Metrorail** and **Metrobus** (www.wmata.com), but visitors will greatly benefit from having access to a car.

The city of Fairfax offers the **CUE Bus System** (703/385-7859, www.fairfaxva.gov, Mon.-Fri. 6am-11pm, Sat. 8:30am-8:30pm, Sun. 9:30am-6pm, $1.75) for public transportation around town. Buses accept exact change and SmarTrip cards. They also sell ticket books. Students and seniors can receive discounts. A bus schedule is available on the website.

Additional bus service in the county is provided by the **Fairfax Connector** (703/339-7200, www.fairfaxcounty.gov, $1.75). This service is countywide. Please consult the website for routes and schedules.

Prince William County

Prince William County is approximately 35 miles southwest of Washington DC. It stretches from the foothills of the Appalachian Mountains to the banks of the Potomac River and contains primarily suburban commuter communities but with a bit more rural feel than neighboring Fairfax County. The county has a number of historical landmarks, including the famous Manassas battlefield. It also offers outdoor recreation along the river and in several large parks.

For many years, the population in Prince William County was focused in Manassas, which was a large railroad junction, and Woodbridge, near the Potomac River. In recent decades the population has expanded significantly throughout the county, making it one of the most populated counties in the state.

SIGHTS

★ Manassas National Battlefield Park

The premier attraction in Prince William County is **Manassas National Battlefield Park** (6511 Sudley Rd., Manassas, 703/361-1339, www.nps.gov/mana, daily dawn to dusk, $3). This historic battlefield was established as a national park in 1940 to preserve the site of two well-known Civil War battles: the First Battle of Bull Run (July 21, 1861), which was the first major land battle in the war; and the Second Battle of Bull Run (August 28-30, 1862), which was the biggest simultaneous mass assault of the Civil War and signaled the height of the Confederate army's power. The battles are also referred to as the First and Second Battles of Manassas. The reason there are two names for each battle is because the North usually named a battle after a nearby body of water (creek, river, or stream) and the South named battles after towns and railroads. So the Confederate army named the battles after Manassas Junction and the Union army named them after the Bull Run stream. It was at this site that Confederate general Thomas J. Jackson was nicknamed "Stonewall" Jackson.

The park encompasses more than 5,000 acres of meadows, woods, and streams. When visiting the battlefield, you can see the site where the battles took place and also visit three buildings: the **Henry Hill Visitor Center,** the **Brawner Farm Interpretive Center,** and the **Stone House.**

The **Henry Hill Visitor Center** (daily 8:30am-5pm) is on Sudley Road near the southern park entrance. It houses exhibits and information on the First Battle of Bull Run that include uniforms from the era, weapons, and field gear. It also offers an electronic battle map that visitors can interact with for a quick lesson in field strategy and tactics. Take the time to watch the 45-minute orientation film offered at the center; it is interesting and informative. It is shown on the hour. There is also a bookstore.

The **Brawner Farm Interpretive Center** (daily 9am-5pm) is the location of the opening phase of the Second Battle of Bull Run. There are exhibits and audiovisual programs that give a detailed overview of the second battle. There is a parking lot off of Pageland Lane on the western side of the park.

The **Stone House** (weekends only 10am-4:30pm) is a two-story brick house that was built in 1848 and served as a hospital during both battles at Bull Run. It is near the intersection of Sudley Road and Lee Highway.

Other attractions in the park include the **Stone Bridge,** which the Union army retreated across after both battles; **Battery Heights,** where Confederate batteries fired on the attacking Union troops at the Brawner Farm; **Matthews Hill,** the site of the opening phase of the first battle; and **Groveton,** the remains of a Civil War-era village. There are many other points of interest in the park as well. A great way to see many of them is by taking a self-guided walking tour of the one-mile **Henry Hill Loop Trail** that begins at the Henry Hill Visitor Center.

More than 900,000 people visit the battlefield yearly. Guided tours running 30 to 45 minutes are available from the Henry Hill Visitor Center.

National Museum of the Marine Corps

The **National Museum of the Marine Corps** (18900 Jefferson Davis Hwy., Triangle, 877/635-1775, www.usmcmuseum.com, daily

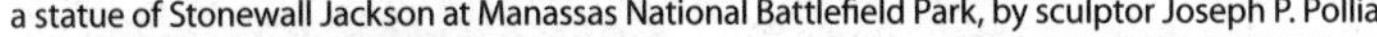

a statue of Stonewall Jackson at Manassas National Battlefield Park, by sculptor Joseph P. Pollia

9am-5pm, free) is in Triangle, adjacent to the **Marine Corps Base Quantico.** The museum was built to serve as an ongoing tribute to U.S. Marines of the past, present, and future. The beautiful soaring 210-foot design can be seen from I-95, and it is reminiscent of the famous Iwo Jima flag-raising image from World War II. The museum opened in 2006 and continues to expand. It houses interactive exhibits using innovative technology and shows visitors what it is like to be a marine. An example of this is the Legacy Walk, which uses lifelike cast figures of individual marines, photographs, maps, and artifacts to illustrate the evolution of the Marine Corps. Artifacts on display in the museum include aircraft, vehicles, weapons, uniforms, and personal items. A small fee is charged to experience the flight simulator.

Ben Lomond Historical Site & Old Rose Garden

Those looking for a historical site with a new twist will enjoy the **Ben Lomond Historical Site & Old Rose Garden** (10311 Sudley Manor Dr., Manassas, 703/367-7872, www.pwcgov.com, house hours May-Oct. Thurs.-Mon. 11am-4pm, $5). This is a hands-on historical experience with a focus on medicine. The federal-style manor house, built in 1837, is within five miles of Manassas National Battlefield Park, and it served as both a Confederate and Union hospital during the Civil War. The site includes the main house (where visitors can learn about medical techniques used during the Civil War and even see fake blood), slave quarters, and a smokehouse. Original graffiti written by Union soldiers in 1862 can still be seen on the walls. There is also an heirloom rose garden on the property with rare and antique plants. The garden is one of the largest public rose gardens in the country with approximately 160 different cultivars. This is a great museum for kids and teenagers. Tours are given on the hour.

Occoquan Waterfront

More than 50 shops and restaurants line the quaint streets along the Occoquan River on the historic **Occoquan Waterfront** (www.occoquanwaterfront.com). The town began as a site for public tobacco warehouses as early as 1734, and its name means "at the end of the water." With a mostly industrial past due to its water access, the town has transformed into a residential community served by small businesses. Antiques stores, galleries, gift shops, and boutiques are just some of the shops visitors will find. Many festivals and events are held throughout the year on the streets and even in the water. Check out the website to see what is happening when you're in town.

ENTERTAINMENT AND EVENTS

Jiffy Lube Live

A bustling venue for summer outdoor concerts is **Jiffy Lube Live** (7800 Cellar Door Dr., Bristow, 703/754-6400, www.livenation.com). This 25,000-capacity pavilion hosts many big-name bands, artists, and other performers. Reserved seating is underneath an overhang and protected from weather, while general admission is out on the lawn. Past performances include the Dave Matthews Band, The Who, Aerosmith, Jimmy Buffett, and Kelly Clarkson. Traffic entering and exiting the pavilion is notorious for being very slow, so plan accordingly.

Hylton Performing Arts Center

The **Hylton Performing Arts Center** (10960 George Mason Circle, Manassas, 703/993-7550, www.hyltoncenter.org) is a modern performing arts center at the Prince William Campus of George Mason University. The center includes 85,000 square feet of performance space including an elegant opera house, a family theater, and an art gallery. Performances include concerts, theater, comedy, dance, and other performing arts. Visit the website for a list of upcoming events.

Fairs and Festivals

The **Occoquan Craft Show** (www.occoquancraftshow.com) is an annual event held in June on the streets of historic downtown Occoquan. The show is hosted by the town of Occoquan and has been in existence for more than 25 years. Vendors include local merchants, crafters, and food, and there is live music. During the event, the roads are closed to traffic to make room for vendors and visitors. Information on parking and shuttle service can be found on the website.

The annual **Manassas Heritage Railway Festival** (9366 Main St., Manassas, 703/361-6599, www.visitmanassas.org) takes place in June and draws more than 30,000 visitors each year. Enjoy a day of train-oriented activities including train rides, model train displays, music, train memorabilia vendors, and other performances.

Another popular festival held in Manassas in June is the **Manassas Wine and Jazz Festival** (9101 Prince William St., 703/361-6599, www.visitmanassas.org, $30). This festival is held on Father's Day on the Manassas Museum Lawn in Old Town Manassas.

SHOPPING

Keeping in step with the rest of Northern Virginia, Prince William County offers a multitude of strip malls with many national retailers. The most well-known shopping area, however, is **Potomac Mills** (2700 Potomac Mills Circle, Woodbridge, 703/496-9330, www.simon.com, Mon.-Sat. 10am-9pm, Sun. 11am-6pm), right on I-95 near Woodbridge. Potomac Mills is the largest outlet mall in Virginia, with more than 200 stores. It is an indoor mall and also offers 25 food retailers and movie theaters.

Manassas Mall (8300 Sudley Rd., Manassas, 703/368-0181, www.manassasmall.com, Mon.-Sat. 10am-9:30pm, Sun. 11am-7pm) is a traditional mall with more than 100 stores.

SPORTS AND RECREATION

Splashdown Water Park

Splashdown Water Park (7500 Ben Lomond Park Dr., Manassas, 703/792-8200, www.splashdownwaterpark.com, Memorial Day-mid-June weekends only 11am-6pm, mid-June-mid-Aug. daily 11am-7pm, mid-Aug.-Labor Day daily noon-6pm, $14.95) is the largest water park in Northern Virginia. It features five unique water areas and a variety of food options. Some of the fun activities it offers include waterslides, a lazy river, a 25-meter lap pool, bubblers, fountains, cannonball slides, and a beach. They also offer swimming lessons.

Prince William Forest Park

Prince William Forest Park (18100 Park Headquarters Rd., Triangle, 703/221-7181, www.nps.gov/prwi, daily sunrise-sunset, $5-7) is a 15,000-acre all-season destination. It offers hiking, mountain biking, fishing, birdwatching, and cross-country skiing. There are 37 miles of hiking trails (the most extensive hiking network in Northern Virginia) and 21 miles of mountain biking roads and trails. Road biking on a 12-mile scenic stretch of road is also permitted, and the path has light traffic and great natural scenery. The visitors center is open daily 9am-5pm.

Leesylvania State Park

Leesylvania State Park (2001 Daniel K. Ludwig Dr., Woodbridge, 703/730-8205, www.dcr.virginia.gov, Mon.-Fri. 6am-8:30pm, Sat.-Sun. 5am-8:30pm, $5) is in southeast Prince William County, approximately 25 miles from Washington DC. The park is the site of the former Leesylvania Plantation where General Robert E. Lee's

canoe and kayak launch at Leesylvania State Park

father, Henry Lee III (aka Light Horse Harry), was born. Created in 1992, the park encompasses 542 acres on a peninsula bordered by the Potomac River, Neabsco Creek, and Powells Creek. The park has five hiking trails, including a segment of the **Potomac Heritage National Scenic Trail.** There are also many scenic overlooks to the Potomac River, and the one at Freestone Point is on the remains of a gun battery used by the Confederates in the Civil War. Fishing and boating are popular sports in the park. There is a boat ramp, a cartop launch for canoes and kayaks, and a 300-foot fishing pier. There is a large visitors center with nature displays, information on the history of the park, and a gift shop. Canoe tours, nature walks, and children's fishing tournaments are available, and a summer music concert series is held May-September. Picnic shelters are also available for rent.

A fun kayaking option is to launch from the park and paddle south on the Potomac River a short way to **Tim's Rivershore Restaurant & Crabhouse** (1510 Cherry Hill Rd., Dumfries, 703/441-1375, www.timsrivershore.com, $9-29) for a seafood lunch on their deck. The restaurant is visible from the cartop launch, and there's a beach at Tim's to land your kayaks. A short paddle north to Neabsco Creek will take you past a shoreline of cute houses by the railroad tracks.

Largemouth bass are plentiful in the Potomac River near Leesylvania State Park. Other sport fish include catfish, perch, and striped bass. Overnight boating and fishing pier usage are allowed March-October.

G. Richard Pfitzner Stadium

The **G. Richard Pfitzner Stadium** (7 County Complex Ct., Woodbridge, 703/590-2311) is a minor league baseball stadium and the home field of the Potomac Nationals, a Class A affiliate of the Washington Nationals. The stadium holds 6,000 spectators.

Golf

The **Old Hickory Golf Club** (11921 Chanceford Dr., Woodbridge, 703/580-9000, www.golfoldhickory.com, $70-92) is an upscale golf and banquet facility in Woodbridge. The 18-hole, par-72 course was designed by Tim Freeland and is the sister course to Raspberry Falls in Leesburg. It is a well-maintained course with fast greens.

The **Osprey's Golf Club at Belmont Bay** (401 Belmont Bay Dr., Woodbridge, 703/497-1384, www.ospreysgolf.com, $59) is an 18-hole, par-70 championship golf course along the Occoquan River. It is an Audubon

Certified course designed for golfers of all abilities. It has an on-site golf shop and restaurant.

There are four public golf courses run by the **Prince William County Park Authority.** The first is the **Prince William Golf Course** (14631 Vint Hill Rd., Nokesville, 703/754-7111, www.princewilliamgolf.com, $34-42) in Nokesville. This course was built in the 1960s by local farmers. It is an 18-hole, par-70 course geared toward beginner and intermediate golfers and offers wide fairways and gentle knolls. There is also a driving range, a large putting and chipping green, a practice bunker, and PGA instruction.

The second is the **General's Ridge Golf Course** (9701 Manassas Dr., Manassas, 703/335-0777, www.generalsridge.com, $29-39), a scenic 18-hole, par-72 championship course in Manassas. This course is geared toward players of all abilities as it rambles over hills and through trees. The course also includes a two-tier, all-grass driving range with 10 covered bays, a large putting and chipping green, and PGA instruction. A golf shop, clubhouse, and restaurant are also on-site.

The third, **Forest Greens Golf Club** (4500 Poa Annua Ln., Triangle, 703/221-0123, www.forestgreens.com, $57) in Triangle, offers resort amenities. This 18-hole, par-72 course was given four stars by *Golf Digest* and features gently rolling terrain, tree-lined fairways, and protected greens. Designed by architect Clyde Johnston, the course offers an interesting layout with elevated tees, large landing areas, and few blind shots. This facility also includes a driving range, a pro shop, a putting and chipping green, PGA instruction, and a beverage cart on the course.

The fourth golf course is the 9-hole, par-3 **Lake Ridge Park Golf Course** (12350 Cotton Mill Dr., Woodbridge, 703/494-5564, www.lakeridgegc.com, $14-18) in Woodbridge. This course is an affordable novice course designed to help improve players' short games.

Bird-Watching

There are two prime birding locations in Prince William County. The first is the **Manassas National Battlefield Park** (6511 Sudley Rd., Manassas, 703/361-1339, www.nps.gov/mana, $3), which was recently named an Audubon Important Bird Area. Park residents include the eastern meadowlark, barn owl, northern harrier, Savannah sparrow, and the grasshopper sparrow.

The second is the **Prince William Forest Park** (18100 Park Headquarters Rd., Triangle, 703/221-7181, www.nps.gov/prwi, daily sunrise to sunset, $5-7), a 15,000-acre national park in Triangle. The park is known as one of the premier birding habitats in Northern Virginia and has residents such as cedar waxwings, warblers, and kingfishers.

FOOD

American

The ★ **Philadelphia Tavern** (9413 Main St., Manassas, 703/393-1776, www.thephiladelphiatavern.com, daily 11am-2am, $6-16) is the place in Manassas to go for cheesesteaks, brews, and a little bit of everything else. The signature "Build Your Own Original Cheesesteak" is a local favorite. Try it with American cheese and Cheese Whiz. With daily specials like Monday Mexican, Wing Wednesday, and Home Cookin' on Thursdays (featuring homemade pot roast and meat loaf), every day is a little different at the tavern. Located in the historic district, the building was constructed in 1940 and was formerly a liquor store and storehouse. It was converted to the tavern in the 1990s as a replica of the common corner bar found in Philadelphia neighborhoods. Breakfast is also served on Sunday.

For casual seafood in a lovely setting, try **Madigans Waterfront** (201 Mill St., Occoquan, 703/494-6373, www.madiganswaterfront.com, Mon.-Thurs. 11am-10pm, Fri. 11am-11pm, Sat. 10:30am-11pm, Sun. 10:30am-9pm, $6-24). Madigans is right on the waterfront in historic Occoquan and offers a large deck with a tiki bar, many seafood selections, steak, pasta, and oysters year-round. They also have a sandwich menu with favorites such as shrimp salad, crab cakes, and an assortment of wraps. If you're looking for decent food and a relaxing waterfront setting, Madigans is a good choice.

French

The **Bistro L'Hermitage** (12724 Occoquan Rd., Woodbridge, 703/499-9550, www.bistrolhermitage.com, lunch Thurs.-Fri. 11:30am-3pm, dinner Tues.-Thurs. and Sun. 5pm-10pm, Fri.-Sat. 5pm-11pm, brunch Sat.-Sun. 11:30am-2:30pm, $31-60) is a cozy French bistro located in Woodbridge but near the charming and historic Occoquan Waterfront. They serve fine French cuisine for brunch, lunch, and dinner. Dinner entrées include many seafood dishes as well as roasted duck, steak, roasted chicken, and veal liver. The restaurant offers delicious, well-presented food, good ambience, and friendly service.

the Philadelphia Tavern

Greek

For great Greek food go to **Katerina's Greek Cuisine** (9212 Center St., Manassas, 703/361-4976, www.katerinasgreekcuisine.com, Sun.-Thurs. 11am-9pm, Fri.-Sat. 11am-10pm, $6-13) in Manassas. This impressive little restaurant combines family recipes with fresh ingredients. If you're not sure what to order, try the Taste of Greece combination dinner or a traditional gyro platter. If someone in your party isn't keen on Greek food, they also offer burgers.

Mexican

Wonderful authentic Mexican food can be found in Haymarket at ★ **El Vaquero West** (14910 Washington St., Haymarket, 703/753-0801, Mon.-Thurs. 11am-10pm, Fri. 11am-11pm, Sat. 11am-10pm, Sun. 11am-9pm, $7-20). People travel from all parts of Northern Virginia to enjoy the white queso and the dozens of freshly prepared menu items (most from family recipes). The chips and salsa are average, but the rest of the food will keep you coming back. The huge burritos are a favorite and come in all varieties. The restaurant is small and very family friendly. The waitstaff is extremely nice, and both staff and patrons are lively and always seem to enjoy themselves. Try a Texas-style margarita, which comes in three sizes, and then order your entrée by the menu item number. Don't be thrown by the numbering system; there really isn't one. You'll understand when you see the menu. The portions are big, the food is consistent, and the prices are very reasonable. This is easily one of the best Mexican restaurants in the region.

Farmers Markets

Haymarket's Farmers Market (Town

Hall parking lot, 15000 Washington Street, 703/753-2600, www.townofhaymarket.org, May-Oct., Sat. 8am-2pm) is a Virginia producer-only weekly market featuring fresh produce, specialty items, and baked goods.

ACCOMMODATIONS

Accommodations in Prince William County are primarily national chain hotels. Some good choices are available near the county's favorite spots for visitors.

$100-200

The **Hampton Inn Manassas** (7295 Williamson Blvd., Manassas, 703/369-1100, www.hamptoninn3.hilton.com, $139-159) is a reasonably priced hotel near Route 66. It is approximately 20 minutes from Washington Dulles International Airport. The hotel offers 125 pleasant, clean rooms, a fitness center, and free Internet. Complimentary breakfast is available each morning.

The **Holiday Inn Manassas Battlefield** (10424 Balls Ford Rd., 571/292-5400, www.ihg.com, $130-225) is convenient to Route 66 and the Manassas Battlefield. This modern hotel offers visitors 104 spacious guest rooms with a few extra touches such as nice hair products in the bathrooms and an attentive staff. Breakfast is included each morning with your stay. A pleasant indoor pool and hot tub and small fitness room are also on-site.

The **SpringHill Suites Potomac Mills** (14325 Crossing Pl., Woodbridge, 703/576-9000, www.marriott.com, $116-139) in Woodbridge is conveniently located off exit 158 of I-95 near the Potomac Mills shopping area. There are 98 spacious guest rooms. The hotel is modern, and the staff goes out of its way to make guests comfortable. Breakfast is included, and there is a pool, fitness center, and a free laundry facility on-site. Free high-speed Internet and parking are included.

A good value near I-95 is the **Country Inn & Suites Woodbridge** (2621 Prince William Pkwy., Woodbridge, 703/492-6868, www.countryinns.com, $118-179, check for Internet specials). This hotel offers 100 nice guest rooms, complimentary coffee and cookies, and friendly service. The rooms have comfortable beds, microwaves, and refrigerators. Breakfast is included. There is also an indoor pool. The hotel is convenient for Potomac Mills shopping.

CAMPING

Prince William Forest Park (18100 Park Headquarters Rd., Triangle, 703/221-7181, www.nps.gov/prwi, $4.52-58.76) has four campgrounds and more than 100 campsites a half mile from the park entrance. Cabin camping is available in five cabins, four of which were built during the Great Depression and are now listed in the National Register of Historic Places. Cabin rentals are available May-October. One cabin can accommodate large groups.

INFORMATION AND SERVICES

The **Historic Manassas Visitor Center** (9431 West St., Manassas, 703/361-6599) is housed in an early-20th-century train depot in the center of town. Another good resource for Manassas information is www.visitmanassas.org.

For additional information on Prince William County in general, visit www.pwcounty.org.

GETTING AROUND

The **OmniLink** (703/730-6664, www.prtc-transit.org/local-bus, times vary by location, $1.40) is a local bus service in Prince William County. The service is unique because buses are able to alter their routes to accommodate additional service locations when there is available time in their schedules.

Loudoun County

It is hard to believe that at one time Loudoun County was considered the northwestern frontier of Virginia. Loudoun became a county in 1757 during the French and Indian War. It was named after John Campbell, the fourth earl of Loudoun (of Ayrshire, Scotland), who was the commander in chief of the British and colonial troops. Leesburg became the county seat around 1760. When the British invaded Washington DC during the War of 1812, the county clerk in Loudoun hid the Constitution and the Declaration of Independence in a family vault in a home just southeast of Leesburg.

President James Monroe had a home in Loudoun County called Oak Hill. Located in Aldie (13 miles south of Leesburg), it was there that he wrote the Monroe Doctrine in 1823. Oak Hill is currently a private residence and not open to the public.

Loudoun was a divided county during the Civil War. Sitting on the border between the North and the South, it became a thoroughfare of sorts for both Union and Confederate troops. Communities in Loudoun were often stripped of their horses and resources as the troops came through, leaving many residents in dire straits. Some residents began to fight back as members of John Singleton Mosby's partisan rangers, and Mosby became known as the "Gray Ghost of the Confederacy" after experiencing success with his hit-and-run strategy.

After the war, the railroad expanded west through Loudoun and new communities sprang up. The county saw the development of many farms and summer homes for Washingtonians. In the 1960s, the county began to blossom into a full-fledged suburb of Washington DC and experienced a population growth of 600 percent during a 40-year span. Today substantial growth continues, and many homes and businesses are built in the county yearly, making it one of the wealthiest and most populous counties in the state.

Visitors to Loudoun County will find large housing developments and strip malls, but despite incredible growth, the area is also known as "Virginia hunt country" for its history of foxhunting and for the many wineries that grace its rolling terrain. The historic towns of Leesburg and Middleburg have maintained their charm and should be high on the list of places to visit.

GETTING THERE AND AROUND

Loudoun County Transit (703/771-5665, www.loudoun.gov) provides commuter bus service from Loudoun County to Washington DC, the Pentagon, and Rosslyn (Arlington) for $9 one-way and to the Wiehle-Reston Metrorail station for $1.50 one-way. Service begins at multiple park-and-ride lots throughout Loudoun County. For a map of parking lot locations, visit www.loudoun.gov.

LEESBURG

Leesburg is a historic town 45 miles west of Washington DC and 15 minutes from Washington Dulles International Airport. Its roots stretch back more than 250 years, but this bustling town has seen tremendous growth over the past two decades as suburban sprawl found its way into Loudoun County and then continued to explode. Spend a day or a weekend exploring historic downtown Leesburg, watch a point-to-point horse race sponsored by the Loudoun Hunt, or spend an afternoon shopping at the Leesburg Outlets.

Sights

HISTORIC DOWNTOWN LEESBURG

Leesburg was established in 1758 and is the seat of Loudoun County. At the outbreak of the Civil War, the town was prospering and had approximately 1,700 residents. Leesburg is just two miles south of the Potomac River, which at the time divided the North and South. During the war, the town suffered frequent raids and fighting in its streets, and it changed hands nearly 150 times. Following the war, Leesburg's proximity to Washington DC helped it recover economically, and it eventually became a primary stop for the railroad. Today, visitors to **Historic Downtown Leesburg** (www.visitloudoun.org) can see beautiful 18th- and 19th-century architecture, walk its brick sidewalks, visit many unique shops, eat in trendy restaurants, and partake in special events and festivals. Blue tourist information signs direct the way to the **visitors center** (112-G South St., 703/771-2170, daily 9am-5pm), which is a great place to begin exploration.

OATLANDS HISTORIC HOUSE AND GARDENS

A National Trust Historic Site and National Historic Landmark, **Oatlands Historic House and Gardens** (20850 Oatlands Plantation Ln., 703/777-3174, www.oatlands.org, April-December Mon.-Sat. 10am-5pm, Sun. 1pm-5pm, $12) is a lovely example of a Virginia plantation. Just six miles south of downtown Leesburg, Oatlands was built in the early 19th century and was a thriving 3,408-acre wheat plantation. It was owned by George Carter, a descendant of one of Virginia's most well-known families. A large federal-style mansion was started near the southern border of the property but ended up being finished in the 1820s in the Greek revival style. Many outbuildings were added including a smokehouse, greenhouse, and barn. The plantation prospered until the time of the Civil War, but the family's wealth declined after the war and the plantation became a girls school and boardinghouse.

In 1897, the mansion and 60 acres were sold to *Washington Post* founder Stilson Hutchins, although he never actually lived there. In 1903, the property was purchased by William and Edith Eustis, who were avid outdoors lovers and saw the potential for restoring the home and neglected gardens and using the property for foxhunting. In 1964, after Edith's passing, her daughters donated the mansion (furnished) and 261 acres to the National Trust for Historic Preservation.

Oatlands is now open to the public

Historic Downtown Leesburg

April-December. Forty-minute interpretive guided tours of the first floor are available, and self-guided tours of the second floor are encouraged. They also offer Enslaved Community Tours and Paranormal Tours.

The formal terraced Oatlands Gardens and grounds are open to visitors. These 200-year-old gardens were designed in the Tidewater Virginia style and have multiple terraces carved into a hillside. Box hedges, trees, vegetables, shrubs, and flowers are part of the plantings, and the beautiful stonework was quarried locally. There are also many sculptures in the gardens (thanks to the Eustis's son-in-law, who was the first director of the National Gallery of Art). Be sure to take in the wonderful view of Bull Run Mountain.

Many events are held at Oatlands throughout the year. Concerts, murder-mystery dinner theater, point-to-point horse races, art shows, an annual harvest festival, summer camps, wine-tasting, dog shows, and footraces are just some of the events scheduled at this beautiful venue. A traditional afternoon tea is held regularly; check the website for information.

There's a gift shop on-site but no food facilities. However, there are plenty of places to enjoy a relaxing picnic on the grounds.

★ MORVEN PARK

Morven Park (17263 Southern Planter Ln., 703/777-2414, www.morvenpark.org, grounds open dawn-dusk, free) is a special place in Loudoun County. This 1,200-acre estate was home to Virginia governor Westmoreland Davis, who served as governor from 1918-1922, for 40 years. The site now offers the original mansion (Governor's Residence), two museums, a farmhand house, an equestrian center, historic gardens, sports fields, hiking trails, and beautiful country scenery. Many public events are held at Morven Park throughout the year including Civil War reenactments, equestrian competitions, and festivals. It is also the "forever home" to pardoned White House turkeys.

All-inclusive tours of the Mansion, Carriage Museum, Museum of Hounds and Hunting of North America, and Farmhand House are available for $10 ($5 for children). Tour days and hours change throughout the year so check the Morven Park website before planning a visit.

The **Governor's Residence** is worth a trip itself. It evolved from a fieldstone farmhouse built in 1781 into a beautiful turn-of-the-20th-century mansion. The stately home with its white exterior and columned facade sits on a rise surrounded by a blanket of pristine lawn. It supports an unusual mix of architectural styles that includes a Greek Revival portico, a Jacobean dining room, French drawing room, and a renaissance great hall. The furnishings are also an eclectic mix that includes pieces from the Renaissance, neo-Renaissance, and 16th-century Belgian tapestries. A terraced, formal garden sits just behind the house and can be toured at leisure with admission to the Governor's Residence. Forty-five-minute tours of the mansion are offered on the half hour.

Other museums on-site include the **Carriage Museum,** which houses an assortment of antique vehicles; the **Museum of Hounds & Hunting** (inside the Governor's Residence), which preserves art and memorabilia of foxhunting in Virginia; and the **Farmhand House,** which interprets the lives of farmhands who made it possible to operate large farms in the early 1900s. Other points of interest include information on Morven Park during the Civil War (offered on the grounds through permanent historical markers and periodic living-history programs, free) and the beautiful parklike grounds surrounding the mansion (free).

The **equestrian center** at Morven Park (41793 Tutt Ln.) hosts local, regional, national, and international equestrian events including horse trials, schooling shows, trail rides, clinics, polo events, races, and dressage events. It includes indoor and outdoor arenas, a series of stunning cross-country courses, and sporting fields. Morven Park is two miles north of downtown Leesburg.

LOUDOUN MUSEUM

The **Loudoun Museum** (16 Loudoun St. SW, 703/777-7427, www.loudounmuseum.org, Fri.-Sat. 10am-5pm, Sun. 1pm-5pm, $3) is dedicated to Loudoun County's rich and diverse heritage. It offers educational exhibits that are a little different from other museums since the artifacts displayed are authentic items formerly owned by county residents. The museum's goal is to tell the stories of the people from the county. Exhibits include original documents, photographs, maps, furniture, and toys. There are also exhibits geared specifically toward kids.

LEESBURG ANIMAL PARK

A fun place to take the kids is the **Leesburg Animal Park** (19270 James Monroe Hwy., 703/433-0002, www.leesburganimalpark.com, Tues.-Sun. 10am-5pm, $11.95), a 21-acre family petting zoo. It offers an animal petting and feeding area with residents such as llamas, bunnies, deer, lambs, pigs, and camels, and exotic animal exhibits with animals such as lemurs, gibbons, zebras, porcupines, and tortoises. Kids of all ages can participate in many park activities. They offer pony and camel rides, wagon rides, and other activities too. The favorite event of the year at the park is **Pumpkinfest** (www.pumpkinfestleesburg.com), which is open daily between late September and early November. Visitors can enjoy a kid's hay maze, slides, an obstacle course, face and pumpkin painting, and many more seasonal activities.

THOMAS BALCH LIBRARY

The **Thomas Balch Library** (208 W. Market St., www.leesburgva.gov, hours vary daily) features collections on Loudoun County, Virginia history, genealogy, military history, and the American Civil War. The library is operated by the town of Leesburg. The library is also a designated Underground Railroad research site.

BALL'S BLUFF BATTLEFIELD REGIONAL PARK

Ball's Bluff Battlefield Regional Park (Ball's Bluff Road, 703/737-7800, www.nvrpa.org, daily dawn-dusk, free) preserves the site where the first Civil War engagement in Loudoun County took place, the Battle of Ball's Bluff, in October 1861. Visitors can enjoy seven miles of marked hiking trails and read interpretive signs that describe the battle.

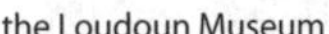

the Loudoun Museum

The park surrounds **Ball's Bluff National Cemetery,** the third-smallest national cemetery in the country. A small monument dedicated to a Confederate soldier who was killed in the battle, Clinton Hatcher, may be found in the cemetery. A second memorial is dedicated to the memory of a Union colonel, Edward D. Baker, who was also killed in the battle. Baker was a U.S. Senator at the time he was killed. Efforts are underway to restore the battlefield to its original appearance. Guided tours are offered May-mid-October on Saturday and Sunday at 11am and 1pm.

WINERIES

Wine lovers shouldn't miss a tasting at the **Fabbioli Cellars** (15669 Limestone School Rd., 703/771-1197, www.fabbioliwines.com, daily 11am-5pm, tastings $15). This small, family-owned boutique vineyard and winery grows and makes high-quality red wines (and only red wines). The atmosphere is different from many other wineries since it is located in the owner's home, but the ambience and service are wonderful. Tastings include a food pairing (chocolate or savory), and the staff does a great job (additional food and wine can be enjoyed outside after your tasting). The staff is very knowledgeable and goes out of its way to make everyone feel welcome. This is an ideal outing for a small group. Groups with more than eight people should make a reservation.

Tarara Winery (13648 Tarara Lane, 703/771-7100, www.tarara.com, Mon.-Thurs. 11am-5pm, Fri.-Sun. 11am-6pm, tastings $10) is a popular winery near the Potomac River. The property is beautiful, with a large deck for when the weather is nice. On a rainy day, follow the stone "tunnel" to the tasting room in the spacious-yet-cozy basement. The wines are delicious and the staff does a great job of making everyone feel welcome.

Fabbioli Cellars and Tarara Winery are just two of many wineries on the **Loudoun Wine Trail.** Loudoun County boasts more wineries than any other county in Virginia, and directions to other wineries can be found on the county's Wine Growers Association website (www.loudounwine.com). **Point to Point Winery & Vineyard Tours** are also available through **Point to Point Limousine** (703/771-8100, www.pointtopointlimo.com, tour prices start at $40 per person).

Entertainment and Events

The **Loudoun Hunt Point to Point Races** are held annually in mid-April at the historic **Oatlands Historic House and Gardens** (20850 Oatlands Plantation Ln., 703/777-8480, www.loudounhunt.com, $25 per car). The races were first held in 1966 and are known for featuring challenging timber and hurdle courses that test the abilities of the local and global competitors.

Classic-car enthusiasts won't want to miss the annual **Leesburg Classic Car Show** (King St., 571/237-2888, www.novarodsn-classics.org, free). This event, hosted by the Northern Virginia Rods and Classics Car Club and usually held the first Saturday in June, takes place in downtown Leesburg. More than 200 classic cars are on display, including street rods and muscle cars. The event is free to spectators, but donations are appreciated.

Music lovers will enjoy the free **Acoustic on the Green** (Town Hall Green, 25 W. Market St., www.acousticonthegreen.com) summer concert series in downtown Leesburg. Concerts are held on Saturday evenings 7pm-9pm June-August.

The **Leesburg Air Show** (1000 Sycolin Rd., 703/737-7125, www.leesburgairshow.com, free) is a much-anticipated free annual air show that is held at the **Leesburg Executive Airport** at the end of September. The show features many types of planes including experimental aircraft and warbirds from World War II. The show has air performances and tarmac attractions, and food is available for purchase.

Shopping

Historic Downtown Leesburg offers

antiques stores, art galleries, and other specialty shops. The primary shopping area is on Market, Loudoun, and King Streets.

In recent years, Leesburg has become synonymous with outlets. People travel from all over the region to shop at the **Leesburg Corner Premium Outlets** (241 Fort Evans Rd., 703/737-3071, www.premiumoutlets.com, Mon.-Sat. 10am-9pm, Sun. 10am-7pm). The mall houses 110 outlets including stores for designer fashion, shoes, children's clothes, leather, jewelry, housewares, and gifts. There is also a food court, and other national chain restaurants are nearby.

The **Village at Leesburg** (1602 Village Market Blvd., 571/291-2288, www.villageatleesburg.com) is a modern 57-acre open-air shopping plaza with upscale retailers and restaurants. The anchor store is **Wegmans** food market.

The **Dulles Town Center** (21100 Dulles Town Circle, Dulles, 703/404-7120, www.shopdulletowncenter.com) is one of the newest indoor malls in Northern Virginia. It offers many national-brand stores and restaurants with ample free parking. It is located at the intersection of Route 7 and Route 28, 10 miles east of Leesburg.

Sports and Recreation

GOLF

The **Raspberry Falls Golf and Hunt Club** (41601 Raspberry Dr., 703/779-2555, www.raspberryfalls.com, $85-105) is a beautiful and challenging 18-hole, par-72 course that is open to the public. The award-winning course was designed by Gary Player to evoke the feeling of the British Isles. This is evident in the rolling terrain, stone walls, rambling streams, and bunkers. The course has elevated tee boxes and lush bent grass greens. The course is set against the backdrop of the Catoctin Mountains and holes 3 and 18 have particularly nice views. This is one of the most popular daily-fee courses in Northern Virginia but is not for those on a budget.

PARKS

If you're looking for a nice short hike with good views of the Potomac River, visit **Red Rock Wilderness Overlook Regional Park** (43098 Edwards Ferry Rd., 703/737-7800, www.nvrpa.org, daily dawn to dusk, free). This 67-acre park is four miles east of downtown Leesburg and offers a two-mile loop trail through the woods and over hills to a panoramic view of the river. Trail terrain varies from moderate to strenuous in some places. Dogs are allowed on leashes, and there are no restroom facilities in the park.

Food

AMERICAN

One part wine-tasting, one part farm-to-table experience, **The Wine Kitchen** (7 S. King St., 703/777-9463, www.thewinekitchen.com, Tues.-Thurs. 11:30am-9pm, Fri.-Sat. 11:30am-10:30pm, Sun. 11:30am-9pm, $15-29) is a small, cozy restaurant with a modern vibe. Wine is served with clever and humorous description cards, and the food selection is interesting and beautifully presented. The staff is very knowledgeable about the wine and food and make excellent recommendations. If you are unsure what to order, try a wine flight. The mussel appetizer is delicious as is the butternut squash soup.

Tuscarora Mill (203 Harrison St., 703/771-9300, www.tuskies.com, Mon.-Thurs. 11am-11pm, Fri.-Sat. 11am-midnight, Sun. 11am-9pm, $18-38) is a local institution in Leesburg. The food is consistent and delicious, and the warm historic ambience is inviting. The owners of this establishment really care about the food and guests at their restaurants (they own another great restaurant in nearby Purcellville called **Magnolias at the Mill,** which is equally wonderful). There's an informal bar area to grab a casual drink (they have a great wine list), and the dining area is good for groups. This is a good place for a date or to visit with friends. Tuscarora Mill is also known for their beer- and wine-pairing dinners. They are fantastic. The chef goes out of his way to prepare delicious and unexpected combinations. Check the website for a schedule.

Lightfoot Restaurant (11 N. King St., 703/771-2233, www.lightfootrestaurant.com, Mon.-Thurs. 11:30am-11pm, Fri.-Sat. 11:30am-midnight, Sun. 11:30am-10pm, $10-24) serves contemporary food in a great atmosphere. The building is a restored turn-of-the-20th-century bank building with many interesting and original architectural features and artifacts as well as original French posters from the 1920s. There are two bars, one with a grand piano, and an open kitchen with a chef's table. If you are unsure what to order, the onion soup, fried green tomatoes, crab cakes, and filet are all excellent choices. There is a private parking lot in back of the restaurant and street parking out front.

Lightfoot Restaurant

ITALIAN

Fireworks Pizza (201 Harrison St., 703/779-8400, www.fireworkspizza.com, opens daily at 11am, $9-19) was a quick-rising star in the Leesburg restaurant scene when it opened a few years ago. This popular restaurant housed in the former Leesburg Freight Depot has fantastic pizza (try the Smokey Blue Pizza) and a great beer selection. The sandwiches are good too. The ambience is warm and inviting, and on nice days, the porch adds much-needed seating. If you come on the weekend, expect a wait. A friendly atmosphere, great food, and reasonable prices make this place a gem in the heart of historic Leesburg. Their patio is dog friendly.

TREATS

When your sweet tooth is acting up, stop in **Mom's Apple Pie** (220 Loudoun St. SE, 703/771-8590, www.momsapplepieco.com, Mon.-Fri. 7:30am-6:30pm, Sat. 8am-6pm, Sun. 8am-5pm), at the fork in the road between Loudoun Street and Market Street. As the name implies, they have fantastic pie, cookies, cupcakes, bread, and other baked goods. A Leesburg tradition, this establishment is known for baking natural, preservative-free pies. They even grow much of their own fruit.

FARMERS MARKETS

Leesburg hosts several great farmers markets featuring local producers such as **Shenandoah Seasonal** (www.shenandoahseasonal.com) from Boyce, Virginia.

The **Leesburg Saturday Summer Farmers Market** (Virginia Village Shopping Center on Catoctin Circle SE, 540/454-8089, www.loudounfarmersmarkets.org, Nov.-Apr. 9am-noon, May-Oct. 8am-noon) is open year-round. There is also a seasonal Wednesday market in the same location (May-Oct. 2:30pm-6:30pm).

The **Ashburn Farmers Market** (One Loudoun, north end of Exchange Street, Ashburn, www.loudounfarmersmarkets.org) also runs May-October. It is held Saturday 8am-noon.

The **Brambleton Market** (Emberbrook Circle, in front of Regal Cinemas,

The Gray Ghost

Throughout American Civil War history, the operatives of one man in particular continue to fascinate scholars and history buffs alike. Colonel John Singleton Mosby, known as "the Gray Ghost," was a free-thinking man whose dislike for routine military life eventually led him to develop an independent guerrilla group that made forays throughout Loudoun County.

An attorney by profession, and a graduate of the University of Virginia, Mosby joined his local militia unit as a private soldier in 1861. With the outbreak of the Civil War, his cavalry unit joined the Confederate forces. Mosby's strength was in scouting and patrolling duties, and he became a member of J. E. B. Stuart's personal staff.

In 1863, with nine men from his regiment, Mosby began guerrilla attacks on isolated Union posts in Northern Virginia and Maryland. Mosby led lightning-quick cavalry strikes aimed at disrupting supply lines and communication.

Mosby's men swelled in numbers and soon became known as "Mosby's Rangers." Many of Mosby's Rangers were volunteers who never had any formal military training. Many brought their own uniforms and weapons. Their two most important items were their pistols and their horses. They often assembled near a blacksmith's shop so their horses' feet could be tended to.

When things became dangerous, the Rangers would melt into the night. They'd stay with friends, family, or simply camp out in the hills. Loudoun became known as Mosby's Confederacy, and Union commanders were furious with his success. Because of their guerrilla tactics and tendency to keep their spoils, the Rangers were often viewed by Federal officials as criminals rather than soldiers.

On March 9, 1863, Mosby led 29 Rangers through Federal lines at the Fairfax Courthouse and captured General Edwin Stoughton, 33 men, and 58 horses. A sack of gold and silver coins worth $350,000 was also taken, but Mosby was forced to bury it when chased by Union troops. Allegedly, he was never able to recover the loot, and it is still said to be buried between two tall pine trees in a shallow hole between Haymarket and New Baltimore.

By April 1865, Mosby had been promoted to colonel, had been wounded seven times, and was in command of eight companies. His last raid was on April 10, the day after Robert E. Lee surrendered at Appomattox. At that time, he had more than 700 men in his command.

After the war, Mosby continued to practice law in Warrenton. Mosby wrote two books while serving terms as U.S. consul to Hong Kong and assistant attorney in the Justice Department. They are titled *Mosby's War Reminiscences and Stuart's Cavalry Campaigns (1887)* and *Stuart's Cavalry in the Gettysburg Campaign (1908)*. He died on May 30, 1916, in Washington DC.

Brambleton, www.loudounfarmersmarkets.org, Sunday 9am-1pm) is held seasonally on Sunday.

Information and Services

Visitor information on Leesburg can be found at www.leesburgva.gov and www.visitloudoun.org, or visit the **Loudoun County Visitors Center** (112-G South St., 703/771-2170, www.visitloudoun.org, daily 9am-5pm).

Accommodations

There is a wide assortment of national chain hotels in Leesburg. Many are on the newer side, part of the rapid growth in Loudoun County over the past decade. If you're looking for someplace unique, there are several good options.

$100-200

The Country Comfort Bed and Breakfast (19724 Evergreen Mills Rd., 703/926-6994, $150-175) offers two suites that are more like apartments near downtown Leesburg. Guests are treated to a scrumptious home-cooked breakfast of their choice delivered each morning. Refrigerators are stocked with sodas, water, juice, and snacks, which are available throughout the stay. The suites have king beds, private bathrooms, a work area, high-speed Internet, and a living/dining area. The Evergreen Suite also has a private deck. Picnic lunches can be arranged as well as cooking and woodworking classes (for a fee).

$200-300

Lansdowne Resort (44050 Woodridge Pkwy., 703/729-8400, www.lansdowneresort.com, $235-720) has 305 guest rooms in the Potomac River valley, approximately four miles east of Leesburg. Amenities at the resort include a golf course, spa, health club, tennis courts, indoor and outdoor pools, and on-site restaurants. This resort offers beautiful grounds, a great view, and a quiet atmosphere. It is a popular location for business conferences.

UNIQUE ACCOMMODATIONS

The beautiful **Idyll Time Farm, Cottage & Stabling** (43470 Evans Pond Rd., 703/443-2992, www.bbonline.com, call for pricing) offers guests the opportunity to rent a fully restored historic log home. Visitors can enjoy the entire cottage instead of just one room and even bring their horses (there is long- and short-term stabling on-site). This is a wonderful getaway for long or short stays and was featured in *This Old House Magazine*. The kitchen comes stocked with breakfast items, and special requests can be accommodated. Guests can bring their own food to cook during their stay or go out to the many local restaurants. The house is pet friendly.

MIDDLEBURG

Middleburg is an oasis in Northern Virginia just 42 miles west of Washington DC. Its stunning landscape, rich Civil War history, and beautifully restored buildings make it a very special place for visitors to explore. The area truly has the look of the English countryside: ribbons of low stone walls wind across lush pastures, and acres and acres of pristine farmland blanket the foothills of the Blue Ridge Mountains. Middleburg has over 160 historic buildings, and nearly every one has a unique story. Some housed troops during the Civil War, others were shot at, and some hid well-known figures such as John Singleton Mosby (aka the Gray Ghost) and his band of raiders.

Middleburg is horse and hunt country. Many of its residents have family histories in equine sports competitions, and many U.S. Olympic riders live and train in the Middleburg area. As such, equine events and festivals attract visitors from all over the country.

Sights

THE VILLAGE OF MIDDLEBURG

Middleburg was developed in the mid-1700s and was later named for its location midway between Alexandria and Winchester. The town (with a local population between 500 and 600 people) was established in 1787 and has many Civil War roots. It is beautifully preserved as a quaint, colonial island in an otherwise busy Northern Virginia. The main attraction is the village of Middleburg itself. This charming, historic section is lined with family-owned shops, inns, and restaurants and is well worth a day trip from Washington DC or other parts of Virginia and Maryland. Take a stroll down Washington Street, and you'll feel miles and possibly centuries away from the busy nation's capital, as you become part of the historic landscape. The people are friendly, the pace is relaxed, and the merchandise is often rare and unusual.

NATIONAL SPORTING LIBRARY & MUSEUM

The **National Sporting Library & Museum** (102 The Plains Rd., 540/687-6542, www.nationalsporting.org, Wed.-Sat. 10am-5pm, Sun. 1pm-5pm, library free, museum $10) is a beautiful site dedicated to preserving equestrian, angling, and field sports literature, art, and culture. It is a research facility and art museum (located in two buildings)

The War Horse

There is something beautiful and haunting about the three-quarters life-size bronze sculpture that stands in the courtyard of the National Sporting Library & Museum in Middleburg. It depicts a thin, exhausted, war-weary Civil War horse wearing authentic Civil War-style tack.

This sculpture was created in the mind of Paul Mellon, a well-known American philanthropist, Thoroughbred racehorse breeder, and coheir to the Mellon Bank fortune who lived in nearby Upperville. Mellon was profoundly moved by Robert F. O'Neill Jr.'s book, *The Cavalry Battles of Aldie, Middleburg and Upperville, June 10-27, 1863,* which told of human and horse bloodshed during a 17-day period in the American Civil War. After reading the book, Mellon felt compelled to do something for all the horses that died during the war.

To that point no monuments had been erected to honor the war's tremendous equine losses. The idea of a memorial came up one day while Mellon was speaking with the director and others at the National Sporting Library. The idea grew into a vision for an extraordinary bronze sculpture to honor all mules and horses from both the Union and Confederate armies.

Extensive research was conducted on the number of equine fatalities and also on the type of leather tack and gear they wore during battle. Mellon then took the idea to sculptor Tessa Pullan from Rutland, England, whom he had worked with earlier on a statue of his 1993 Kentucky Derby winner, Sea Hero.

A tremendous amount of time was spent consulting with many sources to create a design that was completely authentic. An example is the horse's stance, with his back leg bent, which is how horses stand when they are tired. Another is the scabbard worn by the horse. It is shown without a sword to indicate that the horse's rider was lost in battle. Care was also taken to fit the horse with gear that could have been from either the Union or Confederate side.

More extensive research showed that a realistic estimate of equine losses during the war was between 1,350,000 and 1,500,000, an astonishing and unsettling number. This number is reflected in the inscription at the bottom of the statue.

The library's Civil War horse was completed in 1997 and is now one of the most visited landmarks in the area. Local residents feel a personal attachment to the statue and often place horse blankets over it when the weather is cold.

National Sporting Library & Museum

with more than 24,000 books and pieces of art. Be sure to look closely at the beautiful, haunting horse statue in front of the library. It is a memorial to the horses who lost their lives in the Civil War.

MOUNT DEFIANCE CIDERY & DISTILLERY

Mount Defiance Cidery & Distillery (207 W. Washington St., 540/687-8100, www.mt-defiance.com, Wed.-Sat. noon-6pm, Sun. 1pm-6pm, tastings $5) is located right on West Washington Street. They create small-batch, handcrafted, classic hard cider and spirits. Their cidery produces farmhouse blends and a single-variety cider, but is also known for unique infused and co-fermented ciders (honey, five-pepper, blueberry, etc.). The distillery focuses on classic spirits from both colonial America and Europe, such as apple brandy, apple liqueur, rum, and absinthe.

WINERIES AND VINEYARDS

Middleburg is on the edge of Virginia wine country and home to a number of good wineries, vineyards, and tasting rooms that are worth visiting for their relaxing atmosphere and, of course, wine.

The beautiful **Boxwood Estates Winery** (2042 Burrland Rd., 540/687-8778, www.boxwoodwinery.com, Fri.-Sun. 11am-6pm) is owned by former Washington Redskins owner John Kent Cooke. They produce red wine only in three styles in the Bordeaux tradition (from five grape varieties). Tastings by the glass or flight are available by appointment at the winery in Middleburg, but they also have several tasting rooms throughout the Washington DC area called **The Tasting Room Wine Bar & Shop** (www.thetastingroomwinebar.com).

Chrysalis Vineyards (39025 John Mosby Hwy., Middleburg, 540/687-8222, www.chrysaliswine.com, April-Oct. Mon.-Thurs. 10am-6pm, Fri.-Sun. 10am-7pm, Nov.-Mar. daily 10am-5pm, tastings $10 for 10 wines) is located just west of Aldie on Route 50 in the Ag District Center. They specialize in unusual French and Spanish grape varietals and also in the native Virginia Norton grape.

The **Barrel Oak Winery** (3623 Grove Ln., Delaplane, 540/687-6111, www.barreloak.com, May-Nov. Mon.-Thurs. 11am-6pm,

Fri.-Sat. 11am-9pm, Sun. 10am-6pm, Dec.-Apr. Sun. 10am-6pm, Mon.-Thurs. 11am-6pm, Fri. 11am-9pm, Sat. 11am-6pm, tastings start at $7) is located 14 miles southwest of Middleburg. They are dog and kid friendly. They also offer activities and events such as horseback rides.

For something a little bit different, visit **Quattro Goomba's Winery** (22860 James Monroe Hwy., Aldie, 703/327-6052, www.goombawine.com, Thurs. and Sat.-Sun. noon-6pm, Fri. noon-9pm, tastings $7) in nearby Aldie (six miles east of downtown Middleburg). This winery is very casual and offers a signature white-and-red-wine-swirl slushy. It might sound a little unusual, but don't knock it until you try it. The slushies are refreshing and delicious, and nearly everyone there is drinking them. Goomba's also serves fantastic bread and cheese and old-school pizza (made with their own bread and cheese). The atmosphere is fun, the clientele often stays for hours, and the establishment is very dog friendly.

Entertainment and Events

CHRISTMAS IN MIDDLEBURG

One of Loudoun County's largest annual events is **Christmas in Middleburg** (Washington St., 571/278-5658, www.christmasinmiddleburg.org), held annually on the first Saturday in December. This daylong celebration in horse country includes a unique parade with more than 700 horses, llamas, alpacas, and hounds. An assortment of troops, bands, and floats also join the march down Washington Street along with fire trucks and, of course, Santa in a horse-drawn coach. Other festivities include performances, hayrides, a flower and greens show, and craft show. The final phase of the celebration is a wine crawl where adults can enjoy samples from area vineyards and food in local restaurants.

HUNT COUNTRY STABLE TOUR

The **Hunt Country Stable Tour** (540/592-3711, www.trinityupperville.org/hunt-country-stable-tour, $30) is a 55-plus-year tradition in Middleburg and neighboring Upperville. This self-driven stable tour takes visitors through some of the most impressive private horse stables in the region. The tour is held over Memorial Day weekend and includes Thoroughbred breeding farms, foxhunting barns, and show hunter barns. A remarkable experience for horse lovers and non-equestrians alike, this is a great way to spend a day in the beautiful Virginia countryside.

UPPERVILLE COLT & HORSE SHOW

The **Upperville Colt & Horse Show** (Upperville Show Grounds, on Rte. 50 between Middleburg and Upperville, 540/687-5740, www.upperville.com, $10) is the longest-running horse show in the country. It was founded in 1853 and is held each year at the **Upperville Show Grounds.** More than 2,000 horses and riders compete each year over seven days at the beginning of June under towering oak trees in a beautiful storybook setting. Young riders on ponies and Olympic and World Cup riders and horses are all part of this well-known event.

THE MIDDLEBURG SPRING RACES AND THE VIRGINIA FALL RACES

The Middleburg Spring Races (www.middleburgspringraces.com) and **The Virginia Fall Races** (www.vafallraces.com) are two annual point-to-point (steeplechase) horse races with a long tradition in Middleburg. Both are held at **Glenwood Park** (36787 Glenwood Park Ln., www.glenwoodpark.org), less than two miles north of downtown Middleburg. The spring races are in April, and the fall races are in October.

VIRGINIA GOLD CUP RACES

The premier event at the premier equestrian venue in Northern Virginia is the **Virginia Gold Cup Races** (540/347-2612, www.vagoldcup.com) at Great Meadows. This event is held eight miles south of downtown Middleburg in a nearby village called The

Plains. The grand point-to-point race is held the first Saturday in May (rain or shine) and brings out the best gourmet tailgates in town. The day of racing dates back to 1922, and now more than 50,000 spectators from all over the Washington DC area descend on hunt country to enjoy this festive eating, drinking, people-watching, and yes, horse-watching event. The race itself is extremely demanding with horses running more than four miles and jumping over four- to five-foot solid rail fences. The **International Gold Cup Races** are held at the same venue in October. Tickets to both events must be purchased well in advance.

Shopping

The village of Middleburg is an elegant and historic shopping area right on Route 50 (John S. Mosby Highway). Unique boutiques housed in beautiful old buildings line the streets and offer goods from all over the world. Most stores are individually owned and operated specialty shops with hand-selected merchandise. It is obvious the owners take great pride in these establishments.

The Fun Shop (117 W. Washington St., 540/687-6590, www.thefunshop.com, Mon.-Sat. 9:30am-5:30pm, Sun. 1pm-5pm) is a regional favorite. This inspiring store sells a little of everything. Whether you need candles, kitchen accessories, holiday decor, lampshades, picture frames, or picnic accessories, this store has it all. They even have party accessories, toys, and an area for kids to play in.

Duchessa (100 E. Washington St., 540/687-8898, www.duchessaofmiddleburg.com, Tues.-Sat. 10am-5pm, Sun. 11am-5pm) is an elegant boutique selling upscale designer women's collections. The displays are eye-catching, the selection is wonderful, and the owner and staff are delightful to work with. The expertise that goes into running this shop is obvious, making it an inviting atmosphere for all who walk through the doors.

The Shaggy Ram (3 E. Washington St., 540/687-3546) sells European furnishings, antiques, and some newer items. Local artwork is also displayed.

Second Chapter Books (10 S. Liberty St., 540/687-7016) is a local favorite for both general-interest books and titles on Middleburg topics.

The **Middleburg Antique Emporium** (107 W. Washington St., 540/687-8680, www.middleburgantiqueemporium.com, daily 10am-5pm) sells authentic, one-of-a-kind antiques. The owners are very knowledgeable about their products, and items are reasonably priced.

Sports and Recreation

HORSEBACK RIDING

It seems like everyone in Middleburg owns a pair of riding boots. Most of the farms are privately owned and don't offer riding to the public, but if you are interested in giving it a try, **FlyAway Stables** (1625 Brookhill Ln., 703/622-4230, www.tteamva.com), a few miles west of Middleburg off Route 50, and **FoxholeFarm** (22064 Sam Fred Rd., 540/687-5953, www.foxholefarmva.webs.com), four miles northeast of downtown Middleburg, offer lessons. Another option is to visit the **Middleburg Polo Academy** (20221 Foggy Bottom Rd., Bluemont, 540/272-3820, www.middleburgpoloacademy.org) in nearby Bluemont (13 miles northwest of downtown Middleburg). They offer lessons for kids and adults in the sport of polo (no riding experience is necessary).

Glenwood Park (36787 Glenwood Park Ln., www.glenwoodpark.org) is an equestrian-oriented park that hosts many events throughout the year including point-to-point races, dressage shows, horse trials, and pony club events. Refer to the website for a list of upcoming events.

BIKING

Road cycling and mountain biking are very popular in Middleburg. The beautiful and rolling country roads draw bikers from all over Northern Virginia, and the incredible scenery keeps them coming back. This has caused some friction between the local residents and the visiting bikers. The roads in

Middleburg do not have bike lanes, so traffic is shared between bikes and cars. Although there is little traffic compared to the rest of the region, the hairpin turns and low shoulders can create a dangerous situation for both drivers and bikers. Use extreme caution when biking in Middleburg and be sensitive to traffic. A good resource for finding bike routes in the area is www.mapmyride.com.

HOT-AIR BALLOONING

For high-flying adventure, try a hot-air balloon ride with **Balloons Unlimited** (23217 Meetinghouse Ln., Aldie, 703/327-0444, www.balloonsunlimited.com, adults $225, children $125). Rides begin in several locations depending on the weather. Two flights are scheduled daily.

Food

AMERICAN

The Red Fox Inn and Tavern (2 E. Washington St., 540/687-6301, www.redfox.com, Mon.-Fri. breakfast 8am-10am, lunch 11:30am-2:30pm, dinner 5pm-8:30pm, Sat. lunch 11:30am-2:30pm, dinner 5pm-8:30pm, Sun. prix fixe brunch 10am-2:30pm, dinner 5pm-7:30pm, $26-52) is a historic tavern in the heart of Middleburg that serves traditional Virginia-style food using cooking techniques such as roasting, smoking, and braising. Hearty breakfasts, relaxing lunches, and cozy candlelight dinners draw people to the tavern from all over the region. The stone fireplace and handcrafted furnishings are a good complement to the seasonal menus featuring indigenous Southern and Virginia ingredients. If you've never tried peanut soup, this is the place to order it. The wine list includes both imported and domestic wines and includes many local Virginia wines. The restaurant offers great ambience, consistently good food, and friendly service.

If you're looking for breakfast, a gourmet sandwich, or a picnic to take with you on a country outing, or you need to purchase gourmet ingredients, the **Market Salamander** (200 W. Washington St., 540/687-8011, www.marketsalamander.com, Mon.-Thurs. 11am-6pm, Fri.-Sat. 8am-6pm, Sun. 8am-4pm, extended hours in summer, sandwiches $7-15) is the place to visit. It is a chef's market, complete with an in-house café (order at the counter), catering services, and custom cake

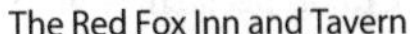
The Red Fox Inn and Tavern

making. The market sells produce, prime aged meat, seafood, artisanal cheese, home-baked bread, pastries, wine, and a variety of imported packaged goods. The focal point in the market is the open display kitchen where the chef's daily selections are prepared.

If a local bar is more your style, stop in the **Red Horse Tavern** (118 W. Washington, Street, 540/687-6443, daily 11am-10pm, $10-25). They offer basic pub fare and a large patio.

ENGLISH

About eight miles west of Middleburg on Route 50 is **Hunter's Head Tavern** (9048 John S. Mosby Hwy., Route 50, Upperville, 540/592-9020, www.huntersheadtavern.com, Mon.-Sat. 11:30am-9:30pm, Sun. 11am-9:30pm, $11-36). This authentic English pub is in a cute, old crooked house right on the road. Look for the red English telephone box out front. Hunter's Head offers local organic farm meat and produce and was the first restaurant in the country to receive a certified humane designation. When you enter the pub, you immediately realize you're going to have a unique dining experience. Original log cabin walls, "settled" floors, and mismatched wooden tables are all part of the charm. Read the extensive menu off the chalkboard and place your order at the window next to the bar (even if you have reservations, which is advised). The menu includes hearty pub fare and fine-dining options, and the offerings change frequently. Then, take your number to your table where traditional table service will commence (you can order additional drinks and dessert from your server). Tables are located in many different rooms. If the macaroni and cheese is on the menu, it's worth ordering in spite of the calories. The calamari is also good and very tender. Hunter's Head Tavern has good beer on tap as well (they even have Lambick from time to time). The desserts are fabulous, so save room.

FRENCH

The French Hound (101 Madison St., 540/687-3018, lunch Wed.-Sun. 11:30am-2:30pm, dinner Tues.-Thurs. 5:30pm-9:30pm, Fri.-Sat. 5:30pm-10pm, $10-31) is a wonderful little bistro tucked into a neighborhood on a side street in the village. The staff is warm and friendly, and since the dining area is split between several rooms in the house, it feels like you're an invited guest in someone's home. As the name implies, they offer simple French cuisine and a casual atmosphere. The menu is limited but offers delicious choices with enough variety. They have good steak frites and a knowledgeable sommelier (with a carefully selected wine list). They also have a cute hound logo.

The **Goodstone Inn & Restaurant** (36205 Snake Hill Rd., 540/687-3333, www.goodstone.com, Mon.-Sun. noon-2:45pm and 5:30pm-8:45pm, à la carte entrées $29-55, prix fixe $59-85) deserves accolades for both its inn and restaurant. The small restaurant serves outstanding "modern American French country cuisine" in a superb country setting. The chef only uses fresh ingredients, and many of them are sourced from the inn's private organic herb and vegetable gardens. Sample menu items include braised rabbit ragout, filet mignon, and crab cakes. It is a charming place full of simple elegance for a special date or to just get away from it all.

TREATS

Curb your sweet tooth while helping homeless animals. What could be better? Stop in **Scruffy's Ice Cream & Coffee Parlor** (6 W. Washington St., 540/687-3766) for some delicious ice cream. A portion of the proceeds benefits local homeless animals at the Middleburg Humane Society. Try the chocolate ice cream or the mango sherbet. This is a small place, but there are a few stools inside and some benches outside.

A wonderful local bakery is the **Upper Crust** (2 N. Pendleton Street, 540/687-5666). They serve breakfast and lunch but are known for their pastries and fresh pies. You'll likely smell cookies baking as you approach. They do not take credit cards.

Scruffy's Ice Cream & Coffee Parlor

Accommodations

Middleburg is one of the few places in Northern Virginia where you'll have a good selection of private inns and bed-and-breakfasts to choose from. Truly a stay in the country, spending a night in Middleburg can make you feel light-years away from the city.

$100-200

The stately **Welbourne** (22314 Welbourne Farm Ln., 540/687-3201, www.welbourneinn.com, $147) is an authentic historical treasure in Virginia hunt country. The house was built in the 1700s and has been in the same family ever since. A stay there will take you back to Civil War times (the owners refer to it as "faded elegance"). There are five primary guest rooms with private baths and fireplaces. Relax in a rocking chair on the back porch, or take a hike around the property. Complimentary cocktails (served each evening at 6:30pm) and a wonderful, hearty breakfast are just some of the amenities that make visitors feel like family. Many dogs and horses live at this several-hundred-acre property, so be prepared for four-legged company. The estate is decorated with family heirlooms and antiques. The property is dog friendly.

Another lovely bed-and-breakfast a few miles from town is the **Briar Patch Bed and Breakfast Inn** (23130 Briar Patch Ln., 703/327-5911, www.briarpatchbandb.com, $95-295). This historic home (built in 1805) was damaged during the Civil War and still shows a few scars today. The main house offers eight guest rooms decorated with antiques and colonial quilts. Six of the rooms can be combined into two-bedroom suites. There is also a small cottage and three "chicken coop" rooms. A good buffet breakfast is served daily, and plentiful snacks are available all day. There are resident horses, and the inn is dog friendly.

$200-300

One of the best-known inns in Middleburg is **The Red Fox Inn and Tavern** (2 E. Washington St., 540/687-6301, www.redfox.com, $215-525). This iconic inn and restaurant sits prominently at the center of Middleburg on the corner of East Washington Street and North Madison Street. The tavern is famous as a meeting spot for Confederate colonel John Singleton Mosby and his Rangers. The Red Fox Inn is a complex consisting of several buildings and cottages that house 15 guest rooms. The tavern is located in the main building, and there is event space on the first and second floors. Six of the guest rooms are also in the main building on the upper two levels. The rooms are cozy and cleanly appointed in a colonial style, yet not overstuffed. A hunt country breakfast is served each day. The inn is very convenient to shopping and restaurants in the village.

The **Middleburg Country Inn** (209 E. Washington St., 540/687-6082, www.middleburgcountryinn.com, $170-255) in downtown Middleburg is elegant but personal. The seven lovely rooms have king-size beds, private bathrooms, bathrobes, television, phone, and Internet access. Guests have access to the inn's beautiful porches. The breakfast room is warm and filled with smells of delicious breakfast items such as waffles and eggs Benedict. Complimentary ice cream is also available. The innkeepers are helpful with advice on local attractions. There is a surcharge on rooms rented for one night on Saturday. Easy parking is available, and the inn is within walking distance to shopping and restaurants.

OVER $300

The charming and luxurious ★ **Goodstone Inn & Restaurant** (36205 Snake Hill Rd., 540/687-3333, www.goodstone.com, $325-825) is a wonderful choice for an upscale country getaway. The inn has a highly regarded restaurant with a noted chef, and the service is friendly and genuine. There is also an on-site spa. The property is large (265 acres) and scenic with views of the Blue Ridge Mountains. The 18 tastefully decorated guest rooms and suites are housed in six buildings around the farm (which actually has farm animals). You can hike around the property on a trail that is several miles long and very relaxing. Canoeing is also available.

The **Salamander Resort and Spa** (500 North Pendleton St., 540/687-3600, www.salamanderresort.com, $383-975) opened in 2013 and is one of the first luxury destination resorts in the nation to be LEED (Leadership in Energy and Environmental Design) certified. This stately 168-room resort sits on 340 acres in the heart of Virginia's wine and horse country, just outside the historic district of Middleburg. The modern, spacious guest rooms are 545-575 square feet and include sitting areas and a private balcony or terrace. Guests can enjoy a 23,000-square-foot spa, cooking studio, wine bar, billiards room, pool complex, tennis courts, and a two-acre culinary garden that supplies the resort's restaurant. There is also a full-service, 22-stall equestrian center on-site with an arena, riding trails, and instructional classes.

Information and Services

Middleburg's information center, the **Pink Box** (12 N. Madison St., 540/687-8888) is a good place to pick up brochures. They also offer information on a self-guided walking tour of the town. Downloadable driving maps are also available from the **Mosby Heritage Area Association** (www.mosbyheritagearea.org).

Coastal Virginia

Look for ★ to find recommended sights, activities, dining, and lodging.

Highlights

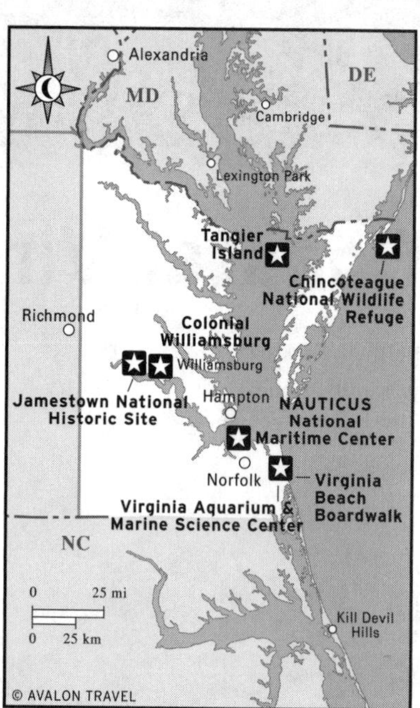

★ **Colonial Williamsburg:** A living museum that is unmatched nationwide, Colonial Williamsburg takes visitors back in time. It's one of America's most popular family destinations (page 171).

★ **Jamestown National Historic Site:** The original site of the Jamestown settlement spans centuries of history. Founded in 1607, it was the first permanent English settlement in the New World (page 181).

★ **NAUTICUS National Maritime Center:** This nautical-themed science and technology center in Norfolk is also home to the battleship USS *Wisconsin* (page 201).

★ **Virginia Beach Boardwalk:** The most popular beach resort in the state offers enough activity to keep visitors busy for days—and provides access to miles of wonderful sand and surf (page 206).

★ **Virginia Aquarium & Marine Science Center:** Hundreds of exhibits, live animals, and hands-on learning make this amazing aquarium one of the most popular attractions in the state (page 208).

★ **Tangier Island:** This remote island in the middle of the Chesapeake Bay feels like another country. The residents even have their own language (page 219).

★ **Chincoteague National Wildlife Refuge:** This 14,000-acre wildlife refuge protects thousands of birds and a herd of wild ponies. Visitors can enjoy miles of natural beaches and hike or bike through the marsh (page 223).

Coastal Virginia sounds like a simple concept: the place where the Atlantic Ocean meets the land. It's actually much more complicated than that. The Chesapeake Bay is a defining feature along the coast, and the area where it opens into the Atlantic Ocean has developed into one of the world's largest and busiest natural ports. Several large rivers empty into the Chesapeake Bay as well, including the Potomac, Rappahannock, James, and York Rivers.

The coastal region can be divided into five main areas. The first is the Northern Neck, which sits between the Potomac and Rappahannock Rivers, both of which flow into the bay. The Northern Neck is quiet and flat, and farms line the riverbanks. The area is home to several notable historic sites including George Washington's birthplace. The second area is known as the Historic Triangle, which includes the colonial cities of Williamsburg, Jamestown, and Yorktown. These cities sit along the James and York Rivers, which also flow into the Chesapeake Bay. Next is the huge area of Hampton Roads. This is where everything converges. The rivers flow into the bay just to the north, and the Chesapeake Bay flows into the Atlantic Ocean just to the east. The main cities in this area are Newport News, Hampton, and Norfolk. Then we have Virginia Beach. The Virginia Beach resort area is truly on the Atlantic coast. Our final region, Virginia's Eastern Shore, is sandwiched between the Chesapeake Bay on the west and the Atlantic Ocean on the east. It is sparsely populated compared to its mainland neighbors and offers charming historic towns and ample bird-watching and fishing.

PLANNING YOUR TIME

Visiting Coastal Virginia requires some planning, a love of water, and no fear of bridges. Although there is some public transportation between specific cities, the easiest way to get around is by car. I-64 runs from Richmond down to the Historic Triangle and Hampton Roads areas, while Routes 17 and 3 traverse the Northern Neck. Route 13 runs the length of the Eastern Shore.

Previous: the Public Hospital of 1733 in Colonial Williamsburg; docks on Tangier Island. **Above:** Assateague Island Lighthouse in Chincoteague National Wildlife Refuge.

Coastal Virginia

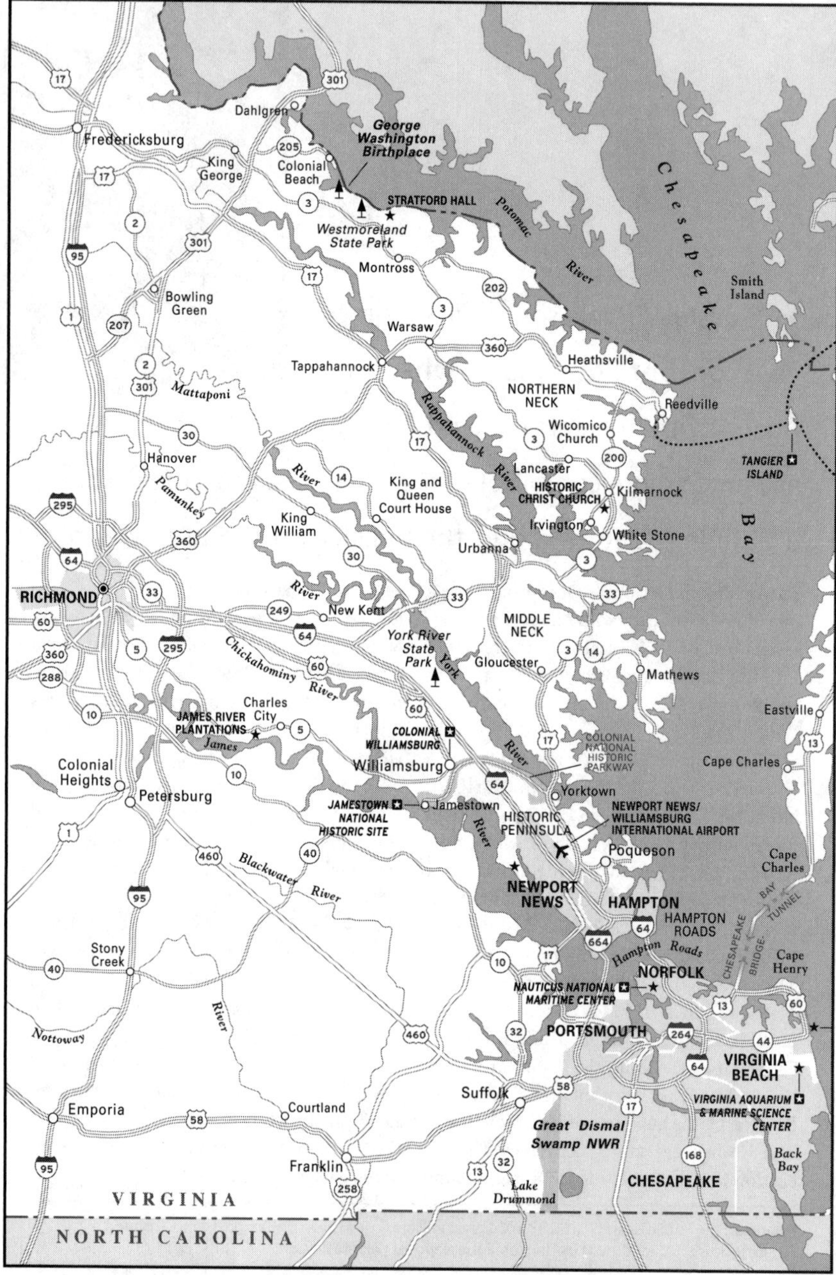

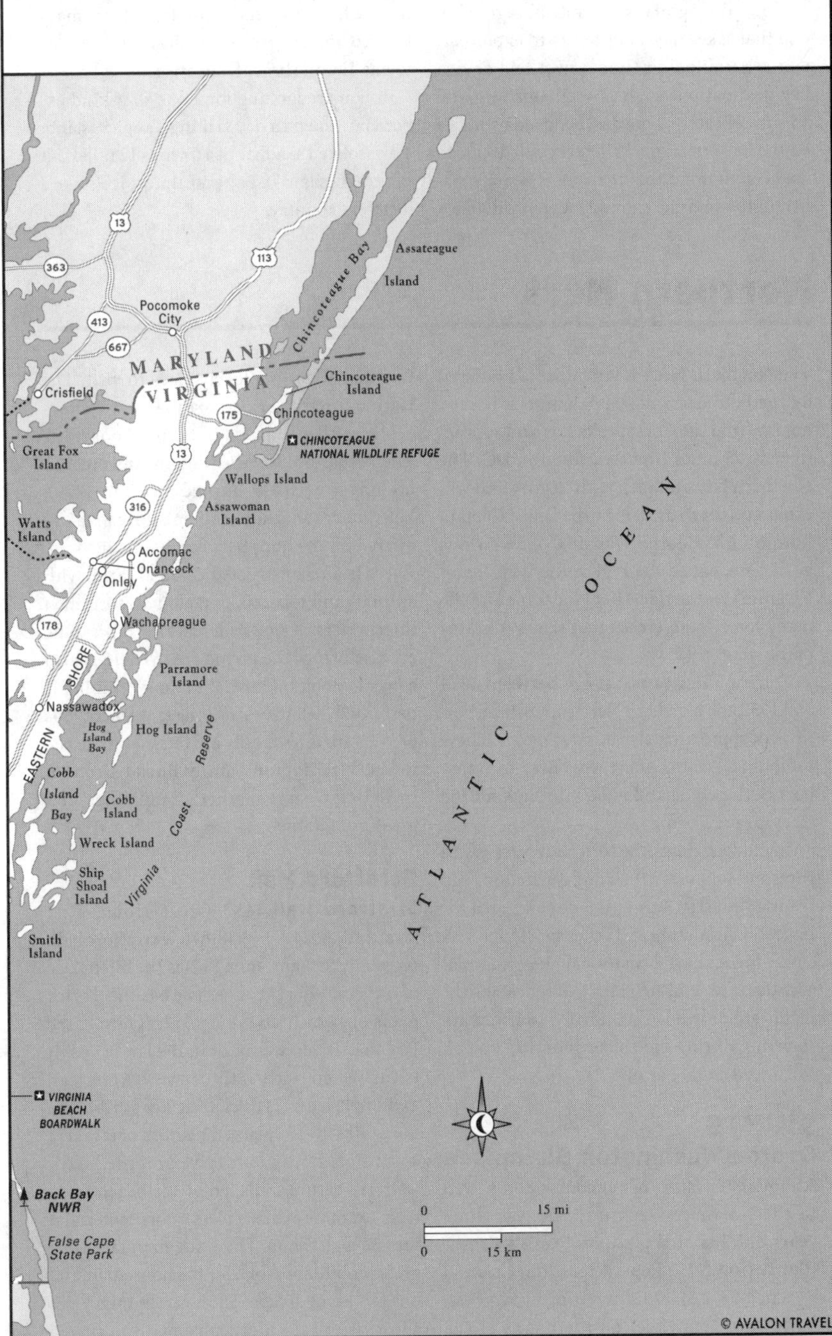

13
363
113
Assateague
Island
Chincoteague Bay
Pocomoke
City
413
667
MARYLAND
VIRGINIA
Crisfield
Chincoteague
Island
175
Chincoteague
CHINCOTEAGUE
NATIONAL WILDLIFE REFUGE
Great Fox
Island
13
Wallops Island
316
Assawoman
Island
Watts
Island
Accomac
Onancock
Onley
ATLANTIC OCEAN
178
Wachapreague
EASTERN SHORE
Parramore
Island
Nassawadox
Hog
Island
Bay
Hog Island
Virginia Coast Reserve
Cobb
Island
Bay
Cobb
Island
Wreck Island
Ship
Shoal
Island
Smith
Island
VIRGINIA
BEACH
BOARDWALK
Back Bay
NWR
False Cape
State Park
0
15 mi
0
15 km

Coastal Virginia is a beautiful region but one that takes days, not hours to explore. If you are limited on time, select one or two key destinations such as Williamsburg and Virginia Beach, or maybe spend a day or two on the Eastern Shore. Wherever you decide to go, keep in mind that the area is heavily visited in the summer months, so you will likely have a few thousand close friends to share the experience with, especially in the historic towns and the beachfront areas.

If you are looking for a one-of-a-kind experience, spend a day visiting Tangier Island. This isolated sandbar of a town is 12 miles out in the Chesapeake Bay and almost feels like a different country.

Northern Neck

The Northern Neck is a peninsula bordered by the Potomac and Rappahannock Rivers, not far from the Chesapeake Bay and approximately 75 miles from Washington DC. The Northern Neck is laden with history and was explored as early as 1608 by the famed Captain John Smith. George Washington, who was born here, called the region the "Garden of Virginia" for the tidewater landscape and the many forests and creeks that shape this area of the state.

During the steamboat era between 1813 and 1937, the Northern Neck supported a network of approximately 600 steamboats. These mechanical works of art were used to transport both people and goods throughout the Chesapeake Bay area.

In modern times, the Northern Neck is still rural and supports a thriving, generations-old fishing industry. It is also a popular area for recreational boating and water sports. It offers small-town charm, historical sites, colonial architecture, and marinas. Many establishments are only open seasonally, so if you are traveling during the colder months, a quick call ahead could pay off.

SIGHTS

George Washington Birthplace

Although the father of our country only lived in the Northern Neck until he was three years old, his birthplace on **Pope's Creek Plantation** (1732 Popes Creek Rd., Colonial Beach, 804/224-1732, www.nps.gov/gewa, daily 9am-5pm, free) on the banks of the Potomac River is a lovely place to visit. The National Park Service maintains a visitors center with a film, exhibits, and bookstore. The actual house Washington was born in no longer exists (it burned down in 1779), but ranger talks about the historic area are offered on the hour between 10am and 4pm. There is a reconstructed colonial farm, with animals and tobacco, operated by costumed interpreters. A one-mile nature trail can be accessed from the picnic area. There is also a beach along the river, but no swimming is permitted. Relatives spanning five generations of Washington's family are buried on the site in the Washington Family Burial Ground, including George's father, grandfather, and great-grandfather.

Stratford Hall

Stratford Hall (483 Great House Rd., Stratford, 804/493-8038, www.stratfordhall.org, daily 9:30am-4pm, $12) is the birthplace of General Robert E. Lee. The beautiful brick mansion, which sits on 1,900 acres next to the Potomac River, was built in the late 1730s. It is furnished with 18th-century American and English pieces (including Lee's crib). The home has 16 fireplaces. Visitors can take a 45-minute house tour (given on the hour), walk six nature trails, enjoy the beach overlook, examine exhibits in a visitors center, and browse a gift shop. There site maintains two great mobile apps, one for the house tour and one for the landscape. The house tour includes a fun historical education component geared for kids called the SquirrelLee University. The on-site dining room can be reserved for groups of 15 or more for a special buffet.

Reedville

Reedville is a little gem of a town founded in 1867 and a jumping-off point to **Tangier Island** in the Chesapeake Bay. It is known for its thriving Atlantic menhaden fishing industry (menhaden are small, oily fish found in the mid-Atlantic) and in the early 20th century was the wealthiest city per capita in the country. (Millionaire's Row, a string of Victorian mansions along the water, attests to this affluence.) Reedville remains a major commercial fishing port in terms of weight of catch, second behind Kodiak, Alaska.

Don't miss the **Reedville Fishermen's Museum** (504 Main St., 804/453-6529, www.rfmuseum.org, hours change often, call ahead for information, $5) on Cockrell's Creek. There are several parts to the museum: the **William Walker House,** a restored home built in 1875 that represents a watermen's home; the **Covington Building,** which houses temporary exhibits and a permanent collection; and the **Pendleton Building,** which contains a boatbuilding and model shop. In addition, there are two historic boats at the museum, a skipjack and deck boat. Both are in the National Register of Historic Places.

Irvington

The historic village of **Irvington** (www.irvingtonva.org) was established in 1891 during the steamboat era. A busy port on the well-traveled Norfolk-Baltimore route, the town thrived during the early 1900s. The Great Fire of Irvington destroyed many businesses in June of 1917, coinciding with the decline of the steamboat era. In 1947, the town was put back on the map with the opening of the **Tides Inn Resort,** and today Irvington is a hip little town with boutique shopping, friendly dining, and several key attractions. It's easy to feel the fun vibe in Irvington. Stroll down Irvington Road and read some of the fun sayings that are posted on signs in the gardens of shops and restaurants. Keep in mind that many establishments are closed on Monday.

The **Steamboat Era Museum** (156 King Carter Dr., 804/438-6888, www.steamboateramuseum.org, Fri.-Sat. 10am-4pm, $5) is a delightful little museum in Irvington that preserves artifacts and information from the steamboat era of the Chesapeake Bay (1813-1937). Steamboats were

the Historic Christ Church

a vital mode of transportation along the bay for both goods and people and the lifeline of the economy connecting the region to cities such as Norfolk, Virginia, and Baltimore, Maryland. This is the only museum fully dedicated to the steamboats of the Chesapeake Bay, and the docents are very entertaining and knowledgeable.

The most treasured historic structure in the Northern Neck is arguably the **Historic Christ Church** (420 Christ Church Rd., Weems, 804/438-6855, www.christchurch1735.org, year-round Mon.-Fri. 10am-4pm, Apr.-Nov. Sat. 10am-4pm, Sun. 1pm-4pm, weekends by appointment the rest of the year, $5). Less than two miles north of Irvington, the church was finished in 1735 and remains one of the few unaltered colonial churches in the United States. It was a center of social and political activity during colonial times, and Sunday service was a big event. In addition to being a place or worship, it was a place to exchange news and the cornerstone of the community. The detailed brickwork in the tall walls and a vaulted ceiling help make it one of the best-crafted Anglican parish churches of its time. Services are still held there, and the interior boasts a triple-decker pulpit, walnut altar, and high-backed pews. **The Carter Reception Center** houses a museum dedicated to the church and its founder, Robert Carter. Guided tours are available from the center, and there is also a gift shop.

ENTERTAINMENT AND EVENTS

Many of the events in the Northern Neck revolve around water and nature. The **Blessing of the Fleet** is an annual event in Reedville that opens the fishing season on the first weekend of May. There is a parade of boats and the official blessing service. The **Reedville Bluefish Derby** is a large fishing tournament held annually in mid-June that features substantial cash prizes.

Mid-September brings the **Reedville Antique and Classic Boat Show** (www.acbs.org), featuring an antique boat parade. And mid-November is the time for the much-anticipated **Reedville Fishermen's Museum Oyster Roast** (www.rfmuseum.org). Tickets go on sale in October and sell out quickly for this mouthwatering event.

Wine enthusiasts will enjoy the **Kilmarnock Wine Festival** (www.northernneckwinefestival.com) held annually at the end of June. It offers tastings and sales from local wineries along the **Chesapeake Bay Wine Trail** (www.chesapeakebaywinetrail.com), including more than a dozen wineries in Virginia in the Chesapeake Bay area that can be visited year-round. Each offers wine tastings, sales, gift shops, and tours.

SPORTS AND RECREATION

Westmoreland State Park

Westmoreland State Park (1650 State Park Rd., Montross, 804/493-8821, www.dcr.virginia.gov, open 24 hours, $5) along the Potomac River offers riverfront beaches, hiking trails, a public pool, kayak and paddleboat rentals, a pond, and cliffs housing fossils. It became one of Virginia's first state parks in 1936. This 1,300-acre park also provides camping cabins for rent year-round and 133 seasonal campsites. The Potomac River Retreat is a lodge that is available for rent; it holds 15 overnight guests and up to 40 people for meetings. There is a small camp store, but it's best to bring your own food because they stock only limited drinks and snacks. Dogs and cats are allowed in the park and cabins for an additional fee. Take in the great view of the Potomac from **Horsehead Cliffs,** and don't miss a stroll down fossil beach where you might even find some ancient shark's teeth. There is a visitors center that is open daily 8am-4:30pm.

Westmoreland Berry Farm

If picking berries makes you feel connected to colonial times, stop by the **Westmoreland Berry Farm** (1235 Berry Farm Ln., Colonial

The Steamboat Era

the Steamboat Era Museum

Steamboats came on the scene in the Chesapeake Bay in the early 1800s. As their popularity rose, they quickly became as important to the cities along the bay as the railroad was to the rest of the country. By the mid-1800s, steamboats were used to transport passengers, mail, and goods.

By the turn of the 20th century, nearly 600 steamboats cruised the bay, carrying thousands of passengers to the cities of Norfolk, Virginia, and Baltimore, Maryland, and every place in between. Steamboat excursions became extremely popular, and commerce flourished. Farms grew as their potential for distributing goods expanded, and many canneries were built near the shore. At one time, 85 percent of the world's oyster trade came from the Chesapeake Bay, and these little delicacies were shipped via steamboat.

The 20th century brought the development of the automobile and the slow demise of the steamboat. As cars became affordable and more common, passenger traffic on the steamboats began to dwindle. Still, the boats were used for commerce until the 1930s, when a hurricane in 1933 wiped out many of the Chesapeake Bay wharfs.

The final excursion of a popular steamboat named the *Anne Arundel* was made on September 14, 1937. That day is still celebrated in Virginia as "Steamboat Era Day."

Visit the **Steamboat Era Museum** (156 King Carter Dr., 804/438-6888, www.steamboateramuseum.org, Fri.-Sat. 10am-4pm, $5) in Irvington to learn more about the steamboat era of the Chesapeake Bay. Additional information on the era can be found on the museum's website.

Beach, 804/224-9171, www.westmorelandberryfarm.com, May-Nov. daily 10am-5pm). This farm on the banks of the Rappahannock River offers visitors the opportunity to pick their own fruit and berries (depending on what's in season). Or you can browse their country store for fresh produce or have lunch at the country kitchen.

Canoeing and Kayaking

The country's first national water trail, the **Captain John Smith Chesapeake National Historic Trail** (www.smithtrail.net) includes 3,000 miles of routes through the Chesapeake Bay, Northern Neck, Middle Neck, and their tributaries in Virginia and Maryland. The route was inspired by the regions explored in the 17th century by Captain John Smith.

Two-hour interpretive kayak trips are offered at **Westmoreland State Park** (800/933-7275, $19 solo kayak, $25 tandem) and include basic instruction and a guided trip along the shoreline.

Fishing

Captain Billy's Charters (545 Harveys Neck Rd., Heathsville, 804/580-7292, www.captbillyscharters.com) runs boat charters for both fishing and cruising from the **Ingram Bay Marina** into the Chesapeake Bay. **Crabbe Charter Fishing** (51 Railway Dr., Heathsville, 804/761-0908, www.crabbescharterfishing.com, $600 for up to six people) is another charter fishing company in the Northern Neck. They offer outings year-round.

Bird-Watching

Bird-watchers have many opportunities to view songbirds, waterfowl, eagles, and wading birds along the **Northern Neck Loop** birding trail (www.dgif.virginia.gov). This driving trail passes by historical sites and through an area known to have the largest population of bald eagles on the Eastern Seaboard.

FOOD

Reedville

The Crazy Crab Restaurant (902 Main St., 804/453-6789, www.reedvillemarina.com, $11-24), at the Reedville Marina, is a casual joint offering an abundance of local seafood choices and a few land-based choices. The waterfront view from the restaurant is nice, the atmosphere is fun, and outdoor seating is available. Hours vary greatly each season.

Cockrell's Seafood (567 Seaboard Dr., 804/453-6326, www.smithpointseafood.com, Mon.-Thurs. 11am-3pm, Fri.-Sat. 11am-4pm, $8-10) is a seafood deli on the waterfront. The atmosphere is very casual, with diners sitting at picnic tables. They serve delicious crab dishes.

Satisfy your sweet tooth at **Chitterchats Ice Cream** (846 Main St., 804/453-3335, www.chitterchatsicecream.com, $5-10). This family-oriented ice cream shop offers delicious homemade ice cream in roughly 20 flavors.

Nate's Trick Dog Café

Irvington

Nate's Trick Dog Café (4357 Irvington Rd., 804/438-6363, www.trickdogcafe.com, Tues.-Sat. 5pm-close, $21-35) is a trendy little find in a town full of fun surprises. A statue of the "Trick Dog" guards the entrance and brings good luck to those who pet it. The statue, which depicts a terrier, was found in the basement of the local opera house after a devastating fire in 1917 that destroyed many local businesses. The statue was sooty and dirty, and was called the Trick Dog since it didn't need food or water. It is an institution at this fine little spot and, judging by the good times and laughter flowing out of the restaurant's doors, seems to be working its magic. The menu offers tasty entrées such as jumbo crab cakes, fillet of yellowfin tuna, and shrimp and grits. There's also a bar menu of interesting finger food, burgers, and sandwiches. This place is worth a stop.

★ **The Local** (4337 Irvington Rd., 804/438-9356, www.thelocalblend.com, daily 7:30am-3pm, under $10) is a good choice for a grabbing a sandwich at lunchtime. This friendly little restaurant has cute decor and a good selection of sandwiches and salads, including a unique menu of panini and wraps. A personal recommendation is the "Tom" wrap, which has turkey, brie, apples, and honey mustard. It goes well with a Northern Neck soda. They also serve ice cream, great coffee, and beer and wine.

ACCOMMODATIONS

$100-200

Ma Margaret's House (249 Greenfield Rd., Reedville, 804/453-9110, www.mamargaretshouse.com, $110-210) is a cozy, recently renovated 4,000-square-foot home built in 1914 that belonged to the owner's grandparents. It offers several guest suites, a lot of privacy, and a wonderful staff.

$200-300

★ **The Hope and Glory Inn** (65 Tavern Rd., Irvington, 804/438-6053, www.hopeandglory.com, $240-395) is a boutique inn with 6 rooms and 10 cottages. Lavish and romantic, with a little sense of humor, the inn was originally a schoolhouse built in 1890. The school had two front doors, one for girls and one for boys. The building now boasts beautifully appointed rooms, lush gardens, and even a moon garden with flowers that only bloom in the evening. There's a spa, meeting facilities, and a dock for boating, kayaking, or canoeing on-site as well as an outdoor pool and an outdoor bath (that is not a typo, there really is a claw-foot tub in an enclosed area outside). Tennis and three golf courses are a short distance away. The town of Irvington, which sits on the Chesapeake Bay, offers trendy shopping and a fun atmosphere.

Wine lovers won't want to miss visiting **The Dog and Oyster,** the Hope and Glory Inn's vineyard. It's named for the establishment's rescue dogs who guard the grapes from area wildlife and also in honor of the local oysters, which pair well with the wines. If the weather is nice, enjoy a bottle of wine on the porch.

The **Tides Inn** (480 King Carter Dr., Irvington, 804/438-5000, www.tidesinn.com, $265-575) is a well-known resort bordered by the Potomac and Rappahannock Rivers and

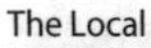

The Local

the Chesapeake Bay. This romantic waterfront inn hangs on the banks of Carters Creek as a little oasis of red-roofed buildings offering peace and relaxation to visitors of all ages. It features luxurious waterfront accommodations, golf, a marina, and a spa. There is also a sailing school with many options for lessons and family sailing activities. Packages include some geared toward golf, family vacations, and romance. There are also several good restaurants on-site and the inn is dog friendly.

CAMPING

Westmoreland State Park (1650 State Park Rd., Montross, 804/493-8821, www.dcr.virginia.gov, open 24 hours) offers 133 campsites and a handful of camping cabins. Camping sites feature a fire ring grill or box grills. Forty-two sites offer electric and water hookups for $30 per night; sites without these amenities are $20 per night. There is also one group tent site that can accommodate up to 40 people ($122). Camping cabins have a maximum capacity of four and require a two-night minimum stay. Cabins do not have bathrooms, kitchens, heat, air-conditioning, or linens. Bathhouses are available on-site for all campers.

INFORMATION AND SERVICES

For additional information on the Northern Neck, visit www.northernneck.org.

Williamsburg and the Historic Triangle

The "Historic Triangle," as it is known, consists of Williamsburg, Jamestown, and Yorktown. These three historic towns are just minutes apart and are the sites of some of our country's most important Revolutionary War history.

The **Colonial Parkway,** a scenic, 23-mile-long, three-lane road, connects the points of the Historic Triangle. Millions of travelers drive the road between Williamsburg, Jamestown, and Yorktown each year. The parkway is maintained by the National Park Service and was designed to unify the three culturally distinct sites while preserving the scenery and wildlife along the way. The construction of the parkway took more than 26 years and stretched through the Depression and World War II. It was completed in 1957. The parkway enables motorists to enjoy the surrounding landscape and has a speed limit of 45 miles per hour.

The National Park Service also maintains the **Colonial National Historical Park,** which contains two of the most historically significant sites in the country, the **Jamestown National Historic Site** (which is jointly administered by Preservation Virginia) and **Yorktown National Battlefield.** These sites are connected by the Colonial Parkway.

WILLIAMSBURG

The original capital of the Virginia Colony, Jamestown, was founded in 1607. It was located on the banks of the James River with a deepwater anchorage on a peninsula between the York and James Rivers. By 1638, an area called Middle Plantation (named for its location halfway across the peninsula) was settled about 12 miles away on higher ground. In 1676, Jamestown burned down and the government seat was temporarily moved to Middle Plantation. The statehouse was rebuilt, but burned down again in 1698. Once again, the capital was relocated to Middle Plantation. Finding the temporary location to be safer and less humid than Jamestown, the House of Burgesses permanently moved the colonial capital there in 1699. A village was planned in the new location and the name Middle Plantation was changed to Williamsburg in honor of King William III of England.

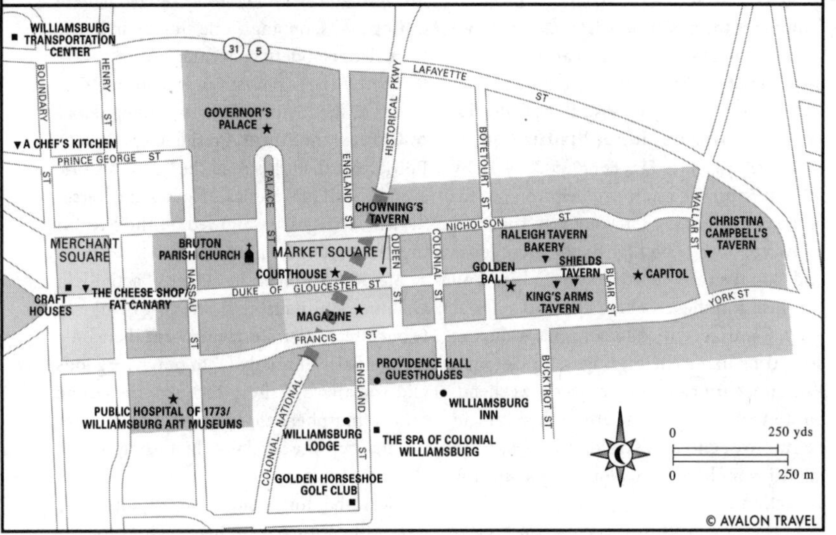

Williamsburg is one of America's earliest planned cities. It was designed as the capital of the Virginia Colony, which was the most populous of the British colonies in America in 1699. As such, Williamsburg had the oldest legislative assembly in the New World, and a series of elaborate capitol buildings were erected as the city developed into the thriving center of Virginia. Williamsburg remained the capital of Virginia until 1780, when the seat of government was moved to its current location in Richmond.

Today, when people speak of Williamsburg, they most often are referring to the area known now as **Colonial Williamsburg.** This original capital city is the country's prime example of not only the preservation of American colonial history but also its interpretation. However, although Colonial Williamsburg is the best-known attraction in the Williamsburg area, there are many other attractions nearby including the historic **College of William & Mary** and a number of popular theme parks.

Sights

★ COLONIAL WILLIAMSBURG

Colonial Williamsburg (888/965-7254, www.colonialwilliamsburg.com, one-day ticket $40.99, three-day ticket $50.99) is the largest living museum in the country, and it is truly a historical marvel. It is open 365 days a year and run by the private, not-for-profit **Colonial Williamsburg Foundation.** The museum encompasses the restored 18th-century colonial Virginia capital city, which was the center of politics in Virginia for 80 years, and includes the real city streets and buildings that were erected during that time. There are historical exhibits, taverns, shops featuring original trades, and many other sites within the museum area. Ticketholders gain access to the historical buildings, theatrical performances, 15 site tours, 35 exhibitions, and museums. It is free to wander the streets themselves.

Although Colonial Williamsburg is open all year, if you are flexible in choosing when to visit, spring and fall can be the most rewarding. This is when crowds are less dense and the temperatures are the most moderate (plan to do a lot of walking around the city). Summer is the busiest tourist season because school is out of session, and it can also be very hot and humid, especially in August.

It is best to begin your visit at the **Colonial Williamsburg Regional Visitor Center** (101 Visitor Center Dr., 888/965-7254, daily 9:15am-5pm). The staff can help you put together an itinerary for your stay that will allow you to hit the highlights and choose additional sites you are interested in. You can also purchase tickets and learn about events and activities taking place during your time here. The highlights in Colonial Williamsburg can be seen over a weekend, but to really soak in the atmosphere, it can be fun to spend an extra day or two, or to make it your base for exploring other nearby attractions.

Everything within the museum area is neat, clean, well-maintained, and historically correct. The staff is dressed in period clothing and plays their roles very seriously. Conversations between staff members and the public are always in character. Visitors become "Residents of the City" and are immersed in history—and can enjoy authentic colonial-era dining and shopping while staying in hotels with all the modern conveniences.

There's a large pedestrian area through the center of the historical enclave along **Duke of Gloucester Street.** President Franklin D. Roosevelt called this road the "most historic avenue in all of America." Horses and horse-drawn carriages are allowed on the street if they are part of the museum.

Market Square, the center of activity in Colonial Williamsburg, straddles Duke of Gloucester Street. Residents went there on a regular basis (if not daily) to purchase goods and socialize. Visitors can experience the same atmosphere along Duke of Gloucester Street, where the official Williamsburg-brand shops are located.

Ticket-holding visitors can explore a variety of historical buildings such as the reconstructed **Capitol,** which sits at the east end of Duke of Gloucester Street (daily 9am-5pm). The current building is the third capitol to stand on the site, but it is very much

a shop in Colonial Williamsburg

the same as the original completed in 1705. A trip through this tall brick building is like a history lesson on the government in colonial Virginia and the contributions the colony made to the American Revolution. Evening programs in the Capitol include reenactments of political and social events that actually occurred here in the 18th century. One day a year, a naturalization ceremony is carried out at the Capitol for immigrants becoming Americans, carrying on a tradition that began nearly 300 years ago.

The impressive **Governors Palace,** built between 1706 and 1722 at the end of Palace Green Street off of West Duke of Gloucester Street, was home to seven royal governors, as well as Thomas Jefferson and Patrick Henry. After many decades as a symbol of the power of royal England, the home served as a military headquarters and twice as a wartime hospital (156 soldiers and 2 women are buried in the garden, casualties of the Battle of Yorktown). The original structure burned to the ground in 1781, but the building was reconstructed to its current grandeur in the 1930s. Since then, the home has been furnished with American and British antiques in the colonial revival style. This is perhaps the most popular site in Colonial Williamsburg, so make it first on your list, early in the day, before the crowds set in.

The **Courthouse** (Duke of Gloucester Street) is a focal point of Market Square and one that no doubt put fear in the hearts of many criminals in its day. Built in 1770, it is one of Williamsburg's original 18th-century buildings, and it housed the municipal and county courts until 1932. The building's T-shaped design is common to many Virginia courthouses, but an octagonal cupola and several other formal design elements (such as a weather vane, arched windows, and a cantilevered pediment) make it distinct in appearance. The signing of the Treaty of Paris (ending the Revolutionary War) was announced at the Courthouse.

A small but fascinating building is the **Magazine** (Duke of Gloucester Street). It was constructed in 1715 at the request of Governor Alexander Spotswood, who wanted a solid-brick house in which to store and protect weapons and ammunition. The

the Courthouse in Colonial Williamsburg

Magazine is well known for its role in the **Gunpowder Incident** on April 20, 1775, an episode that occurred in the opening days of the Revolutionary War between the royal governor, Lord Dunmore, and the militia (led by Patrick Henry). Lord Dunmore gave orders to remove all the gunpowder from the Magazine and move it to a Royal Navy ship. This led to unrest in Virginia and the movement of Patrick Henry's militia toward Williamsburg to secure the gunpowder for the colonial troops. The matter was resolved peacefully, but Dunmore retreated to a naval ship, thus ending royal governance of the colony. The incident helped move Virginia toward revolution.

Many craftspeople, some who have spent years learning the trade, create colonial-era crafts in dozens of shops throughout Colonial Williamsburg. Visitors can watch blacksmiths and armorers shape tools, weapons, and hardware out of iron and steel at **Anderson's Blacksmith Shop & Public Armoury** (E. Duke of Gloucester Street) or visit the **Wigmaker** (E. Duke of Gloucester Street) to learn the importance of 18th-century wigmakers and barbers and how these trades were essential to the social structure of the day. Other crafters include the **Shoemaker** (W. Duke of Gloucester Street), the **Weaver** (W. Duke of Gloucester Street), and the **Bindery** (E. Duke of Gloucester Street).

A number of historic taverns and restaurants are also located in Colonial Williamsburg and serve authentic colonial-style food. Look for the colonial flags out in front of the buildings. If a flag is out, it means the establishment is open.

More than 20 tours, both guided and self-led, are included in a Colonial Williamsburg admission ticket. The visitors center is the best place to find out what tours are offered on the day(s) you are there and what time they leave. Some popular tours include the **Freshest Advices for Travelers, Archaeology Walking Tours,** and the **Tavern Ghost Walk.** Dates and times change daily.

WILLIAMSBURG ART MUSEUMS

Two top-notch art museums, the **DeWitt Wallace Decorative Arts Museum** (326 Francis St. W, 888/965-7254, daily 10am-7pm) and the **Abby Aldrich Rockefeller Folk Art Museum** (326 Francis St. W, 888/965-7254, daily 10am-7pm) are located in the same building and can be reached by walking through the **Public Hospital of 1773** (326 Francis St. W, admission is included with the Colonial Williamsburg ticket). The DeWitt Wallace Decorative Arts Museum opened in 1985, funded by a generous donation from DeWitt and Lila Wallace, the founders of *Readers Digest.* It houses a large collection of American and British art and antiques, including the world's most extensive collection of southern furniture. The Abby Aldrich Rockefeller Folk Art Museum features a colorful variety of paintings, sculptures, and other art forms. Each work created by self-taught artists and shows an imaginative array of details and color selections. There is also a kid-friendly animal-themed exhibit called Down on the Farm. While you're there, take in the exhibits at the Public Hospital. It was the first facility in North America dedicated to caring for the mentally ill. In this day and age, the hospital is seen as part jail, part infirmary, and the treatments used in the 18th and 19th centuries are thankfully just part of history.

THE COLLEGE OF WILLIAM & MARY

Early on, Williamsburg developed into a hub for learning. **The College of William & Mary** (200 Stadium Dr., www.wm.edu), which is the second-oldest college in the country, was founded in 1693. It is just west of Colonial Williamsburg and an easy walk from the colonial city. William & Mary turned out many famous early political leaders including Thomas Jefferson, John Tyler, and James Monroe. Today, the 1,200-acre campus is bustling with students. Visitors can enjoy a handful of historical attractions right on campus, including the **Sir Christopher Wren Building,** which was built 1695 and is known for being the oldest college building in the country. It was named for a royal architect, although concrete evidence has not been found that Wren actually designed it.

WILLIAMSBURG WINERY

Wine lovers will want to stop in for a tour and tasting at the **Williamsburg Winery** (5800 Wessex Hundred, 757/229-0999, www.williamsburgwinery.com, Jan.-Feb. Mon.-Fri. 11:30am-4:30pm, Sat.-Sun. 10:30am-5:30pm, Mar.-Dec. daily 10:30am-5:30pm, $8), about a 10-minute drive from the Colonial Williamsburg visitors center. The winery is Virginia's largest and accounts for one-quarter of all the wine produced in the state. Tours are available daily on the half hour.

BUSCH GARDENS WILLIAMSBURG

Busch Gardens Williamsburg (1 Busch Gardens Blvd., 800/343-7946, www.seaworldparks.com, mid-May-Labor Day Mon.-Thurs. 10am-6pm, Fri. 10am-9pm, Sat. 10am-10pm, Sun. 10am-9pm, reduced schedule the rest of the year, $77) is a theme park with rides, re-created European villages, shows, exhibits, and exclusive tours. The park is less than five miles southeast of Williamsburg and is owned by SeaWorld. Hair-raising roller coasters, water rides, authentic food, and special attractions for little kids are just part of the fun at this beautiful park. Test your nerves on the Griffon, a 205-foot dive coaster (the tallest in the world), where brave riders free-fall at 75 miles per hour. Thrill seekers will also enjoy the Verbolten, one of the park's newest additions, an indoor/outdoor multi-launch coaster set in Germany's Black Forest. This coaster winds through the dark and ends with a heart-pounding plunge toward the Rhine River. The park's classic ride is the Loch Ness Monster, a 13-story, double-loop roller coaster that made Busch Gardens famous 30 years ago. This popular park also offers an Oktoberfest Village, a high-tech simulator that takes passengers over Europe, and animal attractions such as Jack Hanna's Wild Reserve, where visitors can see and learn about endangered and exotic animals. A combined Busch Gardens Williamsburg and Water Country USA ticket can be purchased for $87.

WATER COUNTRY USA

Busch Gardens Williamsburg's sister park **Water Country USA** (176 Water Country Pkwy., 800/343-7946, www.watercountryusa.com, Memorial Day-Labor Day daily 10am-close, $52) is the largest water theme park in the mid-Atlantic. It is approximately three miles southeast of Williamsburg, just north of Busch Gardens. The park offers waterslides, pools, and more than 30 rides for kids of all ages as well as restaurants and live entertainment. A combined Busch Gardens Williamsburg and Water Country USA ticket can be purchased for $87.

Entertainment and Events

Colonial Williamsburg doesn't shut down after dark. A variety of tours are available, including the "Original Ghost Tour" given by **The Original Ghosts of Williamsburg Candlelight Tour** (345 W. Duke of Gloucester St., 877/624-4678, www.theghosttour.com, Apr.-Aug. daily 8pm, reduced schedule the rest of the year, $12). This is a family-friendly candlelit walking ghost tour of the town and taverns that offers a relaxing end to a day of sightseeing. The **Kimball Theatre** (428 W. Duke of Gloucester St., 757/565-8588, www.colonialwilliambsburg.com) is a film and stage venue right in the middle of Colonial Williamsburg in Merchants Square. It offers programming in alliance with the College of William & Mary, including foreign, classic, and documentary films along with live concerts.

Outside of the historic center—but only minutes away—visitors can play pool and enjoy live music on some nights at **The Corner Pocket** (4805 Courthouse St., 757/220-0808, www.thecornerpocket.us, Mon.-Tues. 11:30am-1am, Wed.-Sat. 11:30am-2am, Sun. 3pm-1am), an upscale pool hall.

Many festivals are held throughout

the year in Williamsburg. The **Colonial Williamsburg Early Music Festival** (Historic Area, www.colonialwilliamsburg.com) happens over four days at the end of September and showcases musical instruments that were popular in colonial Virginia. The fifes and drums play daily in the historic area, but during the festival many other instruments are featured and lectures explain their origins.

Busch Gardens Williamsburg hosts an annual **Howl-O-Scream** (1 Busch Gardens Blvd., www.seaworldparks.com) event starting at 6pm daily in mid-September and running all through October. During Howl-O-Scream the park becomes a horrorfest for brave souls, featuring scary shows, creepy creatures lurking about the park, and fun characters. It is not advisable to take young children.

The holiday season is a very popular time to visit Colonial Williamsburg. The **Grand Illumination,** held on the Sunday of the first full weekend in December, is an eagerly awaited street festival where the entire historic area is decorated with traditional natural adornments for the season such as pinecones, evergreen branches, and candles. The area flickers at night by candlelight as carols are sung, concerts are held, and fireworks light up the night. Holiday festivities continue until the **First Night** celebration on New Year's Eve.

Shopping

Williamsburg offers endless shops. Strip malls and outlet stores can be found in much of the area surrounding Colonial Williamsburg. For unique souvenirs, try stopping in the **Williamsburg Craft House** (420 W. Duke of Gloucester St., 757/220-7747) run by the Colonial Williamsburg Foundation. Pewter and ceramic gifts, jewelry, and folk art are for sale. Other favorite shops in the historic district include **The Prentis Store** (214 E. Duke of Gloucester St., 757/229-1000), which sells handcrafted leather pieces, pottery, furniture, ironware, and baskets; the **Market House,** an open-air market on Duke of Gloucester Street that sells hats, toys, and other handmade items; and the **Golden Ball** (406 E. Duke of Gloucester St., 757/229-1000), which sells one-of-a-kind jewelry.

Sports and Recreation

GOLF

The **Golden Horseshoe Golf Club** (401 S. England St., 757/220-7696, www.colonialwilliamsburg.com, $52-79) is part of Colonial Williamsburg and offers 45 walkable holes. This scenic course is well maintained and has received accolades from publications such as *Golf Magazine* and *Golfweek*.

The **Kingsmill Resort** (1010 Kingsmill Rd., 757/253-1703. www.kingsmill.com, $60-165) offers three championship 18-hole courses that are open to the public (one of which was ranked in the top 10 for women by *Golf Digest*).

The award-winning **Williamsburg National Golf Club** (3700 Centerville Rd., 757/258-9642, www.wngc.com, $69-89) has two 18-hole courses.

SPAS

The **Spa of Colonial Williamsburg** (307 South England St., 757/220-7720, www.colonialwilliamsburg.com) is behind the Williamsburg Inn. Enjoy treatments made from botanicals used by the early settlers or a variety of soaks and massages. Packages are available.

HORSEBACK RIDING

If horseback riding seems appropriate while visiting Williamsburg, contact **Lakewood Trails** (575/566-9633, www.lakewoodtrailrides.com, $75) for one-hour guided trail rides.

GO APE TREETOP ADVENTURE

For something completely different, try a **Go Ape** (5537 Centerville Rd., 800/971-8271, www.goape.com, $58) Treetop Adventure. This adventure course is appropriate for ages 10 and up (who are taller than 4'7") and includes high wires, ladders, tunnels, zip lines, and a lot of treetop excitement. A junior course is available for children under 10 who are 3'3" or taller.

Food

AMERICAN

If you just need to grab a quick sandwich or you'd like to enjoy a gourmet cheese platter and a glass of wine, stop in **The Cheese Shop** (410 Duke of Gloucester St., 757/220-0298, www.cheeseshopwilliamsburg.com, Mon.-Sat. 10am-6pm, Sun. 11am-6pm, under $15) in Merchants Square. They make custom cheese plates (from 200 varieties of imported and domestic cheese) at their cheese counter (to the left) and deli sandwiches at the back of the store (try their chicken salad; it has just enough bacon to taste wonderful but not enough to feel guilty). The store also carries fresh-baked bread and a variety of snacks and drinks. Their wine cellar has more than 4,000 bottles of wine. There's seating outside (pay before you exit).

The ★ **Fat Canary** (410 Duke of Gloucester St., 757/220-3333, www.fatcanarywilliamsburg.com, daily 5pm-10pm, $28-39) in Merchants Square is named for the wine brought to the New World by ships that stopped in the Canary Islands for supplies. The wine was called a "canary," and this wonderful restaurant knows its wine. Widely considered one of the top dining spots in Williamsburg, The Fat Canary is an upscale restaurant that delivers an interesting menu of mouthwatering entrées such as quail, scallops, lamb, and beef tenderloin. They also have delicious desserts. The restaurant has a romantic ambience with soft pendant lighting and friendly service. This is a great place for a date or to relax after a day touring Colonial Williamsburg. Reservations are strongly suggested.

For a unique dining experience, make reservations at **A Chef's Kitchen** (501 Prince George St., 757/564-8500, www.achefskitchen.biz, Tues.-Sat. seating 6:30pm, $85) in the heart of Williamsburg. This food destination allows guests to learn about the fare they are eating and how it's prepared while being entertained by a talented chef. The fixed-price menu is for a multicourse meal in which recipes are prepared, served, and paired with great wines. Diners sit at elegant long tables in tiered rows. The menu changes monthly, but sample dishes include asparagus and sweet pea soup, scallion and lime Gulf shrimp cake, roast rack of lamb, and strawberries sabayon in lace cup cookie. This small restaurant only seats 26 people, and it only offers one seating per night, so reservations are a must. Plan for 2-3 hours of dining time.

TREATS

To satisfy a craving or pick up an afternoon snack, stop in the **Raleigh Tavern Bakery** (Duke of Gloucester Street, behind the Raleigh Tavern, under $10). They offer a selection of fresh cookies, muffins, rolls, sandwiches, drinks, and other treats. Try the sweet potato muffins and the gingerbread cookies, which are done to perfection and are much better than the peanut butter and chocolate chip cookies. Casual seating is available in the courtyard outside. Alcohol must be consumed in the courtyard and cannot be taken out on Duke of Gloucester Street. A cookbook with the recipes is available for purchase, and this writer knows firsthand that almost nothing has changed in this historical little bakery in the past 30 years—but then again, that's the idea here.

The **Jamestown Pie Company** (1804 Jamestown Rd., 757/229-7775, www.buyapie.com, Sun. 10am-9pm, Mon.-Sat. 9am-9pm, $5-23) sells everything round including pizza, potpie, and dessert pie. They also offer a small selection of sandwiches. Pies are also available to go.

COLONIAL TAVERNS

There are four taverns in the historic area of Williamsburg, and dining in one is a great way to get into the spirit of the town. Costumed servers bring authentic dishes from two centuries ago to wooden tables in flickering candlelight. Don't be hesitant to try some 18th-century staples such as spoon bread and peanut soup. There are a few featured items available in all four taverns, but aside from that, each specializes in its own dishes. Make reservations when you book your hotel. The same phone number (757/229-2141) can be used for all four taverns (www.colonialwilliamsburg.com). These restaurants are very popular.

Christiana Campbell's Tavern (101 S. Waller St., Tues.-Sat. 5pm-close, $24-37) is noted as George Washington's favorite tavern. It specializes in seafood dishes. The tavern was re-created from artifacts excavated on-site and from a sketch of the building found on an original insurance policy. George and other famous colonial figureheads often met here for business and pleasure, and private rooms could be reserved alongside public chambers where travelers sometimes shared beds with complete strangers when the tavern was full. The crab cakes are a signature dish.

Chowning's Tavern (109 E. Duke of Gloucester St., lunch daily 11:30am-2pm, dinner daily 5pm-9pm, lunch $7-13, dinner $24-33) is a casual alehouse where lively singing and other reenactments of 18th-century life are common. Light fare is served at Chowning's for lunch, including soups and sandwiches, and more substantial entrées are available for dinner (such as pork and Brunswick stew). Outdoor seating is available behind the tavern in the garden where light meals and pints are served.

The King's Arms Tavern (416 E. Duke of Gloucester St., lunch Thurs.-Mon. 11:30am-2:30pm, dinner Thurs.-Mon. 5pm-close, $33-37) is a genteel tavern serving southern food and decadent desserts. This chophouse-style tavern offers entrées such as chicken, pork chops, venison, and prime rib. The peanut soup is a signature dish.

Shields Tavern (422 E. Duke of Gloucester St., daily 11:30am-9pm, $7-30) is the largest of the taverns, and it specializes in comfort food such as bangers and mash and barbecue ribs. Try the potato leek pie or a sample plate. The ale-potted beef is also a favorite.

Accommodations

If Colonial Williamsburg is the focus of your Williamsburg trip, and you'd like to be immersed in the Revolutionary City, book a room in one of the Colonial Williamsburg Foundation hotels or guesthouses. These are conveniently located near the museum sites and have a historic feel to them. Reservations, especially during the peak summer months, should be made in advance.

COLONIAL WILLIAMSBURG FOUNDATION

The **Colonial Williamsburg Foundation** maintains 5 hotels/lodges and 26 guesthouses. Each offers a different atmosphere and price range. Hotel guests have access to a terrific fitness facility located behind the Williamsburg Inn that includes a spa, state-of-art fitness room, indoor lap pool, and two gorgeous outdoor pools. Hotel guests also receive the best rate on general admission passes and discounts on special events. Reservations are handled through the foundation (www.colonialwilliamsburg.com).

The **Colonial Houses** (888/965-7254, $199-459) are individual colonial homes and rooms, each with a unique history. The number of rooms per house varies, but all are decorated with authentic reproductions of period pieces such as canopy beds and all have modern amenities. Look out over Duke of Gloucester Street, or sleep in the home where Thomas Jefferson lived while attending The College of William & Mary. Some homes are original historic buildings and others are replicas.

The luxurious ★ **Williamsburg Inn** (136 E. Francis St., 757/220-7978, www.colonialwilliamsburg.com $449-669) was built in 1937 by John D. Rockefeller Jr., and the decor and furnishings in the lobby are still arranged exactly the way his wife, Abby Aldrich Rockefeller, designed it. This stately, upscale hotel has hosted many heads of state including President Dwight D. Eisenhower, Queen Elizabeth II, and Sir Winston Churchill. In 1983, the inn welcomed the

Economic Summit of Industrialized Nations, hosted by President Ronald Reagan. It is listed in the National Register of Historic Places, but offers modern first-class accommodations in its 62 guest rooms. The hotel was the first in the United States to have central air-conditioning. Each elegant and spacious room is furnished similar to an English country estate. The setting and decor are charming, and the service is excellent. Mrs. Rockefeller wished for guests to feel at home in the inn and as such instilled a warmth throughout the staff that still radiates today. Every last detail is attended to in the luxurious rooms, from beautifully tiled temperature-controlled showers to a fresh white rose in the bathroom (the rose is the official inn flower) and little comforts like vanity mirrors and nightlights. The hotel is centrally located adjacent to Colonial Williamsburg. The Golden Horseshoe Golf Club is behind the inn, and daily participatory events such as lawn bowling are offered to guests. There are two restaurants on-site (one formal dining room and a more casual lounge), and the hotel is very family friendly.

The **Williamsburg Lodge** (310 S. England St., 757/220-7976, www.colonialwilliamsburg.com $199-289) is decorated in the classic Virginia style. Colorful fabric, leather, and warm woods give this hotel a lodge feel. This 300-room hotel hosts many conferences, and its unique garden gives it a relaxing focal point. The rooms are spacious, the lodge is conveniently located near Colonial Williamsburg, and it's an easy walk to the attractions.

The **Providence Hall Guesthouses** (305 S. England St., 757/220-7978, www.colonialwilliamsburg.com, $229-279) is in a quiet area near the Williamsburg Inn. It offers 43 large, bright rooms in a quiet, parklike setting with a more modern look to it. The hotel is pet friendly.

The **Williamsburg Woodlands Hotel and Suites** (105 Visitor Center Dr., 757/220-7978, www.colonialwilliamsburg.com, $139-209) is next to the visitors center for Colonial Williamsburg. This 300-room hotel offers contemporary rooms in a wooded setting. It is one of the least expensive options of the Colonial Williamsburg Foundation hotels.

The **Governor's Inn** (506 N. Henry St., 757/253-2277, www.colonialwilliamsburg.com, $85-100) is a short walk from historic Colonial Williamsburg and the visitors center. This 200-room hotel offers economy accommodations and a seasonal outdoor pool.

OUTSIDE COLONIAL WILLIAMSBURG

There are quite a few choices for accommodations outside Colonial Williamsburg. Many are within an easy drive of the historical area.

The **Marriott's Manor Club at Ford's Colony** (101 St. Andrews Dr., 757/258-1120, www.marriott.com, $129-305) is in the private community of Ford's Colony and offers colonial architecture, deluxe guest rooms, and one- and two-bedroom villas. Each villa has a kitchen, living/dining area, washers and dryers, a balcony or patio, and a fireplace. This is a great place for families or groups who need a bit more space or plan an extended stay. Colonial Williamsburg and the College of William & Mary are about a 15-minute drive away, and Busch Gardens is about 20 minutes. There's a spa and golf course in the community, a fitness center, indoor and outdoor pools, and a sport court. Rooms are nicely appointed, and the buildings are spread out on a well-manicured property.

The **Wedmore Place** (5810 Wessex Hundred, 757/941-0310, www.wedmoreplace.com, $195-575) offers 28 individually decorated rooms in a variety of price ranges. Each room is designed after a European province and a different time in history, including all the furnishings and wall hangings. The 300-acre farm is also the site of the Williamsburg Winery and is about a 10-minute drive to the Colonial Williamsburg visitors center.

If you're looking for a kid-oriented hotel, the **Great Wolf Lodge** (549 E. Rochambeau Dr., 757/229-9700, www.greatwolf.com,

$239-410) provides endless amusement for the little ones. This Northwoods-themed lodge offers 405 guest rooms and a huge indoor water park complete with waterslides, a wave pool, and a tree house. It is a four-season resort.

The **Kingsmill Resort and Spa** (1010 Kingsmill Rd., 757/253-1703, www.kingsmill.com, $179-399) offers 425 luxurious rooms and suites (with up to three bedrooms) as well as breathtaking views of the James River. It also has golf, a spa, an indoor pool, and summer children's programs. This is a great place for a romantic getaway or to spend time with friends playing golf or taking a spa day.

Camping

There are several good options for camping in Williamsburg. The **Anvil Campground** (5243 Mooretown Rd., 757/565-2300, www.anvilcampground.com, $40-155) is open year-round and offers 77 campsites and two cottages. It has been in operation since 1954 and is close to Colonial Williamsburg with shuttle service available to attractions, restaurants, and shopping. The **Williamsburg KOA Campground** (4000 Newman Rd., 757/565-2907, www.williamsburgkoa.com, starting at $46) is another good option close to Colonial Williamsburg and the theme parks. They offer 180 acres of wooded sites and patio sites (with more than 100 sites total). They also offer bus service to attractions in the peak season. Two additional campgrounds in Williamsburg are the **Williamsburg RV Resort and Campground** (4301 Rochambeau Dr., 757/566-3021, $49), with 158 sites, and the **American Heritage R.V. Park** (146 Maxton Ln., 757/566-2133, www.americanheritagervpark.com, $38), with 103 sites.

Information and Services

The best information on Colonial Williamsburg can be obtained from the **Colonial Williamsburg Foundation** (800/447-8679, www.history.org) and at the **Colonial Williamsburg Regional Visitor Center** (101 Visitor Center Dr., 757/220-7645, daily 8:45am-5pm). For additional information on Williamsburg, contact the **Greater Williamsburg Chamber and Tourism Alliance** (www.williamsburgcc.com) or visit www.visitwilliamsburg.com.

Getting There

Most people arrive in Williamsburg by car. The city is off I-64 and approximately 1 hour from Richmond, 1 hour from Norfolk, and 2.5 hours from Washington DC.

The **Newport News/Williamsburg International Airport** (PHF, 900 Bland Blvd., Newport News, www.flyphf.com) is off I-64 at exit 255B. Williamsburg is a 20-minute drive from the airport.

Amtrak (468 N Boundary St., 800/872-7245, www.amtrak.com) offers train service into Williamsburg.

Getting Around

Getting around Colonial Williamsburg requires a lot of walking. The pedestrian area where you'll find many of the attractions is preserved as it was during Revolutionary times when there were no cars. If you are not staying at one of the Colonial Williamsburg hotels, you will want to arrive early during peak season to park outside the pedestrian area. Parking spaces can be difficult to come by, but designated areas are clearly marked. The important thing to remember is not to park in private lots or at the College of William & Mary (even in the summer). Parking restrictions are strictly enforced.

Williamsburg has a reliable bus system called the **Williamsburg Area Transit (WATA)** (www.gowata.org), which offers bus service seven days a week and stops at many of the local hotels. An all-day pass is $2.

Shuttle service between the Colonial Williamsburg Regional Visitor Center and select hotels is available for free to those who have a Colonial Williamsburg ticket. Shuttle tickets can also be obtained at the visitors center.

From mid-March through October, the **Historic Triangle Shuttle** (www.nps.gov/colo, daily every 30 minutes, 9am-3:30pm) provides transportation service between the Colonial Williamsburg Regional Visitor Center and Jamestown via the scenic Colonial Parkway. There is no charge if you have purchased a ticket to either historical area. Boarding passes can be obtained from the Colonial Williamsburg Regional Visitor Center.

JAMESTOWN

Jamestown was the first permanent English settlement in America. It was founded in 1607, more than a decade prior to the Pilgrims' arrival at Plymouth. Three small ships carrying 104 men made landfall at Jamestown (which is actually an island) on May 13, 1607. They moored the ships to trees, came ashore the following day, and never left. The newly formed town served as the capital of Virginia during the 17th century.

★ Jamestown National Historic Site

The **Jamestown National Historic Site** (1368 Colonial Pkwy., 757/856-1200, www.nps.gov/jame, daily 8:30am-4:30pm, $14) occupies the site of the original Jamestown settlement on the banks of the James River. It is run by the National Park Service and Preservation Virginia. The site was also the location of a military post during the American Revolution where prisoners were exchanged from both sides.

Purchase your admission ticket at the visitors center (your ticket also grants access to Yorktown National Battlefield), which shows an informative 18-minute video that is a good start to orienting yourself with the site. From there, continue to "Old Towne," the original settlement site, and explore it on foot. Highlights include the original Memorial Church tower (the oldest structure still standing in the park, dating to 1639), a burial ground (many of the first colonists died here), a reconstructed sample of a "mud-and-stud" cottage, and the foundations of several buildings. Another don't-miss sight is the Jamestown Rediscovery excavation, where remains of the original James Fort built in 1607 are being uncovered at an archaeological dig site open to visitors. History programs and children's events are held in the summer months.

Continue on to "New Towne," where you can explore the part of Jamestown that was developed after 1620. The foundations of many homes were excavated in the 1930s and 1950s and replicas can be seen throughout the site. Next, take a cruise along the Loop Drive, a five-mile wilderness road. Be sure to stop to read the interpretive signs and view the paintings along the route to learn how inhabitants used the island's natural resources, or visit the **Glasshouse** to see artisans creating glass products as glassblowers did back in the early 1600s.

Jamestown Settlement

The **Jamestown Settlement** (2110 Jamestown Rd., 757/253-4838, www.historyisfun.org, daily 9am-5pm, $17) is one of the most popular museums in Coastal Virginia. It is a living museum that re-creates and honors the first permanent English-speaking settlement in the country and takes visitors back to the 1600s. Costumed guides share facts about a Powhatan Village, and there are replicas of the three ships that sailed from England under the command of Captain Christopher Newport and eventually landed at Jamestown. The ships are a highlight of the museum, and the costumed crew does an excellent job of answering questions and showing off every nook and cranny of the ships. The **James Fort** is another main attraction. There, visitors can see authentic meals being prepared, witness arms demonstrations, and even try on armor. Ninety-minute tours of the outdoor interpretive areas are available several times a day. Thanksgiving is a great time to visit because special events are held in the museum. Combined-entry tickets to Colonial Williamsburg and the Yorktown

historical building and artifacts at Jamestown Settlement

Victory Center can be purchased, and bus service between the sites is offered during the summer season.

Getting There

Jamestown is nine miles southwest of Colonial Williamsburg along the Colonial Parkway.

From mid-March through October, the **Historic Triangle Shuttle** (www.nps.gov/colo, daily every 30 minutes 9am-3:30pm) provides transportation service between the Colonial Williamsburg Regional Visitor Center and Jamestown via the Colonial Parkway. There is no charge if you have purchased a ticket to either historical area. Boarding passes can be obtained from the **Colonial Williamsburg Regional Visitor Center** (101 Visitor Center Dr., Williamsburg, 757/220-7645, daily 8:45am-5pm).

YORKTOWN

The quaint waterfront village of Yorktown was established in 1691 and is most famous as the site of the historic victory in the American Revolutionary War. It was also an important tobacco port on the York River where crops were exported from local plantations. During its peak in the mid-1700s, it had nearly 2,000 residents and several hundred buildings. It was a thriving city of primarily merchants, planters, shopkeepers, and indentured servants.

There are many earthworks surrounding Yorktown. These were first built by British troops in 1781, when nearly 80 percent of the town was damaged or destroyed during the Siege of Yorktown. These earthworks were built over with new fortifications by Confederate troops during the Civil War. During the **Siege of 1862,** the Union army was held back by the Confederates for more than a month in this area. After the Confederates left town, Union troops settled in for the rest of the war.

In addition to learning about history, visitors can enjoy art, shopping, special events, and water sports.

Sights

YORKTOWN NATIONAL BATTLEFIELD AND VISITOR CENTER

The **Yorktown National Battlefield** (757/898-2410, www.nps.gov/york) is a national park that marks where, on October 19, 1781, the British army, led by General Charles Lord Cornwallis, surrendered to General George Washington, ending the

Yorktown

Revolutionary War. Visitors can see the battlefield, Washington's Headquarters and tent, and the actual surrender field.

The **Yorktown National Battlefield Visitor Center** (1000 Colonial Pkwy., 757/898-2410, reservations 757/898-2411, daily 9am-5pm, $7) is a great place to begin your exploration of the battlefield and town. It is a living-history museum where re-creations are staged by historical interpreters in costume. Two self-guided driving tours allow visitors to learn about the Siege of Yorktown at a relaxed pace. Guided group tours are also available for a fee (rates vary depending on the number of participants), and reservations should be made two months in advance.

The entrance fee is paid at the visitor centers, where maps are available as well as an informative orientation film that should be your first order of business if you're a first-timer to the site. The admission fee at Yorktown includes entrance into historic houses, entrance to the battlefield, and access to a variety of interpretive programs and is good for seven days. Your pass can be upgraded to visit Jamestown Settlement at the Historic Jamestown Visitor Center for an additional $7.

The 84-foot-tall **Yorktown Victory Monument** and the **Moore House,** where the surrender terms were negotiated, are fascinating sites at the battlefield. The Victory Monument was not erected until 100 years after the end of the war. Its purpose was to "keep fresh in memory the all decisive successes that had been achieved." The four-sided base has an inscription on each side: one for victory, one for a succinct narrative of the siege, one for the treaty of alliance with France, and one for the resulting peace treaty with England. The pediments over the inscriptions feature emblems of nationality, war, alliance, and peace. The monument's podium is a "symbol of the birth of freedom." The column (coming out of the podium) symbolizes the greatness and prosperity of the United States after a century. On top of the monument's shaft is a sculpture of Liberty, which attests to the existence of a nation governed by the people, for the people.

YORKTOWN VICTORY CENTER

Next to the battlefield is the **Yorktown Victory Center** (Rte. 1020 near Colonial Pkwy., 757/253-4838, www.historyisfun.org, daily 9am-5pm with extended summer hours, $9.75), an informative museum dedicated to

Yorktown National Battlefield

the American Revolution that chronicles the entire era beginning with unrest in the colonies and ending with the creation of a new nation. Visitors can view 1,300 artifacts, enjoy artillery demonstrations, explore a re-created Continental Army encampment featuring live historical interpreters, and join seasonal celebrations such as the Yorktown Victory Celebration in October honoring the anniversary of the end of the Revolutionary War.

Summer is the best time to visit since there are outdoor living-history exhibits (you might even be asked to help load a cannon). Indoor exhibits are also offered year-round. A free shuttle runs between the Victory Center and historic Yorktown as well as other Williamsburg-area attractions. A combination admission ticket for the Yorktown Victory Center and the Jamestown Settlement can be purchased for $21.25.

If you're lucky enough to be here on the Fourth of July, you can experience the **Liberty Celebration** firsthand. What better location to celebrate American's independence than where it all began? The celebration includes a plethora of reenactments, military drills, and food demonstrations. This event complements the **Yorktown Fourth of July Celebration** that takes place in the evening on July 4.

HISTORIC YORKTOWN

Yorktown still has a sparse population of full-time residents. Its streets are lined with historic homes, some more than two centuries old. There's Yorktown Beach, a pleasant sandy beach along the York River, and overall, Yorktown offers a relaxing place to explore history, shop, and dine.

Riverwalk Landing (425 Water St., 757/890-3370, www.riverwalklanding.com) is a pedestrian walkway along the York River. This quaint area includes retail shops and dining. Take a stroll on the mile-long River View path that runs along the York River from the Yorktown Battlefield to the Yorktown Victory Center. Riverwalk Landing is a great place to take a walk, go shopping, or grab an ice cream cone on a hot day.

The **Watermen's Museum** (309 Water St., 757/887-2641, www.watermens.org, Apr.-Dec. 23 Tues.-Sat. 10am-5pm, Sun. 1pm-5pm, closed the rest of the year, $5) highlights the role that watermen on the Chesapeake Bay's rivers and tributaries had in the formation of our country. This is done through

Riverwalk Landing

displays illustrating the methods of their trade and craft. Visitors learn what it means to earn a living harvesting seafood from the Chesapeake Bay watershed. The museum offers educational programs and a waterfront facility that can be rented for events.

The **Nelson House** (Main St., 757/898-2410, www.nps.gov/york, open as staffing permits, $10) is a prominent 18th-century structure on Main Street. It was built in the Georgian manor style by the grandfather of Thomas Nelson Jr., one of Yorktown's most famous residents. The younger Nelson was the governor of Virginia in 1781 and the commander of the Virginia militia during the siege. He was also a signer of the Declaration of Independence. Damage from the siege is still evident at the Nelson House. Informal tours are available throughout the year. It's best to call for hours because the house is not open continuously.

Entertainment and Events

The **Lighted Boat Parade** (Yorktown Beach) kicks off the holiday season in early December with a festive procession featuring power- and sailboats adorned with holiday lights. Musical performances and caroling are held on the beach by the light of a bonfire, and hot cider is served. The event is free to the public.

The **Yorktown Wine Festival** (425 Water St. at Riverwalk Landing, tastings $30) is held in October and features wines from throughout Virginia. Art and food vendors also share their wares at the festival.

Shopping

Yorktown's Main Street in the Historic Village is lined with unique shops and galleries. There are antiques stores, galleries, and jewelry and glass shops to name a few. Down by the water at Riverwalk Landing are additional shops featuring colonial architecture and offering art, home items, jewelry, quilts, and clothing.

Sports and Recreation

Yorktown is a waterfront town and outdoor recreation haven. The mile-long **Riverwalk** is a great place for a power walk or to stretch your legs after travel. The two-acre beach near the Riverwalk offers a great location for launching a kayak, swimming, and beachcombing.

There are also kayak and canoe launches at nearby **Wormley Creek Landing** (1110 Old Wormley Creek Rd.) with access to Wormley

the Watermen's Museum

Creek and the York River, **Rodgers A. Smith Landing** (707 Tide Mill Rd.) with access to the Poquoson River and the lower Chesapeake Bay, and **New Quarter Park** (1000 Lakeshead Dr., Williamsburg, 757/890-5840, www.yorkcounty.gov) with access to Queens Creek and the York River.

The **Riverwalk Landing Pier** is a pleasant place to enjoy a day of fishing, and visitors can dock their boats there.

For bicycle rentals ($7.50 per hour or $25 for four hours), kayak and paddleboard rentals ($30 for two hours), or guided Segway tours ($39 for one hour or $65 for two hours), contact **Patriot Tours & Provisions** (757/969-5400, www.patriottoursva.com).

If sailing on a romantic schooner sounds appealing, **Yorktown Sailing Charter** (757/639-1233, www.sailyorktown.com, $37 for two hours) docks its beautiful sailing vessel, the schooner ***Alliance,*** at the pier at Riverwalk Landing April-October. They offer daily sailing trips during the day and at sunset. Daytime trips leave at either 11am or 2pm. Sunset cruise times vary by month. Its sister schooner, ***Serenity,*** offers pirate cruises (Sun., Mon., Wed., Fri., and Sat. 11:30am-1pm, $37), educational trips, and charters for those looking for a bit of adventure.

Food

The ★ **Carrot Tree Kitchen** (323 Water St., Suite A-2, 757/988-1999, www.carrottreekitchens.com, Mon.-Thurs. 10am-5pm, Fri.-Sat. 8am-5pm, $8-20) is a small, casual lunch spot on the waterfront with delightful food. Don't be turned off by the paper plates and plastic utensils; the Carrot Tree offers delicious lunches of sandwiches and comfort food. Save room for the carrot cake—it's their signature dessert.

The **Riverwalk Restaurant** (323 Water St., Suite A-1, 757/875-1522, www.riverwalkrestaurant.net, daily 11am-9pm, $12-32) provides diners with a scenic view of the York River through large glass windows and a cozy fireplace for cool evenings. The fare is primarily seafood, but they offer selections from the land as well. This is a great place to relax after a day of sightseeing.

If fresh seafood and cold beer right on the beach sound like a good ending to a day of exploration in Yorktown, stop in at the **Yorktown Pub** (540 Water St., 757/886-9964, www.yorktownpub.com, Sun.-Thurs. 11am-midnight, Fri.-Sat. 11am-2am, $7-16). The atmosphere is very casual, but the food and service are good. The pub burger, local oysters, and hush puppies are among the best choices. The place is crowded on the weekends, so plan ahead.

For a quick sandwich, pizza, or burger, stop in the **Beach Delly** (524 Water St., 757/886-5890, www.beachdellyandpizzaria.com, daily 11am-9pm, $7-20). This little restaurant is across from the beach and offers good food and friendly service.

Accommodations

The **Duke of York Hotel** (508 Water St., 757/898-3232, www.dukeofyorkmotel.com, $149-199) is an older hotel with a great location right on the water. This family-run establishment has all river-view rooms (some have balconies and some open to landscaped grounds), an outdoor pool, and an on-site café and restaurant. The Yorktown Trolley stops in front of the hotel.

The **York River Inn Bed & Breakfast** (209 Ambler St., 757/887-8800, www.yorkriverinn.com, $135-165) sits on a bluff overlooking the York River and offers two rooms, a suite with private bathrooms, and all the hospitality you can imagine from its friendly owner (who is also a knockout breakfast chef). This is a wonderful colonial-style inn with elegant rooms.

The ★ **Hornsby House Inn** (702 Main St., 757/369-0200, www.hornsbyhouseinn.com, $149-285) offers five beautiful guest rooms with private modern bathrooms in an exquisite colonial home. The inn is in the heart of Yorktown and offers a great view of the York River. It is also just a short walk from the Yorktown Battlefield. The inn is run by two friendly brothers who grew up in the house and provide exemplary service, wine and cheese, and a delicious fresh breakfast each morning. The owners take the time to eat breakfast with and get to know their guests as well as share the history of their home. They also make recommendations for attractions in the area and the best strategy for enjoying them. The house is beautifully appointed and is a warm and inviting home away from home. Book the Monument Grand Suite and enjoy a private outdoor terrace overlooking the York River and Yorktown Victory Monument.

The **Marl Inn Bed & Breakfast** (220 Church St., 301/807-0386, www.marlinnbandb.com, $99-139) is two blocks from the Riverwalk. This colonial-style home is a private residence and inn offering four guest rooms; rates can be booked with no breakfast or with full breakfast. The owner is a great-grandson of Thomas Nelson Jr.

Information and Services

For additional information on Yorktown, visit www.visityorktown.org and www.yorkcounty.gov.

Getting There and Around

Yorktown is 13 miles southeast of Williamsburg along the Colonial Parkway. The **Yorktown Trolley** (757/890-3500, www.yorkcounty.gov, daily 11am-5pm, extended service hours June-Aug., free) is a free seasonal trolley service with stops in nine locations around Yorktown. It runs every 20-25 minutes from the end of March until November.

JAMES RIVER PLANTATIONS

Between Richmond and Williamsburg (in Charles City County) along Route 5 are four stunning plantations that survived the Revolutionary War, War of 1812, and Civil War. These treasures, which span three centuries, are all privately owned National Register properties that are open to the public. For additional information on all four plantations, visit www.jamesriverplantations.org.

Sherwood Forest

Sherwood Forest (Rte. 5, 14501 John Tyler Hwy., Charles City, 804/829-5377, www.sherwoodforest.org, grounds open daily 9am-5pm) sounds like a place out of a fairy tale, and it

James River Plantations

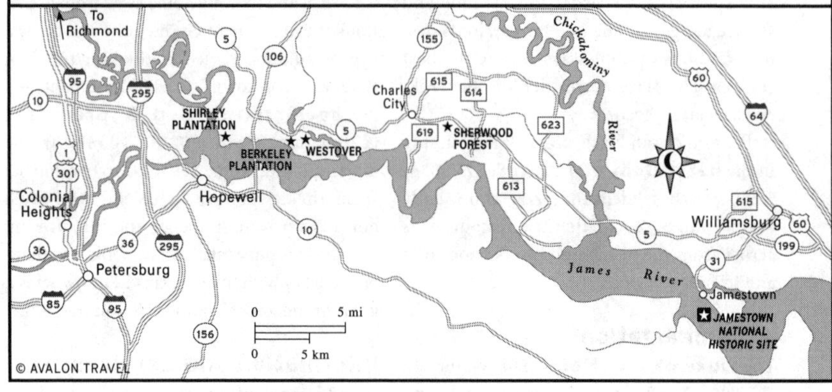

kind of is. This beautiful plantation was the home of President John Tyler for 20 years. The home has been the residence of the Tyler family continuously since he purchased it in 1842.

At more than 300 feet in length—longer than a football field—Sherwood Forest is the longest frame house in the country. The home evolved from a modest 17th-century English-style home (circa 1660) into a substantial 19th-century "Big House" that features a ballroom designed specifically for dancers to engage in the Virginia reel. There is also a resident ghost.

Self-guided walking tours of the grounds are available for $10 per person. The tour features 21 numbered stations on 25 acres with information on the 19th-century plantation. The grounds include terraced gardens, quiet woodlands, and lush lawn. A printed guide is available at a kiosk at the main entrance and features descriptions and history information for each station. House tours are only available by appointment and cost $35.

Westover

Speaking of fairy tales, **Westover** (off Rte. 5, 7000 Westover Rd., 804/829-2882, www.jamesriverplantations.org, grounds open daily 9am-6pm, $5) could have come straight off the pages of one. William Byrd II, who founded the city of Richmond, built the home in 1730. Westover is known for its architectural details, but kids of all ages will love it for its secret passages and enchanting gardens. The mansion is widely considered to be one of the top examples of Georgian architecture in the country. The house itself is not open to the public, but there are still many interesting things to see on the grounds, which offer wide views of the James River. The icehouse and another small structure to the east of the mansion contain a dry well and passageways leading under the house and down to the river. These were created as an escape route from the house during attacks.

Shirley Plantation

Shirley Plantation (501 Shirley Plantation Rd., 804/829-5121, www.shirleyplantation.com, Dec.-Mar. daily 10:30am-4pm, longer summer hours, $11) was the first plantation built in Virginia. It was established in 1613, just six years after Jamestown, and construction was completed in 1738. This property has a legacy of 11 generations of one family (descendants of Edward Hill I) who still own and operate the colonial estate. It has survived attacks, war, and the Great Depression and remains the oldest family-owned business in the United States.

Admission includes a guided house tour that showcases original furnishings, artwork, silver, and hand-carved woodwork. Special architectural features include a "flying staircase" and a Queen Anne forecourt. A self-guided grounds tour features gardens and original outbuildings. Allow at least one hour for your visit.

Berkeley Plantation

Berkeley Plantation (12602 Harrison Landing Rd., 888/466-6018, www.berkeleyplantation.com, daily Jan.-mid-Mar. 10:30am-3:30pm, mid-Mar.-Dec. 9:30am-4:30pm, $11) is famous for being the site of the first official Thanksgiving in 1619, although substantiated claims for the first Thanksgiving also belong to locations in Florida, Texas, Maine, and Massachusetts. It is also the birthplace and home of Declaration of Independence signer Benjamin Harrison and President William Henry Harrison. The beautiful Georgian mansion, which was erected in 1726, sits on a hilltop overlooking the James River. The brick used to build the home was fired on the plantation.

Guided tours are conducted in the mansion and feature a nice collection of 18th-century antiques. An audiovisual presentation is included in the tour as is access to a museum collection of Civil War artifacts and unique paintings by artist Sydney King. Visitors can then tour the grounds on their own and explore five terraces of boxwood and flower gardens. Allow approximately 1.5 hours for the house tour and to roam the gardens.

Hampton Roads

The Hampton Roads region is all about water. In sailors' terms, "Roadstead" means a safe anchorage or sheltered harbor. The word "Hampton" came from an English aristocrat, Henry Wriothesley, who was the third earl of Southampton. Hence, Hampton Roads.

Hampton Roads, which used to be known as Tidewater Virginia, contains one of the largest natural deepwater harbors in the world. The harbor is where the James, Elizabeth, and Nansemond Rivers meet the Chesapeake Bay. Pioneers first settled the area in 1610, after disease struck nearby Jamestown. The area was a throughway for goods from both the colonies and England and, as such, drew merchants and pirates. One of history's most famous pirates, Blackbeard (Edward Teach), plundered the port and waters of Hampton Roads, which was just a short distance from his base in North Carolina.

The port in Hampton Roads is the country's second largest to New York City, and is notable for remaining ice-free year-round. It is also the birthplace of the modern U.S. Navy.

Defining the Hampton Roads area can be a bit confusing. Technically, the Historic Triangle is considered part of Hampton Roads, but the coastal cities from Newport News to Virginia Beach are more commonly thought of as the Hampton Roads area.

NEWPORT NEWS

Newport News is a short drive from Williamsburg, Virginia Beach, and the Atlantic Ocean. There are several versions of whom Newport News was named for, but the most widely accepted is that it was named for Captain Christopher Newport, who was in charge of the three ships that landed in Jamestown in 1607. The "news" part of the name came from the news that was sent back to England on the ships' safe arrival.

Sights

THE MARINERS' MUSEUM

The Mariners' Museum (100 Museum Dr., 757/596-2222, www.marinersmuseum.org, Mon.-Sat. 9am-5pm, Sun. 11am-5pm, $13.95) is one of the largest maritime history museums in the United States. It has more than 60,000 square feet of gallery space showing maritime paintings, artifacts, figureheads,

Northern Hampton Roads

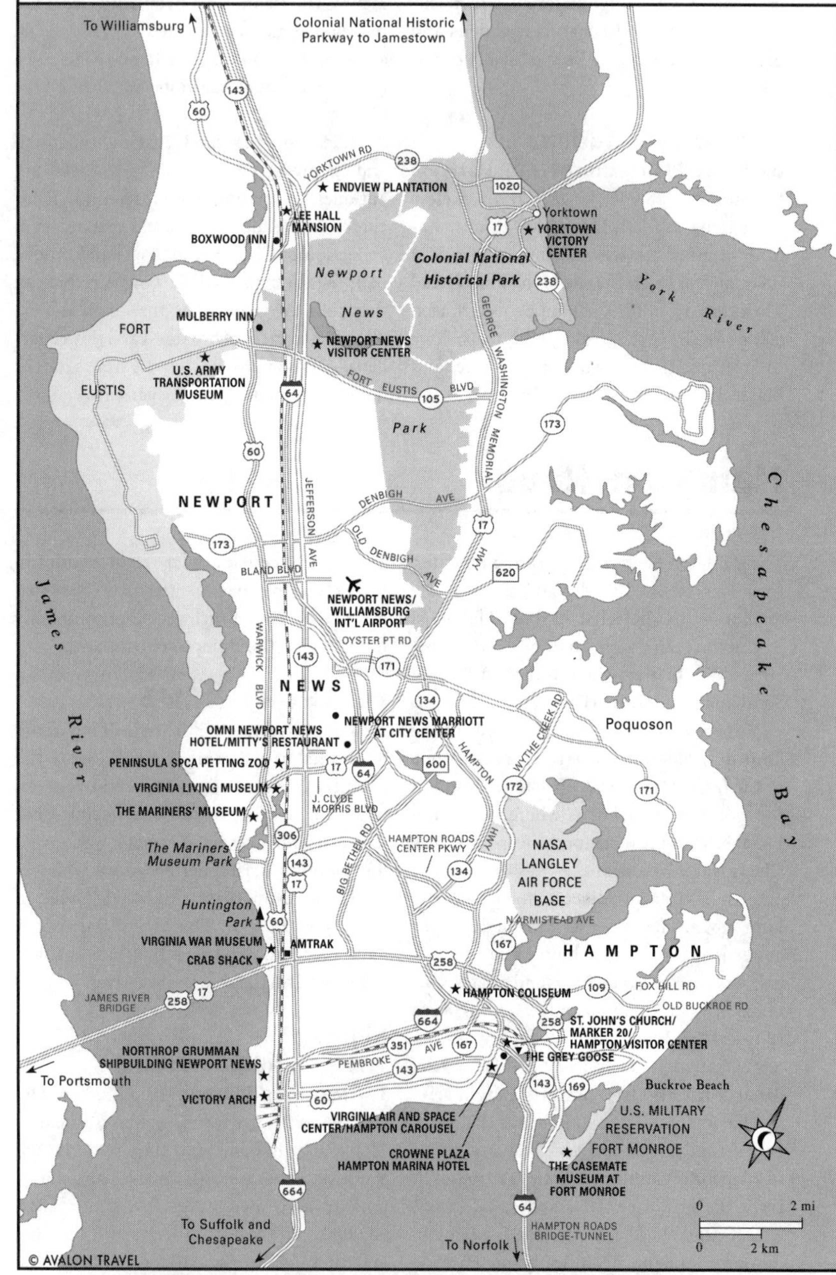

Shipbuilding in Newport News

Newport News is home to the largest privately owned shipyard in the country, **Northrop Grumman Shipbuilding Newport News,** on Washington Avenue along the James River. The facility was built in 1886 for a sum of $7 million and was called the Newport News Ship Building and Dry Dock Company. Its 4,000 employees repaired the many vessels that came to use the ever-growing transportation hub in the Hampton Roads area. The yard produced its first tugboat (named *Dorothy*) in 1891. By 1897, the company had produced three additional tugboats for the U.S. Navy.

Business took off with the onset of the Great Naval Race of the early 1900s. At the start of World War I, shipbuilding was in full swing and the company constructed 6 dreadnoughts and 25 destroyers for the U.S. Navy. The company has been going full force ever since, with its achievements including building the first nuclear-powered submarine and the famous ocean liner the SS *United States*.

Today, the company is the largest private employer in Hampton Roads. The 21,000 employees (many of whom are third- and fourth-generation shipbuilders) turn raw steel into some of the world's most complex ships. The shipyard is the country's sole designer and builder of nuclear-powered aircraft carriers and also one of only two companies that design and build nuclear submarines.

ship models, and small craft from around the world. Exhibits include vessels for warfare, exploration, pleasure, and fishing. A highlight of the museum is the **USS Monitor Center,** where a full-scale replica of the Civil War battleship USS *Monitor* is housed. In 1862 the *Monitor* battled the CSS *Virginia* in what went down in history as the first engagement of steam-powered iron warships (aka The Battle of the Ironclads). Visitors can learn about the historic encounter in the Battle Theater. The center is also home to recovered parts of the original battleship, which sank off the coast of Cape Hatteras, North Carolina, in December 1862.

The museum offers countless other collections including the **Crabtree Collection of Miniature Ships.** The museum is very kid

The Mariners' Museum

friendly and offers numerous events, lectures, and even a concert series. Check the website for upcoming events.

THE VIRGINIA LIVING MUSEUM

Endangered red wolves, loggerhead turtles, and moon jellyfish are just some of the amazing animals you can get close to at **The Virginia Living Museum** (524 J. Clyde Morris Blvd., 757/595-1900, www.thevlm.org, daily 9am-5pm, extended summer hours, $17). This is a wonderful place to learn about Virginia's natural heritage. Indoor exhibits, outdoor exhibits, four interactive discovery centers, and gardens showcase Virginia's geographical regions and the more than 250 species of plants and animals that live in the state. The 30,000-gallon aquarium is a focal point for kids of all ages. Many hands-on activities are also offered such as touch tanks and live feedings, and there is even a planetarium.

VIRGINIA WAR MUSEUM

The **Virginia War Museum** (9285 Warwick Blvd., 757/247-8523, www.warmuseum.org, Mon.-Sat. 9am-5pm, Sun. noon-5pm, $8) explains the development of the U.S. military from 1775 to modern times. Its many exhibits showcase war efforts throughout our country's history. Weapons, artifacts, and uniforms are displayed from the Revolutionary War through the Vietnam War and exhibits explain the evolution of weaponry, the role of women in the military, contributions made by African Americans to military history, and provide a tribute to prisoners of war.

ENDVIEW PLANTATION

Endview Plantation (362 Yorktown Rd., 757/857-1862, www.endview.org, Apr.-Dec. Mon. and Thurs.-Fri. 10am-4pm, Sat. 10am-5pm, Sun. noon-5pm, Jan.-Mar. Thurs.-Sat. 10am-4pm, Sun. 1pm-5pm, $8) was a privately owned estate that was used briefly as a Confederate hospital during the 1862 Peninsula Campaign. The small, white, T-frame Georgian-style home was later occupied by Federal troops. The house sits on top of a knoll, and a spring flows at the base of the hill. This, coupled with the beautiful rolling farmland that surrounds the place has made it an attractive location for centuries. The city

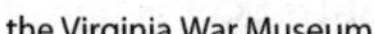

the Virginia War Museum

of Newport News purchased the plantation in 1995 and restored it to its original configuration. School programs are held at the plantation, and guided tours of the house and grounds are offered periodically but not on a published schedule.

LEE HALL MANSION

Lee Hall Mansion (163 Yorktown Rd., 757/888-3371, www.leehall.org, Apr.-Dec. Mon. and Thurs.-Fri. 10am-4pm, Sat. 10am-5pm, Sun. noon-5pm, Jan.-Mar. Thurs.-Sat. 10am-4pm, Sun. 1pm-5pm, $8) is the only remaining large antebellum plantation on the lower Virginia peninsula. The 6,600-square-foot structure is a blend of several architectural styles, including Italianate, Georgian, and Greek revival. The primary style, however, is Italianate. The redbrick home was built on a rise in the 1850s and was home to wealthy planter Richard Decatur Lee. Due to the mansion's commanding view, the home served as headquarters for Confederate generals John Magruder and Joseph E. Johnston during the 1862 Peninsula Campaign. Visitors can take a step back in time to the mid-Victorian period and view hundreds of artifacts in the mansion's authentically furnished rooms. Combination admission tickets for Lee Hall Mansion, Endview Plantation, and the Virginia War Museum can be purchased for $21.

PENINSULA SPCA PETTING ZOO

The **Peninsula SPCA Petting Zoo** (523 J. Clyde Morris Blvd., 757/595-1399, www.peninsulaspca.com, Mon.-Fri. 11am-6pm, Sat. 10am-5am, $2) is a fun place to bring the kids for a hands-on experience with barnyard animals. The zoo is run by the nonprofit Peninsula Society for the Prevention of Cruelty to Animals (SPCA). Visitors can enjoy the company of sheep, goats, chickens, ducks, and other friendly animals.

VICTORY ARCH

The **Victory Arch** (25th St. and West Ave., 757/247-8523, www.newport-news.org) was built in 1919. Troops returning from World War I marched through the arch in victory parades after disembarking from their ships. The arch was reconstructed in 1962, and an

the Victory Arch

The Peninsula Campaign of 1862

The Peninsula Campaign of 1862 was an aggressive plan designed by Union forces during the Civil War to outsmart Confederate defenses in Northern Virginia by moving 121,000 troops by sea to the Virginia Peninsula between the York and James Rivers. This would place them to the east of Richmond, the Confederate capital. Having bypassed the Northern Virginia forces, the army, led by General George B. McClellan, would be able to advance on Richmond without meeting entrenched opposition.

The failure of this plan remains a highly debated episode in the war. Union troops moved slowly and never made a serious attack on Richmond, despite their strategic placement. Although they were met by small Confederate forces, McClellan blamed the failure on Washington for not providing men and support for the effort, even though his troops outnumbered the Confederates throughout the campaign.

From the Confederate standpoint, the Peninsula Campaign of 1862 resulted in the emergence of two great commanders, Stonewall Jackson and Robert E. Lee, who jointly kept the Union forces out of Richmond.

eternal flame was added to it on Memorial Day in 1969. Today the arch stands as a memorial to all men and women of the armed forces.

Entertainment and Events

FERGUSON CENTER FOR THE ARTS

The **Ferguson Center for the Arts** (1 Ave. of the Arts, 757/594-8752, www.fergusoncenter.org) at Christopher Newport University is a performance hall that also houses the university's theater, arts, and music departments. The center opened in 2005 and contains a 1,725-seat concert hall and a 200-seat studio theater. It offers a wide range of performances. Check the website for upcoming events.

PENINSULA FINE ARTS CENTER

The **Peninsula Fine Arts Center** (101 Museum Dr., 757/596-8175, www.pfac-va.org, Tues.-Sat. 10am-5pm, Sun. 1pm-5pm) is dedicated to the promotion of the fine arts. It offers exhibits, a studio art school, an interactive gallery, educational programs, and hands-on activities for children.

EVENTS

The **Newport News Fall Festival of Folklife** (www.nngov.com) is held on the first weekend in October and has been running for approximately four decades. The festival draws 70,000 visitors annually and has more than 230 exhibitors featuring trade demonstrations, crafts, and food.

The **Newport News Children's Festival of Friends** (www.nngov.com) is held at the beginning of May and offers a variety of themed areas for children. Activities, rides, entertainment, and food are all part of the fun of this popular festival that's been going on for more than a quarter century.

Shopping

The **City Center at Oyster Point** (701 Town Center Dr., 757/873-2020, www.citycenteratoysterpoint.com, Mon.-Sat. 10am-9am, Sun. noon-6pm) is an outdoor town center with retail stores, gourmet eateries, spas, and salons.

The **Patrick Henry Mall** (12300 Jefferson Ave., 757/249-4305, www.shoppatrickhenrymall.com, Mon.-Sat. 10am-9am, Sun. noon-6pm) is the largest mall on the peninsula with more than 120 stores in a single-level, indoor configuration.

Sports and Recreation

PARKS

The **Newport News Park** (13560 Jefferson Ave., 757/886-7912, www.nnparks.com) is one of the largest municipal parks in the country, encompassing nearly 8,000 acres. Boat and bike rentals are available in the park as are hiking and biking trails, picnicking, canoeing, archery, disc golf, and fishing. The park's Discovery Center has many hands-on activities and historical artifacts.

Huntington Park-Beach, Rose Garden & Tennis Center (361 Hornet Cir., 757/886-7912) offers a public beach with lifeguards, a playground, baseball, boating, swimming, and tennis.

King-Lincoln Park (600 Jefferson Ave., 757/888-3333) overlooks the Hampton Roads Harbor and provides fishing, tennis, picnicking, playgrounds, and basketball.

Riverview Farm Park (100 City Farm Rd., 757/886-7912) has two miles of multiuse paved trails, a 30,000-square-foot community playground, biking, hiking, and soccer fields.

The Mariners' Museum Park (100 Museum Dr., 757/596-2222, www.marinersmuseum.org) offers a five-mile trail along Lake Maury. There is also boating and hiking.

GOLF

Golfers can get their fix at two local courses: **Kiln Creek Golf Club and Resort** (1003 Brick Kiln Blvd., 757/874-2600, www.kilncreekgolf.com, $32-42) and **Newport News Golf Club at Deer Run** (901 Clubhouse Way, 757/886-7922, www.nngolfclub.com, $34-38).

FISHING

Fishing enthusiasts will enjoy the **James River Fishing Pier** (2019 James River Bridge, 757/274-0364, $9), which is made entirely of concrete and has LED lights. It is one of the longest fishing piers on the East Coast.

BOATING

Boaters can make the **Leeward Marina** (7499 River Rd., 757/274-2359, www.nngov.

Huntington Park-Beach, Rose Garden & Tennis Center

com, May-Oct. daily 7am-7pm, Nov.-Apr. daily 8am-5pm) a base for exploration of the Hampton Roads Harbor and the Chesapeake Bay.

Food

AMERICAN

★ **Circa 1918 Kitchen & Bar** (10367 Warwick Blvd., 757/599-1918, Tues.-Sat. 5pm-10pm, $10-28) offers delicious food, a lovely wine list, friendly, professional service, seasonal selections, and wonderful specials. Sample menu items include duck meat loaf, Prince Edward Island mussels, and grilled lamb burgers. The restaurant is in the historic, two-block-long Hilton Village neighborhood. The atmosphere is relaxed and comfortable, and separate groups of patrons actually talk to each other. Don't shy away from interacting—you could get a great tip for what to order. This is a small restaurant with only about a dozen tables, so reservations are highly recommended.

Fin Seafood (3150 William Styron Sq., 757/599-5800, www.finseafood.com, daily 11am-10pm, $28-90) is a great choice for a romantic dinner or a large gathering. It is a local favorite for delicious seafood. They use mostly organic and sustainable produce and proteins, as well as seasonal ingredients.

Second Street American Bistro (115 Arthur Way, 757/234-4448, www.secondst.com, Mon.-Thurs. 11:30am-10pm, Fri.-Sat. 11:30am-12am, Sun. 11am-10pm, $8-27) is an upscale yet casual restaurant with a wide menu selection, including small plates, pizza, burgers, steak, chicken, ribs, fish, and pasta. They offer a three-course prix fixe dinner for $20.16 and a two-course prix fixe lunch for $10.16. There is also a wonderful wine selection, including a private-label petite sirah grown in Napa Valley.

Brickhouse Tavern (141 Herman Melville Ave., 757/223-9531, www.brickhouse-tavern.com, daily 11am-2am, $7-16) is a casual restaurant serving a variety of pub food, including burgers and pizza. **Chic N Fish** (954 J. Clyde Morris Blvd., 757/223-6517, Mon.-Sat. 11am-9pm, $5-26) serves up a little bit of everything including burgers, seafood and Korean fried chicken.

One of the best views in town is from the **Crab Shack** (7601 River Rd., 757/245-2722, www.crabshackonthejames.com, Sun.-Thurs. 11am-11:30pm, Fri.-Sat. 11am-12:30am, $9-21) on the James River waterfront. This casual seafood restaurant serves sandwiches and entrées in a window-lined dining room or on an outdoor deck.

ITALIAN

For good mid-priced Italian food, try **Al Fresco** (11710 Jefferson Ave., 757/873-0644, www.alfrescoitalianrestaurant.com, lunch Mon.-Fri. 11am-3am, dinner daily 5pm-10pm, $12-24).

Accommodations

UNDER $100

The **Mulberry Inn & Plaza at Fort Eustis** (16890 Warwick Blvd., 757/887-3000, www.mulberryinnva.com, $65-115) is a 101-room hotel offering standard rooms, efficiencies, and studios that can hold up to four people. It is close to I-64 and has amenities such as an outdoor pool, a fitness center, and a business center. Hot breakfast is included.

The **Magnuson Hotel and Convention Center at Oyster Point** (1000 Omni Blvd., 757/873-6664, www.omnihotels.com, $55-99) is only a few blocks from the city center and has a heated indoor pool, a fitness room, free parking, and free Internet.

$100-200

The **Newport News Marriott at City Center** (740 Town Center Dr., 757/873-9299, www.marriott.com, $159-259) is a 256-room hotel near shopping and many restaurants. It offers a pool and workout facility.

The **Comfort Suites Airport** (12570 Jefferson Ave., 757/947-1333, www.choicehotels.com, $134-154) is the hotel closest to the Newport News/Williamsburg International Airport. It offers all suite accommodations, a free airport shuttle, an indoor pool, and a spacious workout facility.

The **Hilton Garden Inn Newport News** (180 Regal Way, 757/947-1080, http://hiltongardeninn3.hilton.com, $118-139) offers 122 guest rooms, an indoor heated pool and spa, an airport shuttle, and easy access to the city center and military bases.

For those seeking more privacy, **The Boxwood Inn** (10 Elmhurst St., 757/888-8854, www.boxwood-inn.com, $105-145) is a historic bed-and-breakfast built in 1897. It offers two rooms and two suites with genuine southern hospitality. Each room in the gracious white home has a theme: The Captain's Quarters is named for the area's rich maritime history; Miss Nana's Room is named for the former owner of the home; the Politician Suite is named for many political gatherings held at the home; and General Pershing's Suite is named for General John Pershing, who often stayed in the home while on hunting trips. Friday dinners are available by reservation.

Camping

Year-round camping is available in the **Newport News Park** (13564 Jefferson Ave., 757/888-3333, www.nnva.gov and www.nnparks.com, $31.50-40). This is one of the biggest municipal parks on the East Coast, and it has 188 campsites with hot showers and restroom facilities. The 8,000-acre park is a combination of woods, meadows, and lakes (campsites are wooded).

Information and Services

For additional information on Newport News, visit www.newport-news.org or stop by the **Newport News Visitor Center** (13560 Jefferson Ave., 757/886-7777, daily 9am-5pm), off I-64 at exit 250B.

Getting There and Around

Newport News is located along I-64 and U.S. Route 60.

The **Newport News/Williamsburg International Airport** (PHF, 900 Bland Blvd., www.flyphf.com) is off I-64 at exit 255B. Downtown Newport News is a 15-minute drive from the airport.

Amtrak (9304 Warwick Blvd., 757/245-3589, www.amtrak.com) has a station in Newport News at Huntington Park. Consult the website for schedules and fares.

Newport News, Hampton, Norfolk, and Virginia Beach are connected by **Hampton Roads Transit** (757/222-6100. www.gohrt.com). Consult the website for schedules and fares.

HAMPTON

Hampton is the oldest continuously inhabited English-speaking community in the United States, with a history dating back to 1607. It is also home to Langley Air Force Base. Hampton was partially destroyed during three major wars—the Revolutionary War, the War of 1812, and the Civil War—but was rebuilt each time and continues to undergo renovations even today. The city now offers an attractive waterfront filled with modern sailing and fishing boats and a variety of attractions for visitors and residents.

Sights

VIRGINIA AIR & SPACE CENTER

The **Virginia Air & Space Center** (600 Settlers Landing Rd., 757/727-0900, www.vasc.org, Sept.-Mar. Tues.-Sat. 10am-5pm, Sun. noon-5pm, extended summer hours, $18 includes IMAX) houses more than 100 interactive exhibits that detail the historic achievements of NASA. Topics include space travel, aircraft development, communications, and a hands-on space gallery. Hampton was the birthplace of the space program in the United States and has played an important role in the 100-plus-year history of flight. Displays include more than 30 historic airplanes, the Apollo 12 command module, a passenger jet, moon rocks, and many replicas.

THE HAMPTON CAROUSEL

The Hampton Carousel (602 Settlers Landing Road, Carousel Park, 757/727-1610, www.visithampton.com, seasonally

the Virginia Air & Space Center

Tues.-Sun. 11am-8pm, $1) was originally built for an amusement park at Buckroe Beach, where it resided between 1921 and 1985. It is now on the waterfront in downtown Hampton, fully restored and protected from the elements. The merry-go-round's 48 horses and chariots were hand-carved out of hardwood, and it is adorned with original paintings and mirrors. It also still plays the original organ music. The carousel is open from the end of March through early September, but it is best to check the website because there are scheduled closures each month.

THE CASEMATE MUSEUM AT FORT MONROE

The Casemate Museum (20 Bernard Rd., 757/788-3391, www.tradoc.army.mil, Tues.-Sun. 10:30am-4:30pm, free) on the grounds of Fort Monroe shares many exhibits about the fort, which was built in 1834 to protect the Chesapeake Bay, James River, and Hampton River. This is the largest stone fort in the country. The museum contains the prison cell where Confederate president Jefferson Davis was held and also the living quarters of Robert E. Lee while he was stationed there from 1831 to 1834. Other displays include military uniforms and supplies. The grounds at Fort Monroe are open year-round for walking and other outdoor activities.

ST. JOHN'S CHURCH

St. John's Church (100 W. Queens Way, 757/722-2567, www.stjohnshampton.org) is the oldest English-speaking parish in the United States. The church was founded in 1610, and the current structure was built in 1728. The church was designed in the shape of a Latin cross and boasts beautiful colonial-style brickwork, two-foot-thick walls, and stained glass windows. The church survived the Revolutionary War, the War of 1812, and the Civil War. The silver used for communion dates back to 1618 and is considered to be the most valuable relic in the American Anglican Church. Services are still held here; consult the website for details.

Entertainment and Events

The **Hampton Coliseum** (1000 Coliseum Dr., 757/838-4203, www.hamptoncoliseum.org) is the premier venue in Hampton for concerts, performances, and sporting events. A list of upcoming events can be found on the website. The Coliseum is convenient to I-64 and offers free parking.

The annual **Hampton Jazz Festival** (www.hamptonjazzfestival.com) has been going on for almost 50 years. It is held for three days at the end of June in the Hampton Coliseum. Information on the lineup and tickets can be found on the website.

The **Hampton Cup Regatta** (www.hamptoncupregatta.com) is billed as the "oldest continually run motorsport event in the world." It is held for three days in mid-August in Mill Creek, between Fort Monroe and the East Mercury Boulevard Bridge. Another fun water festival is the **Blackbeard Pirate Festival** (www.blackbeardfestival.com) held at the beginning of June each year. The Hampton waterfront is overrun with pirate reenactors as visitors are taken back to the 18th century. There is live music, children's activities, vendors, fireworks, and arts and crafts.

Sports and Recreation

Buckroe Beach (100 1st St. South) is a wide, sandy, eight-acre beach on the Chesapeake Bay. There is a playground, picnic shelters, a bike path, and certified lifeguards on duty. Concerts are held in the summer months, as is an outdoor family movie series.

Grandview Nature Preserve (State Park Drive) is a local secret. This nature preserve and beach at the end of Beach Road in Grandview is great for families and allows dogs in the off-season.

Hampton is located at the entrance to the Chesapeake Bay and is a convenient stopping point for boaters. Those traveling by boat can stop at the **Blue Water Yachting Center** (15 Marina Rd., 757/723-6774, www.blueyachtsales.com), which offers daily dockage.

If you don't have your own boat but wish to take a relaxing sightseeing cruise, board the double-decker ***Miss Hampton II*** (757/722-9102, www.misshamptoncruises.com, $26 for 2.5-3 hours), a motorized vessel that offers cruising in Hampton Harbor and on the Chesapeake Bay.

Golf enthusiasts can play at the **Woodlands Golf Course** (9 Woodlands Rd., 757/727-1195, www.hampton.gov, $13-19) or the **Hamptons Golf Course** (320 Butler Farm Rd., 757/766-9148, www.hampton.gov, $14-21).

Food

AMERICAN

Surf Rider Bluewater (1 Marina Rd., 757/723-9366, www.surfriderrestaurant.com, $6-23) is a family-owned seafood restaurant in the Blue Water Yachting Center off Ivy Home Road. This is a great place for local seafood, which you can tell by the number of local residents eating here. Their crab cakes are famous as are the oysters, tuna, and hush puppies.

Another local favorite is **Marker 20** (21 E. Queens Way, 757/726-9410, www.marker20.com, Mon.-Fri. 11am-2am, Sat.-Sun. 10am-2am, $7-25). This downtown seafood restaurant has a large covered outdoor deck and inside seating. Enjoy a casual menu of soups, salads, sandwiches, and seafood specials, along with dozens of types of beer.

The cute **Grey Goose** (118 Old Hampton Way, 757/723-7978, www.greygooserestaurant.com, lunch Mon.-Sat. 11am-3pm, $6-10) serves homemade soups, salads, sandwiches, and bakery items made from fresh ingredients.

SPANISH

The **Six Little Bar Bistro** (6 E. Mellen St., 757/722-1466, www.littlebarbistro.com, daily 5pm-2am, tapas $3-14) serves an eclectic assortment of tapas including herbed sausage, seaweed salad, pork, and chipotle crab cakes. There is also a large bar that is notorious for mixing potent cocktails. The food is delicious and the atmosphere is fun, but they do not split checks, so be prepared for this if you're with a group.

Accommodations

UNDER $100

The **Candlewood Suites Hampton** (401 Butler Farm Rd., 757/766-8976, www.

candlewoodsuites.com, $90-119) offers 98 reasonably priced, spacious rooms in a quiet location. The hotel is geared toward extended-stay guests and offers per diem rates for members of the armed services. The service is good, and the staff is caring and friendly. The rooms are well stocked, and the hotel is pet friendly. There are also free laundry facilities on-site.

$100-200

The **Crowne Plaza Hampton Marina** (700 Settlers Landing, 757/727-9700, hwww.hamptonmarinahotel.com, $120-149) is a riverfront hotel in downtown Hampton. It is within walking distance to the Virginia Air & Space Center and a short drive to Langley Air Force Base, Fort Monroe, and Northrop Grumman.

OVER $200

The **Embassy Suites by Hilton Hampton Hotel Convention Center & Spa** (1700 Coliseum Dr., 757/827-8200, www.embassysuites3.hilton.com, $219-475) offers 295 suites with kitchenettes. The hotel has a warm decor with an attractive atrium, and the staff provides good, reliable service. There's a restaurant and a nicely appointed fitness center. Spa service is also available.

Information and Services

For additional information on Hampton, visit www.hampton.gov and www.visithampton.com or stop in at the **Hampton Visitor Center** (120 Old Hampton Ln., 757/727-1102, daily 9am-5pm).

Getting There and Around

Hampton is approximately 10 miles southeast of Newport News.

The **Newport News/Williamsburg International Airport** (PHF, 900 Bland Blvd., Newport News, www.flyphf.com) is off I-64 at exit 255B. Hampton is a 20-minute drive from the airport.

Greyhound (2 W Pembroke Ave., 757/722-9861, www.greyhound.com) offers bus service to Hampton.

Hampton Roads Transit (www.gohrt.com) is a public transit service that serves the Hampton Roads area including Hampton. It currently offers transportation by bus, light-rail, ferry, and Handi-ride (a service for people with disabilities).

NORFOLK

Norfolk is the second-largest city in Virginia and home to the largest naval base in the world. A longtime navy town, the city has an appealing downtown area and a nice waterfront. The city has undergone a rebirth in recent history that is most evident in the delightful restaurants and shops in the trendy Ghent village, located just northwest of downtown, not far from the Elizabeth River. The city also boasts numerous universities, museums, and a host of other attractions including festivals and shopping.

Sights

CHRYSLER MUSEUM OF ART

The **Chrysler Museum of Art** (One Memorial Pl., 757/664-6200, www.chrysler.org, Tues.-Sat. 10am-5pm, Sun. noon-5pm, free) is one of Virginia's top art museums with 62 galleries and 30,000 pieces of artwork including paintings, textiles, ceramics, and bronzes. The art on display spans thousands of years and comes from around the world. A highlight is the glass museum (a museum within a museum) that is entirely devoted to glass art and features 10,000 glass pieces (spanning 3,000 years) and a glass art studio. Other collections include European painting and sculpture, American painting and sculpture, modern art, a gallery of ancient and non-Western art, contemporary art, photography, and decorative arts.

NORFOLK BOTANICAL GARDEN

Something is always in bloom at the **Norfolk Botanical Garden** (6700 Azalea Garden Rd., 757/441-5830, www.norfolkbotanicalgarden.org, daily 9am-7pm, $11). This 155-acre garden contains more than forty different themed areas and thousands of plants. It is open to visitors year-round. Inside the garden is the

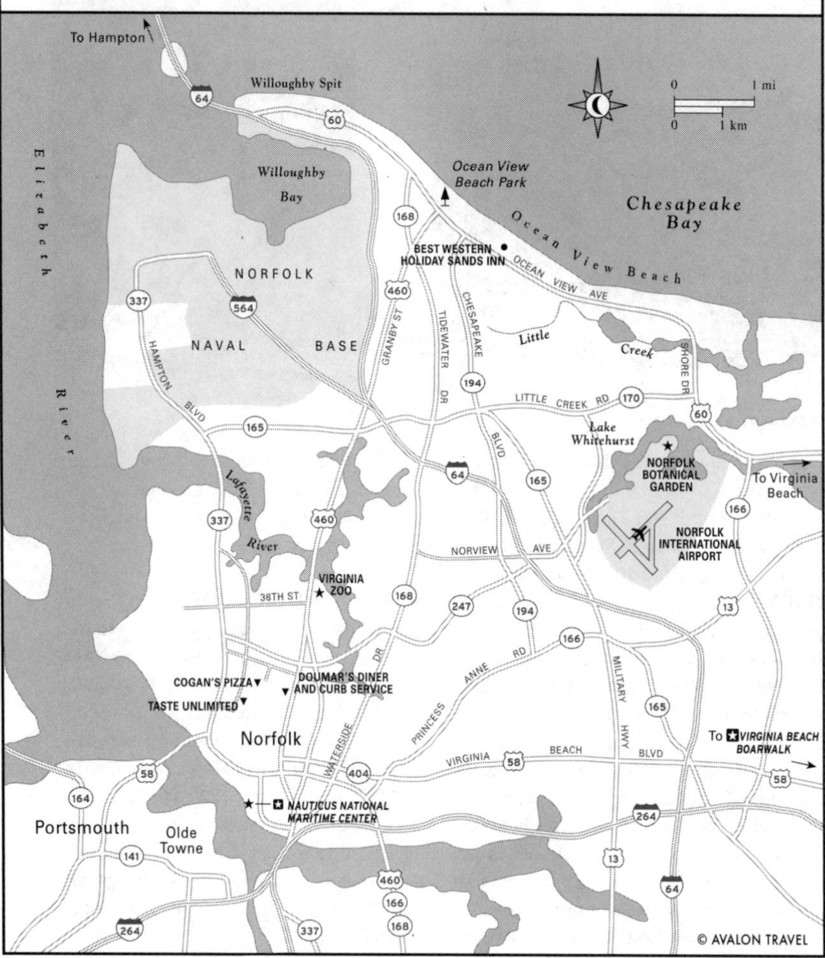

three-acre **World of Wonders Children's Garden,** which is geared toward children and families and houses several learning areas.

★ NAUTICUS NATIONAL MARITIME CENTER

The **NAUTICUS National Maritime Center** (1 Waterside Dr., 757/644-1000, www.nauticus.org, daily Memorial Day-Labor Day 10am-5pm, rest of the year Tues.-Sat. 10am-5pm, Sun. noon-5pm, $15.95) is an incredible interactive science and technology center. They have a great floor plan with a lot of interesting permanent and rotating exhibits including hands-on activities for children (they will love the Morse code exhibit). Be sure to catch *The Living Sea* movie featured on a large panoramic screen that opens to a view of the water.

The ***Battleship Wisconsin*** is one of the prime on-site attractions, and the center features many exhibits related to the ship. It is

the Chrysler Museum of Art

one of the biggest and also one of the last battleships built by the U.S. Navy. The ship served in World War II, the Korean War, and Operation Desert Storm. Admission to the ship is included with admission to NAUTICUS, and visitors can take a self-guided tour of the deck. For $35.95 (which includes NAUTICUS admission), guided **Battleship Wisconsin Topside Tours** (11am, 1pm, and 3pm) are available. These tours include the administration area, radio room, main deck with enlisted berthing, the captain's cabin and sleeping quarters, the flag bridge, and the combat engagement center. Participants must be at least eight years old and have the ability to climb stairs to four decks and be comfortable in small spaces.

The **Hampton Roads Naval Museum** (free admission) is also located inside the NAUTICUS National Maritime Center on the second floor. The museum is run by the U.S. Navy and details the 237-year history of the Hampton Roads region fleet. Exhibits in the museum include an 18-pounder cannon from 1798, artifacts from the cruiser **CSS *Florida*** and the sloop-of-war **USS *Cumberland,*** a World War II Mark 7 undersea mine, and a torpedo warhead from a German submarine.

Allow at least 2-4 hours to explore the center and the ship. The facility includes a casual restaurant serving sandwiches, salads, beverages, and snacks.

NAVAL STATION NORFOLK

Norfolk offers a unique opportunity to tour the largest naval base in the world. The **Naval Station Norfolk** sits on 4,300 acres on Sewells Point and is home to 75 ships and 134 aircraft. The 45-minute bus tour leaves from the **Naval Tour and Information Center** (9079 Hampton Blvd., 757/444-7955, www.norfolkvisitor.com) next to Gate 5. The tour rides past destroyers, aircraft carriers, frigates, amphibious assault ships, and the airfield. Tour times change frequently so call for a current schedule.

VIRGINIA ZOO

The **Virginia Zoo** (3500 Granby St., 757/441-2374, www.virginiazoo.org, daily 10am-5pm, $14.95) occupies 53 acres adjacent to Lafayette Park. It opened in 1900 and houses more than 400 animals including elephants, giraffes, orangutans, otters, and birds. The zoo is operated by the City of Norfolk and the Virginia Zoological Society. It offers many educational and children's programs.

ST. PAUL'S CHURCH

St. Paul's Church (201 St. Paul's Blvd., 757/627-4353, www.saintpaulsnorfolk.com) is the oldest building in Norfolk, dating back to 1739. A cannonball that was fired into the church on the night before the Revolutionary War began is still lodged in its southwestern wall. Tombstones in the church's historic cemetery date back to the 17th and 18th centuries. Episcopalian services are still held at St. Paul's.

Entertainment and Events

Chrysler Hall (215 St. Paul's Blvd., 757/644-6464, www.sevenvenues.com) is the top performing arts venue in the Hampton Roads area. It hosts Broadway shows, concerts, theatrical performances, the **Virginia Symphony** (www.virginiasymphony.org), the **Virginia Arts Festival** (www.vafest.org), and the **Virginia Ballet.**

The **Virginia Opera** (www.vaopera.org, 866/673-7282) performs in three locations throughout Virginia (Norfolk, Richmond, and Fairfax). The Norfolk venue, the **Harrison Opera House** (160 E. Virginia Beach Blvd., 757/627-9545), is a beautifully renovated World War II USO theater that seats just over 1,600 people.

The **Scope Arena** (201 E. Brambleton Ave., 757/644-6464, www.sevenvenues.com) is a 12,000-seat complex that hosts concerts, family shows, and conventions. It is also the home of the **Norfolk Admirals** of the ECHL.

Norfolk also has a number of quality small venues featuring good nightlife and entertainment. The **NorVa** (317 Monticello Ave., 757/627-4547, www.thenorva.com) is a 1,500-person concert venue the hosts a variety of artists such as Ingrid Michaelson, Citizen Cope, and The Legwarmers. **The Banque** (1849 E. Little Creek Rd., 757/480-3600, www.thebanque.com) is a popular, award-winning country-and-western nightclub and restaurant offering a large dance floor and well-known artists.

Norfolk Festevents (757/441-2345, www.festevents.org) presents more than 65 days of events including concerts and festivals in **Town Point Park** (on the Elizabeth River in the center of the business district in downtown Norfolk) and **Ocean View Beach Park** (at the end of Granby Street at Ocean View Avenue) from February through October. One of the most popular events, the **Norfolk Harborfest** is held annually for four days at the beginning of June and attracts more than 100,000 people. This large festival covers more than three miles on the Norfolk waterfront and offers visitors three sailboat parades, tall ships, the largest fireworks display on the East Coast, and seemingly endless entertainment. Another Festevent, the **Norfolk Jazz Festival** is a two-day festival held in mid-July. Tickets are $30-69. The **Town Point Virginia Fall Wine Festival** is held in Town Point Park for two days in October. More than 200 Virginia wines are featured. Tickets start at $20 and can be purchased online.

Shopping

The **MacArthur Center** (300 Monticello Ave., 757/627-6000, www.shopmacarthur.com, Mon.-Sat. 10am-9pm, Sun. noon-6pm) is a large shopping mall with close to 150 retail stores and restaurants. There is also a movie complex.

A trendy little shopping area worth checking out is **The Palace Station & Shops of Ghent** (Llewellyn Ave. and 21st St., www.ghentnorfolk.org) in the historic Ghent neighborhood. Thirty-five unique shops and restaurants line this retail shopping complex near downtown Norfolk. Boutiques, antiques stores, gift stores, and craft stores are just some of the establishments found in this interesting area.

Sports and Recreation

Harbor Park (150 Park Ave., www.milb.com) is home to the **Norfolk Tides,** the Class AAA affiliate of the Baltimore Orioles. The park is considered one of the best minor league baseball facilities in the country, boasting a practical design and a terrific view of downtown Norfolk. The park opened in 1993 on the Elizabeth River.

The **Norfolk Admirals** (www.norfolkadmirals.com) take to the ice seasonally at the **Scope Arena** to compete in the ECHL. Consult the website for schedules and tickets.

Those looking for a little local adventure can take in a **sand wrestling** (www.sandwrestling.com) competition. Sand wrestling, which is also known as beach wrestling, is a version of traditional wrestling. Established as an international style of amateur wrestling in 2005, it is quickly gaining popularity and offers competition for males and females of all ages.

Beachgoers can enjoy miles of public beach at **Ocean View Beach Park** (www.norfolk.gov). The park offers a boardwalk, bandstand, beach access ramp for people with disabilities, commercial fishing pier, and open recreation space. There is a bathhouse, and parking is free. Dogs are allowed on leashes in the off-season.

A trip with **American Rover Sailing Cruises** (333 Waterside Dr., 757/627-7245, www.americanrover.com, $20) is a relaxing way to tour the Hampton Roads Harbor and the Elizabeth River. The *American Rover*'s red sails are a distinctive sight in the Hampton Roads area. From April through October, they offer 1.5- and 2-hour narrated cruises. Guests can help out with sailing the ship or just sit back and relax.

Food

AMERICAN

★ **Freemason Abbey Restaurant** (209 W. Freemason St., 757/622-3966, www.freemasonabbey.com, Mon.-Thurs. 11am-9:30pm, Fri.-Sat. 11am-10:30pm, Sun. 9:30am-9:30pm, $9-30) is a local favorite in downtown Norfolk for fresh seafood, steak, and pasta. It is housed in a 140-year-old renovated church and has been a restaurant for more than two decades. The atmosphere is friendly, elegant, and casual with a beautiful decor that retains a church-like feel yet has cozy seating. Try the award-winning she-crab soup. Reservations are highly recommended on the weekends.

Freemason Abbey Restaurant

Doumar's Barbeque & Curb Service (1919 Monticello Ave., 757/627-4163, www.doumars.com, Mon.-Thurs. 8am-11pm, Fri.-Sat. 8am-midnight, $2-5) is a legendary diner that was featured on the show *Diners, Drive-Ins and Dives*. Its origin was an ice-cream stand that opened in 1907 in Ocean View Amusement Park. The business moved to its current location in 1934 and is still owned by the same family. Famous for barbecue and ice cream, they bake their own ice-cream cones in the original cone machine. Take a seat inside the diner, or dine from your car and enjoy their carhop service. This is a fun, genuine, old-school diner that is inexpensive and has a great history.

Seafood lovers can get their fix at **A. W. Schuck's** (2200 Colonial Ave., 757/664-9117, daily 11am-2am, $8-15). They seem to be firm believers that any meal can include seafood. Try their burger topped with lump crab, or a po'boy; both are well seasoned, huge, and delicious. Finding the place can be a bit tricky—look on 22nd Street in the plaza rather than along Colonial Avenue. The staff is friendly and attentive, and the atmosphere is social. This is a good choice for reasonably priced, yet tasty food.

ITALIAN

Razzo (3248 E. Ocean View Ave., 757/962-3630, www.razzo-norfolk.com, daily 5pm-10pm, $8-19) is a big hot spot in a small package. This tiny Italian restaurant on Ocean View only has a handful of tables, but waiting for one is worth your time (and there's a well-stocked bar that can make that wait more enjoyable). The food is outstanding, with daily specials and homemade bread. When in doubt, order the chicken marsala.

Accommodations

$100-200

There are many chain hotels in Norfolk. A few stand out for above-average accommodations, good service, and proximity to downtown attractions and the airport, such as the **Courtyard Norfolk Downtown** (520 Plume St., 757/963-6000, www.marriott.com, $149-179), the **Holiday Inn Express Hotel & Suites Norfolk International Airport** (1157 N. Military Hwy., 757/455-5055, www.hiexpress.com, $149-162), and the **Residence Inn Norfolk** (227 W. Brambleton Ave., 757/842-6216, www.marriott.com, $149-239).

In addition to the selection of large chain hotels, there are some very nice bed-and-breakfasts and historic hotels in Norfolk. The **Page House Inn** (323 Fairfax Ave., 757/625-5033, www.pagehouseinn.com, $170-245) is a historic bed-and-breakfast (circa 1899) next to the Chrysler Museum of Art in the Ghent Historic District. This stately redbrick mansion has four guest rooms and three guest suites, decorated with 19th-century furniture, antiques, and art. A delicious full breakfast is served each morning, and refreshments are served each afternoon. The innkeepers are warm and welcoming.

The ★ **Freemason Inn Bed and Breakfast** (411 W. York St., 757/963-7000, www.freemasoninn.com, $160-225) is known for its tasteful interior, spacious rooms, comfortable beds, and incredible food (they serve a three-course breakfast). Four elegant guest rooms and a friendly host make this a top choice in Norfolk. The inn is centrally located in a charming neighborhood near the harbor.

Information and Services

For additional information on the Norfolk area, visit www.visitnorfolktoday.com.

Getting There and Around

Norfolk is 16 miles south of Hampton.

The **Norfolk International Airport** (ORF, 2200 Norview Ave., www.norfolkairport.com) is convenient for those traveling by air to the Norfolk area. It is one mile east of I-64 (exit 279) and just minutes from downtown Norfolk.

The city is serviced by **Amtrak** (130 Park Ave., www.amtrak.com) rail service and by **Greyhound** (701 Monticello Ave., 757/625-7500, www.greyhound.com) bus service.

Norfolk Electric Transit (www.virginia.org) is part of Hampton Roads Transit and offers free bus service around town and stops at major attractions. It operates weekdays 6am-6:15pm at 15-minute intervals and 6:15pm-11pm at 30-minute intervals. Saturday service is 6am-12:15am at 30-minute intervals, and Sunday service is 7am-11:15pm at 30-minute intervals.

Hampton Roads Transit also offers additional bus routes around Norfolk (www.gohrt.com, $1.75) and **Paddlewheel Ferry** (www.gohrt.com, $1.75) service on three passenger paddle-wheel boats. Each boat holds 150 passengers and runs between downtown Norfolk (at the Waterside) and Portsmouth. The ferry operates every 30 minutes Monday-Thursday 7am-9:45pm, Friday 7am-11:45pm, Saturday 10am-11:45pm, and Sunday 10am-9:45pm. Extended service kicks in during peak summer weeks. Passengers are allowed to bring bicycles on board.

Virginia Beach

Virginia Beach is the state's premier beach destination, with sand, surf, and ice cream. It is a thriving year-round city with more than 437,000 full-time residents as well as a bustling tourist destination, with nearly three million visitors annually. Everyone coming to town is greeted by ***Neptune,*** a 24-foot-tall statue by Paul DiPasquale. He stands on the boardwalk and invites children and adults alike to enjoy the wonders of the ocean responsibly. The resort area runs along more than 20 miles of beach, which is maintained and replenished on a regular basis. The area is booming with commercialism and has more than its share of touristy gift shops and oversize hotels, but also offers a variety of attractions, events, parks, and wildlife refuges. The farther north you travel, the quieter it gets, and the northern reaches are mostly residential.

The three-mile-long boardwalk is the center of activity, and the aquarium, water sports, fishing, and parks keep visitors coming back year after year. Accommodations are plentiful but also book quickly during the peak summer season, especially those right on the beach. The beach is busiest not only in the summer but also during March and April, when thousands of college students arrive for spring break. Keep this in mind when planning your trip since it may be best to avoid these windows unless you are joining in the fun.

Tourism in Virginia Beach began with the opening of the first hotel in 1884. The boardwalk was built just four years later. The strip has been growing ever since, and a few historic landmarks such as the Cavalier Hotel (circa 1927) still stand today.

A population boom in the 1980s resulted in some bad press for the beach area, which experienced some pains from the onslaught of visitors and the hard partying that came with them. Since then, the municipality has made a concerted effort and spent millions of dollars to revamp the beach's reputation as a family resort. They've succeeded on most levels by encouraging more high-end businesses to come to the beach and by making the main thoroughfares more visually pleasing to visitors with fresh lighting and landscaping. The area is now known for its excellence in environmental health, and as more and more sporting events are booked for the beach, it is becoming a destination for the fitness-minded. In a nutshell, Virginia Beach is a modern and affordable vacation destination that offers a little bit of everything.

SIGHTS

★ Virginia Beach Boardwalk

No trip to Virginia Beach is complete without a stroll along the 28-foot-wide boardwalk running parallel to the ocean for three miles (between 1st Street and 42nd Street) on one of the longest recreational beach areas in the world. The boardwalk is perfect for getting some exercise with a view. There are lanes for walkers and bicycles, and many running events utilize

Neptune greets visitors to Virginia Beach.

Virginia Beach

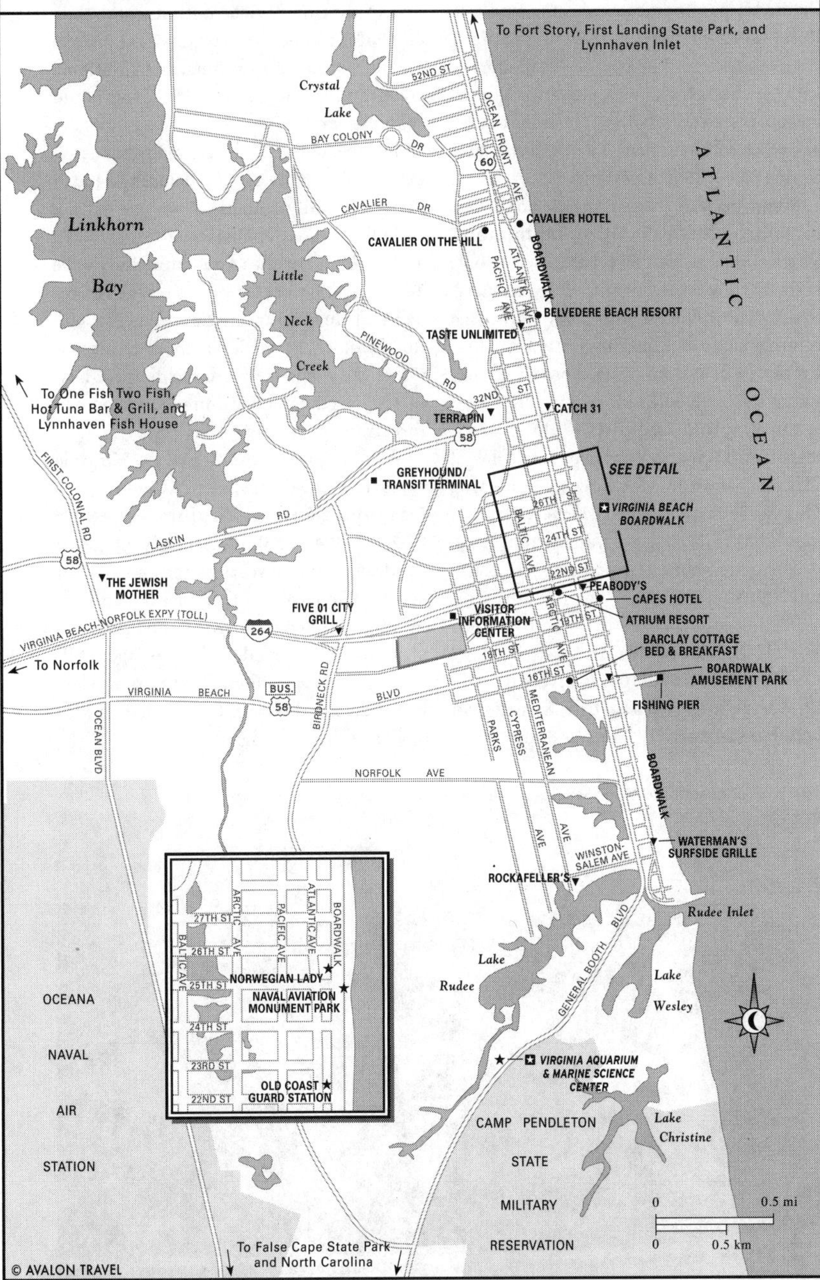

a portion of the boardwalk on their route, including the **Shamrock Marathon** (www.shamrockmarathon.com) and the **Rock 'n' Roll Marathon Series** (www.runrocknroll.competitor.com). The boardwalk is adorned with benches, grassy areas, play areas, amusement parks, arcades, hotels, restaurants, shops, and other entertainment. There is also a large fishing pier at 15th Street.

Some special features along the boardwalk include the **Naval Aviation Monument,** which stands at 25th Street and pays tribute to the navy, Marine Corps, and Coast Guard. Nearby is the ***Norwegian Lady*** statue that commemorates the lives lost during the shipwreck of a boat from Moss, Norway (a sister statue was erected in Moss). At 13th Street is the **Virginia Legends Walk,** a landscaped walkway that pays tribute to some of Virginia's most famous citizens, including Thomas Jefferson, Robert E. Lee, Captain John Smith, Ella Fitzgerald, and Arthur Ashe.

There are public restrooms at 17th, 24th, and 30th Streets.

★ Virginia Aquarium & Marine Science Center

The **Virginia Aquarium & Marine Science Center** (717 General Booth Blvd., 757/385-3474, www.virginiaaquarium.com, daily 9am-5pm, $22) is a must-visit attraction in Virginia Beach. With its more than 800,000 gallons of aquariums, live animal habitats, numerous exhibits, and a National Geographic 3-D Theater ($8), you could spend several hours or an entire day here and not get bored. There are many hands-on experiences in the center, including a touch pool of friendly animals. A unique exhibit called *Stranded* enables visitors to learn about the Virginia Aquarium Response Team and the work they do to rescue and rehabilitate marine animals in need. Through this exhibit, visitors learn about recent patients the response team has helped, how they track rehabilitated animals, and human threats to marine mammals.

Another great attraction at the Virginia Aquarium & Marine Science Center is the **Adventure Park at Virginia Aquarium** (757/385-4947, $55). It offers adventure for children over five years of age and also for adults. The park is a trail of wooden platforms connected by zip lines and bridges. A play area is also available for younger children. This is a wonderful attraction when you need a break from the beach, and kids of all ages find it compelling.

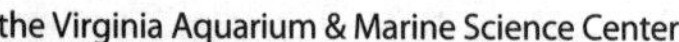
the Virginia Aquarium & Marine Science Center

Old Coast Guard Station

The **Old Coast Guard Station** (2401 Atlantic Ave., 757/422-1587, www.oldcoastguardstation.com, May-Oct. Mon.-Sat. 10am-5pm, Sun. noon-5pm, Nov.-Apr. Tues.-Sat. 10am-5pm, Sun. noon-5pm, closed Mon., $4) houses more than 1,800 artifacts and 1,000 photographs that honor Virginia's maritime heritage. Two galleries relate the history of the U.S. Life-Saving and Coast Guard Services, along with shipwrecks off the Virginia coast. The building itself was constructed in 1903 and is the only one of five original life-saving stations built that year along the Virginia coast that remains standing. It now resides on the boardwalk at 24th Street, and the rooftop "Towercam" enables guests to look at ships in the Atlantic.

The Old Cape Henry Lighthouse

The Old Cape Henry Lighthouse (583 Atlantic Ave., Fort Story, 757/422-9421, www.preservationvirginia.org, Nov. 1-Mar. 15 daily 10am-4pm, Mar. 16-Oct. 31 daily 10am-5pm, $8) is part of the Fort Story military base. It once protected the entryway to the Chesapeake Bay at the northern end of Virginia Beach. Construction of the lighthouse was authorized by George Washington as one of the first acts of the newly organized federal government, and it was the first federal construction project. Alexander Hamilton oversaw its construction. The lighthouse was completed in 1792. This octagonal sandstone edifice remains one of the oldest surviving lighthouses in the country and is a National Historic Landmark. Visitors can climb to the top of the lighthouse and enjoy commanding views of the Chesapeake Bay and the Atlantic Ocean. Guided tours of the grounds are also available, and there's a gift shop. To reach the lighthouse, you must drive through a security gate at Fort Story. Photo identification is required to enter, and car searches are frequently made.

ENTERTAINMENT AND EVENTS

Endless entertainment can be found on the Virginia Beach boardwalk, including concerts, athletic events, and performances.

Nightlife

Virginia Beach doesn't sleep when the sun goes down. In fact, in the summer it doesn't seem to sleep at all. Live music can be found at the **Hot Tuna Bar & Grill** (2817 Shore Dr., 757/481-2888, www.hottunavb.com, daily from 4pm). They offer Top 40 dance music starting at 10pm. Another dance bar is **Peabody's** (209 21st St., 757/422-6212, www.peabodysvirginiabeach.com). They've been around since 1967 and have one of the largest dance floors in the area.

If a game of pool is more your speed, try **Q-Master II Billiards** (5612 Princess Anne Rd., 757/499-8900, www.q-masters.com). They are the premier billiards room in the region and have 72 tables. They also host competitions.

For those wishing to kick back for some live folk, jazz, or blues, stop in **Jewish Mother & VB Tap House** (211 21st St., 757/222-1818, www.jewishmother.com). They offer live entertainment and a large menu that includes delicious deli sandwiches. If comedy is more up your alley, catch a show at the **Funny Bone Comedy Club & Restaurant** (217 Central Park Ave., 757/213-5555, www.vabeachfunnybone.com). They host well-known comics and offer tables with a full dinner and bar menu during the show. Shows are for ages 21 and older.

Events

Some popular annual events include the **American Music Festival** (5th St. and Atlantic Ave., www.beachstreetusa.com, $40), the largest outdoor music event on the East Coast. It runs for three days over Labor Day weekend and features local and national artists. Sounds of rock, jazz, country, blues, and R&B flow out to the oceanfront from a huge stage on the beach at 5th Street and

The Great Dismal Swamp

The **Great Dismal Swamp National Wildlife Refuge** (3100 Desert Rd., Suffolk, free) is a 112,000-acre refuge southwest of Virginia Beach. The refuge is primarily forested wetlands and is home to numerous birds and animals. It also encompasses 3,100-acre Lake Drummond, which is the largest natural lake in Virginia. One hundred miles of trails are open daily for hiking, walking, and biking (sunrise to sunset).

Although humans first occupied the swamp as much as 13,000 years ago, there was not much interest in the area until Lake Drummond was discovered by William Drummond (a governor of North Carolina) in 1665. The area was later surveyed, and the state line between Virginia and North Carolina was drawn through it in 1728. The name of the land was recorded as the Great Dismal (dismal was a common term at the time for a swamp). Shortly thereafter, George Washington visited the swamp and developed the Dismal Swamp Land Company, with designs on draining and logging parts of it. The name "great" was likely added to the swamp's name due to its large size. Logging continued in the swamp until 1976, with all parts of the swamp having been logged one or more times.

The dense forests in the swamp have traditionally been a refuge for animals, but have also been used by people for a similar reason. The swamp was at one time a haven to fleeing slaves, and as a result, the swamp was the first National Wildlife Refuge to be recognized officially as part of the Underground Railroad.

Today, more than 200 species of birds live in the refuge either permanently or seasonally. Perhaps an even more impressive fact is that 96 species of butterflies have also been recorded here. More than 47 mammals live in the refuge, including black bears, bobcats, white-tailed deer, river otters, and mink.

For more information, visit www.fws.gov/refuge or contact the park headquarters at 757/986-3705.

from stages in many parks along the water. Another favorite is the **Boardwalk Art Show and Festival** (http://virginiamoca.org) held annually for four days in mid-June. This event began in 1956 and is one of the oldest and best outdoor art shows on the East Coast. It is held on the boardwalk between 17th Street and 24th Street.

Runners won't want to miss the annual **Shamrock Marathon** (www.shamrock-marathon.com) weekend in mid-March. The Shamrock Marathon has been around since 1973 and is now a premier running event with numerous races that draw more than 24,000 participants.

SPORTS AND RECREATION

Parks and Wildlife

First Landing State Park (2500 Shore Dr., 757/412-2300, www.first-landing-state-park.org, daily 8am-dusk, $5) is the site where the first permanent English settlers landed in 1607. This 2,888-acre park offers 20 miles of hiking trails, biking, fishing, a boat ramp, and camping.

Mount Trashmore Park (310 Edwin Dr., 757/473-5237, www.vbgov.com, 7:30am-dusk, free) is a famous land-reuse park that was built on an old landfill. The 165-acre park was created by compressing multiple layers of waste and clean soil. The park includes playgrounds, picnic areas, volleyball courts, and a large skate park.

Back Bay National Wildlife Refuge (4005 Sandpiper Rd., 757/301-7329, www.fws.gov/backbay, daily during daylight hours, $5) includes approximately 9,000 acres of beach, marsh, and woods. It is a haven for many migratory birds. There is both fresh- and saltwater fishing, a canoe and kayak launch, biking, and hiking.

False Cape State Park (4001 Sandpiper Rd., 757/426-7128, www.virginiastateparks.

gov, 24 hours, $4) is an ocean-to-brackish water area that is only accessible by boat, bike, or on foot. The land trail leading in is five miles long. A tram from the Back Bay National Wildlife Refuge visitors center is also available (call for a schedule). Primitive camping is allowed.

Boat Ramps

The **Owl Creek Boat Ramp** (701 General Booth Blvd.) is a free launch facility next to the Virginia Aquarium & Marine Science Center. Other boat ramps include **First Landing State Park** (2500 Shore Dr., www.virginiastatparks.gov), **Bubba's Marina** (3323 Shore Dr., www.bubbasseafoodrestaurant.com), and **Munden Point Park** (2001 Pefley Ln., www.vbgov.com/parks).

Kayaking and Boat Tours

There are many local outfitters in the Virginia Beach area offering seasonal kayak tours, rentals, and eco-tours. **Chesapean Outdoors** (757/961-0447, www.chesapean.com) provides an exciting guided dolphin kayak tour ($60) where guests can paddle with bottlenose dolphins at the north end of Virginia Beach. They also offer guided sunset paddle tours ($55) and rentals (single kayak, one hour $20, two hours $30; tandem kayak, one hour $25, two hours $35). **Kayak Nature Tours** (757/480-1999, www.kayaknaturetours.net) also has guided dolphin kayak tours (2.5 hours, $60) and flat-water guided trips (2.5 hours, $50).

Explore the creeks near the **Virginia Aquarium & Marine Science Center** (www.virginiaaquarium.com) on a guided pontoon boat or ride along with aquarium staff on a 90-minute seasonal dolphin-watching excursion ($21). The aquarium also offers ocean collections boat trips, when a variety of sea creatures are brought on board, and winter wildlife boat trips (75 minutes, $19).

Kayaking tours are also available through **Back Bay Getaways** (757/721-4484, www.backbaygetaways.com, $35-45) and **Ocean Eagle Kayak** (757/589-1766, www.oceaneaglekayak.com, $70).

Fishing

The Virginia Beach coastline and inshore waterways are thoroughfares for many species of fish including tuna, bluefin, blue marlin, Atlantic mackerel, red drum, and flounder. Private fishing charters are available through a number of companies including **Dockside Seafood and Fishing Center** (3311 Shore Dr., 757/481-4545, www.fishingvabeach.com), **Rudee Inlet Charters** (200 Winston Salem Ave., 757/425-3400, www.rudeeinletcharters.com), **Virginia Beach Fishing Center** (200 Winston Salem Ave., 757/491-8000, www.virginiafishing.com), and **Fisherman's Wharf Marina** (524 Winston Salem Ave., 757/428-2111, www.fishermanswharfmarina.com).

There are also several fishing piers that are great for dropping a line, including the **Virginia Beach Fishing Pier** (15th Street), the **Little Island Fishing Pier** (3820 S. Sandpiper Rd., www.sandbridgepier.com), the **Lynnhaven Fishing Pier** (2350 Starfish Rd., www.lynnhavenpier.com), and the **Sea Gull Fishing Pier** at the Chesapeake Bay Bridge-Tunnel (www.cbbt.com).

Amusement Park

The **Atlantic Fun Park** (233 15th St., 757/422-0467, www.atlanticfunpark.com) has a yesteryear vibe that is nostalgic for parents and pure fun for the kiddies. The park offers thrill rides, family rides, and kiddie rides, including a 100-foot Ferris wheel. Single ride tickets ($3-5) or unlimited ride wristbands ($20-30) can be purchased.

FOOD

American

Firebrew Bar & Grill (1253 Nimmo Pkwy., Suite 117, 757/689-2800, www.fire-brew.com, Mon.-Thurs. 11am-10pm, Fri. and Sat. 11am-11pm, Sun. 11am-9pm) is a casual bar and grill with a few twists. Most menu items (flatbread, steak, tacos, etc.) are prepared on an open-flame fire deck, and the restaurant proudly states that they do not use microwaves or fryers. Their extensive bar includes local craft brews and a self-service wine station.

If you're looking for a good place to grab a sandwich, stop in **Taste Unlimited** (36th St. and Pacific Ave., 757/422-3399, www.tasteunlimited.com, Mon.-Sat. 10am-6pm, Sun. 11am-5pm, $6-11). This pleasant sandwich shop and specialty food store, a block from the beach, has ample seating, good variety, and a friendly atmosphere. They also sell wine, cheese, and other gourmet snacks, and at times there's even a little farmers market outside.

Seafood

★ **One Fish Two Fish** (2109 W. Great Neck Rd., 757/496-4350, www.onefish-twofish.com, dinner daily from 5pm, $22-30) is an elegant but fun seafood and steak restaurant on Long Creek (in the Pier House building at the Long Bay Pointe Marina). It is comfortably away from the hubbub of the strip, and diners can enjoy a panoramic view of the water or be entertained by the activity in the exhibition kitchen. There's also an open patio. Seafood combinations are expertly and imaginatively prepared, and they offer an excellent selection of wine.

Catch 31 (3001 Atlantic Ave., 757/213-3474, www.catch31.com, Mon.-Fri. 6am-2am, Sat.-Sun. 7am-2am, $25-43) is inside the Hilton Virginia Beach Oceanfront and is one of the finest restaurants along the main strip. They are known for offering at least 15 types of fresh fish, and their signature dish is the seafood towers that include crab legs, mussels, lobster, and shrimp. The restaurant's high ceilings, ocean-blue walls, and indoor/outdoor bar add to the ambience. If the weather is nice, dine outside on their beachfront terrace. They serve breakfast, lunch, and dinner.

A restaurant popular with Virginia Beach residents is **Rockafeller's** (308 Mediterranean Ave., 757/442-5654, www.rockafellers.com, Mon.-Sat. 11am-10pm, Sun. 10am-10pm, $16-33). This dependable local favorite offers seafood, steaks, pasta, and salads in a large three-story home on Rudee Inlet. Double-decker porches provide lovely seating, or you can dine inside. There's a bar and raw bar and nice views from indoors as well.

Lynnhaven Fish House (2350 Starfish Rd., 757/481-0003, www.lynnhavenfishhouse.net, Sun.-Thurs. 11:30am-9pm, Fri.-Sat. 11:30am-9:30pm, $11-33) serves up fresh surf dishes with a nice view of the oceanfront. They have a large fish selection on their dinner menu and creative lunch entrées such as seafood omelets and quiche.

Waterman's Surfside Grille (5th St. and Atlantic Ave., 757/428-3644, www.watermans.com, lunch daily 11am-4pm, dinner daily 4pm-10pm, $10-25) is one of the few freestanding restaurants left on the strip that isn't connected to a hotel. It offers a lively atmosphere, good seafood, and outstanding cocktails.

ACCOMMODATIONS

$100-200

The **Belvedere Beach Resort** (3603 Atlantic Ave., 800/425-0612, www.belvederebeachresort.com, $175-200) is a privately owned hotel on the oceanfront on the northern end of Virginia Beach. The light-filled, wood-paneled rooms offer private balconies with views of the beach. The hotel has adult-size bicycles for guest use and direct access to the boardwalk. Rooms are quiet, and the staff is very friendly and helpful. The **Wave Trolley** stops in front of the hotel for easy access to many places on the beachfront. This is not a luxurious resort, but a very pleasant, comfortable choice in a fantastic location. The hotel is open seasonally, normally April through the beginning of October. Minimum stays may be required. Coffeepots are available upon request.

$200-300

The **Capes Hotel** (2001 Atlantic Ave., 757/428-5421, www.capeshotel.com, $192-277, closed Oct.-Mar.) is a pleasant oceanfront hotel on the boardwalk. It has an indoor pool with a view of the ocean and nicely kept grounds. The hotel is convenient to all the beach attractions. The 59 oceanfront rooms are cozy rather than large, but all are comfortable with an airy feel and good views. The service is also very dependable. There is a small café on-site with an oceanfront patio. This is not a luxurious resort, but it doesn't attempt to be; it's a good value in a great location, with a friendly staff.

The **Atrium Resort** (315 21st St., 757/491-1400, www.vsaresorts.com, $250-330) is a comfortable hotel a few blocks from the boardwalk. They offer 90 suites with well-appointed kitchenettes, an open-air lobby, and a small indoor pool. The rooms are well-kept, with updated televisions and comfortable beds. The hotel is owned by VSA Resorts, along with two others in Virginia Beach (Ocean Sands Resort and the Ocean Key Resort). They offer room rentals and vacation ownership (similar to a timeshare). Grocery delivery is available upon request. Orders can be placed online and delivered to your room upon arrival.

Over $300

★ **The Cavalier Hotel** (4200 Atlantic Ave., www.cavalierhotel.com, $299 and up during off-season, $499 and up in peak season) is a historic hotel that opened in 1927. A Virginia Beach icon and a National Register of Historic Places property, the grand hotel was built on a hill overlooking the ocean and has welcomed seven U.S. presidents, celebrities such as Frank Sinatra, Judy Garland, and Bette Davis, and international dignitaries. It was also used as a naval training center during World War II. The hotel underwent a $70 million renovation from 2015 to 2017, at which point it became a member of Marriott International's Autograph Collection. Today the hotel portrays the bygone age of grand hotels as it sits majestically above the hubbub of activity on the oceanfront. The Cavalier Hotel offers 85 guest rooms and suites, three restaurants, a spa, a bourbon distillery and tasting room, a museum, ballroom, meeting space, poolside vistas and loggias, and a fitness center. At the time of publication, the hotel was closed for renovations, but is expected to reopen in April 2017.

The imposing 21-story **Hilton Virginia Beach Oceanfront** (3001 Atlantic Ave., 757/213-3000, www.hiltonvb.com, $329-599) offers oceanfront luxury with amenities such as a rooftop infinity pool, an indoor pool, the Sky Bar, a fully equipped fitness center, and

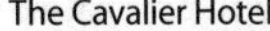
The Cavalier Hotel

bicycle rentals. There are 289 modern rooms and suites, outfitted with a beach décor and offering a choice of city or ocean views. There are several on-site restaurants and convenient parking ($10 for self-park and $16 for valet per day).

Bed-and-Breakfasts and Inns

The **Barclay Cottage Bed and Breakfast** (400 16th St., 757/422-1956, www.barclaycottage.com, $115-189) is a beautiful B&B offering five comfortable guest rooms. Three rooms have private bathrooms, and two others share bath facilities. Each room is individually decorated with its own colors and theme (such as nautical or floral). The white, two-story, porch-wrapped cottage (complete with rocking chairs) is within walking distance of many attractions and a few blocks from the beach.

The **Country Villa Bed and Breakfast** (2252 Indian River Rd., 757/721-3844, www.countryvillainn.com, $299-379) is a charming B&B on four acres in Virginia Beach. They offer two private guest rooms and personalized in-room spa services. Guests are served three-course gourmet breakfasts with outstanding personalized service. The inn is eight minutes driving from Sandbridge Beach and will provide beach chairs, towels, coolers, and umbrellas. There is also an outdoor hot tub and swimming pool.

House and Condo Rentals

There are several local real estate offices in Virginia Beach that offer rentals for a week or longer. **Sandbridge Realty** (800/933-4800, www.sandbridge.com) is in southern Virginia Beach and offers a property search feature on its website, as does **Siebert Realty** (877/422-2200, www.siebert-realty.com), which is also in southern Virginia Beach.

CAMPING

First Landing State Park (2500 Shore Dr., 757/412-2300, www.first-landing-state-park.org, $24-32) on the north end of Virginia Beach offers 200-plus beach campsites near the Chesapeake Bay. There are also 20 cabins for rent ($94-139).

INFORMATION AND SERVICES

For additional information on Virginia Beach, visit www.virginiabeach.com or stop by the **Visitor Information Center** (2100 Parks Ave., 757/437-4882, daily 9am-5pm). There are also two kiosks run by the Visitor Information Center that are available from May to September; they are on the Boardwalk at 17th Street and on Atlantic Avenue at 24th Street.

GETTING THERE

Most people arrive in Virginia Beach by car. I-64 connects with the Virginia Beach-Norfolk Expressway (I-264) which leads to the oceanfront at Virginia Beach.

The **Norfolk International Airport** (ORF, 2200 Norview Ave., Norfolk, www.norfolkairport.com) is approximately 17 miles from Virginia Beach. Daily flights are available through multiple commercial carriers.

Rail service does not run to Virginia Beach, but **Amtrak** (800/872-7245, www.amtrak.com) serves Newport News with connecting bus service to 19th Street and Pacific Avenue in Virginia Beach. Reservations are required. Bus service is also available to Virginia Beach on **Greyhound** (971 Virginia Beach Blvd., 757/422-2998, www.greyhound.com).

GETTING AROUND

There are plenty of paid parking lots in Virginia Beach. The cost per day ranges about $5-8. Municipal parking lots are located at 4th Street, 9th Street, 19th Street, 25th Street, and 31st Street. **Hampton Roads Transit** (www.gohrt.com, $1.75-3.50) operates about a dozen bus routes in Virginia Beach.

Virginia's Eastern Shore

Visiting Virginia's Eastern Shore can be a bit like stepping back in time. The long, narrow, flat peninsula that separates the Chesapeake Bay from the Atlantic Ocean has a feel that's very different from the rest of the state. The pace is more relaxed, the people take time to chat, and much of the cuisine centers on extraordinary seafood fished right out the back door.

Traveling from the Virginia Beach area to the Eastern Shore requires passage over and through one of the great marvels of the East Coast. The **Chesapeake Bay Bridge-Tunnel** (www.cbbt.com) spanning the mouth of the Chesapeake Bay is an engineering masterpiece. The four-lane, 20-mile-long bridge-and-tunnel system is a toll route and part of Route 13. It takes vehicles over a series of bridges and through two-mile-long tunnels that travel under the shipping channels. Five-acre artificial islands are located at each end of the two tunnels, and a fishing pier and restaurant/gift shop were built on one.

Upon arrival on the Eastern Shore, you are greeted by endless acres of marsh, water, and wildlife refuge areas. Agriculture and fishing are the primary sources of revenue on the peninsula, and tourism in the towns provides a nice supplement.

There are a handful of charming towns that dot the coastline on both bodies of water, and most have roots prior to the Civil War. In fact, many beautiful 19th-century homes have been refurbished, as have the churches, schools, and public buildings.

The first town on the southern end of the Eastern Shore is Cape Charles, and the northernmost is Chincoteague Island. Bus transportation runs between the two on the **Star Transit** (www.vatransit.org, Mon.-Fri.).

CAPE CHARLES

Cape Charles is the southernmost town on Virginia's Eastern Shore, 10 miles from the Chesapeake Bay Bridge-Tunnel. The town was founded in 1884 as the southern terminus of the New York, Philadelphia, & Norfolk Railroad. It was also a popular steamship port for vessels transporting freight and passengers across the Chesapeake Bay to Norfolk.

Today, Cape Charles is primarily a vacation town. It is not large, nor is it particularly well known, but this is part of the charm. It offers a quiet historic district, sandy beaches, golfing, boating, and other outdoor recreation.

Sights

The **Historic District** (757/331-3259) in Cape Charles is approximately seven square blocks and boasts one of the largest groups of turn-of-the-20th-century buildings on the East Coast. The area offers a pleasant atmosphere of shops and eateries near the Chesapeake Bay waterfront. Route 184 runs right into the historic district and ends at the beach.

Cape Charles Beach (Bay Avenue, www.capecharles.org) has a pleasant, uncrowded atmosphere and wonderful sunsets over the Chesapeake Bay. The beach is clean, family oriented, and free to the public. The water is generally shallow with little to no waves.

The **Cape Charles Museum and Welcome Center** (814 Randolph Ave., 757/331-1008, www.smallmuseum.org, mid-Apr.-Nov. Mon.-Fri. 10am-2pm, Sat. 10am-5pm, Sun. 1pm-5pm, free, donations appreciated) is a nice place to begin your visit to Cape Charles. It is housed in an old powerhouse and has a large generator embedded in the floor. Visitors can view boat models, pictures, and decoys as they learn about the history of Cape Charles.

Kiptopeke State Park (3540 Kiptopeke Dr., 757/331-2267, www.dcr.virginia.gov, daily 6am-10pm, $5) is approximately 10 miles south of the Historic District in Cape Charles. It encompasses a half-mile of sandy beach open to the public during the summer. There are no lifeguards on duty, so swimming is at your own risk. There are also hiking trails, a fishing pier, a boat ramp, and a full-service campground. The park is known for its robust bird population. Many bird studies are conducted here by the U.S. Fish and Wildlife Service. Some of the birds encountered in the park include hawks, kestrels, and ospreys.

Sports and Recreation

SouthEast Expeditions (239 Mason Ave., 757/331-2680, www.southeastexpeditions.com, starting at $45) offers kayaking tours in Cape Charles. Trips of different lengths are available, and paddlers of all experience levels are welcome.

Golfers will enjoy the beautiful atmosphere and two challenging courses designed by Arnold Palmer and Jack Nicklaus at the **Bay Creek Golf Club** (1 Clubhouse Way, 757/331-8620, www.baycreekgolfclub.com, $70-115).

A big annual event in the Cape Charles area is the **Eastern Shore Birding & Wildlife Festival** (www.esbirdingfestival.com). The area is one of the most important East Coast migration stops for millions of birds each year, and festivalgoers can observe the spectacle firsthand in early October.

Food

AMERICAN

★ **The Oyster Farm Seafood Eatery** (500 Marina Village Circle, 757/331-8660, www.kingscreekmarina.com, Sun. 11:30am-8pm, Mon.-Thurs. 11:30am-9pm, Fri.-Sat. 11:30am-10pm, $12-38) is the top choice for food and ambience in Cape Charles. The modern beachfront building offers a trendy "water-to-table" eating experience in a comfortable waterfront dining room. The food is delicious, with creative seafood items, entrees from the land, burgers, and tacos. The scene is semi-upscale with a lively clientele. This is a great place to bring the family or relax with friends for an unrushed and tasty meal. There is a beautiful waterfront patio and lawn games for entertainment.

The Bay Creek Resort's **Coach House Tavern** (1 Clubhouse Way, 757/331-8631, www.baycreekresort.com, Sun.-Thurs. 7am-8pm, Fri.-Sat. 7am-9pm, winter hours Sun. 7:30am-8pm, Mon. 8am-8pm, Tues.-Thurs. 8am-5pm, Fri. 8am-9pm, Sat. 7:30am-9pm, $8-15) is at the golf clubhouse and overlooks the golf course. The rustic ambience of the beautifully appointed building is due in part to the use of reclaimed wood and bricks from a farmhouse that once stood on the property. The restaurant offers traditional pub fare with exquisite soups and sandwiches. There is patio seating, and the atmosphere is upscale and inviting.

For a quick and casual breakfast, burger, or seafood meal, stop in **Sting Ray's Restaurant** (26507 Lankford Hwy., 757/331-1541, www.cape-center.com, weekdays 6:30am-8pm, weekends 6:30am-8:30pm, $5-18). This restaurant shares a roof with a gas station and offers a full breakfast menu featuring homemade biscuits and omelets. The lunch menu includes hot dogs, burgers, and barbecue while the dinner menu offers a large variety of local seafood. Order at the counter, and the server will bring the food to your table.

Accommodations

$100-200

The **Fig Street Inn** (711 Tazewell Ave., 757/331-3133, www.figstreetinn.com, $160-200) is a year-round boutique bed-and-breakfast offering four comfortable guest rooms with private bathrooms. Each room has memory foam mattresses, lush towels, flat-screen televisions, wireless Internet, and a jetted tub or gas fireplace. The house has been renovated and is decorated with antiques. The beach and shops are within walking distance.

The **King's Creek Inn** (3018 Bowden Landing, 757/678-6355, www.kingscreekinn.com, $150-210) is a beautiful historic plantation home that has offered guest accommodations since 1746. The home has been fully renovated and has four guest rooms with private bathrooms. The inn sits on 2.5 acres and overlooks Kings Creek (with access to the

Chesapeake Bay). A private dock is available for guest use. The cozy salon offers a great ambience for breakfast, or guests can enjoy meals on their balconies. The home has a long and exciting history and some interesting legends that include stories of the Underground Railroad and a possible resident ghost.

OVER $300

★ **Bay Creek Resort** (3335 Stone Rd., 757/331-8742, www.baycreek.net, $400-900) is the premier resort community in Cape Charles. The resort offers rentals of vacation homes, villas, and condos in a well-landscaped waterfront and golf community on more than 1,700 acres. Golf packages are available, and golf condos offer three-bedroom, two-bath units with garages and a balcony or patio. Single-family homes are also available overlooking the golf course. Those who prefer a water view will enjoy the Marina District. Rental options include single-family villas with views of the Chesapeake Bay or the Kings Creek Marina. One- and two-bedroom suites are also available. Nightly and longer-term stays can be accommodated. Visitors can stay in luxurious accommodations or dock their own boat in the large, modern marina. Two delicious restaurants are on the property, one at the marina and the other on the golf course. The staff is extremely helpful and friendly.

Camping

Camping is available at **Kiptopeke State Park** (3540 Kiptopeke Dr., 757/331-2267, www.dcr.virginia.gov). The park has tent sites ($24), rental RVs ($120), a yurt ($120), and a six-bedroom lodge ($434). There is a two-night minimum stay required at the lodge during the peak summer season and a seven-night minimum at the yurt and rental RVs. There are sites for those driving their own RVs as well. All facilities except the yurt allow pets ($10 fee nightly). There is at $5 reservation fee.

Information

For additional details on Cape Charles, contact the **Northampton County Chamber of Commerce** (757/678-0010, www.northamptoncountychamber.com).

ONANCOCK

Thirty-eight miles north of Cape Charles is the picturesque town of Onancock. The town sits on the shore of Onancock Creek and has a deepwater harbor. Cute 19th-century homes with gingerbread trim line the streets, and visitors can shop, visit art galleries, partake in water sports, or just relax and enjoy the tranquil atmosphere. The town was founded in 1680 by English explorers, but its name is derived from the Native American word *auwannaku,* which means "foggy place."

Onancock was one of the colonies' 12 original "Royal Ports." Its deepwater access to the Chesapeake Bay made it appealing for ships, and its port provided safety during storms. For more than 250 years, Onancock was the trade center on the Eastern Shore and was closely connected (in terms of commerce) to Norfolk and Baltimore.

The homes along Market Street belonged to sea captains who worked on the Chesapeake Bay. These homes harken back to a time during the steamboat era when Onancock was a stop on the way to bustling Baltimore.

Today, Onancock retains a small working harbor and offers a pretty port of call for recreational boaters. It has modern boats in its harbor, and outdoor enthusiasts paddle colorful kayaks around its waters. Its wharf is also the jumping-off point for a small ferry that goes to and from Tangier Island. The town is a pleasant place to spend a day or two, and about 1,500 people make it their permanent home. There are free parking areas located around town and by the wharf.

Sights

The key sight in Onancock is **Ker Place** (69 Market St., 757/787-8012, www.shorehistory.org, Mar.-Dec. Tues.-Sat. 11am-3pm, admission by donation), one of the finest federal-style manors on the Eastern Shore. John Shepherd Ker was the owner and a renaissance man of his time. He was a successful merchant, lawyer, banker, and farmer. His estate was built in 1799 and originally comprised 1,500 acres. The home is now restored to its original appearance and features period furniture, detailed plasterwork, and rich colors throughout. The headquarters for the **Eastern Shore of Virginia Historical Society** are in the house, and the second floor contains a museum, the society's library, and archives space. A smaller, newer section of the house serves as a welcome center with a museum shop. Visitors can view Eastern Shore artwork throughout the home and rotating exhibits are displayed regularly. Guided tours are given on the hour; reservations should be made by calling ahead.

Sports and Recreation

A public boat ramp at the wharf has a launch for canoes and kayaks ($5 launch fee). **SouthEast Expeditions** (2 King St., 757/354-4386, www.southeastexpeditions.com) offers kayak rentals ($20-55) and tours ($45-125) from the wharf. Guided kayak trips are also offered by two local travel writers and kayak guides through **Burnham Guides** (www.burnhamink.com). Visitors arriving by boat can dock at the Town Marina but should call the **harbormaster** (757/787-7911) for reservations.

Free self-guided walking tours are a fun way to learn about the town. Pick up a tour brochure at the visitors center (located on the wharf) and learn about Onancock's historic homes and gardens.

Food

Mallards Restaurant (2 Market St., 757/787-8558, www.mallardsllc.com, Sun.-Thurs. 11:30am-9pm, Fri.-Sat 11:30am-10pm, $8-25) is on the wharf. The menu includes fresh seafood, ribs, duck, pasta, and many more delicious entrées. Don't be surprised if chef Johnny Mo comes out of the kitchen with his guitar to play a few tunes. He's a local legend.

The **Blarney Stone Pub** (10 North St., 757/302-0300, www.blarneystonepubonancock.com, Tues.-Thurs. 11am-9pm, Fri.-Sat. 11am-10pm, Sun. 11am-7pm, closed Mon.$8-24) is an Irish pub three blocks from the wharf serving traditional pub fare. It has indoor and outdoor seating and frequent live entertainment.

the Yellow Duck Bakery

If you're making the drive between Onancock and Cape Charles and need a sugary snack, drive through Exmore on Business Route 13 and stop at the **Yellow Duck Bakery** (3312 Main St., Exmore, 757/442-5909, www.yellowduckcafe.com, Mon.-Wed. 7am-3pm, Thurs.-Fri. 7am-5pm, Sat. 8am-3pm, under $10). They offer amazing sweet potato biscuits, shortbread "Yellow Duck" cookies, other types of cookies, and delicious muffins. You can drive through town and pick up Route 13 again on the other side.

Accommodations

★ The Charlotte Hotel and Restaurant (7 North St., 757/787-7400, www.

The Charlotte Hotel and Restaurant

thecharlottehotel.com, $130-180) is a boutique hotel with eight guest rooms. The owners take great pride in this lovely hotel and even made some of the furnishings by hand. There is an award-winning restaurant on-site that can seat more than 30 people, and the American cuisine served is made from products supplied by local watermen and farmers.

The Inn at Onancock (30 North St., 757/787-7711, www.innatonancock.com, $185-205) is a luxurious bed-and-breakfast with five guest rooms, each offering stylish modern bathrooms and feather top beds. Full-service breakfasts are served in their dining room, or guests can choose to eat on the porch in nice weather. A wine hour is also hosted every evening. Soda and water are available to guests all day.

The **Colonial Manor Inn** (84 Market St., 757/787-2564, www.colonialmanorinn.com, $109-139) offers six spacious rooms decorated with period furnishings. The home was built in 1882 and is the oldest operating inn on the Eastern Shore in Virginia. A delicious full breakfast is served daily.

The Inn & Garden Café (145 Market St., 757/787-8850, www.theinnandgardencafe.com, $110-130) has four guest rooms and was built in 1880. The on-site restaurant serves American food and guests can choose to eat in the cozy dining room (with a fireplace) or in an all-season gazebo with broad garden views.

Information and Services

Additional information on Onancock can be found at www.onancock.org. There is also a small, seasonal visitors center at the wharf.

★ TANGIER ISLAND

Tangier Island is a small 3.5-mile-long island, 12 miles off the coast of Virginia in the middle of the Chesapeake Bay. It was first named as part of a group of small islands called the Russell Isles in 1608 by Captain John Smith when he sailed upon it during an exploration of the Chesapeake Bay. At the time the island was the fishing and hunting area of the Pocomoke Indians, but it was allegedly purchased from them in 1666 for the sum of two overcoats. Settlers were drawn to the island for the abundant oysters and crabs.

The unofficial history of the island states that John Crockett first settled here with his eight sons in 1686. This appears to be accurate since most of the 600 people who live on Tangier Island today are descendants of the Crockett family and the majority of the tombstones on the island bear the Crockett name. The island was occupied by British troops during the Revolutionary War, and it has also survived four major epidemics, with the most devastating being the Asian cholera epidemic of 1866. So many people died in such a short period of time that family members buried their dead in their front yards. Cement crypts can still be seen in many yards on the island.

There is a tiny airstrip, used primarily for the transport of supplies, but most visitors come by ferry (without their cars). There are no true roads on the island and golf carts and bicycles are used to get around.

Tangier Island is only five feet above sea level, and it is known as the "soft-shell crab capital" for its delectable local crabs. It is also known for the unique dialect the people on Tangier Island speak. They converse in an old form of English and have many euphemisms that are unfamiliar to visitors. It is thought that the island's isolation played a role in preserving the language that was spoken throughout the Tidewater area generations ago.

Tangier Island can be toured in a couple of hours. The ferry schedules are such that they allow enough time to cover the sights on the island, grab lunch, and head back the same day. If you enjoy the slow pace of the island, limited overnight accommodations are available, but be aware there is not much, if any, nightlife and the island is "dry." Addresses aren't frequently used when describing how to get to a place on Tangier Island. Basically, you can see the whole island from any given point. The ferry dock drops visitors off in the heart of the small commercial area, and if you can't see the establishment you are looking for immediately, take a short walk or ride down the main path and you'll find it. The island residents are also very friendly, so if in doubt, just ask someone walking by.

There are very limited services on Tangier Island. The island hasn't changed much in the last century, and it looks much as it did 30 or 40 years ago. There is a post office and one school that all local children attend (most go on to college elsewhere in the state). There is spotty cell service on the island, but some establishments do offer wireless Internet. More important, there are no emergency medical facilities on the island; however, there is a 24-hour clinic, **The Tangier Island Health Foundation** (www.tangierclinic.org), where a physician's assistant is available.

Many establishments do not accept credit cards, so it's best to bring cash and checks. There are no banks or ATMs on the island.

Sights

TANGIER HISTORY MUSEUM AND INTERPRETIVE CENTER

The **Tangier History Museum and Interpretive Center** (16215 Main Ridge, 757/891-2374, www.tangierisland-va.com/water_trail_brochure, mid-May-mid-Oct. daily 10am-5pm, other times by appointment, $3) is a small museum down the street from the ferry dock. It is worth a visit and the small fee to learn about life on Tangier Island and its interesting heritage. View island artifacts and a rare five-layered painting of the island that illustrates the erosion it has experienced since 1866. Visitors can also learn about the many sayings that are common on the island but completely foreign to those on the mainland, such as "He's adrift," which means, "He's a hunk," and the term "snapjack" which means "firecracker." A handful of kayaks are available behind the museum for visitors to borrow (for free) for exploring the surrounding waterways.

TANGIER BEACH

At the south end of Tangier Island is the nice, sandy public **Tangier Beach.** Rent a golf cart from **Four Brothers** and head out of the village on the winding paved path and over the canal bridge. The beach is at the very end of the path on the left side of the island. There's a small parking area for carts and a sandy path to the beach. There is no lifeguard on duty so swimming is at your own risk. Bring plenty of water with you since there are also no services at the beach. Water machines and soda machines can be found along the golf cart paths on the island if you need to pick up beverages on your way. There is also a very small grocery store near the ferry dock with a few bare essentials, but it's best to bring provisions with you.

Shopping

There are two small gift shops on Tangier Island: **Wanda's Gifts** (757/891-2230) and **Sandy's Gifts** (757/891-2367). Both are on the main path not far from the ferry dock. They sell souvenir T-shirts and trinkets.

Sports and Recreation

Kayaking the waterways of Tangier Island is a wonderful way to explore the marshes. Kayaks can be borrowed from the Tangier History Museum, and a listing of water trail routes can be found at www.tangierisland-va.com. The marshes also offer a terrific opportunity for bird-watching. Black skimmers, great blue herons, common terns, double-crested cormorants, Forster's terns, clapper rails, and ospreys are just some of the birds living on the island.

Since there are no roads on Tangier—only paved paths—the place is very conducive to casual biking. Bikes can be brought over on the ferry on weekdays only (call ahead to schedule) and a fleet of older-model cruising bikes can be rented from **Four Brothers** (www.fourbrotherscrabhouse.com) on the island. Since the island is only 3.5 miles long, it is easy to cover the entire length by bicycle in a short time.

For a unique local experience, take a **Crab Shanty Tour** (757/891-2269, ask for Ookire). This 30- to 45-minute tour is led by a Chesapeake Bay waterman. Other island tours are available outside the ferry dock. Tour guides wait in golf carts for guests when the ferries arrive and offer guided tours in their vehicles.

Food

Visitors arriving by ferry will likely see the **Waterfront** (757/891-2248, mid-May-Nov. 1 Mon.-Sat. 10am-4pm, Sun. 1pm-4pm, under $15) as they depart the ferry. This small, seasonal restaurant is right by the dock and offers a variety of casual food including burgers, fried seafood baskets, and crab cakes.

Four Brothers Crab House & Ice Cream Deck (757/891-2999, www.fourbrotherscrabhouse.com, lunch and dinner daily) will likely be the next establishment you see when you take the short path from the dock to the main path in the small commercial area. While this is the place to rent golf carts, crabbing equipment, and bicycles, they also serve a casual menu of seafood and sandwiches on their deck, along with 60 soft-serve ice-cream flavors. Four Brothers also offers free wireless Internet; however, they do not accept credit cards. Another fun place for ice cream is **Spanky's Place** just down the path.

A short walk from the ferry terminal is **Lorraine's Restaurant** (757/891-2225, lunch Mon.-Sat. 10am-2pm, dinner Mon.-Fri. 5pm-10pm, Sat. 5pm-11pm, Sun. noon-5pm, under $15). Take a right on Main Street, and the restaurant is on the right. They serve snacks, lunch, and dinner. Like all the restaurants on the island, local, fresh seafood is the specialty, and this place is known for its soft-shell crabs. Lorraine's also delivers to any of the inns on the island.

Across from Lorraine's, **Fisherman's Corner Restaurant** (757/891-2900, www.fishermanscornerrestaurant.com, daily 11am-7pm, $15-26) has a wide menu with steaks and seafood. Sandwiches and a kid's menu are also available. It's no surprise that fresh crab is a highlight, and their crab cakes contain large, succulent blue crab meat with little filler.

The best-known and oldest restaurant on the island is ★ **Hilda Crockett's Chesapeake House** (757/891-2331, breakfast daily 7am-9am, lunch/dinner daily 11:30am-5pm, breakfast $10, lunch/dinner $22). They offer an all-you-can-eat breakfast with selections such as scrambled eggs, fried bread, and potatoes. They are most famous, however, for the family-style lunch and dinner. For $22, guests can enjoy unlimited homemade crab cakes, clam fritters, ham, potato salad, coleslaw, pickled beets, applesauce, green beans, corn pudding, and rolls. The family-style setting means you may share a table with other guests.

Accommodations

It is difficult to find more friendly innkeepers than those at the **Bay View Inn** (757/891-2396, www.tangierisland.net, $125-150). This family-run bed-and-breakfast offers seven motel-style rooms, two cottages, and two guest rooms in the main house. A scrumptious homemade breakfast is included with your stay. The inn is on the west side of the island and has lovely views of the Chesapeake Bay and decks to watch the sunset from. The inn is open year-round. They do not take credit cards.

Hilda Crockett's Chesapeake House (757/891-2331, www.tangierisland-va.com, $100-155) is the oldest operating bed-and-breakfast on the island and was established in 1939 as a boardinghouse. It is in the small commercial area not far from the ferry dock. There are eight guest rooms in two separate buildings.

Those arriving by private boat can rent a slip at the **James Parks Marina** (16070 Parks Marina Ln., 757/891-2581). They offer 25 slips and showers, but no pump-outs. Docking fees start at $25.

Information and Services

For additional information, visit www.tangier-island.com.

Getting There

Getting to Tangier Island is half the fun. There are three seasonal ferries that travel to and from the island May-October. The first is the ***Chesapeake Breeze*** (804/453-2628, www.tangiercruise.com, $27 round-trip for same-day service, $40 for overnight), a 150-person passenger boat that leaves at 10am daily from Reedville for the 1.5-hour trip. The ship heads back to Reedville at 2:15pm. The second is the ***Steven Thomas*** (410/968-2338, www.tangierislandcruises.com, $27 round-trip for same-day service, $35 for overnight), a 90-foot, 300-passenger boat that leaves from Crisfield, Maryland, daily (May 15-Oct. 15) at 12:30pm and arrives on Tangier at 1:45pm. The return voyage departs Tangier at 4pm. The third ferry is the ***Joyce Marie II*** (757/891-2505, www.tangierferry.com, Tues.-Sun., $25 round-trip for same-day service, $30 for overnight), a small fiberglass lobster boat that holds 25 people and runs from Onancock, Virginia, to Tangier Island. The trip takes 65 minutes. Ferry service is offered twice a day with departures from Tangier Island at 7:30am and 3:30pm and departures from Onancock at 10am and 5pm.

Getting Around

There are no cars on Tangier Island. The best way to get around is by renting a golf cart from

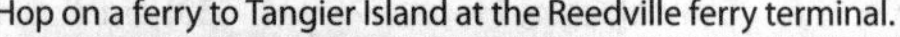
Hop on a ferry to Tangier Island at the Reedville ferry terminal.

Four Brothers Crab House & Ice Cream Deck ($50 for 24 hours, $25 for a half day) or a bicycle ($10 a day). The owners will make you feel welcome immediately, and Tommy is sure to put you in a good mood for your ride around town.

CHINCOTEAGUE ISLAND

Chincoteague Island is 7 miles long and just 1.5 miles wide. It is nestled between the Eastern Shore and Assateague Island. Chincoteague is famous for its herd of wild ponies, and many children and adults first became familiar with the island through the popular book *Misty of Chincoteague,* which was published in 1947. Many local residents made appearances in the movie that followed.

The island is in the far northeastern region of the Eastern Shore in Virginia and has a full-time population of 4,300 residents. It attracts more than one million visitors each year to enjoy the pretty town and to visit the Chincoteague National Wildlife Refuge and the beautiful beach on nearby Assateague Island.

Chincoteague is a working fishing village with world-famous oyster beds and clam shoals. It is also a popular destination for bird-watching. During the summer, the town is bustling with tourists, but in the off-season things slow down considerably and many establishments close.

The town of Chincoteague is accessed via Route 175. A scenic causeway spans the water and marsh and ends on Main Street, which runs along the western shore of the island. Maddox Boulevard meets Main Street and runs east to the visitors center and Chincoteague National Wildlife Refuge.

Sights

★ CHINCOTEAGUE NATIONAL WILDLIFE REFUGE

The **Chincoteague National Wildlife Refuge** (8231 Beach Rd., 757/336-6122, www.fws.gov, May-Sept. daily 5am-10pm, Mar.-Apr. and Oct. daily 6am-8pm, Nov.-Feb. daily 6am-6pm, $8) is a 14,000-acre refuge consisting of beach, dunes, marsh, and maritime forest on the Virginia end of Assateague Island and was established in 1943. The area is a thriving habitat for many species of waterfowl, shorebirds, songbirds, and wading birds. The popular herd of wild ponies that Chincoteague is known for also lives in the refuge.

Assateague Island itself extends south from Ocean City, Maryland, to just south

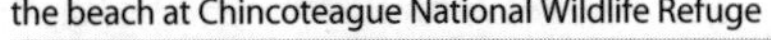

the beach at Chincoteague National Wildlife Refuge

of Chincoteague Island. It is a thin strip of beautiful sand beach, approximately 37 miles long. The entire beach is a National Seashore, and the Virginia side is where the Chincoteague National Wildlife Refuge is located. The refuge entrance is at the end of Maddox Boulevard. A visitors center is situated near the beach, and is where information and trail brochures can be obtained. One of the main attractions is the **Assateague Island Lighthouse,** which visitors can hike to. The lighthouse is painted with red and white stripes and is 142 feet tall. It was completed in 1867 and is still operational. There are also 15 miles of woodland trails for hiking and biking (the wild ponies can often be seen from the trails).

The road ends at the Atlantic Ocean where there's a large parking area for beachgoers. Parts of the beach are open to swimming, surfing, clamming, and crabbing.

To get to the refuge, travel east on Route 175 onto Chincoteague Island and continue straight at the traffic light onto Maddox Boulevard. Follow the signs to the refuge.

OYSTER AND MARITIME MUSEUM

The only oyster museum in the country is in Chincoteague. The **Oyster and Maritime Museum** (7125 Maddox Blvd., 757/336-6117, Tues.-Sun. 11am-5pm, $3) is on Maddox Boulevard just prior to the entrance to the National Wildlife Refuge. The museum is dedicated to sharing the history of the island and details of the oyster trade and the local seafood industry. One of the most noteworthy exhibits in the museum is the Fresnel lens that was part of the Assateague Island Lighthouse. This lens helped guide ships as far out to sea as 23 miles for nearly 96 years.

CHINCOTEAGUE PONY CENTRE

For those wishing to see the local ponies up-close, the **Chincoteague Pony Centre** (6417 Carriage Dr., 757/336-2776, www.chincoteague.com/ponycentre, Mon.-Sat. during summer) has a herd of ponies from the island in their stable and a field facility for visitors to enjoy. The center offers pony rides, riding lessons, shows, day camps, and a large gift shop.

a foal at the Chincoteague Pony Centre

Entertainment and Events

The premier event on Chincoteague Island is the annual **Wild Pony Swim** (www.chincoteaguechamber.com) that takes place each year in late July. At "slack tide," usually in the morning, the herd of wild ponies is made to swim across the Assateague Channel on the east side of Chincoteague Island (those ponies that are not strong enough or are too small to make the swim are ferried across on barges). The first foal to complete the swim is named "King" or "Queen" Neptune and is given away in a raffle later that day. After the swim, the ponies are given a short rest and are then paraded to the carnival grounds on Main Street. The annual Pony Penning and Auction is then held, in which some foals and yearlings are auctioned off. Benefits from the auction go to support the local fire and ambulance services. The remaining herd then swims back across the channel.

Another big event in town is the **Chincoteague Island Oyster Festival** (8128 Beebe Rd., www.chincoteagueoyster-festival.com, $45). This well-known event has been happening for more than 40 years and offers all you can eat oysters prepared every which way imaginable. It is held in early October, and tickets are available online.

Sports and Recreation

Kayaks can be launched on the beach on Assateague Island, but not in areas patrolled by lifeguards. Kayak tours are available through **Assateague Explorer** (757/336-5956, www.assateagueexplorer.com, $49-$59). **Snug Harbor Resort** (7536 East Side Rd., 757/336-6176, www.chincoteagueaccommodations.com) also offers tours ($49) and rents kayaks (single kayak half day $38, full day $48, tandem kayak half day $48, full day $58).

Jus' Bikes (6527 Maddox Blvd., 757/336-6700, www.jus-bikes.com) rents bicycles ($4 per hour or $12 per day), scooters ($15 per hour or $45 per day), surreys ($20 per hour or $75 per day), tandems ($5 per hour or $25 per day), three-wheelers ($3 per hour or $18 per day), and low-speed vehicles ($45-$199).

Fishing enthusiasts can have all their needs met at several fishing and tackle establishments including **Capt Bob's Marina** (2477 Main St., 757/336-6654, www.captbobsmarina.net) and **Capt Steves Bait & Tackle** (6527 Maddox Blvd., 757/336-0569, www.stevesbaitandtackle.com).

For an interactive cruise, contact **Captain Barry's Back Bay Cruises** (6262 Main St., 757/336-6508, www.captainbarry.net). They offer hands-on, interactive "Sea Life Expeditions" ($40) and "Champagne Sunset Cruises" ($40) leaving from the Chincoteague Inn Restaurant at 6262 Main Street.

Food

AMERICAN

If you like a casual beach environment, eating outside, and lounging in hammocks, then **Woody's Beach Barbeque and Eatery** (6700 Maddox Blvd, Mon.-Sat. 11am-8pm, Sun. 1pm-8pm, $6-20) is worth checking out. They offer delightful barbecue and crab sandwiches, yummy sweet potato fries, and peach tea. The restaurant is dog friendly and there are outdoor games for the kids.

For a quick bite to go, stop at the ★ **Sea Star Café** (6429 Maddox Blvd., 757/336-5442, http://www.seastarcafeci.com, Thurs.-Mon. 11am-6pm, daily July and Aug., $5-10). They have yummy sandwiches and wraps to go (order at the window; be sure to know what you're ordering before going up when there's a crowd). Everything is fresh and made to order, and they have a large vegetarian menu. The café sits back off the road a little and offers a few picnic tables but no restrooms. The menu is handwritten on a chalkboard and items contain whatever is fresh that day.

SEAFOOD

Seafood is the mainstay on Chincoteague Island, and the local oysters and crabs are especially delicious. Many restaurants are only open seasonally; so visiting in the off-season can pose a bit of a challenge in finding open eateries.

AJ's on the Creek (6585 Maddox Blvd., 757/336-5888, www.ajsonthecreek.com, Mar.-Dec. Mon.-Thurs. 11:30am-8:30pm, Fri.-Sat. 11:30am-9:30pm, $14-30) is the longest-operating restaurant on the island under one management. They are one of a few upscale restaurants on the island, and they serve delicious seafood menu items such as crab imperial, shellfish bouillabaisse, crab cakes, and grilled scallops. The restaurant is owned by two spunky sisters originally from Pittsburgh.

Don't let the plain exterior of **Bill's Seafood Restaurant** (4040 Main St., 757/336-5831, www.billsseafoodrestaurant.com, daily from 6am for breakfast, lunch, and dinner, $12-27) fool you. They offer delightful seafood entrées such as lobster tail, scallops, oysters, and crab cakes, as well as pasta selections. This is one of the few restaurants in town that is open all year.

TREATS

The **Island Creamery** (6243 Maddox Blvd., 757/336-6236, www.islandcreamery.net, year-round Sun.-Thurs. 11am-9pm, Fri.-Sat. 11am-10pm) is "the" place to go for ice cream. The place is large for an ice-cream joint and offers friendly smiles, samples, and dozens of flavors. It's a popular stop, so the line can be long and parking difficult, but it's worth it.

Accommodations

$100-200

If you're looking for a charming bed-and-breakfast, spend a night at ★ **Miss Molly's Inn** (4141 Main St., 757/336-6686, www.missmollys-inn.com, $110-200) on Main Street. This beautiful Victorian B&B offers seven delightful guest rooms and five porches with rocking chairs. The home overlooks the bay and has a pretty English garden. Marguerite Henry stayed at the bed-and-breakfast when she wrote the famous book *Misty of Chincoteague,* and the room she stayed in has since been named after her. A full breakfast is included. The sister inn to Miss Molly's is the **Island Manor House Bed and Breakfast** (4160 Main St., 757/336-5436, www.islandmanor.com, $165-210), which offers eight guest rooms and plenty of common areas. This house was built in the popular Maryland-T style, which borrows from both federal and Georgian architecture. Refreshments are available 24 hours a day. They provide a gourmet breakfast each day and easy are within access to Main Street attractions.

The **Dove Winds** (7023 Maddox Blvd., 757/336-5667, www.dovewinds.com, $89-160) is a nice, clean hotel offering mini townhouses for rent with two-bedroom guest accommodations. The units aren't fancy, but they are comfortable and offer more privacy than a typical hotel. Each includes a kitchen, living room, and two bathrooms. The Dove Winds also offers two- and three-bedroom cottages. An indoor pool and hot tub are on-site.

$200-300

The ★ **Hampton Inn & Suites Chincoteague Waterfront** (4179 Main St., 757/336-1616, www.hamptoninnchincoteague.com, $239-312) is known as one of the premier Hampton Inns in the country. Its bayfront location offers beautiful views, and it is close to many shops and restaurants in town. The rooms are well appointed with light wood furniture, and everything is oriented toward

Island Creamery

the water. The landscaping is appealing, the breakfasts are better than standard chain fare, and there is a boat dock next to the hotel. Amenities include a large indoor heated pool, a fitness center, laundry facilities, a waterfront veranda, and wireless Internet. The staff and owner are also very friendly. Ask for a room on the third floor with a balcony looking over the water and don't be surprised if you spot dolphins swimming by.

Camping

Camping is available on Chincoteague Island at several campgrounds. The **Maddox Family Campground** (6742 Maddox Blvd., 757/336-3111, www.chincoteague.com, $40-$50) has 550 campsites and 361 utility hookups March-November. **Tom's Cove Campground** (8128 Beebe Rd., 757/336-6498, www.tomscovepark.com, $33-53) has waterfront campsites near the pony swim, three fishing piers, and a pool. They are open March-November. **Pine Grove Campground** (5283 Deep Hole Rd., 757/336-5200, www.pinegrovecampground.com, $33-43) offers campsites on 37 acres April-November. There are six ponds on the property.

Information and Services

For additional information on Chincoteague Island, visit www.chincoteaguechamber.com or stop by the **Chincoteague Island Visitor's Center** (6733 Maddox Blvd., 757/336-6161, Mon.-Sat. 9am-4:30pm).

Getting There

Visitors should arrive on Chincoteague Island by car; the surrounding waters are shallow and difficult to navigate by boat. The closest airport is **Wicomico Regional Airport** (410/548-4827), which is 52 miles away in Salisbury, Maryland.

Shenandoah and Northwestern Virginia

Bounded to the east by the Blue Ridge Mountains and to the west by the Appalachians, Northwestern Virginia and the Shenandoah Valley make up one of the prettiest regions in the nation.

From the charming town of Winchester, with its historic homes, apple orchards, and inviting pedestrian area, south to Staunton, one of the oldest cities in the Shenandoah Valley, this area is filled with history and charm. Civil War battlefields, forts, and other military-related structures dot the landscape, and ghosts of fallen soldiers are said to haunt many of the towns.

Nature fans can get their fill of outdoor bliss with stunning mountain vistas, intricate caverns, rolling foothills, and lush forests. Virginia's pride and joy, Shenandoah National Park, makes up a large part of the region, covering more than 200,000 acres. Its highest point is 4,051 feet. The wide and picturesque Shenandoah River winds through the park, nearly 40 percent of which is protected wilderness. This long, narrow park is home to Skyline Drive, one of the most scenic stretches of road in the nation.

The town of Luray is another prime destination. It is home to the world-famous Luray Caverns, the largest caverns in the eastern United States. This landmark has drawn millions of visitors since it was discovered in 1878. It comprises vast chambers up to 10 stories tall that contain natural columns, stalactites, stalagmites, mudflows, and pools.

Other towns in this region include Harrisonburg, home of James Madison University, and the quaint town of New Market, which is the site of the New Market Battlefield, a 300-acre historical park.

PLANNING YOUR TIME

Shenandoah National Park and northwestern Virginia can be covered by car in a long weekend, but nature lovers will want to allot more time to truly explore the region. The park itself deserves a couple of days to fully appreciate by cruising Skyline Drive, taking

Previous: Shenandoah National Park; New Market Battlefield State Historical Park. **Above:** pipe organ in the Luray Caverns.

Look for ★ to find recommended sights, activities, dining, and lodging.

Highlights

★ **Museum of the Shenandoah Valley:** This impressive complex in Winchester focuses on the art, history, and culture of the Shenandoah Valley (page 232).

★ **Skyline Drive:** This stunning 105-mile road takes travelers from vista to vista through beautiful Shenandoah National Park (page 237).

★ **Old Rag Mountain:** Visitors to Shenandoah National Park can enjoy this challenging and rewarding nine-mile hike (page 238).

★ **Luray Caverns:** Enter a subterranean world of mystery that took more than four million centuries to create (page 246).

★ **New Market Battlefield State Historical Park:** This 300-acre park was the site of a historic 1864 battle that forced Union troops out of the Shenandoah Valley (page 251).

★ **Grand Caverns Regional Park:** Grand Caverns is the oldest continuously operating "show" cave in the country (page 253).

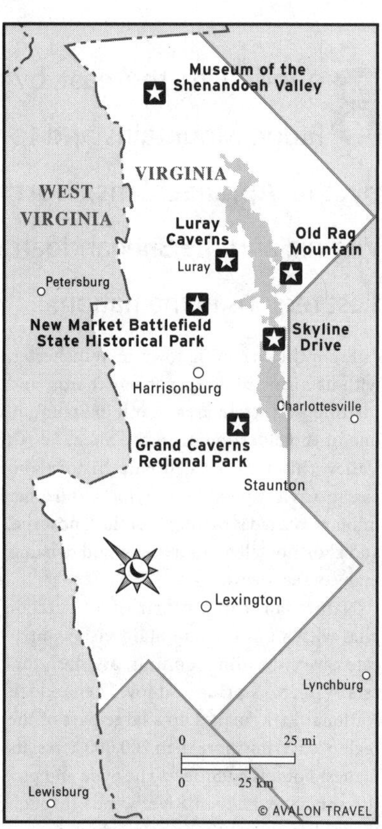

a hike or two, and staying at one of the park lodges. If you plan to visit the park to see the fall foliage, keep in mind that Skyline Drive can be very crowded and you may have to wait in a line of traffic to access it. Those wishing to relax in the Hot Springs area may want to plan on a day or two just for that, especially if you book a room at The Omni Homestead Resort. The cities along I-81—Winchester, New Market, Harrisonburg, and Staunton—can be visited in a few hours each, but you should plan on incorporating a bit more time into your schedule for Luray, especially if you plan to go down into the famous Luray Caverns, which can take at least two hours to tour if you also visit the aboveground attractions.

Winchester

Lying in the northwest corner of the state, Winchester is one of the loveliest towns in Virginia. Founded in 1744, Winchester is also the oldest Virginia city west of the Blue Ridge Mountains. It is the county seat of Frederick County and has a population of around 26,000. It is known mostly for its Civil War history (General Stonewall Jackson had his headquarters here during the winter of 1861-1862), its apple blossoms, acres of orchards, and its charming downtown area with many historic buildings and tree-lined streets.

Although industry has developed in Winchester during the past decades with employers such as Rubbermaid, Kraft, and American Woodmark, many people make the daily commute into Washington DC or the Northern Virginia area and then enjoy their little slice of heaven when they get home.

The downtown area has a very pleasant mall lined with shops and restaurants, with a pedestrian section located on Loudoun Street between Piccadilly and Cork. Winchester is also home to Shenandoah University.

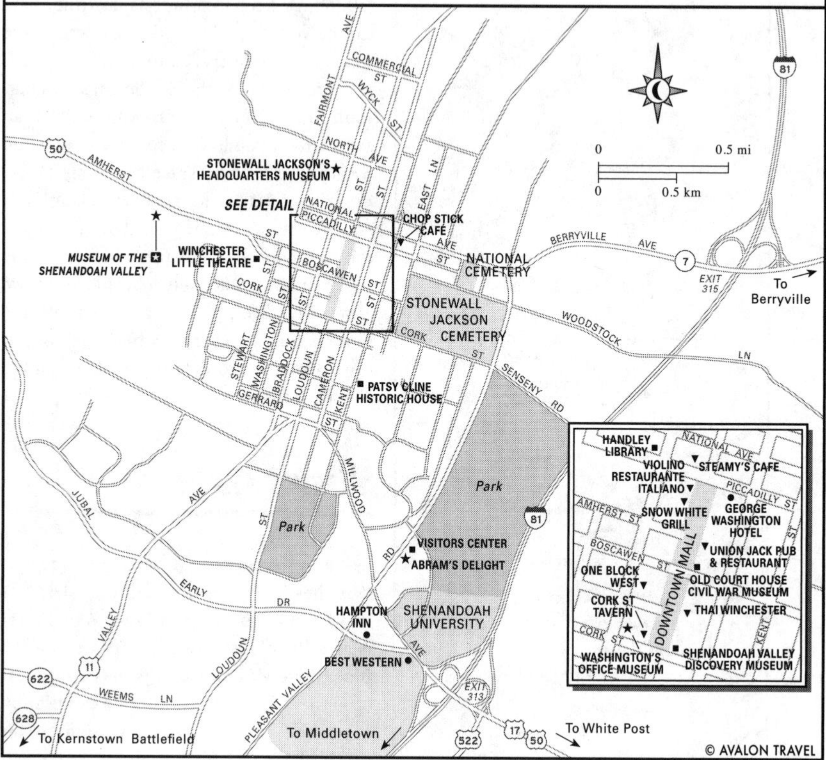

SIGHTS

★ Museum of the Shenandoah Valley

The **Museum of the Shenandoah Valley** (901 Amherst St., 540/662-1473, www.shenandoahmuseum.org, Tues.-Sun. 10am-4pm, $10) is a complex that focuses on the art, history, and culture of the Shenandoah Valley and also features historical information on Winchester. The well-landscaped site includes multiple collections on display in three venues. The first is the 18th-century Glen Burnie House, which exhibits paintings, furniture, and decorative items. The second is six acres of gardens, and the third is a 50,000-square-foot museum made up of four galleries.

The museum itself is reason enough to visit the complex. This is an outstanding facility with comprehensive and well-thought-out exhibits. The **Shenandoah Valley Gallery** is where the history of the valley comes to life through multimedia presentations and dioramas. The **Founders Gallery** features rotating exhibits of fine art and antiques. The **R. Lee Taylor Miniatures Gallery** displays the work of more than 70 artists through fully furnished miniature houses and rooms. The fourth gallery is the **Changing Exhibition Gallery,** where a new exhibit is featured every 3-6 months.

The historic house and gardens welcome the public April to October, but the museum is open all year. The hours of operation are the same year-round. The complex can be explored in a few hours. There is a café and gift store on-site.

Stonewall Jackson's Headquarters Museum

Stonewall Jackson's Headquarters Museum (415 N. Braddock St., 540/667-5505, www.winchesterhistory.org, Mon.-Sat. 10am-4pm, Sun. noon-4pm, $5) is nestled in a neighborhood on Braddock Street. It is a lovely little Hudson River gothic revival-style home that was used by General Jackson over the winter of 1861-1862. Jackson occupied two rooms in the home, including an office on the lower level. The house features a large collection of authentic Jackson belongings, as well as personal items that belonged to his staff. His office remains much as it looked when he used it. Allow about an hour to tour the home.

George Washington Office Museum

From September 1755 to December 1756, George Washington used a small log building in Winchester as an office while he supervised the construction of Fort Loudoun on the north side of town. Today, that office is the middle room of the **George Washington Office Museum** (32 W. Cork and Braddock Sts., 540/662-4412, www.winchesterhistory.org, Mon.-Sat. 10am-4pm, Sun. noon-4pm, $5). Visitors can see some of Washington's personal items on display, along with surveying equipment and a model of Winchester circa 1755. A cannon that General Edward Braddock left in Alexandria is also displayed on the museum grounds.

Site of Historic Fort Loudoun

During 1755 and 1756, George Washington oversaw the construction of Fort Loudoun from his small office in Winchester. The log fort was considered the "most formidable fort on Virginia's colonial frontier" and was the command center for a series of fortifications. Washington is said to have brought his personal blacksmith from Mount Vernon to craft the ironwork at the fort, which housed 14 mounted cannons on half an acre. The fort held barracks for 450 men and had its own well, which remains there still. Today, the fort is no longer standing, but the **Site of Historic Fort Loudoun** (419 N. Loudoun St., 540/678-4041, daily 8am-5pm, free) can be visited during daylight hours. A marker between the sidewalk and a fenced yard recounts the fort's history.

Old Court House Civil War Museum

A nice little Civil War exhibit is the **Old Court House Civil War Museum** (20 N. Loudoun St., 540/542-1145, www.civilwarmuseum.org, Mon.-Sat. 10am-5pm, Sun. 1pm-5pm, closed Mon.-Tues. Nov.-Apr., $5) on the downtown mall. The courthouse was designed in the Georgian style and was used by both armies during the war. It served as a hospital, prison, and barracks. One of the unique features of the house is the original graffiti from both Union and Confederate soldiers that is still visible. The museum displays more than 3,000 Civil War items.

Patsy Cline Historic House

Patsy Cline fans will enjoy the **Patsy Cline Historic House** (608 S. Kent St., 540/662-5555, www.celebratingpatsycline.org, Apr.-Oct. Tues.-Sat. 10am-4pm, Sun. 1pm-4pm, winter weekend hours through Dec., $8). Cline lived in the little house with her family between 1948 and 1953. The house is furnished with some Cline family personal items and is decorated as it was when the singer lived there. The admission price includes a 45-minute guided tour of the house.

Shenandoah Valley Discovery Museum

The **Shenandoah Valley Discovery Museum** (19 W. Cork St., 540/722-2020, www.discoverymuseum.net, Tues.-Sat. 9am-5pm, Sun. 1pm-5pm, $8) offers many hands-on exhibits for children. This little museum right near the downtown mall is a fun place to go on a rainy day and is particularly interesting for children under 10. Some activities include rock climbing,

Winchester's Sweetheart

It is hard to make your way around Winchester without bumping into a photo or poster of **Patsy Cline.** Patsy was born as Virginia Patterson Hensley in Winchester Memorial Hospital on September 8, 1932. Her family moved around Virginia many times during her early years, but in 1948, after her parents separated, she returned to Winchester with her mother and siblings. "Ginny," as she was known, dropped out of school to help support the family and went to work in a local poultry plant. She later held a number of different jobs around town and began singing in the evenings and on weekends for additional income.

Over the next few years, Ginny's singing career grew as she won contests, was featured on local radio, and sang with several local bands. In 1952, Ginny was hired by a bandleader named Bill Peer to sing on a regional music circuit. He gave her the stage name Patsy.

In 1953 she married Gerald E. Cline and became Patsy Cline. Her big break came in 1954, when she signed a contract with a record company and produced her first titles in Nashville. Her first songs included "Hidin' Out," "Honky-Tonk Merry-Go-Round," "Turn the Cards Slowly," and "A Church." Cline's first single was released in July 1955. Her most recognizable song, a cover of Willie Nelson's "Crazy," was released in 1961.

Cline died in 1963 and is buried in Winchester.

touching real dinosaur bones, working in a mock emergency room, stepping into a kaleidoscope, and playing in a sandbox.

Abram's Delight

The oldest home in Winchester, built in the mid-1700s, is **Abram's Delight** (1340 S. Pleasant Valley Rd., 540/662-6519, www.winchesterhistory.org, Apr.-Oct. Mon.-Sat. 10am-4pm, Sun. noon-4pm, $5). The stone house was home to five generations of the Hollingsworth family, spanning 200 years. Tours give visitors a great look into life between the colonial period and the Civil War. The antiques furnishing the home include rope beds that had to be tightened each night by crank (which some believe to be the origin of the phrase, "Sleep tight"). The friendly ghost of Abraham Hollingsworth is said to haunt the house. Combo tickets to the George Washington Office Museum, Stonewall Jackson's Headquarters Museum, and Abram's Delight can be purchased at any of the three museums for $10.

RECREATION AND EVENTS

If you visit Winchester during apple season, you'll be missing out if you don't sample the local produce. Stop in at a "pick-your-own" orchard before leaving town. A good place to pick and sample these delights is **Marker-Miller Orchards** (3035 Cedar Creek Grade, www.markermillerorchards.com). Pick-your-own apple time begins September 1.

The premier event in Winchester is the spring **Shenandoah Apple Blossom Festival** (www.thebloom.com). This ten-day event takes place in April/May and features music, parades, parties, celebrities, and a lot of tradition. The first festival was held back in 1924. There is even a 10k race and the coronation of the Apple Blossom Queen. Many local businesses close on the first Friday of Apple Blossom weekend.

Local theater fans will thoroughly enjoy the **Winchester Little Theatre** (315 W. Boscawen St., 540/662-3331, www.wltonline.org), which produces several shows throughout the year including dramas, mysteries, comedies, and even musicals. The cast and staging are professional, and it is clear everyone involved is very passionate about their performance. The stage itself is set in an old train station, which adds to the fun.

FOOD

American

One block west of the downtown mall is

the appropriately named **One Block West** (25 S. Indian Alley, 540/662-1455, www.oneblockwest.com, Tues.-Sat. lunch 11am-2pm, dinner Tues.-Thurs. 5pm-8:30pm, Fri.-Sat. 5pm-9pm, $21-36), which serves creative American cuisine and is known for using very fresh ingredients and local products in its dishes. The chef/owner is very hands-on and speaks with guests, takes reservations, and does much of the cooking. The menu changes daily based on what is available in local markets, generally split between seafood and meat. Sample items include trout, bison, crab cakes, and shepherd's pie. They also offer a seven-course chef's tasting menu ("menu of the moment") for $75.

Grab a mini-burger and dine where Patsy Cline did at the **Snow White Grill** (159 N Loudoun St., 540/662-5955, Mon.-Wed. 11am-6pm, Thurs. 10am-7pm, Fri.-Sat. 10am-2am, closed Sun. except during the summer, under $10). This historic burger joint opened in 1949 and hasn't changed much since. Their famous mini-burger is a small ground beef patty with mustard, a pickle, and grilled onions. It's served on a steamed bun just like Patsy had it when she dined here "daily." They also serve sandwiches and ice cream. Grab a seat at the counter (there are no tables) and enjoy the nostalgia. This is the complete 1950s experience—and probably one of the few restaurants in the country with no bathroom.

For a beer and a burger and cozy ambience, try **Union Jack Pub and Restaurant** (101 N Loudoun St., 540/722-2055, www.theunionjackpub.com, Sun.-Thurs. 11am-midnight, Fri. and Sat., 11am-2am, $9-25). This multilevel restaurant serves good pub food, including gluten-free and vegetarian options. The long wooden bar is a focal point and the friendly staff helps to create the warm atmosphere.

Good coffee and delicious handmade bagels can be found at **Steamy's Cafe** (38 E. Piccadilly St., www.thecoffeemademedoit.com, Mon.-Fri. 7am-2pm, Sat.-Sun. 8am-3pm, under $10).

A good lunch stop is **Bonnie Blue Southern Market and Bakery** (334 W. Boscawen St., 540/686-7490, www.bonnieblue.us, Mon.-Thurs. 8am-6pm, Fri. 8am-8pm, Sat. 8am-5pm, Sun. 10am-4pm, $9-15), housed in a former gas station at the corner of Boscawen Street and Amherst Street. They offer tasty sandwich selections and also carry locally made goods and excellent homemade bakery items. There is only outdoor seating, but it's a fun place to stop on a sunny day. This is more of a market than a restaurant, but they have good food.

Italian

★ **Violino Restaurant** (181 N. Loudoun St., 540/667-8006, www.violinorestaurant.com, lunch Mon.-Fri. 11:30am-2pm, Sat. noon-2pm, dinner Mon.-Sat. 5pm-9pm, $16-32) is known for its delicious northern Italian dishes and hearty sauces. The staff is friendly, professional, and very good at suggesting wine pairings. The food is downright superb, and it is also consistent. The menu includes many specialty dishes such as lobster *pansotti gondoliera* (Mediterranean lobster ravioli sautéed in a lemon parmesan sauce) and *galletto al limone* (grilled Cornish hen marinated and pressed with rosemary, garlic, and lemon). They also offer a wonderful selection of authentic Italian desserts. The restaurant is on the north end of the downtown mall.

Thai

A great little place to grab some Thai food is the **Chop Stick Café** (207 N. Kent St., 540/450-8691, www.chopstickcafe.biz, Mon.-Thurs.11am-9pm, Fri. 11am-10pm, Sat. noon-10pm, Sun. noon-8pm, $9-14). They serve traditional Thai food, sushi, and even a few burgers. The place is a little cramped, but don't let that fool you: It's friendly, slightly funky on the inside, and even has good music. They also specialize in home-baked pies—unusual for a Thai place, but they're delicious.

ACCOMMODATIONS

$100-200

Comfortable lodging choices include the **Holiday Inn SE Historic Gateway** (333 Front Royal Pike, www.ihg.com, $94-113), just off I-81. This friendly hotel was built in 2008 and has 130 nicely appointed rooms with comfortable beds. There is an indoor pool, fitness center, Internet, and an on-site restaurant. Another good option is the **Country Inn & Suites Winchester** (141 Kernstown Commons Blvd., 540/869-7657, www.countryinns.com, $112-220). This pet-friendly hotel (additional $20) offers an indoor pool, fitness room, free wireless Internet, and a complimentary breakfast. The hotel is a 10-minute drive from the historic downtown area. A third comparable option is the **Candlewood Suites Winchester** (1135 Millwood Pike, 540/667-8323, www.candlewoodsuites.com, $93-112). This extended-stay hotel is near I-81 and offers 70 guest suites with fully equipped kitchens, 32-inch TVs, workspace, and free high-speed Internet. There are also free laundry facilities, a convenience store, and a 24-hour fitness center on-site.

$200-300

The most historic and luxurious hotel in town is ★ **The George Washington Hotel** (103 E. Piccadilly St., 540/678-4700, www.wyndham.com, $209-349). This downtown treasure was built in 1924 and features 90 guest rooms and a unique indoor swimming pool designed to look like a Roman bath complete with columns and statues. The soaring ceilings, beautiful marble floors, antique front desk (the original), and traditionally decorated rooms help make the atmosphere inviting and elegant. The staff is exceptional, and guests are treated with the utmost respect. The hotel restaurant serves breakfast, lunch, and dinner, and there is a bar in the lobby. There is also a spa, fitness room, business center, and high-speed Internet access. The hotel is within walking distance of most downtown attractions and was originally built near the B&O Railroad depot to accommodate train travelers. Famous guests have included Lucille Ball and Jack Dempsey.

The George Washington Hotel

INFORMATION AND SERVICES

For additional information on Winchester, contact the **Winchester-Frederick County Convention and Visitors Bureau** (1400 S. Pleasant Valley Rd., 540/542-1326, www.visitwinchesterva.com).

GETTING THERE AND AROUND

Winchester is 75 miles northwest of Washington DC off Route 50 and I-81. The local **Winchester Transit** (540/667-1815, www.winchesterva.gov, Mon.-Fri. 6am-8pm, Sat. 9am-5pm, $1) provides bus service throughout the city during the day.

Shenandoah National Park

Seventy-five miles west of Washington DC is 200,000 acres of protected parkland known as **Shenandoah National Park** (540/999-3500, www.nps.gov/shen, $20 per vehicle or $10 per person, admission good for 7 days). The park is a popular escape for people living in the densely populated areas of Northern Virginia and Maryland, and for good reason: It offers superb outdoor recreation, stunning mountain scenery, and the lovely Shenandoah River.

The park stretches 105 miles from north to south and has four primary entrances: from Front Royal (via I-66 and U.S. 340), at Thornton Gap (via U.S. 211), at Swift Run Gap (via U.S. 33), and at Rockfish Gap (via I-64 and U.S. 250).

Shenandoah National Park is a prime location for hiking. There are more than 500 miles of trails here, mostly through lush forests. Trail maps are available at entrance stations and visitors centers. The park is also a great place to view wildlife. Some of the resident animals include coyote, black bear, bald eagles, and the timber rattlesnake. Dogs are welcome in the park as long as they are leashed.

★ SKYLINE DRIVE

One of the most beautiful stretches of road in the East, **Skyline Drive** (540/999-3500, www.nps.gov/shen, $20 per vehicle) is the most popular attraction in Shenandoah National Park. This 105-mile road takes travelers from vista to vista along a stunning byway that runs the entire length of the park from north to south. It is the only public road that goes through the park. Access to Skyline Drive is from four entry points: from Front Royal at the northern terminus (near I-66 and U.S. 340), at Thornton Gap (U.S. 211), at Swift Run Gap (U.S. 33), and near Waynesboro at Rockfish Gap at I-64 and U.S. 250 (at the southern terminus). Skyline Drive ends where the **Blue Ridge Parkway** begins. It takes approximately three hours to drive the entire road.

The most popular time to visit Skyline Drive

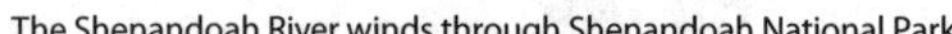
The Shenandoah River winds through Shenandoah National Park.

Skyline Drive

is during the fall foliage. Virginia is known for having one of the most spectacular leaf displays in the country, and this route showcases the best of the best. Unfortunately, this can often mean long lines leading into the park when the colors are at peak. So expect to have a lot of company, especially on a weekend. Inclement weather can also close the road at any time during the year. Call or visit the park's website for a status if the forecast calls for fog, snow, or heavy rain. The road is also closed at night during deer-hunting season (mid-November through early January). Hikers are allowed into the park on foot even if the road is closed.

RVs, camping trailers, and horse trailers are allowed on Skyline Drive, but will need to use a low gear. There is also a low tunnel (Marys Rock Tunnel) south of the entrance at Thornton Gap off U.S. 211 that is 12 feet 8 inches high. The speed limit on Skyline Drive is 35 miles an hour. This is partly because of the curves and steep inclines and partly to protect wildlife in the area.

Mileposts demarcate the entire length of Skyline Drive on the west side of the road starting with 0.0 in Front Royal. All park maps use these as location references.

There are 75 overlooks along the route. Visitors can see the beautiful Shenandoah Valley to the west and the piedmont to the east. Wildflowers and other stunning blooms keep the area colorful throughout the warmer months.

HIKING

★ Old Rag Mountain

The most popular hike in Shenandoah National Park is **Old Rag Mountain** (www.nps.gov/shen). It is also the most challenging and dangerous. A day at Old Rag is an experience to remember, as summiting the peak requires a vigorous uphill ascent and many rough areas of scrambling near the top.

The hike is a 9-mile circuit that can take up to seven or eight hours. The route at the top changes periodically but always involves a hefty scramble requiring good upper body strength. Children and shorter adults may need assistance to get through some sections.

Several search-and-rescue missions are required each year at Old Rag, but this shouldn't deter you from the hike. It is a fun way to spend the day and the views from the top are very rewarding. There is a safety

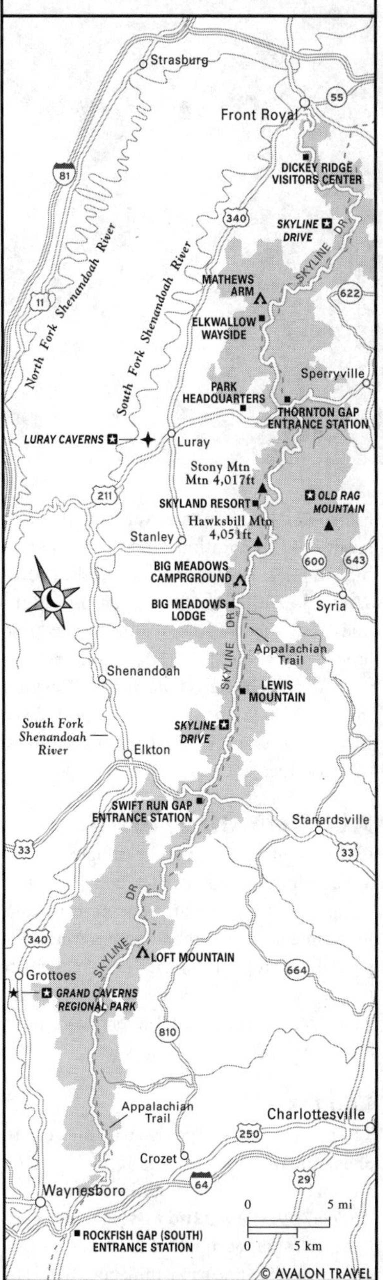

video on the park website that should be viewed prior to your hike. Bring food and water (at least two quarts per person) with you. Arrive early in the morning to ensure you can get a parking space; this is a very popular hike and can be crowded on nice days, especially on weekends.

Most people arrive at Old Rag Mountain from the eastern park boundary near Sperryville. From the intersection of U.S. 211 and U.S. 522 in Sperryville, take Route 522 south for 0.8 mile. Turn right on Route 231 and go eight miles. Turn right on Route 601. Continue three miles, follow the signs to the parking lot. Parking can be tough on weekends. Hikers must use the designated parking area at the Old Rag Fee Station and then walk to the trailhead; the small parking lot at the trailhead is not open for public parking. This is not a pet-friendly hike, and pets are not allowed on parts of the trail. A valid Shenandoah National Park entrance pass is required.

White Oak Canyon

At milepost 42.6 on Skyline Drive, just south of Skyland Resort, is the parking lot and trailhead for the popular **White Oak Canyon** hike (www.nps.gov/shen). This moderate hike offers one of the premier waterfall views in the park and treats hikers to spectacular scenery as they walk down a steep gorge past boulders, pools, and six waterfalls (35-85 feet in height). This hike is steep in sections (there is an elevation gain of 1,200 feet), but the trail is well used and maintained. It can also be very crowded in peak season. Allow four hours for this 4.8-mile up-and-back hike.

Dark Hollow Falls

A scenic, family-friendly hike near Skyline Drive is the 1.5-mile round-trip route to **Dark Hollow Falls.** The trail begins just north of Big Meadows at mile 50.7. The trail follows the Hogcamp Branch stream out of the Big Meadows spring to the falls. The hike to the 70-foot waterfall is downhill, which means it is uphill on the way back. The trail

hiking on Old Rag Mountain

is especially pretty in the spring when the mountain laurel along the path blooms a vibrant pink. The trail is shaded by the tree canopy, keeping it relatively cool in the summer.

FOOD

There are two park-operated dining facilities in Shenandoah National Park. The first is the **Pollock Dining Room** (dinner entrées $13-25) at Skyland Resort. They serve breakfast, lunch, and dinner and offer regional cuisine (such as rainbow trout and beef tenderloin). Be sure to try the Mile-high Blackberry Ice Cream Pie. The **Mountain Taproom** is also at Skyland Resort and has family-friendly entertainment and adult drinks. Visitors can also purchase boxed lunches to go. Just ask the hostess for a "picnic to go."

The second dining facility is the **Spottswood Dining Room** (dinner entrées $13-23) at Big Meadows Lodge. They are open for breakfast, lunch, and dinner and serve regional cuisine such as roasted turkey and steak. The **New Market Taproom** is also on-site with live music and specialty drinks.

In addition to the two sit-down restaurants, the park operates three **Wayside Food Stops** along Skyline Drive. **Elkwallow Wayside** (milepost 24.1, open mid-Apr.-Oct.) has carryout food in addition to groceries, camping supplies, and gasoline. **Big Meadows Wayside** (milepost 51.2, open mid-Mar.-mid-Nov.) offers full-service meals (breakfast, lunch, and dinner), groceries, camping supplies, and gasoline. **Loft Mountain Wayside** (milepost 79.5, open May-Oct.) provides a snack counter, groceries, camping supplies, and gasoline.

ACCOMMODATIONS

Park-operated lodges and campgrounds in Shenandoah National Park can provide a unique base for exploration. Reservations for prime seasons such as summer and especially during fall foliage (mid-September to mid-October) should be made well in advance. Many places accept reservations up to a year in advance.

Lodges

There are three park-run lodges in Shenandoah National Park. Information on all can be found at www.goshenandoah.com (877/847-1919). **Skyland Resort** (open Apr.-Nov., $90-445) occupies 36 acres at the highest point on Skyline Drive (milepost 41.7). The resort sits at an elevation of 3,680 feet and has incredible views of the Shenandoah Valley. It offers 179 rooms, multiunit lodges, rustic cabins, and modern suites for rent in 28 buildings. Skyland Resort is not luxurious; there are no phones or wireless Internet access in the rooms. It is geared toward the enjoyment of the surrounding nature.

Big Meadows Lodge (open mid-May-Oct., $115-255) is near the center of the park at milepost 51.2. This is the largest developed area of the park, and it is named after a beautiful large meadow near the lodge where deer come to graze. The exterior of the main lodge is made of stones cut from Massanutten Mountain back in 1939, while the interior structure was constructed from chestnut trees (now extinct in the area).

The main lodge at Big Meadows has 29 guest rooms. There is a full-service dining room offering breakfast, lunch, and dinner, a taproom with light fare and nightly entertainment, and a gift shop. Five cabins and six multiunit buildings are also near the lodge.

Big Meadows is close to the Shenandoah River and the Shenandoah Valley. There are no phones or wireless access in the lodge rooms, but free wireless Internet is available in the Great Room of the main building.

Lewis Mountain (open Apr.-mid-Nov., $124-126) offers cabins for rent in a quiet wooded setting near milepost 57.5. Cabins have electricity, private bathrooms, heat, towels, linens, and an outdoor grill pit. There are no phones or wireless access in the cabins. The Shenandoah River and the town of Luray are nearby.

Camping

Most of Shenandoah National Park is open to backcountry camping (a free permit is required). In addition, there are four park-operated campgrounds with a variety of amenities (877/444-6777, www.goshenandoah.com) that are open from spring to fall. They are located at milepost 22.1 (**Mathews Arm Campground,** mid-May-Oct., $15), milepost 51.2 (**Big Meadows Campground,** late Apr.-Dec., $20), milepost 57.5 (**Lewis Mountain Campground,** May-Nov., $15), and milepost 79.5 (**Loft Mountain Campground,** mid-May-Oct., $15). Mathews Arm Campground has approximately 178 sites (tent, generator-free, and group sites), restrooms, water, and a trash and recycle center. Big Meadows Campground has more than 200 sites (tent, generator-free, and group sites), restrooms, showers, and a trash and recycle center. Lewis Mountain Campground has approximately 30 tent sites, restrooms, a camp store, and a trash and recycle center. Loft Mountain Campground has more than 200 sites (tent, generator-free, and group sites), restrooms, showers, and a trash and recycle center. Reservations are taken (and advised) at all the campgrounds except Lewis Mountain Campground, which only operates on a first-come, first-served basis.

INFORMATION AND SERVICES

There are two visitors centers in Shenandoah National Park. **Dickey Ridge Visitor Center** (milepost 4.6 on Skyline Drive, 540/999-3500, open on weekends Apr.-mid-May 9am-5pm and daily mid-May-Nov. 9am-5pm) has an information desk, restrooms, an orientation movie, maps, permits, first aid, and publications. **Harry F. Byrd, Sr. Visitor Center** (milepost 51 on Skyline Drive, 540/999-3500, open on weekends Apr.-mid-May 9am-5pm and daily mid-May-Nov. 9am-5pm) has an information desk, restrooms, publications, maps, permits, and first aid.

Front Royal

The northern gateway to the popular **Skyline Drive** in Shenandoah National Park is **Front Royal** in Warren County. The town has a population of around 14,000.

The Shenandoah River runs through Front Royal, offering opportunities for fishing, canoeing, and tubing. The downtown area is worth a visit in itself, with a **Town Hall** that looks like it came from a movie set, many cute stores, and several first-rate restaurants. The two main roads in downtown Front Royal are Royal Avenue and East Main Street. The Village Commons off of East Main Street house Front Royal's trademark gazebo, a large red caboose, and the visitors center. Front Royal is also known for a series of elegant murals painted on buildings in the downtown area.

SIGHTS

Warren Rifles Confederate Museum

The **Warren Rifles Confederate Museum** (95 Chester St., 540/636-6982, www.vaudc.org, Apr. 15-Nov. 1 Mon.-Sat. 9am-4pm, Sun. noon-4pm, open by appointment the rest of the year, $5) is in a plain brick home and offers displays of Civil War relics such as weapons, battle flags, uniforms, photos, and rare documents. Memorabilia of famous Civil War players in the Front Royal area (such as Belle Boyd, John S. Mosby, General Robert E. Lee, and General Stonewall Jackson) are also on exhibit. There is a book and gift shop.

Belle Boyd Cottage

Nearly across the street from the Warren Rifles Confederate Museum, in one of the oldest buildings in Front Royal, is the **Belle Boyd Cottage** (101 Chester St., 540/636-1446, www.warrenheritagesociety.org, June-Oct. Mon.-Fri. 10am-4pm, Sat.-Sun. 10am-4pm, $3). Belle Boyd was a charming female spy who helped Stonewall Jackson capture Front Royal in May 1862. Boyd was well known among Union forces and had been reported no fewer than 30 times, arrested a

Front Royal's Town Hall

half-dozen times, and even spent time in jail. For a time during the war, Front Royal was her home base, and she stayed in this cottage owned by her relatives. Visitors can learn more about Boyd's life and her spy adventures.

Skyline Caverns

A wonderful underground experience, **Skyline Caverns** (10334 Stonewall Jackson Hwy., 540/635-4545, www.skylinecaverns.com, June 15-Labor Day daily 9am-6pm, Mar. 15-June 14 and Labor Day-Oct. Mon.-Fri. 9am-5pm, Sat.-Sun. 9am-6pm, Nov. 1-Mar. 14 daily 9am-4pm, $20) opened to the public in 1939. Visitors are led by professional guides through a maze of living caverns on a one-hour tour. Expect to see magical cave formations, three underground streams, and a 37-foot waterfall. A fun mirror maze is also offered for both children and adults for an additional $6. Skyline Caverns is just southwest of town.

RECREATION

The Shenandoah River is ideal for float trips. A handful of outfitters offer gear and shuttle service for visitors wishing to spend a day on this normally peaceful river. The **Front Royal Canoe Company** (8567 Stonewall Jackson Hwy., 540/635-5440, www.frontroyalcanoe.com, open Apr. 1-Oct. 31) offers self-guided trips down the river (3-11 miles) in canoes ($45-60), kayaks ($33-41), four-person rafts ($80-100), and six-person rafts ($120-150). They offer three-mile tubing trips (complete with a tube for your cooler) for $23.74 per person. They also rent paddleboards and fishing kayaks. **Skyline Canoe Company** (540/305-7695, www.skylinecanoe.com) offers self-guided canoe ($40-50) and kayak ($30-35) trips of 3-12.5 miles. They also offer three-mile tubing trips ($20).

Mountain bikers can challenge themselves on trails that go up to 3,300 feet in elevation, traversing deep valleys and wooded slopes. A popular expert trail is the **Elizabeth Furnace** trail, approximately 11 miles west of Front Royal in the **George Washington National Forest** (www.singletracks.com). The 15-mile trail starts with a long uphill climb on a fire road, followed by a long, bumpy ride downhill. It is very challenging and offers many water crossings, outcrops, technical sections, and rock gardens. Another

Warren Rifles Confederate Museum

Blue Ridge Whiskey Wine Loop

The Front Royal and Northern Blue Ridge Mountains area is home to many lovely vineyards and wineries. The Blue Ridge Whiskey Wine Loop is a driving tour through scenic country roads with stops at wineries, a whiskey distillery, and other attractions. A map of the tour and recommended stops can be downloaded at the Discover Shenandoah website (www.discovershenandoah.com). Some popular wineries along the tour include:

- **Chester Gap Cellars** (4615 Remount Rd., Front Royal, 540/636-8086, www.chestergapcellars.com)
- **Desert Rose Winery** (3726 Hume Rd., Hume, 540/635-3200, www.desertrosewinery.com)
- **DuCard Vineyards** (40 Gibson Hollow Ln., Etlan, 540/923-4206, www.ducardvineyards.com)
- **Gadino Cellars** (92 Schoolhouse Rd., Washington, 540/987-9292, www.gadinocellars.com)
- **Rappahannock Cellars** (14437 Hume Rd., Huntly, 540/635-9398, www.rappahannockcellars.com)
- **Sharp Rock Vineyards** (5 Sharp Rock Rd., Sperryville, 540/987-8020, www.sharprockvineyards.com)
- **Wisteria Farm and Vineyard** (1126 Marksville Rd., Stanley, 540/742-1489, www.wisteriavineyard.com)

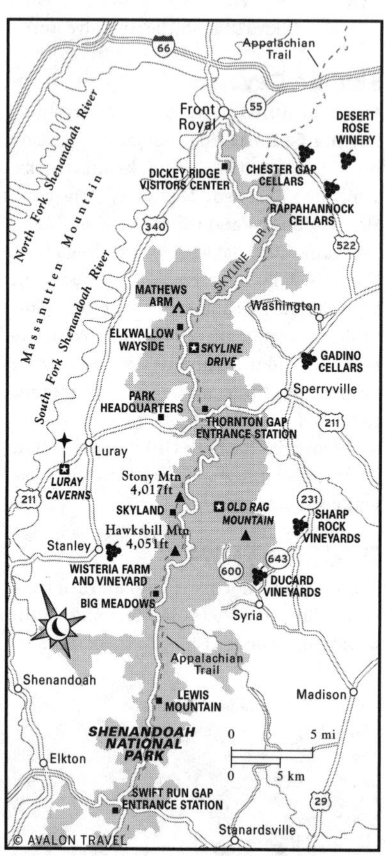

local favorite is the 13-mile network of trails in the **Shenandoah River State Park** (350 Daughter of Stars Dr., Bentonville, www.virginiaoutdoors.com), nine miles southwest of Front Royal. The trails are wide and smooth and not nearly as daunting as the Elizabeth Furnace trail, but there are moderate climbs. There are also scenic views of the river.

Equine enthusiasts may enjoy a trail ride with **Double H Stable** (5197 Reliance Rd., 540/636-4523, www.doublehstable.com, starting at $30). They offer trail rides for riders of all levels of experience.

FOOD

There are a few restaurants in Front Royal that have grabbed the attention of weekend visitors. The first is ★ **Apartment 2g** (206 S. Royal Ave., 540/636-9293, www.jsgourmet.com, open Sat. 6:30pm for a five-course American prix fixe menu for $50). This small restaurant and wine store is a favorite among visiting foodies and offers a first-class dining experience. The atmosphere is relaxed and intimate, and guests can watch their food being prepared on a video monitor. Examples of items on the five-course menu include saffron and shrimp risotto, grilled filet mignon, and seared sea scallops. The chef and his wife are the restaurant owners, and they are nearly always happy to answer questions and speak with their customers. The experience is similar to dining at a friend's house—that is, a friend who happens to be an excellent chef. Reservations are a must.

As if the owners of Apartment 2g don't "wow" patrons enough, they also own the popular **Element** (206 S. Royal Ave., 540/636-9293, www.jsgourmet.com, lunch Tues.-Sat. 11am-3pm, dinner Tues.-Sat. 5pm-9pm, $12-21) in the same building. Element is a casual sister to Apartment 2g, with a delectable menu of salads, veggie selections, seafood, beef, pork, and starters. They also serve lunch. The atmosphere is modern, and there is a full bar and handpicked wine list. The menu changes regularly.

Another favorite is **Ben's Family Cuisines** (654 West 11th St., 540/551-3147, www.bensfamilycuisines.com, Tues.-Thurs. 11am-9pm, Fri.-Sat. 11am-10pm, Sun. noon-8pm, $10-22). This unassuming family restaurant is a bit hidden in a small brick building in a residential neighborhood. They offer Thai, Cambodian, Vietnamese, Korean, Japanese, and American dishes. All meals are made to order and the staff is warm and delightful. Try the Ben's Family Pancake Wrap; it is unique and scrumptious.

If you're craving a burger and frozen custard, stop in at **Spelunker's Frozen Custard and Cavern Burgers** (116 South St., 540/631-0300, www.spelunkerscustard.com, daily 11am-10-pm, under $10). They offer dine-in and drive-through service.

ACCOMMODATIONS

Several hotels provide rooms in Front Royal for around $100, such as the **Holiday Inn Hotel & Suites Front Royal Blue Ridge Shadows** (111 Hospitality Dr., 540/631-3050, www.ihg.com, $144-180). The hotel is next to the Blue Ridge Shadows Golf Club, and offers 124 guest rooms on seven floors, with free high-speed Internet, a heated indoor pool, a 24-hour fitness center, and a 24-hour business center.

Another good option is the **Hampton Inn Front Royal** (9800 Winchester Rd., 540/635-1882, www.hamptoninn3.hilton.com, $139-149). This pleasant, 102-room hotel is located just off I-66 and is a short drive from town. Guests can enjoy a complimentary breakfast, free wireless Internet, and a fitness room.

For those who prefer to stay in a bed-and-breakfast, the **Woodward House on Manor Grade** (413 S. Royal Ave., 540/635-7010, www.acountryhome.com, $110-225) is a cozy spot with a homey feel. This charming home has seven guest rooms and one cabin (all with private bathrooms). A delightful breakfast is served daily, and each room comes with snacks, fresh-baked cookies, and water. They also offer complimentary beer or wine for guests in their on-site pub. The house sits on a hill above town and has nice views.

INFORMATION AND SERVICES

For additional information on Front Royal, contact the **Front Royal-Warren County Visitor Center** (414 E. Main St., 540/635-5788, www.discoverfrontroyal.com, daily 9am-5pm).

GETTING THERE

Front Royal is 70 miles west of Washington DC and is easily accessed from I-66.

Luray

The town of Luray is nestled in the scenic Shenandoah Valley in Page County. The town is less than five square miles and has a population of fewer than 5,000 people. Luray is a western gateway to Shenandoah National Park and is a two-hour drive from Washington DC. The charming downtown area along Main Street is the focal point of Luray and offers visitors a choice of restaurants and shops. The streets are decorated with seasonal flowers and the lovely Shenandoah Valley scenery is everywhere. Luray is a great day or overnight trip from many areas of Virginia and Maryland and offers small-town charm, friendly residents, outdoor recreation, and the world-famous Luray Caverns.

SIGHTS

★ Luray Caverns

There are many cavern attractions in the Blue Ridge Mountains, but the cream of the crop is **Luray Caverns** (970 U.S. 211 West, GPS 101 Cave Hill Rd., 540/743-6551, www.luraycaverns.com, opens daily at 9am with tours beginning every 20 min., closing hours vary by season: Apr. 1-June 14 6pm, June 15-Labor Day 7pm, day after Labor Day-Oct. 31 6pm, Nov. 1-Mar. 31 weekdays 4pm, weekends 5pm, $26). This incredible natural wonder has been awing visitors since it was first discovered in 1878. Upon entering the caverns, you are transported into a subterranean world of mystery that took more than four million centuries to create. A series of paved walkways guide visitors through massive cavern "rooms" filled with natural stalagmites, stalactites, and when the two join, columns or pillars. Some of the chambers have ceilings that are 10 stories high.

There are many attractions along the paved route in the caverns, including the famous **Stalacpipe Organ.** It is considered the world's largest musical instrument and is made up of stalactites covering 3.5 acres. The organ produces symphonic-quality sounds when the stalactites are tapped (electronically) by rubber-tipped mallets. It took 36 years to perfect the organ, but visitors can hear its haunting melodies played on every tour.

The general admission rate includes the entrance fee to the caverns, a cavern tour (tours depart every 20 minutes and are one hour), a self-guided tour of the **Car and Carriage Caravan Museum,** which displays restored cars, carriages, and coaches from 1725 to 1941, and entrance to the **Luray Valley Museum,** which interprets early Shenandoah Valley culture from as far back as pre-contact native people and includes a Swiss Bible (in the German vernacular) from 1536. Visitors can also enjoy displays of thousands of toys and train-related artifacts at **Toy Town Junction.**

the town of Luray

Underground Adventures

Luray Caverns

The mountains of Virginia harbor some of the nation's best caverns. Many are open to the public and can be explored in a couple of hours.

- **Luray Caverns** (page 246) is the granddaddy of all caverns. This awe-inspiring natural wonder in Luray, Virginia, transports visitors into an underground world of mystery and adventure that took more than four million centuries to create (yes, *centuries*).
- **Skyline Caverns** (page 243) near Front Royal, Virginia, offers kids of all ages a magical subterranean experience. With cave formations, three streams, and a 37-foot waterfall, this is another top cavern experience in rural Virginia.
- **Grand Caverns Regional Park** (page 253) near Harrisonburg, Virginia, is the oldest continuously operating "show" cave in the nation. It opened to the public in 1806 and at one time hosted elaborate balls in its 5,000-square-foot "Grand Ballroom."
- **Natural Bridge Caverns,** along the Blue Ridge Parkway, is 34 stories below ground. Visitors can see this natural wonder during a trip to a unique aboveground attraction, **Natural Bridge Park** (page 302).

Other attractions at the caverns can be enjoyed for an additional fee, including the **Rope Adventure Park,** a challenging multilevel ropes course with trails consisting of several poles connected by acrobatic elements, and the **Stonyman Mining Company Gem Sluice,** a re-created operational mining station.

Another interesting sight opposite Luray Caverns is the **Belle Brown Northcott Memorial,** which is also known as the **Luray Singing Tower.** This beautiful 117-foot-tall bell tower was built in 1937 and contains 47 bells (the largest of which is 7,640 pounds with a diameter of six feet). The tower holds regular recitals from spring through fall.

Luray Zoo

The **Luray Zoo** (1087 U.S. 211, 540/743-4113, www.lurayzoo.com, Apr.-Oct. daily 10am-5pm, Nov.-Mar. weekends 11am-4pm and weekdays by appointment, $10) is a small zoo that rescues exotic animals. The more than 250 animals that live there have all been taken from sad and harmful situations and given a permanent home. The zookeepers are friendly and interact with both the animals and the visitors and are happy to answer any questions. The zoo's reptile center has one of the largest collections of snakes on the East Coast. There is a petting section of the zoo for children; it includes animals such as goats, deer, a burro, and a potbellied pig.

SPORTS AND RECREATION

Luray is an outdoor town. Tucked into the Shenandoah Valley, Luray offers visitors a wonderful home base for hiking, fishing, canoeing, tubing, and kayaking. **Shenandoah River Outfitters** (6502 S. Page Valley Rd., 540/743-4159, www.shenandoah-river.com) is a great place to rent or purchase boats and gear. They rent white-water and flat-water canoes and kayaks ($36-56 per day) and offer 3-4-mile tubing trips ($22). They also rent furnished log cabins ($115-180 per night).

Those wishing to hike can take the **Stony Man Mountain Hike** (www.hikingupward.com), in Shenandoah National Park. This short (less than four miles) loop hike is pleasant, easy, and offers stunning views of the park. Just under the main peak is a fun rock-climbing area known as **Little Stony Man.** The trailhead is off of Skyland Drive (between mileposts 41 and 42).

If biking is more your thing, **Hawksbill Bicycles** (20 W. Main St., 540/743-1037, www.hawksbillbicycles.com) offers mapped routes of scenic rides in and around Luray. Triathletes can compete in the annual **Luray Triathlon** (luraytriathlon.com), which is held over two days in August and features both international- and sprint-distance races.

FOOD

55 East Main Brew House and Grill (55 E. Main St., 540/743-2739, www.lurayvabrewgrill.com, daily 11am-9pm, $11-20) serves up delicious burritos, bowls, and vegan options. The restaurant draws a big crowd of both locals and tourists. They have homemade chips, a good beer selection, and reasonable prices. It is located in a lovely building with large plate-glass windows and tin ceilings.

Outstanding New York-style pizza, pasta, and delicious cheesesteaks can be found at **Gennaro's Pizza and Italian Restaurant** (42 W. Main St., 540/743-2200, Sun.-Thurs. 11am-10pm, Fri.-Sat. 11am-11pm, $8-$18). The owner is from Napoli and many of the recipes are family heirlooms.

For a cup of coffee or casual sandwich, stop in the **Gathering Grounds Patisserie and Cafe** (24 E. Main St., 540/743-1121, www.ggrounds.com, Mon.-Thurs. 7am-6pm, Fri. 7am-8pm, Sat. 8am-8pm, Sun. 11am-3pm, $10-15). They serve a variety of paninis, wraps, quiche, soup, salads, homemade baked treats (different every day), and of course, delicious coffee. They also have an espresso bar. The atmosphere is warm and friendly.

ACCOMMODATIONS

There are many cabins for rent in and around Luray. Some overlook the Shenandoah River while others are mountain-view retreats. The **Luray & Page County website** (www.luraypage.com) has an extensive listing of available cabins and is a good resource for private accommodations. Click on "places to stay" for an alphabetical listing.

There are also several inns and motels in town. The **Mimslyn Inn** (401 W. Main St., 540/743-5105, www.mimslyninn.com, $169-329) is the premier overnight location in

Destination Dining

One of the premier dining destinations in Virginia is the famous **Inn at Little Washington Restaurant** (309 Middle St., Washington, 540/675-3800, www.theinnatlittlewashington.com). This extremely high-end restaurant is renowned for its incredible food, scenery, and service. Located in the town of Washington, between Front Royal and Luray and not far off U.S. 211 and 522, the inn sits on a historic street that hasn't changed much since George Washington himself named the town roads in 1749 (he was only 17 at the time).

The inn was founded in 1978 and the main building (where the restaurant is) occupies the space of a former garage, dance hall, and general store. It has since grown into a campus of sorts, incorporating many additional properties in the village (some dating back to the 1700s). The inn comprises guest rooms, the Claiborne House (a 3,600-square-foot cottage), a cutting garden (where fresh herbs and vegetables are grown), a walking path, a ballroom, and a gift shop.

The inn describes itself as an "unassuming dark blue building festooned with flags on the corner of Middle and Main Streets." This may be true, but once you step inside and see the crackling fire and tables adorned with silver and crystal, you will know you've entered a very special restaurant that is renowned for its exquisite food. Not only do they purchase food from local farmers, but the inn also has its own gardens and orchards. Main course selections can include items such as pan-roasted Maine lobster, juniper-crusted venison loin, and seared rare tuna crusted with mustard seeds, while desserts may include choices such as a southern butter pecan ice-cream sandwich, lemon-meringue tartlet with toasted pistachios, or cocoa nib napoleon with caramelized bananas.

Dinner reservations are accepted up to a year in advance. Prices vary during holidays and special events, but are generally $178 per person Monday through Thursday, $188 per person on Friday and Sunday, and $208 per person on Saturday. These prices do not include beverages, tax, or gratuity. Two chef's tables are also available and can accommodate up to six guests at each. These tables can be reserved any night of the week and carry the following surcharges: Monday through Thursday $395 per table, Friday and Sunday $495 per table, and Saturday $595 per table. Guests at the chef's tables can watch the action in the inn's stunning kitchen. Not only is the food preparation a sight to behold, but the kitchen, with its hand-painted tiles and a huge Vulcan range, is an attraction on its own.

Accommodations at the inn include 18 guest rooms, suites, and cottages ($655-1,325 per night). All are located on the inn's campus and are luxurious masterpieces designed by a stage and set designer from London. Many of the furnishings were purchased in England.

Luray. The colonial-style inn is just a short walk from the historic downtown area and strives to offer "vintage Southern hospitality." Visitors enter the property on a circular driveway leading to a portico lined with columns. The winding staircase in the lobby is reminiscent of those found in grand homes of the Old South, and each guest is warmly greeted by the attending staff. The inn has 45 guest rooms, each individually decorated. Rooms are available in a variety of sizes in several price ranges. There is a spa, fitness room, and business center on-site as well as a formal dining room and casual tavern.

The **Inn of the Shenandoah** (138 E. Main St., 540/300-9777, www.innoftheshenandoah.com, $150-210) is a nice three-suite inn with antique glass windows and European accents. The house has a pretty front porch and second-story balcony. Behind the inn is a renovated farmhouse called the **Cottage of the Inn,** which offers two additional suites.

The very similar **Luray Caverns Motel East** (at the east entrance to Luray Caverns across from the Luray Singing Tower) and the **Luray Caverns Motel West** (at the west entrance to Luray Caverns) offer

Mimslyn Inn

standard accommodations. Both have free wireless Internet and a swimming pool. Rates for both range from $72-95 per night and reservations can be made by calling 540/743-6551.

CAMPING

Several local campgrounds are convenient to Luray including **Yogi Bear's Jellystone Park** (2250 U.S. 211, 540/743-4002, www.campluray.com, camping $65-109, cabins $113-594), which offers camping and cabin rentals three miles east of downtown off U.S. 211; and **Camp Roosevelt** (540/984-4101, $12), 8.5 miles northwest of Luray on Route 675.

INFORMATION AND SERVICES

Begin your visit to Luray at the **Luray Train Depot and Visitor Center** (18 Campbell St., 540/743-3915, www.luraypage.com, daily 9am-5pm). This lovely building houses knowledgeable staff, brochures, and clean bathrooms amid a parklike setting. It is downtown about a block off Main Street and is within easy walking distance to shops and restaurants.

GETTING THERE

Luray is 93 miles southwest of Washington DC on U.S. 211. U.S. 340 also runs through Luray.

New Market

Fourteen miles west of Luray is the town of New Market. It was established in 1796 and became known for its printing and publishing industry in the early 1800s. During the Civil War, the town was a key thoroughfare in the Shenandoah Valley and witnessed Stonewall Jackson's troops marching through at four different times. The historic Battle of New Market took place in 1864 and is reenacted annually in mid-May.

Visitors to New Market will find a cozy, quiet downtown area on the east side of I-81, and the historic battlefield on the west side of the interstate. Explore the battlefield or take in a show at the **Schultz Theatre and School of the Performing Arts** (9357 N. Congress St., 540/740-9119, www.schultztheatre.com). They offer a full schedule of theater performances including stage shows, musicals, youth productions, and dinner theater.

SIGHTS

★ New Market Battlefield State Historical Park

The main attraction in New Market is the **New Market Battlefield State Historical Park** (8895 George R. Collins Pkwy., 866/515-1864, www.vmi.edu/vmcw, daily 9am-5pm, $10). This 300-acre park occupies the site of a Civil War battle on May 15, 1864, famous for being the only occasion in American history when college cadets were responsible for victory in combat. During the battle, cadets from the Virginia Military Institute in Lexington fought alongside Confederate soldiers to force Union troops out of the Shenandoah Valley.

Today visitors can explore nine structures at the 19th-century **Bushong Farm** that provided shelter to the Bushong family as the battle unfolded around them on their property (primarily in the orchard right behind the house). After the battle, the farmhouse was used as a field hospital for a week (bloodstains can still be seen in the parlor).

Another on-site attraction is the **Virginia Museum of the Civil War.** This museum has information and exhibits on the entire Civil War, but focuses on the conflict in Virginia. The museum is housed in the **Hall of Valor,** a monument building dedicated to young people who have served in the military during times of national need. Plan to watch the Emmy Award-winning film *Field of Lost Shoes* during your visit.

The park also offers walking trails, scenic overlooks of the Shenandoah River, and wonderful picnic areas. The park is a National Historic Landmark.

It is important to note that the nearby New Market Battlefield Military Museum, on the way to the battlefield park, is not part of the state-run battlefield facility (despite its official looking Greek revival exterior with large white columns). It offers a private collection of relics, many of which are not Civil War related.

FOOD

New Market isn't known as a foodie's paradise, but good comfort food can be found on Congress Street. A local favorite with an old-fashioned ambience is the **Southern Kitchen**

Southern Kitchen

(9576 S. Congress St., 540/740-3514, daily 7am-9pm, $5-12). They serve simple, southern cooking (think country ham, pork barbecue, burgers, and fried chicken) in a friendly atmosphere. Look for the neon sign and crowded parking lot; it is hard to miss in small downtown New Market. They are open for breakfast, lunch, and dinner.

Another popular choice is **Jalisco Mexican Restaurant** (9403 S. Congress St., 540/740-9404, www.jalisconewmarket.com, Mon.-Thurs. 11am-10pm, Fri.-Sat. 11am-10:30pm, Sun. 11am-9:30pm, $5-15). This eatery serves traditional Mexican food from an extensive menu. The atmosphere is lively (for New Market), and the place has a friendly vibe. They have good chorizos and a lot of vegetarian options as well as dishes with shrimp.

ACCOMMODATIONS

There aren't many choices for hotels in New Market. There are a few inexpensive chain hotels such as the **Quality Inn Shenandoah Valley** (162 W. Old Cross Rd., 540/740-3141, www.qualityinn-shenandoahvalley.com, $90-95), with 100 rooms and an adjoining restaurant, and the **Days Inn New Market Battlefield** (9360 George Collins Pkwy., 540/740-4100, www.daysinn.com, $65-76), which has a continental breakfast, free wireless Internet, and a seasonal pool.

Another option is the **Shenvalee Golf Resort** (9660 Fairway Dr., 540/740-3181, www.shenvalee.com, $92). Accommodations here include a guesthouse and motel less than three miles from New Market Battlefield Park. The 42 rooms are not luxurious, but they offer balconies with golf course or pool views, free Wi-Fi, and mini-fridges. The guesthouse has four bedrooms, a kitchen, and a mountain view. There is also a restaurant on-site.

The **Rosendale Inn Bed and Breakfast** (17917 Farmhouse Lane, 540/325-4544, www.1790rosendaleinn.com, $135-145) is a good choice for a quiet getaway. The historic home was built in 1790 and has two lovely 60-foot verandas (with rocking chairs and benches) and a two-story front porch. Accommodations include four rooms in the main house and a separate cozy cottage that has a fireplace. The owner is an author and has many interesting stories to share about the area. He goes out of his way to make sure each guest has a good experience. There is a barn on the property that can accommodate guests' horses.

If you'd prefer a bed-and-breakfast that includes the entire house with your stay, the **Jacob Swartz House** (574 Jiggady Rd., 540/740-9208, www.jacobswartz.com, Feb.-Dec. $150) is for you. The house is a lovely historic cottage and renovated cobbler shop that sits on a river bluff. It has a master bedroom and a second loft bedroom as well as a living room (with a woodstove), dining area, and full kitchen (stocked with staples). The house has wireless Internet and is located outside of town on a long country road.

INFORMATION AND SERVICES

Additional information on New Market can be found at www.newmarketvirginia.com and www.shenandoahvalleyweb.com.

GETTING THERE

New Market is 113 miles (approximately two hours) southwest of Washington DC off U.S. 211 and I-81.

Harrisonburg

Harrisonburg, tucked away in the Shenandoah Valley, is part of Rockingham County and has a population of around 46,000. It is best known as the home of **James Madison University.** The historic section of its downtown area includes 10 blocks of locally owned restaurants, galleries, and museums.

Harrisonburg is an active town, due in part to the large population of students that live here much of the year and also to its proximity to the Blue Ridge Mountains. The town was named as a top location for families to "beat nature deficit disorder" by *Backpacker Magazine.*

SIGHTS

James Madison University

James Madison University (JMU) (800 S. Main St., 540/568-6211, www.jmu.edu) is the largest attraction in Harrisonburg. The school was founded in 1908 and offers 124 degree programs. With almost 20,000 students and 112 buildings on 721 acres, the school dominates the Harrisonburg landscape. JMU has earned many national rankings and recognitions, and is considered to be one of the most environmentally responsible colleges.

The beautiful campus is a pleasure to walk around, with the focal point being the large grassy quadrangle on South Main Street where students can be seen lounging, reading, or playing ball when the weather is nice. This is also the location of the stately **Wilson Hall,** which houses a 1,372-seat auditorium under its red roof and was named after President Woodrow Wilson. It is said that on a clear day, it is possible to see Staunton, Virginia—the birthplace of its namesake—from its cupola.

The campus is split by I-81, with the original buildings on the west side and the newer **College of Integrated Science and Technology** on the east side (along with other academic and resident buildings). A bridge and a tunnel connect the two sides.

A highlight of the campus is the **Edith J. Carrier Arboretum** (540/568-3194, open daily dawn to dusk, free) on University Boulevard. This beautiful 125-acre landscaped area offers nature trails and guided tours by appointment.

Explore More Discovery Museum

For those traveling with children, the **Explore More Discovery Museum** (150 S. Main St., 540/442-8900, www.iexploremore.com, Tues.-Sat. 9:30am-5pm, $6) is a great stop that has interactive exhibits geared toward children under 10 on topics such as health, construction, art, science, mechanics, theater, farms, the outdoors, and much more.

Virginia Quilt Museum

The **Virginia Quilt Museum** (301 S. Main St., 540/433-3818, www.vaquiltmuseum.org, Tues.-Sat. 10am-4pm, $7) is a small specialty museum that features a wonderful permanent collection of nearly 300 quilts, antique sewing machines, and a gift store. They also have a handful of rotating exhibits throughout the year. The museum is housed in a pretty home that was built in 1856. Tours are self-guided, but guided group tours can be arranged.

★ Grand Caverns Regional Park

Approximately 15 miles southeast of Harrisonburg is **Grand Caverns Regional Park** (5 Grand Caverns Dr., Grottoes, 540/249-5705, www.grandcaverns.com, Nov.-Mar. daily 10am-4pm, Apr.-Oct. daily 9am-5pm, $18). Discovered in 1804 and opened to the public in 1806, Grand Caverns is the oldest continuously operating "show" cave in the country. The caverns are made up of an impressive network of caves including Cathedral Hall, one of the most massive underground rooms on the East Coast, as well as the Grand

Ballroom, which is 5,000 square feet and literally was the site of balls in the early years after the caverns were discovered. Many famous people have visited the caverns, including Thomas Jefferson and both Confederate and Union soldiers (of which more than 200 signed their names on the cave walls). This is a great attraction for both adults and children. Seventy-minute tours are given on the hour. Admission to the caverns is by guided tour only.

RECREATION

The nearby **Massanutten Resort** (1822 Resort Dr., McGaheysville, 540/289-9441, www.massresort.com) is a 6,000-acre four-season family destination that offers lodging, skiing, golfing, fishing, horseback riding, a water park, a spa, and hiking around Massanutten Peak as well as panoramic views of the Blue Ridge Mountains. Best known as a ski resort, Massanutten has 14 trails (all with lights for night skiing) with 1,110 feet of vertical drop. The resort offers skiing, snowboarding, and snow-tubing (lift tickets are $40-70). Massanutten is about 15 miles southeast of Harrisonburg.

Cycling is big in Harrisonburg. Both road biking and mountain biking are popular, and many events are scheduled throughout the year. For information on cycling in the area visit the **Harrisonburg Tourism** website (www.visitharrisonburgva.com) or the **Shenandoah Valley Bicycle Coalition** website (www.svbcoalition.org). Bike rentals are available at Massanutten Resort April to October ($10-26).

FOOD

Fresh local ingredients, beautiful exposed brick walls, white tablecloths, and great food are some of the key ingredients to the success of the ★ **Local Chop and Grill House** (56 W. Gay St., 540/801-0505, www.localchops.com, Tues.-Thurs. 5pm-9pm, Fri.-Sat. 5pm-10pm, $15-33). This wonderful restaurant occupies the former building of Harrisonburg's Old City Produce Exchange, which is perfect for this modern establishment whose menu features fresh, handpicked local and seasonal foods. They specialize in steak and seafood and have a large selection of savory house-made sauces.

Another local favorite is **Vitos Italian Kitchen** (1047 Port Republic Rd., 540/433-1113, vitositaliankitchen.com, Sun.-Thurs. 11am-10pm, Fri.-Sat. 11am-11pm, $8-16). This wonderful Italian restaurant is a great place to bring the family. The atmosphere is warm and inviting, the food is delicious, and the staff is friendly. The menu has traditional Italian items, house specials, and pizza. Their house Italian salad dressing deserves accolades on its own.

ACCOMMODATIONS

Charming lodgings can be found at the **Joshua Wilton House** (412 S. Main St., 540/434-4464, www.joshuawilton.com, $145-160). This lovely inn and restaurant has five beautiful guest rooms in an elegant Victorian home. Each offers feather top queen-size beds, private bathrooms, ceiling fans, antique furniture, robes, and free wireless Internet. A gourmet breakfast is included with each stay. The inn is also known for its restaurant and wonderful seasonally inspired menu. They offer beer- and wine-tasting dinners and more than 100 bottles of wine on their wine list. The Joshua Wilton House is where actor Richard Dreyfuss spent his honeymoon in 2006.

The **Stonewall Jackson Inn** (547 E. Market St., 540/433-8233, www.stonewalljacksoninn.com, $139-189) is a delightful bed-and-breakfast with 10 guest rooms (all named for Civil War notables). The 1885 restored mansion is within walking distance of downtown Harrisonburg. The staff is warm and welcoming, and the breakfast is delightfully creative.

INFORMATION AND SERVICES

For additional information on Harrisonburg, visit the **Harrisonburg Tourism** website at www.harrisonburgtourism.com or stop by **Harrisonburg Tourism and Visitor Services** (212 South Main Street, daily 9am-5pm).

GETTING THERE

Harrisonburg sits right on I-81 and is 132 miles (about a 2.25-hour drive) southwest from Washington DC.

Staunton

Founded in 1747, Staunton is the self-proclaimed "Queen City of the Shenandoah." It sits in Augusta County and has just fewer than 24,000 residents.

The focal point of Staunton is the charming and compact historic downtown area. Beautiful Victorian architecture, unique restaurants, local galleries, and independent shops lend the area to exploration on foot. Staunton was lucky that it escaped destruction during the Civil War and many of its original 18th- and 19th-century homes still stand today. The city does a wonderful job preserving the town's heritage and visual appeal by disallowing power lines and cell towers within view in the historic districts.

If you hear someone mention the "Wharf," don't look around for water. The Wharf is the neighborhood surrounding the train station. The name dates back to the 19th century when the warehouses in this historic neighborhood resembled those commonly seen in port towns.

Staunton was President Woodrow Wilson's birthplace. It is also the home of **Mary Baldwin College, Stuart Hall** (a private prep school), and the **Virginia School for the Deaf and Blind.**

SIGHTS

Frontier Culture Museum

The **Frontier Culture Museum** (1290 Richmond Rd., 540/332-7850, www.frontiermuseum.org, Mar. 14-Nov. 30 daily 10am-5pm, Dec. 1-Mar. 13 daily 10am-4pm, $10) is a popular family destination that tells the fascinating story of the thousands of immigrants who settled colonial America. The fun and informative museum explores the lives of people from England, Germany, Ireland, and West Africa and how they all contributed to the success of our country. The museum is a collection of original and reproduced buildings that represent the Old World and America. Each features interpretive signage, period furnishings, food, animals, and living-history demonstrations presented by costumed interpreters.

Woodrow Wilson Presidential Library and Museum

The **Woodrow Wilson Presidential Library and Museum** (18-24 N. Coalter St., 540/885-0897, www.woodrowwilson.org, Mon.-Sat. 9am-5pm, Sun. noon-5pm, shorter winter hours, $14) tells the story of our country's 28th president. Self-guided tours lead visitors through seven galleries depicting different phases of Wilson's life. A highlight is the president's restored Pierce-Arrow limousine from 1919. He liked it so much his friends bought it for him when he left office. There is also a section of the museum geared specifically to children.

At the same address is the **Woodrow Wilson Birthplace.** This wonderfully restored Greek Revival home offers guided tours and a window into what life was like back in 1856, the year Wilson was born. The home contains period furniture and artifacts from the Wilson family. Behind the house is a beautiful Victorian-style garden that was created in the 1930s.

ENTERTAINMENT AND RECREATION

The **Blackfriars Playhouse** (10 S. Market St., 540/851-1733, www.

Haunted Staunton

There are many stories of hauntings throughout Virginia and Maryland, a number of which center on towns where Civil War battles were fought. Staunton is no exception, and in fact, seems to have more than its fair share of tales of the paranormal.

The most famous haunting in Staunton is at the train station. This is where a member of an opera troupe, Myrtle Knox, was killed in 1890 when a train carrying her troupe derailed and demolished Staunton's C&O depot. The 18-year-old actress bled to death at the site after multiple injuries. It has been reported many times by eyewitnesses that Knox's spirit now haunts the rail station and was even seen looking through windows at the former Pullman Restaurant (which is now closed). It is interesting to note that the train station has been featured in several movies, including *The Love Letter* in 1998.

Another well-known haunting is at the Thornerose House at Gypsy Hill. The home was built in 1912. Shortly after, the owner's 10-year-old son became very ill. His dedicated nurse, Caroline, spent day and night by the boy's side trying desperately to keep him alive, but he eventually died. It is said that Caroline now roams the house looking for him. The house served as a bed-and-breakfast for many years, and guests reported meeting Caroline in what was called the Canterbury Room (where she had lived), at which point she would introduce herself and then disappear. She was also known to play tricks on people by stealing their keys and bringing them to her room.

The Selma House was built in approximately 1848 and is the site of another famous Staunton haunting. In 1864, when Union troops were stationed in Staunton, they were said to have chased a young Confederate soldier into the house. He stopped in front of the fireplace, turned toward the door, and was shot and killed. The young man's blood flowed onto the wooden floor and caused a rather disturbing bloodstain that became a permanent mark on the floor despite numerous efforts to remove it. In addition to his blood, the soldier's spirit is said to have never left the house, and is described by the many who have seen him as a "polite man in uniform" who listens intently to conversations going on in the home. One hundred years after his death, he is said to have pushed a woman out of her bed in the middle of the night. The Selma House is a private residence, but it is easily spotted at the top of Selma Boulevard near the park.

Many additional ghost sightings have been reported in Staunton locations, including at the Stonewall Jackson Hotel, Emilio's restaurant, the Clock Tower, Mary Baldwin College, the grounds of the DeJarnette Center, and in private homes.

americanshakespearecenter.com) is a widely popular local theater in Staunton. Run by **The American Shakespeare Center,** the theater is said to be the only re-creation of Shakespeare's indoor theater in the world. It may sound small, with just 300 seats, but the performances are greatly entertaining and energetic. Balcony seats are sold as general admission, but offer a terrific view. Aim to get there early (they have entertainment before the show) so you can grab a balcony seat in the front row. This is a fun theater with a relaxed atmosphere.

Gypsy Hill Park (600 Churchville Ave., daily 6am-11pm) is a lovely 214-acre public park with an outdoor gym, walking paths, ball fields, playgrounds, a duck pond, tennis courts, a small train, and an outdoor pool. Pets are allowed, but they must remain on a leash.

FOOD

American

★ **Zynodoa** (115 E. Beverley St., 540/885-7775, www.zynodoa.com, Wed.-Sat. 5pm-10:30pm, Sun.-Tues. 5pm-9:30pm, $20-34) offers wonderful contemporary southern cuisine. This farm-to-table restaurant has an ever-changing menu (depending on what fresh ingredients are available). They even have their own 50-acre farm from which they harvest many ingredients for their dishes (including fresh eggs). Examples of menu items include Chesapeake seafood gumbo, duck confit ravioli, and roasted whole rainbow trout. The service is outstanding; servers are well versed in the details of the menu and are also helpful with suggestions and wine pairings. This is one of the few restaurants open late on Sunday nights.

For great ribs and delicious steak and burgers, stop in the **Mill Street Grill** (1 Mill St., 540/886-0656, www.millstreetgrill.com, Mon.-Thurs. 4pm-9:30pm, Fri.-Sat. 4pm-10:30pm, Sun. 11am-9pm, $8-30). The restaurant is housed in a former turn-of-the-20th-century flour mill. It has a loyal client base and can be crowded on weekends. The menu also includes seafood, pasta, sandwiches, and vegetarian choices. If you happen to be in town during Mardi Gras, they offer jazz entertainment and go all out with their decorations.

The slightly out-of-the-way **Depot Grille** (42 Middlebrook Ave., 540/885-7332, www.depotgrille.com, open daily for lunch and dinner, Sun.-Thurs. 11am-9pm, Fri.-Sat. 11am-10pm, $10-26) is a unique little restaurant in the historic freight train station in Staunton. The atmosphere is train oriented, cozy, and fun. The main dining room maintains the original hardwood floors from the station, and the dining booths were once church pews. There is also a 40-foot Victorian bar that came from a historic luxury hotel in Albany, New York. They offer a lot of variety on their menu (including ribs, chicken, prime rib, salads, sandwiches, and seafood), and there is an enclosed deck with views of the downtown area.

A downtown restaurant offering a flavorful southern menu is **Byers Street Bistro** (18 Byers St., 540/887-6100, www.byersstreetbistro.com, daily 11am-midnight, $9-27). This upbeat favorite has a large patio and live entertainment many nights. The menu includes selections such as shrimp and grits, fish tacos, ribs, steak, gourmet pizza, and mac and cheese.

Italian

A large dining establishment with a small-restaurant feel is **Emilio's** (23 E. Beverley Street, 540/885-0102, www.emiliositalianrestaurant.com, Tues.-Thurs. 11am-9:30pm, Fri.-Sat. 11am-10:30pm, Sun. 11am-8:30pm, $15-26). This wonderful, friendly Italian eatery has terrific food and great ambience with its downtown location, lounge, four fireplaces, and a rooftop patio. Fresh pasta, wonderful specials, wine tastings, and live entertainment many nights in the lounge help make this a fun place to spend an evening.

ACCOMMODATIONS

Under $100

The **Red Roof Inn Staunton** (42 Sangers Ln., 540/885-3117, www.redroof.com, $63-76) is just off I-81 (six miles from downtown Staunton) and also offers free continental breakfast and wireless Internet. They are pet friendly with no additional fee.

$100-200

The **Stonewall Jackson Hotel and Conference Center** (24 S. Market St., 540/885-4848, www.stonewalljacksonhotel.com, $161-270) was built in 1924 and has since been fully restored. It has 124 guest rooms, a heated indoor pool, a fitness center, and a business center. The rooms aren't large, but they are comfortable and well appointed. The public areas are nice also. A big plus for this hotel is its location in downtown Staunton, convenient to attractions and dining. The hotel is also pet friendly.

The ★ **Inn at Old Virginia** (1329 Commerce Rd., 540/248-4650, www.innatoldvirginia.com, $145-225) is a cozy bed-and-breakfast just north of town. The inn was built prior to the Civil War and has 10 guest rooms in two buildings. The Main House contains the common areas including an English-style conservatory, living room (with a library and fireplace), meeting room, breakfast room, and outdoor patios. A beautifully renovated barn contains eight guest rooms, a common area living room, and decks overlooking the valley. The house and grounds are elegant and well maintained. A delicious and plentiful breakfast is served each morning by delightful hosts, and specific dietary needs are accommodated.

INFORMATION AND SERVICES

For additional information about visiting Staunton, go to www.visitstaunton.com or visit the downtown **Staunton Visitor Center** (35 S. New St., 540/332-3971, daily 9am-5pm).

GETTING THERE

Staunton is located in the Shenandoah Valley off I-81, 28 miles south of Harrisonburg and 36 miles north of Lexington.

Allegheny Highlands

The western reaches of the state toward the West Virginia border include Highland County, Bath County, and parts of Augusta and Allegheny Counties. The Allegheny Mountains spill into West Virginia, and the area is split by river valleys. This region is scenic and sparsely populated. **Route 220** from Monterey to Covington is a particularly scenic drive. Part of the enjoyment of a trip to this region can be the drive there and back.

HOT SPRINGS

The village of Hot Springs is in a beautiful area of Bath County that offers visitors a blend of resort atmosphere and natural scenery. Bath County is one of the wealthiest in Virginia, thanks to several resorts that have taken advantage of numerous natural thermal springs. Native tribes originally hailed their healing powers, but wealthy Virginians quickly learned what a wonderful retreat the mountain air and springwaters made. The area became the site of lavish resorts, and to this day remains a destination for vacationers.

Hot Springs is quaint, small, and contains many buildings that have existed for more than 150 years. The population is just over 700 people. During the summer months, Hot Springs hosts a local farmers market, and its **Garth Newel Music Center** (403 Garth Newel Ln., 540/839-5018, www.garthnewel.org) is a popular venue for chamber music, blues, and jazz performances.

Hot Springs is known as home to one of Virginia's premier resorts, ★ **The Omni Homestead Resort** (7696 Sam Snead Hwy., 540/839-1766, www.omnihotels.com/hotels/homestead-virginia, $255-782), off U.S. 220. This enormous 480-room resort has origins dating back to 1766 and was built around magnificent warm springs. The crystal-clear springs are still a focal point of the resort and maintain a uniform temperature and flow all year long. The mineral content of the springs is also very high, making them easy to float in. The spring pools are named for President Thomas Jefferson, who visited them in 1818.

The resort encompasses 2,000 manicured acres and has impressive stately brick buildings and two premier golf courses. It offers elaborate lodging, dining, and many year-round recreational opportunities. It is also a popular conference site for Virginia businesses.

The resort is nothing short of a self-contained campus, with many restaurants, stores, a first-class European-style spa, and countless guest activities including a trout stream, a shooting club, and a small ski resort.

Additional information on Hot Springs can be found at www.discoverbath.com.

DOUTHAT STATE PARK

About 26 miles southeast of Hot Springs (much less as the crow flies) is one of the oldest state parks in Virginia, **Douthat State Park** (14239 Douthat State Park Rd., Millboro, 540/862-8100, www.dcr.virginia.gov, $5 entrance fee). The park is just under 4,500 acres and offers all of the following: 40 miles of hiking trails; a 50-acre lake for swimming, boating, and fishing; rental cabins ($115-146); camping ($26-30); horseback riding; nature programs; picnic areas; a camp store; laundry facilities; and a restaurant. This is a wonderful park for families and outdoor enthusiasts.

GETTING THERE

The Allegheny Highlands are approximately 200 miles from Washington DC. Much of the trip is on major highways such as I-66 and I-81, but the last 60 miles are in more rural, mountainous areas. This part of the trip is slow going but very scenic.

Central and Southern Virginia

Central and Southern Virginia is teeming with both history and natural beauty. It's a place in which breathtaking byways and small country roads lead to state parks and country inns, and Civil War battlefields and presidential homes attest to the land's deep roots and historical importance.

The region encompasses a vast amount of acreage, but is much less densely populated than Northern Virginia and Coastal Virginia. This part of the state is home to many colleges and universities, including the University of Virginia and Virginia Tech, and the state capital, Richmond.

From the Civil War battlefields in Fredericksburg to Robert E. Lee and Stonewall Jackson's final resting place in Lexington, Central Virginia offers visitors many opportunities to learn firsthand about the conflicts fought on the nation's soil and the many soldiers who gave their lives in those wars. Thomas Jefferson also had strong ties to Central Virginia, and his influence can be seen in many places. His home, Monticello, is a popular attraction in Charlottesville and is close to the University of Virginia, which was founded by Jefferson himself.

Southern Virginia is home to the scenic Blue Ridge Parkway and vast tracts of farmland and mountains that provide a deep contrast to the more populated regions of the state. Business suits are traded for fishing waders and limousines for tractors. Visitors can sample a slower pace of life through small towns and historic cities such as Lynchburg and Roanoke and gain an appreciation for the natural beauty of the state.

PLANNING YOUR TIME

You could easily spend weeks exploring Central and Southern Virginia. The drive time alone between Fredericksburg and Abingdon is approximately five hours. Since most of the cities in this region are about an hour away from each other, it is best to focus on a handful of destinations over a few days and to go from one to the next hitting the highlights.

If Civil War history is your passion, then

Previous: Mabry Mill; Blue Ridge Parkway. **Above:** downtown Roanoke.

Look for ★ to find recommended sights, activities, dining, and lodging.

Highlights

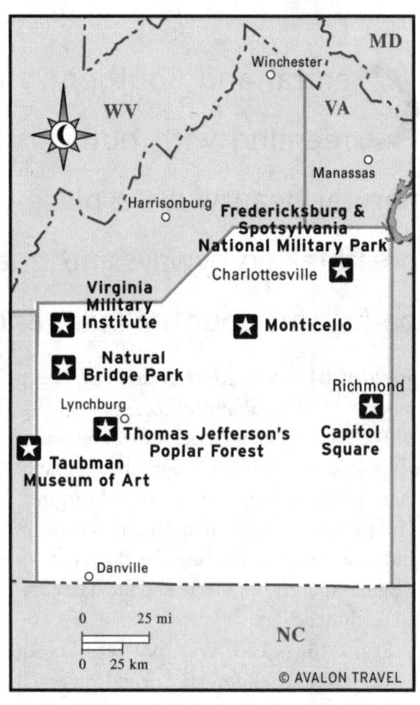

★ **Fredericksburg & Spotsylvania National Military Park:** The second-largest military park in the world tells the story of four important Civil War battles that resulted in more than 100,000 casualties (page 267).

★ **Capitol Square:** This beautifully landscaped 12-acre parcel in the heart of Richmond is home to several state buildings including the Virginia State Capitol (page 276).

★ **Monticello:** This amazing 5,000-acre plantation was the home of Thomas Jefferson, our nation's third president, author of the Declaration of Independence, and the University of Virginia's founder (page 291).

★ **Natural Bridge Park:** This 20-story solid limestone arch is an impressive act of nature (page 302).

★ **Thomas Jefferson's Poplar Forest:** The president's personal retreat is an architectural masterpiece and the first octagonal house in the country (page 303).

★ **Virginia Military Institute:** The oldest state-supported military college in the country was founded in Lexington, Virginia in 1839 (page 309).

★ **Taubman Museum of Art:** This popular museum in Roanoke highlights the culture of the Roanoke Valley and Southern Virginia (page 324).

Fredericksburg is a must. If you're fascinated with the accomplishments of Thomas Jefferson, then Charlottesville will be on your list.

If it's beautiful mountain scenery you seek, then a ride down the Blue Ridge Parkway should be on your agenda—especially during the fall. The parkway's Virginia portion stretches 218 miles and can be driven in one day, but is best experienced over two days. This allows time to explore the unique sights and towns along the way and take in some of the best scenery the state has to offer.

The best way to move between cities is by car. The highways in Virginia are easy to navigate and are generally in excellent shape. I-95 and I-64 are the primary routes through Central Virginia, while I-81 is the main highway in Southern Virginia.

Fredericksburg

Fredericksburg is a far-reaching suburb of Washington DC and the largest city between Washington and Richmond. It is easily accessed from I-95, and the quaint historic district is a popular day trip from many locations in Virginia and Maryland.

Fredericksburg is known for its extensive history. It was established in 1728 and named after the Prince of Wales and the father of King George III. Fredericksburg was a prominent port during the colonial era and home to George Washington during his boyhood. It also has an extensive Civil War history due in part to its location halfway between the Union and Confederate capitals.

Although the Fredericksburg area is home to many commuters who drive north for work, it is also home to the **University of Mary Washington** (www.umw.edu) and several large employers (such as GEICO). The city sits within the county lines of Spotsylvania, but is an independent city with approximately 25,000 residents.

SIGHTS

Old Town Fredericksburg

Old Town Fredericksburg takes visitors back to the Civil War era. The town was built along the Rappahannock River and includes several blocks of tree-lined streets with historic residences from the 18th and 19th centuries. A few of the homes still bear scars from Civil War battles and have cannonballs stuck in their exterior walls.

The historic district boasts many galleries, restaurants, and shops. It's a lovely place to window-shop, take a walk, grab a bite, and enjoy some of the history in this famous town.

The students from the University of Mary Washington provide much of the workforce for the charming stores and eateries along Princess Anne Street and neighboring roads in the historic district. Most of the businesses are privately owned and operated.

RISING SUN TAVERN

The **Rising Sun Tavern** (1304 Caroline St., 540/373-1494, www.washingtonheritagemuseums.org, Mar.-Oct. Mon.-Sat. 10am-5pm, Sun. noon-4pm, Nov.-Feb. Mon.-Sat. 11am-4pm, Sun. noon-4pm, $5) is a historic site (they do not serve food) that used to be Charles Washington's home (George's younger brother). The home was built in 1760 and made a popular overnight stop for weary travelers. It hosted such famous people as George Mason, James Madison, Thomas Jefferson, and John Paul Jones. The home became a "proper" (high-class) tavern in 1792. Visitors are treated to a lively introduction to tavern life in the 18th century. Costumed interpreters lead the way through the taproom, dining room, and public and private quarters.

HUGH MERCER APOTHECARY SHOP

The **Hugh Mercer Apothecary Shop** (1020 Caroline St., 540/373-3362, www.

Central and Southern Virginia

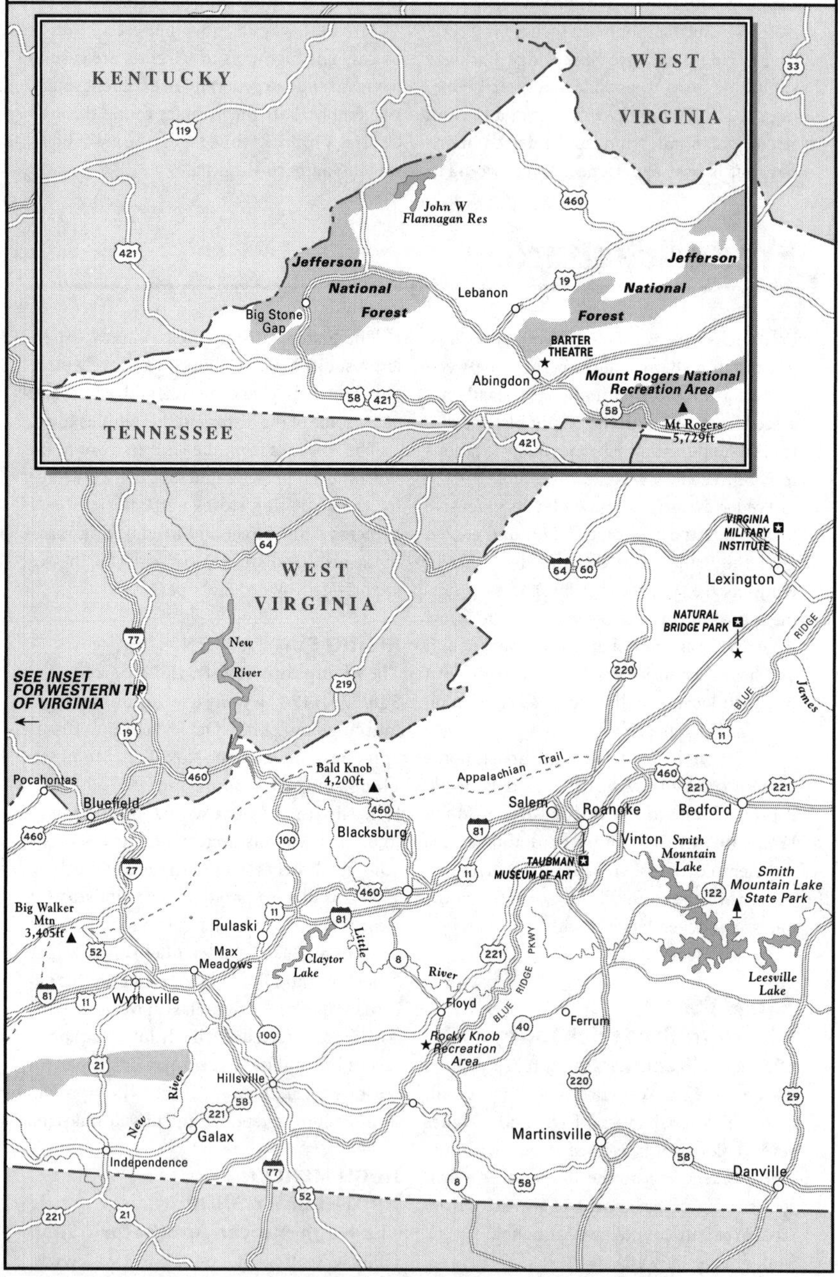

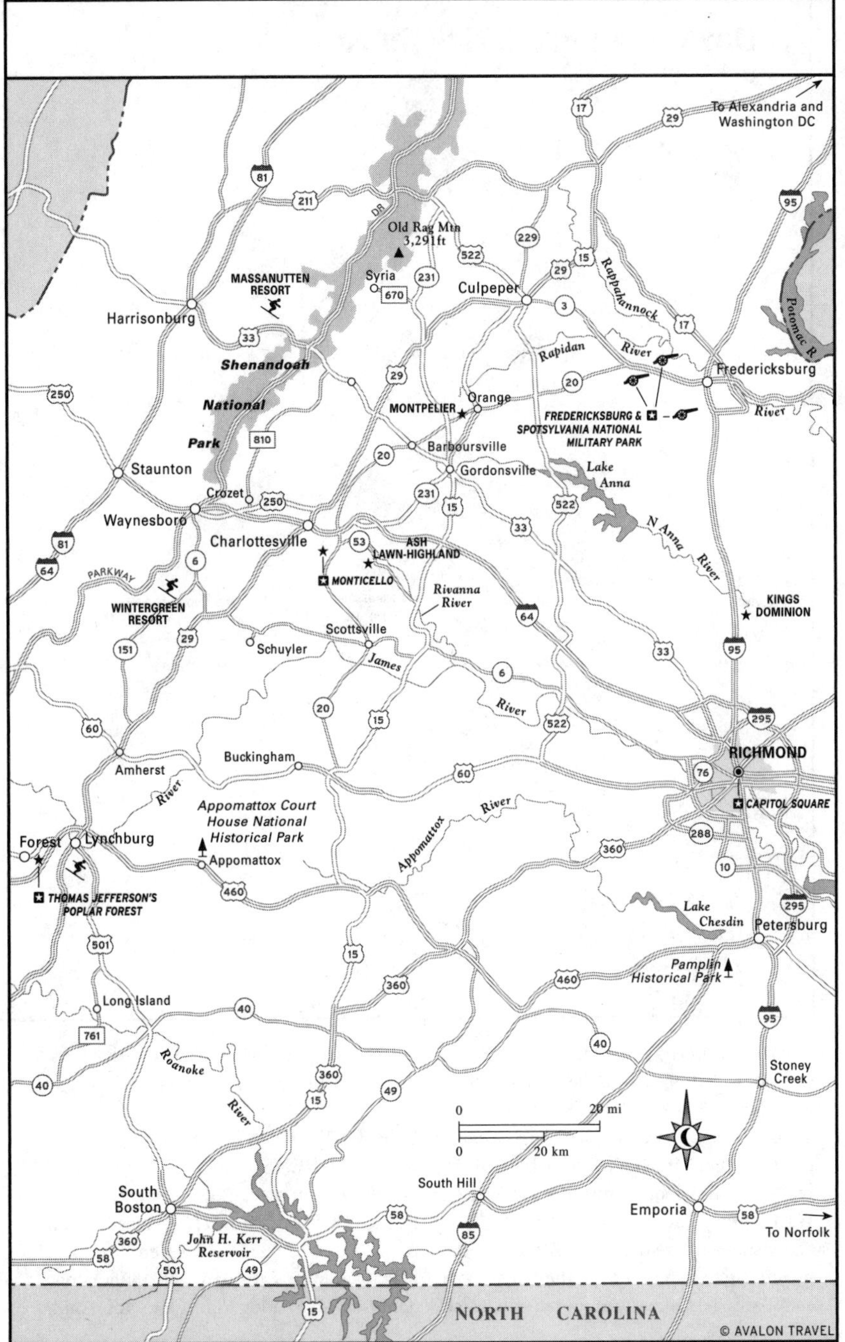
To Alexandria and Washington DC
Old Rag Mtn
3,291ft
MASSANUTTEN RESORT
Syria
Culpeper
Harrisonburg
Shenandoah National Park
Rappahannock
River
Rapidan
Potomac R
Fredericksburg
River
MONTPELIER
Orange
FREDERICKSBURG & SPOTSYLVANIA NATIONAL MILITARY PARK
Barboursville
Staunton
Gordonsville
Lake Anna
Crozet
Waynesboro
Charlottesville
N Anna River
ASH LAWN-HIGHLAND
PARKWAY
MONTICELLO
WINTERGREEN RESORT
Rivanna River
KINGS DOMINION
Scottsville
Schuyler
James
River
RICHMOND
Buckingham
Amherst
CAPITOL SQUARE
River
Appomattox Court House National Historical Park
River
Appomattox
Forest
Lynchburg
Appomattox
THOMAS JEFFERSON'S POPLAR FOREST
Lake Chesdin
Petersburg
Pamplin Historical Park
Long Island
Roanoke
River
Stoney Creek
0
20 mi
0
20 km
South Hill
South Boston
Emporia
To Norfolk
John H. Kerr Reservoir
NORTH CAROLINA
© AVALON TRAVEL

Downtown Fredericksburg

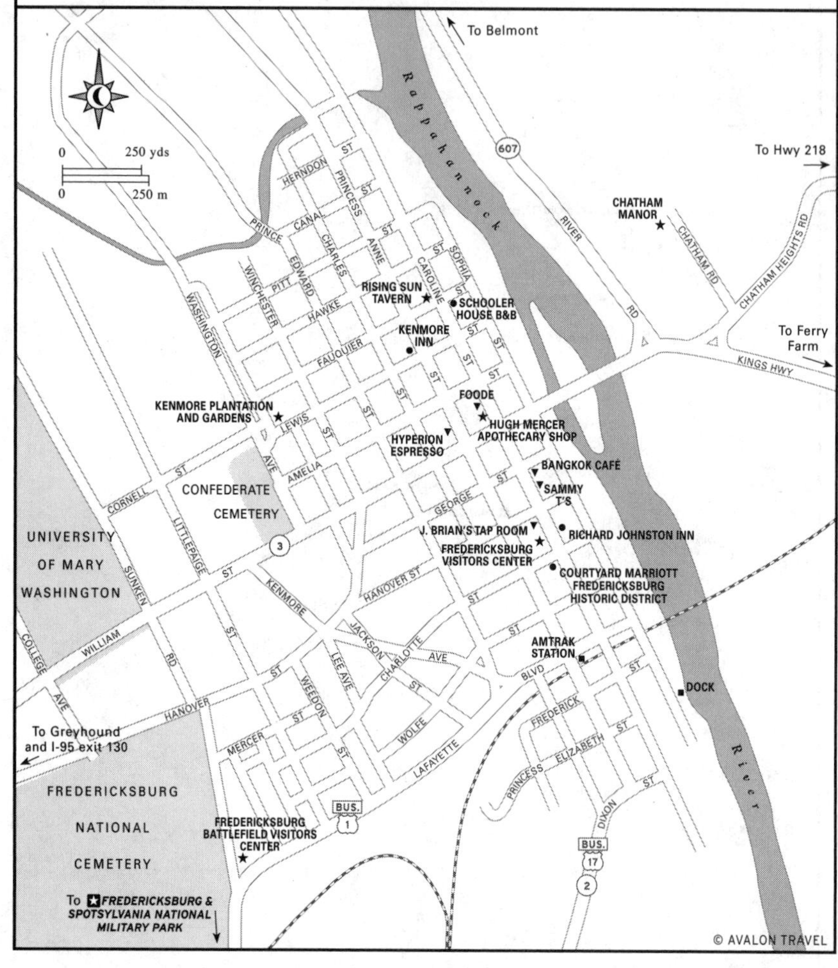

washingtonheritagemuseums.org, Mar.-Oct. Mon.-Sat. 9am-4pm, Sun. noon-5pm, Nov.-Feb. Mon.-Sat. 11am-4pm, Sun. noon-4pm, $5) makes for a fun visit. Hugh Mercer practiced medicine in Fredericksburg for 15 years, and his list of clients included Martha Washington. This shop dates back to 1742, and visitors are treated to lively tours of the reconstructed shop where they can learn about a variety of natural ingredients (such as leeches, crab claws, and lancets) that were used to cure common ailments.

KENMORE PLANTATION AND GARDENS

On the western edge of Old Town is the **Kenmore Plantation** (1201 Washington Ave., 540/373-3381, www.kenmore.org, Mar.-Oct. Mon.-Sat. 10am-5pm, Sun. noon-5pm, Nov.-Dec. Mon.-Sat. 10am-4pm, Sun.

noon-4pm, $10). The estate was built by Betty Washington (George Washington's sister) and her husband Fielding Lewis. Lewis owned a mercantile business but lost money during the Revolutionary War because he could no longer trade with England. He died while the state of Virginia still owed him the money that he had lent it to build a gun factory in Fredericksburg.

The Georgian-style brick home sits on three acres and is open for tours. It is elegant inside and out and noted for having stunning decorative plaster ceilings. Tours begin at the **Crowninshield Museum,** to the left of the front gate. Decorative arts and antique furnishings are on display there. Next, guides lead a 45-minute tour of the mansion's first floor and kitchen. The gardens are then available to explore on your own. Visitors who wish to visit both Kenmore and Ferry Farm can purchase a combination ticket for $15.

★ Fredericksburg & Spotsylvania National Military Park

Between 1862 and 1864, four Civil War battles were fought on the streets of Fredericksburg and in the fields and forests surrounding the city. The result was more than 100,000 casualties. The **Fredericksburg & Spotsylvania National Military Park** (540/693-3200, www.nps.gov/frsp, free) is the second-largest military park in the world. It can take two days to fully explore or visitors can choose to see specific sights. There are two visitors centers: the **Fredericksburg Battlefield Visitors Center** (1013 Lafayette Blvd., 540/693-3200, ext. 4040, daily 9am-5pm) and the **Chancellorsville Battlefield Visitor Center** (9001 Plank Rd., Spotsylvania, 540/693-3200, ext. 4050, daily 9am-5pm). Orientation films are available at both locations, as are maps to trails and driving tours.

The most important and well-known battle of the four that occurred here was the Battle of Fredericksburg, which took place on December 11-15, 1862. The battle was one of the largest (nearly 200,000 soldiers) and deadliest of the war and is known for being the "first major opposed river crossing in American military history." It was also the first time Union and Confederate troops fought right on city streets and as such is considered the first location of urban combat.

The Union's plan for the battle was for General Burnside's command to defeat General Lee's southern flank at Prospect Hill, while also holding the Confederate First Corps at Marye's Heights. The bloody battle raged for several days, eventually resulting in a Confederate victory and Burnside's troops retreating back across the river. Four generals were killed in the battle (two from each side).

The **Fredericksburg National Cemetery** was placed on Marye's Heights as the final resting place of more than 15,000 soldiers. Approximately 20 percent of the soldiers buried there have been identified.

A driving tour can be made of Prospect Hill and Marye's Heights. The route is five miles long. Directions for self-guided walking trails for a 400-yard walk around the Sunken Road, a short loop through the Fredericksburg National Cemetery, and several other short walks can be downloaded at the National Park Service website (www.nps.gov/frsp).

Across the Rappahannock from Fredericksburg is **Chatham Manor** (120 Chatham Ln., 540/693-3200, daily 9am-4:30pm), which served as a hospital during the battle. The home was built between 1768 and 1771. Five of the 10 rooms of this 12,000-square-foot Georgian estate are open for touring. Interior exhibits provide information on the home's 15 owners and the mansion's role in the Civil War.

Another Civil War battle that took place near Fredericksburg was the **Battle of Chancellorsville** (Apr. 30-May 6, 1863). It is best known as General Lee's "perfect battle," since his risky move of dividing his army against much greater enemy forces ended in a Confederate victory. During this battle

The Angel of Marye's Heights

During the horribly bloody Battle of Fredericksburg, more than 8,000 Union soldiers were wounded or killed in front of Marye's Heights at the Sunken Road on December 13. As dawn came on the morning of the 14th, many wounded soldiers who were not able to walk to the field hospital lay moaning and crying on the battlefield suffering from their wounds and a lack of water. Both armies had ceased fire and were forced to sit and listen to the agony.

A young soldier from the Confederate army, Richard Rowland Kirkland, finally requested permission to help the wounded Union soldiers by giving them water. He was first denied, but later was given permission at his own risk. The young man collected canteens, filled them with water, and risked his own life walking out on the battlefield. Realizing what he was doing, soldiers from both sides watched in silence and not one shot was fired.

Kirkland spent an hour and a half running between his lines and the wounded, bringing them water, blankets, and warm clothing. Wounded soldiers cried out for water as Kirkland performed his task, and he did not stop until he had helped each one that lay on the Confederate side of the field.

Kirkland was killed in battle only a year later. However, he will always be known as the Angel of Marye's Heights. A statue of him by artist Felix De Weldon (who also created the U.S. Marine Corps War Memorial) was erected in front of the stone wall at the Sunken Road and unveiled in 1965.

Stonewall Jackson was mortally wounded by friendly fire. He died eight days later at age 39.

The third is the **Battle of the Wilderness** (May 5-6, 1864). This engagement marked the start of the Overland Campaign, known as the bloodiest campaign of the war. It was also the first battle between Robert E. Lee and Ulysses S. Grant.

The fourth was a continuation of the Battle of the Wilderness, known as the **Battle of Spotsylvania Court House.** This conflict marked a sea change in the war: the Union army moved forward to Spotsylvania, and continued to push forward for the rest of the war.

Ferry Farm

Ferry Farm (268 Kings Hwy., 540/370-0732, www.kenmore.org, Mar.-Oct. Mon.-Sat. 10am-5pm, Sun. noon-5pm, Nov.-Dec. Mon.-Sat. 10am-4pm, Sun. noon-4pm, $8) was George Washington's childhood home. The 80-acre park is in Stafford, across the river from Fredericksburg. It is so named because people (including the Washingtons) used to cross the river by ferry from the farm to reach Fredericksburg. Washington lived there between the ages of 6 and 20, and this is where he is rumored to have chopped down the cherry tree and thrown a penny across the Rappahannock River. Not much remains of the original house, but there is a visitors center where colonial and Civil War artifacts that were found on the property are on display (there is an archaeological lab on-site where scientists work on weekdays). There are also gardens to explore featuring plants commonly grown in the 18th century. Visitors who wish to visit both Kenmore and Ferry Farm can purchase a combination ticket for $15.

Gari Melchers Home and Studio at Belmont

The **Gari Melchers Home and Studio at Belmont** (224 Washington St., Falmouth, 540/654-1015, www.garimelchers.umw.edu, Apr.-Oct. Thurs.-Tues. 10am-5pm, Nov.-Mar. Thurs.-Tues. 10am-4pm, $10) is the estate of one of the most sought-after painters of the late 1800s and early 1900s, Gari Melchers. Located in Falmouth, two miles north of Fredericksburg, visitors can tour the home where Melchers and his wife lived between 1916 and 1932 and enjoy the site's beautiful

27-acre grounds. There are four stunning art galleries with 1,677 paintings and drawings by Melchers and approximately 3,000 of his personal furnishings and decorative objects. There are also gardens and trails to enjoy. The home (originally built around 1790) and studio are one of just 30 artists spaces named in the National Trust for Historic Preservation's Historic Artists' Homes and Studios consortium. Tours of the estate, which run throughout the day, take 90 minutes and include a 12-minute film.

TOURS

Trolley Tours of Fredericksburg (540/898-0737, www.fredericksburgtrolley.com, $17) last 75 minutes and depart from the **Fredericksburg Visitor Center** (706 Caroline St.). Reservations are recommended during the summer months.

Old Towne Carriage Tours (540/318-7455, www.oldetownecarriages.com, $15) carries visitors around Fredericksburg in horse-drawn carriages. They offer daily tours in the historic district and can arrange private evening tours. Tours depart from the Fredericksburg Visitor Center (706 Caroline St.), and tickets can be purchased there.

Another interesting tour is aboard the 100-foot paddle-wheel boat called the ***City of Fredericksburg*** (804/453-2628, $30-50). The two-level boat cruises the Rappahannock starting from the dock at 201 Sophia Street. Trips include a buffet meal, and there's also a full bar and dance floor on board.

Additional tours of Fredericksburg can be arranged through the **Living History Company** (540/899-1776, www.historyexperiences.com, $15-60). Costumed actors accompany you on a personal walking or driving tour (different locations available) and provide a firsthand historical experience.

SHOPPING

In the past decade or two, the Fredericksburg area has seen tremendous growth as an exurb of Washington DC. As sprawling housing developments sprang up along the I-95 corridor, so did numerous strip malls. Many national chain stores can be found along Route 3 and farther north into Stafford County.

Old Town Fredericksburg, however, has remained a fun and charming place to shop. Art galleries and independently owned gift shops and boutiques line the historical streets, offering a nice break from the chain stores and the opportunity to buy one-of-a-kind merchandise. Princess Anne Street is the main shopping area, and contains several blocks of stores and restaurants. This is a pleasant area to window-shop or to look for a special Civil War-era gift or items made in Virginia.

SPORTS AND RECREATION

Fredericksburg sits on the banks of the Rappahannock River. As such, it lends itself to canoeing, kayaking, and boating in a relaxed and mostly pristine environment. At the southern end of Old Town is the **Fredericksburg City Dock.** The boat ramp there offers the best access to the Rappahannock River. Follow the river east along Sophia Street; the road dead-ends at the ramp. There is a nice parking area in which to leave your car. Be aware that water levels fluctuate a lot on the river. Springtime can bring massive floods, while late summer and fall can offer low, slow-moving water. The Chesapeake Bay can be reached via the Rappahannock River. Head downstream if you are in anything other than a kayak or canoe (away from the railroad bridge). Upstream can be very rocky, especially in low water.

Two local outfitters that can arrange outdoor instruction and rentals are the **Virginia Outdoor Center** (3219 Fall Hill Ave., 540/371-5085, www.playva.com) and **Clore Brothers Outfitters** (5927 River Rd., 540/786-7749, www.clorebros.com).

Mountain bikers can learn about local trails and events by visiting the

Fredericksburg City Dock

Fredericksburg Area Mountain Bike Enthusiasts website (www.fambe.org).

FOOD

American

Yummy pub fare with a healthy twist is what **Sammy T's** (801 Caroline St., 540/371-2008, www.sammyts.com, daily 11:30am-9:30pm, $7-13) is known for. A local favorite, this friendly place has a lot of atmosphere and a fun vibe. Sit at the bar and chat with new friends or grab a table and be treated to good service. They serve a wide variety of dishes and have many vegetarian and vegan entrées. There are a few outdoor seats right on Caroline Street.

J. Brian's Tap Room (200 Hanover St., 540/373-0738, www.jbrianstaproom.com, Sun.-Thurs. 11am-10pm, Fri.-Sat. 11am-11pm, $8-22) is a great local eatery in the historic district that's been around since 1961. They have delicious food at reasonable prices and offer a friendly atmosphere in an old building that has a lot of character. They have outdoor seating that is dog friendly (they even provide water bowls). The crab bisque is a winner, but their pizza and sandwiches are also good choices. This is a fine place to grab a drink with friends or enjoy a casual meal.

The popular **Foode** (1006 C/D Caroline St., 540/479-1370, www.foodeonline.com, lunch Tues.-Fri. 11am-3pm, dinner Tues.-Thurs. 4:30pm-8pm, Fri. 4:30pm-9pm, brunch Sat. 10am-2:30pm, Sun. 10am-2pm, $14-24) describes itself as "gourmet for the rest of us," and they believe the "freshest, cleanest ingredients make the best dishes." Apparently many people agree, because this nontraditional restaurant has become a favorite in Fredericksburg. The idea is simple: You order and pay at the counter, and then you sit at either the communal or individual tables. There is no table service, and they do not expect tips. The menu changes seasonally and highlights local products and produce and organic ingredients. The dinner menu includes items such as burgers, grilled sausage on polenta, oven-roasted chicken, and pork chops. There is also a wine and beer list, a kids' menu, and desserts. They also offer a five-course tasting dinner each night to a limited number of guests (reservations required).

Italian

A favorite local Italian eatery is **Castiglia's Italian Restaurant and Pizzeria** (10705 Courthouse Rd., 540/891-7300, www.mycastiglias.com, Mon.-Thurs. 11am-9:30pm,

Fri.-Sat. 11am-10pm, Sun. noon-8:30pm, $12-16). They serve authentic homemade dishes that are "made by real Italians, born in Italy." The menu includes scrumptious pasta, classic Italian entrées, seafood, sandwiches, wood-fired pizza, and a few surprises (such as Italian fried chicken). There is even a lunch buffet during the week 11am-3pm for $5.99 that features pizza, stromboli, soup, and salad. Their house salad dressing alone is worth the trip. They offer coupons online.

Coffee and Treats

Hyperion Espresso (301 William St., 540/373-4882, www.hyperionespresso.com, Mon.-Thurs. 7am-8pm, Fri.-Sat. 7am-10pm, Sun. 8am-8pm, under $10) is the local favorite for coffee lovers. It is a comfortable, unpretentious place to grab a good cup of coffee and a light meal or snack. Sit outside (you can bring your pooch) and watch the world go by. This is a hometown coffee place that will please even the pickiest travelers.

No trip to Fredericksburg is complete without a stop at ★ **Carl's** (2200 Princess Anne St., open seasonally, under $10). Carl's is perhaps the most famous ice-cream stand in the state and is truly a landmark. Don't be scared off if the line of eager patrons is wrapped around the building (which will no doubt include everyone from your grandmother to police officers, small children, and tattoo-clad bikers). The line will move quickly—just have your money and your order ready when it's your turn at the window.

ACCOMMODATIONS

There are many large hotels in the Fredericksburg area, but in the historic district visitors can choose from among a handful of lovely and historic bed-and-breakfasts.

Under $100

Comfort Suites Fredericksburg (4615 Southpoint Pkwy., 540/891-1112, www.choicehotels.com, $119-124) is an all-suite hotel offering 85 guest rooms with two double beds or one king bed. All suites have a parlor with a sofa bed. The hotel is near I-95 and a short drive to the historic district. The hotel lobby welcomes guests with a five-story atrium and a large stone fireplace. A complimentary hot breakfast is included, and there is an indoor pool and fitness room.

$100-200

The **Hampton Inn & Suites Fredericksburg South** (4800 Market St., 540/898-5000, www.

Carl's

hamptoninn3.hilton.com, $96-114) offers 121 guest rooms and is a five-minute drive from the historic district. There is an indoor pool, and a hot breakfast is included.

The **Schooler House Bed and Breakfast** (1303 Caroline St., 540/374-5258, www.schoolerhouse.com, $160-175) is a small Victorian-style home built in 1891. It offers two guest rooms with private fireplaces and bathrooms. Original pine floors and trim are still in place throughout much of the house, and the four fireplaces have restored antique tile. The home is decorated with many antiques (even the wicker furniture on the front porch is antique). A full breakfast is included. Pets and children are discouraged.

The historic ★ **Kenmore Inn** (1200 Princess Anne St., 540/371-7622, www.kenmoreinn.com, $130-225) offers nine well-appointed guest rooms with private bathrooms in a historic home on Princess Anne Street. The rooms are not terribly large, but they are beautiful and cozy. Luxury rooms are located in the original portion of the home, which was built in 1793. These rooms have high ceilings, hardwood floors, and wood-burning fireplaces. Deluxe rooms are located in an addition that was put on the home in 1933 and have antique furniture and wall-to-wall carpeting. The inn has a comfortable porch with chairs and swings. Some street parking is available. Breakfast is served in the main dining room, and evening meals can be taken in the wonderful restaurant downstairs. Ask for a room in the front of the house.

The **Richard Johnston Inn** (711 Caroline St., 540/899-7606, www.therichardjohnstoninn.com, $150-300) was built in 1770 and during the 1800s was home to Richard Johnston, the mayor or Fredericksburg. The inn has seven guest rooms and two suites, all with private bathrooms. A continental breakfast is served during the week, and a full breakfast is served on weekends. The inn has two pet-friendly rooms. It is located three blocks from the train station, and parking is available on-site.

The **Courtyard Marriott Fredericksburg Historic District** (620 Caroline St., 540/373-8300, www.marriott.com, $159-244) offers 94 comfortable, modern rooms in the historic district.

INFORMATION AND SERVICES

The **Fredericksburg Visitor Center** (706 Caroline St., 540/373-1776, www.visitfred.com, daily 9am-5pm) provides wonderful

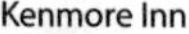
Kenmore Inn

information on touring the Fredericksburg area. Maps, brochures, parking information, tickets, and lodging information are just some of the things visitors can learn about from the helpful staff. A short orientation film about the city is shown there.

GETTING THERE AND AROUND

Fredericksburg is about 50 miles south of the nation's capital. A **Virginia Railway Express** (703/684-1001 or 800/743-3873, www.vre.org) and **Amtrak** (800/872-7245, www.amtrak.com) station may be found at 200 Lafayette Boulevard. Commuter service runs to Alexandria and Washington DC.

The local bus system, called the **Fredericksburg Regional Transit (FRED)** (540/372-1222, www.ridefred.com, $1), provides local bus transportation on weekdays year-round and on weekends during the school year.

Richmond

Richmond is the capital of the Commonwealth of Virginia. The city is independent, but the Richmond area encompasses part of Henrico and Chesterfield Counties.

The city was founded in 1737 and is significant in both Revolutionary and Civil War history. During the Revolutionary War, Richmond was the site of Patrick Henry's famous "Give me liberty or give me death" speech, and it became the capital of Virginia in 1780. During the Civil War, Richmond was the Confederate capital.

Richmond was known in the early 20th century as home to one of the first successful streetcar systems. It was also a center of African American culture.

Today, Richmond is a vibrant, ever-changing city. Many neighborhoods have undergone major revitalizations over the past decades, although some are still waiting for their turn. Outdoor recreation is gaining popularity, even in the shadow of the downtown buildings. This is due in part to the James River flowing through the city limits and the plethora of activities it allows for.

The Richmond economy is fueled by the presence of federal, state, and local government agencies, banking firms, and legal agencies. The U.S. Court of Appeals for the Fourth Circuit and the Federal Reserve Bank of Richmond are located in Richmond. Many private companies, large and small, also call Richmond home.

Richmond is a city of colleges and universities. The University of Richmond (UR), Virginia Commonwealth University (VCU) and its Medical College of Virginia branch, Virginia Union University, and the Union Theological Seminary all call the city home.

Safety can be an issue on the downtown streets after dark. It is best to drive through town at night rather than walk. Many hotels offer shuttles around the city, but if yours does not, drive or call a cab.

SIGHTS

Richmond is carved up geographically into five primary sections: Downtown, the East End, West End, North Side, and South Side. It sounds simple at first, but Richmonders like to further distinguish areas of the city by neighborhood names. This becomes confusing to visitors who have no frame of reference for each neighborhood and is further complicated by the loosely defined boundaries. For simplicity's sake, the sights in this guide are broken out by the directional distinctions, and additional information is provided on specific neighborhoods that are either commonly known or have distinct characteristics that might be of interest to visitors.

Central Richmond

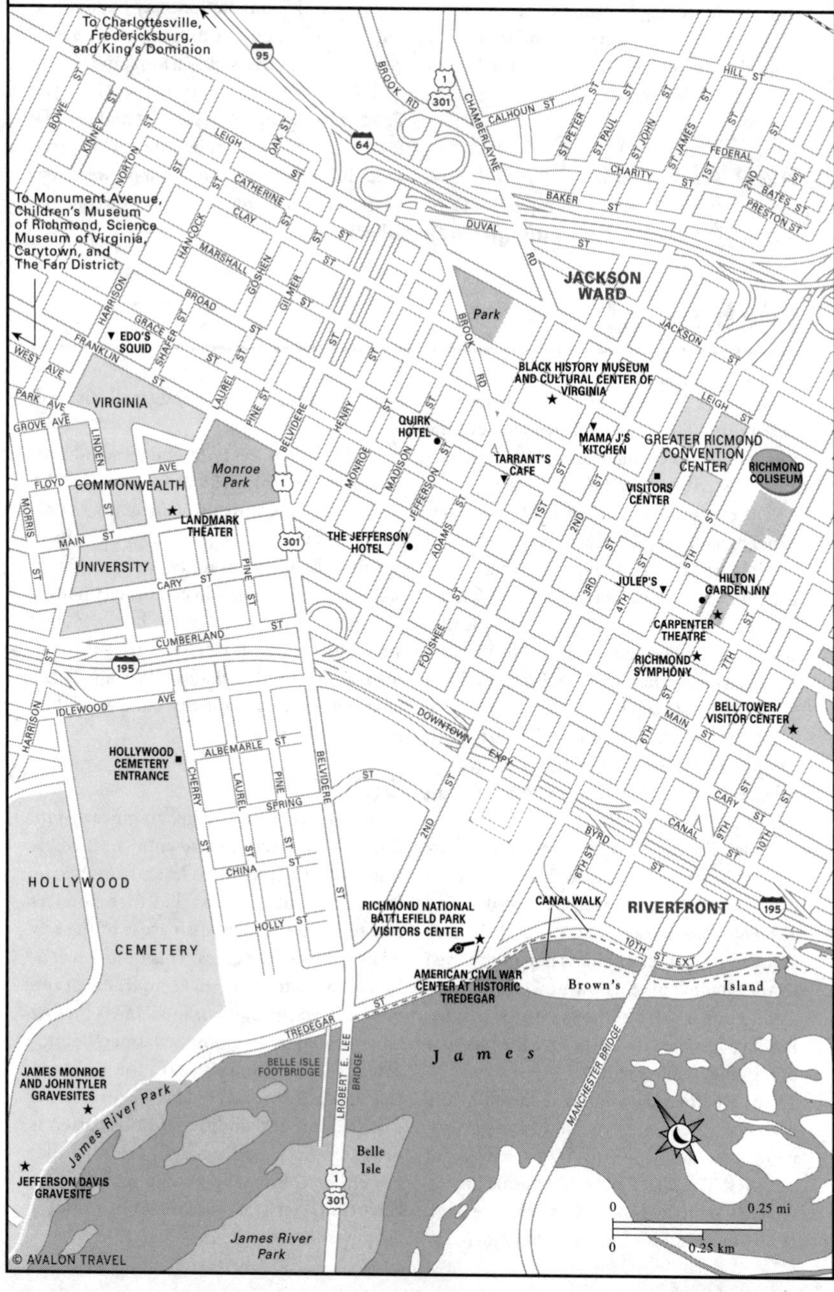

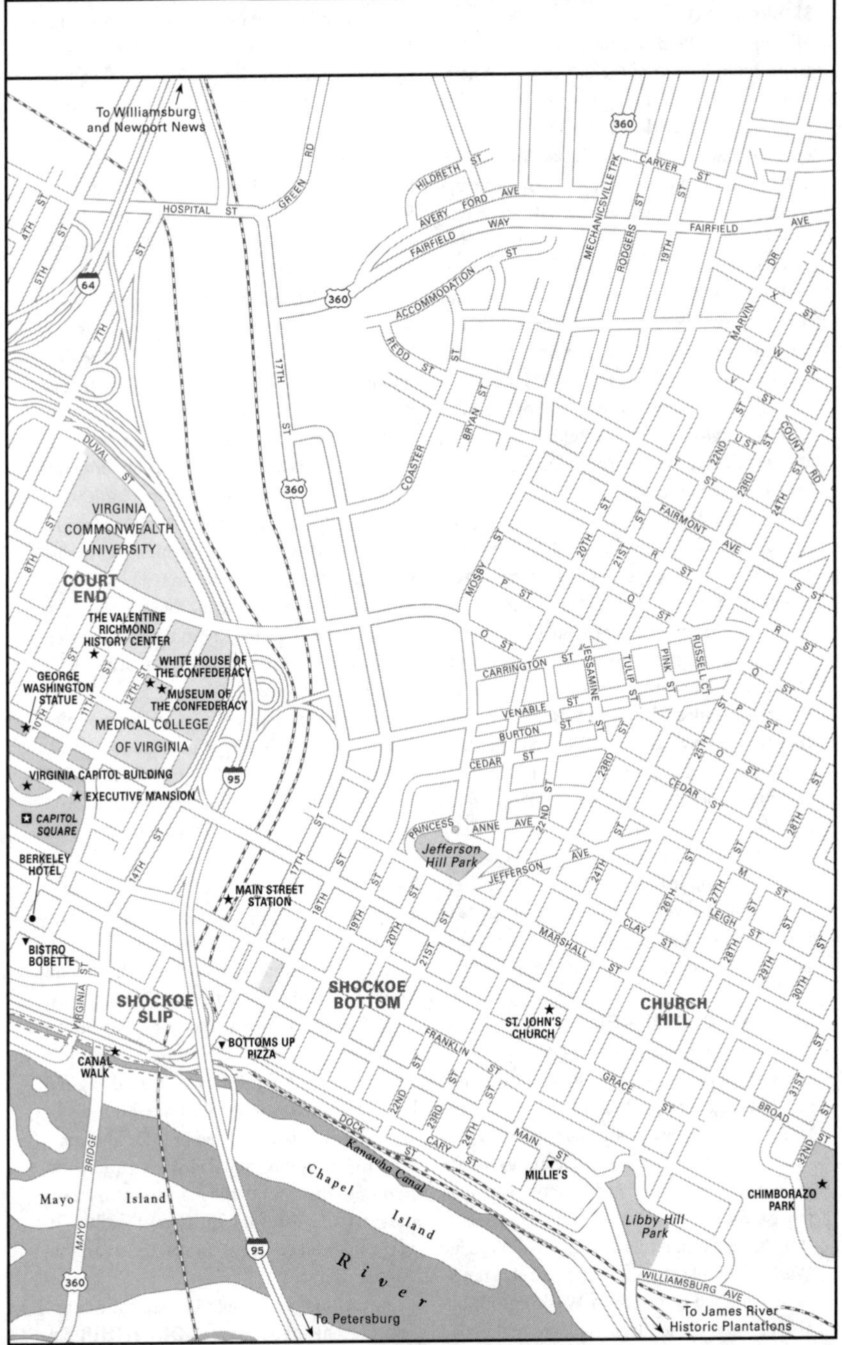
To Williamsburg and Newport News
HOSPITAL ST
GREEN RD
HILDRETH ST
AVERY FORD AVE
FAIRFIELD WAY
FAIRFIELD AVE
CARVER ST
MECHANICSVILLE TPK
ROGERS ST
19TH ST
ACCOMMODATION ST
REDD ST
MARVIN DR
BRYAN ST
COASTER ST
17TH ST
4TH ST
5TH ST
7TH ST
8TH ST
DUVAL ST
VIRGINIA COMMONWEALTH UNIVERSITY
COURT END
THE VALENTINE RICHMOND HISTORY CENTER
WHITE HOUSE OF THE CONFEDERACY
MUSEUM OF THE CONFEDERACY
GEORGE WASHINGTON STATUE
MEDICAL COLLEGE OF VIRGINIA
VIRGINIA CAPITOL BUILDING
EXECUTIVE MANSION
CAPITOL SQUARE
BERKELEY HOTEL
BISTRO BOBETTE
MAIN STREET STATION
SHOCKOE SLIP
SHOCKOE BOTTOM
CHURCH HILL
BOTTOMS UP PIZZA
CANAL WALK
ST. JOHN'S CHURCH
MILLIE'S
CHIMBORAZO PARK
Jefferson Hill Park
Libby Hill Park
PRINCESS ANNE AVE
JEFFERSON AVE
MOSBY ST
FAIRMONT AVE
CARRINGTON ST
JESSAMINE ST
TULIP ST
PINK ST
RUSSELL CT
VENABLE ST
BURTON ST
CEDAR ST
MARSHALL ST
CLAY ST
LEIGH ST
FRANKLIN ST
GRACE ST
BROAD ST
MAIN ST
CARY ST
DOCK ST
WILLIAMSBURG AVE
COUNT RD
Kanawha Canal
Mayo Island
Chapel Island
River
MAYO BRIDGE
VIRGINIA ST
To Petersburg
To James River Historic Plantations
360
64
95

Downtown

Downtown, like it sounds, is at the heart of Richmond. The area includes the financial district and several popular neighborhoods such as **Court End,** which sits to the north of Capitol Square and East Broad Street. This neighborhood was developed during the federal era, just after the state capital was moved to Richmond. The area is a combination of historic mansions and modern office space.

Jackson Ward is historically the center for African American commerce and entertainment. It is less than a mile from the Capitol, west of Court End and north of Broad Street. Many famous people such as Duke Ellington, Ella Fitzgerald, Lena Horne, Billie Holiday, and James Brown frequented the neighborhood.

Monroe Ward is a historic district (east of the Fan District) that is now home to many VCU students. The historic **Jefferson Hotel** is located there.

Not far from the financial district is a charming neighborhood of cobblestone streets and alleys that runs along the James River. It is called **Shockoe Slip** after a creek that ran through the area. "Shacquohocan" was a Native American word for the large flat rocks that collected at the mouth of the creek, and the word "Slip" refers to boat slips. The neighborhood consists mainly of Italianate-style brick and iron-front structures, including restored taverns and warehouses. It is Richmond's most fashionable district and is now known for its dining and shopping.

★ CAPITOL SQUARE

Capitol Square is a historic 12-acre parcel of grassy, beautifully landscaped public grounds that house government buildings, serve as the site for inauguration and commemoration events, and function as a civic campus for the governing of Virginia. A distinctive cast-iron fence built in 1818 surrounds the grounds.

A giant equestrian statue of George Washington sits at the formal square entrance. It was erected in honor of Washington, but also to hail the role Virginia played in the road to independence. More than 130 paintings and statues honor distinguished American figures inside the buildings in Capitol Square and also outdoors. Living memorial trees are also part of the square's landscape.

The focal point of Capitol Square is the **Virginia Capitol Building** (10th and Bank Sts., 804/698-1788, www.virginiacapitol.gov, Mon.-Sat. 8am-5pm, Sun. 1pm-5pm, free). It has been the home of the General Assembly since 1788. The stunning monumental classical-style structure was the handiwork of Thomas Jefferson, who designed it as the first public building in the New World. Jefferson modeled it after the Maison Carrée, a 1st-century Roman temple at Nîmes in southern France that has been the inspiration for many other capitol buildings, municipal buildings, and courthouses throughout the country.

In the Capitol's central rotunda is a marble sculpture of George Washington. It is said to be the most valuable marble statue in the United States because George himself posed for it. Seven portrait busts of other U.S. presidents who were natives of Virginia and one of Lafayette, who fought for the colonies in the Revolutionary War, are also displayed.

House and Senate chambers were added to the Capitol in 1904, and additional renovations were made between 2005 and 2007.

Free guided tours are held Monday-Saturday 9am-4pm and Sunday 1pm-4pm. Self-guided tours are also available daily.

East of the Capitol, but still within Capitol Square, stands the **Executive Mansion** (804/786-2211). This federal-era mansion is the oldest continually inhabited governor's residence in the country. It was designed by architect Alexander Parris (who lived in Boston) and was completed in 1813. The home is a Virginia and National Historic Landmark. Rooms in the front of the mansion still retain most of the original ceilings, woodwork, and plaster cornices. Tours are available Tuesday-Thursday.

Additional buildings in Capitol Square include the neoclassical **Oliver Hill Sr.**

Building (Virginia's first state library, to the east of the Capitol), the 12-story **Washington Building** (in the southeast corner), and the brick **Bell Tower** (in the southwest corner).

MUSEUM OF THE CONFEDERACY

The **Museum of the Confederacy** (1201 Clay St., 804/649-1861, www.acwm.org, daily 10am-5pm, $10) houses the largest collection of Confederate artifacts in the country. The museum's mission is to be the center for the "display, study, interpretation, commemoration, and preservation of the history and artifacts of the Confederate States of America." It is easy to see that they have accomplished this: The museum holds more than 130,000 relics and documents spread out over three floors. Appropriately located in the Confederate capital, the museum does a good job of presenting the collection in an objective manner (mostly). Display highlights include Stonewall Jackson's revolver, General Robert E. Lee's sword and coat, and the pen Lee used to sign the Confederate army's surrender.

Right next door to the Museum of the Confederacy is the **White House of the Confederacy** (guided tours only, $10). It is Jefferson Davis's former executive mansion, which served as the political, social, and military center of the Confederacy. The house has been fully restored to its original appearance.

A combination admission fee of $15 is charged for both the Museum of the Confederacy and the White House of the Confederacy.

BLACK HISTORY MUSEUM AND CULTURAL CENTER OF VIRGINIA

The **Black History Museum and Cultural Center of Virginia** (122 W. Leigh St., 804/780-9093, www.blackhistorymuseum.org, Tues.-Sat. 10am-5pm, $10), is a permanent repository for artifacts as well as visual, oral, and written records that commemorate the accomplishments of African Americans in Virginia, with detailed exhibits on Richmond's African American history. The museum is housed in the historic Leigh Street Armory.

CANAL WALK

Richmond's **Canal Walk** (14th and Dock Streets) was completed in 1999 and stretches for 1.25 miles through downtown Richmond near in the Shockoe Slip area along the Haxall Canal and James River & Kanawha Canals. The walk can be accessed from 5th Street, 7th Street, Virginia Street, 14th Street, 15th Street, and 17th Street. Four centuries of history can be explored along the walk as it passes by monuments and exhibits and also the popular **Brown's Island,** a park that hosts festivals, art exhibits, and concerts.

RICHMOND NATIONAL BATTLEFIELD PARK

The **Richmond National Battlefield Park** (www.nps.gov/rich, daily sunrise to sunset, free) is a collection of 13 individual sites that preserve more than 1,900 acres of Civil War history. The sites are located in Hanover, Henrico, and Chesterfield counties as well as the city of Richmond. The park tells the story of Richmond's involvement in the war between 1861 and 1865.

The **Tredegar Visitor Center** (470 Tredegar St., daily 9am-4:30pm) is the main visitor center for the park. It is housed inside the former Tredegar Ironworks building, which was an important asset to Confederate troops since it produced their cannons and ammunition. The center offers three floors of displays and an orientation film. The **Chimborazo Medical Museum** (3215 East Broad Street, daily 9am-4:30pm) is another visitor center for the park that contains exhibits that focus on Confederate medical equipment and hospitals. This building is also the park headquarters. There are three additional visitor centers in the park: **Cold Harbor Battlefield Visitor Center** (5515 Anderson-Wright Drive, 9am-4:30pm), which offers a book store, ranger programs in the summer, and electric map programs that provide information on the 1862 Battle of Gaines' Mill and the 1864 Battle of Cold Harbor; the **Fort Harrison Visitor Center** (8621 Battlefield Park Road, daily during summer 9am-4:30pm), which offers a self-guided walking trail, a relief map of the fort, and a short informational film; and the **Glendale/Malvern Hill Battlefields Visitor Center** (8301 Willis Church Road, June, July and early August, daily 9am-4:30pm), which offers information on the final two battles of the 1862 Seven Days campaign.

Also on the RNBP site is the **American Civil War Center at Historic Tredegar** (500 Tredegar St., 804/780-1865, www.acwm.org, daily 9am-5pm, $8). Located on the James River, this center is the first museum to interpret the American Civil War from the Union, Confederate, and African American viewpoints. The center is a National Historic Landmark and consists of five buildings from the ironworks era sitting on eight acres. Although the National Park Service's visitor center is located in one of the buildings, this center is operated independently from the rest of the park.

East End

The East End of Richmond is a collection of neighborhoods loosely defined as the area north of the James River and east of the historic Virginia Central Railroad-Chesapeake & Ohio Railway line.

Church Hill, one of the largest existing 19th-century neighborhoods in the country, is located at the end of Broad Street, a primary east-west road through Richmond. It retains numerous examples of period architecture.

Fulton Hill runs roughly from Gillies Creek to the Richmond city limits. This is an urban neighborhood that is finally seeing renovations after years of neglect, which can be credited in part to the dedication of its community in dealing with criminal activity in the area.

Major nightlife can be found in **Shockoe Bottom,** just east of downtown near the James River. This is one of Richmond's oldest neighborhoods, and although it has a history of flooding from the James River, it has become a hot spot for dining, entertainment, and partying. Just east of Shockoe Bottom is **Tobacco Row,** so named for a group of multistory brick tobacco warehouses and factories producing cigarettes. The buildings were vacated in the 1980s, but many of the warehouses have since been converted into loft apartments, condos, retail space, and offices. The neighborhood sits adjacent to the James River and was the site of two famous Confederate prisons, **Libby Prison** and **Castle Thunder.**

One of the most historic neighborhoods in Richmond is **Union Hill,** an area bordered to the south by Jefferson Avenue, to the north by Venable Street, to the east by 25th Street, and to the west by Mosby Street. Union Hill sits high on a bluff above Shockoe Bottom. Its mix of antebellum, Victorian, classical revival, and modern architecture has landed the neighborhood in the National Register of Historic Places and the Virginia Landmarks Register.

SAINT JOHN'S CHURCH

Saint John's Church (2401 E. Broad St., 804/648-5015, www.historicstjohnschurch.org, Mon.-Sat. 10am-4pm, Sun. 1pm-4pm), in Church Hill, was built in 1741 and served as a place of worship but also as a local meeting hall. When the assembly of the Second Virginia Convention moved from Williamsburg to Richmond, Saint John's was its meeting place. In March of 1775, as things heated up between Virginia and England, many prominent historical figures, such as George Washington, Thomas Jefferson, and Richard Henry attended the meeting where Patrick Henry gave his famous "Give me liberty or give me death" speech. Services are still held in Saint John's Church, and visitors are welcome.

CHIMBORAZO PARK

Chimborazo Park (3200 E. Broad St., open sunrise to sunset), in Church Hill, is the former site of the Chimborazo Hospital,

the largest American Civil War hospital. The hospital served the Confederate army between 1862 and 1865. During that time, more than 76,000 soldiers were treated there, and it had a 20 percent mortality rate. The National Park Service now owns the site. The 30-acre park offers a 180-degree view of the city and is home to the headquarters of Richmond National Battlefield Park. There is a small house on the east side of the park that is available to rent for events. The **Church Hill Dog Park** is also located on the east side of the park and includes an area for large dogs and one for small dogs.

West End

The boundaries of the West End are most commonly considered to be north of the James River, west of I-195, and south of Broad Street.

Byrd Park is a residential neighborhood north of a park with the same name and south of the Downtown Expressway. The neighborhood contains row homes from the 1920s and bungalows, ranch houses, Cape Cods, and American foursquare homes from the 1930s and 1940s.

Carytown is a thriving and eclectic cluster of 1920s homes, restaurants, antiques stores, clothing stores, and cafés. The 2800-3500 blocks of Cary Street, west of the **Boulevard** (a historic street that provides entrance to Byrd Park and divides Carytown and the Museum District from the Fan District), are the most active. The neighboring **Museum District** is just north of Carytown. This neighborhood (also known as West of the Boulevard) is home to a number of large institutions such as the **Virginia Museum of Fine Arts** and the **Virginia Historical Society.**

On the eastern edge of the West End of town is the **Fan District.** It is named simply for the "fan" formed by the streets that run west from Belvidere Street. The area is bordered to the north by Broad Street and to the south by Route 195. The neighborhood is mostly residential and includes late-19th-century and early-20th-century homes. Historic **Monument Avenue** is located there, as are numerous cafés.

South of Cary Street, west of Belvidere Street, and north of the James River and Canal is **Oregon Hill,** a neighborhood of affordable housing that is a popular location for students to live. The Cowboy Junkies rock band released a song in 1992 called "Oregon Hill," the lyrics of which describe this neighborhood.

BYRD PARK

Byrd Park (600 S. Boulevard, www.richmondgov.com) is a 287-acre public park just south of the Byrd Park neighborhood. It has a one-mile trail, an amphitheater, three small lakes, tennis courts, baseball fields, and a playground. Pedal boats are available for rent during the summer. The park is named after William Byrd II, whose family owned a large portion of the land in Richmond when it was founded in 1737.

VIRGINIA MUSEUM OF FINE ARTS

The **Virginia Museum of Fine Arts** (200 N. Boulevard, 804/340-1400, www.vmfa.museum, Sat.-Wed. 10am-5pm, Thurs.-Fri. 10am-9pm, free) first opened its doors in the middle of the Great Depression in 1936. Its purpose was to become the flagship art museum in Virginia and to lead an educational network throughout the state to bring the best of world art to Virginia. Today, the museum is state-supported and privately endowed. It is known for its wide range of world art collections and their exceptional aesthetic quality.

The building and grounds are lovely, and the exhibits are first-rate. Permanent exhibits cover topics such as African art, American art, ancient art, East Asian art, European art, English silver, Fabergé, and modern and contemporary art. The upstairs restaurant in the museum is wonderful, with a sculpture garden that can be viewed while eating. The museum is located in the Museum District.

VIRGINIA HISTORICAL SOCIETY

The **Virginia Historical Society** (428 N. Boulevard, 804/358-4901, www.vahistorical.org, daily 10am-5pm, free), in the Museum District, is a research and teaching center for Virginia history as well as a large repository. The Virginia Historical Society offers many award-winning exhibits in 13 galleries. It is the official state historical society and has the largest display of artifacts from Virginia.

MONUMENT AVENUE

The most recognized street in Richmond is Monument Avenue. It runs through the northern border of the Fan District and is known as one of the most beautiful boulevards in the world. The tree-lined street with a large grass median and six grand statues along a 1.5-mile section is a fantastic example of the "Grand American Avenue" style of city planning. The first statue was of Robert E. Lee and was erected in 1890. Other famous Americans honored on the street include Civil War figures J. E. B. Stuart, Jefferson Davis, and Stonewall Jackson, as well as Matthew Fontaine Maury (a Richmond native known as the "Father of the Seas"), and tennis star Arthur Ashe.

Monument Avenue is lined with beautiful historic homes and churches and a one-mile segment is still surfaced with original cobblestones. The avenue is listed in the National Register of Historic Places and has been named one of 10 "great" streets in America by the American Planning Association.

HOLLYWOOD CEMETERY

Just west of Oregon Hill is the **Hollywood Cemetery** (412 S. Cherry St., 804/648-8501, www.hollywoodcemetery.org, daily 8am-5pm, free). Jefferson Davis, James Monroe, and John Tyler may be the most famous "residents" in this forever home, but many others such as J. E. B. Stuart and more than 20 additional Confederate generals, two Supreme Court justices, six Virginia governors, and the very first battle casualty of the Civil War keep them in good company. The cemetery sprawls over 135 acres and has stunning views of the James River.

North Side

The North Side of Richmond has a diversity of residential neighborhoods with a wide mix of architectural styles represented. Portions of Henrico County and Hanover County are broadly regarded as part of the North Side.

The most noted neighborhood on the North Side is **Three Corners,** which sits north of Broad Street and east of the Boulevard. The triangle-shaped area (hence the name) has notable landmarks situated near each corner. Near the north point is **The Diamond** baseball stadium (3001 North Boulevard), home to the VCU Rams and the Richmond Flying Squirrels (a minor league baseball team). Near the west corner is the **Science Museum of Virginia,** and near the east corner is the **Sauers Vanilla Factory,** which displays one of the country's oldest moving lightbulb billboards.

SCIENCE MUSEUM OF VIRGINIA

To the west of Three Corners is the **Science Museum of Virginia** (2500 W. Broad St., 804/864-1400, www.smv.org, Tues.-Sat. 9:30am-5pm, Sun. 11:30am-5pm, exhibits only $11, IMAX only $9, exhibits and IMAX $16). Housed in the former Broad Street Station (built in 1919) and established in 1970, the museum includes many exciting permanent exhibits on space, electricity, health, and the earth and also has unique visiting exhibits from around the globe. Some of the things you can expect to see include the world's largest analemmic sundial (located in the parking lot), the largest exhibit in the world on crystallography, the world's first aluminum submarine, the world's first solar airplane, a state-of-the-art IMAX theater and planetarium, live animals (including a basketball team of rats), and the world's largest kugel ball. You can't miss the green copper dome that sits on top of the building. This is a great stop for both children and adults.

The Grand Kugel

kugel ball at the Science Museum of Virginia in Richmond

The word *kugel* is a German term for ball or sphere. A kugel ball is a large, heavy, perfectly spherical sculpture made of granite that is supported by a thin film of water. Although it can weigh thousands of pounds, the ball spins on top of the water due to the lubrication provided by the water.

Kugel balls are found in many parts of the world. One popular kugel ball is at the Science Museum of Virginia in Richmond, and is famous for its enormous size. The ball currently on display is actually their second ball; the first, the "Grand Kugel" unveiled in 2003, was carved from South African black granite, was more than eight feet in diameter, and cost approximately $1.5 million. However, shortly after its installation, the Grand Kugel cracked, eventually preventing it from floating. In 2005, a replacement kugel ball was installed. It is recognized as the world's largest floating-ball sculpture by the *Guinness Book of World Records*. The original can be found on display behind the museum.

South Side

The South Side refers to areas that are south of the James River.

Manchester is both a residential and industrial neighborhood across the James River from the Canal Walk. This is an area of new development where modern homes, loft condos, and businesses are part of the revitalization process.

Westover Hills, an established neighborhood also south of the James River, sits at the intersection of Route 161 and the Boulevard Bridge. It is home to many restaurants, churches, and businesses.

The **Woodland Heights** neighborhood was built in the early 1900s along the James River. It is listed in the National Register of Historic Places and also in the Virginia Landmarks Register.

ENTERTAINMENT AND EVENTS

Tours

Richmond History Tours are provided

through the **Valentine Richmond History Center** (804/649-0711, ext. 301, www.richmondhistorycenter.com). They offer more than 370 tours by foot, bus, and even with your dog. Professional guides lead all tours.

Performing Arts

The **Landmark Theater** (6 N. Laurel St., 804/592-3368, www.landmarktheater.net) first opened in 1927 as a Shriner facility and was called the Mosque Theater. The City of Richmond purchased the theater in 1940. This popular stage on the VCU campus west of downtown hosts concerts, lectures, comedians, commencements, and fashion shows.

The **Richmond CenterStage** (804/592-3330, www.richmondcenterstage.com) is a performing arts complex in downtown Richmond offering a wide array of performances in three venues. The primary venue is the **Carpenter Theatre,** a beautifully renovated grand theater that is more than 80 years old.

The **Richmond Symphony** (612 E. Grace St., 804/788-1212, www.richmondsymphony.com) was founded in 1957 and gives more than 200 appearances each year. Consult the website for a list of upcoming performances.

The **Virginia Opera** (866/673-7282, www.vaopera.org) is the premier opera performance company in Virginia. They offer 40 performances in three markets (Richmond, Fairfax, and Norfolk). Consult the website for a schedule of events.

The largest ballet company in town is the **Richmond Ballet** (804/344-0906, www.richmondballet.com), one of the best ballet companies on the East Coast. The **Concert Ballet of Virginia** (804/798-0945, www.concertballet.com) is another wonderful local ballet company.

Theater

A beautiful historic movie palace called the **Byrd Theater** (2908 W. Cary St., 804/353-9911, byrdtheatre.com) in Carytown was built in 1928 at the astronomical cost of $900,000 (which would be more than $11 million today). Movie tickets were 50 cents. It now shows second-run movies for $1.99. The original manager of the theater, Robert Coulter, remained there until 1971 and is rumored to now haunt the theater.

Nightlife

Richmond is an active city with a large population of students and twentysomethings. There's no shortage of nightlife, especially around the Shockoe neighborhood. Establishments in Virginia are required by law to serve food if they serve alcohol, so much of the action can be found in local restaurants. As with many cities, it is safer to drive or take a cab after dark in Richmond.

A popular hip-hop dance club in Shockoe Slip is **Infuzion** (1401 Roseneath Rd., 804/447-6852, www.clubinfuzion.com, Fri.-Sat. 10pm-2am, $10-15 cover). They call themselves the "most elaborate dance facility in Richmond," and have three dance floors, extensive lighting, video projectors, televisions, and an outdoor smoking area. The decor is modern, and the crowd is generally in the 25- to 35-year-old range. They also offer VIP rooms.

The **Tobacco Company** (1201 E. Cary St., 804/782-9555, www.thetobaccocompany.com, no cover) is a Shockoe Slip restaurant that includes a classy lounge and bar area featuring live entertainment Thursday-Sunday. They are known for quality jazz, blues, rock, and acoustic performances on Friday and Saturday and local entertainers on Sunday. Shows begin at 9:30pm.

It is difficult to beat the atmosphere at **Havana 59** (16 N. 17th St., 804/780-2822, www.havana59.net, Mon.-Sat. bar opens at 4:30pm) in Shockoe Bottom. They strive to re-create a feeling of Havana in the 1950s and do a great job with strung lights, wood floors, high ceilings, ironwork, and the famous rooftop bar (where you can salsa dance on Thursday nights). Cigars are allowed on the second floor. You can purchase them there or bring your own. The club is known for delicious drinks and friendly service.

More than 200 types of bottled beers can be ordered at the **Capital Ale House** (623 E. Main St., 804/780-2537, www.capitalale-house.com, daily 11am-1:30am) in the heart of Downtown Richmond. This classic ale-house, housed in a century-old building half a city block long, also has 51 taps, two cask-conditioned ale hand pumps, and a gaming area with pool tables and darts. They also have a beer garden. This is a great place for serious beer lovers to share their passion with other like-minded souls.

Events

The **State Fair of Virginia** (www.statefairva.org) in nearby Doswell is a 10-day fair full of tradition. There are rides, food, livestock, music, arts, and even a circus. The fair started back in 1854 and is held annually at the end of September and beginning of October.

SHOPPING

Shopping in Richmond offers everything from quaint boutiques, antiques shops, and specialty stores to upscale modern shopping malls. A unique area to shop is **Carytown,** where nine blocks of West Cary Street (between Thompson Street and Boulevard) are alive with stores selling clothing, furniture, jewelry, and toys, along with many independent eateries.

The **Shoppes at Bellgrade** (11400 W. Huguenot Rd.) include clothing stores, specialty shops, and stores selling athletic gear. Two additional shopping areas are **Shockoe Slip** (E. Cary Street) between 11th and Virginia Streets and **Shockoe Bottom** between Broad and Dock Street from 14th to 21st Streets.

SPORTS AND RECREATION

Spectator Sports

There are many sporting events throughout the year at the University of Richmond and VCU. A list of events can be obtained through both athletic departments at www.richmond-spiders.com and www.vcuathletics.com.

The **Richmond Coliseum** (601 E. Leigh St., 804/780-4970, www.richmondcoliseum.net) hosts numerous professional and college sporting events such as football, basketball, wrestling, and monster-truck events. A list of events is available on the website.

Five miles north of Richmond, the **Richmond International Raceway** (600 E. Laburnum Ave., 866/455-7223, www.rir.com) hosts NASCAR racing on weekends in April and September. The raceway is the largest sports facility in Virginia. Additional events are held at the raceway throughout the year.

If horse racing is more your thing, then **Colonial Downs** (804/966-7223, www.colonialdowns.com) in New Kent offers a pari-mutuel betting racecourse with a five-level grandstand and some of the nicest amenities of any track in the country.

Outdoor Recreation

Runners, walkers, climbers, and boaters can enjoy the **James River Park** (www.jamesriverpark.org), which includes more than 500 acres of parkland in the city and several islands on the James River. Access to the park is from 22nd Street, 43rd Street, and at Reedy Creek where the park headquarters and a canoe launch are located.

Cyclists will find a lot of company both on and off road in the Richmond area. The **Richmond Area Bicycling Association** (www.raba.org) has information on local group rides for road cyclists, while the **Mid-Atlantic Off Road Enthusiasts** (www.more-mtb.org) has information on local mountain biking.

White-water rafting is a big sport in Richmond. The James River runs right through the city and offers rapids up to Class IV. Visitors can book a guided raft trip through a handful of outfitters including **Riverside Outfitters** (804/560-0068, www.riversideoutfitters.net, $84).

Hot-air ballooning is popular in Central Virginia. When in Richmond, contact **Richmond Hot Air Balloons** (888/994-9275, www.richmondhotairballoons.com) for piloted balloon rides.

Amusement Parks

A half hour north of Richmond off I-95 is one of the mid-Atlantic's favorite theme parks, **Kings Dominion** (16000 Theme Park Way, Doswell, 804/876-5134, www.kingsdominion.com, June-Aug. daily, late May and Sept.-Oct. weekends, $66). This 400-acre park first opened in 1975 and offers more than 60 rides. It is known for its large collection of roller coasters (14), including classic wooden coasters like the original Rebel Yell and the Grizzly as well as many new steel coasters. The Intimidator 305 plunges riders 305 feet at more than 90 mph. The park holds special events and a fun Halloween Haunt in October. There is also a 20-acre water park on-site.

FOOD

American

The stunning Jefferson Hotel in downtown Richmond is the venue of one of the nicest restaurants in town: ★ **Lemaire** (101 W. Franklin St., 804/649-4629, www.lemairerestaurant.com, daily 5pm-10pm, $11-30). This "Virginia Green Certified" restaurant not only offers farm-to-table-influenced menu items, but also exceptional service. The menu isn't extensive but certainly offers a little of everything (including small plates, burgers, and lobster). The wine list, however, has more than 200 selections, including a significant selection of bottles under $30 and wines offered by the glass. They also have a creative list of cocktails and a lovely lounge to enjoy them in. Ask for a table by the window so you can see both the dining room and the view onto Franklin Street. A great time to go is around the holidays when the hotel is festively decorated.

For some true southern-style comfort food and a healthy dose of city atmosphere in downtown Richmond, grab a bite at **Mama J's Kitchen** (415 N. 1st St., 804/255-7449, www.mamajskitchen.com, Mon.-Thurs. 11am-9pm, Fri.-Sat. 11am-10pm, Sun. noon-7, under $10). Between Clay and Marshall Streets, this feel-good restaurant full of food made from family recipes serves wonderful cocktails and gut-warming selections such as fried chicken, country fried steak, catfish, and mac and cheese. They also have cobbler and bread pudding for dessert. Their slogan is "welcome home," and it's easy to see why.

Southern-style cooking can also be found downtown at the upscale **Julep's** (420 E. Grace St., 804/377-3968, www.juleps.net, Mon.-Sat. 5pm-10pm, $25-34). Their "New Southern Cuisine" puts a fancy spin on some old favorites such as shrimp and grits, roasted breast of duck, and pan-seared black grouper. The restaurant was relocated in 2015 after a decade in Shockoe Bottom. It is now housed in the historic Shields Shoes building on the first floor. The dress is equivalent to business casual, and you'll want to make a reservation.

The former Tarrant Drug Company building at the corner of Foushee and Broad Streets now houses one of Downtown's most popular eateries. **Tarrant's Café** (1 W. Broad St., 804/225-0035, www.tarrantscaferva.com, Mon.-Thurs. 11am-11pm, Fri.-Sat. 11am-midnight, Sun. 10am-11pm, $19-30) is a quaint restaurant with an upscale feel. It is quite dark inside but has nice paintings, exposed brick walls, and a hip and pleasant atmosphere. It has a long, full-service bar and two dining areas with booths and tables. Reminders of the building's pharmacy past are in the form of signs noting Prescriptions, Soda, Drugs, and Tobacco. The huge menu includes a number of Italian dishes, southern comforts, seafood, ribs, beef, salads, sandwiches, pizza, and wraps. Portions are generous, the service is excellent, and there's a large Sunday brunch menu.

What do you call a deep-fried, bacon-wrapped jumbo beef hot dog topped with hand-pulled pork, barbecue sauce, and coleslaw? At the **HogsHead Café** (9503 W. Broad St., Henrico, 804/308-0281, www.thehogsheadcafe.com, Tues.-Sat. 11:30am-9pm, $6.50-28), they call it a "Hog Dog." Build-your-own hot dogs, ribs, barbecue, seafood, and beer served in mason jars—it's all part of the fun atmosphere at this southern restaurant. The food is authentic, the service is friendly and quick, and the patrons are lively. They also offer takeout and catering.

For those wanting the comfort of a diner with more upscale food, visit ★ **Millie's** (2603 E. Main St., 804/643-5512, www.milliesdiner.com, Tues.-Fri. 11am-2:30pm and 5:30pm-10:30pm, Sat. 9am-3pm and 5:30pm-10:30pm, Sun. 9am-3pm and 5:30pm-9:30pm, $18-27), on the edge of Shockoe Bottom (look for the black-and-white dog out front). For starters, don't wait to be given a menu—it's on the chalkboard. You'll most likely have to wait for a table, so plan on having a mimosa and people watching. Their brunch is legendary (example: lobster in a puff pastry with lightly scrambled egg and hollandaise sauce for $14). The 44-seat restaurant serves upwards of 300 brunch customers on Sunday. The lunch and dinner menu is wonderful too. Be sure to take a look at the vintage jukeboxes (they have an impressive collection of 45s).

French

Those yearning for a little French bistro need look no further than **Bistro Bobette** (1209 E. Cary St., 804/225-9116, www.bistrobobette.com, lunch Tues.-Fri. 11:30am-2:30pm, dinner Mon.-Sat. 5pm-10pm, $22-36) in trendy Shockoe Slip. They serve Provençal food in a casual yet elegant atmosphere, and the owners do a wonderful job at making guests feel welcome. The menu stands up to the most seasoned foodie and offers a diverse, yet creatively prepared choice of entrées and sides. Fresh ingredients are clearly standard in this establishment and contribute to an overall delightful dining experience.

Greek

Everyone feels like family at a hidden gem called **Stella's** (1012 Lafayette St., 804/385-2011, www.stellasrichmond.com, Mon.-Thurs. 11am-3pm and 5pm-10pm, Fri. 11am-3pm and 5pm-11pm, Sat. 5pm-11pm, Sun. 10am-3pm, $9-25). The modern and traditional Greek cuisine is exquisite, and the atmosphere in this mostly residential neighborhood establishment makes guests feel like they are visiting friends (there is even a communal table). There is a meze menu (the Greek equivalent of tapas), full entrées, and numerous sides to choose from. There are also delicious desserts. Stella's has many loyal customers, so make a reservation if you plan on dining here on a weekend evening.

Italian

No city is complete with a favorite pizza joint. **Bottoms Up Pizza** (1700 Dock St., 804/644-4400, www.bottomsuppizza.com, Mon.-Wed. 11am-10pm, Thurs. and Sun. 11am-11pm, Fri.-Sat. 11am-midnight, large pizza $15-26) may be under the I-95 overpass, but it serves fantastic pizza with a thick sourdough crust. They have great specialty pies with unique toppings (crab, artichoke, spinach, etc.) and two outdoor decks to enjoy when its nice out.

ACCOMMODATIONS

Under $100

The **Candlewood Suites Richmond Airport** (5400 Audubon Dr., 804/652-1888, www.candlewoodsuites.com, $88-104) is a good value near the airport. The hotel caters to a business clientele with a business center, free wireless Internet, complimentary laundry service, and a 24-hour fitness center, but vacationers can also enjoy the apartment-style suites and proximity to the downtown area. Candlewood even offers a library of DVDs that guests can borrow.

$100-200

The **Grace Manor Inn** (1853 W. Grace St., 804/353-4334, www.thegracemanorinn.com, $150-225), one block from Monument Avenue in the Fan District, is within walking distance of museums and cafés. The inn has 7,500 square feet of living space, high ceilings, decorative crown moldings, and 10-foot-tall pocket doors. There are four two-room suites with private bathrooms and common areas that include a parlor, music room, and dining room with an original Tiffany chandelier. Guests enjoy a gourmet three-course breakfast, an outdoor saltwater pool, high-speed Internet, and a business center. Three Yorkshire terriers live at the inn.

A pretty little European-style hotel in the Shockoe Slip is the **Berkeley Hotel** (1200 E. Cary St., 804/780-1300, www.berkeleyhotel.com, $167-209). This charming boutique hotel has 55 elegant guest rooms with traditional furniture. Many rooms have great views of downtown Richmond. The service is excellent, and rooms come with free wireless Internet, coffeemakers, terry robes, a morning paper, and access to a health club. Laundry and dry cleaning services are available as is valet parking.

A good hotel on the far northwest side of Richmond (near where I-64 and I-295 meet) is the **Hyatt House Richmond-West** (11800 W. Broad St., Henrico, 804/360-7021, www.richmondwest.house.hyatt.com, $171-211). The hotel can accommodate long stays and offers 134 spotless guest rooms and suites. They provide a complimentary hot breakfast, a 24-hour fitness room, and an indoor heated pool. Next door, the Short Pump Town Center is home to many shops and restaurants.

$200-300

The **Hilton Richmond Downtown** (501 E. Broad St., 804/344-4300, http://hiltongardeninn3.hilton.com, $269-394) is a good choice for staying right in the city. They offer 250 modern rooms and suites in a historic downtown building. Each room has a mini fridge, microwave, free wireless Internet, and access to an indoor pool, a modern fitness center, and a business center. There is a restaurant on-site. Valet parking is available for $21 a day.

The **Westin Richmond** (6631 W. Broad St., 800/937-8461, www.westinrichmond.com, $170-349) is a modern hotel with 250 rooms just off I-64 on the west side of town. The hotel has comfortable beds and nice bathrooms (most king rooms have a stand-up shower while most double rooms have a bathtub shower). There is an extra charge for Internet access.

Located a few blocks from Virginia Commonwealth University, **Quirk Hotel** (201 W. Broad St., 804/340-6040, www.destinationhotels.com/quirk-hotel, $215-259) is a fun boutique hotel occupying the former J. B. Mosby Department Store, built in 1916. The hotel offers 74 guest rooms and has an art-driven theme. The 13-foot ceilings and original wood floors reveal the building's roots, but the rest of the hotel's charm is in the details—for one, the rooms are pink. It may sound unusual (and it is), but it works for this hotel. Rooms are decorated with regional and local artwork. Each floor features a unique papier-mâché portrait of an animal or human and the lobby features art made from used coffee lids (they have their own custom blend of coffee). All the beds are made of reclaimed wood and floor joists. The rest of the details you'll need to see for yourself. There is a $6.99 nightly fee for the following hotel services: telephone calls, Wi-Fi, newspapers, and use of the fitness facility, lobby, coffee bar, and in-room water and caffeine bar.

Over $300

The grand ★ **Jefferson Hotel** (101 W. Franklin St., 804/649-4750, www.jeffersonhotel.com, $305-535) first opened on Halloween in 1895 and has a long and interesting history. It has hosted 12 U.S. presidents, numerous actors, musicians, and politicians, and even had alligators living in the marble pools of its Palm Court for a period of time (the last one died in 1948). This downtown hotel has undergone many changes, the most recent being a full renovation of all guest rooms and suites in 1992 and the addition of an indoor swimming pool in 2000.

The public areas in the hotel are tremendous. The center attraction is the 36-step polished marble staircase that many believe was the model for the one shown in *Gone with the Wind*. The staircase leads to the Palm Court, which has a beautiful Tiffany stained glass dome and a life-size statue of

Jefferson Hotel

Thomas Jefferson. The court had, at one time, a grass lawn surrounding marble pools, but both have long since been removed.

The many amenities in the hotel include a large fitness center, massage treatments, a salon (offering Aveda products), and an extensive business center. There are 240 guest rooms, which come in a variety of sizes, but all are nicely furnished with comfy triple-sheeted beds and well-equipped bathrooms.

There are two restaurants on-site, the upscale Lemaire and the more casual T. J.'s Grill and Bar.

INFORMATION AND SERVICES

There are three **Richmond Region Visitors Centers** (804/783-7450, www.visitrichmondva.com). The main location is 405 North 3rd Street at the **Greater Richmond Convention Center.** A second is found at the **Richmond International Airport** (804/236-3260) on the lower level near baggage claim, and the third is inside the **Bass Pro Shops** (11550 Lakeridge Pkwy., Ashland, 804/615-5412). Staff at each can provide local maps and make hotel reservations.

Another visitors center (that has information on the entire state) is located in the southwest corner of **Capitol Square** inside the Bell Tower (9th and Franklin Streets).

GETTING THERE AND AROUND

Richmond is 98 miles south of Washington DC. The city sits at the intersection of I-95 and I-64.

Air service to Richmond is through the **Richmond International Airport** (RIC, 1 Richard E. Byrd Terminal Dr., 804/226-3000, www.flyrichmond.com), approximately nine miles east of downtown. This is the busiest airport in Central Virginia and has eight carriers that provide service to 21 cities.

Amtrak (800/872-7245, www.amtrak.com) provides train service to the **Main Street Station** (1500 E. Main St.) in Shockoe Slip and also the **Staples Mill Road** station (7519 Staples Mill Rd.). There is a **Greyhound** (800/231-2222, www.greyhound.com) bus terminal at 2910 North Boulevard.

The **GRTC Transit System** (804/358-4782, www.ridegrtc.com) provides local bus service in the Richmond area. They offer 23 routes and operate daily in the city between 5am and 1am.

PETERSBURG

Petersburg, twenty-five miles south of Richmond, served as an important supply hub for the Confederate capital during the Civil War. It had five railroad lines and several key roads running through it, and General Grant knew that if he could cut off this resource to General Lee's army, the Confederates would be forced out of Richmond.

Petersburg National Battlefield

The Siege of Petersburg was the longest single Civil War military event. It lasted more than nine months and produced 70,000 casualties.

In June 1864, the Union army began using force against Petersburg, thus beginning a long tough fight for control of the city. By February 1865, General Lee had only 60,000 troops against Grant's 110,000, and finally on April 2, Lee's army was forced out of the strategic location.

Today, visitors to the **Petersburg National Battlefield** (804/732-3531, ext. 204, www.nps.gov/pete) can follow a 33-mile route that includes 13 battlefield sites and three visitors centers. It takes an entire day to fully explore the park.

The **Eastern Front** (5001 Siege Rd., 804/732-3531, ext. 200, daily 9am-5pm, $5 per car) visitors center is a great place to begin exploration of the battlefield. It has audiovisual programs and standing exhibits that explain the progression of the siege and its overall impact on the Civil War.

At **Grant's Headquarters at City Point** (1001 Pecan Ave., Hopewell, 804/458-9504, daily 9am-5pm, free) visitors can learn about the huge Union supply base and field hospital. There is also information on a plantation that sat on the battlefield before the war overtook the area.

The western side of the tour route is where the **Five Forks Battlefield** (9840 Courthouse Rd., Dinwiddie, 804/469-4093, daily 9am-5pm, free) is located. The Union victory here sealed the fate of Petersburg and Richmond.

The park hosts a number of special events throughout the year including tours, lectures, and living-history demonstrations. Downloadable brochures are available on the website.

Pamplin Historical Park

Pamplin Historical Park (6125 Boydton Plank Rd., 804/861-2408, www.pamplinpark.org, daily 9am-5pm, weekends only in winter, $12.50) is a 422-acre historical campus that features multiple indoor and outdoor exhibits.

A primary attraction in the park is one of the nation's best-known Civil War museums, the **National Museum of the Civil War Soldier.** This 25,000-square-foot building features a seven-gallery exhibit called "Duty Called Me Here" that allows visitors to follow the personal experiences of Civil War soldiers through an MP3 audio player, video, interactive computers, original artifacts, dioramas, and a multisensory battlefield simulator. Another popular feature is the Remembrance Wall, which displays the names of people who "responded to the call of duty during the Civil War."

The **Tudor Hall Plantation** is another popular attraction in the park. Just a short walk from the National Museum of the Civil War Soldier, this circa 1815 house is fully restored and furnished with period antiques. The house was used by Confederate general Samuel McGowan as his headquarters. Visitors can also tour the **Field Quarter,** the area of the plantation where the agricultural slaves lived. Elements common to field quarters of the time have been re-created to give a sense of slave life at the plantation. Guided tours of the plantation are available. To find out specific tour dates, call 804/861-2408.

Be sure to also make time to visit the **Field Fortifications Exhibit.** This unusual exhibit is the only one of its kind and features 60 yards of re-created late-war field fortifications. Other exhibits in the park include a military encampment, a battlefield center with a theater and fiber-optic battle map, a battlefield walk with three loop trails (0.3-1.25 miles long), and the historic **Banks House,** which served as General Grant's headquarters in 1865. Plan for a minimum of 2-4 hours to explore the park.

Charlottesville

Charlottesville (aka C-ville) is an independent city in the foothills of the Blue Ridge Mountains that is surrounded by, but not included in, Albemarle County. Charlottesville was established in 1762 and encompasses 10.4 square miles.

Charlottesville was home to two U.S. presidents: Thomas Jefferson and James Monroe. James Madison also lived nearby in Orange. Monticello, Jefferson's home, hosts nearly 500,000 visitors each year and is one of the top attractions in the area. Ash Lawn-Highland, James Monroe's home, is just down the road from Monticello. Both Jefferson and Monroe also served terms as the governor of Virginia, during which time each traveled the 71-mile historic **Three Notch'd Road,** a popular east-west route across Virginia, back and forth to Richmond.

Despite the city's small size, there are many attractions and historic sites in and near Charlottesville. Right in town on West Main Street between 6th Street East and 2nd Street East is the **Downtown Mall.** This beautiful outdoor pedestrian section of the city is one of the longest of its type in the nation. It is a pleasant mix of trees, statues, benches, shops, restaurants, and vendors. There is also a movie theater and ice rink at the west end. At the east end is the **Charlottesville Pavilion,** where concerts and the popular free "Fridays after Five" concerts featuring local talent are held. A large white tent marks the pavilion.

The **University of Virginia (UVA)** also calls Charlottesville home. The main grounds of UVA along University Avenue are next to a neighborhood known as **The Corner,** which is full of bars, restaurants, and UVA-related stores. Greek life abounds on nearby Rugby Road and adds to the buzz of social life at the local bars. A commercial district that runs from The Corner to the Downtown Mall along West Main Street is home to more restaurants, bars, and private businesses.

Across the train tracks from downtown Charlottesville is the Belmont neighborhood. It is a short walk (about 10 minutes) from the east side of downtown. Belmont used to be a farm but has undergone several transformations over the years. It is now an area of great restaurants and the home of the **Bridge Progressive Arts Initiative** (209 Monticello Rd., 434/984-5669, www.thebridgepai.com), a small nonprofit arts organization that provides space to working artists.

SIGHTS

University of Virginia

The **University of Virginia** (434/924-0311, www.virginia.edu) is one of the top-rated state universities in the nation, with 11 schools in Charlottesville and one in southwest Virginia. The university, founded by Thomas Jefferson, opened in March 1825 with 123 students. Jefferson was heavily involved with the students and faculty for the first year of operation, but he passed away on July 4, 1826. UVA now adds more than 20,000 students to the local population in Charlottesville during the school year.

The main grounds are situated on the west side of Charlottesville. Thomas Jefferson's Academical Village, also referred to as "The Lawn," is its focal point. The Academical Village reflects Jefferson's vision that daily life at college should be infused with learning. He designed 10 pavilions, each focused on a different subject that had faculty living quarters upstairs and classrooms downstairs and were attached to rows of student housing. The Lawn is a long esplanade with two premier buildings: the elegant early republic-style **Rotunda** (which Jefferson designed, standing 77 feet tall with a diameter of 77 feet) and the stately **Old Cabell Hall** (which faces the Rotunda and has a pediment sculpture that reads, "Ye shall know the truth, and the truth shall make you free.").

Charlottesville

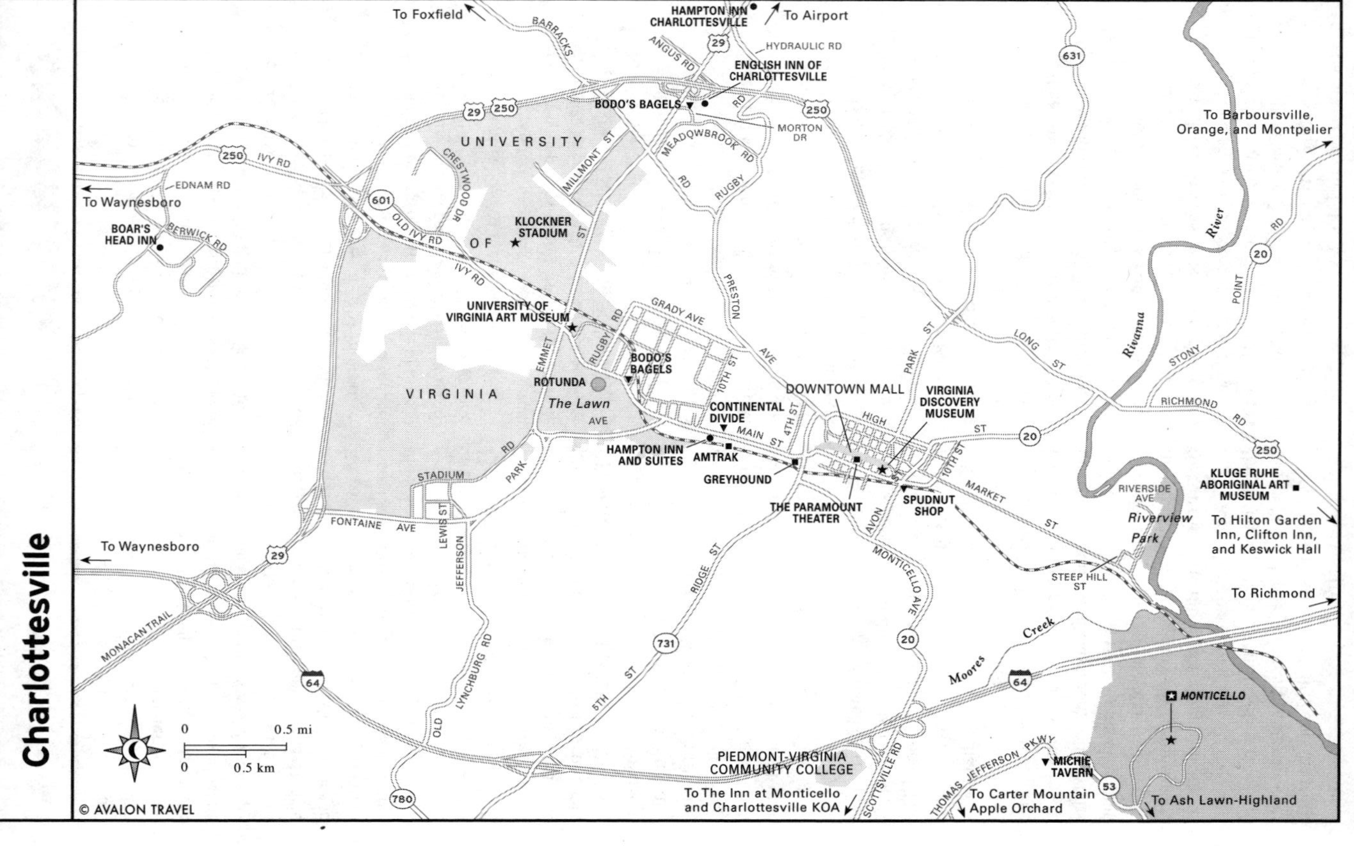

Free guided tours of the Rotunda and Lawn (www.virginia.edu) are offered daily at 10am, 11am, 2pm, 3pm, and 4pm. They depart from the Rotunda's Lower East Oval Room.

UNIVERSITY OF VIRGINIA ART MUSEUM

The **University of Virginia Art Museum** (155 Rugby Rd., 434/924-3592, www.virginia.edu, Tues.-Sun. noon-5pm, free) is one block north of the Rotunda. It houses a permanent collection of more than 10,000 artifacts. Exhibits include 15th- to 20th-century European and American painting and sculpture, Asian art, American figurative art, and photography. There is a special focus on the "Age of Thomas Jefferson" (1775-1825), and temporary exhibits change often throughout the year.

Kluge Ruhe Aboriginal Art Museum

The **Kluge Ruhe Aboriginal Art Collection of the University of Virginia** (400 Worrell Dr., 434/244-0234, www.kluge-ruhe.org, Tues.-Sat. 10am-4pm, Sun. 1pm-5pm, free) is the only museum in the nation fully dedicated to Australian Aboriginal artwork. The museum collaborates with artists, scholars, and art professionals to advance the knowledge of Australia's indigenous people and to provide learning opportunities for the university community. The museum houses one of the premier Aboriginal art collections in the world. It is located approximately three miles east of the UVA campus.

★ Monticello

Monticello (931 Thomas Jefferson Pkwy., 434/984-9880, www.monticello.org, daily 10am-5pm, entrance with tour $25), located on a mountaintop approximately four miles southeast of Charlottesville, is one of the most visited historic sites in the region. The 5,000-acre plantation was the home of Thomas Jefferson, our nation's third president, author of the Declaration of Independence, and the University of Virginia's founder.

Jefferson inherited the land Monticello sits on from his father and began building the house at the age of 26. He maintained and lived in Monticello the rest of his life, always working on and expanding the beautiful home.

Monticello, the home of Thomas Jefferson

Jefferson conceived of his home as a functioning plantation house. Although the design was influenced by Italian Renaissance architecture, it included many elements that were fashionable in late 18th-century Europe and even more elements that were entirely Jefferson's own.

Monticello has one of the most recognized exteriors of any home in Virginia. The large brick structure has a facade adorned by columns and a dramatic octagonal dome. Two large rooms anchor the interior: an entrance hall that Jefferson used to display items of science and a music room. The dome, which sits above the west front of the building, had a room beneath it that is perhaps the most famous part of the house. This "dome room" has yellow octagonal walls and a green wooden floor. Each wall contains a circular window. The top of the dome (the oculus) also has a window that is made of brown glass. The room functioned as an apartment but is said to not have been used much. Visitors are prohibited from entering the room today due to fire regulations.

Jefferson never sat idle. He is said to have told his daughter in a letter, "Determine never to be idle . . . It is wonderful how much may be done, if we are always doing." As such, he created many unusual contraptions in his home and some are still on display today. Fascinated with time, Jefferson put a clock in nearly every room of his mansion. One notable clock is the Great Clock in the entrance hall. He designed the Great Clock to tell both the time and day of the week, and it has both an interior face, which faces the hall, and an exterior face that looks outside over the plantation. The exterior face bears a huge hour hand so workers on the plantation could read it. It also contained a gong that sounded so loudly that the time could be heard three miles away. Another fun invention was Jefferson's clothing rack. Instead of climbing a ladder to reach the top of his tall closet, he created a large spiral rack with 50 arms to hold his clothing. He then turned the rack with a stick to make his outfit selection.

Thomas Jefferson was a terrific gardener and grew many varieties of plants and vegetables. There are three main gardens on the grounds of Monticello for flowers, fruits, and vegetables.

Monticello is the only house in the country included on the United Nations' World Heritage List. Visitors can take a guided, 35-minute tour of the first floor of this beautiful mansion and see original furnishings and personal items that belonged to Jefferson.

Monticello offers tours on a timed ticketing basis. To ensure you get a tour time that's convenient for you, purchase your ticket online. Be sure to arrive 30 minutes ahead of your ticketed time since it takes 30 minutes to submit tickets and ride the shuttle bus from the ticketing area to the house. Allow two hours for your visit. Tours run throughout the day, April through October, and tours of the grounds and gardens are included in the price of the house tour (visitors are welcome to walk the grounds on their own at other times of the year). Interpreters lead these 45-minute walking tours and provide plant identification, stories, and historical insight into the extensive gardens.

Several additional tours are offered, such as the "Behind the Scenes" tour (daily, $42) visiting the upstairs of the mansion, and the "Hemings Family Tour" (Fri.-Sun. Feb, Apr.-Nov. $27), which shows Monticello through the eyes of the best-documented enslaved family in the country.

Ash Lawn-Highland

James Monroe's home, **Ash Lawn-Highland** (2050 James Monroe Pkwy., 434/293-8000, www.ashlawnhighland.org, Apr.-Oct. daily 9am-6pm, Nov.-Mar. daily 11am-5pm, $14) is 2.5 miles south of Monticello. Ash Lawn-Highland is not a grand mansion like Monticello; instead, it is a 535-acre working farm, a performing arts site, and a historic home museum. James Monroe and his wife, Elizabeth Kortright Monroe, owned the estate from 1793 to 1826 and lived there most of the time. The estate is now open to the public and displays examples of Victorian and early American architecture, features period craft demonstrations, showcases decorative arts, and is the site of special events and a summer music festival. Original period furnishings are on display in the main house including some the Monroes had while living in the White House. There are even rumors of a resident ghost.

Visitors can come year-round and can even cut their own Christmas trees in December. Ash Lawn-Highland hosts many events and workshops throughout the year. The College of William & Mary (Monroe's alma mater) now maintains the estate.

Virginia Discovery Museum

A great place to bring the little ones is the **Virginia Discovery Museum** (524 E. Main St., 434/977-1025, www.vadm.org, Mon.-Sat. 10am-5pm, $8). This children-oriented museum at the east end of the Downtown Mall is small compared to other children's museums in large cities, but it is still a wonderful little attraction, especially on a rainy day. The interactive exhibits are excellent for little kids (under 10) and offer crafts, science, and opportunities to run around. Don't miss the beehive in the back of the museum.

Montpelier

Another presidential home, **Montpelier** (11350 Constitution Hwy., 540/672-2728, www.montpelier.org, daily 9am-5pm, $18) was home to the "Father of the Constitution," James Madison, and the country's first first lady, Dolley Madison. Madison spent six months in the library of the home performing research and designing the principles for a representative democracy. These ideas first became the "Virginia Plan" and were later used to frame the Constitution.

Today the estate features Madison's mansion, a garden, archaeological sites, and other historical buildings. The Madisons frequently hosted guests at the estate, and the central feature of the compound is their stately brick mansion. Admission tickets include a guided tour of the mansion, highlighting the dining room that was used to host dinner parties, the drawing room, and the presidential library. A self-guided tour of additional exhibits on the second floor of the home, the cellars, gardens, and grounds is also covered by admission. Plan on spending at least two hours at the mansion.

Wineries and Vineyards

October is officially "wine month" in Charlottesville, but any of the 30 local vineyards can be enjoyed year-round. Part of the reason for the success of vineyards in this part of the state is the topography. The eroded mountains create wonderful growing conditions, which in turn yield beautifully complex wines. Following are a few vineyards in and around Charlottesville that should be included on any wine tour.

Barboursville Vineyards (17655 Winery Rd., Barboursville, 540/832-3824, www.barboursvillewine.net, daily 10am-5pm, $7) is a popular stop on the local wine tour scene. It's on a beautiful 18th-century estate, less than a half hour from Charlottesville. They were the first in the region to seriously develop European wine varietals and offer daily tastings.

Blenheim Vineyards (31 Blenheim Farm, Charlottesville, 434/293-5366, www.blenheimvineyards.com, daily 11am-5:30pm, $6) was established in 2000 by Dave Matthews, of Dave Matthews Band fame. The vineyard is a family-owned and operated business 20 minutes southeast of the city. They have two vineyard sites and grow chardonnay, viognier, cabernet franc, petit verdot, and cabernet sauvignon. The timber-frame tasting room ($6 per person) has cool glass flooring that allows visitors to look into the tank and barrel room below.

First Colony Winery (1650 Harris Creek Rd., Charlottesville, 434/979-7105, www.firstcolonywinery.com, Mon.-Fri. 11am-5pm, Sat.-Sun. 11am-6pm, $7) offers

Brew Ridge Trail

Grapes aren't the only things growing in Charlottesville. Hop vines love the Central Virginia climate. In fact, once upon a time, Virginia was the hop capital of the world. Albemarle County and nearby Nelson County are home to many small-batch brewhouses that produce a wide variety of handcrafted beers. The Brew Ridge Trail (www.brewridgetrail.com) gives beer lovers a chance to tour a small number of these breweries. Simple fare and live music accompany the special brews.

The six breweries along the trail are listed below. Maps of the trail and additional information about upcoming events are available on the trail website.

- **Blue Mountain Barrel House** (495 Cooperative Way, Arrington, 434/263-4002, www.bluemountainbarrel.com)
- **Blue Mountain Brewery** (9519 Critzer's Shop Rd., Afton, 540/456-8020, www.bluemountainbrewery.com)
- **Devils Backbone Brewing Company** (200 Mosbys Run, Roseland, 434/361-1001, www.dbbrewingcompany.com)
- **South Street Brewery** (106 W. South St., Charlottesville, 434/293-6550, www.southstreetbrewery.com)
- **Starr Hill Brewing Company** (5391 Three Notched Rd., Crozet, 434/823-5671, www.starrhill.com)
- **Wild Wolf Brewing Company** (2461 Rockfish Valley Hwy., Nellysford, 434/361-0088, www.wildwolfbeer.com)

state, national, and internationally awarded wines. They produce chardonnay, viognier, merlot, cabernet franc, and cabernet sauvignon. They have tastings, a gift shop, a beautiful 2,000-square-foot event room, and picturesque grounds for picnicking.

Jefferson Vineyards (1353 Thomas Jefferson Pkwy., Charlottesville, 434/977-3042, www.jeffersonvineyards.com, daily 11am-5pm) sits on the site between Monticello and Ash-Lawn where Thomas Jefferson and Filippo Mazzei of Italy first decided to establish a vineyard. The vineyard produces between 6,000 and 8,000 cases annually and makes wine entirely from grapes grown in Virginia. Daily tours and tastings are $10 and include a crystal Riedel glass.

Keswick Vineyards (1575 Keswick Winery Dr., Keswick, 434/244-3341, www.keswickvineyards.com, daily 9am-5pm, $10) specializes in the production of small lots of wine. Their international award winners include viognier, verdejo, chardonnay, cabernet franc, cabernet sauvignon, merlot, petite verdot, syrah, norton, chambourcin, and touriga. Their wines are all produced from their own fruit. Tastings are available daily.

Pippin Hill Farm and Vineyard (5022 Plank Rd., North Garden, 434/202-8063, www.pippinhillfarm.com, Tues.-Sun. 11am-5pm) is a boutique winery and vineyard just outside Charlottesville. It offers a sustainable viticulture program, an exquisite event space, and landscaped gardens. The tasting room features signature wines and food pairings ($6), which can be enjoyed at a beautiful hand-carved bar or out on a stone terrace.

ENTERTAINMENT AND EVENTS

Live Music

The music scene in Charlottesville is surprisingly active. The best-known local talent is the Dave Matthews Band. Dave was a bartender at **Miller's Downtown** (109 W. Main St.,

434/971-8511, www.millersdowntown.com, daily 11:30am-2am), a local restaurant where they have a full schedule of live music (jazz and otherwise). It is on the Downtown Mall and used to be a hardware store.

The **Southern Café and Music Hall** (103 S. 1st St., 434/977-5590, www.thesoutherncville.com) is another truly local establishment. They feature locally sourced ingredients on their menu, have local artwork on their walls, and host great live music nearly every night. There's not a bad spot in the house. Visitors enter through a brick patio in this nearly belowground establishment.

The **Jefferson Theater** (110 E. Main St., 800/594-8499, www.jeffersontheater.com) is one of the best live venues in Charlottesville and attracts better-known acts like Eric Hutchinson and Amos Lee. They have a more advanced sensory experience with improved lighting and sound systems.

The **Paramount Theater** (215 E. Main St., 434/979-1333, www.theparamount.net) is a historic theater on Main Street that first opened in 1931. It became an icon and local landmark immediately, and flourished during the Great Depression and even as the era of the American movie palace declined. The venue closed in 1974 but was refurbished and reopened in 2004. It now hosts larger acts as well, such as Lyle Lovett and Natalie Cole.

Paramount Theater

The **nTelos Wireless Pavilion** (700 E. Main St., 434/245-4910, www.thenteloswirelesspavilion.com) also hosts nationally known talent such as the Counting Crows and Avett Brothers in an outdoor concert series from spring until fall. It was previously known as the Charlottesville Pavilion.

Performing Arts

Charlottesville's number one performance company is **Live Arts** (123 E. Water St., 434/977-4177, www.livearts.org). They are a volunteer theater offering a rounded schedule of drama, comedy, dance, music, and performance arts.

Events

The annual **Dogwood Festival** (www.charlottesvilledogwoodfestival.org), held each spring in mid-April, is the largest festival in the city and lasts for two weeks. It is a great celebration of the city itself and features fireworks, a carnival, food, and a parade.

The **Virginia Film Festival** (617 W. Main St., 2nd fl., 434/982-5277, www.virginiafilmfestival.org) is an annual event hosted by the University of Virginia at the beginning of November. The festival features more than 70 films and more than 80 guest artists and presenters at a variety of venues. Free panel discussions take place on topics important to both high-and low-budget film processes. Featured guests in the past have included big-name actors such as Sandra Bullock, Anthony Hopkins, and Sigourney Weaver.

SHOPPING

The Downtown Mall is Charlottesville's premier browsing district and is considered one of the best urban parks in the nation.

There are more than 120 independent shops on or near Main Street, with delightful surprises such as rare bookstores, funky boutiques, galleries featuring local artists, craft stores, wine shops, and many others.

Farm-fresh produce can be found seasonally at the **Charlottesville City Market** (www.charlottesvillecitymarket.com, Apr.-Dec. Sat. 7am-noon). This market, which started in 1973, is held on Saturdays in the parking lot at 1st and Water Streets.

SPORTS AND RECREATION

Spectator Sports

There are no professional sports teams in Charlottesville, but a plethora of sporting events take place at **UVA** (434/924-8821, www.virginiasports.com). Whether it's football at **Scott Stadium,** basketball at the **John Paul Jones Arena,** or soccer and lacrosse games at **Klockner Stadium,** you can catch the Wahoo spirit most anytime during the school year.

Spring and fall steeplechases are held annually at **Foxfield** (2215 Foxfield Track, 434/293-9501, www.foxfieldraces.com). A full day of tailgating, people watching, and of course, horse racing is a tradition on the last Saturday in April and the last Sunday in September. Infield and invitation tickets are available online, but rail parking and sponsor tickets must be purchased in person at the race office. Patrons who drink are encouraged to leave their cars on the property and may do so for up to 48 hours after the race.

Outdoor Recreation

Intermediate and advanced mountain bikers should check out the five-mile single-track trail at **Walnut Creek Park** (4250 Walnut Creek Park Rd., North Garden, 434/296-5844) about 10 miles southwest of Charlottesville. This challenging loop runs through a hardwood forest surrounding a 23-acre lake. The trail is twisty, tight, and technical. Less experienced riders may enjoy the easier trail along the water. There are 15 miles of trails in this 525-acre park.

Fishing and boating (electric motors only) are popular pastimes on **Beaver Creek Lake** (4365 Beaver Creek Park Rd., Crozet, 434/296-5844). This 104-acre lake is stocked with sunfish, channel catfish, and largemouth bass. A Virginia state fishing license is required.

Mint Springs Valley Park (6659 Mint Springs Park Rd., Crozet, 434/296-5844, www.albemarle.org, daily during daylight hours, $4.50) in nearby Crozet is a 520-acre park with an 8-acre lake. It offers a beach with swimming during the summer (daily 11am-7pm), four hiking trails ranging from .5 miles to 1.8 miles, fishing (license required), and boating (electric motors only).

Pick your own apples and peaches (depending on the season) at **Carter Mountain Apple Orchard** (1435 Carters Mountain Trail, 434/977-1833, www.chilesfamilyorchards.com/orchards/carter-mountain-orchard/, open daily mid-Apr.-Dec.) next to Michie Tavern near Monticello.

FOOD

Breakfast and Snacks

For a tasty Italian treat, stop in **Splendora's Gelato** (317 E. Main St., 434/296-8555, www.splendoras.com, Mon.-Thurs. 7:30am-9pm, Fri. 7:30am-10pm, Sat. 9am-10pm, Sun. noon-10pm, under $10) on the Downtown Mall. They offer between 24 and 36 flavors of delectable gelato every day as well as espresso and other desserts.

The **Spudnut Shop** (309 Avon St., 434/296-0590, www.spudnutshop.com, Tues.-Fri. 6am-2pm, Sat. 6am-6pm, under $10) is what it sounds like: a doughnut shop where the doughnuts are made from potatoes. These mouthwatering treats are a local staple in Charlottesville, and they sell out quickly each morning. Be forewarned, after tasting these babies, you may never go back to regular doughnuts.

Bodo's Bagels (www.bodosbagels.com) serves top-notch bagels at three locations (1418 Emmet St., 434/977-9598; 505 Preston Ave., 434/293-5224; 1609 University Ave., 434/293-6021; all day breakfast, lunch, and dinner Mon.-Sat., breakfast and lunch Sun., hours vary by location). Their New York-style "water" bagels are simply delicious, and they have great bagel sandwiches, salads, and soups.

American

The ★ **Ivy Inn** (2244 Old Ivy Rd., 434/977-1222, www.ivyinnrestaurant.com, daily 5pm-9:30pm, $11-32) is an elegant restaurant serving "locally inspired seasonal American cuisine." The restaurant is just one mile from UVA in a beautiful home built in 1816; the business itself was established in 1973. The food is excellent. They offer limited choices, but all are done exceptionally well. Examples of the menu include wild-caught rockfish fillet, beef tenderloin, and jumbo lump crabmeat and fettuccini. The atmosphere is genteel and refined, but not pretentious. The staff is friendly and very knowledgeable about the food and wine list.

For some colonial charm and old-world atmosphere, the **Michie Tavern** (683 Thomas Jefferson Pkwy., 434/977-1234, www.michietavern.com, Apr.-Oct. daily 11:15am-3:30pm, Nov.-Mar. daily 11:30am-3pm, $17.95) offers a bountiful lunch buffet in a tavern that was built in 1784. The tavern is a half mile from Monticello and was a popular lodging option for travelers more than 200 years ago. Today they offer a southern-style buffet lunch with fried chicken, pork barbecue, baked chicken, black-eyed peas, corn bread, stewed potatoes, and other colonial favorites, served by staff dressed in period clothing. The cider ale is wonderful, and the tavern does beer and wine tastings in the evening. The food is served in five dining rooms known as **The Ordinary.** Meals are eaten on steel/pewter plates to add to the experience. Tours of the tavern are also available.

The Local (824 Hinton Ave, 434/984-9749, www.thelocal-cville.com, Sun.-Thurs. 5:30pm-10pm, Fri.-Sat. 5:30pm-11pm, $8-22) showcases products produced by local farmers, artisan cheese makers, distilleries, vineyards, and breweries. They serve trout, chicken, beef, and pasta entrees and offer an extensive wine list and a good variety of desserts. The brick and wood building dates back to 1912, when it housed a shoe-repair shop (the proprietor lived upstairs in what is now part of the restaurant). The building has served as a church, general store, furniture store, pool hall, motorcycle shop, and a photography studio. Start with the crispy shrimp appetizer; it is a unique and delicious dish.

Good burgers, fries, and beer can be found at **Citizen Burger Bar** (212 East Main St., 434/979-9944, www.citizenburgerbar.com, Sun.-Thurs. 11:30am-midnight, Fri.-Sat. 11:30am-2am, $6-15). This lively spot is a popular choice when students, visitors, and locals crave a meal on a bun (gluten-free buns are available). The portions are large, the food is locally sourced, the beef is grass-fed, and the cheese is made in Virginia. They also offer vegan burgers. Sides such as cheese fries and sweet potato fries are big enough to share. Their bar is well stocked with interesting cocktails and more than 110 types of beer.

Italian

The rustic **Tavola** (826 Hinton Ave., 434/972-9463, www.tavolavino.com, Mon.-Sat. 5pm-10pm, $20-26) is a cozy little Italian restaurant that is big on taste. This isn't a typical American Italian place; the meals are freshly prepared and full of authentic flavor. The atmosphere is lively and fun (aka noisy), but it is charming at the same time and feels like a European bistro. They don't take reservations, so put your name on the list and go to one of the neighboring bars for a drink while you wait. The restaurant is in the Belmont district.

Tex-Mex

The Get in Here sign may be the only clue to the entrance to the **Continental Divide** (811 W. Main St., 434/984-0143, www.eatdivide.com, Mon.-Thurs. 5pm-10:15pm, Fri.-Sat. 5pm-10:45pm, Sun. 5pm-9:45pm, $5-14). This little hole-in-the-wall is known for incredible tuna tostados and the best margaritas in town. The atmosphere is lively and noisy (and not family friendly), so be ready for a party when you finally find the front door. The food is fantastic and cheap, and there's normally a line out the door on weekends. The restaurant is in Midtown across from the Amtrak station.

Turkish

Excellent kabobs are a staple at **Sultan Kabob** (1710 Seminole Trail, 434/981-0090, www.sultancville.com, daily 11am-9pm, $7-15). The atmosphere is comfortable, the prices are reasonable, and the staff is friendly. This is a quiet, relaxing place where the food takes center stage. For something different, try the hummus casserole. They also have vegan and gluten-free options.

ACCOMMODATIONS

$100-200

The **English Inn of Charlottesville** (2000 Morton Dr., 434/971-9900, www.englishinncharlottesville.com, $100-280) is an independent hotel with 106 rooms and suites. Built in the Tudor style, this friendly hotel offers wireless access, a fitness room, an indoor pool, and a free hot breakfast.

The **Hampton Inn Charlottesville** (2035 India Rd., 434/978-7888, www.hamptoninn3.hilton.com, $119-159) has 123 guest rooms, an outdoor pool, free breakfast, and wireless Internet. The hotel is a few miles from the downtown area, but there are chain restaurants and stores within walking distance. The staff is exceptionally friendly and helpful.

The **200 South Street Inn** (200 W. South St., 434/979-0200, www.southstreetinn.com, $170-260) has 19 rooms and suites just two blocks from the pedestrian mall, one mile from the University of Virginia, and four miles from Monticello. The inn is made up of two restored homes, one built in 1856 and the other in 1890. It is decorated with antiques, and many rooms have fireplaces, whirlpool baths, and canopy beds. Larger suites with living rooms are available. All rooms have private baths. Guests can enjoy a continental breakfast in the library or, in nice weather, on the veranda. Cookies, wine, and cheese are served in the afternoon. Rooms are comfortable but lack some of the modern conveniences of large hotel chains. Still, the personal attention given by the innkeepers, the charming atmosphere, and proximity to the downtown area make this a good choice in Charlottesville.

The **Hilton Garden Inn** (1793 Richmond Rd., 434/979-4442, www.hiltongardeninn3.hilton.com, $152-249) is on the east end of town (three miles from the historic area and four miles from UVA) and has 124 guest rooms. There's an indoor pool and fitness center and free wireless Internet.

$200-300

The ★ **Clifton Inn** (1296 Clifton Inn Dr., 434/971-1800, www.clifton-inn.com, $229-449) is a luxurious inn with 17 rooms and suites. This romantic establishment sits on 100 acres and was built and used by Thomas Jefferson's son-in-law, Thomas Mann Randolph Jr., who was also the governor of Virginia. During the Civil War, the family of Colonel John Singleton Mosby stayed at Clifton after fleeing their home near Middleburg in Northern Virginia. Mosby had a secret hiding area outside the main house where he is said to have left supplies for his family when Union troops were nearby. Today, guests enjoy first-rate service in the serene environment of this charming inn. The many extras include an infinity pool and complimentary wine with historical significance—the varietal was used in a toast by Thomas Jefferson upon the signing of the Declaration of Independence.

Two miles west of town is the highly acclaimed ★ **Boar's Head Inn** (200 Ednam Dr., 434/296-2181, www.boarsheadinn.com, $185-385). The 573-acre estate is a destination in itself, with 175 rooms and suites, a fitness club, a spa, 20 tennis courts, a lap pool, golf course, biking, fishing, hiking, and even hot-air balloon rides. There are also four restaurants and 20 event spaces.

Wintergreen Resort

Forty minutes southwest of Charlottesville is **Wintergreen Resort** (39 Mountain Inn Loop, 434/325-2200, www.wintergreenresort.com). This beautiful year-round destination is perched on the eastern side of the Blue Ridge Mountains. Unlike traditional mountain resorts, Wintergreen is built at the top of the mountain ridges instead of at the base of the mountain. The elevation is approximately 4,000 feet.

There is a large full-service spa on-site, 40,000 square feet of meeting space, and 300 choices of condos and homes for rent. There is also an aquatics center with indoor and outdoor pools.

Skiing and snowboarding ($39-89 for lift tickets) are popular on the 26 trails (14 of which are lit for night skiing). There are also a 900-foot tubing trail with 12 lanes and a terrain park. There are five chairlifts and the resort can make snow on 100 percent of its trails.

During the summer, there are 45 holes of championship golf, tennis, hiking on 30 miles of trails, and many family activities such as mini golf, a climbing tower, and a bungee trampoline.

The inn is a certified "Virginia Green" establishment. Rooms are decorated with antique furnishings and have beautiful bathrooms with modern conveniences. Premium bath items, plush bathrobes, and high-quality bedding are standard. The service is top-rate. The inn is close enough to downtown attractions to be convenient, but far enough away that you feel like you're out in the country. Rooms are spread out over several buildings. Ask for one in the main inn building.

The award-winning ★ **Keswick Hall** (701 Club Dr., Keswick, 434/979-3440, www.keswick.com, $310-1,000) at Monticello is a 1912 Italianate villa that was turned into a grand resort by the widower of designer Laura Ashley. Guests are welcomed into this extravagant home in a comfortable lounge opening onto a patio that overlooks the 600-acre estate grounds. Guests in its 48 rooms can enjoy access to the Keswick Club, where they can play golf or tennis, swim in the saltwater pool, and use the spa. The resort is beautifully decorated in Laura Ashley's style and with many personal antiques and artwork. The resort won't disappoint for those who can afford its lofty price tag. It is about 15 minutes from Charlottesville in Keswick.

A second Hampton Inn in Charlottesville is the **Hampton Inn & Suites Charlottesville at the University** (900 W. Main St., 434/923-8600, www.hamptoninn3.hilton.com, $229-259). It has 100 guest rooms and suites near UVA and complimentary breakfast.

INFORMATION AND SERVICES

The **Charlottesville-Albemarle Convention and Visitors Bureau** (610 E. Main St., 434/293-6789, www.visitcharlottesville.org, daily 9am-5pm) provides visitors with maps and brochures about Charlottesville and the surrounding area. They are on the Downtown Mall.

GETTING THERE AND AROUND

Charlottesville is 115 miles southwest of Washington DC. The main highways running through Charlottesville are I-64, U.S. 250, and U.S. 29.

The **Charlottesville-Albemarle Airport** (CHO, 100 Bowen Loop, 434/973-8342, www.gocho.com) is a public airport with commercial service eight miles north of Charlottesville. Four airlines provide service to six cities, and more than 40 flights are scheduled daily. Rental cars are available on-site.

Amtrak (800/872-7245, www.amtrak.com) provides service to Charlottesville at 810 West Main Street (not far from the UVA campus), and **Greyhound** (800/231-2222, www.greyhound.com) bus service is also available at 310 West Main Street.

Charlottesville Area Transit (CAT) (434/970-3649, www.charlottesville.org, Mon.-Sat. 6am-11:45pm, times vary by route, $0.75) offers 11 bus routes throughout the city. CAT also provides free trolley services daily from the Downtown Transit Station (615 E. Water St.) along Main Street. It also goes through the grounds of UVA.

Blue Ridge Parkway

The **Blue Ridge Parkway** (www.blueridgeparkway.org) is one of the most popular units of the national park system. The parkway is 469 miles long and connects **Great Smoky Mountains National Park** in North Carolina and Tennessee with **Shenandoah National Park** in Virginia. The parkway was designed during the Great Depression, and its creators took advantage of the beautiful terrain and followed the natural contours of the ridgeline. Outstanding scenery is the key ingredient to this outstanding park, and visitors can enjoy overlooks of the Blue Ridge Mountains, countless vistas, beautiful old meadows, and picturesque farmland.

217 miles of the Blue Ridge Parkway are in Virginia, with the prettiest stretch being the 114 miles between Waynesboro and Roanoke. This section follows the crest of the Blue Ridge Mountains.

Attractions and landmarks along the parkway are announced by mileposts (mp). Milepost 0 is at the northern end of the parkway at Rockfish Gap. This is also the southern end of Shenandoah National Park. Milepost 218 is at the North Carolina border. The speed limit along the entire Blue Ridge Parkway is 45 miles per hour. Visitors should expect slower traffic during peak foliage in the fall and also during the summer months.

PLANTS AND ANIMALS

Wildflower meadows, colorful leaves, spotted fawns, and black bear cubs can all be seen at times along the Blue Ridge Parkway. There

the famed Blue Ridge Parkway, a 469-mile scenic drive

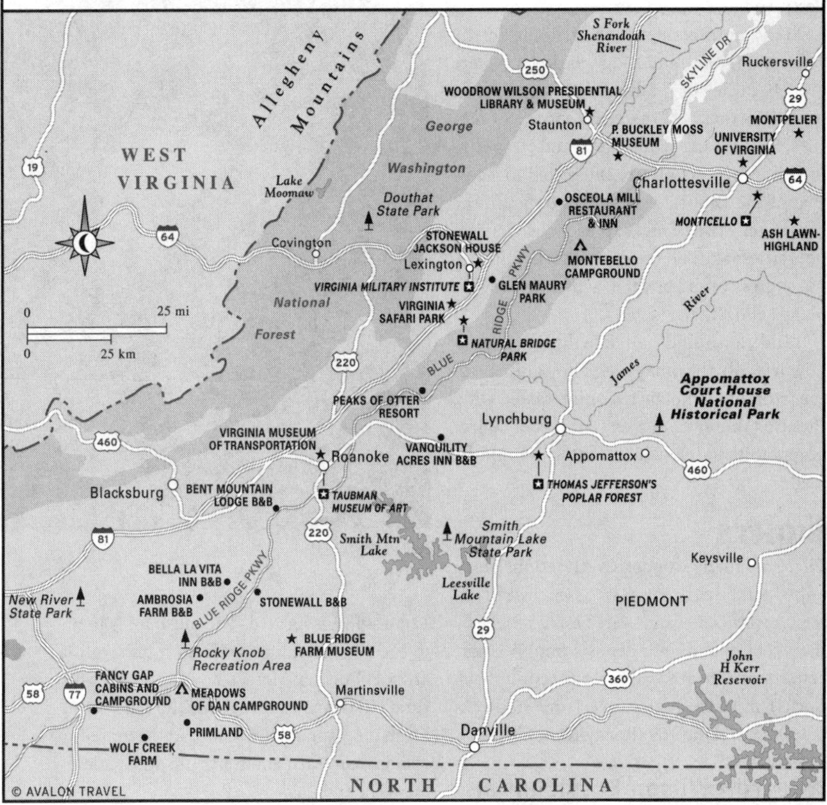

are millions of varieties of flora and fauna that can be found on this famed stretch of road.

There are more than 130 species of trees growing along the parkway (as many as are found in all of Europe). Some of the most popular types include evergreens such as Virginia pine, white pine, spruce, fir, and hemlock. The altitude along the entire parkway varies from just under 650 feet to 6,047 feet. Because of this, the fall foliage season is rather long since the fireworks of colored leaves burst at slightly different times at each altitude. A current **Fall Color Report** can be heard by calling 828/298-0398 (press 3).

Dogwood, sourwood, and black gum leaves change to deep red, while hickory and tulip tree leaves turn bright yellow. Red maples produce multicolored leaves, while sassafras trees add orange leaves to the mix. The fall is an amazing time to explore the parkway. There's nothing quite like the autumn foliage in Virginia, and the Blue Ridge Parkway offers the crème de la crème of this incredible spectacle.

There are many types of flowers along the parkway. The Blue Ridge Parkway website (www.blueridgeparkway.org) has a helpful **Bloom Schedule** that gives tentative blooming periods for many popular flowers. There is also a **Wildflower Report** available on the Parkway Information Line (828/298-0398) during the spring and summer. It should be noted that all plants along the parkway are protected and should not be picked or destroyed.

Many animals make their home in the wilds along the Blue Ridge Parkway. There are 74 species of mammals, 250 species of birds (159 that nest there), 35 species of reptiles, 50 types of salamanders, and 50 species of fish. Many people are interested to know that of the 22 species of snakes living in the region, only two types are poisonous: the timber rattlesnake and the copperhead. Both are not aggressive and prefer to avoid contact with people altogether.

Wildlife should be left wild. No matter how friendly they may seem, any animals in the park should not be fed or interacted with. Picture taking, from a distance, is of course acceptable, but no close contact should be made.

Natural Bridge Park

SIGHTS

There are many wonderful attractions along or just off the parkway as it passes close to numerous towns. Locations are best described by their corresponding mileposts (mp). Visitors centers are located at mp 5.8 (Humpback Rocks), mp 63.6 (James River), mp 86 (Peaks of Otter), and mp 169 (Rocky Knob).

Woodrow Wilson Presidential Library and Museum

The **Woodrow Wilson Presidential Library and Museum** (mp 0, 18-24 N. Coalter St., Staunton, 540/885-0897, www.woodrowwilson.org, Mon.-Sat. 9am-5pm, Sun. noon-5pm, $14) is a historical destination and the former home of Woodrow Wilson. It offers multiple attractions such as the Woodrow Wilson Museum (self-guided tours are available through seven galleries), a state-of-the-art World War I trench experience, a research library, gardens, and a hands-on kids' corner.

Milepost 0 is also where the **P. Buckley Moss Museum** (329 West Main St., Waynesboro, 540/949-6473, www.pbuckleymoss.com, Tues.-Sat. 10am-5pm, Sun. 12pm-4pm) is located. The museum is home to the permanent art collection of Virginia artist P. Buckley Moss, who is known for her rural landscape paintings and those depicting life in the Shenandoah Valley. At the museum, visitors can learn about her life and achievements in art.

Stonewall Jackson House

The **Stonewall Jackson House** (mp 45.6, 8 E. Washington St., Lexington, 540/464-7704, www.stonewalljackson.org, Mon.-Sat. 9am-5pm, Sun. 1pm-5pm, $8) is the former home of the Civil War general. It has been beautifully restored and contains some original Jackson family furnishings. Guided tours, a garden, and museum shop are part of the offerings.

★ Natural Bridge Park

The **Natural Bridge Park** (mp 61.6, U.S. 11, Natural Bridge, www.naturalbridgeva.com, daily 9am-4pm, extended summer hours $20) is a National Historic Landmark that was once owned by Thomas Jefferson. The 20-story solid limestone rock arch created by nature is an awesome sight and one that has inspired people for generations. A variety of other attractions are also at the Natural Bridge, including the **Natural Bridge Caverns** (daily 9am-4pm, Nov.-mid-March Fri.-Sun. only, $18), which sit 34 stories below ground. A combo bridge and caverns ticket can be purchased for $28.

Virginia Safari Park

Four miles north of the Natural Bridge is the **Virginia Safari Park** (mp 61.6, 229 Safari Ln., Natural Bridge, 540/291-3205, www.virginiasafaripark.com, mid-Mar.-Nov. daily 9am-5pm, extended weekend and summer hours, $18). This 180-acre drive-through zoo houses more than 1,000 animals that are free to roam in a natural setting. Three miles of roads meander through woods and fields, allowing visitors to see animals such as deer, zebras, elk, antelope, giraffe, camels, and bison. The free-roaming animals literally stick their heads inside your car waiting to be fed. Buckets of feed are available at the entrance to the park. There is also a walk-through area where visitors can feed giraffes, goats, pigs, and baby llamas.

Another attraction at the same milepost is a frightfully accurate replica of Stonehenge called **Foamhenge** (mp 61.6, U.S. 11 South, Natural Bridge, 800/533-1410, www.enchantedcastlestudios.com, free). This life-size foam replica sits on a bluff and can be seen from the southbound lanes of U.S. 11 one mile north of the Natural Bridge.

★ Thomas Jefferson's Poplar Forest

Thomas Jefferson's Poplar Forest (mp 86, 1542 Bateman Bridge Rd., Forest, 434/525-1806, www.poplarforest.org, Mar. 15-Dec 30, daily 10am-5pm, $15) was Thomas Jefferson's personal retreat. He originally inherited the land from his father-in-law as a working tobacco farm, and it offered him a nice source of income. Ten miles west of Lynchburg, the home is an architectural masterpiece built in 1806 and one of only two that Jefferson designed and constructed for his personal use. It was also the first octagonal house in the country. It was a three-day ride for Jefferson between Monticello and Poplar Forest, but he went there several times a year and stayed from two weeks to two months each visit. Visitors to Poplar Forest learn about life in the early 19th century, the architecture of the home, and its preservation. They also witness ongoing excavation of the property and can

Thomas Jefferson's Poplar Forest

see authentic artifacts from the plantation. Admission includes a guided 40-minute tour of the house and a self-guided tour of the grounds.

Virginia Museum of Transportation

Farther south, in Roanoke, is the **Virginia Museum of Transportation** (mp 112.2, 303 Norfolk Ave. SW, Roanoke, 540/342-5670, www.vmt.org, Mon.-Sat. 10am-5pm, Sun. 1pm-5pm, $8). This large museum is mostly outdoors and holds more than 50 railway exhibits, road vehicle exhibits, and air exhibits. It is best known for its exhibits on the Norfolk & Western Class J-611 and Class A-1218 modern steam locomotives.

Mill Mountain Star and Park

The **Mill Mountain Star and Park** (mp 120, 210 Reserve Ave., Roanoke, 540/853-2000) is famous for the huge illuminated star that sits on top of Mill Mountain. Roanoke is nicknamed "the Star City of the South," which was the inspiration for the construction of the massive star, erected in 1949. It is the largest man-made illuminated star in the world at 88.5 feet tall. It is lit by 2,000 feet of neon tubes channeling 17,500 watts of power. The star is lit each evening but is turned off at midnight.

Blue Ridge Farm Museum

For a lesson on farm life, check out the **Blue Ridge Farm Museum** (mp 152, 20 Museum Dr., Ferrum, 540/365-4416, www.blueridgeinstitute.org/farm, mid-May-mid-Aug. Sat. 10am-5pm, Sun. 1pm-5pm). The farm takes visitors back to 1800 to experience what life was like on a Virginia German farmstead. Interpreters dressed in period clothing complete numerous farm chores such as cooking, driving oxen, and blacksmith work. Call for admission prices.

Mabry Mill

The most photographed location on the Blue Ridge Parkway is **Mabry Mill** (mp 176.1). This charming water-powered mill (built in 1867) is visited by several hundred thousand people each year. The gristmill and sawmill have been restored, and visitors can see a working miller demonstrate the milling process. The mill grounds are lovely and tranquil, although crowded in the summer months, and include interpretive media.

ENTERTAINMENT

The **Blue Ridge Music Center** (mp 213, Blue Ridge Parkway, Galax, 276/236-5309, www.blueridgemusiccenter.org) is a modern performing arts venue that was constructed for the purpose of promoting historical Blue Ridge music. Old-time and bluegrass music frequently flood the facility and surrounding area. Visitors can take in a show, explore the visitors center, and check out the views of Fisher Peak.

SPORTS AND RECREATION

The Blue Ridge Parkway has numerous attractions and recreational opportunities along its winding route. Campgrounds, hiking trails, interpretive centers, and picnic areas are just some of the possibilities for a break when traversing this gorgeous roadway. The famed **Appalachian Trail,** which runs 2,184 miles from Maine to Georgia, meanders along the parkway from Rockfish Gap (at the northern end) down to Roanoke.

Near the northern end of the parkway is a beautiful area known as **Humpback Rocks** (mp 5.8). Visitors can see a number of farm buildings from the 19th century and enjoy numerous hiking trails suitable for all abilities. Interpretive programs in which park rangers demonstrate local mountain craftmaking are held during the summer months.

At mp 64, a section of the **James River** can be explored. Visitors can see one of the restored canal locks from the James River and Kanawha Canal, a prime commercial route in Virginia in the mid-1800s, and also go fishing from a public dock. There are plenty of areas for picnicking.

The popular **Peaks of Otter** area at mp 86 offers incredible views and an abundance of natural beauty. The area has been a popular tourist attraction since 1834. Ranger programs are offered at the visitors center, and a lovely picnic area along Little Stoney Creek provides tables, grills, and restroom facilities. There are six hiking trails at Peaks of Otter, and Abbott Lake is open to the public for fishing (with a Virginia or North Carolina fishing license).

Virginia's Explore Park (mp 115, 540/427-1800, www.explorepark.org/231/Explore-Park), located near Roanoke, is a 1,200-acre park with nine miles of mountain bike trails, a one-mile interpretive trail, fishing, canoeing, and kayaking.

The **Smart View Trail** (mp 154.5) is a popular 2.6-mile loop hiking trail around the Smart View Picnic Area. It is a level trail through the woods with nice views.

The beautiful **Rocky Knob** area at mp 169 offers several great hiking trails of different lengths. The Rock Castle Gorge Trail (blazed in green) is a moderate-to-strenuous 10.8-mile loop with elevation ranges from 1,700 feet to 3,572 feet. Sections are steep and rocky on this National Scenic Trail. The Black Ridge Trail (blazed in blue) is a moderate 3-mile loop hike with good views to the north from the top of Black Ridge. This trail joins the Rock Castle Gorge Trail on the return trip. The Rocky Knob Picnic Area Trail (blazed in yellow) is an easy 1-mile loop walk through mature forest.

FOOD

At milepost 27 (halfway between Staunton and Lexington) is the **Osceola Mill Restaurant & Inn** (mp 27, 352 Tye River Tpke., Steeles Tavern, 540/377-6455, www.osceolamill.com, Fri. and Sat. 5pm-10pm, $14-32). This elegant but casual restaurant serves seafood, steak, and veal. The menu varies weekly depending on what is in season. The Mill Stone dining room has huge chestnut beams, original millworks, and views of the mill's waterwheel.

The **Liberty Station Restaurant** (mp 86, 515 Bedford Ave., Bedford, 540/587-9377, www.oldelibertystation.com, Mon.-Thurs. 11am-10pm, Fri. 11am-11pm, Sat. noon-10pm, $8-20) in Bedford is housed in a former railroad station. It serves traditional American food and is known for its cheesecake.

Seven miles from the parkway at milepost 121 is the **Roanoker Restaurant** (mp 121, 2522 Colonial Ave., Roanoke, 540/344-7746, www.theroanokerrestaurant.com, Tues.-Sat. 7am-9pm, Sun. 8am-9pm, $10-17). They serve American home-style food and are open for breakfast, lunch, and dinner. Their menu includes a variety of seafood, salads, and sandwiches at reasonable prices.

If you're looking for food near milepost 164, the **Blue Ridge Restaurant** (mp 164, 113 E. Main St., Floyd, 540/745-2147, Mon.-Wed. 6am-9pm, Thurs.-Sat. 6am-10pm, Sun. 8am-4pm $7-25) is a good stop for traditional diner food. This no-frills place across from the courthouse in Floyd, six miles from the parkway, will satisfy your appetite in a casual, friendly environment. They are open for breakfast, lunch, and dinner.

The **Mabry Mill Restaurant** (mp 176, 266 Mabry Mill Rd. SE, Meadows of Dan, 276/952-2947, www.mabrymillrestaurant.com, May-Oct. Mon.-Thurs. 7:30am-5pm, Fri.-Sun. 7:30am-6pm, under $10) offers home-style cooking and is known for its buckwheat cakes, country ham, and Virginia barbecue. They serve breakfast all day. The restaurant is located next to the **Mabry Mill.**

Not far from milepost 199.5 is the **Gap Deli at the Parkway** (mp 199.5, 7975 Fancy Gap Hwy., Hillsville, 276/728-3881, www.thegapdeli.com, Mon.-Thurs. 11am-5pm, Fri.-Sun. 11am-7pm, under $10). They serve a nice variety of sandwiches, wraps, salads, and dessert.

ACCOMMODATIONS

There are many wonderful independent inns, lodges, and bed-and-breakfasts nestled in the mountains along the Blue Ridge Parkway. Most are family owned and operated and offer reasonable rates. Book early when visiting during peak season.

At a town called Steeles Tavern (between

Staunton and Lexington) is the **Osceola Mill Restaurant & Inn** (mp 27, 352 Tye River Tpke., Steeles Tavern, 540/377-6455, www.osceolamill.com, $105-200). The inn offers bed-and-breakfast accommodations, cabin rentals, and a restaurant. There are four rooms in the inn and two individual cabins for rent in a peaceful, beautiful six-acre compound. Another good option near mp 27 is the **Sugar Tree Inn** (mp 27, 145 Lodge Trail, Steeles Tavern, 540/377-2197, www.sugartreeinn.com, closed Jan., $148-248). This peaceful log inn offers accommodations in the main lodge (three rooms) and four additional cabins/houses. There are 13 guest rooms total. It has expansive views and wood-burning fireplaces in all guest rooms. A full breakfast is included with your stay.

A nice bed-and-breakfast in Bedford near mp 86 is the **Vanquility Acres Inn Bed and Breakfast** (mp 86, 105 Angus Terrace, Bedford, 540/587-9113, www.vanquility-acresinn.com, $85-175). This 10-acre farm has wonderful views of the Blue Ridge Mountains, fishing, fireplaces, wireless Internet, and suites with private bathrooms. There are five guest rooms. The better known, **Peaks of Otter Resort** (mp 86, 85554 Blue Ridge Pkwy., Bedford, 540/586-1081, www.peaksofotter.com, $159) sits between two mountains on the parkway and looks over tranquil Abbott Lake. It offers 63 rooms and has a restaurant on-site.

Unique accommodations can be found at the ★ **Depot Lodge Bed and Breakfast** (mp 112.2, Route 311, Paint Bank, 540/897-6000, www.thedepotlodge.com, $129-279), about an hour from Roanoke in the Jefferson National Forest. This restored train depot was built in 1909 as the final stop on the Potts Valley Branch line of the Norfolk & Western Railroad. They offer nine guest rooms and cabins in the depot and surrounding historic buildings, including a romantic restored caboose.

The **Bent Mountain Lodge Bed and Breakfast** (mp 136, 9039 Mountain View Dr., Copper Hill, 540/651-2500, www.bentmountainlodgebedandbreakfast.com, $120-150) has 10 guest suites with private bathrooms. This 15,000-square-foot lodge is between Floyd and Roanoke (20 minutes away from each). Room rates include continental breakfast. The lodge is pet friendly.

The **Bella La Vita Inn Bed and Breakfast** (mp 161, 582 New Haven Rd. SE, Floyd, 540/745-2541, www.bellalavitainn.com, $149-160) is less than two miles from the Blue Ridge Parkway and offers four delightful European-style guest rooms and in-house massage therapy.

A good overnight stop near mp 165 is the **Stonewall Bed and Breakfast** (mp 165.2, 102 Wendi Pate Trail SE, Floyd, 540/745-2861, www.stonewallbed.com, $70-130). They have six guest rooms in the main house and two cabins for rent. This lovely three-level log house is in the woods and has a warm and inviting atmosphere.

The **Ambrosia Farm Bed and Breakfast** (mp 171.5, 271 Cox Store Rd., Floyd, 540/745-6363, www.ambrosiafarm.net, $90-135) is housed in a restored log farmhouse that is 200 years old. It now contains four cozy guest rooms. The home has lovely views, porches to enjoy them from, and an on-site pottery studio.

Just 200 yards from the Blue Ridge Parkway near milepost 174 is the **Woodberry Inn** (mp 174.1, 182 Woodberry Rd. SW, Meadows of Dan, 540/593-2567, www.woodberryinn.com, $99). They offer 16 simply appointed rooms (each with a private bathroom), free wireless Internet, and a restaurant on-site. They are pet friendly.

For stunning upscale accommodations, treat yourself to a stay at ★ **Primland** (mp 177.7, 2000 Busted Rock Rd., Meadows of Dan, 866/960-7746, www.primland.com, $300-1,890). Primland offers 62 units that include lodge rooms, suites, cottages, treehouses, and mountain homes. There is a mile-long list of amenities and activities offered on the premises, including a spa, fitness center, and golf course. Turn east at milepost 177.7 to take Route 58/Jeb Stuart Highway for 4.5 miles to Busted Rock Road.

The **Wolf Creek Farm** (mp 192, 688 Gid

Primland

Primland (2000 Busted Rock Road, Meadows of Dan, 276/222-3800, www.primland.com, $300-1,890) might be the best-kept secret in all of Virginia. Nestled in the beautiful Blue Ridge Mountains on more than 12,000 acres, this LEED-certified, upscale resort offers complete relaxation, as well as stunning scenery, plentiful activities, great food, and attention to every last detail.

Unpretentious, yet classy in every respect, this unique four-season property is the perfect getaway for a range of occasions, from family vacations to business conferences and even honeymoons. In addition to its luxurious suites, the main lodge offers a formal dining room, a cozy pub, a conference space, a beautiful spa, an indoor swimming pool, a fitness center, a game room, a common space, and a large deck with a fire pit. The lodge also features a unique observatory with a Celestron CGE Pro 1400 series telescope, and nightly tours of the universe are offered by a local astronomer. Additional accommodations include stunning secluded tree houses, golf-course view cottages, pinnacle cottages, and individual homes.

The list of amenities and activities available at Primland includes the highly ranked Highland Golf Course, hiking, sporting clays, fly fishing, ATV rides, hunting, kayaking, horseback riding, disc golf, geocaching, nature walks, tree climbing, mountain biking, and an authentic Virginia moonshine experience. They also offer a Tesla charger, a smoking house, and eco-conscious extras throughout the resort.

Collins Rd., Ararat, 800/416-9653, www.wolfcreekfarmva.net, $135-160) offers two guest rooms and one cabin for rent in the town of Ararat. It sits on 102 acres and has a fishing lake and swimming pool.

CAMPING

Camping and fishing can be found three miles from the parkway at mp 27 and the **Montebello Camping and Fishing Resort** (mp 27, 15072 Crabtree Falls Hwy., Montebello, 540/377-2650, www.montebellova.com, $28-40). This full-service campground accommodates RVs, trailers, and tent camping. There's a four-acre lake and cabins on-site.

The **Glen Maury Park Campground** (mp 45.6, 101 Maury River Dr., Buena Vista,

540/261-7321, www.glenmaurypark.com, $22-35) is five miles from the parkway on 315 acres. They have 52 sites and modern facilities. A few miles down the parkway is the **Lynchburg NW/Blue Ridge Parkway KOA** (mp 61.5, 6252 Elon Rd., Monroe, 434/299-5228, www.koa.com, $28-49.50), sitting just one mile from the parkway and open all year. They have RV and tent camping and also rent cabins ($60-75).

Visitors can pitch a tent at one of 74 tent sites in the **Roanoke Mountain Campground** (mp 120.4, Blue Ridge Dr., Roanoke, 540/342-3051, $20). Facilities include 30 RV/trailer sites, comfort stations, water, flush toilets, and sinks (no showers).

Near milepost 177.7 is the **Meadows of Dan Campground** (mp 177.7, 2182 Jeb Stuart Hwy., Meadows of Dan, 276/952-2292, www.meadowsofdancampground.com, $30). They have full hookups, a separate tent area, a bathhouse, and a dumping station. They also offer log cabin rentals.

The **Fancy Gap Cabins and Campground** (mp 199.5, 202595 Blue Ridge Pkwy., Fancy Gap, 484/560-9119, www.fancygapcabinsandcampground.com, $21-68) is right on the Blue Ridge Parkway in Fancy Gap. They offer tent sites, RV sites, camping cabins ($21-53), and motel rooms ($68) with scenic views. They are pet friendly.

INFORMATION AND SERVICES

For additional information on the Blue Ridge Parkway, visit www.blueridgeparkway.org, or stop by the **Humpback Rocks Visitor Center** (mp 6, Park Information Line 828/298-0398, daily 10am-5pm) or the **Peaks of Otter Visitor Center** (mp 85.6, Park Information Line 828/298-0398, daily 10am-5pm).

Lexington

Lexington is a popular tourist stop due to its lovely location in the southern part of the Shenandoah Valley, vibrant military history, and the fact that it is home to **Washington and Lee University** and the **Virginia Military Institute (VMI).** Lexington is part of Rockbridge County. Buena Vista is the closest town (15-minute drive), and Natural Bridge near the Blue Ridge Parkway is about 20 minutes away.

Many historic residences are preserved along the town's tree-lined streets and in the downtown area, making Lexington a charming mix of homes, shops, and restaurants. There are numerous cozy inns and bed-and-breakfasts to choose from, and many are within walking distance to local attractions.

Two of the most famous Confederate heroes, Robert E. Lee and Stonewall Jackson, are buried in Lexington. Both lived and worked in Lexington and their legacies live on in this somewhat quiet community.

downtown Lexington

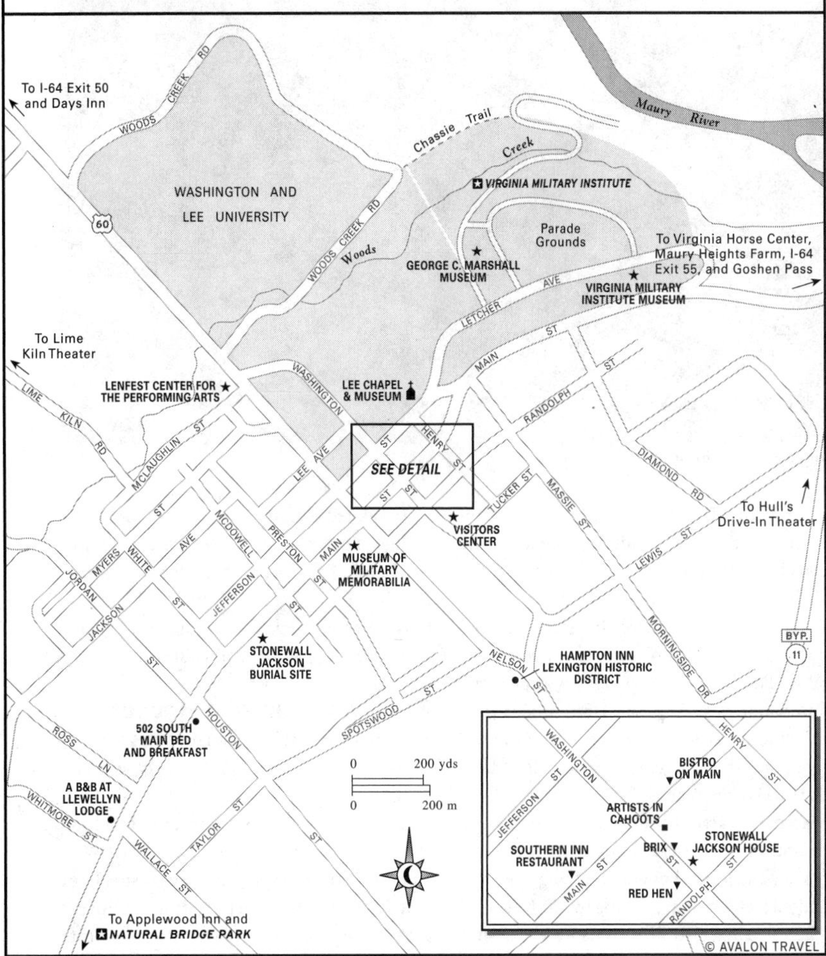

Lexington was founded in 1777 and was destroyed by fire in 1796. It was quickly rebuilt but was again partly destroyed in 1864 by Union gunfire. Today it is a lovely southern town, steeped in history, where cadets in uniform can be seen strolling down the streets, and tourists enjoy leisurely meals in local eateries.

SIGHTS

★ Virginia Military Institute

The **Virginia Military Institute** (Letcher Avenue, 540/464-7230, www.vmi.edu) is the oldest state-supported military college in the country (founded in 1839). Many famous leaders have graced its doorstep including General Stonewall Jackson, who was a professor there

Virginia Military Institute

prior to the Civil War. Be sure to check the VMI website for the cadet parade schedule. This is a highlight of any trip to the institute. Cadet-led tours of campus are also available.

One of the most interesting sights on campus is the **George C. Marshall Museum** (VMI Parade, 540/463-7103, www.marshallfoundation.org, Tues.-Sat. 11am-4pm, $5), an informative space dedicated to the life of a legendary five-star general who rose to fame during World War II. The museum follows Marshall's career beginning as a young lieutenant. Visitors can get a short dose of military history and learn about the evolving role of the United States military during the 20th century. The museum also illustrates how Marshall learned to be such a strong leader. Items featured in the museum include Marshall's Nobel Peace Prize, a narrated World War II map, and a Jeep from 1943. A good place to begin is by watching the video presentation on Marshall's life. Allow 1-2 hours to visit. The museum is in the southwest corner of campus, and there is plenty of parking behind it.

Another VMI museum is **The Virginia Military Institute Museum** (Jackson Memorial Hall, 415 Letcher Ave., 540/464-7334, www.vmi.edu/museum, daily 9am-5pm, $3 suggested donation) in Jackson Memorial Hall. Visitors can learn about the history of VMI and hear stories of its alumni. Special features include a statue of Stonewall Jackson's horse, his field desk, and his uniforms. There is also an antique firearms collection.

Stonewall Jackson House

The **Stonewall Jackson House** (8 E. Washington St., 540/464-7704, www.stonewalljackson.org, Mon.-Sat. 9am-5pm, Sun. 1pm-5pm, $8) offers an interesting look at life in Lexington prior to the Civil War. Visitors can learn about many aspects of Stonewall Jackson's life including his time as a professor at the Virginia Military Institute (VMI), his role as a leader in his church, his time as a businessman, and his private affairs. The museum first opened in 1954 and was meticulously restored to its original appearance in 1979. Owned by VMI, the museum contains many of Jackson's personal belongings. Guided tours are available on the hour and half hour.

Stonewall Jackson Burial Site

General Stonewall Jackson was laid to rest in Lexington in May 1863 following his

Stonewall Jackson

Stonewall Jackson's burial site in Lexington

Thomas Jonathan Jackson was born in western Virginia (in Clarksburg, which is now part of West Virginia) in 1824 and was orphaned at the age of seven. Raised by extended family, Jackson was a constable and a teacher prior to his appointment to the U.S. Military Academy at West Point. After graduation, he served in the U.S. Army and fought in the Mexican-American War before being stationed in New York and Florida.

In 1851 Jackson was appointed as a professor at the Virginia Military Institute in Lexington, where he taught natural and experimental philosophy and was an artillery instructor. Some of his methods are still passed on there today. While in Lexington, he married Elinor Junkin in 1853 and joined the Lexington Presbyterian Church. After only one year of marriage, Elinor died in childbirth. The child was stillborn, and Jackson was suddenly alone.

In 1857, Jackson married Mary Anna Morrison, and the couple bought a home on Washington Street. They lived there quietly until 1861 when Jackson went off to fight in the Civil War just weeks after it began.

Jackson entered the war as an infantry colonel, but was soon promoted to brigadier general. During the First Battle of Bull Run on July 21, 1861, Jackson and his brigade provided reinforcements to Confederate lines that were under heavy Union fire. As other Confederate troops began to flee the battle, Jackson and his troops held their ground. Seeing this, General Barnard E. Bee Jr. yelled, "There is Jackson, standing like a stone wall," and thus, Jackson earned the nickname "Stonewall."

Jackson became known for his superb leadership skills and was promoted to major general. His most noted accomplishment was the Valley Campaign of 1862, during which Jackson's army of 17,000 marched 646 miles in 48 days and won five big victories against forces numbering around 60,000. It is thought of as one of the most brilliant campaigns in history.

In May 1863 at Chancellorsville, Virginia, Jackson's troops won a great victory. During the battle, Jackson was accidently fired on by Confederate troops, killing two of his aides and seriously wounding the general's left arm and right hand. Doctors in a field hospital decided to amputate his left arm. As Jackson lay in bed, Robert E. Lee looked at him and said, "He has lost his left arm, but I have lost my right."

Jackson put up a good fight but was overcome with pneumonia and died on May 10.

death from pneumonia. His remains were moved to their current resting place in 1890. A statue marks his tomb on the south end of Main Street, which is surrounded by grave sites of other prominent Civil War soldiers and citizens. The grounds are open dawn to dusk.

Museum of Military Memorabilia

The **Museum of Military Memorabilia** (122 S. Main, 540/464-3041, Apr.-Oct. Wed.-Fri. noon-5pm, Sat. 9am-5pm, Nov.-May by appointment, $3, cadets free) is a wonderful personal collection of artifacts dedicated to uniformed servicemen and women. It features items such as flags, weapons, and uniforms from the United States, the United Kingdom, and several European countries. A tour is available.

Washington and Lee University

Washington and Lee University (204 W. Washington St., 540/458-8400, www.wlu.edu) is the ninth-oldest institution of higher learning in the United States. It was founded in 1749 as the Augusta Academy. The school has undergone four name changes in the past 250 years and is now named for George Washington (who gave the school its first endowment) and Robert E. Lee (who served as president of the school and is now buried there). It is a private liberal arts school that was originally all male. The first women were admitted to the university's top-ranked law school in 1972, but it wasn't until 1985 that they were allowed in undergraduate programs. The charming campus full of Georgian-style buildings with redbrick facades and multistory porticos is right in downtown Lexington.

LEE CHAPEL & MUSEUM

The **Lee Chapel & Museum** (100 North Jefferson St., Washington and Lee University, 540/458-8768, www.wlu.edu, Apr.-Oct. Mon.-Sat. 9am-5pm, Sun. 1pm-5pm, Nov.-Mar. Mon.-Sat. 9am-4pm, Sun. 1pm-4pm, $5 suggested donation) was built in 1867 at the request of Robert E. Lee. At the time, Lee was the university president of what was then called Washington College. Lee was a regular at weekday services in the chapel and had his office in the lower level of the building. When he died in 1870, he was buried under the chapel, but his remains were moved in 1883 into a family crypt that was added to the lower level of an addition to the building. Other members of Lee's family are also buried in the crypt, and the remains of his horse Traveller were laid to rest just outside the entrance to the museum. Today the chapel hosts concerts, lectures, and other events in an auditorium on the main level. There is seating for 500 people. The lower level houses an informative museum that discusses the contributions both George Washington and Robert E. Lee made to education and features Lee's office. There is also a museum shop. The museum plays a part in many university events, so it is best to call ahead prior to visiting.

Virginia Horse Center

The enormous **Virginia Horse Center** (487 Maury River Rd., 540/464-2950, www.horsecenter.org) is a 600-acre equestrian compound three miles north of downtown Lexington. The beautiful grounds house a coliseum that holds 4,000 spectators, eight barns that hold 1,200 horses, 17 outdoor riding rings, two indoor arenas, a cross-country and combined carriage driving course, a campground, and food services. The center hosts many horse events throughout the year but also hosts non-horse-related events such as dog shows, agricultural programs, the Regional Fair and Farm Show, and BMX competitions.

ENTERTAINMENT AND EVENTS

Lexington is a charming city to explore. Free walking tours of the historic downtown area are available April-November at the **Visitors Center** (106 E. Washington St., 540/463-3777, www.lexingtonvirginia.com). Tours leave on Friday at 3pm and go through historic downtown and through the campus of Washington and Lee University. Tours conclude at the Virginia Military Institute.

Starting each Memorial Day and running through Halloween, visitors can take the **Haunted Tales** (540/464-2250, $13) tour of Historic Lexington. This 90-minute tour by candlelight follows in the footsteps of Generals Lee and Jackson. Costumed guides reveal ghost stories about the city and will likely raise the hair on your neck or at least make you shiver. Reservations are required and tours begin at the Visitors Center.

For those who prefer to let a horse do the walking, the **Lexington Carriage Company** (540/463-5647, www.lexcarriage.com, $16) offers horse-drawn carriage tours April through October. Tours last 40-45 minutes and are narrated by a professional guide. Tours pass through historic residential streets and go by the Stonewall Jackson House, Lee Chapel, Washington and Lee University, and the Stonewall Jackson Cemetery.

Theatergoers will love the unique **Lime Kiln Theater** (607 Borden Rd., 540/463-7088, www.limekilntheater.org). This beautiful outdoor venue was erected out of the ruins of a 19th-century kiln. The theater is set among the vine-covered stones of the ruins and has three stages (two that are open to the stars). The theater hosts classic theater, concerts, and civic celebrations April to October.

Concerts and theater performances can also be found at the **Lenfest Center for the Performing Arts** (100 Glasgow St., 540/458-8000, www.wlu.edu) at Washington and Lee University. The center hosts more than 250 performances a year by both students and professionals.

Moviegoers can take in the action from the comfort of their cars at **Hull's Drive-in Theater** (2367 N. Lee Hwy., 540/463-2618, www.hullsdrivein.com, $7), a seasonal drive-in theater that first opened in 1950. Its first showing was of John Wayne's *The Wake of the Red Witch.*

A yearly celebration is held to honor the birthdays of General Robert E. Lee and General Stonewall Jackson on **Lee-Jackson Day** (www.leejacksonday.webs.com) in mid-January. The celebration actually spans two days and features a variety of speakers, an annual memorial service, a parade, a luncheon, and a ball. Free tours of Jackson's home are also given during the celebration.

Another much-anticipated annual event is the **Fourth of July Balloon Rally** (540/461-0402, www.sunriserotarylexva.org). This free event lasts for three days over the Fourth of July and is a spectacular gathering of brightly colored hot-air balloons. Visitors can purchase piloted balloon rides during the event.

SHOPPING

Lexington is an antiques collector's dream. There seems to be at least one antiques store on every block. The largest is **Duke's Lexington Antique Center** (1495 N. Lee Hwy., 540/463-9511, www.lexingtonvirginia.com/directory/shopping, daily 10am-6pm). This impressive 20,000-square-foot space features more than 200 antiques dealers and consignments. It is open 365 days a year and has ample parking for cars and RVs.

A wonderful local gallery run by an artist cooperative is **Artists in Cahoots** (21 W. Washington St., 540/464-1147, www.artistsincahoots.com, Apr.-Dec. Mon.-Sat. 10:30am-6pm, Sun. 10:30am-3:30pm). The cooperative was founded in 1983, and the gallery features paintings, jewelry, pottery, ironwork, woodwork, furniture, bird carvings, decoys, photography, sculpture, printmaking, fabric art, and more.

SPORTS AND RECREATION

Lexington is surrounded by the **George Washington and Jefferson National Forests,** which encompass land in the Appalachian Mountains of Virginia, West Virginia, and Kentucky. The two forests are managed jointly by the U.S. Forest Service. Together at 1.8 million acres they form one of the largest public land areas in the eastern part of the country. Easy access to this large wilderness area provides ample possibilities for outdoor recreation near Lexington.

The seven-mile **Chessie Nature Trail** (www.traillink.com) links Lexington with the neighboring town of Buena Vista. The trail begins at Route 631 in Lexington and follows the north bank of the Maury River along mile markers on the former Chesapeake & Ohio Railroad route. Travelers can expect to see scenic Virginia countryside along the way and a variety of wildlife and farm animals. Be aware that cattle gates are sometimes closed along the trail.

Local streams are teeming with trout. Expert fly-fishing guides and instruction can be found at **Fly Fishing Adventures** (540/463-3235, www.vatrout.com). They offer fishing trips and instruction for beginners and experienced fly fishers.

Lexington is horse country. The pristine Virginia Horse Center is a prime example of this; however, there are also 65 miles of **horse trails** that wind through the George Washington and Jefferson National Forests near Lexington (U.S. Forest Service, 540/291-2188, www.usfs.gov/gwj). Multiple trailheads with room for trailer parking are located in the forest.

Canoeing, kayaking, and float trips on tubes on the James and Maury Rivers can be arranged through **Twin Rivers Outfitters** (653 Lowe St., 540/261-7334, www.canoevirginia.net). They are a full-service livery in Buchanan (about 25 miles from Lexington) and have been in business since 1978.

Take a shot at some sporting clays at **Quail Ridge Sporting Clays** (336 Murat Rd., 540/463-1800, $30 per round of 100, $23 per round of 50). They offer a challenging course with multiple types of targets at different speeds and distances.

FOOD

American

A favorite farm-to-table restaurant right in town is the ★ **Red Hen** (11 E. Washington St., 540/464-4401, www.redhenlex.com, Tues.-Sat. 5pm-9:30pm, $24-30). This cozy little restaurant in a little red house serves imaginative, well-planned entrées that have great flavor combinations. The menu changes daily depending on what produce and meat is fresh. Whether it is local steak or fresh beet risotto, there is always something new to try. The wine list is also carefully picked to pair well with the current menu, and they focus on serving natural wines that come from vineyards using organic growing methods. The staff is wonderful and helps make this a great place to celebrate an occasion or to bring a special someone.

For comfort food with a southern touch, dine at the **Southern Inn Restaurant** (37 S. Main St., 540/463-3612, www.southerninn.com, Mon.-Sat. 11:30am-10pm, Sun. 10am-9pm, $12-35). They serve contemporary American food (such as stuffed butternut squash and roasted duck breast) along with classic American dishes such as meat loaf, rainbow trout, and fried chicken. There is also a good wine list and homemade desserts. The restaurant was established in 1932 but has been updated by the current owners cosmetically, functionally, and with a refreshed menu. A seat at the bar invites a casual evening with locals, as this is a popular place with visitors and residents alike.

Another contemporary American restaurant that is well worth a visit is the **Bistro on Main** (8 N. Main, 540/464-4888, www.bistro-lexington.com, Tues.-Sat. lunch 11:30am-2:30pm, dinner 5pm-9pm, Sun. brunch 11am-2pm, $12-29), which has a great little bar and serves creative dishes with a variety of influences. Try the shrimp and grits, duck breast with blackberry sauce, or jambalaya; each dish is different, yet delicious. Their brunch menu is also good (a personal favorite is the smoked salmon omelet paired with a Bloody Mary). The atmosphere is comfortable, intimate, and has an upscale feel to it, yet the food is reasonably priced. There is a plate charge for split dishes.

Mediterranean

If wine and a small-plate menu sound appealing, visit **Brix** (4 E. Washington St., 540/464-3287, www.brix-winebar.com, Wed.-Sat. 5pm-10pm, Sun. 11am-3pm, small plates $5-13) in downtown Lexington. This lovely little wine bar and restaurant serves pan-Mediterranean small plates and has a full bar and a grand selection of wine by the glass. The food is prepared with fresh, local ingredients, and the small-plate menu allows diners to be adventurous and try a variety of dishes.

The menu changes frequently, but expect to see items such as shrimp bobo, lamb ragout, and salumi. The atmosphere is quaint with a European feel.

ACCOMMODATIONS

Lexington is known for its lovely bed-and-breakfasts and inns. There are dozens of them in and around the town. Some offer visitors a piece of history, some offer stunning landscape views, and some offer both. Although there are more than 1,500 rooms to rent, these can fill up quickly when there's an event going on in town or at the area's universities. It is best to book a room as early as possible if you know you'll be competing with many other out-of-town guests.

$100-200

While you explore Lexington, **502 South Main Bed and Breakfast** (502 S. Main, 540/460-7353, www.502southmain.com, $159-229) is a great place to get spoiled. The refurbished home was built in 1885 and is classically furnished with European flair. It has three large guest rooms with either a king or queen bed and modern private bathrooms. Guests are met with genuine hospitality and are pampered with many extras such as plentiful snacks and luxurious bath products. The house is in downtown Lexington and within walking distance to many attractions.

Another wonderful bed-and-breakfast is **A Bed and Breakfast at Llewellyn Lodge** (603 S. Main St., 540/463-3235, www.llodge.com, $129-249). They offer six guest rooms with private bathrooms, high-speed Internet, and air-conditioning in a charming gray-brick colonial home. The lodge is in a residential area of Lexington, just a short walk from shops, restaurants, and attractions. The innkeepers are experts in hospitality and serve a delicious full breakfast (from a menu). They are also experts on the Lexington area and eager to share their knowledge.

An eco-friendly bed-and-breakfast is the **Applewood Inn & Llama Trekking** (242 Tarn Beck Ln., 540/463-1962, www.applewoodbb.com, $155-172). They offer "green" lodging in a three-story passive solar home built in 1979. The inn is south of town, at the end of a dirt road in a private setting on 37 acres. They have three lovely rooms with wood floors and private bathrooms. One

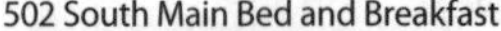

502 South Main Bed and Breakfast

room comes with a private hot tub. Guests can use the pool and kitchen. The inn also offers guided llama trekking, which can be arranged at the house. Treks last about two hours.

The **Comfort Inn Virginia Horse Center** (62 Comfort Way, 540/463-7311, www.choicehotels.com, $109-134) offers clean, comfortable rooms at a good value near the Virginia Horse Center. They have 80 guest rooms, a small heated indoor pool, a sundeck, and a picnic area for guest use.

$200-300

The **Brierley Hill Bed and Breakfast** (985 Borden Rd., 540/464-8421, www.brierleyhill.com, $149-399) offers five guest suites and one cottage, all with private bathrooms. The inn was built in 1993 specifically as a bed-and-breakfast and was named after the antique clock that hangs in the foyer. Located just outside Lexington, the B&B has wonderful views of the Shenandoah Valley landscape, and the house is meticulously maintained. They serve wonderful gourmet breakfasts, and the staff is very friendly.

The **Hampton Inn Lexington—Historic District** (401 E. Nelson St., 540/463-2223, www.hamptoninn3.hilton.com, $179-249) is an unusual chain hotel that is in part a historic manor house called the Col Alto Mansion. There are 10 rooms in the restored manor house and 76 hotel rooms. The hotel sits on seven acres and is within walking distance of many attractions in downtown Lexington. The grounds are nicely kept, and there are beautiful old trees on the property. There is a fitness center and outdoor pool for guest use, free high-speed Internet, and free breakfast.

CAMPING

Lake Robertson Park (106 Lake Robertson Dr., 540/463-4164, $24-28) offers 56 tent and full hookup camping sites. The 581-acre park has a lake, boat rentals, tennis courts, a swimming pool, a picnic pavilion, and hiking trails. Pets are welcome, and there is a laundry facility on-site.

Lee Hi Campground (2516 N. Lee Hwy., 540/463-3478, www.leehi.com, $15-35) has 40 sites, most with full hookups, a restaurant, playground, laundry facility, and a dump station. Pets are welcome.

The **Virginia Horse Center** (487 Maury River Rd., 540/464-2950, $25-40) also offers camping. They have 86 full-hookup sites and 10 tent sites.

INFORMATION AND SERVICES

Lexington has a great **Visitors Center** (106 E. Washington St., 540/463-3777, www.lexingtonvirginia.com, daily 9am-5pm). They provide an information video, a small museum, and very helpful employees. They offer free walking tours of the historic downtown area and the campus of Washington and Lee University. Tours conclude at the Virginia Military Institute.

GETTING THERE AND AROUND

Lexington is in central Virginia off I-81 and I-64, 185 miles southwest of Washington DC and approximately 55 miles east of the West Virginia border and 50 miles north of Roanoke. There is no direct air or rail service to Lexington.

Lynchburg

Lynchburg is a city of 50 square miles in the foothills of the Blue Ridge Mountains and along the James River. It sits near the geographic center of Virginia.

Lynchburg was settled in 1757 when 17-year-old John Lynch began a ferry service across the James River to a 45-acre parcel of land he owned. In 1786, he was granted a charter for the town, and in 1805 Lynchburg was incorporated.

Early Lynchburg relied on tobacco and iron as its primary sources of revenue. Due in part to the Lynch's ferry system, the town became one of the largest tobacco markets in the country. During the Civil War, Lynchburg was a major storage depot and burial spot for soldiers. Many Confederate generals were laid to rest here. Lynchburg was the sole major city in Virginia that was not overtaken by the Union during the Civil War.

Lynchburg is nicknamed the "City of Seven Hills," and each hill has a historical reference behind its name, including Franklin Hill, which was probably named after Ben Franklin, and College Hill, which was named after a military college that existed prior to the Civil War.

Lynchburg is also known as the core of Virginia's conservative religious community and is sometimes referred to as the "Buckle in the Bible Belt." Jerry Falwell's Liberty University is here, as are more than 130 places of worship. As such, many businesses (including restaurants) are closed on Sunday. The city is also considered to have a strong network of safe neighborhoods and good schools, and its residents enjoy a high quality of life.

SIGHTS

Historic Districts

Lynchburg has five historic districts. **Court House Hill** overlooks the James River and downtown Lynchburg. The main street, Court Street, is home to the historic **City Court House,** a Greek revival building that is the main attraction in this small district. Many churches with distinctive steeples also line the street, which is otherwise a mix of government and private offices. **Daniel's Hill** is a linear district that contains the high-traffic Cabell Street. The area was developed for residential use in the 1840s and overlooks the James River and Blackwater Creek.

The most diverse historical district is **Diamond Hill.** This 14-block area contains a large variety of architectural styles including Georgian revival and colonial revival homes. The district is bounded by steep hills and the Lynchburg Expressway. Major streets in the district include Washington Street, Church Street, Harrison Street, and Grace Street. Diamond Hill is the largest historic district and encompasses more than 100 historic structures. Most of the homes were built during the late 19th and early 20th century. The area is well maintained, and extensive renovations are apparent throughout its streets.

Federal Hill offers views toward downtown. The primary street is Federal Street. Many houses in the district were constructed in the 1820s, and the area is known for the fine craftsmanship of its buildings. Many of the homes in the district face maintenance issues, but retain most of their original character.

One of the best-preserved neighborhoods in Lynchburg is the historic **Garland Hill** district. The district begins off 5th Street and runs along the tree-lined Madison Street to its end overlooking Blackwater Creek, and includes Harrison and Clay Streets. The neighborhood was built between the early 19th century and the early 20th century and includes architectural styles such as gothic revival, Victorian, and Queen Anne. The area

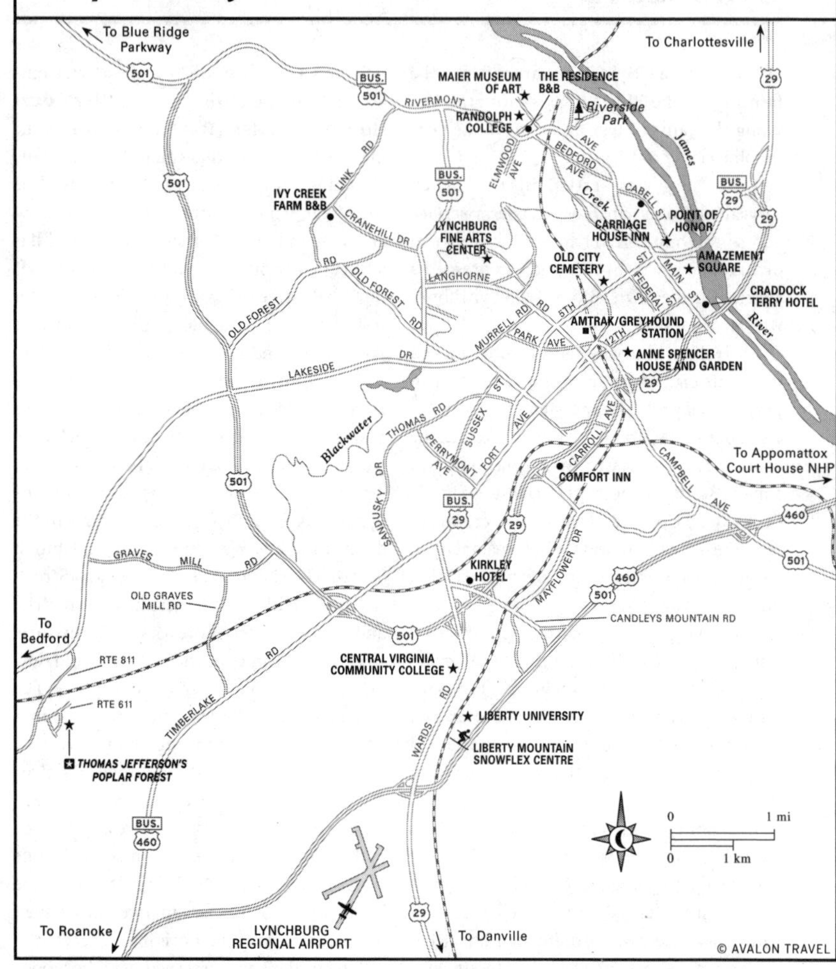

was home to many distinguished residents who worked in the tobacco industry.

Amazement Square

Amazement Square (27 9th St., 434/845-1888, www.amazementsquare.org, Tues.-Sat. 10am-5pm, Sun. 1pm-5pm, $9) is a hands-on museum for children with a happy atmosphere. It is the first multidisciplinary, interactive children's museum to be established in Central Virginia, and it has set a high standard. Kids make their way through four floors of exciting exhibits where they can climb, slide, and participate in a variety of programs and activities on the topics of art, the humanities, science, and health. Allow at least two hours to explore the museum. The staff is excellent.

Old City Cemetery

A fascinating historical spot in Lynchburg is the **Old City Cemetery** (401 Taylor St.,

434/847-1465, www.gravegarden.org, daily dawn to dusk, free). It is the oldest public cemetery in Virginia that is still in use, and it has an estimated 20,000 "residents." Civil War notables, artists, inventors, civil servants—all are buried here, including 2,200 Confederate graves. A stroll through the grounds is a history lesson and a look at a who's who of Lynchburg. There are five small free museums on-site that interpret the history of the area, the city, and the cemetery itself. Four are designed for self-guided tours and can be viewed whenever the cemetery gates are open. The fifth, the **Mourning Museum,** is inside the Cemetery Center, a visitors center for the cemetery (Mon.-Sat. 10am-3pm). A scatter garden for human and pet ashes and a rose garden are also in the cemetery. A looped trail beginning at Taylor and 4th Streets takes visitors around the plots. Guided tours are available for a small fee.

Point of Honor

Perched on a hill overlooking the James River is **Point of Honor** (112 Cabell St., 434/455-6226, www.pointofhonor.org, Mon.-Sat. 10am-4pm, Sun. noon-4pm, $6), a gorgeous federal-style mansion. The home was built in 1815 and has been meticulously restored. It is not certain how it got its name, but there are two theories. The first is that duels were fought here for honor, as was the custom in centuries past; the second theorizes that the name refers to the prominent point of land the home sits on looking out on the James River. The **Diggs Gallery** inside the home provides interesting information on the families who lived in the house. House tours are given daily on the half hour.

Maier Museum of Art

A few blocks away from Point of Honor is the **Maier Museum of Art** (1 Quinlan St., 434/947-8136, www.maiermuseum.org, academic year schedule Tues.-Sun. 1pm-5pm, May-Aug. Wed.-Sun. 1pm-4pm, free, donations appreciated). This nationally recognized art museum at Randolph College features works by 19th- and 20th-century American artists. The museum's permanent collection includes thousands of paintings, photographs, and drawings, with a focus on American impressionism and early 20th-century realism. They have a large collection of works by visionary modernist Arthur B. Davies and painter, printmaker, and photographer Ben Shahn. Special exhibits and programs are offered year-round as well as internships and

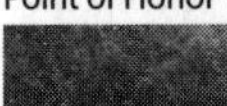

Point of Honor

class visits. The museum is located on campus, behind the athletic fields, and offers a great opportunity to see an amazing collection of artwork without the crowds.

Anne Spencer House and Garden

The **Anne Spencer House and Garden** (1313 Pierce St., 434/845-1313, www.annespencermuseum.com, tours $15) is a two-story Queen Anne-style home that once belonged to poet Anne Spencer (1882-1975). Spencer's work is considered to be part of the Harlem Renaissance, and she wrote of love and beauty. While living in the home, the author entertained many famous guests such as Martin Luther King Jr., Thurgood Marshall, and George Washington Carver. The gardens are open daily from dawn to dusk, and visitors can pick up a brochure at the garden cottage. There is no fee to visit the garden. Tours of the house ($15) are given Saturdays between 1pm and 4pm, or by appointment. The house is closed November-March.

Appomattox Court House National Historical Park

Twenty-two miles east of Lynchburg is **Appomattox Court House National Historical Park** (113 National Park Dr., 434/352-8987, ext. 223, www.nps.gov/apco, daily 8:30am-5pm, $10 per vehicle). The park is the site of General Lee's surrender at the close of the Civil War on April 9, 1865. The park consists of numerous historic structures in the village of Appomattox and sits on 1,700 acres. Begin your exploration at the visitors center, a reconstructed courthouse building that also serves as a museum offering exhibits that include artifacts from the surrender (including surrender documents and a pencil used by General Lee). The three-story **McLean House-Surrender Site** is the reconstructed house where the actual surrender took place approximately 150 yards west of the visitors center. The parlor inside the house, where the surrender meeting occurred, is furnished with both original and reproduced items. Park ranger interpretation is offered daily at the house, and tours are offered seasonally on the hour. Several outbuildings are also open to visitors, including the kitchen, outhouse, and slave quarters. Living-history programs are offered daily during the summer and feature historical interpretations from the 1860s.

Walton's Mountain Museum

Die-hard fans of *The Waltons* television series will enjoy the **Walton's Mountain Museum** (6484 Rockfish River Rd., Schuyler, 434/831-2000, www.waltonmuseum.org, daily 10am-3:30pm, $8), 50 miles northeast of Lynchburg in Schuyler. See Earl Hamner's childhood home (creator of *The Waltons*) and replicas of John Boy's bedroom, Ike Godsey's Store, the Waltons' kitchen and the Waltons' living room. There's a good 30-minute video featuring Earl Hamner and stars of the television show.

ENTERTAINMENT AND EVENTS

Options for live entertainment are less than abundant in Lynchburg. Live music can be found on most weekends at **Phase 2 Dining & Entertainment** (4009 Murray Pl., 434/846-3206, www.phase2club.com). They offer a restaurant, concert hall and banquet facilities. Concerts feature mostly country and rock. There's also a sports bar and lounge. The **Academy of Fine Arts** (600 Main St., 434/846-8499, www.academyfinearts.com) offers live music, classes, and theatrical events. They have a list of upcoming events on the website. The **Lynchburg Symphony Orchestra** (621 Court St., 434/845-6604, www.lynchburgsymphony.com) offers performances in a variety of locations in Lynchburg.

SPORTS AND RECREATION

Ski enthusiasts can indulge year-round at the **Liberty Mountain Snowflex Center** (1971 University Blvd., 434/582-3539, www.

liberty.edu, skiing and snowboarding $8 per hour, tubing $13 for the first hour, $8 for each additional hour). This unusual ski complex opened on the campus of Liberty University six miles south of Lynchburg in 2009 as the first facility in the United States to offer skiing and snowboarding on simulated snow. The 5,000-acre mountain has a bunny slope, intermediate and advanced slopes, and even a freestyle park. A tubing chute and ski lodge complete the simulated ski experience. Rental equipment is $14.

Liberty Mountain also offers 65 miles of trails for mountain biking, hiking, and running. Trails are open to the public daily dawn to dusk. Visit www.liberty.edu/snowflex/trails-maps for trail maps.

Another popular, well-marked trail is the **James River Heritage Trail,** an eight-mile-long trail combining two smaller trails, the **Blackwater Creek Bikeway** and **RiverWalk.** The trail passes through downtown Lynchburg and also lush forest areas. The RiverWalk section is one of the most popular. Its 3.5 miles of paved trail begin on Jefferson Street and run east along the waterfront. To reach the Blackwater Creek Bikeway trailhead, take Route 501 north from the Lynchburg Expressway. Turn right onto Old Langthore Road. The trailhead is on the right.

A favorite park in Lynchburg, **Riverside Park** (2270 Rivermont Ave., 434/455-5858, www.lynchburgva.gov) offers 47 acres of recreation area with views of the James River. Walking trails, tennis, basketball, a large playground, and a seasonal "sprayground" are some of the main attractions. There is also a transportation exhibit that features a train locomotive, tender, and caboose.

The **James River Canoe Ramp** (7th Street) is a good place to launch hand-carried watercraft on the James River. It is located at the end of the 7th Street.

FOOD

American

You may not associate shoes with food, but at ★ **Shoemakers American Grille** (1312 Commerce St., 434/455-1510, www.shoemakersdining.com, Mon.-Sat. 4:30pm-10pm, $13-35) shoes are part of the history. The restaurant is housed in a building that used to be home to the largest shoe manufacturer in the country. The exposed brick is a nod to the building's factory roots, while the interior decor is modern and welcoming. The taste-bud-pleasing menu includes a wide variety of salads, sandwiches, steak, seafood, and a nice selection of scrumptious desserts (try the "Shookie"). They also have a good wine list. The restaurant is the perfect place for a date or to relax with friends. The atmosphere is lively and comfortable, and the service is some of the best in town. There's an outdoor patio that is perfect when the weather is nice.

The **Main Street Eatery and Catering Company** (907 Main St., 434/847-2526, www.mainsteatery.com, Mon.-Sat. 4:30pm-9:30pm, $16-24) serves a delicious menu of seafood, pasta, beef, veal, and poultry. The menu isn't large, but they rotate offerings seasonally so there's always something new. In addition, each item is uniquely prepared with flavorful touches, and the wine and drink menus are extensive. Don't skip the dessert tray; it will tempt you even if you think you're full. Exposed brick and hardwood floors make a cozy atmosphere, and the owner frequently visits tables to check on his customers.

The sister eatery to the Texas Tavern in Roanoke, the **Texas Inn** (422 Main St., 434/846-3823, under $10) is a local icon that stays open late, is cheap, and serves greasy food. Grab a spot at the counter (it's your only choice for seating) and order the Cheesy Western. This signature dish is a hamburger with cheese and a fried egg topped with a delicious secret mustard relish. The chili is also legendary. Not a date place, not a business place, but a sacred institution nonetheless.

Asian

Kings Island Restaurant (2804 Old Forest Rd., 434/384-0066, www.kingsislandrestaurant.com, Sun.-Thurs. 11:30am-10pm, Fri.

11:30am-11pm, Sat. 4:30pm-11pm, $8-20) is your best bet for Chinese and Japanese food in Lynchburg. It is also the oldest Chinese restaurant in town, first serving customers in 1977. The food is good, with the typical menu items for American Chinese restaurants, and the sushi is a step above. They earn extra points on the atmosphere, which is quiet and cozy without being dark and drab. The food is reasonably priced, and the service is excellent,

Italian

A great choice for pizza is **Waterstone Fire Roasted Pizza** (1309 Jefferson St., 434/455-1515, www.waterstonepizza.com, Sun.-Thurs. 11am-10pm, Fri.-Sat. 11am-11pm, $10-14). This popular pizza joint opened in 2010 and has a loyal following. Natural ingredients and wonderful flavor are the keys to their mouthwatering pizzas. They also have a brewery on-site. If you're lucky to go on a nice day or evening, grab a seat on the patio. The neighboring historic buildings offer a pleasant backdrop and make for an inviting atmosphere.

Mexican

Good Mexican food can be found at **La Carreta** (8004 Timberlake Rd., 434/239-9701, www.lacarretaonline.com, Mon.-Fri. 11am-2:30pm and 5pm-11pm, Sat. noon-10pm, Sun. noon-2:30pm and 5pm-9pm, $6-12), which has four locations throughout Lynchburg and serves flavorful, authentic fare at a very reasonable price. The salsa is fresh and delicious, and the beer is served in frosted mugs. This is a great place to bring a group and it has a loyal local following.

ACCOMMODATIONS

$100-200

The ★ **Craddock Terry Hotel** (1312 Commerce St., 434/455-1500, www.craddockterryhotel.com, $147-214) may well be a first: This trendy boutique hotel is a converted turn-of-the-20th-century shoe factory. The large red lady's shoe out front the brick building might give that away,

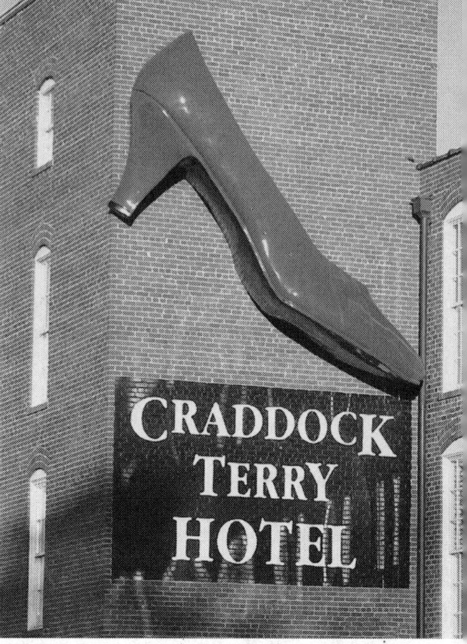

Craddock Terry Hotel

but the interior is far from its factory roots. The renovated space now offers 44 large modern rooms and suites with high ceilings, large windows, comfortable beds, luxurious bathrooms, and eco-friendly bath products. Views from the rooms include downtown, the James River, and the Blue Ridge Mountains. The decor is contemporary with many historical artifacts from the Craddock-Terry Shoe Corporation and modern shoe-themed accents. Complimentary continental breakfast arrives at your room each morning in a wooden shoeshine box and the resident hotel dog, a wirehaired fox terrier, is named Buster Brown.

The ★ **Federal Crest Inn Bed and Breakfast** (1101 Federal St., 434/845-6155, www.federalcrest.com, $165-245) is a peaceful alternative to hotel accommodations. This elegant 8,000-square-foot turn-of-the-20th-century home has four guest rooms with private bathrooms. Completely renovated and decorated with antiques, the Federal Hill home was built in 1909 in the Georgian revival style. Gourmet candlelight breakfasts, snack baskets in each room, evening refreshments, and turndown service are just some of the amenities guests can expect in this beautiful bed-and-breakfast. The kind innkeepers truly make this a home away from home and treat their guests wonderfully.

The **Kirkley Hotel** (2900 Candlers Mountain Rd., 434/237-6333, www.kirkley-hotel.com, $99-136) is a reasonably priced hotel with many recent renovations. They have 168 rooms and suites with free wireless Internet, comfortable beds, two-line telephones with data ports, ironing boards, coffeemakers, desks, and a microwave or refrigerator. Suites have dining rooms, wet bars, and living rooms.

Once the president's residence of Randolph-Macon Women's College (now called Randolph College), **The Residence Bed and Breakfast** (2460 Rivermont Ave., 434/845-6565, www.theresidencebb.com, $150-250) offers three cozy rooms near campus. Once a place where many celebrities were entertained—such as Elizabeth Taylor, President Gerald Ford, and Georgia O'Keeffe—this 1915 home was part of the school until 1983. Now the innkeepers greet visitors with nicely appointed rooms, gourmet breakfasts, free use of bicycles, and warm hospitality.

$200-300

Another lovely bed-and-breakfast is the **Carriage House Inn** (404 Cabell St., 434/846-1388, www.thecarriagehouseinnbandb.com, $179-299) in the Daniel's Hill Historic District. This six-guest-room bed-and-breakfast offers comfortable accommodations in a beautifully renovated 1878 Italianate mansion featuring a grand spiral staircase and many original details such as molding, woodwork, and fixtures. The Carriage House Inn was the first lodging facility in Lynchburg to earn a "green" certification. Rooms are spacious with high ceilings, and the house has a nice porch with rocking chairs. Hiking and biking trails are just six blocks away. The entrance to the bed-and-breakfast is easy to miss from the road, so look carefully for the sign.

INFORMATION AND SERVICES

The **Lynchburg Visitors Information Center** (216 12th St., 434/847-1811, www.

Carriage House Inn

discoverlynchburg.org, daily 9am-5pm) is a great additional resource for information and services in the city.

GETTING THERE

Lynchburg is 180 miles from Washington DC. **Lynchburg Regional Airport** (LYH, 350 Terminal Dr., #100, 434/455-6090, www.lynchburgva.gov) is a small city-owned airport also known as **Preston Glenn Field.** It's about five miles southwest of downtown Lynchburg. The airport has a dozen arriving and departing flights a day through the regional carrier American Eagle. Rental cars are available on-site, and there is free wireless Internet.

Train service runs to the **Amtrak** station (825 Kemper St., 800/872-7245, www.amtrak.com). **Greyhound** (800/231-2222, www.greyhound.com) bus service is also available in the same location.

Local bus service is provided by the **Greater Lynchburg Transit Company** (434/455-5080, www.gltconline.com, $2), with 37 buses traveling 14 routes Monday-Saturday.

Roanoke

Roanoke is the largest city in southwest Virginia. It sits in the picturesque Roanoke Valley and is bisected by the Roanoke River. The history of Roanoke dates back to the 1740s, when the area near natural salt marshes in the center of the valley was first settled. The marshes were called "licks" and served as gathering places for deer, elk, and buffalo. The first village was known as Big Lick.

When the Shenandoah Valley Railroad came to the area, Big Lick was renamed Roanoke, and in the late 1800s Roanoke became a crossroads for the railroad. This spurred the city's growth. A market opened not long after and remains the cornerstone of downtown commerce. Roanoke is now southwest Virginia's thriving center for transportation, manufacturing, trade, and entertainment.

Roanoke is known to offer residents a good quality of life. It is metropolitan, yet has a less stressful pace than many other cities. There is a vibrant downtown area with culture and business, and Roanoke has the largest airport in southwestern Virginia. Roanoke is also easily accessible via I-81.

SIGHTS

★ Taubman Museum of Art

The **Taubman Museum of Art** (110 Salem Ave. SE, 540/342-5760, www.taubmanmuseum.org, Wed.-Sat. 10am-5pm, third Thurs. and first Fri. 10am-9pm, free) attracts visitors with its shiny, modern building that opened in 2008 on Salem Avenue. Between 100,000 and 130,000 people visit the museum each year to take in exhibits on subjects such as art, crafts,

Taubman Museum of Art

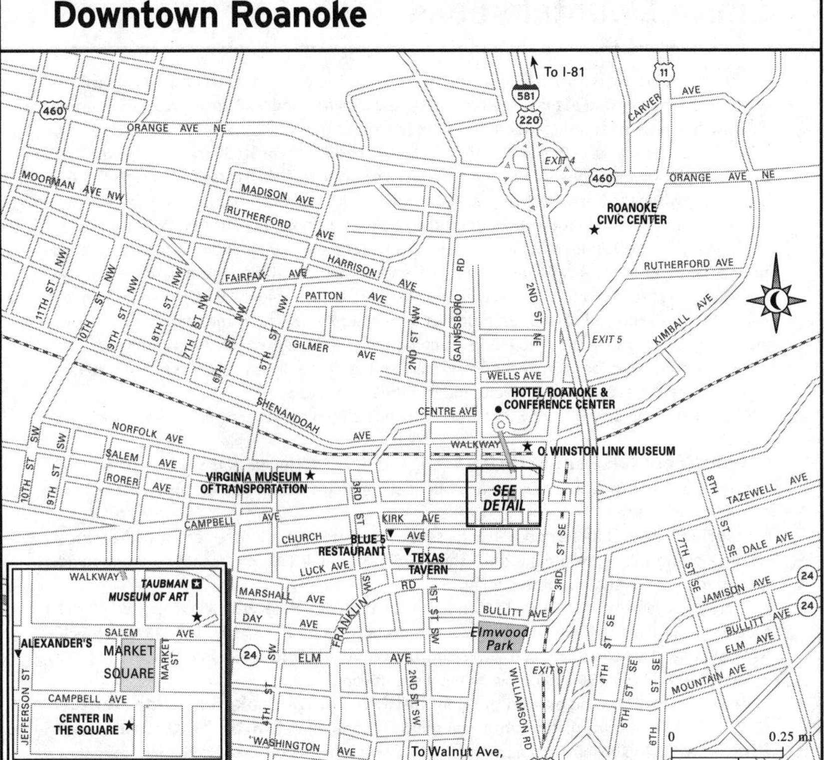

dance, sculpture, graphic arts, photography, poetry, and film. The museum reflects cultural traditions throughout America as well as of a global nature, but it also features local culture from the Roanoke Valley and southern Virginia. There is an arts center at the museum where children and their families can create their own art and learn different artistic techniques. This hands-on gallery offers painting, drawing, theater, sculpture, music, and more. Exhibits change at the museum every six to eight weeks, so there is always something new to experience. The museum houses a store that showcases merchandise related to current exhibits and regional crafts and gifts from around the globe.

Virginia Museum of Transportation

The **Virginia Museum of Transportation** (303 Norfolk Ave. SW, 540/342-5670, www.vmt.org, Mon.-Sat. 10am-5pm, Sun. 1pm-5pm, $8) is a unique, mostly outdoor museum featuring more than 50 exhibits. It provides a wonderful overview of the extensive railway heritage in Virginia and is best known for its exhibits on the Norfolk & Western Class J-611 and Class A-1218 modern steam locomotives. The museum's road exhibits take visitors through the history of road transportation starting with the horse and buggy and ending with modern-day cars and trucks. Air exhibits discuss early aviation, commercial aviation,

Smith Mountain Lake

Smith Mountain Lake is the perfect mountain lake retreat and a favorite among Virginians. This is where the movie *What About Bob?* starring Richard Dreyfuss and Bill Murray was filmed, and it was also featured in the independent film *Lake Effects* in 2012.

Smith Mountain Lake is the largest artificial lake in Virginia; it covers 32 square miles and has 500 miles of shoreline. The average depth of the lake is 55 feet. The lake itself was created in the early 1960s when the Roanoke River was dammed at Smith Mountain Gap. It is equidistant from Lynchburg and Roanoke (about an hour's drive) and is a four-hour drive from Washington DC.

The community of Smith Mountain Lake has approximately 22,000 residents, but the area is a popular destination for vacationers. Residential growth was slow during the initial decades after the lake was created, but has been increasing steadily since the mid-1980s. Upscale residences, condominiums, and golf course communities are the norm now, and commuters from Roanoke and Lynchburg also make their homes in the community. Retirees from Northern Virginia are part of the latest growth trend at Smith Mountain Lake, and the influx of new residents has contributed to recent retail and commercial development in the community.

Route 122 is the only highway that crosses the lake. The area is accessed by Routes 24, 116, and 40.

Smith Mountain Lake State Park (1235 State Park Rd., Huddleston, 540/297-6066, www.dcr.virginia.gov, $5) provides a beach and public swimming on the lake, and there are a handful of public golf courses.

In addition to beautiful scenery and endless opportunities for outdoor recreation in the form of boating, biking, hiking, swimming, and fishing, Smith Mountain Lake offers shopping, antiquing, art, entertainment, and wonderful dining.

There are several marinas on Smith Mountain Lake, including **Parkway Marina** (16918 Smith Mountain Lake Pkwy., 540/297-4412, www.parkwaymarina.com), **Bridgewater Marina** (16430 BT Washington Hwy., 540/721-7800, www.bwmarina.com), and **Mitchells Point Marina** (3553 Trading Post Rd., 540/484-3980, www.mitchellspoint.com).

Vacation rentals can be booked through **Smith Mountain Lake Vacation Rentals** (877/773-2452, www.smithmountainlakerentals.com) and **Smith Mountain Lake Properties** (540/797-0477, www.smithmountainlakeproperties.org). For additional information on Smith Mountain Lake, visit www.smithmountainlake.com.

military aviation, and airports. The museum also features model trains and a gift shop.

Mill Mountain Star and Park

The **Mill Mountain Star and Park** (210 Reserve Ave., 540/853-2200) is famous for its huge illuminated star that sits on top of Mill Mountain. Roanoke is nicknamed "the Star City of the South," which was the inspiration for the construction of the massive star erected in 1949. It is the largest man-made illuminated star in the world. It is 88.5 feet tall and lit by 2,000 feet of neon tubes channeling 17,500 watts of power. The star is lit each evening, but is turned off at midnight.

O. Winston Link Museum

The **O. Winston Link Museum** (101 Shenandoah Ave., 540/982-5465, www.linkmuseum.org, Mon.-Sat. 10am-5pm, Sun. 1pm-5pm, $5) houses the largest exhibit of O. Winston Link's famous photographs depicting life in the 1950s along the railroad in Virginia. Even people who don't know anything about railroads can appreciate the talent of this photographer and the era that is represented in the museum. Each photograph captures a story, and many are accompanied by articles that appeared in a large variety of magazines and textbooks. The museum is housed in a restored passenger train station.

Center in the Square

In the southwest corner of Market Square (a historic market at the intersection of Campbell Avenue and Market Street) is a five-story cultural center called **Center in the Square** (1 Market Sq., 540/342-5700, www.centerinthesquare.org). The center opened in 1983 as the cornerstone of a redevelopment program in an urban area that was once facing economic decline. Several organizations focused on arts and science now call the center home: the **Science Museum of Western Virginia** (540/342-5710, www.smwv.org), **Harrison Museum of African American Culture** (540/857-4395, www.harrisonmuseum.com), **Mill Mountain Theatre** (540/342-5740, www.millmountain.org), and the **Interactive Roanoke Pinball Museum** (540/342-5746, www.roanokepinball.org). Visitors can now enjoy a thriving cultural community in the square and also visit private stores and restaurants. The most famous, perhaps, is the **Roanoke Weiner Stand,** which opened just after the original Center in the Square building (first called the McGuire Building) opened in 1915 and is a city landmark. As the name suggests, they serve outrageously good hot dogs and have a huge local following.

Virginia Tech

Forty miles southwest of Roanoke near I-81 is Blacksburg, home of **Virginia Polytechnic Institute and State University, or Virginia Tech** (210 Burruss Hall, 540/231-6000, www.vt.edu). Virginia Tech was founded in 1872 as an agricultural and mechanical land-grant college and has long had a thriving cadet program. Today, the school provides the largest number of degrees in Virginia with 90 bachelor's degree programs and 150 master's and doctoral degree programs, and has 30,000 full-time students. One of the powerhouse universities in the state, its campus includes more than 2,600 beautiful acres, 125 buildings, and the enormous Lane Stadium. Most of the buildings are neo-Gothic limestone edifices. A large grassy drill field leads up to stately Burruss Hall, the main administration building on campus, which houses a 3,000-plus-seat auditorium where major events and concerts are held.

ENTERTAINMENT AND EVENTS

There's always something going on at the **Berglund Center** (710 Williamson Road, 540/853-5483, www.theberglundcenter.com), formerly known as the Roanoke Civic

Virginia Tech's Lane Stadium

Center. This is the premier venue for concerts, ice hockey, expos, and even public ice-skating. For a more intimate setting, take in a performance at the **Jefferson Center** (541 Luck Ave., 540/345-2550, www.jeffcenter.org), a historic venue that hosts the **Roanoke Symphony Orchestra** (540/343-9127, www.rso.com), **Opera Roanoke** (540/982-2742, www.operaroanoke.org), and other performing arts companies.

The **Roanoke Festival in the Park** (www.roanokefestival.org) is the premier festival in Roanoke. It takes place annually over Memorial Day weekend and spans four days of art, music, and nightly concerts. Daytime events are free, but tickets are required for nighttime concerts ($12-15).

Another popular event is the **Virginia State Championship Chili Cook-Off** (www.virginia.org). The largest chili cook-off in Virginia, the event brings in nearly 8,000 people each year in May. Teams compete for the honor of representing Virginia in the World Championship Chili Cook-Off.

SHOPPING

The heart of downtown Roanoke is **Market Square** (intersection of Campbell Ave. and Market St., 540/342-2028, Mon.-Sat. 8am-5pm, Sun. 10am-4pm). This historic market, first opened in 1882, is the oldest continuously running open-air market in Virginia. It now has 42 permanent tables displaying an incredible selection of local fruits, vegetables, plants, meat, and handcrafted merchandise. The market is open year-round, its tables covered in festive white and yellow awnings. One vendor, Martin's Plant Farm, has been a part of the market since 1904.

SPORTS AND RECREATION

Outdoor recreation is a favorite pastime in Roanoke. Whether your preferred mode of transport is by mountain bike or foot, the Roanoke area has more than 600 miles of trails to explore. **Virginia's Explore Park** (mp 115, Blue Ridge Pkwy., 540/427-1800, www.explorepark.org/231/Explore-Park) is about a 10-minute drive from downtown Roanoke on the Blue Ridge Parkway. This 1,200-acre park has nine miles of mountain bike trails, a one-mile interpretive trail, fishing, canoeing, and kayaking.

Hikers can enjoy numerous trails near Roanoke and even explore parts of the **Appalachian Trail.** One of the most famous trails, the **McAfee Knob Hike** (www.roanokeoutside.com) is a challenging seven-mile round-trip that offers stunning views of the Catawba Valley and more than 1,700 feet of climbing. McAfee Knob itself, a large rocky outcrop, is one of the most photographed areas on the Appalachian Trail. To access the trail, take I-81 south from Roanoke to exit 141. Turn left at the light onto Route 419 (Electric Road) and continue for less than a mile. Take Route 311 north for 5.6 miles up the mountain. The trailhead parking lot is at the top of the mountain on the left. A great ending to this hike includes a stop at **The Homeplace** (4968 Catawba Valley Dr.) for dinner. To get there, continue north on Route 311 for one mile to a large white farmhouse.

Another well-known local trail is **Dragon's Tooth** (www.roanokeoutside.com). This difficult 4.5-mile out-and-back hike travels to its namesake geological feature, a collection of large Tuscarora quartzite spires that jut out of the top of Cove Mountain, the tallest being 35 feet. The Dragon's Tooth summit rewards hikers with great views year-round. The parking lot is about 20 minutes south of downtown Roanoke. Take I-81 south to exit 141. Turn left on Route 419 (Electric Road) and then turn right on Route 311. Continue for 10 miles to the Dragon's Tooth parking lot on the left.

Baseball fans will want to take in a **Salem Red Sox** (1004 Texas St., Salem, 540/389-3333, www.milb.com) home game in nearby Salem. This minor league baseball team is a Class A farm team for the Boston Red Sox. Virginia Tech fans can cheer on the Hokies just 45 minutes south of Roanoke in Blacksburg.

FOOD

American

For a special occasion, a celebration at ★ **The Regency Room** in the Hotel Roanoke & Conference Center (110 Shenandoah Ave., 540/985-5900, www.hotelroanoke.com, Mon.-Sat. 6:30am-10pm, Sun. 7am-2:30pm, $17-38) can help make the evening memorable. This first-class restaurant first opened in 1938 and offers the same candlelit ambience as it did so many decades ago. White tablecloths, heavy drapery, and a baby grand piano give the dining room a cozy, upscale feel. The menu is simple and elegant, offering classics like steak and lobster for entrées, but traditional Virginia menu items such as peanut soup, spoon bread, and bread pudding are also featured. They also offer a sensational crab cake with a Virginia twist: it is served with a corn and leek puree. The restaurant holds 150 people comfortably, and the tables are nicely spaced so you don't hear the conversation next door. Reservations are recommended.

The cosmopolitan atmosphere at **Alexander's** (105 S. Jefferson St., 540/982-6983, www.alexandersva.com, lunch Wed. 11am-2pm, dinner Tues.-Thurs. 5pm-9pm and Fri.-Sat. 5pm-10pm, $31-48) is unique in Roanoke, and the contemporary menu will impress most die-hard foodies. This intimate restaurant uses many ingredients from its own farm and gradually changes the menu with the growing season. Their seafood, steak, lamb, duck, and other entrées are masterfully prepared, and the staff is polite and knowledgeable. The wine list is impressive. Even the vases on their tables are filled with flowers and herbs from their own garden. Small plates, wine, and cocktails are served Tuesday-Saturday at 4pm.

This author first discovered ★ **The Homeplace** (4968 Catawba Valley Dr., Catawba, 540/384-7252, Thurs.-Fri. 4pm-8pm, Sat. 3:30pm-8pm, Sun. 11am-6pm, $14 for two meats, $15 for three, $3 extra for dessert) as a poor student at Virginia Tech. Groups of students would make a pilgrimage of sorts to seek out home-cooked meals sorely missed while living in student housing. The Homeplace is just as it sounds, a great place to dine on wonderful food like you would expect to be served at grandma's house and for a very reasonable price. The restaurant is even inside a beautiful old house on a large property. A set menu of classic Virginia fare is brought out to the entire table, family-style. There is roast beef or country ham, fried chicken, mashed potatoes, gravy, green beans, fresh biscuits, coleslaw, and cobbler for dessert. The best part is, the food keeps coming until you swear your pants will split. This place is an institution in the Roanoke area, but not just for students; friends, family, and even hikers detouring from the Appalachian Trail come together at this comfortable restaurant to share an old-fashioned home-cooked meal. The Homeplace is 16 miles northwest of Roanoke.

The **Blue 5 Restaurant** (312 2nd St., 540/904-5338, www.blue5restaurant.com, Mon.-Tues. 11:30am-11pm, Wed.-Thurs. 11:30am-midnight, Fri. 11:30am-1am, Sat. 4pm-1am, $17-29) offers good food, craft beer, and live music. It's hard to argue with those offerings, and they do all three well. They serve southern cuisine (the shrimp creole and grits is over-the-top delicious) and have 46 beers on tap. They offer live music four nights a week.

Pubs and Diners

The **Texas Tavern** (114 W. Church Ave., 540/342-4825, www.texastavern-inc.com, open 24/7, under $5) is the definition of a dive. This tiny tavern opened on Friday, February 13, 1930, and stays that way 24 hours a day every day of the year except for Christmas. This family business serves breakfast, lunch, and dinner and can seat a handful of people at the bar (there are also shelves by the window if you want to stand). If everyone is very familiar with each other, it might hold 15 people, but more than that would be pretty cozy. One of their slogans is "We seat 1,000 people, 10 at a time."

For a casual sandwich, salad, or burger, visit **Hollywood's Restaurant and Bakery**

the Texas Tavern

(7770 Williamson Rd., 540/362-1812, www.hollywoodsrestaurant.com, Mon.-Sat. 11am-10pm, $8-27). They offer a dine-in menu with a large variety of delicious salads and sandwiches served on freshly made bread. They have many vegetarian options and will also prepare tailgate packages when reserved the day before.

ACCOMMODATIONS

$100-200

The **Cambria Suites Roanoke** (301 Reserve Ave., 540/400-6226, www.cambriasuitesroanoke.com, $127-189) is less than a mile from downtown Roanoke and has 127 nonsmoking suites. The rooms are large and have flat-screen LCD televisions, refrigerators, microwaves, and wireless Internet. There is a lovely indoor pool and fitness center at the hotel, and they offer complimentary shuttle service to the airport and to attractions within a 10-mile radius. There is an on-site bar and a restaurant that serves breakfast and dinner.

For a good night's sleep in a historic bed-and-breakfast, book a room at the **King George Inn** (315 King George Ave. SW, 757/657-4034, www.kinggeorgeinnbandb.com, $140-160), a 1900s colonial revival home fully restored and within walking distance of downtown Roanoke. There are four spacious guest suites with private bathrooms, relaxing common areas, a library and art gallery, and access to a butler's pantry. A separate furnished carriage house is also available for long- or short-term rentals. A gourmet breakfast as well as afternoon refreshments are included with all stays. The innkeepers are warm, helpful, and eager to make recommendations for things to do in the area.

$200-300

The ★ **Hotel Roanoke & Conference Center** (110 Shenandoah Ave., 540/985-5900, www.hotelroanoke.com, $159-384) downtown is the most famous hotel in Roanoke and has been a prime destination since it was built in 1882. The restored historic Tudor hotel was originally supported by the railroad industry as a stop for rail travelers (it was owned by Norfolk and Western), but its popularity as a vacation destination has kept it going long after the railroad heyday. As you stroll past the stunning facade, you will walk where numerous celebrities and presidents have trod, including Amelia Earhart and the King himself, Elvis Presley. The hotel is decorated with artifacts that showcase the hotel's long history and also American history. Portraits of two famous Virginians, George Washington and Robert E. Lee, adorn the lobby walls. Rooms are traditionally decorated but have modern amenities, and a business center is available to guests. The hotel is listed in the National Register of Historic Places and is part of the International Association of Conference Centers with its 35 meeting rooms and two ballrooms. There are 331 guest rooms and suites, which include many types of accommodations to choose from in a variety of price ranges. They also offer allergy-friendly guest rooms.

Owned and operated by Hilton as a DoubleTree Hotel, the Hotel Roanoke is convenient to the Roanoke Regional Airport and many local attractions. A walkway connects the hotel to Market Square. There are two restaurants on-site: **The Regency Room** and **The Pine Room Pub.** There's a seasonal outdoor pool on the property and a fitness center. Spa services are also available in your room. The staff is exceptional at this hotel, and there are many fun little touches, such as the weekday-specific carpets in the elevators such as "Have a pleasant Friday!"

CAMPING

Visitors can pitch a tent at one of 74 tent sites in the **Roanoke Mountain Campground** (mp 120.4, Blue Ridge Parkway, 540/342-3051, $20). Facilities include 30 RV/trailer sites, comfort stations, water, flush toilets, and sinks (no showers).

INFORMATION AND SERVICES

For more information on the Roanoke area, visit www.visitroanokeva.com or stop by the **Roanoke Valley Convention and Visitors Bureau** (101 Shenandoah Ave., 540/342-6025, daily 9am-5pm).

GETTING THERE AND AROUND

Roanoke is 56 miles southwest of Lynchburg and 240 miles southwest of Washington DC. The **Roanoke-Blacksburg Regional Airport** (5202 Aviation Dr. NW, 540/362-1999, www.roanokeairport.com) is the primary regional airport in southwest Virginia. It is five miles north of downtown Roanoke. The airport has more than 50 scheduled daily flights and is served by commercial airlines such as American, Delta, and United. Car rentals are available at the airport.

The **Valley Metro** bus service (540/982-0305, www.valleymetro.com, Mon.-Sat. 6am-8pm, $1.50) provides bus transportation throughout Roanoke. Its main terminal is at Campbell Court (17 W. Campbell Ave.).

Danville

Danville was settled in 1793 and sits just a half hour's drive from the North Carolina border. It has a population of around 42,000, and was formerly one of the most important tobacco auction centers in the country and also had a thriving textile industry. Glimpses of its economic heyday are evident in several historic districts, including **The Danville Historic District** where the popular **Millionaires' Row,** on River Park Drive, is located. Millionaires' Row is where those who were prosperous in the tobacco and textile industries resided in the late 19th century, and it has one of the premier collections of both Victorian and Edwardian architecture in the South. Five architecturally significant

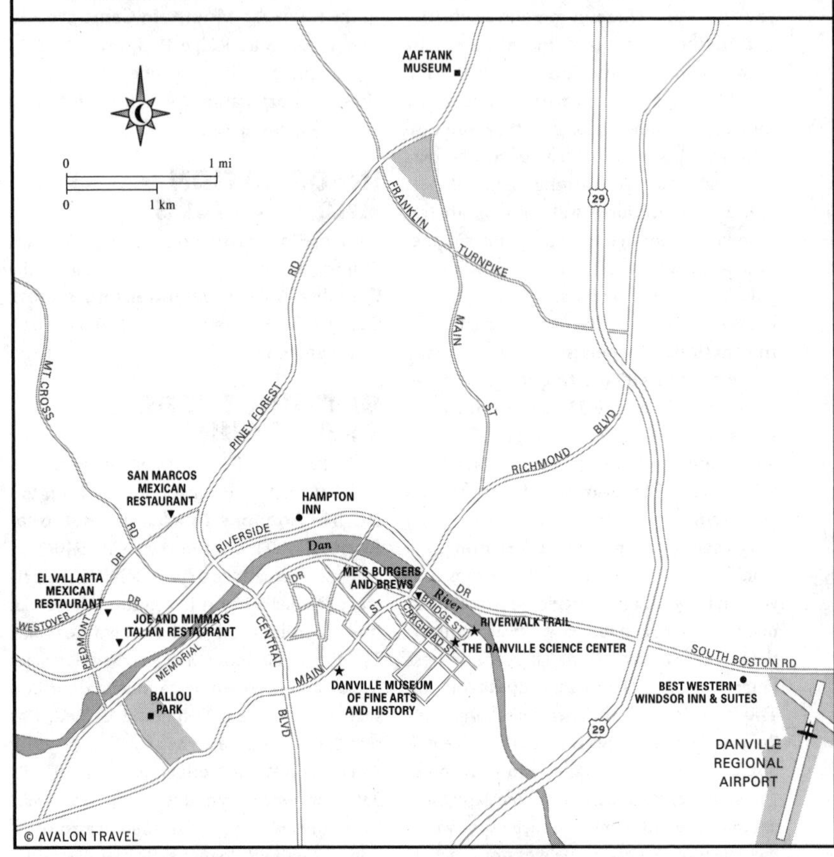

churches grace its streets and helped Danville earn the nickname "City of Churches."

The **Danville Tobacco Warehouse District** is the prime area for new development. Former tobacco warehouses are now home to new businesses, housing, and nanotechnology research. The focal point of the district is the **Crossing of the Dan** complex, which is a restored railroad station that now houses exhibits for the **Danville Science Center** and a community marketplace. The **Carrington Pavilion** is also there and features summer concerts.

The Dan River is a prominent feature in the city and along both sides runs the **Dan River Historic District.** A historic canal, original textile factories from the 1880s, and several beautiful arch bridges can be found in the area.

SIGHTS

Danville Museum of Fine Arts & History

The **Danville Museum of Fine Arts & History** (975 Main St., 434/793-5644, www.danvillemuseum.org, Tues.-Sat. 10am-5pm, Sun. 2pm-5pm, $10) showcases nationally acclaimed and emerging artists, national traveling exhibits, and local and regional artists. The museum is housed in the Italianate Sutherlin Mansion in Millionaires' Row. The home served as the last capitol of the Confederacy for just nine days in April 1865, several weeks before the end of the Civil War. The museum has an impressive collection of Civil War memorabilia, and the history of the mansion itself will be of interest to Civil War buffs.

AAF Tank Museum

Take a trip back in time through the largest private collection of international tank and cavalry artifacts in the world. **The Tank Museum** (3401 U.S. 29 N., 434/836-5323, www.aaftankmuseum.com, Jan.-Mar. Sat. only 10am-4pm, Apr.-Dec. Fri.-Sat. 10am-4pm, $12) has over 30,000 artifacts and 119 tanks and artillery pieces displayed spanning several hundred years. The museum is housed in a large warehouse, and the tanks are displayed on mini sets, complete with sand, woods, rice paddies, and plastic human figures. Additional items on display include helmets, guns, uniforms, and many personal items. This one-of-a-kind museum also offers an annual car-crushing demonstration and a hand grenade-throwing contest.

The Danville Science Center

The Danville Science Center (677 Craghead St., 434/791-5160, www.dsc.smv.org, Mon.-Sat. 9:30am-5pm, Sun. 11:30am-5pm, admission and exhibits $7, exhibits and digital dome $10) is in the Danville Tobacco Warehouse District in the Crossing of the Dan complex. The center is part of the Science Museums of Virginia network, whose facilities aim to make science fun for kids of all ages by offering interactive exhibits and special programs. A butterfly station and garden are open between April and October.

A special collection at the Science Center is the **Estelle H. Womack Natural History Collection.** This exhibit is located in the Science Station (where the local Amtrak station is) and features artifacts donated by local residents of Danville over the years. The museum also features a **Digital Dome Theater** that takes viewers on a journey through the night sky and shows giant-screen films.

EVENTS AND RECREATION

Danville's **Festival in the Park** (Ballou Park, www.danville-va.gov) is an annual event that's been held since 1974. The three-day festival takes place each May in historic Ballou Park.

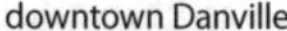
downtown Danville

The festival includes arts and crafts, food, entertainment, a health fair, kids' activities, vendors, rides, and a 5K run/walk/wheelchair race.

The paved eight-mile **Riverwalk Trail** (434/799-5215) that runs along the Dan River is designed for walkers, runners, bikers, and inline skaters. Parking is available at the Crossing at the Dan, the Dan Daniel Memorial Park (302 River Park Drive), Main Street at the Martin Luther King Bridge, and Anglers Park (350 Northside Dr.). A trail map and brochure can be downloaded at www.danville-va.gov.

Mountain bikers should check out the **Anglers Ridge Mountain Bike Trail System** (www.svmba.org). This incredible network of 25 miles of single-track offers a technically challenging ride on sections such as Hot Tamale and Witchback, while novice bikers will likely enjoy the more moderate terrain on Anglers Ridge and the Riverside Drive trails.

Me's Burgers and Brews

FOOD

★ **Me's Burgers and Brews** (215 Main St., 434/792-0123, www.mesburgers.com, Tues.-Thurs. 4pm-11pm, Fri.-Sat. 4pm-midnight, closed Sun.-Mon., $7-15) is a trendy little surprise located downtown at the south end of the Main Street bridge. The mother-daughter owner duo artfully pulled together every little detail to make this beer-and-burger joint a step above the norm. They offer an ever-changing draft brew selection from local Virginia and North Carolina breweries, alongside a scrumptious menu of high-quality burgers named for classic authors like Agatha Christie and P. G. Woodhouse. Burgers are served on potato rolls created by a Mennonite bakery with a sourdough starter. The mouth-watering sweet potato salad is made from a secret family recipe. Be sure to finish off the evening with their glazed doughnut bread pudding.

Tasty Mexican food can be found at **El Vallarta Mexican Restaurant** (418 Westover Dr., 434/799-0506, www.elvallartamexicanrestaurant.net, Mon.-Thurs. 11am-10pm, Fri.-Sat. 11am-11pm, Sun. 11am-9:30pm, $6-20). The cozy décor is upstaged by the friendly staff and delicious menu. With hundreds of choices for lunch and dinner, making a selection can be the hardest part. If you're stumped, try the fajitas, cheese dip, and a margarita.

Another good Mexican choice is **San Marcos Mexican Restaurant** (150 Holt Garrison Pkwy., 434/792-4202, www.sanmarcosrestaurant.com, $6-13). They have a large dining room and offer many traditional Mexican dishes along with a few surprises. This is a nice place to bring the family since there are so many menu options. They also make a decent margarita.

Joe and Mimma's Italian Restaurant (3336 Riverside Dr., 434/799-5763, www.joeandmimmasdanville.com, Tues.-Thurs. 11am-9:30pm, Fri.-Sat. 11am-10pm, $16-23) is a local favorite for delicious Italian food. They advertise "healthy" ingredients and serve a variety of entrées, pizzas, subs, pastas, and seafood.

That Old-Time Bluegrass

The second week in August marks a very special time in the southern Virginia town of **Galax.** This town, 104 miles west of Danville and 90 miles east of Abingdon, near the North Carolina border, is the home of the largest old-time bluegrass fiddler's convention in the country.

Galax is famous for a long history of "old-timey" music, and that tradition remains strong even with the younger crowd. The **Annual Old Fiddlers' Convention** (276/236-8541, www.oldfiddlersconvention.com) has been a main event in town since 1935. Hundreds of people from all over the country come with their instruments to compete for prize money totaling more than $10,000. Thousands more fans converge on the town to witness the contest and to hear up-and-coming bluegrass musicians.

The goal of the convention hasn't changed over time. It is dedicated to "Keeping alive the memories and sentiments of days gone by and make it possible for people of today to hear and enjoy the tunes of yesterday." Instruments featured in the competition include everything from mouth harps to bull fiddles. Some competitors have attended nearly every convention since 1935.

Tickets to the event are only sold at the gate and range $6-12 per day. Attendees are advised to bring rain gear and boots since rain is common at that time of year and the fields where the performance stages are can get muddy.

Camping is available for $80, but spaces are only sold at the gate. Recordings of the highlights of each year's events are produced by Heritage Records and can be purchased by calling 276/236-9249.

ACCOMMODATIONS

Under $100

Fall Creek Farm (2556 Green Farm Rd., 434/791-3297, www.fall-creek-farm.com, $80-100) offers a unique bed-and-breakfast experience. Guests stay in individual log cabins, complete with fireplaces, period antiques, and continental breakfast delivered to their doorstep. The farm sits on 50 acres and offers a heated pool, hiking trails, and stream and pond fishing. There are also miniature donkeys at the farm.

For a clean, quite stay, the **Best Western Windsor Inn & Suites** (1292 S. Boston Rd., 434/483-5000, www.book.bestwestern.com, $80-115) is a centrally located all-suite hotel. They offer 74 guest suites with refrigerators, microwaves, work desks, and sitting areas. The rooms are spacious and there's a whirlpool, indoor pool, and fitness room on-site. Breakfast is included with your stay, and fresh-baked complimentary cookies are available in the evening.

Another good option is the 58-room **Hampton Inn Danville** (2130 Riverside Drive, 434/793-1111, www.hamptoninn3.hilton.com, $119-128). It offers free breakfast, a fitness room, business center, and outdoor pool.

$100-200

The **Courtyard Danville Marriott** (2136 Riverside Dr., 434/791-2661, www.marriott.com, $124-169) has 89 modern rooms, a fitness room, and an outdoor pool. The staff is exceptionally pleasant and helpful. This is one of the nicest hotels in the area and is good for business and leisure travel.

INFORMATION

Additional information on Danville can be found at the **Welcome Center** (645 River Park Dr., www.danville-va.gov, Mon.-Fri. 8:30am-5pm, Sat.-Sun. 9am-5pm).

GETTING THERE

Danville is 80 miles southeast of Roanoke and 248 miles southwest of Washington DC. Most visitors arrive by car, but train service through **Amtrak** (677 Craghead St., 800/872-7245) and bus service through **Greyhound** (515 Spring St., 434/792-4722) are available.

Abingdon

Abingdon (named for Martha Washington's home parish in England) was incorporated in 1778 and is the oldest English-speaking town west of the Blue Ridge Mountains. It is hard to believe the town is still in Virginia, as it is a six-hour drive from Washington DC and is as far west as Cleveland. Abingdon, however, is a Virginia Historic Landmark and offers a 20-block historic district with beautiful tree-lined streets, brick sidewalks, and quaint 19th-century homes. The town is also known for its performing and visual arts.

Main Street in Abingdon is a collection of historic treasures. There are galleries, museums, inns, eateries, and a theater. The land the town occupies was originally surveyed in the mid-1700s. Daniel Boone named the area "Wolf Hill" after his hunting dogs were attacked by a pack of wolves nearby. The location of the attack is known as **Courthouse Hill.** In past years, 27 wolf sculptures could be seen around the town, but most have been sold and moved.

SIGHTS

The Arts Depot

One of the most popular sights in Abingdon is **The Arts Depot** (314 Depot St., 276/628-9091, www.abingdonartsdepot.org, Wed.-Sat. 10am-4pm and by appointment, free). Visitors can watch artists at work, walk through galleries, attend workshops, and listen to lectures in this former railroad freight station that is now dedicated to the arts.

Fields-Penn 1860 House Museum

The **Fields-Penn 1860 House Museum** (208 W. Main St., 276/676-0216, Wed.-Thurs. noon-5pm, Fri.-Sat. 9am-5pm, Sun. 1pm-5pm, free) is a delightful historic home decorated with period furnishings. Visitors can take a short and informative tour and learn how a middle-class family lived in 1860 in Abingdon.

White's Mill

A short drive north of town brings you to **White's Mill** (12291 White's Mill Rd., 276/628-2960, www.whitesmill.org, Wed.-Sun. 10am-5pm, closed Jan. and Mar., free), the only remaining water-powered gristmill in southwest Virginia. The mill was built in the late 18th century and provided flour and meal for the community. It was also a gathering place for local residents. The mercantile (store) at the mill sold goods to residents and now offers handmade arts and crafts, local books, and regional music.

Abingdon Vineyard and Winery

Wine enthusiasts can visit **Abingdon Vineyard and Winery** (20530 Alvarado Rd., 276/623-1255, www.abingdonwinery.com, Mar. 15-Dec. 15 Tues.-Sat. 10am-6pm, Sun. noon-6pm) to sample local wine in a welcoming, rustic atmosphere. They are closed on Thanksgiving.

ENTERTAINMENT AND EVENTS

The unique **Barter Theatre** (127 W. Main St., 276/628-3991, www.bartertheatre.com, Mon. and Wed. 9am-5pm, Tues. and Thurs.-Sat. 9am-8pm, Sun. 1pm-5pm) was opened in 1933 by a young actor named Robert Porterfield. Porterfield came up with a unique idea during the Depression to barter produce from local farms in exchange for a ticket to the theater. It opened under the slogan, "With vegetables you cannot sell, you can buy a good laugh." The price of a ticket was 40 cents or the equal in produce. Most patrons gained entrance in this manner and also bartered with dairy products and livestock. The town jail was beneath the stage and is now used for dressing rooms. Today, the theater hosts drama, comedy, musicals, and mystery performances much as it has done for

Abingdon

To White Birches Inn and White's Mill
To Meadowview
0 200 yds
0 200 m
COURT ST
CHURCH ST
OAK HILL ST
TANNER ST
WHITES ALLEY
THE TAVERN RESTAURANT
VALLEY ST
CHINCAPIN ALLEY
PECAN ST
TROOPERS ALLEY
ALLEY
PARK ST
Creek
BARTER THEATRE
EAST MAIN
PARK PL
To Alpine Motel and I-81 exit 19
VIRGINIA CREEPER TRAIL BIKE SHOP
58
RUSSELL RD
PLUMB
MARTHA WASHINGTON HOTEL & SPA
A
ST
ACADEMY DR
WALL ST
FIELDS-PENN 1860 HOUSE MUSEUM
CUMMINGS
GREEN SPRING RD
Eighteen Mile
DEPOT SQUARE
THE ARTS DEPOT
Virginia Creeper Trail
To I-81 exit 14
WEST MAIN
FULLER ST
11
To Visitor Center, I-81 exit 17, and Damascus
© AVALON TRAVEL

more than 70 years, only it no longer accepts produce as payment.

Abingdon hosts one of the top 100 annual tourist events in the country. The **Virginia Highland Festival** (www.vahighlandsfestival.org) is a 10-day event held in August that showcases music, art, crafts, and writing indigenous to the Appalachians. The festival began in 1948 and was founded by the same man who set up the Barter Theatre, Robert Porterfield. It started as a weeklong festival geared toward Appalachian arts and crafts

Barter Theatre

and evolved into ten days of festivities in a variety of venues. A large antiques market is also featured at the festival, and there is wine tasting, gardening instruction, and even a hot-air balloon rally.

Those who like ghost stories won't want to miss taking an **Abingdon Spirit Tour** (276/706-6093, www.abingdonspirittours.com). Since 1998, this popular two-hour walking tour has sent chills down visitors' spines as they learn Abingdon history including where skeletons are buried and local ghost lore. Tours are animated and fun and depart from many different locations (check website for more information).

SHOPPING

One of the oldest crafts cooperatives in the nation, **Holston Mountain Artisans** (214 Park St., 276/628-7721, www.holstonmtnarts.com, Mon.-Sat. 9:30am-5pm) offers a large assortment of traditional arts and crafts from the region including home decor items, gifts, musical instruments, art, books, and photographs. The cooperative began in 1971 and represents more than 100 local artists. They are located in the historic jailhouse on Park Street.

A unique shopping stop on Main Street is the **Abingdon Olive Oil Company** (152 E. Main St., 276/525-1524). This fun tasting gallery and shop features a large variety of organic, extra virgin, and naturally infused oils and balsamic vinegars. The friendly staff gives free tours and tastings.

SPORTS AND RECREATION

The **Virginia Creeper Trail** (www.vacreepertrail.org) is a 34-mile recreation trail that starts in Abingdon (off Pecan Street across the train tracks), runs through Damascus, Virginia, and ends at the North Carolina border. The trail is a former railroad bed and is now a shared-use trail, which means mountain bikers, hikers, and horses can all partake in the trail. There are three visitors centers on the trail (Damascus Caboose, the Old Greene Cove Station, and the Whitetop Station) that are open on weekends May-October. Restrooms are provided in Damascus, the Straight Branch parking lot, Creek Junction parking lot, Green Cove train station, Whitetop train station, and at the parking lot in Abingdon. The **Virginia Creeper Trail Bike Shop** (201 Pecan St. SE, 276/676-2552, www.vacreepertrailbikeshop.com, $10-20) offers bike rentals.

Sixteen miles northeast of Abingdon (north on I-81) is **Greenway Creek Golf Course** (36012 Lee Hwy., Glad Spring, 276/429-2626, $23-26). This public, 18-hole course is a par 68 and features 5,552 yards of golf from the longest tees. The course has a rating of 65.6 and a slope rating of 98.

Twenty-four miles southwest of Abingdon, across the Tennessee state line in Bristol, is the **Bristol Motor Speedway** (151 Speedway Blvd., Bristol, 423/989-6900, www.bristolmotorspeedway.com), a NASCAR short-track venue and a highly popular one at that. The track is known for its steep banking as well as for being one of the loudest venues. The speedway celebrated its 55-year birthday in 2016.

FOOD

American

The **Rain Restaurant and Bar** (283 E. Main St., 276/739-2331, www.rainabingdon.com, Sun.-Mon. 9am-11pm, Tues.-Sat. 11am-11pm, $22-29) is a wonderful place to spend an evening. This modern, colorful restaurant has good food, friendly and attentive staff, and lovely cocktails (try the cucumber martini). The menu includes steak, pork, seafood, and chicken with an interesting and delicious assortment of soups and starters (try the buffalo crawfish).

Sisters at the Martha (150 W. Main St., 276/628-3161, www.marthawashingtoninn.com, Tues.-Fri. 5pm-9pm, Sat.-Sun.

Mount Rogers National Recreation Area

Thirty-five miles northeast of Abingdon is the beautiful **Mount Rogers National Recreation Area** (3714 Hwy. 16, Marion, 276/783-5196, www.fs.usda.gov). This 200,000-acre recreation paradise is part of the George Washington and Jefferson National Forests, which stretch from one end of Virginia to the other along the ancient Appalachian Mountains.

The area includes sprawling rural countryside and the 5,000-acre Crest Zone, which features mountains over 4,000 feet, large rock outcrops, mountain balds, forest, and even a herd of wild ponies.

The area also offers just about any kind of outdoor activity you can dream up in the mountains including camping, horseback riding (there are four horse camps), hiking, biking, cross-country skiing, and wildlife viewing. There are hundreds of miles of trails and seven campgrounds to choose from (call 877/444-6777 for reservations). Cabin rentals are also available.

Mount Rogers itself is the focal point of the region. This 5,729-foot-high mountain is the highest natural point in Virginia. The peak is named after the first Virginia state geologist, William Barton Rogers, who taught at both the College of William & Mary and the University of Virginia.

The **Mount Rogers Scenic Byway** runs through the Mount Rogers National Recreation Area. The first section of this scenic, curvy, hilly byway begins in Troutdale, Virginia. It runs west for 13.2 miles over Virginia Route 603 and on to Konnarock, Virginia, as a paved, two-lane road. The second section runs 32.5 miles east from Damascus, Virginia, to Volney, Virginia, following U.S. Route 58, also a two-lane paved road.

5pm-11pm, $24-33), within the Martha Washington Hotel and Spa, has a lovely menu of southern-style seafood, steaks, and poultry. This is a classy but casual setting, perfect for a quiet or romantic evening out. Reservations are recommended.

For fresh doughnuts or soup and a sandwich, swing by the **Dunk and Deli** (924 E. Main St., 276/628-5150, Mon. 6am-4pm, Tues.-Sat. 6am-8pm, Sun. 8am-4pm, under $12). This cute little shop serves delightful fresh doughnuts and homemade lunch items. It's popular with the locals, so get there early for the best selection.

To sample local beer, go to **Wolf Hills Brewery** (350 Park St., 276/451-5470, www.wolfhillsbrewing.com, Mon.-Fri. 5pm-8pm, Sun.1pm-5pm) in the old ice house near the Virginia Creeper Trail and the train tracks. They do not have a restaurant, but they hold special beer events.

Intercontinental

★ **The Tavern Restaurant** (222 E. Main St., 276/628-1118, www.abingdontavern.com, Mon.-Sat. 5pm-9pm, $19-40), housed in the oldest building in Abingdon, was originally a tavern and inn for stagecoach travelers. The doors and wood floors of this 1779 building lean a little, but that adds to the charm of this landmark. The delicious menu includes seafood, steak, and poultry with German, Austrian, and Swiss influences (the owner's background is German). There's a cozy bar on the first floor and nice dining areas upstairs. The beer menu is inspiring, as is the wine menu. This is a great place for families as well as a great place for a date, and the atmosphere is warm and inviting.

ACCOMMODATIONS

Under $100

For a classic, no-frills motel experience, the **Alpine Motel** (882 E. Main St., 276/628-3178, www.alpinemotelabingdon.com, $70-80) is a good choice. This well-maintained, clean motel sits against a hillside overlooking woods and farmland. It is comfortable and offers 19 spacious rooms.

$100-200

The five-room **White Birches Inn** (268 White's Mill Rd., 276/676-2140, www.whitebirchesinn.com, $159-179) is a lovely and reasonable choice for accommodations in Abingdon. All guest rooms are named after famous playwrights who bartered their work at Abingdon's Barter Theatre. There is a lovely porch out back and a small pond. Breakfast is included with your stay.

A good-quality chain hotel near I-81 is the **Quality Inn & Suites** (930 E. Main St., 276/676-9090, www.choicehotels.com, $109-139). They offer 75 clean rooms with refrigerators, ironing boards, coffeemakers, hair dryers, and cable television. A free hot breakfast, a fitness center, and a seasonal outdoor pool are also available to guests.

The **Hampton Inn Abingdon** (340 Commerce Dr., 276/619-4600, www.hilton.com, $135-145) is another solid choice for a chain hotel in Abingdon. It is off I-81, within walking distance to the historic district. The property is nice, and the staff is warm and friendly. There are 68 guest rooms, and breakfast is included. The hotel offers walking trails, a fitness center, and an outdoor pool.

$200-300

The ★ **Martha Washington Hotel and Spa** (150 W. Main St., 276/628-3161, www.themartha.com, $195-595) is a beautiful historic hotel with a lot of charm. Guests are drawn in by the beautiful, sprawling front porch and the friendly staff, but they stay because of the relaxing atmosphere. The hotel has 55 rooms and eight suites and is decorated with some antiques but offers comfortable furnishings throughout. All rooms are fully renovated and have flat-screen TVs and wireless Internet. The hotel was once a private residence, then a women's college. It is across from the Barter Theatre on Main Street and convenient to many attractions. The rooms are nicely decorated and plenty large, and there is a spa, fitness room, heated saltwater pool, bikes, and tennis courts onsite. You can also schedule a carriage ride. The Sisters restaurant offers an incredible American breakfast with wonderful southern grits. The hotel offers bike rides on the Virginia Creeper Trail, where they will drive you out 17 miles, drop you off with a box lunch, and then let you ride downhill back to the inn. There is free valet parking for guests.

The **Cooper Lantern Boutique Inn** (133 E. Valley St., 276/525-1919, www.copperlanterninn.com, $215-250) was built in 1873 and is conveniently located within walking distance to many attractions in Abingdon. Warm southern hospitality comes with your room in this cozy bed-and-breakfast. The Georgian colonial-style home has a beautiful stained glass front door and offers eight individually named and furnished rooms, all with their own special history. Rooms are outfitted with Egyptian combed-cotton towels and fine bed linens with comfortable mattresses. Relax on the front porch or swing in the love seat in this friendly, comfortable setting. The food is also wonderful and homemade.

CAMPING

Scenic camping can be found approximately 10 miles south of Abingdon on the shores of South Holston Lake and in the surrounding area.

The **Lakeshore Campground** (19417 County Park Rd., 276/628-5394, www.virginia.org, Apr.-Nov.) on South Holston Lake offers 200 campsites, a sanitation facility, swimming, boating, boat storage, fishing, a game room, and telephones. Most of their sites are rented for a full season rather than nightly.

Seven miles north of Abingdon is **Riverside Campground** (18496 N. Fork River Rd., 276/623-0340, www.riversidecampground.org, Apr.-Nov., $40). They have more than 100 tent and RV sites along the North Fork of the Holston River. The campground is family oriented.

Washington County Park (9482 County Park Rd., 276/628-9677, Apr.-Sept., $18-22) is another campground on South Holston Lake. They offer 140 campsites with electric hookups, water, and sanitation facilities. They also offer 10 tent sites. They have a playground, picnic shelters, boating, fishing, and telephone access.

INFORMATION AND SERVICES

For additional information on Abingdon, stop by the **visitors bureau** (335 Cummings St., 276/676-2282) or visit www.abingdon.com.

GETTING THERE

Most people arrive in Abingdon by car. It is just off I-81 in the southwestern corner of Virginia. The public **Tri-Cities Regional Airport** (2525 Hwy. 75, Blountville, TN, 423/325-6000, www.triflight.com) in Sullivan County, Tennessee, is 33 miles southwest of Abingdon. Carriers such as American, Delta, and United offer service to the airport.

Maryland's Capital Region

Bordering Washington DC to the north, Montgomery County is trendy and urban, with cultural and historical sights and attractions. To the east of DC is Prince George's County, more suburban and rich in natural beauty.

Montgomery County has easy access to Washington DC via road and the Metrorail service. It is one of the most affluent counties in the country, with trendy city centers and a variety of restaurants, shopping areas, and hotels.

Prince George's County is a hub for federal government agencies. It includes the National Harbor, an area along the Potomac River that has become a hot spot for tourism, dining, and nightlife. It's also home to the stadium for the Washington Redskins and one of the best fossil parks in the eastern United States.

PLANNING YOUR TIME

Cities in Maryland's Capital Region are relatively close together, so it is advantageous to select the sights you are most interested in seeing to determine where and how long you will stay. Many sites can be visited as a half- or full-day trip when staying in Washington DC, or the Capital Region can be your home base while exploring DC. Accommodations in Montgomery and Prince George's Counties are generally less expensive than those in DC, yet are still convenient to the major downtown sites.

Commercial air service to Maryland's Capital Region is provided at **Ronald Reagan Washington National Airport (DCA)** (703/417-8000, www.mwaa.com) in Arlington, Virginia; **Washington Dulles International Airport (IAD)** (703/572-2700, www.mwaa.com) in Dulles, Virginia; and **Baltimore Washington International Thurgood Marshall Airport (BWI)** (410/859-7111, www.bwiairport.com) near Baltimore, Maryland.

Train service is available on **Amtrak** (www.amtrak.com) to Rockville in Montgomery County and to Landover in Prince George's County.

The **Washington Metropolitan Area Transit Authority (WMATA)** (www.wmata.com) provides **Metrorail** and **Metrobus** service to both counties. Montgomery County is serviced by Metrorail's Red Line, while Prince

Previous: rural area near Sugarloaf Mountain; Montpelier Mansion. **Above:** National Harbor.

Look for ★ to find recommended sights, activities, dining, and lodging.

Highlights

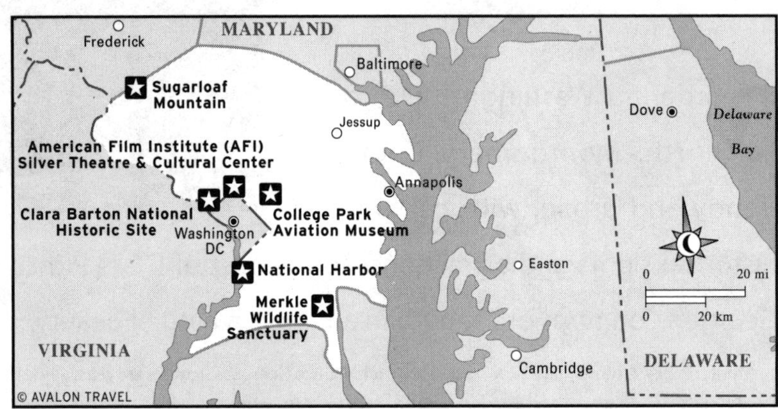

★ **Clara Barton National Historic Site:** This beautiful home was the residence of the pioneering woman who founded the American Red Cross (page 348).

★ **American Film Institute (AFI) Silver Theatre & Cultural Center:** This state-of-the-art film center grew out of the restored art deco Silver Theatre, built in 1938 (page 359).

★ **Sugarloaf Mountain:** This popular recreation area offers hiking, picnicking, and rock climbing (page 363).

★ **National Harbor:** Built right on the Potomac River, this harbor hosts a range of restaurants, shops, and entertainment options for both adults and kids (page 364).

★ **Merkle Wildlife Sanctuary:** This wildlife sanctuary is the wintering ground for thousands of Canada geese (page 367).

★ **College Park Aviation Museum:** This great little museum set in a historic airport focuses on the earliest days of mechanical flight (page 372).

Maryland's Capital Region

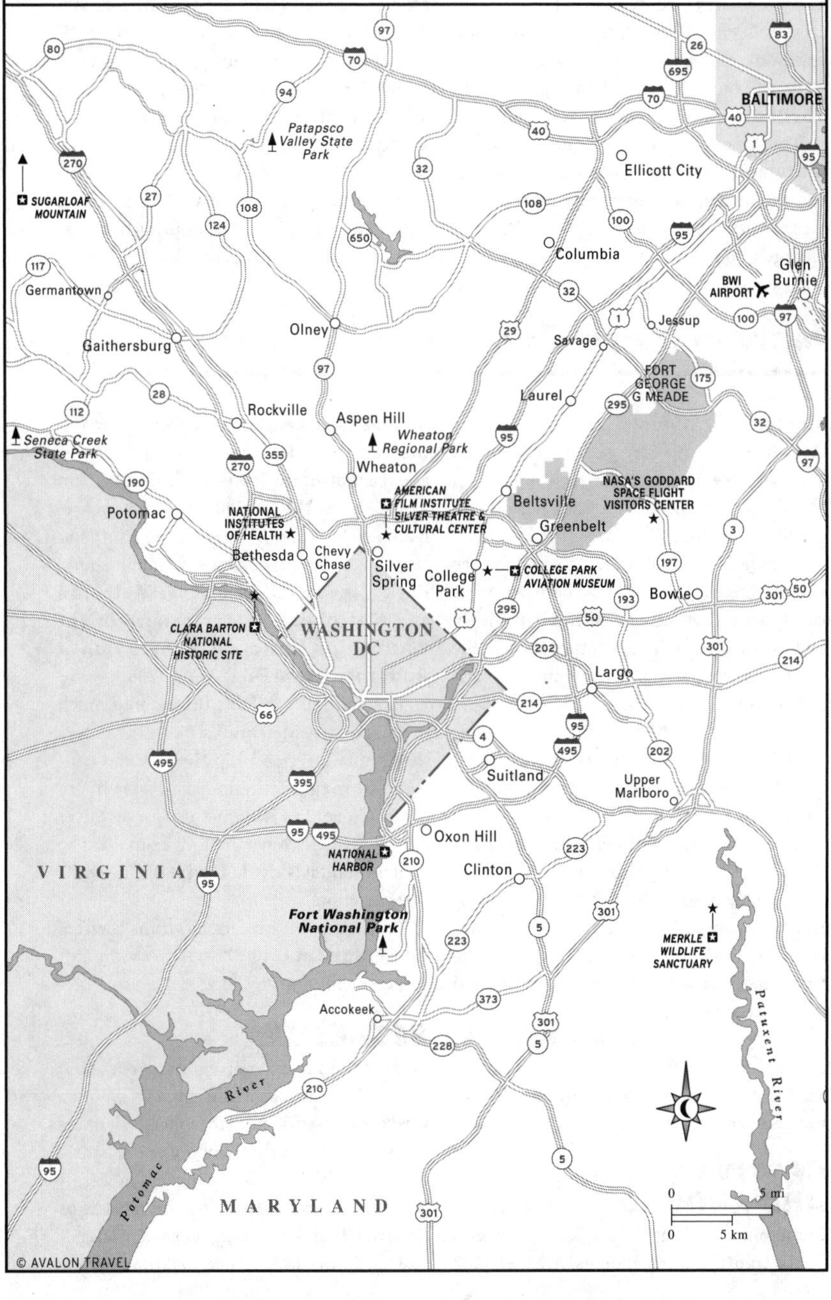

BALTIMORE
Patapsco Valley State Park
SUGARLOAF MOUNTAIN
Ellicott City
Columbia
Germantown
Glen Burnie
BWI AIRPORT
Jessup
Olney
Gaithersburg
Savage
FORT GEORGE G MEADE
Laurel
Rockville
Aspen Hill
Wheaton Regional Park
Seneca Creek State Park
Wheaton
NASA'S GODDARD SPACE FLIGHT VISITORS CENTER
AMERICAN FILM INSTITUTE SILVER THEATRE & CULTURAL CENTER
Beltsville
Potomac
NATIONAL INSTITUTES OF HEALTH
Greenbelt
Bethesda
Chevy Chase
Silver Spring
College Park
COLLEGE PARK AVIATION MUSEUM
Bowie
CLARA BARTON NATIONAL HISTORIC SITE
WASHINGTON DC
Largo
Suitland
Upper Marlboro
Oxon Hill
NATIONAL HARBOR
VIRGINIA
Clinton
Fort Washington National Park
MERKLE WILDLIFE SANCTUARY
Accokeek
Potomac River
Patuxent River
MARYLAND
0 5 mi
0 5 km

George's County is serviced by the Green, Blue, and Orange Lines.

Montgomery County has a public bus transit system called **Ride On** (www.montgomerycountymd.gov/dot-transit/) and Prince George's County has a public bus system called **TheBus** (www.princegeorgescountymd.gov).

The Maryland Transit Administration's **Maryland Area Rail Commuter (MARC)** (http://mta.maryland.gov) rail runs train service to both Montgomery County and Prince George's County.

Travel by car around the Capital Region is easy if you are prepared to deal with traffic. I-270 is a primary northwest-southeast roadway that connects to the Capital Beltway (I-495). Montgomery County, in particular, is known for its use of automated speed cameras and red-light cameras, especially on secondary roads, so keep this in mind when traveling by car. Rush hour throughout the Capital Region is spread out over many hours. For the best chance of missing traffic during the week, travel between the hours of 10am and 2pm.

Montgomery County

Montgomery County is named after Revolutionary War general Richard Montgomery and was the first county in Maryland not named after royalty. As a densely populated metropolitan area, the boundaries between cities and towns in Montgomery County are blurred at best. There are a few clearly defined city centers, such as in Bethesda and Rockville, but in many other parts of the county one neighborhood runs into the next.

Just north of Washington DC is the bustling business hub of Silver Spring. Its once-tired downtown area recently realized a grand rebirth and now offers a vibrant city center for entertainment and shopping.

The I-270 Technology Corridor runs through Rockville, Bethesda, and Gaithersburg and is home to many biotechnology and software companies. Northwest of Gaithersburg is the fast-growing suburb of Germantown, which encompasses many neighborhoods and suburban communities.

In the farther western reaches of the county, along the Potomac River, rural routes are still detectable, and towns are loosely connected by private farmland.

GETTING THERE AND AROUND

Montgomery County is serviced by several public transportation systems. **Amtrak** (307 S. Stonestreet Ave., 800/872-7245, www.amtrak.com) provides train service to Rockville, and the **Maryland Transit Administration** MARC train (410/539-5000, http://mta.maryland.gov) has three Montgomery County stations on the Brunswick Line in Gaithersburg, Rockville, and Silver Spring. **Metrorail** and **Metrobus** service, operated by the **Washington Metropolitan Area Transit Authority (WMATA)** (202/637-7000, www.wmata.com), is available throughout much of the county. Metrorail's Red Line enters the county at Friendship Heights and continues through Bethesda past Rockville to Shady Grove. The Red Line also serves Silver Spring through Wheaton to Glenmont. The Amtrak station is also housed at the Rockville Metro station.

The county has a public bus transit system called **Ride On** (240/777-0311, www.montgomerycountymd.gov, $1.75).

BETHESDA

Bethesda is a busy metropolitan area about seven miles north of Washington DC. With a local population of more than 60,000, it offers a bustling downtown shopping and business district and dozens of restaurant choices. It is also home to the **National Institutes of Health (NIH)** (www.nih.gov) headquarters.

The Bethesda Metrorail station (in the

A Golf-Crazy County

Montgomery County is known for its golf. As host to the annual **Quicken Loans National** (www.tigerwoodsfoundation.org), held at the Congressional Country Club in Bethesda in June, the area draws national attention from the golfing community.

Visitors can enjoy many public golf courses in Montgomery County, including the following:

- **Blue Mash Golf Course** (5821 Olney-Laytonsville Rd., Laytonsville, 301/670-1966)—18 holes/driving range
- **Falls Road** (10800 Falls Rd., Potomac, 301/299-5156)—18 holes/driving range
- **Hampshire Greens** (616 Firestone Dr., Silver Spring, 301/476-7999)—18 holes
- **Laytonsville Golf Course** (7130 Dorsey Rd., Gaithersburg, 301/948-5288)—18 holes
- **Little Bennett Golf Course** (25900 Prescott Rd., Clarksburg, 301/253-1515)—18 holes
- **Needwood Golf Course** (6724 Needwood Rd., Derwood, 301/948-1075)—18 holes
- **Northwest Golf Course** (15711 Layhill Rd., Silver Spring, 301/598-6100)—27 holes
- **Poolesville Golf Course** (16601 W. Willard Rd., Poolesville, 301/428-8143)—18 holes
- **Rattlewood Golf Course** (13501 Penn Shop Rd., Mt. Airy, 301/607-9000)—18 holes/driving range
- **Sligo Creek Golf Course** (9701 Sligo Creek Pkwy., Silver Spring, 301/585-6006)—9 holes

For additional information on golfing in Montgomery County, visit www.mcggolf.com.

center of the downtown area) moves more than 15,000 passengers on a normal weekday.

Sights

RATNER MUSEUM

The **Dennis & Phillip Ratner Museum** (10001 Old Georgetown Rd., 301/897-1518, www.ratnermuseum.org, Sun. 10am-4:30pm, Mon.-Thurs. noon-4pm, closed Aug., free) is a lovely and unique art museum with both permanent and traveling exhibits. The upper level of the museum features a permanent collection of artwork by contemporary artist Phillip Ratner that depicts stories from the Bible through sculpture, drawings, paintings, and other graphics. Visitors can literally take a walk through the Bible by looking at the displays. The lower level, where exhibits change monthly, features work from both established and upcoming local artists. Mediums include painting, photography, glass, wood, and silk panels. Other traveling exhibits are also featured. A children's art and literature museum is housed in another building called the Resource Center. Additional activities held at the museum complex include lectures, concerts, and readings. Phillip Ratner is perhaps best known for being the artist of five sculptures at the Statue of Liberty and 40 sculptures at Ellis Island. Dennis Ratner is Phillip's second cousin and owner of the nation's largest privately owned salon chain, the Hair Cuttery. The two established the museum together.

BE WITH ME CHILDREN'S PLAYSEUM

The **Be With Me Children's Playseum** (7000 Wisconsin Ave., 301/807-8028, www.playseum.com, Mon.-Fri. 10am-5pm, Sat. 9am-7pm, $9) is a great play space for young kids offering many rooms with individual themes such as a grocery store, kitchen, and princess dress-up, all of which kids can enjoy at their leisure. There is also an arts and crafts room (some projects cost extra) and an open play area with a stage and musical instruments. This is a fun and entertaining place to spend an afternoon.

MCCRILLIS GARDENS

A little-known treasure in a quiet residential neighborhood near downtown Bethesda is **McCrillis Gardens** (6910 Greentree Rd., 301/962-1455, daily 10am-sunset, free). This lovely garden and the home that sits on the grounds were donated to the Maryland National Capital Park and Planning Commission in 1978 by its former owners. The gardens are considered a premier shade garden and offer beautiful ornamental trees, shrubs (including many azalea bushes), annuals, ground covers, perennials, and other flowers. There is a pavilion and benches on the grounds. There is also no parking on the grounds, but some street parking is available during the week. On weekends (and after 4pm on weekdays), parking is available across the street at the Woods Academy.

AUDUBON NATURALIST SOCIETY

The **Audubon Naturalist Society's Woodend Sanctuary** (8940 Jones Mill Rd., Chevy Chase, 301/652-9188, www.audubonnaturalist.org, trails open daily dawn to dusk, free) in nearby Chevy Chase is the headquarters for the Audubon Naturalist Society. The sanctuary is one of the few grand old estates remaining in the area and sits on 40 acres. The Woodend Mansion, which was designed in the 1920s and bequeathed to the Audubon Naturalist Society in 1968, is a beautiful example of Georgian revival architecture. Visitors can enjoy self-guided nature trails, a wildflower meadow, and a pond on the grounds. No pets are allowed in the sanctuary. Free beginner bird walks are offered at 8am on Saturday mornings September-November and March-June. They are offered monthly in December-February. A bookshop sells nature and birding books and gifts.

★ CLARA BARTON NATIONAL HISTORIC SITE

Just southwest of Bethesda in Glen Echo is the **Clara Barton National Historic Site** (5801 Oxford Rd., Glen Echo, 301/320-1410, www.nps.gov/clba, open daily with guided home tours on the hour between 10am and 4pm, free). Clara Barton was a pioneer among American women who is credited with founding the American Red Cross. The historical site was established at the home where Barton spent the last 15 years of her life (1897-1912). This National Park

Audubon Naturalist Society's Woodend Sanctuary

Clara Barton: Angel of the Battlefield

Clara Barton National Historic Site

Clara Barton was born on Christmas Day in 1821 in Massachusetts. She is known as a pioneer for her work as a teacher, patent clerk, nurse, and humanitarian, all during a time when very few women held jobs outside the home.

Barton was dedicated to helping others and always held a passion for nursing. At a young age she nursed her injured dog back to health when he hurt his leg, and later saved her brother's life by nursing him back to health after he fell off their family's barn roof.

Barton first became a schoolteacher and later opened a free school in New Jersey. Although attendance at her school rapidly grew to more than 600 students, the school's board hired a man to head the operation instead of Barton. After this insult, Barton moved to Washington DC and became a clerk at the U.S. Patent Office. She was the first woman to receive a salary equal to a man in a substantial clerkship position in the federal government.

During the Civil War, Barton was put in charge of the hospitals at the front of the Army of the James (a Union army that included units from Virginia and North Carolina). She soon became known as the "Angel of the Battlefield."

After the war, Barton lead the Office of the Missing Soldiers in Washington DC and gained wide recognition for giving lectures across the country on her experiences during the war. During this time, she began a long association with the women's suffrage movement and also became an activist for African American civil rights.

During a trip to Geneva, Switzerland, Barton became acquainted with the Red Cross and provided the society assistance during the Franco-Prussian War. Barton also engaged in additional humanitarian work throughout Europe for a couple of years. Upon returning to the United States, Barton started a movement for recognition by the U.S. government of the International Committee of the Red Cross. After much effort, Barton succeeded by arguing that the American Red Cross could assist with crisis situations other than just war. She became the president of the American branch of the Red Cross and held the first branch meeting in her home in Washington DC in 1881.

Clara Barton died at her home in Maryland on April 12, 1912. She was buried in Massachusetts.

Service site is a tribute to her accomplishments and one of the first National Historic Sites dedicated to a woman. The home also shares the early history of the American Red Cross, and was the first headquarters for the organization. The restored home can be visited by guided tour only and offers visitors the chance to see 11 of the original 30 rooms including Barton's bedroom, the parlors, and the Red Cross offices. Tours last approximately one hour. The site is seven miles northwest of Washington DC sitting on a bluff looking over the Potomac River.

At the time of publication, this site was closed to the public for a rehabilitation project. It is expected to reopen in late 2016.

Entertainment and Events

The **Strathmore** (5301 Tuckerman Ln., North Bethesda, 301/581-5100, www.strathmore.org) is a beautiful concert venue in North Bethesda. The hall itself is a work of art, with contemporary styling, light woodwork, wonderful acoustics, and comfortable seats. World-class performers and international artists make up a full schedule of offerings including folk, rock, blues, pop, R&B, jazz, and classical music. Friendly and professional staff and volunteers make the experience at the Strathmore even better, and parking is free.

The **Imagination Stage** (4908 Auburn Ave., 301/961-6060, www.imaginationstage.org) is a theater arts center for young people in downtown Bethesda and known as the "largest multidisciplinary theater arts organization for young people" in the mid-Atlantic. its shows are professionally prepared, entertaining, and offer a nice break for kids from museums and playgrounds. The theater is open year-round. Pay attention to the target age for each performance.

Live stand-up comedy can be found at the **Laugh Riot at the Hyatt** (7400 Wisconsin Ave., http://standupcomedytogo.com, Sat. 8pm-10pm, $10) on Saturday nights. The shows are R rated, and seating is on a first-come first-served basis. A full bar service is available during the show. Admission is cash only.

The **Round House Theatre** (4545 East-West Hwy., 240/644-1100, www.roundhousetheatre.org) is a professional theater company that produces just under 200 performances a year.

The annual **Bethesda Literary Festival** (www.bethesda.org, free) is held for three days in April throughout downtown Bethesda. It hosts many local and national authors, poets, and journalists during more than 20 events. Authors discuss the craft and their work with other writers and attendees. Writing contests are also held during this free event.

A great weekend-long event held annually in mid-May is the **Bethesda Fine Arts Festival** (www.bethesda.org, free). Visitors can enjoy artwork created by more than 125 national artists, entertainment, and local food in the Woodmont Triangle neighborhood, along Norfolk, Auburn, and Del Ray Avenues.

Shopping

Downtown Bethesda is home to almost 700 retail stores and businesses. Most any shopping need or desire can be met in this destination. Fashion boutiques, art galleries, home furnishings stores, and salons are just a few examples of the types of retailers available. For a searchable list of stores visit www.bethesda.org/shopping-guide.

Sports and Recreation

A great place to bring the little ones (including the four-footed kind) is **Cabin John Regional Park** (7400 Tuckerman Ln., 301/765-8702, daily sunrise to sunset, free). This great park has just about everything, including playgrounds, trails, a little train (spring-fall), picnic tables, an amphitheater, and a dog park. The dog park is split into two areas: one for dogs 20 pounds and over and one for dogs less than 20 pounds. The park is very popular but also has plenty of room.

Just west of Bethesda on the Potomac

Billy Goat Trail

Hikers of all abilities can enjoy the popular Billy Goat Trail, running between the C&O Canal and the Potomac River in Montgomery County near Great Falls. The trail is 4.7 miles long and has three sections.

The northern section (Section A) is 1.7 miles long and the most heavily traveled. It runs through rocky terrain on Bear Island. There is a steep climb along a cliff face bordering the Potomac River in Mather Gorge that requires scrambling in parts. Pets are not allowed on Bear Island. Section A is accessible from the **Great Falls Tavern Visitor Center** (11710 MacArthur Blvd., Potomac, 301/767-3714).

Section B is less strenuous and has only one short segment where scrambling is required. It is 1.4 miles long. Section C is the easiest, with no scrambling. It is 1.6 miles long. Sections B and C can be accessed from **Carderock Recreation Area.** Leashed dogs are allowed on these two sections.

The three sections of the trail are not continuous but are connected by the C&O Canal Towpath. The Billy Goat Trail is marked with light blue blazes. Access to the trail is free, although a small parking fee is charged by the visitors center. There is no fee at Carderock.

River is **Carderock Recreation Area** (off Clara Barton Pkwy., Carderock, daily dawn to dusk, free), a 100-acre park that is part of the **Chesapeake & Ohio Canal National Historical Park** and one of the premier rock-climbing destinations in the Washington DC area with more than 100 established climbing routes and plentiful bouldering. Climbers can enjoy friction slabs, cracks, and overhangs. Most routes are best with a toprope. Climbs range 30-50 feet and have seen such notable climbers as Chris Sharma.

Carderock also offers hiking, biking, and picnicking. A section of the Billy Goat Trail passes through the park, and the C&O Canal Towpath can be accessed via a short wooded trail across the parking lot from the restrooms in the northernmost parking lot. The park is

Carderock Recreation Area

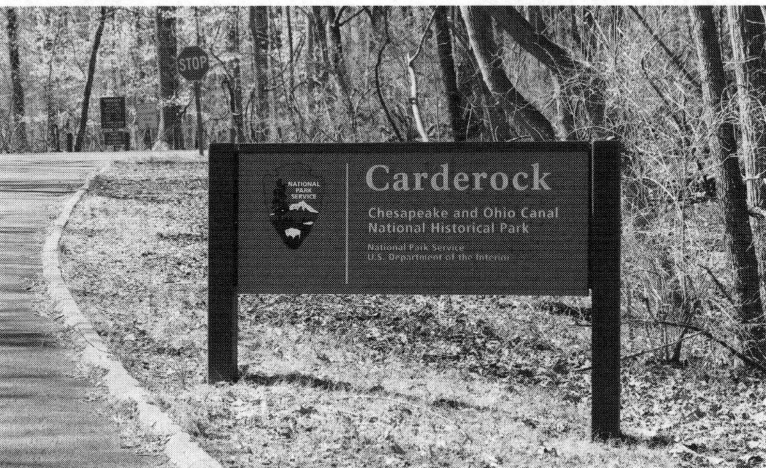

near the Carderock Division of the Naval Surface Warfare Center. Access to the park is free.

Food

There is no shortage of wonderful restaurant choices in Bethesda. In fact, this area is known for its great variety of international cuisine. A stroll through the eight-block "restaurant row" between Rockville Pike/Wisconsin Avenue and Old Georgetown Road will give you a taste of what is available. If you're in the mood for something different, you won't be disappointed.

AMERICAN

Upscale American cuisine that includes burgers, seafood, and steak can be found at **Woodmont Grill** (7715 Woodmont Ave., 301/656-9755, www.hillstone.com/woodmontgrill, Mon.-Sat. 11:30am-10pm, Sun. 11:30am-9pm, $14-52). Their prices may seem high for what sounds like casual fare ($18 for a cheeseburger, $33 for barbecue ribs, etc.) but the quality of the food is excellent, the atmosphere is relaxing, and their bread is made fresh in house. This is a great choice for business, family, and romantic occasions. There is live jazz nightly and free parking on-site. Be sure to make a reservation; the restaurant is very popular.

ASIAN

A good consistent "go-to" restaurant for sushi is **Raku Asian Dining, Sushi and Sake** (7240 Woodmont Ave., 301/718-8680, www.rakuasiandining.com, lunch Mon.-Fri. 11:30am-2:30pm, Sat.-Sun. noon-3pm, dinner Sun.-Thurs. 5pm-10pm, Fri.-Sat. 5pm-10:30pm, $8-40). This is a favorite lunch restaurant among the local business crowd, and that is no accident. They serve great sashimi, sushi, and rolls for all tastes, along with scrumptious soup and bento boxes. They offer a modern, Asian decor and friendly service. The food is freshly prepared and nicely presented. They have been in business for more than a dozen years have quite a following.

ITALIAN

For good, reasonably priced Italian food, dine at **Olazzo** (7921 Norfolk Ave., 301/654-9496, www.olazzo.com, Mon.-Thurs. 11:30am-10pm, Fri. 11:30am-11pm, Sat. 11:30-11pm, Sun. 11:30-10pm, $9-24). This is a very popular restaurant that doesn't take reservations, so plan on a wait during prime time. The food is delicious and consistent, with warm, fresh bread, wonderful martinis, and scrumptious entrées. The rose sauce is delectable. The atmosphere is cozy and rustic with dim lighting and candles on the tables. This is a good value for the quality of the food.

MEDITERRANEAN

Seafood lovers will go wild for the Mediterranean dishes at the family-owned and operated ★ **Chef Tony's** (4926 St. Elmo Ave., 301/654-3737, www.cheftonysbethesda.com, lunch Wed.-Fri. 11:30am-2:30pm, dinner Mon.-Sat. 5pm-10pm, Sun. 11am-8pm, $5-46). The ambience is simple and the food is simply excellent. Sample menu items include pan-roasted PEI mussels, Turkish bronzino, lobster pasta, and grilled surf and turf. Save room for dessert—they have a sizable selection of delicious sweets, including cheesecake, tiramisu, and caramelized sweet potato pie. They also offer a seven-course tasting menu for $65 (advance reservations only). Chef Tony partners with local farmers whenever possible.

PERSIAN

Great Persian food is served at **Kabob Bazaar** (7710 Wisconsin Ave., 301/652-5814, www.kabobbazaar.com, lunch and dinner, $9-19). This authentic restaurant has delicious, flavorful soup, kabobs (prepared on an open-fire grill), and platters, all served with a smile. The rice is perfectly light and fluffy, and the atmosphere is warm with soft, instrumental, traditional Iranian music playing in the background and soft lighting. This restaurant is suited for both business and a romantic evening.

Accommodations

$100-200

The **Golden Tulip Bethesda Court Hotel** (7740 Wisconsin Ave., 301/656-2100, www.bethesdacourtwashdc.com, $159-309) is a European-style hotel in a nice Bethesda neighborhood just eight miles from Washington DC. It offers 74 guest rooms, an English garden, free wireless Internet, a fitness room, and complimentary continental breakfast. The rooms are clean, and the staff is very helpful. Guests can walk to downtown Bethesda, and there are more than 100 restaurants within a two-block radius of the hotel. Parking is available on-site.

$200-300

A good extended-stay hotel is the **Bethesda Marriott Suites** (6711 Democracy Blvd., 301/897-5600, www.marriott.com, $239-279), which is 30 minutes from downtown Washington DC by car and popular for business travel. It offers 272 suites on 11 floors and has 10 meeting rooms. The facility includes a fitness center, an indoor heated pool, and a seasonal outdoor pool.

The **Residence Inn Bethesda Downtown** (7335 Wisconsin Ave., 301/718-0200, www.marriott.com, $189-319) is a modern, friendly facility in a central location near the Metrorail and dining. They offer 187 suites on 13 floors with well-equipped kitchens, wireless Internet, and free breakfast. A seasonal, outdoor, rooftop pool and year-round fitness center are also available to guests. There is a $25 valet parking fee (no self-parking) and a $175 fee for pets.

A short walk from the Bethesda Metro Station (7450 Wisconsin Ave.) is the **Hilton Garden Inn Washington DC/Bethesda** (7301 Waverly St., 301/654-8111, www.hiltongardeninn3.hilton.com, $159-299). They offer 216 large, comfortable rooms with high-speed Internet and good beds. A fitness center and pool are on-site. Self-parking is $16.50 (no valet).

Information and Services

For additional information on Bethesda, visit www.bethesda.org.

Getting Around

There is garage parking in many parts of Bethesda, and it is mostly free on the weekends. Taxi service is also readily available on most streets.

ROCKVILLE

Rockville is the third-largest city in Maryland and encompasses a little more than 13 square miles in central Montgomery County. It is approximately 12 miles north of Washington DC and has always had close connections to the nation's capital. In 1873, the first public transportation between Rockville and Washington was established with the arrival of the Baltimore & Ohio Railroad. Not too long after, trolley service began between Georgetown and Rockville, which continued until the automobile became the preferred mode of transportation.

During the Cold War, Rockville was considered a safe place for evacuation during a nuclear attack, and as such, many bomb shelters were built and I-270 was designated as an emergency landing runway for aircraft. Two Nike missile sites were also located in Rockville until the mid-1970s. The Nuclear Regulatory Commission headquarters is just south of Rockville's corporate limits.

Rockville's downtown area has had ups and downs since the 1960s but in recent years has enjoyed a rebirth with boutique stores, trendy restaurants, and upscale condominiums. It was even featured in REM's popular song released in 1984 titled "(Don't Go Back To) Rockville," written by Mike Mills.

Sights

BEALL-DAWSON HISTORIC HOUSE

The **Beall-Dawson Historic House** (103 W. Montgomery Ave., 301/762-1492, www.montgomeryhistory.org, Wed.-Sun. noon-4pm, $5) was built in 1815 for the county's clerk of the court, Upton Beall. The large, federal-style brick house is impressive both inside and out and remained a private home until the 1960s. At that time, it was purchased by the city as the headquarters for the Montgomery County Historical Society. The home is now a furnished museum that depicts life in the early 19th century, reflecting the lifestyle of both the upper-class homeowners and the enslaved African Americans who lived there with them.

Rotating gallery exhibits are displayed in two rooms and feature collections owned by the historical society. Tours of the home also include a tour of the **Stonestreet Museum of 19th Century Medicine,** a historic one-room doctor's office located on the property. Tours last between 45 minutes and an hour.

GLENVIEW MANSION

Glenview Mansion (603 Edmonston Dr., 240/314-8660, www.rockvillemd.gov, Mon.-Fri. 8:30am-5pm, free) is a beautiful 19th-century home that sits on the grounds of the 153-acre Rockville Civic Center Park. Visitors can take a guided tour (docents are available during business hours) or walk through the pillared, neoclassical mansion that dates back to 1836 on their own. The home can be rented for private events and also features an art gallery on the second floor that showcases local artwork. The mansion grounds offer walking trails and a formal garden.

F. SCOTT AND ZELDA FITZGERALD GRAVE

It may seem odd that F. Scott Fitzgerald and his wife, Zelda, are buried near a busy thoroughfare in Rockville, but Fitzgerald's father's family was from the area, and he visited here many times. Many members of his family are buried in **St. Mary's Catholic Cemetery** (500 Viers Mill Rd.), the oldest cemetery in Rockville. After attending his father's funeral in 1931, Fitzgerald decided that he and his wife would also be buried there. The quote on their joint tombstone is the final line of *The Great Gatsby,* "So we beat on, boats against the current, borne back ceaselessly into the past."

ASPIN HILL PET CEMETERY

One of the oldest pet cemeteries in the country is the **Aspin Hill Pet Cemetery,** also known as the **Aspen Hill Memorial Park & Animal Sanctuary** (13630 Georgia Ave., 240/252-2555, www.ahmemorialpark.org). The cemetery was established in 1921 and is owned by the Montgomery County Humane

Glenview Mansion

Society. The memorial park is the final resting place of General Grant or Jiggs, whom you might know better as Petey from the *Little Rascals*. This cute dog with the circle around one eye lived from 1928 to 1938. He is kept company by J. Edgar Hoover's dogs, and a few dozen humans who are buried with their pets. The cemetery is also the site of a memorial to medical rats. It was originally named after a kennel in England, which explains why the name is sometimes spelled with an "i" rather than an "e" in Aspen.

Entertainment and Events

The **F. Scott Fitzgerald Theatre** (603 Edmonston Dr., 240/314-8690, www.rockvillemd.gov) is a 446-seat performing arts venue in the Rockville Civic Center Park. Both local and professional touring companies offer stage performances at the theater.

One of the most popular annual events in Rockville is the **Rockville Antique and Classic Car Show** (603 Edmonston Dr., www.rockvillemd.gov) at the end of October. It features more than 500 classic automobiles from 25 local car clubs. Live music, food, and a flea market are also part of the festivities.

Shopping

Rockville Town Center (200 E. Middle Ln.) is a pedestrian-friendly town square with locally owned and operated shops and restaurants. It is also a thriving neighborhood with ice-skating in the winter and year-round programs. Shopping is a favorite pastime in the square, with more than 20 stores to choose from. Clothing boutiques, jewelry stores, home furnishing shops, and specialty athletic stores can all be found here, as well as salon and spa services.

There are also plenty of neighborhood shopping areas in Rockville. **Congressional Plaza** (1626 E. Jefferson St., 301/998-8176, www.congressionalplaza.com) has more than 50 stores and restaurants, including national chains, local boutiques, and a gourmet grocery store. **Falls Grove Village Center** (14919-14943 Shady Grove Rd., 301/294-9304, www.fallsgrovevillagectr.com) offers retail, restaurants, and a grocery store. The **King Farm Village Center** (403 Redland Blvd., www.kingfarmvillagecenter.com) is a charming local shopping area with retail stores, a grocery store, and restaurants. **Montrose Crossing** (Montrose Rd. and Rockville Pike, 301/341-8433) is home to mostly chain retail stores that specialize in home furnishings, sports, and clothing. The **Traville Village Center** (9700 Traville Gateway Dr., 703/821-0500, www.travillecenter.com), which is accessible from Darnestown Road and Shady Grove Road, is a neighborhood shopping area that offers a mix of boutique stores, a grocery store, and restaurants. **Wintergreen Plaza** (815-895 Rockville Pike, 301/718-4220, www.wintergreenplaza.com), on Rockville Pike, is home to many specialty stores, restaurants, food providers, and services.

Two popular seasonal **farmers markets** are held in Rockville. The first is at the Rockville Town Center on the corner of Route 28 and Monroe Street on Saturday mid-May to mid-November (9am-1pm). The second is on Wednesday at the Rockville Town Square (200 East Middle Lane) in front of Dawson's Market from the beginning of June through October (11am to 2pm).

Sports and Recreation

Rock Creek Regional Park (6700 Needwood Rd., Derwood, 301/948-5053, www.montgomeryparks.org, daily sunrise to sunset, free) is an 1,800-acre park with two lakes (Lake Needwood and Lake Frank), 13 miles of wooded trails, picnic facilities, a playground, archery range, and nature center. Boat rentals are available on-site ($10 per hour and $35 per day for kayaks, canoes, and rowboats, $8 per half hour for pedal boats), and 30-minute pontoon boat tours are offered on weekends for $2.

The **Chesapeake & Ohio Canal National Historical Park** (301/739-4200, www.nps.gov/choh), a 184.5-mile path that stretches from Georgetown in Washington DC to Cumberland, Maryland, runs along the Potomac River near Rockville. A lovely stretch in Montgomery County is located between Rileys Lock (0.2 miles before milepost 23) and Swains Lock (0.4 miles before milepost 17). The terrain is mostly hard-packed dirt or pebble dirt and the scenery is woodlands with river and canal views. The path is ideal for mountain biking, horseback riding, walking, and running.

Wanna feel like Tarzan? Then an afternoon at **Go Ape** (6129 Needwood Lake Dr., 800/971-8271, www.goape.com, $58) is a must. This incredible treetop adventure is a big obstacle course in the trees that is designed for most age groups. Test your climbing skills and fear of heights on ladders, bridges, walkways, ropes, zip lines, and even tunnels. Safety instruction and all equipment are included.

For something a little different, catch a **Free State Roller Derby** (www.freestaterollerderby.com) competition. This flat-track roller derby league is based in Rockville.

Food

When it comes to food, neighborhood gems are scattered throughout Rockville, mostly camouflaged in drab-looking strip malls. International cuisine is some of the best in the region, if you know where to look.

ECLECTIC

Have you ever tried a waffle sandwich? If not, the place to have your first is ★ **Mosaic** (186 Halpine Rd., 301/468-0682, www.mosaiccuisine.com, Sun.-Thurs. 8am-9pm, Fri.-Sat. 8am-10pm, $7-21), near the Twinbrook Metro station. Mosaic is an eclectic internationally inspired restaurant with a passion for waffles. Their food is loosely based on French cuisine with influences from all over the globe. You'll find pesto soup from Italy, Asian duck rolls, French brie—you get the picture. Now back to the waffles. The chefs at Mosaic searched for a good alternative to using bread or tortillas for their sandwiches. Out of this creative desire to differentiate themselves with a healthy alternative, the waffle sandwich was born. They then spent time perfecting a unique light and crispy waffle recipe suitable for sandwiches, with fewer carbs and more protein. The result is a menu of waffles served all day (breakfast, lunch, and dinner). Breakfast is by far their most popular meal. They offer traditional favorites like eggs Benedict and French toast, but also have an entire menu section devoted to their beloved waffles. With lunch comes salads and a variety of hot and cold sandwiches, available on a choice of breads including their waffles. Dinner is an unusual mix of steak, seafood, pasta, and again, a menu of waffle sandwiches.

GREEK

Scrumptious Greek food can be found at **Cava Mezze** (9713 Traville Gateway Dr., 301/309-9090, www.cavamezze.com, lunch Mon.-Fri. 11:30am-2pm, dinner Mon.-Thurs. 5pm-10pm, Fri.-Sat. 5pm-11pm, Sun. 5pm-9:30pm, $8-15). They serve traditional Greek food in a small-plates format. The restaurant was started by two energetic friends and a chef on a shoestring budget, and their endeavor has blossomed into a five-restaurant success story. The saganaki (flamed cheese) is delightful, as are the scallop risotto, lamb meatballs, and grilled octopus. The atmosphere is energetic yet with a cozy, inviting ambience. Although the service isn't overly friendly, it is prompt. If you're in the mood for very flavorful Greek food, this is a good choice.

LATIN

A plain exterior and average interior atmosphere don't detract from the draw of **La Brasa** (12401 Parklawn Dr., 301/468-8850, www.labrasarockville.com, Mon.-Thurs. 11am-9pm, Fri.-Sat. 11am-10pm, $9-21), which serves great Latin food in an out-of-the-way location. Customers are greeted with warm smiles and fantastic South American dishes. Try the carne asada and the pupusas. They also have great plantains. The dining room is small, but there are a few additional patio seats during the warmer months. This restaurant is family-owned and operated, and they offer takeout service.

MEXICAN

Villa Maya (5532 Norbeck Rd., 301/460-1247, www.villamayarestaurant.com, Mon.-Fri. 11am-midnight, Sat.-Sun. 10am-midnight, $9-18) is a great Mexican restaurant hidden behind a plain exterior in a local strip mall. The food is a step above traditional Mexican, the service is good, and the drinks will make you not care about either. This is a fun place with a large menu of both zesty Mexican fare and mild dishes. The seafood burritos are a favorite, as is the fresh guacamole made at your table. If you're looking for a different appetizer to share, try the yucca con chicharron (tender pork in a savory juice). The place is packed on weekends, so be prepared for a wait. The staff does an excellent job of taking care of the patrons and is particularly accommodating to seniors.

PERUVIAN

★ **La Limena** (765-B Rockville Pike, 301/424-8066, www.lalimenarestaurant.com, Sun.-Thurs. 11am-9pm, Fri.-Sat. 11am-10pm, $8-20) is one of a growing number of Peruvian restaurants that are sprouting up throughout the Washington DC suburbs. As the Peruvian culture spreads, wonderful, soul-soothing Peruvian food is making its way into many people's "go-to" restaurant rotation. At first glance, La Limena appears to be a hole-in-the-wall eatery in a strip mall. Once you step inside, it's clear this little bistro is a blend of sophisticated cuisine in a casual, family atmosphere. The food is simply delicious and features dishes such as ceviche with soft sweet potatoes, fried trout with sliced garlic, and a strip steak topped with a fried egg. They also serve Cuban dishes.

Accommodations

Accommodations in Rockville are primarily chain hotels. There is a big variety, so it is best to select a hotel based on location. If you do not need to be near the Metrorail or the center of town, cheaper rates can be found on the outskirts of the city.

$100-200

The **Sheraton Rockville Hotel** (920 King Farm Blvd., 240/912-8200, www.starwoodhotels.com, $94-199) is in the King Farm development near I-270. It has 152 guest rooms with comfortable beds, 32-inch flat-screen televisions, high-speed Internet, and work desks. Amenities include a fitness center, indoor lap pool, whirlpool, on-site restaurant, and gift shop. The hotel is about eight miles north of downtown Rockville, but it is reasonably priced for the quality of the facility.

Another solid choice in this price range is the **Best Western Plus Rockville Hotel and Suites** (1251 W. Montgomery Ave., 301/424-4940, www.bestwestern.com, $159-189). They have 164 guest rooms and are close to I-270. They offer a complimentary breakfast, a fitness center, a seasonal outdoor pool, free high-speed Internet, and free shuttle to the Metro.

$200-300

The **Homewood Suites by Hilton Rockville-Gaithersburg** (14975 Shady Grove Rd., 240/507-1900, www.homewoodsuites3.hilton.com, $199-269) is a good choice for extended stays or those who want a fully equipped kitchen. Located in the business district, this is a popular hotel for business travel. Complimentary shuttle service to the Shady Grove Metrorail station and other locations within a three-mile radius of the hotel is offered. Each of the 87 suites has a full kitchen, large living area, and free wireless Internet. A full complimentary breakfast is also included. Hotel amenities such as an indoor heated pool, 24-hour fitness center, whirlpool, and kids' entertainment room with books, DVDs, foosball, and air hockey allow guests several options for relaxation outside their studio, one-bedroom, or two-bedroom suites.

The Homewood Suites is joined at the lobby to the **Hilton Garden Inn Rockville Gaithersburg** (14975 Shady Grove Rd., 240/507-1800, www.hiltongardeninn3.hilton.com, $189-229). Both hotels are relatively new and have excellent staff. They also share some amenities.

Information and Services

For additional information on Rockville, visit www.rockvillemd.gov.

SILVER SPRING

Silver Spring is just north of Washington DC and is a prime business hub with numerous office buildings and a dense population. The city is said to be named after a spring that was discovered by Francis Preston Blair, an American journalist and politician, in 1840 when he was thrown from his horse while riding through the countryside looking for an area to build his personal retreat from Washington. As legend goes, the mica and sand around the spring glimmered like silver, and thus the name.

In recent years, the original downtown area, which had paled compared to some of the region's trendy city centers, began a rebirth of sorts. New businesses moved in to stake their claim, including major retail outlets, restaurants, and residential and office developments. Downtown Silver Spring is now a vibrant city center with entertainment, shopping, and other conveniences. One of its most prominent business residents is Discovery Communications, the parent company of Discovery Channel and a dozen other television networks.

Sights

NATIONAL MUSEUM OF HEALTH AND MEDICINE

The **National Museum of Health and Medicine** (2500 Linden Ln., 301/319-3300, www.medicalmuseum.mil, daily 10am-5:30pm, free) is one of the few museums where visitors can see the impact of disease on the human body. The museum is a National Historic Landmark that was established during the Civil War and dates back to 1862. It offers unique exhibits and educational programs, and engages in ongoing medical research.

Instruments used to diagnose and treat disease can be seen as well as the case histories of patients with the diseases (some exhibits may be a bit graphic for young children). The goal of the museum is to promote the understanding of both historic and modern-day medicine.

Children play around the fountain in downtown Silver Spring.

Special attention is given to military medicine. Fascinating artifacts on display include the bullet that killed Abraham Lincoln and bone fragments from Lincoln's skull.

In the museum's initial years, the first curator collected artifacts from doctors treating soldiers in the Union army. Photos of wounded soldiers were also collected that showed the impact of gunshot wounds and the resulting amputations and surgical procedures. Since then much research has been conducted at the museum and a sophisticated method of cataloging was established, which formed the framework for the National Library of Medicine.

At the onset of World War II, the museum began to focus primarily on pathology and became a division of the new Army Institute of Pathology. After several name changes, the museum became known under its current title in 1989.

Adult visitors should be prepared to present photo identification at the entrance and personal belongings may be subject to search for security purposes.

NATIONAL CAPITAL TROLLEY MUSEUM

In the northern reaches of the Silver Spring area is the popular **National Capital Trolley Museum** (1313 Bonifant Rd., Colesville, 301/384-6088, www.dctrolley.org, Sat.-Sun. noon-5pm, $7). This unusual museum strives to preserve artifacts from electric street railways and to help understand their effect on community development in the Washington DC area. There is a visitors center and several exhibit halls, and guests can enjoy authentic streetcar rides through Northwest Branch Park. Many historic trolleys are on display, and educational programs are also offered.

THE *HAND OF NOAA* SCULPTURE

An interesting piece of public art is located outside the National Oceanic and Atmospheric Administration (NOAA) headquarters. Known as the ***Hand of NOAA*** (1325 East-West Hwy.), the sculpture depicts a large bronze hand releasing seagulls to the ocean. The seagulls are part of the agency's logo, and the sculpture symbolizes NOAA's commitment to protecting the environment.

★ AMERICAN FILM INSTITUTE (AFI) SILVER THEATRE & CULTURAL CENTER

The **American Film Institute (AFI) Silver Theatre & Cultural Center** (8633 Colesville Rd., 301/495-6700, www.afi.com) is a state-of-the-art exhibition, education, and cultural center that grew out of the restored 1938 art deco Silver Theatre. It offers multiple stadium-seating theaters in 32,000 square feet of space, along with a reception area, exhibit space, offices, and meeting space. They feature retrospectives, new releases, and tribute shows. A full schedule of films is shown there, and memberships are available. Each June, the center hosts the premier seven-day documentary film festival called **AFI DOCS.** It is considered one of the world's best documentary festivals.

AFI Silver Theatre

Entertainment and Events

The historic **Fillmore Theater** (8656 Colesville Rd., 301/960-9999, www.fillmoresilverspring.com) has brought entertainment to Silver Spring for more than 40 years. With a capacity of 2,000, it offers first-class music and entertainment in the center of the downtown area. A schedule of events can be found on the website.

Shopping

The center of activity in Silver Spring is the **Silver Spring Town Center** (www.silverspringtowncenter.com). Located on Georgia Avenue, it comprises retailers, restaurants, a movie theater, and a Whole Foods grocery store. The town center is the anchor to the newly revitalized downtown area. Year-round activities are held at the center including craft fairs, festivals, and concerts. There is also a seasonal farmers market. A splash fountain is open May-September.

Recreation

The **Capital Crescent Trail** (www.cctrail.org) is an 11-mile off-road rail trail that is designated for shared use by walkers, runners, bikers, and inline skaters. The trail was created in an old railbed of the Georgetown Branch of the B&O Railroad. It runs from Georgetown in Washington DC through Bethesda and ends in west Silver Spring (in Lyttonsville). The trail is heavily used by commuters and recreational users and passes through wooded areas and parks, over four historic bridges, and through two tunnels. Parts of the trail have scenic views of the Potomac River.

Food

The **Sergio Ristorante Italiano** (8727 Colesville Road, 301/585-1040, Mon.-Fri. 11:30am-9:30pm, Sat. 5pm-9:30pm, $13-22) is underappreciated. This cozy little establishment serves authentic Italian fare with a personal touch. The food is consistently delicious and the owner is very involved in making sure each guest has a good experience.

For a classic diner experience, the **Tastee Diner** (8601 Cameron St., 301/589-8171, www.tasteediner.com, open 24/7, under $10) is hard to beat. This landmark diner originally opened in 1946 on Georgia Avenue and was moved to its current location in 1999 when Discovery Communications was built. It remains one of two original diners with a vintage railroad car design in Montgomery County. They are known for their BLTs, but have a wide variety of breakfast, lunch, and dinner menu items.

The historic **Mrs. K's Toll House** (9201 Colesville Rd., 301/589-3500, www.mrsks.com, brunch Sun. 10:30am-3pm, lunch Tues.-Sat. 11:30am-2:30pm, dinner Tues.-Thurs. 5pm-9pm, Fri.-Sat. 4:30pm-9:30pm, Sun. 5pm-8pm, $16-38) offers a quaint country-house atmosphere in one of the last existing tollhouses in the county. Built in the early 1900s, the home was a working tollhouse with living quarters for the keeper and his family. The home was turned into a restaurant in 1930 offering a charming ambience, beautiful gardens, and a variety of interior antiques. The menu offers filet, seafood, venison, lamb, and vegetarian dishes. The menu is not oriented towards children. There is a lovely wine bar in the basement.

A good seafood house that takes pride in its food is **Crisfield Seafood Restaurant** (8012 Georgia Ave., 301/589-1306, www.crisfieldseafood.com, Tues.-Thurs. 11am-9pm, Fri.-Sat. 11am-10pm, Sun. noon-9pm, $15-28). This traditional restaurant has an old-time counter, tiled walls, and a truly retro feel (not a trendy, hip feel—this is the real deal). They serve delicious seafood and some of the best crab cakes in the county. The decor isn't fancy, but the food is simple and fresh.

Accommodations

Silver Spring offers mostly chain hotel accommodations such as the **Hilton Garden Inn Silver Spring North** (2200 Broadbirch Dr., 301/622-3333, www.hiltongardeninn3.hilton.com, $189-199) and the **Courtyard by Marriott Silver Spring Downtown** (8506

Fenton St., 301/589-4899, www.marriott.com, $269-319) in downtown Silver Spring.

A nice bed-and-breakfast alternative is the **Bed & Breakfast at Lansdowne Way** (2009 Lansdowne Way, 301/960-3331, www.bblansdowneway.com, $165-300), on a quiet, tree-lined, neighborhood street. It offers four comfortable guest rooms and suites. A healthy continental breakfast is served to guests.

Getting There and Around

Downtown Silver Spring can be reached from Washington DC by car in less than 20 minutes (using Georgia Avenue or 16th Street). Metrobus service is available in Silver Spring as are Montgomery County's Ride On buses.

GAITHERSBURG

Gaithersburg is in central Montgomery County, five miles north of Rockville, and was incorporated in 1878. It has a population of around 60,000 and is the fourth-largest incorporated city in Maryland. I-270 runs through Gaithersburg, dividing it into east and west sections of the city.

Eastern Gaithersburg is home to a historic business district that is sometimes referred to as "Olde Town" Gaithersburg. The Montgomery County Fair Grounds are also on the eastern side of the city.

The west side of Gaithersburg is primarily neighborhoods, although several major employers are located there such as the National Institute of Standards and Technology (NIST) and several information systems and global services corporations.

Sights

RIO WASHINGTONIAN CENTER

The main center of activity in Gaithersburg is the **Rio Washingtonian Center** (9811 Washingtonian Blvd., 301/921-4686, www.riowashingtonian.com). This premier shopping area is in the heart of the city in combination with the **Waterfront and Rio Entertainment Center.** Together they offer 760,000 square feet of retail space, restaurants, and entertainment venues. The center is set on a lake, and there is a walkway around the lake and paddleboats for rent on the water. Outdoor dining is plentiful, and the area is generally safe and clean. Parking can be a little tough on the weekends.

INTERNATIONAL LATITUDE OBSERVATORY

The only National Historic Landmark in Gaithersburg is the **International Latitude Observatory** (100 DeSellum Ave., 301/258-6350, www.gaithersburgmd.gov, call ahead for tours). This small, 13-square-foot building was constructed in 1899 as part of an international effort to record the earth's wobble on its polar axis. The observatory is one of six in the world (in the United States, Japan, Russia, and Italy) that gathered information still used by today's scientists. The station was in operation until 1982, when its functions were replaced by computers. The original Zenith telescope that was used in the observatory is now on display at the **Gaithersburg Community Museum** (9 S. Summit Ave., 301/258-6160, www.gaithersburgmd.gov, Thurs.-Sat. 10am-3pm, free), which is in the historic 1884 B&O Railroad Station complex and offers exhibits on the city's history.

Recreation

East of Gaithersburg, on the border with neighboring Howard County, are two wonderful recreational lakes: the **Triadelphia Reservoir** and the **Rocky Gorge Reservoir.** They share an information center (2 Brighton Dam Rd., Brookeville, 301/206-7485, www.wsscwater.com) where boat launch permits ($6) and maps can be obtained. The lakes are both dammed portions of the Patuxent River and provide water to Montgomery and Prince George's Counties. There are no natural lakes in Maryland, so without the creation of reservoirs, it would have been difficult to provide water to the many homes and businesses in the state. The Washington Suburban Sanitary Commission, which is more than 85 years old, created both Triadelphia Reservoir and Rocky

Gorge Reservoir and is still responsible for maintaining them. Both are wonderful locations for kayaking and fishing. No gasoline-powered engines are allowed on either lake.

The **Metropolitan Ballet Theatre and Academy** (220 Perry Pkwy, #8, 301/762-1757, www.mbtdance.org) provides training in ballet, jazz, tap, hip-hop, and modern dance. Students perform with the company in professional performances (sometimes with professional artists).

Food

Il Porto (245 Muddy Branch Rd., 301/590-0735, www.ilportorestaurant.com, Mon.-Sat. 11:30am-10pm, Sun. 11:30am-9pm, $10-20) is a delicious, reasonably priced Italian restaurant. They feature traditional Italian dishes and fresh seafood. All food is made to order. The service is outstanding, and this popular restaurant doesn't seem to rest on its laurels despite its excellent reputation. Expect a crowd on weekend evenings.

Good Mediterranean food can be found in the Kentlands area at **Vasilis** (705 Center Point Way, 301/977-1011, www.vasilisgrill.com, Mon.-Thurs. 11am-9pm, Fri.-Sat. 11am-10pm, $8-27). They serve a traditional Greek menu with succulent fresh vegetable side dishes. The lamb is especially savory, meaty, and cooked to perfection. This is a popular restaurant, but they do not take reservations so plan accordingly.

Great beer and upscale pub food can be found at **Dogfish Head Alehouse** (800 W. Diamond Ave., 301/963-4847, www.dogfishalehouse.com, Mon.-Thurs. 11am-11pm, Fri.-Sat. 11am-midnight, Sun. 11am-10pm, $10-20). The restaurant is a little off the beaten path (west of downtown), but is still convenient to many businesses and neighborhoods. They serve sandwiches, pizza, fish, and other pub food, plus a great selection of standard and seasonal beers.

Accommodations

Accommodations in Gaithersburg include many popular chain hotels. The **Comfort Inn Shady Grove** (16216 S. Frederick Rd., 301/330-0023, www.choicehotels.com, $119-129) is one of the nicest Comfort Inns in the area and offers 127 comfortable rooms, good service, and reasonable rates. The **Hyatt House Gaithersburg** (200 Skidmore Blvd., 301/527-6000, www.gaithersburg.house.hyatt.com, $144-175) is a suite hotel in a residential area of Gaithersburg, approximately one mile from the Shady Grove Metro station. It is a good option for extended stays. The hotel is pet friendly.

The **Courtyard by Marriott Gaithersburg Washingtonian Center** (204 Boardwalk Pl., 301/527-9000, www.marriott.com, $159-219) is a lovely hotel on the lake at the Washingtonian Center. It is very convenient to shopping and restaurants and has 203 rooms and seven suites.

GERMANTOWN

Germantown sits 6.5 miles northwest of Gaithersburg along I-270 and is the third-most populous place in Maryland with more than 86,000 people. It is one of Montgomery County's fastest-growing areas and has seen a large increase in the number of neighborhoods, communities, and schools in recent years. Germantown is approximately 25 miles from Washington DC.

Sights and Entertainment

BLACK ROCK CENTER FOR THE ARTS

The center of Germantown is along Middlebrook Road. This is where the **Black Rock Center for the Arts** (12901 Town Commons Dr., 301/528-2260, www.blackrockcenter.org), a cultural center offering shows, classes, camps, and an art gallery, is located, as well as the **Germantown Commons** (13060 Middlebrook Rd.) shopping area.

BLACK HILL REGIONAL PARK

Just north of Germantown and west of I-270 is **Black Hill Regional Park** (20930 Lake Ridge Dr., Boyds, 301/528-3490, www.

montgomeryparks.org, daily sunrise-sunset, free). This lovely 1,843-acre park is home to a scenic recreational lake called **Little Seneca Lake,** a great place to kayak and fish with 505 acres of water and 15 miles of shoreline. The park also features hiking trails and the **Black Hill Visitors Center** (20926 Lake Ridge Dr., 301/528-3488, daily 11am-6pm). Kayak, canoe, and rowboat rentals are available May-September for $8 per hour or $27.50 per day.

★ SUGARLOAF MOUNTAIN

North of Germantown in nearby Frederick County is **Sugarloaf Mountain** (Comus Road, Dickerson, 301/874-2024, www.sugarloafmd.com, daily 8am-one hour prior to sunset, free). Sugarloaf Mountain is a popular recreational area for people in Maryland's Capital Region. It is a small mountain (1,282 feet) that is a designated National Natural Landmark.

Sugarloaf Mountain is a monadnock, which is an isolated mountain that rises sharply from the surrounding ground. Because of this, the mountain can be seen for miles away and is an easily recognizable landmark.

The mountain is a public park that is accessible for recreation at no charge. Activities in the park include hiking, picnicking, and rock climbing. It is also known for its scenic views of the Monocacy Valley.

Sugarloaf Mountain is 15 miles northwest of Germantown and 10 miles south of Frederick. From I-270 take the Hyattstown exit to Route 109 to Comus. Turn right on Comus Road. This will lead to the Sugarloaf Mountain entrance.

WHITE'S FERRY

Sixteen miles west of Germantown on the Potomac River in Dickerson is **White's Ferry** (24801 Whites Ferry Rd., Dickerson, 301/349-5200, $5 one-way or $8 round-trip), the only one of about 100 ferries that used to be in business on the Potomac River that is still in operation. It is the only crossing on the river between the American Legion Bridge on I-495 and the bridge at Point of Rocks in Frederick County, Maryland. Commuters rely on the small ferry for daily transportation, and the ferry is heavily used by recreational travelers on weekends. The ferry runs on a wire cable every 20 minutes year-round 5am-11pm daily unless the river is flooded or there is bad weather. Bicycles ($2) and pedestrians ($1) are welcome aboard.

Prince George's County

Prince George's County was named after Prince George of Denmark (1653-1708), who was married to Queen Anne of Great Britain. Today the county is a hub for federal government agencies.

Part of the Atlantic coastal plain, Prince George's County has a combination of gently rolling hills and valleys. The county borders the Patuxent River on its east side and has some lovely wildlife habitat.

Prince George's County is more city suburb than tourist destination and faces more crime issues and economic challenges than neighboring Montgomery County. However, there are some gems worth visiting while in the area, including the newly established National Harbor, the home stadium for the Washington Redskins, and a well-known site for dinosaur fossils.

GETTING THERE AND AROUND

Amtrak (4300 Garden City Dr., 800/872-7245, www.amtrak.com) provides train service to Landover at the New Carrollton station. The **Maryland Transit Administration** MARC train (410/539-5000, http://mta.maryland.gov) provides weekday-only service to five stations in Prince George's County on the Camden Line (College Park, Greenbelt, Muirkirk,

Laurel, and Riverdale) and three stations on the Penn Line (New Carrollton, Seabrook, and Bowie).

The **Washington Metropolitan Area Transit Authority (WMATA)** (202/637-7000, www.wmata.com) provides **Metrorail** and **Metrobus** service to Prince George's County. The county is serviced by Metrorail's Green Line in College Park and Greenbelt, the Blue Line to Largo, and the Orange Line to New Carrollton.

A local bus system in Prince George's County is **TheBus** (301/324-2877, www.princegeorgescountymd.gov, $1.25), which operates on weekdays only.

★ NATIONAL HARBOR

Twelve miles south of downtown Washington DC, National Harbor sits across the Potomac River from Old Town Alexandria. This trendy addition to the Washington DC metro area is a little oasis in Prince George's County, offering world-class dining, accommodations, and activities. The area was previously a forgotten 350-acre parcel of land on the Potomac River banks that was the site of an abandoned plantation. Then a large local development firm embarked on a seven-year project to create a new hot spot of local and tourist activity. The first phase of the project opened in 2008, and since then, the site has become the location of a convention center, multiple hotels, restaurants, retail space, and condominiums. The area continues to undergo development. Festivals and other outdoor events are also held at National Harbor.

Sights

CAPITAL WHEEL

The **Capital Wheel** (116 Waterfront St., 301/842-8650, www.thecapitalwheel.com, hours vary daily, $15) is a prime attraction at National Harbor. This 180-foot-tall modern Ferris wheel sits on a pier on the Potomac River. The ride offers terrific views of the river and harbor. Each climate-controlled gondola seats up to eight people, with the exception of the VIP gondola, which holds four. The VIP gondola has leather bucket seats and a glass floor ($50). All rides are 12-15 minutes.

CAROUSEL AT NATIONAL HARBOR

The **Carousel at National Harbor** (137 National Plaza, 301/842-8650, www.nationalharbor.com, mid-May-day before Memorial Day Fri.-Sun. noon-8pm, Memorial Day-Labor Day Mon.-Thurs. noon-8pm, Fri.-Sat. noon-10pm, Sun. noon-8pm, $7) is an

National Harbor

Americana-themed carousel, located at the north end of National Harbor on the waterfront. Kids of all ages can enjoy its whimsical animals. There is a playground near the carousel.

THE *AWAKENING* SCULPTURE

The ***Awakening*** is a five-part, 70-foot, cast-iron sculpture that depicts a bearded giant waking up and rising out of the earth. The pieces include the giant's head, hand, outstretched arm, knee, and foot. This impressive artwork by J. Seward Johnson was originally part of a public art exhibition in Washington DC in 1980, when it was installed at Hains Point near the Jefferson Memorial. After the exhibition, the sculpture remained on loan to the National Park Service. The *Awakening* was purchased by the Peterson Companies (which developed National Harbor) in 2008 and moved to the beach at the harbor.

Entertainment and Events

Dinner cruises of 2-4 hours aboard the glass-enclosed ***Odyssey Washington DC*** (866/306-2469, www.odysseycruises.com) leave from National Harbor and provide great views of Washington DC, entertainment, and a full dinner. Reservations can be made for individual seating or the boat can be booked for large functions. Dining cruises can also be booked on the ***Spirit of Washington*** (866/302-2469, www.spiritcruises.com).

If a dueling piano bar sounds like fun, make a reservation at **Bobby McKey's** (172 Fleet St., 301/602-2209, www.bobbymckeys.com, $7-20). This is a two-story venue that holds up to 450 people and hosts regular shows and private parties. Reservations can be made online for standing room or a reserved seat. Due to the popularity of this place as the only live music venue in National Harbor and the only dueling piano bar in the Washington DC area, it's best to reserve a seat. This is a loud but unique show and can be a lot of fun if you're in the mood for it. Tips are expected for requests.

ICE! (www.gaylordhotels.com) is an annual ice sculpture event held at the Gaylord National Resort & Convention Center. Visitors walk through a huge winter wonderland carved from 5,000 blocks of ice shipped in from a factory in Ohio. More than 40 international sculptors work for 30 days prior to the event to produce a themed ice "land" where people can see, touch, and walk inside the amazing works of art. The event has a different theme each year and runs mid-November through early January. Tickets are around $30.

Shopping

The **American Market** (www.americanmarketnh.com, Sat. 10am-4pm) is an upscale farmers market that is held in National Harbor May-October. The market is on American Way, between Waterfront and Fleet Street. The market features locally grown produce and handmade crafts.

Sports and Recreation

National Harbor offers a first-class marina with large floating docks and easy water access to many attractions in the Washington DC area via the Potomac River. Kayak and pedal boat rentals are available right at the dock, and electric boat rentals are available through **Duffy Electric Boat Rentals** (www.experiencetheduffyboat.com, $200 for the first hour, $150 for the second hour, and $100 for each additional hour). Sightseeing cruises are also a popular activity at the harbor and can be booked with **Potomac River Boat Company** (www.potomacriverboatco.com, $32 for 90 minutes). Guided bass fishing is also available through **National Bass Guide Service** (www.nationalbass.com, starting at $295 for four hours).

The harbor is also the site of many annual athletic events. Whether you are looking to do a short fun run, a half marathon, a triathlon, a competitive open-water swimming event, or you simply want to do yoga on the beach, National Harbor is the place. A list of events is available on the website (www.nationalharbor.com).

A nice beachfront walking path along the Potomac connects the National Harbor to a bike trail on the Woodrow Wilson Bridge. This allows walking and cycling into Alexandria across the river.

Food

Upscale dining at the **Old Hickory Steakhouse Restaurant** (201 Waterfront St., 301/965-4000, www.gaylordhotels.com, daily 5:30pm-10:30pm, $28-52) in the Gaylord Hotel is hard to beat. The atmosphere is first-rate, with views of the harbor, and the food is dependable and delicious. This sophisticated restaurant serves 100 percent antibiotic- and hormone-free steak and delicious seafood. They also have an award-winning wine list. Three hours of complimentary parking is available at the Gaylord for dinner guests.

Upscale Mexican food can be found at **Rosa Mexicano** (153 Waterfront St., 301/567-1005, www.rosamexicano.com, Sun.-Thurs. 11:30am-10pm, Fri.-Sat. 11:30am-11pm, $9-27) on the waterfront. They offer indoor and outdoor seating (weather permitting) and a lively decor. The menu consists of fresh Mexican dishes featuring seafood, steak, and other delicious ingredients. The signature Guacamole en Mocajete is made tableside and a great choice for a starter. They have an extensive bar menu (not cheap, but good), and the service is wonderful.

For a quick burger, stop in **Elevation Burger** (108 Waterfront St., 301/749-4014, www.elevationburger.com, Sun.-Thurs. 11am-9pm, Fri.-Sat. 11am-midnight, under $10). This inexpensive dining option offers good gourmet burgers with many choices for patty combinations and toppings. This is one of the few casually priced eateries in National Harbor.

Accommodations

The ★ **Gaylord National Resort and Convention Center** (201 Waterfront St., 301/965-4000, www.marriott.com, $249-399 plus $18 resort fee) is a Marriott-owned hotel that anchors the National Harbor. This massive 18-floor hotel has 1,890 guest rooms, an impressive 18-story glass atrium, indoor gardens, and panoramic views of the Potomac River. A conference center with 89 meeting

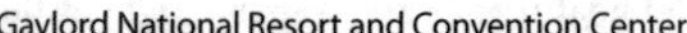
Gaylord National Resort and Convention Center

rooms, the hotel is always bustling, but the staff is friendly and the rooms are very comfortable. There are a fitness center, indoor pool, and spa on-site. Self-parking is available for $26 a day and valet for $39.

The **Residence Inn National Harbor** (192 Waterfront St., 301/749-4755, www.marriott.com, $229-309) is a less expensive alternative to the Gaylord and has 162 suites on seven floors, some with great views of the water. This Marriott hotel offers roomy suites with full kitchens and separate sitting areas. There is a small pool, a small fitness room, a complimentary breakfast buffet, and a manager's reception Monday-Thursday. The hotel is within walking distance of attractions and restaurants in National Harbor, and there is a parking lot near the rear hotel entrance (a discount on parking is offered to hotel guests).

Another good option for accommodations in National Harbor is the **Hampton Inn & Suites National Harbor** (250 Waterfront St., 301/567-3531, www.hamptoninn3.hilton.com, $259-289). This 151-room hotel is welcoming and convenient to the National Harbor attractions. Guests can enjoy a complimentary breakfast buffet, wireless Internet, a pool, and a fitness center. Self-parking is available for $16.

Information and Services

For additional information on National Harbor, visit www.nationalharbor.com or stop by the **National Harbor Visitor's Center** (168 National Plaza, Oxen Hill, 877/628-5427).

Getting There

National Harbor is a 20-minute drive south of Washington DC. The closest major highway is the Beltway (I-495), but from DC, I-295 is the primary route. **Water taxi** service is also available from Old Town Alexandria in Virginia (www.potomacriverboatco.com, $8 each way).

GREATER UPPER MARLBORO

Greater Upper Marlboro is a suburb of Washington DC with approximately 22,000 residents. It is 18 miles west of DC in south-central Prince George's County off Routes 301 and 4. The area encompasses approximately 77 square miles and is primarily residential with many neighborhoods and housing developments. The Patuxent River runs near Upper Marlboro and with it brings protected land for wildlife and recreation near the city.

Sights

★ MERKLE WILDLIFE SANCTUARY

The **Merkle Wildlife Sanctuary** (11704 Fenno Rd., 301/888-1377, www.dnr.state.md.us, daily sunrise to sunset, free) is the only wildlife sanctuary run by the Maryland Department of Natural Resources. It is best known as the wintering ground for the largest concentration of Canada geese on the western shore of the Chesapeake Bay. The sanctuary offers visitors a one-way, self-guided 4.3-mile Critical Area Driving Tour (CADT), open to cars on Sunday 10am-3pm year-round. The CADT is available to hikers, bikers, and horseback riders daily January 1 through September 30, but closed to these users the rest of the year in order to provide a peaceful area for the migrating geese and other waterfowl.

The **Frank Oslislo Visitors Center** (weekends 10am-4pm) sits on a hill overlooking several ponds. This beautiful building has a two-story wall of windows, balconies for viewing the surrounding area, and a large bird feeder viewing area. The center features exhibits on Canada geese and other wildlife and environmental topics. A live animal exhibit with turtles, snakes, and toads is also offered for children.

Four hiking trails at the sanctuary provide access to upland forests and marsh areas. The trails are only open to hikers, and weekly nature hikes are available.

Five fishing ponds are open to the public between April 1 and October 1 for largemouth bass, bluegill, and other types of fishing. Those planning to fish should sign in outside the visitors center.

Merkle Wildlife Sanctuary

PATUXENT RURAL LIFE MUSEUMS

The **Patuxent Rural Life Museums** (16000 Croom Airport Rd., 301/627-6074, http://history.pgparks.com, Apr.-Oct. Sat.-Sun. 1pm-4pm, free) comprises several museums and farm buildings that preserve the heritage of southern Prince George's County. The buildings are in the 7,000-acre **Patuxent River Park** and include a tool museum, a blacksmith shop, a tobacco farming museum, a log cabin (with a smokehouse), a 1923 Sears catalog house, and a hunting, fishing, and trapping museum. Exhibits are on display in the museums, and living-history demonstrations are featured. Guided tours of the museums are available all year by appointment (301/627-6074, $2). Guided nature tours ($2), river ecology boat tours (free), and archaeology presentations (free) are also available and take 45-60 minutes. All-day kayaking/canoeing tours can be scheduled for small groups (8:30am-3:30pm, $20 per person).

DARNALL'S CHANCE HOUSE MUSEUM

Darnall's Chance House Museum (14800 Governor Oden Bowie Dr., 301/952-8010, www.pgparks.com, guided house tours by appointment Tues.-Thurs. 10am-4pm, tours by walk-in Fri. and Sun. noon-4pm, $5) interprets the history and culture of Prince George's County women in the 18th century. The focus is on a longtime resident of the house, Lettice Lee, who lived there prior to the American Revolution. The home is listed in the National Register of Historic Places, the National Underground Railroad: Network to Freedom Trail, and the Star-Spangled Banner National Historic Trail. The home and grounds are portrayed as they were in 1760 when Lee's first husband passed away and the contents of the house were documented room by room. The museum also portrays the lives of the enslaved African American women who worked in the home, and tours address the similarities and differences between their lives and that of Lee.

A rare 17-foot-long burial vault was discovered at the museum in 1987. It contained household garbage from the 18th and 19th century as well as the remains of nine people (three adults and six children).

Recreation and Events

The **Prince George's Equestrian Center** (14900 Pennsylvania Ave., 301/952-7900) is the primary event venue in Upper Marlboro and includes numerous tracks, a schooling ring, and stables for more than 200 horses. The center hosts the annual **Prince George's County Fair** (www.countyfair.org) each September. The fair began in 1842 and is the longest-running fair in Maryland. Other popular events that take place at the center include antique shows and concerts. The center is also the site of the **Show Place Arena** (www.showplacearena.com), which hosts circuses, rodeos, hockey games, conventions, and trade shows.

Six Flags America (13710 Central Ave., 301/249-1500, www.sixflags.com, mid-May-Aug. daily, early May and Sept.-Oct. select weekends, $53 online and $63 at gate) is located between Upper Marlboro and Bowie (near Largo). This large theme park is the only one of its kind in Maryland and features more than 100 rides, a water park (Hurricane Harbor), shows, and other attractions. This is a fun place to bring the kids, but the park is a bit aged and it is not uncommon for some of the rides to be closed due to malfunctions. The park has eight roller coasters and new rides open seemingly every season. They also have specific rides for small kids. The park opens at 10:30am but closing times vary a lot throughout the season; check the website or call ahead for more information.

Watkins Regional Park (301 Watkins Park Dr., 301/218-6700, www.pgparks.com, daily dawn-dusk, free) is a great regional park with an antique carousel, train, nature center, tennis, camping, and miniature golf. The **Old Maryland Farm** (Tues.-Fri. 9am-4pm, Sat. 9am-4:30pm, Sun. 11:30am-4:30pm) is within the park (a short walk from the train station) and features agricultural exhibits, gardens, and live animals.

Food

Jasper's (9640 Lottsford Ct., Largo, 301/883-9500, www.jaspersrestaurants.com, Sun. 10am-midnight, Mon.-Thurs. 11:30am-1am, Fri.-Sat. 11:30am-2am, Sun. 10am-midnight, $7-24) offers seafood, steak, burgers, and sandwiches in an upscale and casual environment. This is a popular restaurant with good food. They are open late and are often very busy on weekends. The entire menu is available to go.

If you're in the mood for a neighborhood dive bar with good pizza, burgers, wings, and a friendly atmosphere, visit **Grizzly's** (9544 Crain Hwy., 301/599-0505, daily 11am-10pm, under $15) off Route 301 in the Marlton Shopping Center.

Accommodations

Upper Marlboro isn't known for its selection of good accommodations. Visitors may prefer to spend the night in neighboring Largo, northwest of Upper Marlboro, where there are a few choices such as the **Holiday Inn Express I-95 Beltway Largo** (9101 Basil Ct., 301/636-6090, www.hiexpress.com, $153-227), which has 89 rooms, an indoor pool, and a fitness center; or the **Hampton Inn Washington I-95, Largo** (9421 W. Largo Dr., 301/499-4600, www.hamptoninn3.hilton.com, $149-159), with 127 guest rooms, free breakfast, a fitness room, and free wireless Internet.

LANDOVER

Landover is a suburban area northwest of Upper Marlboro and Largo. It is 11 miles northeast of Washington DC and is best known as the home of the **Washington Redskins** professional football team. Their home field, **FedEx Field** (1600 FedEx Way, 301/276-6000, www.redskins.com) was built in 1994 and originally called Jack Kent Cooke Stadium after the former owner of the team. When the team was purchased by Daniel Snyder, FedEx Corporation purchased the naming rights. Although FedEx Field is the largest football stadium in terms of seating capacity in the NFL (with seating for 85,000), it sells out all non-premium tickets every year and has a season ticket waiting list of more than 30 years.

FedEx Field has its own exit from I-495 (the Beltway): 16 (Arena Drive).

GREENBELT

Greenbelt, seven miles north of Landover and 30 minutes from Washington DC, is home to **NASA's Goddard Space Flight Visitors Center** (8800 Greenbelt Rd., 301/286-8981, www.nasa.gov, Sept.-June Tues.-Fri. 10am-3pm, Sat.-Sun. noon-4pm, July-Aug. Tues.-Fri. 10am-5pm, Sat.-Sun. noon-4pm, free). The center is a wonderful place to learn about NASA's work in earth science, astrophysics, planetary science, technology development, and other projects. Unique interactive exhibits teach people of all ages about topics such as climate change and space exploration. Exhibits include *Frozen: Cold Matters,* where places on earth are featured where temperatures are generally below freezing all year; *Goddard Rocket Garden,* a collection of artifacts from space; and *Largest,* an exhibit on the planet Jupiter. Visitors can also experience monthly model rocket launches. This is a fun place for kids who are interested in space travel.

Greenbelt: A Planned City

Greenbelt was conceived as a New Deal housing project and will be forever known as the first planned community in the country to be built by the federal government. It was designed in 1935 as a complete city, including housing, businesses, schools, roads, government facilities, and recreational facilities. The city was an experiment in social and physical planning modeled after 19th-century English garden cities. It included one of the first mall shopping centers.

The name came from the area of green forests that surround the city and from the "belts" of natural areas between its neighborhoods that keep residents in contact with nature. Greenbelt is a National Historic Landmark.

BOWIE

Ten miles northeast of Landover is the city of Bowie. With a population of nearly 55,000, the city has blossomed from its beginnings as a small rail stop on the Baltimore & Potomac Railroad to the biggest municipality in the county.

Bowie was originally called Huntington City when it was founded in 1870. The original downtown area is now referred to as "Old Bowie," but some landmarks still bear the Huntington name.

Sights

BELAIR MANSION

The **Belair Mansion** (12207 Tulip Grove Dr., 301/809-3089, www.cityofbowie.org, Tues.-Sun. noon-4pm, free) is a Georgian plantation home that was built in 1745 for the provincial governor of Maryland, Samuel Ogle. In the early 1900s, the mansion became the residence of a noted Thoroughbred horse breeder named William Woodward. The home is listed in the National Register of Historic Places, and the museum interprets the lives of the people who lived there between 1747 and 1950. Visitors can see items such as family silver, a stunning colonial revival card table, paintings, and other artwork. The mansion's stables now operate as the **Belair Stable Museum** (2835 Belair Dr., 301/809-3089, www.cityofbowie.org, Tues.-Sun. noon-4pm, free). Although horse breeding began on the property in the 1740s, the current barn that houses the museum was built in 1907 as part of the Belair Stud Stable, one of the top breeding stables in the country from the 1920s to 1960. The only father/son horses to win the Triple Crown race series (Gallant Fox in 1930 and Omaha in 1935) were raised in the stable. The museum highlights the 200-year Thoroughbred-racing legacy of the Belair's bloodstock and explains other agricultural uses of the property. Both museums are operated by the city of Bowie.

BOWIE RAILROAD MUSEUM

The **Bowie Railroad Museum** (8614 Chestnut Ave., 301/809-3089, www.cityofbowie.org, Tues.-Sun. 10am-4pm, free) sits next to active train tracks at the no-longer-in-service Bowie Railroad Station. The museum features displays on the history of the railroad in Bowie and includes photographs and artifacts in three structures: a switch tower, a passenger waiting shed, and a freight depot. A caboose that dates back to 1922 and was part of the Norfolk and Western Railroad is on the museum grounds.

NATIONAL CAPITAL RADIO AND TELEVISION MUSEUM

Radio and television buffs will enjoy the **National Capital Radio and Television Museum** (2608 Mitchellville Rd., 301/390-1020, www.ncrtv.org, Fri. 10am-5pm, Sat.-Sun. 1pm-5pm, free). This small, two-story museum offers a tour back in time through the evolution of radio and television. There are displays of memorabilia and a large collection of antique receivers. Visitors can hear authentic radio broadcasts and view early television shows on vintage televisions.

Sports and Recreation

A great minor league baseball park (home of the Class AA Bowie Baysox) is **Prince George's Stadium** (4101 Crain Hwy., 301/805-6000, http://bowie.baysox.milb.com). This clean, friendly ballpark offers reasonably priced seats, free parking, and the opportunity to see up-and-coming Baltimore Orioles players.

A pleasant 85-acre, family-oriented park is **Allen Pond Park** (3330 Northview Dr., 301/809-3011, www.cityofbowie.org, daily sunrise to sunset). It has a pond, walking path, playground, skateboard ramp, indoor ice rink (Bowie Ice Arena), amphitheater, basketball courts, fields for baseball, lacrosse, and soccer, and more. The park hosts a great fireworks display each July Fourth.

Food

"Fresh, Casual, and Friendly," is the slogan of the **Chesapeake Grille & Deli** (6786 Race Track Rd., 301/262-4441, www.chesapeakegrille.com, breakfast Sat.-Sun. 8am-11am, lunch and dinner Sun.-Thurs. 11am-9pm, Fri.-Sat. 11am-10pm, $6-17), and they deliver with flavorful sandwiches, seafood, skewers, and steak. This is not a fancy place, but the family-owned restaurant offers good food and dependable service. They are open daily for lunch and dinner.

The only place to find the original "Crab Bomb" is **Jerry's Seafood** (15211 Major Lansdale Blvd., 301/805-2284, www.

the Belair Mansion

jerrysseafood.com, Mon.-Sat. 11:30am-10pm, Sun. noon-8pm, $27-40). This family-owned seafood house is known for its crab dishes (the trademarked Crab Bomb includes 10 ounces of jumbo lump crabmeat), but they also offer other types of seafood and several non-seafood dishes. This restaurant is also known for good service.

Accommodations

For short and extended stays, the **Towne Place Suites Bowie Town Center** (3700 Town Center Blvd., 301/262-8045, www.marriott.com, $154-164) is hard to beat. This Marriott hotel offers 119 suites on four floors, a fitness center, pool, and free on-site parking. The rooms are amply sized and clean. Pets are allowed for an additional fee. It is near shopping and restaurants.

The **Comfort Inn Conference Center** (4500 Crain Hwy., 301/464-0089, www.bowiemdhotel.com, $135-165) offers mini fridges, microwaves, and coffeemakers in each room, complimentary breakfast, and wireless Internet. On-site parking is available, and there is a restaurant and bar at the hotel. This is a good hotel for business travelers. The wireless connection is strong and stable, and the breakfast food is above average for a chain hotel.

Information and Services

For additional information on Bowie, visit www.cityofbowie.org or stop by the **Old Town Bowie Welcome Center** (8606 Chestnut Ave., 301/575-2488, Tues.-Sun. 10am-4pm).

COLLEGE PARK

College Park is 13 miles west of Bowie in the northwestern part of Prince George's County. The city has a population of around 30,000 and is best known as the location of the **University of Maryland, College Park.** The U.S. National Archives and Records Administration also has a facility in College Park known as Archives II.

Sights

UNIVERSITY OF MARYLAND, COLLEGE PARK

The **University of Maryland, College Park** (301/405-1000, www.umd.edu) was founded in 1856 as a public research university. It is the largest university in Maryland, with more than 37,000 students, and it offers more than 120 undergraduate majors and 110 graduate programs. On campus is a 150-acre research park that was honored as an Outstanding Research Park in 2015. The campus also features the Physical Science Complex, which is still in the process of being completed. The building encompasses more than 160,000 square feet and will be a space for collaborative efforts with nearby federal agencies, like NASA.

★ COLLEGE PARK AVIATION MUSEUM

The **College Park Aviation Museum** (1985 Corporal Frank Scott Dr., 301/864-6029, www.collegeparkaviationmuseum.com, daily 10am-5pm, $5) is a nice little museum that is affiliated with the Smithsonian Institution and focuses on the earliest days of mechanical flight. Many of the exhibits in the 27,000-square-foot space are geared toward children and offer a hands-on experience with coloring, video games, puzzles, a flight simulator, and a plane to climb on. There is also information on the Wright Brothers, who made a flight attempt nearby.

The museum is in an open 1.5-story exhibit space on the site of the world's oldest continuously operating airport. The airport opened in 1909 when Wilbur Wright gave flight instruction there to the inaugural group of military aviators in the first army aviation school. The airport has numerous other notable "firsts" in the aviation field, such as the first mile-high flight, the first bomb-dropping test, the first female passenger in the United States, and many more. Visitors can watch planes on the runway from the glass windows inside the museum.

This is a nice family museum, and the volunteers are friendly and informative. There are no food services at the museum, but visitors can picnic outside in nice weather.

Entertainment and Events

The **Clarice Smith Performing Arts Center** (3800 Clarice Smith Performing Arts Center at University Blvd. and Stadium Dr., 301/405-2787, www.theclarice.umd.edu) is part of the University of Maryland, College Park, and offers many free and reasonably priced events such as musical and theatrical performances, lectures, and workshops.

Food

Get the traditional diner experience at the **College Park Diner** (9206 Baltimore Ave., 301/441-8888, open 24/7, under $10). This great little place runs like a well-oiled machine. The breakfast food is the best choice (served all day), but the country-fried steak is also a winner. Patrons can watch their meal being cooked since the kitchen is at the front of the building. This is a good place to come when looking for a local establishment or a late-night eatery. The tables turn over quickly, the servers are friendly and helpful, and you may even be called "Hon."

Good, inexpensive pho can be found at **Pho D'Lite** (8147 Baltimore Ave., 301/982-5599, www.phodlite.com, daily 10:30am-9:30pm, $4-20). They offer good specials on weekday afternoons. Try their Thai iced tea.

Accommodations

There are a handful of national hotels in College Park. For the most part, they are fairly comparable with standard accommodations and conveniences. Three hotels that are convenient to the University of Maryland campus are the **Holiday Inn Washington College Park** (10000 Baltimore Ave., 301/345-6700, www.holidayinn.com, $106-130), which has 220 guest rooms on five floors and free wireless Internet; the **Hampton Inn College Park** (9670 Baltimore Ave., 301/345-2200, www.hamptoninn3.hilton.com, $159-179) with 80 guest rooms, free breakfast, free high-speed Internet, and a fitness room; and the **Best Western Plus College Park** (8419 Baltimore Ave., 301/220-0505, www.bestwestern.com, $130-145), with 40 guest rooms, complimentary full breakfast, a fitness center, and free Wi-Fi.

Information and Services

Additional information on College Park can be found at www.collegeparkmd.gov.

LAUREL

Laurel is 10 miles north of College Park in northern Prince George's County and also spills into Anne Arundel and Howard Counties. It was originally developed as a mill town, its cotton mills utilizing the power of the Patuxent River. It has a population of around 25,000.

Sights

DINOSAUR PARK

You may be surprised to learn that one of the most important dinosaur sites east of the Mississippi River is in Laurel. Most people rush past the site on Route 1 and never have a clue of what lies nearby. At **Dinosaur Park** (13201 Mid-Atlantic Blvd., 301/627-7755, http://history.pgparks.com, daily dawn-dusk, free), rare fossil deposits from the Early Cretaceous period include those from several types of dinosaurs (including *Astrodon johnstoni*), early mammals, and early plants and trees. What makes this location special is that it is part of an exposed layer of the Muirkirk Deposit, a rare fossil-bearing clay found on the East Coast. The park was created to preserve and protect the rare fossil deposits, to provide a natural laboratory for scientists to discover new fossils, and to allow the public the opportunity to work with paleontologists to uncover new findings. The public is welcome to explore an interpretive garden that is open daily and features descriptions of the prehistoric landscape in Maryland and

Maryland's State Dinosaur

Dinosaur bones were found in Maryland as early as the late 1800s. The first dinosaur remains discovered in Maryland were that of a long-necked plant-eater named *Astrodon johnstoni* (think "vegiesaur" from the movie *Jurassic Park*). Astrodon was gigantic (at least 60 feet long) and weighed several tons. One femur was found in the 1990s that weighed 220 pounds and was six feet long. The name Astrodon came from a starburst pattern found in a cross section of the dinosaur's teeth. The species name *johnstoni,* was added later in honor of a Maryland Academy of Sciences dentist, Christopher Johnson, who played a significant role in its identification.

In 1998, the Maryland State Assembly officially designated *Astrodon johnstoni* the official state dinosaur. Only six states (Maryland, Colorado, Wyoming, Missouri, New Jersey, and Texas) and the District of Columbia have official dinosaurs.

the dinosaurs that lived there. A fenced-in fossil area is only accessible during featured programs and during open houses held on the first and third Saturday of each month noon-4pm.

NATIONAL WILDLIFE VISITOR CENTER

The **National Wildlife Visitor Center** (10901 Scarlet Tanager Loop, 301/497-5770, www.fws.gov, daily 9am-4:30pm, free) is a U.S. Fish and Wildlife Service facility that sits on more than 12,000 acres in the **Patuxent Research Refuge.** The center is the largest science and environmental education center within the U.S. Department of the Interior. The center features interactive exhibits that teach the value of wildlife research and also focus on worldwide environmental issues. They also explore migratory bird routes, wildlife habitat, and recovery efforts for endangered species. There are countless opportunities for recreation in the surrounding forests, lakes, and trails.

MONTPELIER MANSION

The **Montpelier Mansion** (9650 Muirkirk Rd., 301/377-7817, www.pgparks.com/parks_and_rec_home.htm, Thurs.-Tues. 11am-3pm, $5) is a Georgian-style mansion that was built in the 1780s for Major Thomas Snowden and his wife. Many noteworthy guests were entertained in the home, including George Washington. The home sits on 70 acres and is a National Historic Landmark. Several rooms in the mansion were refurbished to appear as they did at the close of the 18th century. Both guided and self-guided tours of the home are available. Montpelier Mansion hosts many concerts, festivals, and seminars.

Entertainment and Events

The **Venus Theatre** (21 C St., 202/236-4078, venustheatre.org) is a regional theater with the largest production company in Maryland. Their focus is on the adaptation of classics.

The **Laurel Mill Playhouse** (508 Main St., 301/617-9906, www.laurelmillplayhouse.org) is a local playhouse that is home to the Burtonsville Players, a community theater group that has been around for more than 35 years.

Sports and Recreation

The **Laurel Park Racecourse** (Route 198 and Racetrack Rd., 301/725-0400, www.laurelpark.com) is a Thoroughbred racetrack that opened in 1911. The track has hosted legendary horses such as War Admiral and Secretariat. Races are still held there regularly and a schedule can be found on the website.

The **Fairland Sports and Aquatics Complex** (13820 and 13950 Old Gunpowder Rd., 301/362-6060, www. Rosa Mexicanoparks.com) is part of the **Fairland Regional Park.** The complex includes facilities for swimming, tennis, racquetball, gymnastics, weightlifting, and massage therapy.

The **Gardens Ice House** also within the park offers three ice rinks for skating, hockey, curling, and speed skating.

Food

The **Dutch Country Farmers Market** (9701 Fort Meade Rd., 301/421-1454, www.burtonsvilledutchmarket.com, Thurs. 9am-6pm, Fri. 9am-8pm, Sat. 8am-3pm) is a wonderful market that's open three days a week. Stop in and enjoy the smell of fresh-baked pies and other delectables. There is a good variety of food to purchase including meat, fresh produce, homemade soup, smoothies, and bread. There is also a nice restaurant on-site that serves simple but tasty food and has good service.

Accommodations

Like much of Prince George's County, Laurel primarily offers national chain hotel accommodations. One worth considering is the **Hampton Inn Laurel** (7900 Braygreen Rd., 240/456-0234, www.hamptoninn3.hilton.com, $154-169). It provides 80 guest rooms with strong, free wireless Internet service and complimentary breakfast.

The **Double Tree by Hilton Laurel** (15101 Sweitzer Ln., 301/776-5300, www.doubletreelaurel.com, $159-179) has 208 guest rooms on six floors, a fitness center, and wireless Internet. There's a restaurant on-site.

The **Holiday Inn Express Laurel** (14402 Laurel Pl., 301/206-2600, www.ihg.com, $122-149) has 117 suites, offers complimentary breakfast, is pet friendly, and has free high-speed Internet access, an indoor pool, and a fitness center. Guest laundry services are also available.

Information and Services

For additional information on Laurel, visit www.cityoflaurel.org.

Baltimore

Baltimore has been a major port city since the 1700s. The hardworking city is the birthplace of many industries: the first sugar refinery in the country (1796), the first gaslight company (1819), and the first railroad for commercial transportation (1828). Having spent much of its history as a rough industrial seaport, Baltimore managed to keep its treasures to itself. In the 1970s, outsiders started to recognize the city's hidden charm, and the working-class town was nicknamed "Charm City." Today, after a series of successful urban renewal projects, Baltimore has blossomed into a major mid-Atlantic tourist destination. It flaunts world-class museums, state-of-the-art sports venues, fine dining, and luxury hotels—all while retaining its fierce spirit and authenticity.

ORIENTATION

For simplicity's sake, we're going to focus on six primary sections of Baltimore. They are key areas where popular sights are located, as well as trendy neighborhoods where you can find a delightful selection of food, nightlife, and activities.

Downtown and the Inner Harbor

Most of the beauty shots of Baltimore are taken downtown and at the Inner Harbor. The harbor has long been the center of activity in this port city and was once a thriving destination for visitors and supplies arriving by steamship. Although most people think that Baltimore sits on the Chesapeake Bay, the harbor is actually the mouth of the Patapsco River. The river flows into the bay east of the city, which is why this deepwater yet protected harbor has been popular for centuries. After the collapse of the steamship era, the port still saw industrial action, but lapsed into a state of neglect as the city fell off the radar as a vacation destination.

In the 1970s interest in the city was revived as Baltimore underwent extensive innovative redevelopment. The Inner Harbor benefited greatly from the rejuvenation and

Previous: the view from Federal Hill Park; row houses on Federal Hill. **Above:** the Washington Monument and Museum at Mount Vernon Place.

Look for ★ to find recommended sights, activities, dining, and lodging.

Highlights

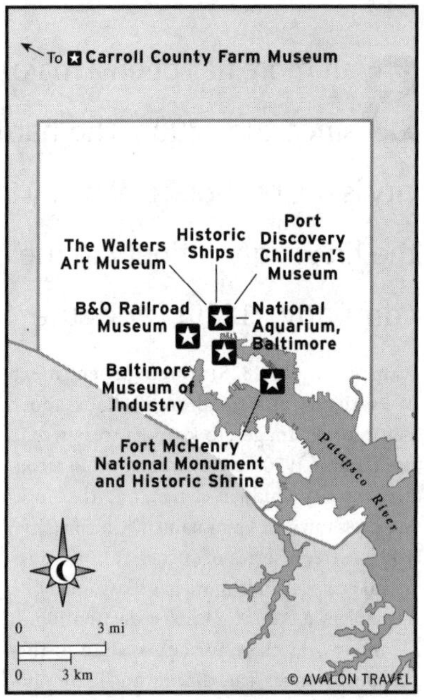

★ **National Aquarium, Baltimore:** The gem of the Inner Harbor, the National Aquarium offers close encounters with sharks, dolphins, and many other sea creatures. Catch a show or sign up for a special slumber party; there's no shortage of awe-inspiring exhibits and activities (page 382).

★ **Historic Ships:** This unique collection on display in the Inner Harbor features four military ships and one lighthouse within easy walking distance of each other (page 384).

★ **Port Discovery Children's Museum:** One of the top children's museums in the country, this educational playground offers three floors of interactive exhibits (page 386).

★ **B&O Railroad Museum:** See the birthplace of the American railroad system and learn about its development in Baltimore. Vintage engines and cars are part of the fun (page 388).

★ **Baltimore Museum of Industry:** Baltimore is the home of many manufacturing firsts. This fascinating museum shares the history of many everyday conveniences (page 393).

★ **Fort McHenry National Monument and Historic Shrine:** This fort dating back to 1802 inspired the poem written by Francis Scott Key that became the U.S. national anthem (page 395).

★ **The Walters Art Museum:** This remarkable collection of 5,000 pieces of work spans 5,000 years and includes a mummy from 1000 BC and two imperial eggs (page 396).

★ **Carroll County Farm Museum:** Glimpse what rural life in the mid-19th century was like on a 142-acre farm (page 429).

Baltimore

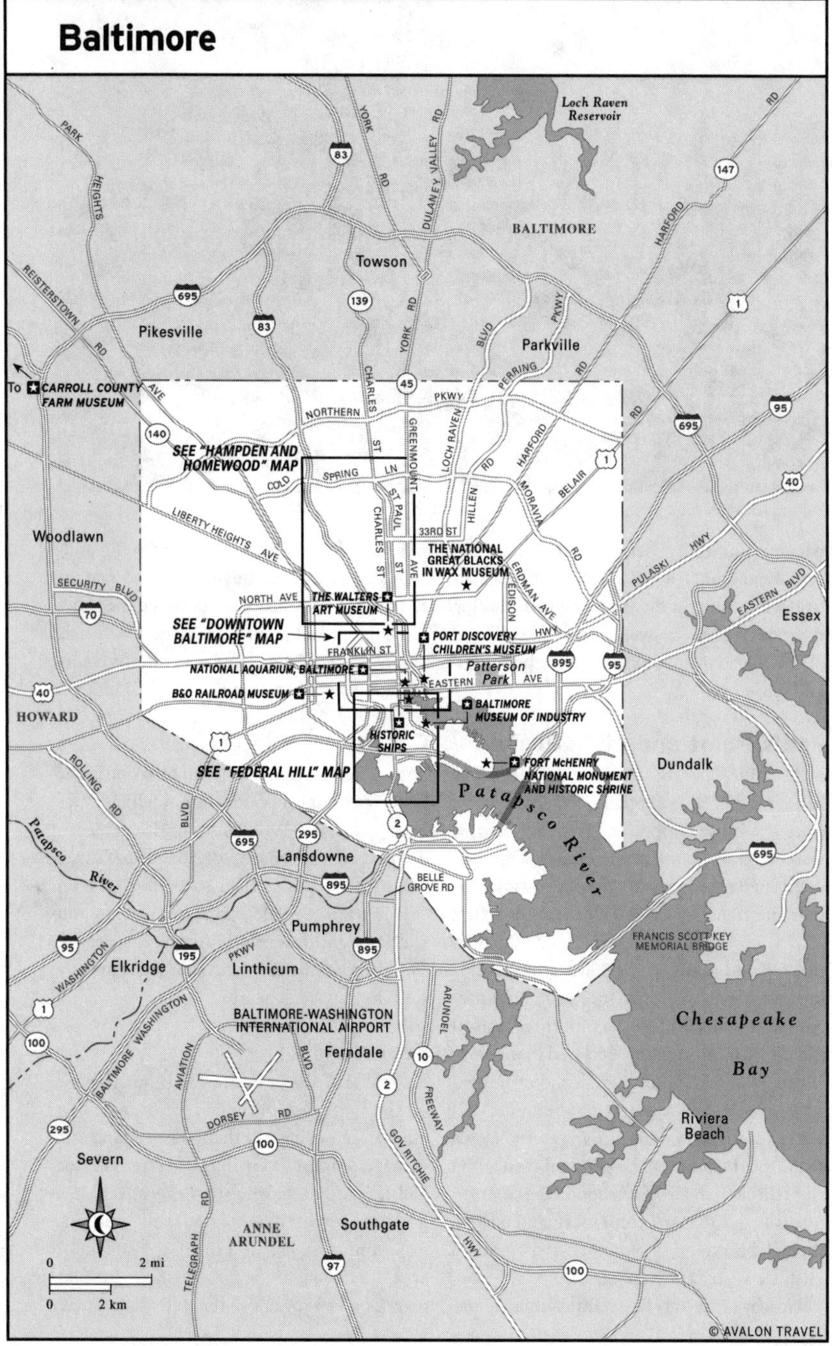
Loch Raven Reservoir
BALTIMORE
Towson
Pikesville
Parkville
To CARROLL COUNTY FARM MUSEUM
SEE "HAMPDEN AND HOMEWOOD" MAP
Woodlawn
THE NATIONAL GREAT BLACKS IN WAX MUSEUM
THE WALTERS ART MUSEUM
SEE "DOWNTOWN BALTIMORE" MAP
PORT DISCOVERY CHILDREN'S MUSEUM
NATIONAL AQUARIUM, BALTIMORE
Patterson Park
B&O RAILROAD MUSEUM
BALTIMORE MUSEUM OF INDUSTRY
HOWARD
HISTORIC SHIPS
SEE "FEDERAL HILL" MAP
FORT McHENRY NATIONAL MONUMENT AND HISTORIC SHRINE
Essex
Dundalk
Patapsco River
Lansdowne
BELLE GROVE RD
Pumphrey
FRANCIS SCOTT KEY MEMORIAL BRIDGE
Elkridge
Linthicum
BALTIMORE-WASHINGTON INTERNATIONAL AIRPORT
Ferndale
Chesapeake Bay
Riviera Beach
Severn
ANNE ARUNDEL
Southgate
0 2 mi
0 2 km
© AVALON TRAVEL

Baltimore's Inner Harbor

became home to many attractions, museums, restaurants, upscale hotels, and a beautiful waterfront promenade. The surrounding downtown area received a boost as well and offers a blend of businesses, historic buildings, and museums.

Fell's Point and Little Italy

Fell's Point is on the harbor to the east of the Inner Harbor. It is about a five-minute drive from the Inner Harbor or can be reached by water taxi. It is one of the oldest neighborhoods in Baltimore, with many historic buildings and trendy eateries. Fell's Point was first settled by William Fell, an English Quaker, in 1726 and many of the 350 historic buildings were constructed before 1800 (200 predate the Civil War). Fell's Point thrived until the need for sailing ships declined in the early 1900s, after which the neighborhood entered a steep decline. The waterfront became a collection of rough saloons, and in the mid-1960s plans for the building of I-95 had it running right through the neighborhood. The community was able to stop the highway, and instead the neighborhood became the first National Historic District in Maryland.

Nearby Little Italy (www.littleitalymd.com) was settled by Italian immigrants in the mid-1800s, who opened businesses and restaurants in the cozy little area between the Inner Harbor and Fell's Point. The area now boasts almost 30 restaurants and also offers visitors vibrant festivals and a bit of old-world Italy.

Canton

East of Fell's Point on the waterfront is the historic community of Canton, which dates back to the late 19th century. Modern condos and old row houses fuse Baltimore's past and present, and lively **Canton Square** on O'Donnell Street offers bars, restaurants, and endless nightlife for the local partying crowd. The Canton waterfront includes views of navy ships as they dock nearby.

Federal Hill

Federal Hill sits opposite the Inner Harbor on the south side of the harbor. It is named after an imposing hill that boasts a fantastic vantage point for viewing the Inner Harbor and downtown Baltimore. Federal Hill has great shopping, bars, restaurants, and entertainment as well as a thriving residential area. It is home to the famed 120-by-70-foot neon Domino Sugar sign that casts a glow over

Little Italy

the city from its 160-foot perch. The sign is a Baltimore icon and has been a fixture in the harbor since 1951.

Mount Vernon

Mount Vernon, north of downtown Baltimore, is the cultural center of the city. Museums and halls provide endless opportunities to take in a show or listen to the symphony. The neighborhood is full of grand 19th-century architecture, and marble-clad homes originally built for wealthy sea captains surround the first monument to honor our first president.

Hampden and Homewood

Northwest of Mount Vernon is the settlement of Hampden. This 19th-century neighborhood was originally a mill town but is now an eclectic mix of bars, restaurants, thrift stores, galleries, and boutiques. The local residents are both hardworking families and young adults, which gives the area a hip yet grounded feel. To the east of Hampden is the neighborhood of Homewood. Homewood is best known as the home of **Johns Hopkins University,** but it also has nice parks and museums.

PLANNING YOUR TIME

You could easily spend a couple of weeks in Baltimore to really see all the city has to offer, but most people pick and choose sights of particular interest to them and explore the city in a long weekend.

People traveling with children may wish to stay at the Inner Harbor so they can visit the **National Aquarium,** the **Maryland Science Center,** and the **Port Discovery Children's Museum,** and see the **Historic Ships** in the harbor. A visit to **Fort McHenry** is another fun option to pique the little ones' interest in history.

History buffs can pick almost any location in the city as their base and from there take in the **Baltimore Civil War Museum,** the **Star-Spangled Banner Flag House and Museum,** the **Washington Monument, Fort McHenry,** and Edgar Allan Poe's grave site at **Westminster Hall Burying Ground & Catacomb.**

Others come to sample the many restaurants and bars in the busy Fell's Point area or to take in a ball game at Camden Yards. No matter what your interests, there is no shortage of exciting itineraries to create. Baltimore is easy to get around and offers many exciting

Best of Baltimore

DAY 1

Start in the popular **Inner Harbor,** where you can get around on foot and visit the **National Aquarium** and the **Historic Ships** collection. Choose one of the restaurants in the busy harbor area for lunch before driving or taking the water taxi to the **Fort McHenry National Monument,** where Baltimore fended off a British attack during the War of 1812 and Francis Scott Key penned "The Star-Spangled Banner." Jump back on the water taxi or drive over to **Fell's Point** for exploration of its charming waterfront streets before having dinner at the **Red Star Bar and Grill.** End your evening at the cozy **Cat's Eye Pub** for some blues, jazz, or folk music, and then turn in for the night at the **Inn at Henderson's Wharf.**

DAY 2

Start your day with breakfast at the popular **Blue Moon Café.** After breakfast, drive or take a cab to the Mount Vernon neighborhood and visit the **Walters Art Museum,** then climb the 228 stairs of the **Washington Monument** for a great view of the city. Grab some pizza at **Joe Squared,** then continue your cultural tour at the **Baltimore Museum of Art** in Homewood. Have dinner at **Woodberry Kitchen** just west of Hampden and finish in time to take in a performance at **Centerstage** in Mount Vernon. Finish up your two-day tour with a drink and a wonderful view of the city at the classy **13th Floor** in the historic Belvedere Hotel building.

sights and activities regardless of how long you have to spend there.

If you have time for a full- or half-day excursion from Baltimore, consider putting Westminster or Havre de Grace on your list of places to visit. Westminster, 45 minutes northwest of Baltimore by car, sits in a rural part of the state and has a history of Civil War battles, spies, and ghosts. An hour car ride north on I-95 will take you to the bayside town of Havre de Grace. Its charming seaside atmosphere at the head of the Chesapeake Bay makes the town a rewarding destination for touring and outdoor recreation.

Sights

DOWNTOWN AND THE INNER HARBOR

★ National Aquarium, Baltimore

The **National Aquarium, Baltimore** (501 E. Pratt St., 410/576-3800, www.aqua.org, Mon.-Thurs. 9am-5pm, Fri.-Sat. 9am-8pm, Sun. 9am-6pm, $39.95) is perhaps the most treasured sight in Baltimore's Inner Harbor. Opening in 1981, it was the anchor venue to the redevelopment plan of the Inner Harbor. The aquarium was one of the first large aquariums in the country and remained independent until it joined with the National Aquarium in Washington DC under the blanket name "National Aquarium" in 2003.

Close to 20,000 animals live at the National Aquarium, representing more than 660 species of fish, amphibians, reptiles, birds, and mammals. See the brilliant coral-filled Blacktip Reef exhibit, which mimics Indo-Pacific reefs and offers stunning floor-to-ceiling "pop-out" viewing windows so visitors can get personal with 65 species of animals. Then watch fearsome sharks swim by in their 225,000-gallon ring-shaped tank in Shark Alley, or see divers feed brightly colored fish as you descend the winding ramp through the

Downtown Baltimore and the Inner Harbor

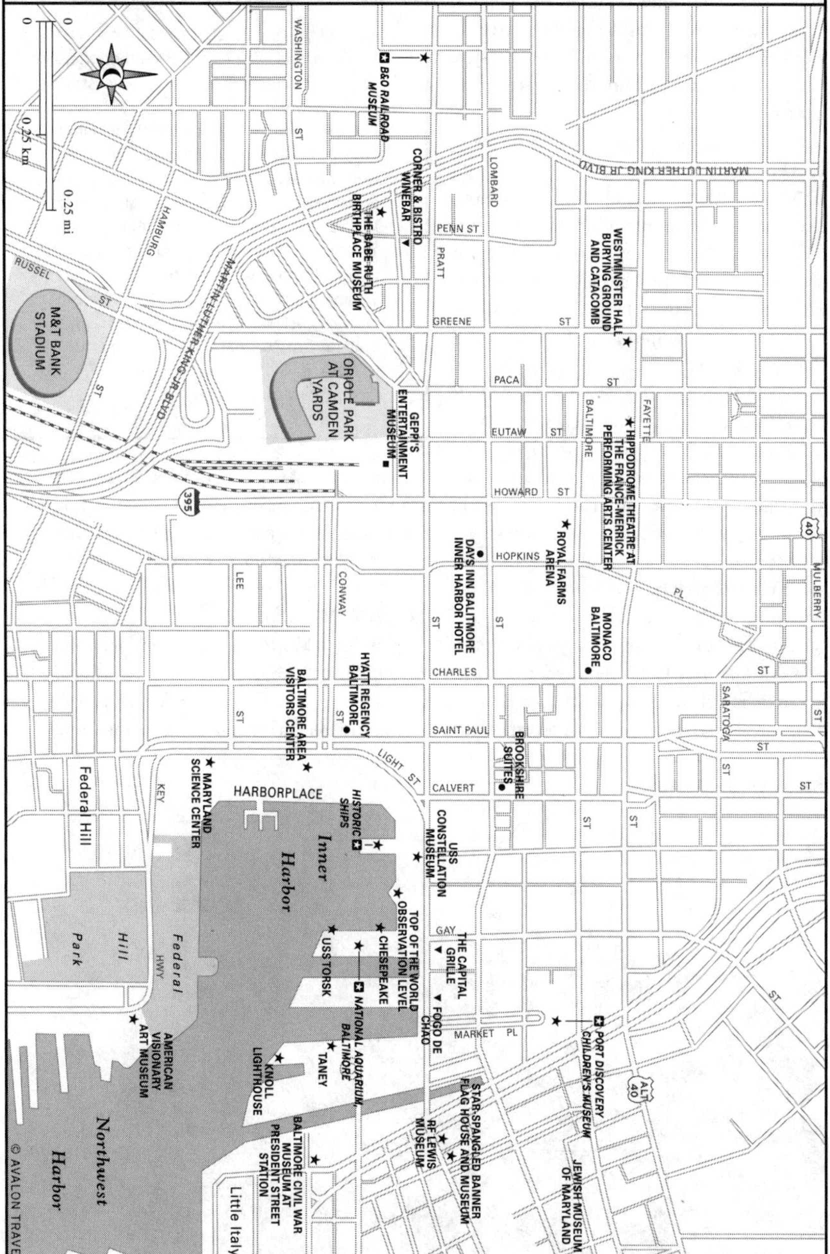

0
0
0.25 km
0.25 mi

WASHINGTON ST
B&O RAILROAD MUSEUM
CORNER & BISTRO WINEBAR
THE BABE RUTH BIRTHPLACE MUSEUM
HAMBURG
RUSSEL ST
M&T BANK STADIUM
MARTIN LUTHER KING JR BLVD
ORIOLE PARK AT CAMDEN YARDS
GEPPI'S ENTERTAINMENT MUSEUM
395
LOMBARD
PENN ST
PRATT
GREENE ST
PACA ST
EUTAW ST
HOWARD ST
HOPKINS PL
DAYS INN BALTIMORE INNER HARBOR HOTEL
ROYAL FARMS ARENA
WESTMINSTER HALL BURYING GROUND AND CATACOMB
HIPPODROME THEATRE AT THE FRANCE-MERRICK PERFORMING ARTS CENTER
BALTIMORE
FAYETTE
40
MULBERRY
MONACO BALTIMORE
SARATOGA ST
LEE ST
CONWAY ST
CHARLES ST
SAINT PAUL ST
HYATT REGENCY BALTIMORE
BALTIMORE AREA VISITORS CENTER
LIGHT ST
BROOKSHIRE SUITES
CALVERT ST
ST
KEY HWY
MARYLAND SCIENCE CENTER
HARBORPLACE
HISTORIC SHIPS
USS CONSTELLATION MUSEUM
Inner Harbor
Federal Hill
Federal Hill Park
TOP OF THE WORLD OBSERVATION LEVEL
GAY ST
CHESEPEAKE
USS TORSK
NATIONAL AQUARIUM, BALTIMORE
THE CAPITAL GRILLE
FOGO DE CHAO
MARKET PL
PORT DISCOVERY CHILDREN'S MUSEUM
TANEY
KNOLL LIGHTHOUSE
AMERICAN VISIONARY ART MUSEUM
ALT 40
STAR-SPANGLED BANNER FLAG HOUSE AND MUSEUM
RF LEWIS MUSEUM
JEWISH MUSEUM OF MARYLAND
BALTIMORE CIVIL WAR MUSEUM AT PRESIDENT STREET STATION
Northwest Harbor
Little Italy

13-foot-deep tropical reef tank in the Atlantic Coral Reef exhibit. Another breathtaking experience can be found in the Upland Tropical Rain Forest. This world-renowned exhibit expertly mimics a real rain forest with live tropical birds, sloths, tamarin monkeys, and even poison dart frogs. A diverse selection of authentic rain forest plant life is also part of this habitat.

The aquarium's award-winning habitats are expertly designed and instantly engage visitors by drawing them into the world of the animals they feature. They also offer demonstrations such as the Dolphin Discovery where visitors can see dolphins feeding, training, and enjoying playtime.

4-D Immersion films ($5) are shown at the aquarium, and behind-the-scenes tours ($15-220) are available. Overnight dolphin and shark sleepovers, in which guests can spend the night at the aquarium ($115), are two of the more popular activities. Reservations for all the behind-the-scenes activities should be purchased well in advance. Tickets to the aquarium are issued on a timed-entry system (allow at least three hours for your visit), so you can purchase tickets online for the time you'd like to visit. The aquarium is a popular attraction year-round, but can be especially crowded during the hot summer days when school is out of session. Try to avoid this time if your schedule allows for it, or visit late in the day after the crowds have thinned out.

Harbor Pass

Many of the popular sights in Baltimore can be accessed with a single ticket that offers discounted entry over individual admission prices. A four-day **Harbor Pass** (877/225-8466, www.baltimore.org, $53.95) includes admission over four consecutive days into four top attractions. Different options are available for the pass, but all include visitation to the National Aquarium and the Top of the World (Observation Level), plus two additional museums such as the Port Discovery Children's Museum, the American Visionary Art Museum, the Reginald F. Lewis Museum of Maryland African American History & Culture, and the Babe Ruth Birthplace Museum.

★ Historic Ships

The **Historic Ships** (Inner Harbor Piers, 301 E. Pratt St., 410/539-1797, www.historicships.org, one ship $11, two ships $15, four ships $18, lighthouse free) in the Inner Harbor form one

National Aquarium, Baltimore

USS *Constellation*

of the most impressive military ship collections in the world. Visitors can not only see four ships and a lighthouse (all within easy walking distance of one another), but also 50,000 photographs, documents, and personal items that relate to the ships. Hours vary between ships and days, but all are open daily March-December (the *Taney* and lighthouse are closed Mon.-Thurs. Jan.-Feb.) 10am-3:30pm at a minimum, with longer hours in the summer months.

The first, the **USS *Constellation*** (Pier 1), was a sloop-of-war ship from 1854 to 1955. The USS *Constellation* was the last all-sail ship built by the U.S. Navy, and it was the flagship of the U.S. African Squadron 1859-1861. Visitors can begin their tour in the museum gallery at the pier to learn about the ship's history through artifacts and personal items that once belonged to the crew. From there, grab a complimentary audio tour wand and go aboard. The "Plan of the Day" will be posted with a list of activities taking place on the day of your visit. If you're lucky, you may get to witness the live firing of the Parrott rifle. Uniformed crew members are on board to answer questions as you explore the ship's four decks.

The second, the submarine **USS *Torsk*** (Pier 3), is the most exciting to visit. It was commissioned in 1944 and was one of just 10 Tench Class submarines to serve in World War II. Visitors can tour the entire boat including the torpedo rooms, operation station, engine room, crew quarters, and navigation station. It is difficult and unnerving to believe that more than 80 navy personnel lived aboard the sub at one time.

The third ship is the lightship ***Chesapeake*** (Pier 3), built in 1930. A lightship is a ship that is moored on a permanent or semipermanent basis and has beacons mounted to it. It is used as a navigational aid. Lightship duty meant long days sitting in place on the water and scary times riding out storms. Visitors can see a unique exhibit on sailors' canine companions.

The fourth ship is the USCG cutter ***Taney*** (Pier 5), built in 1935. A cutter is defined as a Coast Guard ship that is over 65 feet in length and has accommodations for a crew to live aboard. Visitors can tour this authentic cutter that was decommissioned in 1986 and remains pretty much the same as it was when in use.

The **Knoll Lighthouse** (Pier 5), which stands at 40 feet, is one of the oldest Chesapeake Bay-area lighthouses and was erected at the mouth of the Patapsco River on a shallow shoal known as Seven Foot Knoll. It offers a detailed exhibit on how the lighthouse was built back in 1856.

Guided walking group tours of the USS *Constellation* ($14) are available for groups of 10 or more people over age six. Tours include museum admission, presentations, hands-on activities, and a Civil War-era sailor as your guide through the ship. Powder Monkey Tours are offered to children over six. These interactive tours teach the little ones about the young boys (ages 11-18) who served on fighting ships during the Civil War and were responsible for moving gunpowder from the powder magazine of the ship to the artillery pieces. Powder Monkey Tours are available every Saturday and Sunday at 1pm.

The Babe Ruth Birthplace Museum

The Babe Ruth Birthplace Museum (216 Emory St., 410/727-1539, www.baberuthmuseum.com, daily 10am-5pm, closed Mondays Sept.-Mar., $7) is located three blocks west from Oriole Park at Camden Yards. It is inside the home where Babe Ruth was born in 1895 (you can even visit the bedroom where he first entered the world). From the west side of the stadium, look down and follow the 60 painted baseballs on the sidewalk, which will lead you to the museum. Babe Ruth memorabilia is on display in the museum, and visitors can learn little-known information on this legend's private life. The museum also screens a film on the Star-Spangled Banner and has a courtyard for events.

★ Port Discovery Children's Museum

The **Port Discovery Children's Museum** (35 Market Pl., 410/727-8120, www.portdiscovery.org, Memorial Day-Labor Day Mon.-Sat. 10am-5pm, Sun. noon-5pm, shorter hours the rest of the year, $14.95) is one of the top five children's museums in the country and is geared toward children up to age 10. The museum offers three floors of interactive exhibits with the goal of connecting learning and play. Exhibits focus on art, science, and health.

Interactive exhibits draw children into a learning adventure. The Adventure Expeditions area is "part physical adventure and part mental obstacle course," in which children decipher hieroglyphics, look for clues, and are eventually led to a lost pharaoh tomb in Egypt. Another fully interactive exhibit is Kick It Up, an indoor soccer and games stadium. In the stadium, children either play soccer or get involved in interactive, electronic games during which they can compete in a dance competition, ride a bike, and sharpen their balance. Kids and adults can enjoy the KidWorks exhibit together, which is a three-story urban treehouse with rope bridges, slides, and many other exciting surprises. Toddlers (age 2 and up) can "cook" and serve their parents food in Tiny's Diner, a realistic 1950s-style diner.

The museum is geared completely toward children, so adults can take pleasure in the joy on their little ones' faces, but shouldn't expect a lot of exhibits that will capture their own interests. Also, children are free to run through the halls and explore the many fun and entertaining exhibits, so things can get a bit chaotic on busy days. Sneakers are the recommended footwear in order to participate in all the activities. The museum is just north of the Inner Harbor. It gets crowded in the summertime, so going early or late in the day is a good option.

Maryland Science Center

The **Maryland Science Center** (601 Light St., 410/685-2370, www.mdsci.org, Sat.-Thurs. 10am-6pm, Fri. 10am-8pm, shorter hours in winter, $20.95) is a great place to bring the kids for a hands-on learning experience. The Dinosaur Mysteries exhibit is a must-see and will amaze the little ones with life-size models of prehistoric creatures. Your Body: The Inside Story takes kids on an adventure to learn what happens inside a human body in a 24-hour period. In this unique exhibit, visitors can go inside a heart and lungs and feel the heart beat and the lungs breathe. They can also hear a loud concert of digestive noises and interact with germs. Other exhibits include topics such as animal rescue, life on other planets, and a kids' room for children under eight. Other features in the center include Science Encounters, where visitors can see animated data projected on a sphere, or look at the night sky through a telescope in the on-site observatory (free on Fri. nights). There are also a planetarium and an IMAX theater on-site.

The Poe Toaster

Edgar Allan Poe was one of Baltimore's most famous and mysterious citizens. He led a life of tragedy plagued by poverty, illness, and death. Poe was born in 1809 in Boston. The grandson of a Revolutionary War patriot, David Poe Sr., Edgar Allan Poe was orphaned at the age of three. Although he went to live with the Allan family in Richmond, he was never legally adopted and never really accepted fully into the family.

Poe enlisted in the army and after his discharge came to Baltimore to live with his widowed aunt in the neighborhood now known as Little Italy. He left for a brief time to attend West Point, but returned to live with his aunt and a few other family members again, although this time in West Baltimore on Amity Street. It was while here that Poe began writing short stories (prior to that time he had focused primarily on poetry).

Poe was awarded a $50 prize by a Baltimore newspaper for his short story, "MS Found in a Bottle." Many short stories followed including "Berenice," which caused a stir for being too gruesome. In 1835 Poe returned to Richmond. The following year, he married his 13-year-old cousin, Virginia, in Richmond.

In 1847, Virginia died of tuberculosis. Poe only lived another two years before dying a mysterious death back in Baltimore and was buried with his wife and aunt in **Westminster Hall Burying Ground & Catacomb** (519 W. Fayette St., 410/706-2072, www.westminsterhall.org, daily 8am-dusk, free).

The author is still shrouded in mystery, even after death: For 60 years (1949-2009), an unidentified visitor made a yearly trip to Poe's grave in the early hours on his birthday. The visitor was called the "Poe Toaster" because he made a toast of cognac to the grave and left three roses. Although he ended his visits in 2009 for reasons unknown, the Toaster had such an influence that the tradition was resurrected in 2016 with a new Toaster as part of a staged daytime event.

The **Edgar Allan Poe House & Museum** (203 N. Amity St., 410/462-1763, www.poeinbaltimore.org, June-Dec. Sat.-Sun. 11am-4pm, $5) is the house Poe lived in for a short time in West Baltimore. The house itself, which is a 2.5-story, five-room brick duplex (now part of a line of row houses) is the primary attraction of the museum. A few of Poe's personal items including a telescope are featured in the home. The immediate surrounding area is not recommended for sightseeing for safety reasons.

Geppi's Entertainment Museum

Geppi's Entertainment Museum (301 W. Camden St., 410/625-7060, www.geppismuseum.com, Tues.-Sun. 10am-6pm, $10) is a privately owned museum featuring rare collections of American pop culture. The museum showcases a timeline of popular culture and its history in America. Some of the best comic books, cartoons, and memorabilia dating back to the colonial period can be viewed along with posters from 20th-century movies. The museum is in the same building as the Sports Legends Museum at Camden Yards.

Top of the World

For the best view of Baltimore, visit the **Top of the World** (401 E. Pratt St., 410/837-8439, www.viewbaltimore.org, June-Sept. Mon.-Thurs. 10am-6pm, Fri.-Sat. 10am-7pm, Sun. 11am-6pm, reduced hours the rest of the year, $6) on the 27th floor of **Baltimore's World Trade Center.** The Top of the World is a 360-degree observation area with a spectacular view of the city skyline, the harbor, and surrounding areas through expansive windows. Stationary binoculars and photo map guides are available. Visitors are subject to manual searches of personal belongings.

★ B&O Railroad Museum

The **B&O Railroad Museum** (901 W. Pratt St., 410/752-2490, www.borail.org, Mon.-Sat. 10am-4pm, Sun. 11am-4pm, $18) is a National Historic Landmark and the birthplace of the American railroad system. The Baltimore & Ohio Railroad (yes, the one on the Monopoly game board) originated on Pratt Street in Baltimore in 1828. The facility was a station and repair shop that took up 100 acres. Visitors can go inside the 123-foot-tall roundhouse built in the early 1870s that was the turn-around area for large steam engines (they rolled onto a large turntable to reposition). The roundhouse is now a museum for historic train cars. Museumgoers can look at the cars and also take a short ride on the original rail tracks. An exhibition space called the Annex Gallery displays railroad-related artifacts from the museum's collection and those of other institutions such as the Smithsonian. The gallery features small objects such as lanterns, dining car china, tools, fine art, and clocks. Displays on the B&O Railroad's critical role in the Civil War show how the railroad changed the tactics for war and tells personal stories of the people who kept the railroad running during the conflict.

Westminster Hall Burying Ground & Catacombs

What came first, the church or the cemetery? In the case of the **Westminster Hall Burying Ground & Catacombs** (519 W. Fayette St., 410/706-2072, www.westminsterhall.org, daily 8am-dusk, free), the answer is the cemetery by more than 65 years. The cemetery was first used in 1786. Many famous Baltimore residents are interred in the burying ground including Edgar Allan Poe (who was actually buried there twice—his coffin was relocated from his family plot to its current spot near the cemetery gate), General James McHenry, and Francis Scott Key's son, Philip Barton Key. Westminster Hall was built in 1852, at the intersection of Fayette and Greene Streets. The church was constructed above some of the graves on top of brick piers. The result was the creation of catacombs under the church, which visitors can tour. The outside burying ground, where Poe's grave is, is free to tour from 8am-dusk. There is a fee ($5) to tour Westminster Hall and the Catacombs; public tours are offered on the 1st and 3rd consecutive Friday (at 6:30pm) and Saturday (at 10am) of the month, from April to November. At least 15 people are required for a tour.

Baltimore Visitors Center

The **Baltimore Visitors Center** (401 Light St., 877/225-8466, www.baltimore.org, Apr.-Sept. daily 9am-6pm, Oct. 1-Nov. 15 daily 9am-5pm, Nov. 16-Mar. 14 Wed.-Sun. 10am-4pm) is on the waterfront on the Inner Harbor. This large, 8,000-square-foot facility offers information on sights, events, harbor cruises, and other activities to do in Baltimore. Visitors can even purchase tickets here for local attractions. There's a walk-in fountain next to the center where kids of all ages can cool off on hot days.

FELL'S POINT AND LITTLE ITALY

Fell's Point Visitor's Center

A good place to begin exploring Fell's Point and Little Italy is at the **Fell's Point Visitor's Center** (1724 Thames St., 410/675-6750, www.preservationsociety.com/about-us/visitor-center.html, daily 10am-4pm). They offer a great brochure for a walking tour of the neighborhood as well as information on the sights in the area. Seasonal guided historic walking tours also leave from the center, and there is a gift shop.

Frederick Douglass-Isaac Myers Maritime Park

The **Frederick Douglass-Isaac Myers Maritime Park** (1417 Thames St., 410/685-0295, www.douglassmyers.org, Mon.-Fri. 10am-4pm, Sat.-Sun. noon-4pm, $5) is a national heritage site/museum dedicated to African American maritime history. A series of exhibits chronicle the lives of Frederick

Fell's Point and Little Italy

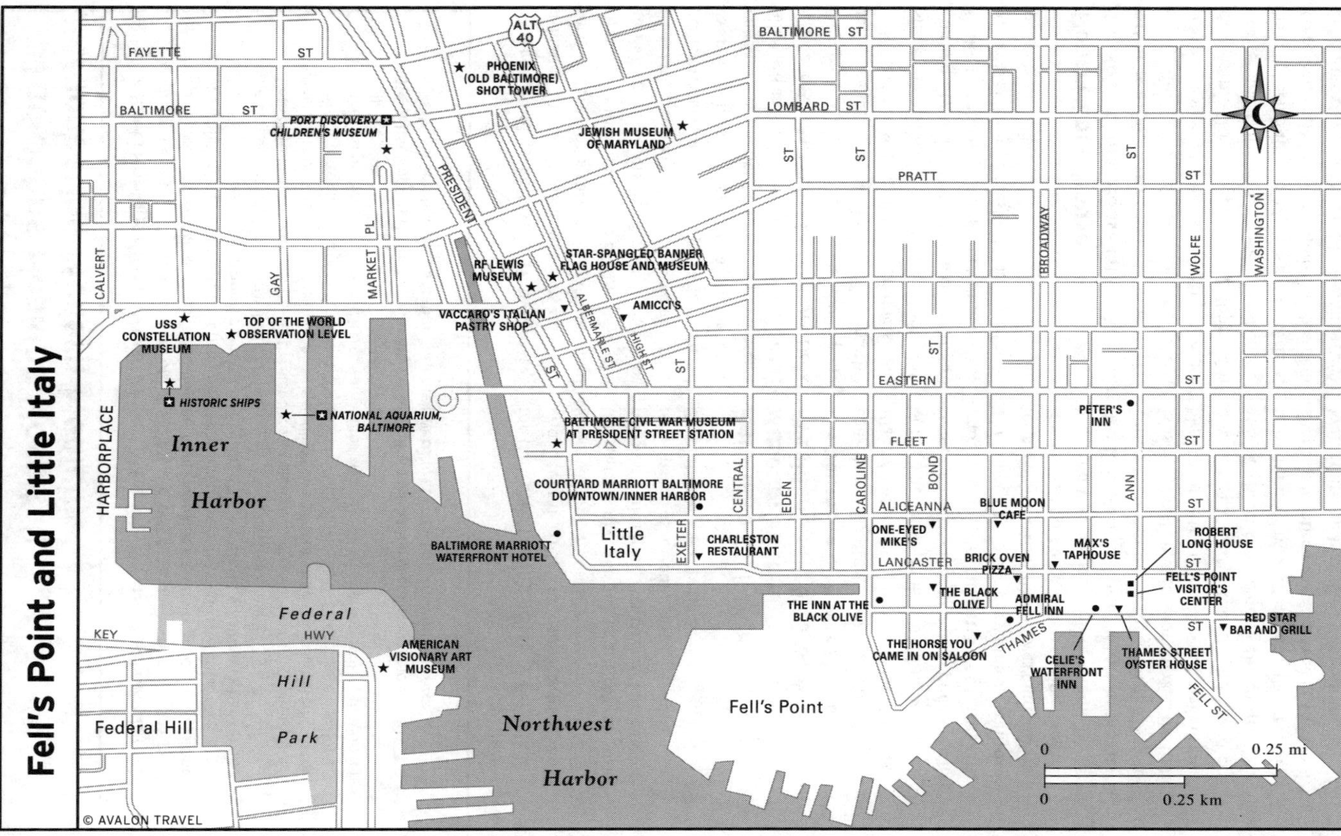

The Johns Hopkins Hospital: Pioneering Modern Medicine

The **Johns Hopkins Hospital** (1800 Orleans St.) is known as one of the best hospitals in the world. In the heart of Baltimore, north of Fell's Point and east of Mount Vernon, this teaching hospital and biomedical research facility for the Johns Hopkins University School of Medicine forms with that institution a $5 billion system of physicians, scientists, and students.

Funding for the hospital and school originally came from a wealthy Baltimore banker and merchant, Johns Hopkins, who willed $7 million in 1873 for their founding.

Both the university and hospital set the standard for many modern American medical practices. Numerous specialties were developed here, including endocrinology and neurosurgery. From the beginning, the goal was to combine research, teaching, and patient care. This concept developed into the first model of its kind, and led to unmatched success and an international reputation for excellence.

The Johns Hopkins Hospital is currently ranked third in the nation overall out of more than 4,700 hospitals. For additional information, visit their website at www.hopkinsmedicine.org.

Douglass and Isaac Myers. Douglass was a leader in the abolitionist movement, a former slave, and a successful statesman and orator. He lived and worked on the docks in Baltimore. Myers was a mason and labor leader who created a first-of-its-kind union for African American caulkers just after the Civil War. Union members ultimately formed a cooperative, and that cooperative purchased a shipyard and railroad in Baltimore called the Chesapeake Marine Railway and Dry Dock Company. The site encompasses 5,000 square feet of gallery space and features interactive exhibits, maps, photos, and artifacts that share the history of the African American community and how it influenced Baltimore in the 1800s. Forty-five-minute guided tours are available for parties of 10 or more for $8 per person.

Robert Long House

The **Robert Long House** (812 S. Ann St., 410/675-6750, www.preservationsociety.com, Mon.-Wed. 9:30am-1:30pm, Thurs. 9:30am-2:30pm, Fri. 9:30am-12:30pm, tours daily Apr.-Nov. at 1pm and 2:30pm, $3) is the oldest city row house in Baltimore, having been built in 1765. It is a symmetrical Georgian-style brick row house with a pent roof and now serves as the headquarters for the Preservation Society of Fell's Point and Federal Hill. The home belonged to Robert Long, who was a quartermaster for the Continental Navy. Visitors can see this restored building and its garden. The interior is furnished as it would have been during the Revolutionary War period.

Baltimore Civil War Museum at the President Street Station

The **Baltimore Civil War Museum** (601 President St., 410/220-0290, Thur.-Mon. 10am-4pm, free) is a great stop for Civil War buffs. The museum is housed in a restored freight and passenger train depot that was known as the **President Street Station.** The depot is the oldest surviving city railroad terminal in the country and was built in 1850. It was an important rail stop during the Civil War and was the location of a famous riot that took place in April 1861 when the first Union troops stopped there on the way to Washington. The altercation marked the first bloodshed of the Civil War and more than a dozen people died in the riot (both soldiers and civilians were among the dead). The museum displays artifacts and pictures that detail Baltimore's involvement in the Civil War. Tours are available by appointment.

the Star-Spangled Banner Flag House and Museum

Star-Spangled Banner Flag House and Museum

The **Star-Spangled Banner Flag House and Museum** (844 E. Pratt St., 410/837-1793, www.flaghouse.org, Tues.-Sat. 10am-4pm, $8) was the home of Mary Pickersgill, the woman who made the enormous and famous flag that flew over Fort McHenry on September 14, 1814, during the War of 1812 and inspired the poem written by Francis Scott Key that eventually became the U.S. national anthem. The house was built in 1793, and visitors can see what it looked like back when Mary lived there. The museum depicts the daily life in the home (that was also used as a business) around 1812, and living-history staff portray members of the Pickersgill family.

Jewish Museum of Maryland

The **Jewish Museum of Maryland** (15 Lloyd St., 410/732-6400, www.jewishmuseummd.org, Sun.-Thurs. 10am-5pm, $10) offers visitors the opportunity to learn about regional Jewish history, culture, and the community. One of the country's leading museums on regional Jewish history, its displays include photographs, papers, and artifacts that are rotated regularly. The museum does a wonderful job of relating Jewish life in early Baltimore and other small towns in Maryland. The museum oversees a modern museum facility and two historic synagogues: the B'nai Israel Synagogue, built in 1876, and the Lloyd Street Synagogue, built in 1845.

Reginald F. Lewis Museum of Maryland African American History & Culture

The **Reginald F. Lewis Museum of Maryland African American History & Culture** (830 E. Pratt St., 443/263-1800, www.africanamericanculture.org, Wed.-Sat. 10am-5pm, Sun. noon-5pm, $8) is the largest museum on the East Coast dedicated to African American culture. Visitors can learn about the contributions of African Americans in Maryland throughout the state's history. The museum includes galleries, a genealogy center, recording studio, theater, café, and gift shop.

Phoenix Shot Tower

The **Phoenix Shot Tower** (801 E. Fayette St., 410/837-5424, $5), which is also known as the **Old Baltimore Shot Tower,** stands nearly 235 feet tall near the entrance to Little Italy. It was built in 1828 out of one million bricks and, at the time, was the tallest structure in the country. The tower was used from 1828 to 1892 to produce lead shot, done by dropping molten lead from a platform at the top of the tower. The lead ran through a sieve and landed in cold water. It is a National Historic Landmark. Tours of the Shot Tower are offered Sat.-Sun. at 4pm.

CANTON

Patterson Park

Patterson Park (27 S. Patterson Park Ave., 410/276-3676, free) is one of the oldest parks in Baltimore. It encompasses 155 acres and has a great view of the harbor. On **Hampstead Hill** inside the park, a pagoda designed in 1890 stands at the site where local residents rallied in 1814 to protect their city from the British. British troops had come up the Patapsco River and attacked Fort McHenry, and on land, they had forces just east of the city at North Point. As they entered Baltimore, the British saw 20,000 troops and a hundred cannons facing them on Hampstead Hill. This caused them to retreat from Baltimore and go back to their ships. The area became a park in 1853, but saw more military activity during the Civil War when a military camp and war hospital were built there.

Today the park offers recreation trails, a lake, pavilions, playgrounds, an ice-skating rink, a public swimming pool, a recreation center, a stadium, and an adult day-care center.

Phoenix Shot Tower

Captain John O'Donnell Monument

The **Captain John O'Donnell Monument** (O'Donnell St. and S. Curley St.) is in the center of Canton Square. John O'Donnell was an Irish sea captain who purchased 1,981 acres in the 1780s in the area that is now Canton. He allegedly named the area after the cargo from his ship, which contained goods from Canton, China. Captain O'Donnell's land included a house near the current-day Boston Street and all the waterfront land east of the northwest branch of the Patapsco River between Colgate Creek and Fell's Point.

the pagoda in Patterson Park

SS *John W. Brown*

The **SS *John W. Brown*** (Pier 1, 2000 S. Clinton St., 410/558-0646, www.ssjohnwbrown.org, Wed. and Sat. 9am-2pm, free, donations appreciated) is one of two remaining Liberty ships out of the 2,700 that were produced by the Emergency Shipbuilding Program during World War II. They were designed for swift construction, and the SS *John W. Brown* was built in just 56 days. The ships were used for sealifts of troops, arms, and gear to all war locations.

The SS *John W. Brown* made 13 voyages and was awarded several honors during the war. Oddly, after the war, the ship served as a vocational high school in New York City from 1946 to 1982. It was acquired in 1988 by the current owner, Project Liberty Ship, and fully restored as a museum and memorial. As the only Liberty ship in operation on the East Coast, the boat hosts six-hour Living History Cruises several times a year. During these cruises, it visits other ports on the East Coast. The ship is part of the National Register of Historic Places and also a recipient of the World Ship Trust's Maritime Heritage Award.

FEDERAL HILL

American Visionary Art Museum

The **American Visionary Art Museum** (800 Key Hwy., 410/244-1900, www.avam.org, Tues.-Sun. 10am-6pm, $16) holds a collection of visionary art—slightly different from folk art in nature, but which to the untrained eye can look similar. The museum defines it as "art produced by self-taught individuals, usually without formal training, whose works arise from an innate personal vision that revels foremost in the creative act itself." In a nutshell, it seems like anything goes in this funky, interesting, and inspiring museum. It has art in all mediums—oil, mosaic, watercolor, toothpicks, and even bras.

★ Baltimore Museum of Industry

The **Baltimore Museum of Industry** (1415 Key Hwy., 410/727-4808, www.thebmi.org, Tues.-Sun. 10am-4pm, $12) is housed in the original 1865 Platt Oyster Cannery building, the only remaining cannery structure in the city, and has exhibits on the history of industry and manufacturing in the Baltimore area. Baltimore has traditionally been a key industrial center and was home to the first passenger train, the world's biggest copper refinery, the first traffic light, and the first gas company. Collections include 100,000 artifacts relating to small business, factory workers, and other citizens whose hard work helped shape the country. Featured fields include the garment industry, automobile industry, pharmaceutical industry, newspaper industry, food industry, and the Maryland Lottery. Many of the exhibits are interactive for both adults and children.

The museum is easy to find—just look for the large red crane out front. Be sure to watch the short introductory video near

a cannon in Federal Hill Park

Federal Hill

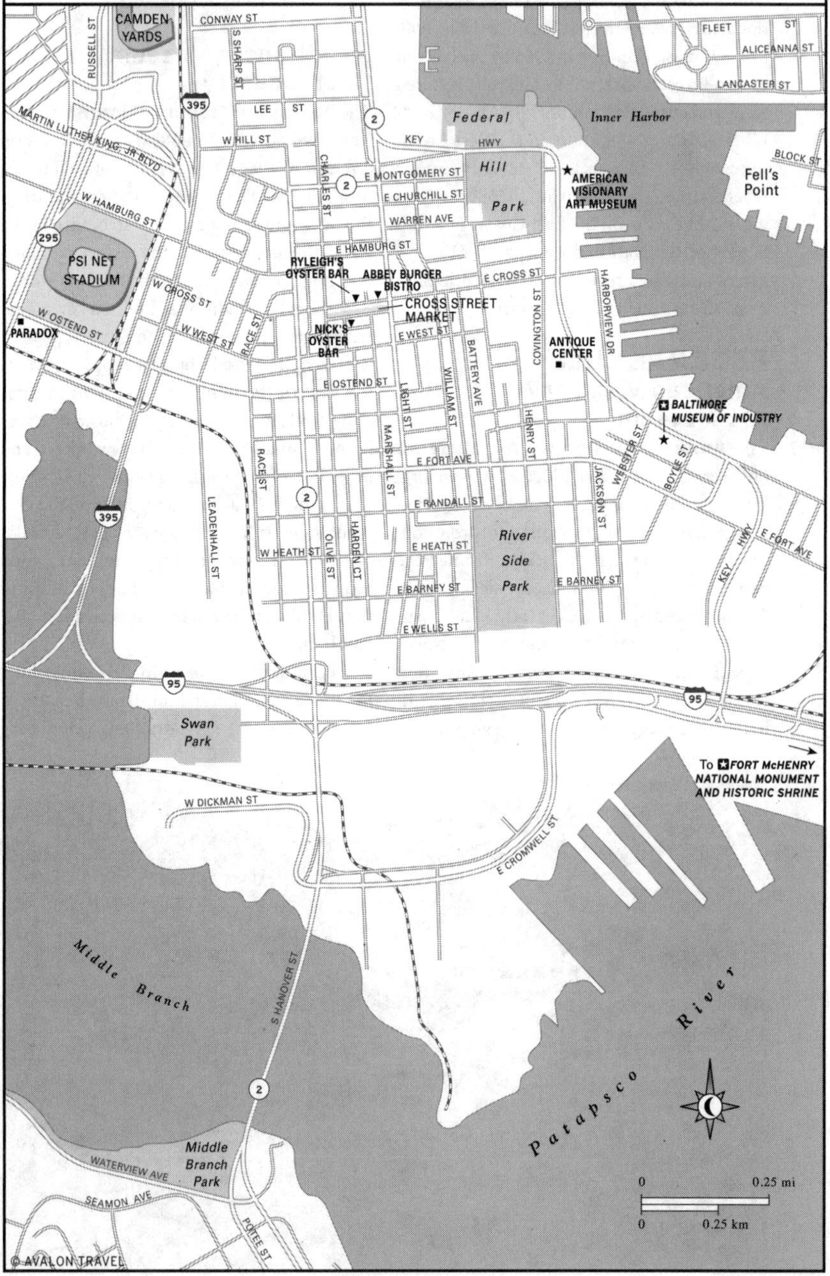

the museum entrance; it provides good insight into the background of the museum. Demonstrations are offered on Saturday and include topics such as printing (you can see how a real Linotype machine operates) and the job of a blacksmith. Exhibits aren't limited to the indoors; visitors can also see the coal-fired SS *Baltimore,* a restored and operational steam tugboat from 1906, just outside the museum. Free 45-minute tours of the museum are available. This is an interesting place for both adults and children over age 10. Plan on spending approximately two hours.

Federal Hill Park

Federal Hill Park (300 Warren Ave., 410/396-5828) is a lovely spot right off the harbor that offers great views of the Inner Harbor and downtown from atop Federal Hill. The park is on the south side of the harbor, and the terrain rises steeply. During the colonial era, the grassy hill was a mine for paint pigment, and the drooping hillside and footpaths indicate where old tunnels remain underground. The area has been a park since the late 1700s and remains a nice recreation and picnic area. There is also a playground on-site. On the northern side of the park are cannons from the Civil War that are symbols of those positioned by Union troops to face the city as a warning to Confederate sympathizers.

★ Fort McHenry National Monument and Historic Shrine

The **Fort McHenry National Monument and Historic Shrine** (2400 E. Fort Ave., 410/962-4290, www.nps.gov/fomc, daily 9am-5pm, extended summer hours, free admission to park, $10 fee for Star Fort/historical area) is a 43-acre national park with a historical area that houses Fort McHenry. It is east of Federal Hill and sticks out into the harbor. The fort was built between 1799 and 1802 and named after James McHenry, who was the secretary of war between 1796 and 1800, and constructed in the shape of a star with five points (aka the Star Fort). The star-shaped design was popular at the time since each point was within view of others to the left and right and the entire fort and surrounding area could be guarded with only five sentries.

Fort McHenry is known as the inspiration for the "Star-Spangled Banner." Francis Scott Key wrote the words to the anthem during the War of 1812 when he was held on a truce ship during the British attack on Baltimore. As the battle went on, Key watched from the water

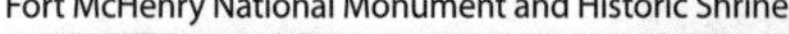
Fort McHenry National Monument and Historic Shrine

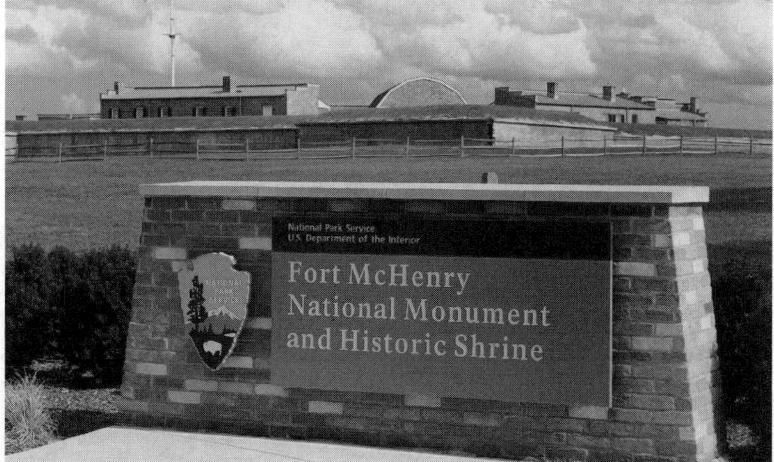

and through a smoke-filled landscape, and at "dawn's early light" on September 14, 1814, he could see the huge 30-by-42-foot American flag still flying above Fort McHenry as a symbol that Baltimore had not surrendered.

Begin your exploration at the visitors center and view the 10-minute video on the fort's history (shown on the hour and half hour). Exhibits on the fort, a gift shop, and restrooms are at the center. Then take a self-guided tour (approximately one hour) of the fort. Inside the fort is a large grassy area, and the rooms of the fort feature displays and authentic artifacts. Continue into the barracks (which include exhibits such as the Enlisted Men's Quarters, weapons, uniforms, Junior Officer's Quarters, the Powder Magazine, Commanding Officer's Quarters, and the 1814 Guard House). Children can participate in the Flag Change Program daily at 9:30am and 4:20pm, when they can assist rangers in raising and lowering a reproduced Star-Spangled Banner flag. Living-history interpreters are available on the weekends in the summer and tell stories about the fort and the people who lived in Baltimore while the facility was active. Allow two hours for your visit. There is no charge to visit the grounds.

MOUNT VERNON

★ The Walters Art Museum

The Walters Art Museum (600 N. Charles St., 410/547-9000, www.thewalters.org, Wed.-Sun. 10am-5pm, Thurs. until 9pm, free) showcases the personal art collection of two men: William Thompson Walters, an American industrialist and art collector, and his son, Henry Walters. Both collected paintings, antiques, and sculptures. Upon Henry Walters's death, their joint collection of more than 22,000 works of art was left to the city of Baltimore for the benefit of the public.

The Walters Art Museum houses a fascinating collection that spans 5,000 years and five continents. It includes pieces from ancient Egypt, Roman sarcophagi, Renaissance bronzes, Chinese bronzes, and art nouveau jewelry. Some must-see items are an ancient Egyptian mummy from 1000 BC, two Fabergé eggs, and one of the best collections of armor in the country (including a child's set of armor).

Be sure to visit the Chamber of Wonders, where the museum has brought to life an intricate scene from a 1620 painting that came from the area that is now Belgium. The scene replicates the painting in detail and

The Walters Art Museum

Mount Vernon

is a re-creation of a chamber of natural history wonders that taps into human ingenuity from all over the globe. A highlight of the room is a 12-foot stuffed alligator. Although general admission to the museum is free, purchased tickets are required for special exhibits.

Washington Monument and Museum at Mount Vernon Place

The **Washington Monument and Museum at Mount Vernon Place** (699 N. Charles St., 410/962-5070, www.mvconservancy.org, Wed.-Fri. 2pm-5pm, Sat.-Sun. 10am-1pm and 2pm-5pm, free) is the site of the first monument planned to honor George Washington. Completed in 1829, the white marble monument stands 178 feet tall and has a rectangular base, a relatively plain column, and a statue of Washington on the top. The monument looks even more imposing than its 178 feet because it sits on a hill. It was a landmark for boats making their way up the river from the Chesapeake Bay. Today, visitors can climb 228 narrow stone stairs to the top and enjoy a great view of Baltimore ($6.35). There is a little museum at the base of the monument.

Baltimore Streetcar Museum

The **Baltimore Streetcar Museum** (1901 Falls Rd., 410/547-0264, www.baltimorestreetcar.org, Sun. Mar.-Dec. noon-5pm, Sat. June-Oct. noon-5pm, $10) details the history of streetcars in the city and their evolution

the Baltimore Streetcar Museum

from horse-drawn transportation to an electricity-driven system. The fun part of this interesting little museum is that a number of original historic streetcars have been salvaged and visitors can actually ride in them (accompanied by volunteer conductors) down the old tracks. Unlimited rides are included with the admission fee. For a taste of what you'll find in the museum, visit the website and click on "Streetcar Memories."

Basilica of the Assumption

The **Basilica of the Assumption** (409 Cathedral St., 410/727-3565, www.baltimorebasilica.org, Mon.-Fri. 7am-4pm, Sat.-Sun. 7am to the conclusion of mass at 5:30pm and 4:30pm respectively, $2 donation for tours) was the first Catholic cathedral built in the United States after the Constitution was ratified, and the building quickly became a symbol of the new country's religious freedom. It was constructed between 1806 and 1821 and the design and architecture were overseen by John Carroll, the first bishop in the country (and later archbishop of Baltimore), and Benjamin Henry Latrobe, who designed the U.S. Capitol. The basilica sits on a hill above the harbor and features a grand dome and what was considered cutting-edge neoclassical architecture to match that of the new federal city of Washington DC. Great effort went into creating an architectural symbol of America rather than using a European gothic design. At the time the cathedral was built, its only architectural rival in terms of scale and size was the U.S. Capitol, and the basilica was considered the most architecturally advanced structure in the country.

The full name of the cathedral is the Basilica of the National Shrine of the Assumption of the Blessed Virgin Mary, in Baltimore. It is ranked as a minor basilica, but is also a national shrine. The basilica is a cultural institution in Baltimore and offers services, tours, concerts, and lectures. It also has a prayer garden nearby on the corner of Franklin and North Charles Streets. The basilica recently underwent an extensive two-year restoration. Forty-five minute tours are offered Monday-Saturday at 9am, 11am, and 1pm, although Saturday tours are sometimes not possible due to weddings and special services. Tours are not required for visitation, but sightseeing is not permitted during mass.

Brown Memorial Presbyterian Church

The **Brown Memorial Presbyterian Church** (1316 Park Ave., 410/523-1542, www.browndowntown.org, daily 9am-6pm, free) is a historic gothic revival-style Presbyterian church that was built in 1870. A unique feature is its 11 Tiffany stained glass windows representing scenes from the Bible, several of which are nearly three stories tall. The windows were added in the early 1900s, which made the church a local art treasure.

The National Great Blacks in Wax Museum

The National Great Blacks in Wax Museum (1601 E. North Ave., 410/563-3404, www.greatblacksinwax.org, hours vary throughout season, $13) is the first wax museum in Baltimore and the first African American-oriented wax museum in the country. It was established in 1983 and displays more than 100 figures. The museum does a nice job of telling the history behind each figure through audio and text displays. Several famous Baltimore residents are depicted in the museum, including Frederick Douglass and singer Billie Holiday.

The Maryland Historical Society

The Maryland Historical Society (201 W. Monument St., 410/685-3750, www.mdhs.org, Wed.-Sat. 10am-5pm, Sun. noon-5pm, museum only with no library hours on Sun., $9) is a great starting point for discovering Baltimore. You can view more than one million objects on display in two museum buildings including photographs, paintings, manuscripts, and lithographs. It also includes a huge library with more than 7 million items, including the most treasured: the historical manuscript to the "Star-Spangled Banner." Exhibits cover a diversity of topics including the War of 1812, African American history, women's history, maritime history, the history of Fell's Point, immigration, furniture, and mining. The Historical Society is easy to spot—the 1,700-pound, 14-foot statue of Nipper the RCA Dog sits on its rooftop facing Park Street.

HAMPDEN AND HOMEWOOD

Druid Hill Park

Druid Hill Park (2600 Madison Ave., 443/281-3538, www.druidhillpark.org, daily dawn to dusk, free) is a 745-acre park developed in 1860. It is approximately two miles from Hampden. It is one of the country's oldest landscaped public parks, along with Central Park in New York City and Fairmount

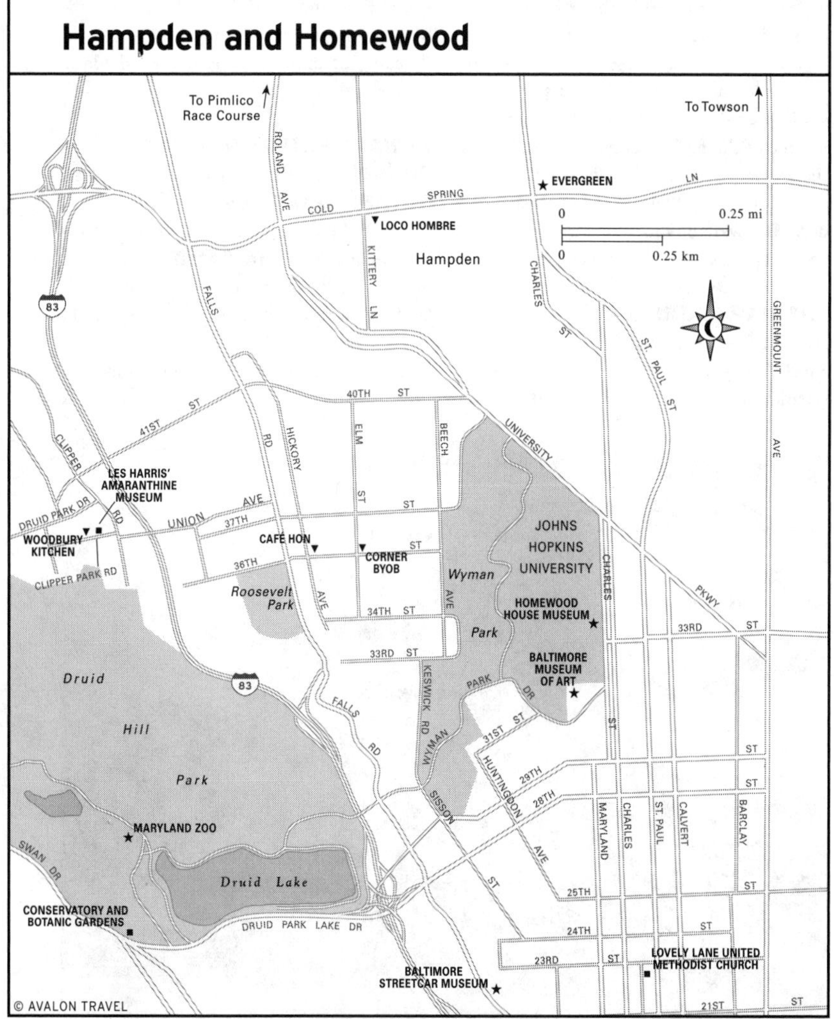

Park in Philadelphia. Druid Park has something else in common with Central Park: It was formed at the northern edges of the city at the time it was established. To this day, the northern end of the park features forest that is some of the oldest in Maryland. The southern end of the park, however, has always been a popular area for those living in the city. Druid Hill Lake was built in 1863 and is one of the biggest earthen dammed lakes in the nation. Many fountains and artificial ponds that were original features in the park have been drained and reclaimed by nature, although their remains can still be found. The park also features tennis courts, a pool, disc golf, and workout equipment. There is also a zoo in the middle of the park, accessible only through the official zoo entrance. Safety can be a concern in the park at any time, but mostly after dark. Be aware of your surroundings, and if you feel uncomfortable, cut your visit short.

THE MARYLAND ZOO IN BALTIMORE

The Maryland Zoo in Baltimore (Druid Park Lake Dr., 410/396-7102, www.marylandzoo.org, Mar.-Dec. daily 10am-4pm, shorter hours Jan.-Feb., $18) is inside the large Druid Hill Park to the west of Hampden. The zoo opened in 1876 and is one of the oldest zoos in the country. It houses more than 1,500 animals. One of the premier exhibits in the zoo is the Polar Bear Watch, where visitors can take a large viewing buggy (like they use on the tundra) to watch three polar bears in their habitat. The zoo also offers other hands-on experiences such as camel rides and a Children's Zoo, where the little ones can pet certain animals. A family camping experience is also available in the spring.

HOWARD PETERS RAWLINGS CONSERVATORY AND BOTANIC GARDENS

The **Howard Peters Rawlings Conservatory and Botanic Gardens** (3100 Swan Dr., Druid Hill Park, 410/396-0008, www.rawlingsconservatory.org, Wed.-Sun. 10am-4pm, free) within Druid Hill Park is the only remaining public conservatory in Baltimore. The complex dates back

Howard Peters Rawlings Conservatory and Botanic Gardens

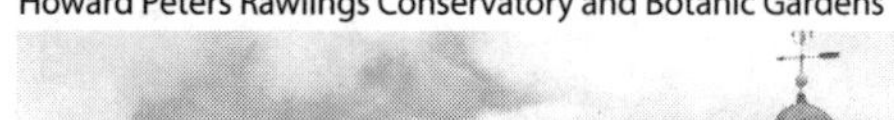

The Dog Who Found His Way Home

You'll find Nipper on the roof of the Maryland Historical Society.

The 14-foot, 1,700-pound RCA Dog, known as Nipper, that sits atop the Maryland Historical Society roof has a long history of adventure. The original Nipper was a stray terrier adopted in the 1880s by a man named Mark Barraud. He named the little black-and-white dog Nipper because he nipped at people's legs. When Barraud passed away, his brother, Francis, who was a painter, adopted the dog.

At the time, the phonograph was the latest technology. Nipper was captivated by the sound of the machine and would sit with his head tilted near its trumpet, listening. Francis thought this would make a great advertisement, and he painted a picture of Nipper and sold it to the Gramophone Company (which made phonographs). A United States patent was issued for the trademark of the image, and after two sales of the company, RCA ended up with the image in 1929.

In 1954, The Triangle Sign Company of Baltimore made the statue of Nipper, and it was placed on top of the D&H Distributing building. D&H Distributing was an RCA distributor. But when the company moved in 1976, they left the statue behind.

A collector from Fairfax, Virginia, wanted the statue and after he spent six years trying to convince D&H Distributing to let him buy it, they finally sold it to him for $1. Baltimore residents and officials were outraged. They felt Nipper was a Baltimore landmark, but a sale is a sale, and Nipper left Baltimore and was moved to Virginia where he sat on the collector's front lawn for 20 years.

In 1996, the collector decided to move, and he sold Nipper to the Baltimore's City Life Museum for $25,000. Two years later, the museum closed, and the Maryland Historical Society took over its collections and, in turn, inherited Nipper and placed him on the roof. Today visitors can still enjoy the 1,700-pound pooch, who found his way home to Baltimore and seems to be here to stay.

to 1888 and consists of two buildings from the Victorian era. There are also three newer buildings. Five different climates are represented in the buildings and there are also beautiful outdoor gardens. The Palm House is one of the most interesting buildings. The Palm House was built in 1888 and was designed by George Frederick (who also designed Baltimore's City Hall). Towering palms reach the upper windows of the impressive five-story house and block some of the natural sunlight in the conservatory.

Les Harris' Amaranthine Museum

It would be a challenge to find another museum comparable to **Les Harris' Amaranthine Museum** (2010 Clipper Park Rd., 410/456-1343, www.amaranthinemuseum.org, Sun. noon-3pm and by appointment, closed July-Aug., $5). This unusual museum, which is open during very limited hours, takes visitors through a maze of the late Baltimore artist Les Harris's work while telling the history of art in chronological order, starting with prehistoric times and going out into the future. The museum is a labyrinth of art history and the creative process, made up of rooms, chambers, and passages, decorated from floor to ceiling with Harris's art. The Amaranthine Museum (the word *amaranthine* means eternally beautiful) itself is a unique art form and a fun deviation from traditional museums.

Baltimore Museum of Art

The **Baltimore Museum of Art** (10 Museum Dr., 443/573-1700, www.artbma.org, Wed.-Fri. 10am-5pm, Sat.-Sun. 11am-6pm, free) is a cultural destination in Baltimore and one of two great art museums in the city (the other is the Walters Art Museum in Mount Vernon). The museum is adjacent to the Homewood campus of Johns Hopkins University.

The museum was founded in 1914 and grew from housing one single painting to offering 90,000 pieces on display. Its collection of 19th-century, modern, and contemporary art is internationally known and includes the famous Cone Collection of over 3,000 pieces by world-famous artists donated by wealthy socialite sisters Claribel and Etta Cone. The Cone Collection is worth approximately $1 billion. The Cone Collection includes the largest single collection of works by Henri Matisse in the world (500 total); 42 oil paintings, 18 sculptures, and 36 drawings are among the Matisse pieces. It also amasses work by Cézanne, Picasso, Degas, Manet, Van Gogh, and Gauguin.

In addition to the Cone Collection (housed in the Cone Wing), the museum features many other galleries. The West Wing for Contemporary Art contains 16 galleries with 20th- and 21st-century art including abstract expressionism, minimalism, conceptual art, and works by Andy Warhol. American galleries feature paintings, sculptures, decorative arts, and works on paper. There is also an African art collection of more than 2,000 pieces with works spanning from ancient Egypt to contemporary Zimbabwe.

The museum also offers visitors two lovely outdoor gardens with 20th-century sculptures.

Johns Hopkins University

Johns Hopkins University (410/516-8000, www.jhu.edu) is a private not-for-profit research university that was founded in 1876 and named for philanthropist Johns Hopkins, its benefactor. The university maintains two main campuses in Baltimore: the Homewood Campus (3400 N. Charles St.) and the Medical Institution Campus (600 N. Wolfe St.). There are secondary campuses in Washington DC, Italy, Singapore, and China. Johns Hopkins developed the concept of a modern research university in the United States and is known throughout the world as one of the best. At least 37 Nobel Prize winners are affiliated with Johns Hopkins.

The Homewood Campus has a parklike setting even though it is located in a large city, with lovely old trees, large grassy areas, stately brick academic buildings, and redbrick residence halls. The Medical Institution Campus is located north of Fell's Point in east Baltimore.

HOMEWOOD HOUSE

The **Homewood House** (3400 N. Charles St., 410/516-5589, www.museums.jhu.edu, Tues.-Fri. 11am-4pm, Sat.-Sun. noon-4pm, $8) on the eastern side of Johns Hopkins University is a wonderful example of federal architecture. Completed in 1808, the house is decorated with well-researched colors, patterns, and furniture from the period, much of it original. The country home was owned by wealthy Baltimore residents during the colonial era and then by the son of Charles Carroll, a signer of the Declaration of Independence.

EVERGREEN MUSEUM & LIBRARY

The **Evergreen Museum & Library** (4545 N. Charles St., 410/516-0341, www.museums.jhu.edu, Tues.-Fri. 11am-4pm, Sat.-Sun. noon-4pm, $8) is a beautiful mansion that was built in the mid-19th century and purchased by the president of the B&O Railroad, John W. Garrett, in 1878. This wonderful exemplar of the Gilded Age sits surrounded by Italian-style gardens on 26 acres. The museum and library hold a collection of rare books, manuscripts, and artwork. The estate's 48 rooms, housing more than 50,000 items from the Garrett family (including a 24K gold-leafed toilet), can be viewed by the public only on guided tours. Tours begin every hour on the hour with the last tour starting at 3pm. Concerts and lectures are also given on the property. The museum is 4.5 miles north of the Inner Harbor.

WALKING TOURS

Historic walking tours around Baltimore are given by the **Preservation Society of Fell's Point and Federal Hill** (410/675-6750, www.preservationsociety.com).

Entertainment and Events

NIGHTLIFE

Whether you're looking for delicious cocktails, a large wine selection, or a wild night of dancing, Baltimore has it all.

One block from the Inner Harbor is a great collection of bars and clubs in an entertainment complex called **Power Plant Live!** (34 Market Place, www.powerplantlive.com). The complex opened in sections between 2001 and 2003 and was named for a neighboring former power plant on Pier 4 that faces the Inner Harbor. Restaurants, bars, and nightclubs line an outdoor plaza where free music is offered May-October on the plaza stage. A popular venue in the complex is **Rams Head Live** (20 Market Pl., 410/244-1131, www.ramsheadlive.com). This general admission, standing-room-only venue features five full-service bars and two food kiosks. A wide variety of groups have played here including Patti Smith, Big Head Todd and the Monsters, They Might Be Giants, and Citizen Cope.

Two blocks north of the Inner Harbor near Power Plant Live! is a slightly upscale nightclub that caters to an older crowd. The **Havana Club** (600 Water St., 410/468-0022, www.havanaclub-baltimore.com, Wed.-Sat. 6pm-2am) is above Ruth's Chris Steak House and features a more intimate atmosphere with leather seating areas, private seating options, an extensive wine list, and a notable cigar selection. They also offer salsa dancing on Friday nights. The dress code is business casual.

Hidden in an industrial warehouse area southwest of the Inner Harbor is a thriving dance club called **Paradox** (1310 Russell St., 410/837-9110, www.thedox.com). People come from all over the region to be part of the serious parties that take place on the wooden dance floor. They feature all types of dance music and do not serve alcohol.

Those looking for a terrific place to catch live jazz won't be disappointed by **An Die Musik Live** (409 N. Charles St., 2nd Fl., 410/385-2638, www.andiemusiklive.com), downtown on the second floor of a town house. This intimate concert venue is for true music lovers. The cool renovated building offers great acoustics, comfortable seating, and a high caliber of artists. There is no elevator, so be prepared to climb some stairs.

Not far away is a popular old-school drinking establishment called **Club Charles** (1724

N. Charles St., 410/727-8815, www.club-charles.us, Mon.-Sun. 6pm-2am). This art deco bar is dark and crowded, but the bartenders are fantastic and the drinks are strong. There's even a resident ghost that plays pranks at the bar.

A classy place to linger over a drink and soak in a gorgeous view of the city is the **13th Floor** (1 E. Chase St., 410/347-0880, www.13floorbelvedere.com, Tues.-Wed. 5pm-10pm, Thurs. 5pm-11pm, Fri.-Sat. 5pm-1am). This Mount Vernon establishment is housed in the historic Belvedere Hotel building, which was known during the early part of the 20th century as the premier hotel in the city; it hosted U.S. presidents, foreign dignitaries, and movie stars. Today, the newly renovated restaurant and bar feature dark hardwood floors, white tabletops, live jazz, and a 360-degree view of the city. This is another place with a dress code, so be prepared so you're not disappointed.

One of the first modern lounges in the city, Mount Vernon's **Red Maple** (930 N. Charles St., 410/547-0149, www.930redmaple.com, Tues.-Fri. 5pm-2am, Sat. 6pm-2am) is still a popular hot spot. It features Asian-inspired tapas and other small plates, and guests can relax in lounge-style seating on the first floor or table seating on the second floor. The indoor dance floor and outdoor patio are popular nightspots.

A local landmark in Fell's Point is the **Cat's Eye Pub** (1730 Thames St., 410/276-9866, www.catseyepub.com, daily noon-2am). It is known for nightly live music despite the close and often crowded space. Music at this cozy pub includes blues, jazz, and folk.

A charming little wine bar on the waterfront in Fell's Point is **V-NO** (905 S. Ann St., 410/342-8466, www.v-no.com, Mon.-Wed. 4:30pm-9pm, Thurs. noon-10pm, Fri.-Sat. noon-midnight, Sun. noon-6pm). They offer indoor and outdoor seating and a lovely wine list with enough of a selection to keep things interesting. This is a great place to unwind away from the crowds.

The Horse You Came In On Saloon

The Horse You Came In On Saloon (1626 Thames St., 410/327-8111, www.thehorsebaltimore.com, open daily at 11:30am, $8-15) is America's oldest continuously operated saloon (it operated before, during, and after Prohibition). It first opened in 1775 and is allegedly the last place Edgar Allan Poe was seen alive. It may be where Poe had his last drink, and it's been rumored that his ghost haunts the saloon. The saloon originally had hitching posts out back to park horses. Menu items include traditional bar food, and there's nightly live entertainment (rock and roll). The saloon's slogan is "Where no one's ugly at 2am." It also has Maryland's only Jack Daniel's club (Old No. 7), where members purchase their own bottles of Jack Daniel's and the saloon stores them in a coveted space in their custom Jack Daniel's case. The saloon sells more Jack Daniel's than any other bar in Maryland.

PERFORMING ARTS

Hippodrome Theatre at France-Merrick Performing Arts Center

The **Hippodrome Theatre at France-Merrick Performing Arts Center** (12 N. Eutaw St., 410/837-7400, www.france-merrickpac.com) is a well-known circa 1914 stage performance theater on the west side of Baltimore. In the 1940s, this part of town had a flourishing arts scene and saw big-time acts such as Frank Sinatra, Bob Hope, and Benny Goodman, but the neighborhood declined in the following decades. This performing arts center is part of the rebirth of the area, and the Hippodrome Theatre was beautifully restored as part of that project. The center now offers musicals, holiday performances, and many other types of performances.

Centerstage

Centerstage (700 N. Calvert St., 410/332-0033, www.centerstage.org) in Mount Vernon is a historic venue with two intimate performance spaces, two rehearsal halls, and three lobbies. The six-story building is a local landmark that has roots as the former Loyola College and High School. It offers a close-up theater experience for classical and contemporary performances and lends itself well to audience interaction. There are no bad seats in the house.

Royal Farms Arena

The **Royal Farms Arena** (201 W. Baltimore St., www.royalfarmsarena.com) is showing its age a bit (it was built in the 1960s), but still hosts musical artists such as Carrie Underwood, well-known shows such as Cirque Du Soleil and Disney on Ice, and sporting events.

Patricia & Arthur Modell Performing Arts Center at the Lyric

The **Patricia & Arthur Modell Performing Arts Center at the Lyric** (140 W. Mount Royal Ave., 410/900-1150, www.lyricoperahouse.com) is a music hall that originally opened in 1894. Today it plays host to a wide variety of talent from kids' shows to top musical artists.

Arena Players

The longest continuously running African American community theater in the country is the **Arena Players** (801 McCulloh St., 410/728-6500, www.arenaplayersinc.com). Founded in 1953, this respected theater supports local actors and writers.

Joseph Meyerhoff Symphony Hall

The **Joseph Meyerhoff Symphony Hall** (1212 Cathedral St., 410/783-8000, www.bsomusic.org) is a 2,443-seat music venue in the Mount Vernon neighborhood. The venue is named for a former president of the Baltimore Symphony, Joseph Meyerhoff, who made a sizable donation for the construction of the hall. The venue is currently home to the **Baltimore Symphony Orchestra.**

EVENTS

The **Baltimore Fun Guide** (www.baltimorefunguide.com) is a great online resource that lists local events throughout the city.

Hundreds of boats (both power and sail) can be found at the **Baltimore Convention Center** (1 W. Pratt St., 410/649-7000, www.bccenter.org) for four days in mid to late January during the **Baltimore Boat Show** (www.baltimoreboatshow.com, $14). The show features exhibits and activities for all ages.

April brings the **Preakness Crab Derby** (400 W. Lexington St, 410/685-6169) to the Lexington Market where fans can watch Baltimore celebrities race crabs for charity. The winner is awarded $500 for donation to their favorite charity.

For something completely different, attend the American Visionary Art Museum's annual **Kinetic Sculpture Race** (www.avam.org/kinetic-sculpture-race/), which takes place on a Saturday in early May. This race showcases completely human-powered works of art that can travel on the land, water, and through mud. These "machines" are often made of old bicycle parts, gears, etc. and can be "driven" by one person or a team. Fun awards are given out such as the "Grand Mediocre East Coast Champion Award (to the vehicle finishing in the middle of the pack)," the "Next to Last Award," and the "Best Bribe" award.

A more serious race that also takes place in May is the **Preakness Stakes** (www.preakness.com). With more than a 140-year history, this second leg of the Triple Crown of Thoroughbred Racing (which consists of the Kentucky Derby, the Preakness Stakes, and the Belmont Stakes) is a big deal in Baltimore and in horse racing overall.

Honfest (www.honfest.net) in Hampden is a major city festival that started out as a neighborhood celebration and blossomed to an international following. The festival takes place in mid-June along 36th Street. The "Hon" is short for "honey" ("hon" is a commonly used term of endearment in Baltimore) and refers to a ladies fashion that evolved in the 1960s. The style included large, brightly colored horn-rim glasses, loud prints, spandex and leopard-print pants, thick makeup, and beehive hairdos. The festival features many Hons in full attire and one is crowned "Miss Hon." There is also the running of the Hons. Hair and makeup can be done by vendors right in the street.

Baltimore's **Fourth of July** celebration (www.baltimore.org) is an annual favorite in the Inner Harbor. It features live music and a fireworks display. The fireworks celebration can be viewed from many vantage points around the city including, Federal Hill, Fell's Point, and Canton.

America's largest free arts festival, **Artscape** (Mount Royal Avenue, www.artscape.org) is held for three days each July and attracts more than 350,000 people. The festival is a rare opportunity for visitors and people from all neighborhoods in Baltimore to interact. More than 150 artists display their craft at this well-known event that began in the early 1980s.

Miracle on 34th Street (www.christmasstreet.com) is the premier holiday extravaganza in Hampden. Throughout December, one block of 34th Street becomes a magical, although somewhat over-the-top display of lights, reindeer, and really any type of decoration you can think of. It's quite the spectacle, but also quite festive, and definitely worth checking out if you don't mind sitting in traffic with the other spectators.

The **Night of 100 Elvises** (www.nightof100elvises.com) is actually a two-day event held in the beginning of December that benefits the Johns Hopkins Children's Center and the Guardian Angels. This ticketed party held at Lithuanian Hall (851-3 Hollins St.) features a dozen bands and multiple Elvis tribute performances.

Shopping

DOWNTOWN AND THE INNER HARBOR

Harborplace

Harborplace (201 E. Pratt St., 410/332-4191, www.harborplace.com, Mon.-Sat. 10am-9pm, Sun. 11am-7pm) is the premier shopping market in downtown Baltimore. It was created in 1980 as a main attraction during the rebirth of the Inner Harbor. The market consists of two pavilions, the **Pratt Street Pavilion** and the **Light Street Pavilion.** National stores and restaurants are abundant at Harborplace, but specialty shops such as **Life in Charm City** (Pratt Street Pavilion, 410/230-2652, Mon.-Sat. 10am-9pm, Sun. noon-6pm), which sells Baltimore-related merchandise; **Sock It To You** (Pratt Street Pavilion, 443/286-8889, Mon.-Sat. 10am-9pm, Sun. noon-6pm), which sells socks; and **Destination Baltimore** (Pratt Street Pavilion, 443/727-5775, Mon.-Sat.

10am-9pm, Sun. noon-6pm), which sells apparel, gifts, and seasonal items, are some of the independent stores located in the market.

The Gallery

The Gallery (200 E. Pratt St., 410/332-4191, www.thegalleryatharborplace.com, Mon.-Sat. 10am-9pm, Sun. noon-6pm) opened a few years after Harborplace in a glass building across Pratt Street (attached to the Renaissance Hotel). The two shopping areas are connected by a skywalk. Many upscale national stores and restaurants are located in the four-story structure, but local merchants running Maryland-themed shops can also be found there.

FELL'S POINT

Some of the most charming shops in Baltimore can be found in Fell's Point. Whether you're in the market for jewelry, home items, music, or clothing, you should turn up plenty to keep you interested if you poke around the historic streets and venture up some side alleys. **B'More Betty** (1500 Thames St., 443/869-6379, www.onlybetty.com, Wed.-Sun. 11am-7pm) is a trendy buyer and seller of designer handbags, shoes, and accessories. **Killer Trash** (602 S. Broadway, 410/675-2449, daily 11am-7:30pm) is a vibrant vintage shop with an eclectic selection of jewelry and clothes for wearing and for costumes. If you are looking for a special piece for your home, or just need a lamp rewired, **Brasswork Co., Inc.** (1641 Thames St., 410/327-7280, www.baltimorebrassworks.com, Mon.-Fri. 8:30am-5pm, Sat. 10am-6pm, Sun. noon-6pm) is the place to go. They offer gifts, lighting, timepieces, candleholders, and many other brass merchandise. For all types of hats, visit **Hats in the Belfry** (813 S. Broadway, 410/342-7480, www.hatsinthebelfry.com, Mon.-Thurs. 10am-6pm, Fri.-Sat. 10am-8pm, Sun. 10am-7pm).

FEDERAL HILL

Charles Street and Light Street are the best areas in Federal Hill to do some window browsing. Small boutiques and shops selling clothes and home goods are scattered through the charming neighborhood. Favorites include **Phina's for the Home** (919 S. Charles St., 410/685-0911, www.phinas.com, Tues.-Sat. noon-6pm, Sun. noon-3pm), a boutique linen store selling home and spa items and gifts; and **Brightside Boutique & Art Studio** (1133 S. Charles St., 410/244-1133, www.shopbrightside.com, Mon.-Sat. 11am-7pm, Sun.11am-5pm), selling clothes, accessories and home items.

HAMPDEN

The "happening place" in Hampden is 36th Street, known locally as "The Avenue." This is especially true for shoppers since there are four blocks of retail stores offering clothing, furniture, antiques, beauty supplies, and some funkier items. The stores are locally owned, and the merchants are helpful if you're looking for a specific item. For starters, visit **Atomic Books** (3620 Falls Rd., 410/662-4444, www.atomicbooks.com, Sun.-Tues. 11am-7pm, Wed.-Thurs. 11am-9pm, Fri. 11am-10pm, Sat. 11am-9pm, Sun. 11am-7pm) to find unique titles and comics, or visit **Ma Petite Shoe** (832 W. 36th St., 410/235-3442, www.mapetiteshoe.com, Mon.-Thurs. and Sat. 11am-7pm, Fri. 11am-8pm, Sun. noon-5pm) for designer shoes and artisan chocolate.

Sports and Recreation

SPECTATOR SPORTS

Oriole Park at Camden Yards

Oriole Park at Camden Yards (333 W. Camden St., 888/848-2473, http://baltimore.orioles.mlb.com) is the home of Major League Baseball's **Baltimore Orioles.** The park opened in 1992 in downtown Baltimore, just a short walk from the Inner Harbor. Camden Yards is consistently rated one of the top professional baseball parks in the country. The train station at the intersection of Howard and Camden Streets services the stadium for the Baltimore Light Rail.

M&T Bank Stadium

A stone's throw from Camden Yards is the **M&T Bank Stadium** (1101 Russell St., 410/261-7283, www.baltimoreravens.com), home to the **Baltimore Ravens** of the National Football League. The multipurpose venue opened in 1998. The Hamburg Street Station of the Baltimore Light Rail services the stadium.

Royal Farms Arena

The **Royal Farms Arena** (201 W. Baltimore St., www.royalfarmsarena.com) is the location for the **Baltimore Blast** (www.baltimoreblast.com) professional indoor soccer team's home games. The team was founded in 1992 and is part of the Major Indoor Soccer League.

BIKING

Baltimore has a large biking community that is working hard to make the city more bike-friendly. Since 2006, 42 on-street bike lane miles have been created in the city, and there are 39 miles of off-road trails.

The **BWI Bike Trail** (www.bikewashington.org) is a 11-mile, asphalt surface, loop trail that circles BWI Airport. It has short sections on city streets, but is mostly level with a few bridge hills and one tougher hill. The trail runs past a light-rail station where a drinking fountain, restrooms, and vending machines are accessible. Parking is available in several spots including the **Dixon Aircraft Observation**

Pimlico Race Course

The second leg of the famed Triple Crown horse races, **The Preakness Stakes,** is held on the third Saturday in May at **Pimlico Race Course** (5201 Park Heights Ave., 410/542-9400, www.pimlico.com), northwest of Hampden. The historic racecourse is the second-oldest in the country, having opened in 1870. The course was built after the governor of Maryland, Oden Bowie, made a proposition over dinner in 1868 to racing gurus in Saratoga, New York. The proposition included a race, to be held two years after the dinner, between horses that were yearlings at the time of the dinner. The American Jockey Club wanted to host the race, but Bowie pledged to build a state-of-the-art racetrack in Baltimore if the race was held there. After the pledge was made, plans were put in place for the birth of Pimlico.

Pimlico (originally spelled "pemblicoe") was a name given to the area west of the Jones Falls, an 18-mile-long stream that runs through the city of Baltimore and into the Inner Harbor, during the colonial era. The Maryland Jockey Club bought 70 acres in the area for $23,500 and constructed the racetrack for $25,000. Race day was always a big event at Pimlico, and horse-drawn carriages made their way through Druid Hill Park toward the course before additional roads were built directly to the track.

Pimlico quickly became an institution. It has survived wars, recession, the Great Depression, fire, and storms. The first Preakness Stakes was held here in 1873 and remains a time-honored tradition.

Area (Route 176 on Dorsey Road) and at the light-rail station (on the west side of Route 648).

The **Baltimore and Annapolis Trail** (410/222-6244) is a 15.5-mile paved trail that runs along a railroad route from Dorsey Road (near BWI Airport) and ends at the Annapolis waterfront. At the north end of the trail is a short connector to the BWI Bike Trail.

The **Gwynns Falls Trail** (www.gwynnsfallstrail.org) covers 15 miles between the I-70 Park and Ride trailhead and the Inner Harbor. The trail connects 30 neighborhoods in west and southwest Baltimore.

Bikes can be rented at **Light Street Cycles** (1124 Light St., 410/685-2234, Mon.-Fri. 10am-7pm, Sat. 10am-6pm, hybrids $30 per day, mountain bikes and road bikes $60 per day).

PADDLEBOATS

Most kids get wide-eyed when they see the lineup of brightly colored "Chessie" the sea monster paddleboats at **Paddleboats Team Chessie** (301 E. Pratt St., www.baltimorepaddleboats.org, Memorial Day-Labor Day daily 11am-10pm, mid-Apr.-day before Memorial Day and day after Labor Day-mid-Nov. daily 11am-6pm, $20 per half hour) on the waterfront. Renting a paddleboat for a half hour or an hour is a fun way to get a new perspective on the harbor. Regular paddleboats are also available for rent ($12 per half hour).

CRUISES

Urban Pirates

Bring the family on a unique 1.5-hour adventure in the harbor. The **Urban Pirates** (Ann Street Pier, Fell's Point, 410/327-8378, www.urbanpirates.com, $22-25) offers pirate cruises out of Fell's Point. Three pirates lead an interactive adventure where guests can dress up, get their faces painted, get a tattoo, and then depart on a cruise complete with songs, games, water cannons, and treasure. Adult cruises are also offered.

Paddle Wheeler Cruise

The Black-Eyed Susan (2600 Boston St., 410/342-6960, www.baltimorepaddlewheel.com) is an authentic paddle wheeler that is docked in Canton but can board passengers at the Maryland Science Center, Pier 5 Hotel, and Broadway Pier in Fell's Point. It is designed for entertainment and can be chartered for corporate or private events, but public events (such as murder mystery dinner cruises for $70) are also offered.

Paddleboats Team Chessie

Food

DOWNTOWN AND THE INNER HARBOR

American

The Capital Grille (500 E. Pratt St., 443/703-4064, www.thecapitalgrille.com, Mon.-Thurs. 11:30am-10pm, Fri. 11:30am-11pm, Sat. 5pm-11pm, Sun. 4pm-9pm, $29-50) on Pratt Street is part of a national chain of restaurants, but still offers a superb dining experience in a great location on the Inner Harbor. Steak and seafood make up the bulk of the menu in this traditional steak house, but the good service and pleasant atmosphere add to its overall appeal.

The **Corner & Bistro Winebar** (213 Penn St., 410/727-1155, www.cbwinebar.com, lunch Tues.-Thurs. 11am-2pm, Fri. 11:30am-2:30pm, dinner Sun. 4pm-10pm, Mon.-Thurs. 5pm-midnight, Fri. 5pm-10pm, Sat. 4pm-1am, $10-17) is a casual little bistro and wine bar that serves a bar menu of tasty appetizers and a small lunch and dinner menu of salads, burgers, and ciabattas. Try the Chesapeake, a ciabatta with grilled marinated chicken breast, crab dip, and grilled tomato and a side of sweet potato fries. The bistro is easy to walk to from attractions such as the Babe Ruth Birthplace Museum and is about a half block off Pratt Street.

Asian

Ban Thai Restaurant (340 N. Charles St., 410/727-7971, www.banthai.us, Mon.-Thurs. 11am-10:30pm, Fri.-Sat. 11am-11pm, Sun. noon-9:30pm, $13-21) opened in 1993, and the same chefs that were here then are still cooking delightful Thai dishes in the kitchen today. The modest restaurant is known for its made-to-order food. They do a nice job with spices and can make each dish as hot or mild as you like. The menu includes a variety of classic and more daring dishes so both beginners and those experienced with Thai cuisine should have no problem finding a suitable dish. Vegetarian dishes are on the menu as well, but some have fish sauce. Try for a seat by the window so you can people-watch on Charles Street.

Brazilian

For die-hard carnivores, it's hard to beat the Brazilian steak house **Fogo De Chao** (600 E. Pratt St., 410/528-9292, www.fogodechao.com, lunch Mon.-Fri. 11:30am-2pm, dinner Mon.-Thurs. 5pm-10pm, Fri. 5pm-10:30pm, Sat. 4pm-10:30pm, Sun. 4pm-9pm, lunch $34.95, dinner $51.95). This dining experience includes a large salad bar with more than 30 items, then an onslaught of 15 cuts of fire-roasted meats brought tableside. Each guest has a card to turn to green when you'd like more meat offered or red when you are taking a break or have had enough. This is a fun place to bring business guests (if they are not vegetarian) and a good place for groups. Although this restaurant is part of a small chain out of Dallas, Texas, this is the only location in Maryland.

Turkish

Cazbar (316 N. Charles St., 410/528-1222, www.cazbar.pro, Mon.-Thurs. 11am-11pm, Fri.-Sat. 11am-midnight, Sun. 4pm-11pm, $16-27) is Baltimore's first authentic Turkish restaurant. They offer consistently good food, a warm and pleasant atmosphere, and friendly staff. As one person sitting close by commented, "I will eat here until my mouth burns like the fires of hell. It's that good." Although the food isn't generally that spicy, it's always good to know someone will take one for the team. The servers know the menu well and can help with tough decisions. Try their hummus or Mohamra walnut dip for a starter. They also have Turkish beer and sangria. On Friday and Saturday nights there are free belly dancing shows—not many places can say that.

FELL'S POINT AND LITTLE ITALY

American

Peter's Inn (504 S. Ann St., 410/675-7313, www.petersinn.com, Tues.-Sun. 6:30pm-10pm, Fri.-Sat. 6:30pm-11pm, $11-30) is a casual contemporary eatery that is known for its innovative dishes and fresh ingredients. It is housed in a farmhouse built in 1799 and the owners live upstairs. The restaurant was mainly known as a biker bar throughout the 1980s and early 1990s but has since transformed into a great food-focused restaurant. The menu changes weekly (look for the chalkboard next to the men's washroom) with the exception of salad, steaks, and garlic bread, which are staples. The restaurant is crowded on weekends so expect a wait (perhaps at their bar). They do not take reservations.

Beer lovers will think they've won the lottery after stepping inside ★ **Max's Taphouse** (737 S. Broadway, 410/675-6297, www.maxs.com, daily 11am-2am $10-12.50). With 140 rotating drafts, 102 taps, 5 casks, and 1,200 bottles in stock, you could spend a lifetime here searching for your favorite beer. This beer-lover's institution is Baltimore's premier beer pub and has been featured in countless magazines and "best of" lists. The friendly owner, expert "beertenders" (many of whom have been here for more than a dozen years), and delicious pub menu make this well-known establishment in the heart of Fell's Point not just a great drinking spot, but also a great place to eat and hang out with new and old friends. For the sports minded, they offer numerous televisions, pool tables, foosball, and dartboards. Private rooms are available with large-screen TVs, custom beer lists, and great sound systems with iPod connections. Weekday specials such as "Monday sucks happy hour" and "Friday big ass draft happy hour" occur weekly in addition to great annual events such as Max's Annual German Beer Fest and the Hopfest.

If you are looking for a classy restaurant with a lovely atmosphere and delicious food, and you don't mind paying for it, then make a reservation at the acclaimed ★ **Charleston Restaurant** (1000 Lancaster St., 410/332-7373, www.charlestonrestaurant.com, Mon.-Sat. 5:30pm-10pm, $79-212). They offer an extensive prix fixe tasting menu with three to six courses and an award-winning wine list of more than 800 labels. Chef Cindy Wolf has been a James Beard Award finalist for best chef, mid-Atlantic, on multiple occasions, and as recently as 2016. She is one of the best-known chefs in the city. Wolf's cooking is a blend of French fundamentals and South Carolina's Low Country cuisine. The restaurant is in Harbor East near Fell's Point. A jacket and tie are recommended but not required.

The **Blue Moon Café** (1621 Aliceanna St., 410/522-3940, www.bluemoonbaltimore.com, daily 7am-3pm, weekends 24 hours, $5-16) is a well-known breakfast café that was featured on Guy Fieri's show *Diners, Drive-Ins and Dives.* Open 24 hours on weekends, this small eatery inside a converted row house has a line out the door on the average Saturday or Sunday. The reason couldn't be that they're serving Captain Crunch—or could it? Captain Crunch french toast is one of their most popular dishes, but Maryland Eggs Benedict and delightful homemade biscuits and gravy are other very convincing reasons.

Exposed brick and beams, high ceilings, and dark wood add to the charm of the **Red Star Bar and Grill** (906 S. Wolfe St., 410/675-0212, www.redstarbar.us, Mon.-Thurs. 11:30am-midnight, Fri. 11:30am-2am, Sat. 10am-2am, Sun. 10am-midnight, $7-20). This fun eatery is a little off the beaten path in Fell's Point but still within easy walking distance of all the action. They serve great sandwiches, pizza, and burgers and also offer a nice selection of beer. This is a fun, casual place with a good vibe and tasty menu. They also have full bar, which is a comfortable place to stop in for a drink or meet friends.

A unique find is **One-Eyed Mike's** (708 S. Bond St., 410/327-0445, www.oneeyedmikes.com, Mon.-Fri. 11am-2am,

Sat.-Sun. 10am-2am, $7-35). This lovely little treasure is one of the oldest operating taverns in Baltimore. It's housed in a tiny space on the edge of Fell's Point in an off-the-beaten-path row house. Walk through the bar and to the lovely little restaurant in the back, where they serve delicious crab cakes and stuffed filet. The staff is fun, the atmosphere is comfortable, and the food is good. The backbar was hand-carved, and they still have the original tin ceiling, both of which were put in during the 1860s. They also offer courtyard seating in nice weather. Ask about their Grand Marnier Club, the world's first.

British Pub

The **Wharf Rat** (801 S. Ann St., 410/276-8304, www.thewharfrat.com, daily 11am-2am, $9-20) harkens back to a day when old seaport taverns were filled with visiting sailors. The name itself is a term used in the 18th century for seafarers and pirates when they came ashore. This is a fun place for great beer and pub food (their specialty is crab dip pizza and fish-and-chips). The bartenders are also the cooks, so be patient with your food. The atmosphere is friendly and inviting, and the pub is allegedly haunted.

Seafood

Thames Street Oyster House (1728 Thames St., 443/449-7726, www.thamesstreetoysterhouse.com, lunch Wed.-Sun. 11:30am-2:30pm, dinner Sun.-Thurs. 5pm-9:30pm, Fri.-Sat. 5pm-10:30pm, raw bar open until 1am, $12-27) is a slightly upscale gem amid the bar scene in Fell's Point. They offer a fun staff and a lively nighttime atmosphere, but can also be a great place for a romantic seafood dinner if you reserve a table early in the evening. This is a classic oyster house with a great raw bar. There's a large bar area, and a water view from the upstairs.

Italian

There is no shortage of great Italian restaurants in Little Italy and the surrounding area. ★ **Amiccis** (231 S. High St., 410/528-1096, www.amiccis.com, Sun.-Thurs. 11am-11pm, Fri.-Sat. 11am-midnight, $14-19) has been a tradition in Baltimore since 1991. It's a self-proclaimed "Very Casual Eatery" whose mission is to provide great homemade Italian comfort food in a relaxed environment. All the menu items are wonderful, but first-timers should try the signature appetizer, the Pane' Rotundo. People in the know call it "that great shrimp and bread thing," and you'll see why after you try it. Amiccis also has a nice bar area that was added as the restaurant expanded from 25 seats to 300, and the original two friends who bought it are still running it today. The atmosphere is lively, and the patrons are a mix of locals and visitors.

Amiccis

★ **Vaccaro's Italian Pastry Shop** (222 Albemarle St., 410/685-4905, www.vaccarospastry.com, café menu $5-10) is *the* place to go in Baltimore for Italian pastries. They are widely known for their incredible cannoli filling but also offer many other delectable baked goods such as rum cake, biscotti, and cheesecake. They also offer a café menu of salads and sandwiches and make cakes, cookie trays, and other items such as tiramisu for parties and other occasions. There are three additional locations throughout the Baltimore area (2919 O'Donnell St., 118 Shawan Rd., and 696A Bel Air Rd.).

For a great slice of pizza pie, stop in **Brick Oven Pizza** (800 S. Broadway, 410/563-1600, www.boppizza.com, Sun.-Thurs. 11am-11pm, Fri.-Sat. 11am-3am, $9-24), another fun, casual restaurant that was featured on *Diners, Drive-Ins and Dives.* The crispy-crust pizza and the list of more than 40 toppings including crab, gyro meat, and even Spam are reason enough dine here, but they also offer wraps, pasta, and salads.

Greek

The Black Olive (814 S. Bond St., 410/276-7141, www.theblackolive.com, $27-40) serves authentic organic Greek food in a cozy section of Fell's Point. This elegant restaurant is family-owned and uses organic produce, dairy, flours, and sugars in all dishes. They have relationships with local farms and also serve fresh fish from all over the world including black sea bass, barbouni, and turbo. They boast the largest wine list in Baltimore. The wine cellar and dining rooms are available for private parties.

CANTON

American

The raven handrails are just one of many "Poe" details at **Annabel Lee Tavern** (601 S. Clinton St., 410/522-2929, www.annabelleetavern.com, Mon.-Sat. 4pm-1am, Sun. 3pm-midnight, $11-25). Baltimore is a natural setting for a restaurant and bar done in "Edgar Allan Poe." This unique little restaurant is a warm, funky place to have a good meal or a house cocktail off the Poe-themed drink list. The walls are inscribed with Poe's work. The tavern serves affordable upscale comfort food from an interesting but not over-the-top menu (try the rosemary beef tenderloin gyro or the roasted orange roughy tacos). They offer many daily specials and nice vegetarian options, but are known for their duck fat fries, which are worth a try if you've never had them.

The **Blue Hill Tavern** (938 S. Conkling St., 443/388-9363, www.bluehilltavern.com, brunch Sat.-Sun. 10:30am-2:30pm, lunch Mon.-Fri. 11:30am-2:30pm, dinner Mon.-Wed. 5pm-9pm, Thurs.-Sat. 5pm-10pm, Sun.

Vaccaro's Italian Pastry Shop

4pm-9pm, $13-29) is a great little modern tavern a few blocks off O'Donnell Street in Canton. Presentation is key in this trendy restaurant, and the food tastes as good as it looks. The menu includes a variety of American food with a heavy lean toward seafood. Try the mushroom Wellington, surf and turf, or yellowfin tuna and shrimp roulade. They also offer a hearty burger and salads. There's a rooftop patio for summertime dining that is one of the best in the city, even though it isn't on the water. They offer free valet parking.

Greek

The **Sip and Bite Restaurant** (2200 Boston St., 410/675-7077, www.sipandbite.com, open 24/7, $5-28) is a Baltimore landmark that was featured on *Diners, Drive-Ins and Dives*. This 1948 original between Fell's Point and Canton is owned by a husband-and-wife team that are the third generation in one family to run this diner. They offer a huge menu of breakfast, lunch, and dinner with a slant toward Greek dishes. They serve classic Greek specialties like gyros, but also have killer crab cakes made from a 60-year-old family recipe.

Seafood

Mama's on the Half Shell (2901 O'Donnell St., 410/276-3160, www.mamasmd.com, Mon.-Fri. 11am-2am, Sat.-Sun. 9am-2pm, $23-35) opened in 2003 and quickly became a tradition in Canton. This classic seafood house sits on the corner of O'Donnell Street and South Linwood Avenue in the heart of the neighborhood. They specialize in large, succulent oyster dishes (oyster stew, fried oysters, grilled oysters—you get the picture) but also have wonderful crab dishes, other seafood favorites, and a filet mignon selection. The two-story restaurant has a dark wood interior, a long bar on the first floor, and patio seating. The staff is warm and friendly, and they offer daily specials.

Mediterranean

The **Speakeasy Saloon** (2840 O'Donnell St., 410/276-2977, Mon.-Thurs. 4:30pm-11pm, Fri.-Sat. 11:30am-11pm, Sun. 10am-10pm, bar daily until 2am, $12-22) is a an elegant saloon with a throwback decor to the Roaring Twenties. A 150-year-old staircase, large murals, mirrors, and a tin ceiling help visitors visualize what things were like when gangsters and flappers frequented the original corner establishment. The upstairs patio boasts beautiful ironwork railings accented with flower boxes and a redbrick exterior. The food is surprisingly good for the reasonable prices they charge, with both seafood and Mediterranean dishes (examples include Mediterranean chicken, veal marsala, lamb scampi, and pork Athena). If you're looking for a quiet spot, sit on the patio, since it can get loud inside on a busy night.

Mama's on the Half Shell

Mexican

If you like good Mexican food and you can put up with a few house rules, such as "Report any Elvis sightings to server," "Be nice or leave," and "Don't feed kitchen staff," then take a table at **Nacho Mama's** (2907 O' Donnell St., 410/675-0898, www.nachomamascanton.com, Mon.-Sat. 11am-2am, Sun. 9am-2am, $11-30) in the heart of Canton. Nacho Mama's has been a hot spot in Baltimore since it opened on Elvis's birthday in 1994. The decor is a mix of the King, Natty Boh, the Orioles, the Baltimore Colts, and everything else Baltimore. The food is delicious, the portions are large, and they have more than a dozen kinds of margaritas. This is a great place to bring visitors to share some Baltimore tradition.

FEDERAL HILL

American

Peanut butter burgers, waffle fry nachos, pretzel roll buns, and homemade chips are just some of the items to try at **The Abbey Burger Bistro** (1041 Marshall St., 443/453-9698, www.abbeyburgerbistro.com, kitchen hours Tues.-Sun. 11:30am-midnight, Mon. 5pm-midnight, $6-17.50). This burger-and-beer-focused eatery has a great menu for both, including a build-your-own burger section and a rotating beer list (they even take requests online). This is a great place to stir your creativity, fill your burger appetite, and wash it all down with a cold brew.

Hull Street Blues Cafe (1222 Hull St., 410/727-7476, www.hullstreetblues.com, lunch Tues.-Sat. 11am-5pm, Mon. 11am-10pm, Sun. brunch 10am-2pm, dinner Tues.-Thurs. 5pm-10pm, Fri.-Sat. 5pm-11pm, Sun. 4pm-9pm, $16-29) has a long history. It got its start as a saloon back in 1889 and is now a lovely neighborhood café. Nestled amid the blocks of row houses in Locust Point, the café is named for its side street address on Hull Street (which was named after a naval hero of the War of 1812, Isaac Hull). The restaurant has two sides: one is a casual barroom (where bar fare is served) with a 40-foot-long bar, and the other is the nautical-themed Commodore Room, where guests can enjoy gourmet meals off linens and stemware in front of the fireplace. Seafood, beef, and poultry are at the heart of the menu, but other options such as the chipotle-lime barbecue pork loin are local favorites.

Seafood

When you're craving good seafood and aren't looking for an upscale atmosphere, **Nick's Oyster Bar** (1065 S. Charles St., 410/685-2020, www.nicksoysterbar.com, Sun.-Thurs. 11am-7pm, Fri. 11am-10pm, Sat. 11am-9pm, $10-22) is the place to go. It is in the west end

Speakeasy Saloon

Natty Boh

The one-eyed, handlebar-mustached Mr. Boh pictured on a gold-and-white National Bohemian Beer can is not just the symbol for **National Bohemian Beer** (aka "Natty Boh"), but also a treasured icon in Baltimore. National Bohemian Beer was first brewed in Baltimore in 1885 by the National Brewing Company. After Prohibition, National Bohemian introduced Mr. Boh, who wears a distinctive smile that has delighted the people of Baltimore for decades.

Now make no mistake, Natty Boh is a cheap, domestic beer (think Pabst Blue Ribbon and Miller High Life); in fact the brand is now owned by Pabst Brewing Company. The beer's slogan is "From the Land of Pleasant Living," which refers to the Chesapeake Bay.

In 1965, Natty Boh became the Baltimore Orioles' official sponsor, and the beer was served at their former home, Memorial Stadium, as "the official beer of Baltimore."

The brand has been sold several times (the first in 1979 to Heileman Brewing Company), and in 1996 its production was moved out of the state. The beer was no longer available on tap in Baltimore. Disappointed fans went for years without their favorite beer being offered fresh from the keg (almost 90 percent of Natty Boh sales are in Baltimore), but in 2011, good news came. Pabst Blue Ribbon announced the return of the famous brew to Baltimore and the rest of Maryland on tap.

Nacho Mama's in Canton was one of the first to tap the newly available kegs, and did so on February 3, 2011. A packed house welcomed Natty Boh back. A total of eight official keg-tapping parties were held throughout the area, and it looks like the people of Baltimore can enjoy their beer on tap for the foreseeable future.

of the Cross Street Market area and has been in business since 1972. It has cement floors, bottles of beer on ice, televisions tuned to sports, and all the local seafood favorites (including a raw bar). The menu includes steamed shrimp, crab, fish-and-chips, mussels, and the famous crab soup. They also have a sushi bar. Pull a stool up to the counter, order a beer, and chat with the crowd that forms on weekends.

Another great seafood restaurant is **Ryleigh's Oyster Bar** (36 E. Cross St., 410/539-2093, www.ryleighs.com, Mon.-Sun. 11am-10pm, $8-29). The atmosphere is more upscale than a bar scene, and they offer really fresh oysters on their old slate oyster bar. There is a gourmet seafood menu with items such as crab cakes, tuna, and shrimp and grits. The crab pretzels are a great way to start, and they also offer salads and sandwiches and other items that aren't seafood.

MOUNT VERNON

Afghan

The Helmand (806 N. Charles St., 410/752-0311, www.helmand.com, Sun.-Thurs. 5pm-10pm, Fri.-Sat. 5pm-11pm, $13-17) looks like a simple restaurant but has been serving incredible Afghan food since 1989. It is one of a handful of eateries owned by a prominent Afghan family that helped bring the cuisine to the United States. Considered by many to be a local treasure, the *kaddo borawni*, a pumpkin appetizer, is a must-try before making the difficult entrée decision.

American

The tuxedoed servers, stuffed leather seats, live piano music, and stiff drinks haven't changed a bit at ★ **The Prime Rib** (1101 N. Calvert St., 410/539-1804, www.theprimerib.com, Mon.-Thurs. 5pm-10pm, Fri.-Sat. 5pm-11pm, Sun. 4pm-9pm, $28-63) since its opening in 1965. Jackets are required, and the place looks like an establishment Sinatra would have frequented. The best part, however, is the food. The Prime Rib has been named one of the best in the country by *Esquire* magazine for its steaks, and it is easy to believe. This is a place to come when you want first-class food and service to match, and you don't mind paying for it.

The funky little pizza shop **Joe Squared** (33 W. North Ave., 410/545-0444, www.joesquared.com, Sun.-Wed. 11am-midnight, Thurs.-Sat. 11am-2am, $11-25) offers coal-fired square pizza, 17 varieties of risotto, an extensive rum list, good beer, and free live music (funk, soul, jazz, old time, etc.). Featured on *Diners, Drive-Ins and Dives,* the restaurant is family-owned, and the food is delicious. The clientele is mainly college-aged, and the area isn't ideal after dark. There is also a location in the Inner Harbor (30 Market Pl.).

Italian

A great choice for pizza in Mount Vernon is **Iggies** (818 N. Calvert St., Ste. 1, 410/528-0818, www.iggiespizza.com, Tues.-Thurs. 11:30am-9pm, Fri-Sat. 11:30am-10pm, Sun. 11:30am-8pm, $10-18). The pizza has a thin, crispy crust and a multitude of interesting topping options (think peaches, gorgonzola, rosemary, etc.). The place is very casual, and you must BYOB if you'd like to drink. When you enter, wait to be seated. Once seated, leave your plate on the table and get in line to order. When your food is ready, the staff will call your name and order number. The pizza is excellent, and the crowd is young and lively. It's a great place to grab a bit before heading to Centerstage.

HAMPDEN AND HOMEWOOD

American

★ **Woodberry Kitchen** (2010 Clipper Park Rd., 410/464-8000, www.woodberrykitchen.com, brunch Sat.-Sun. 10am-2pm, dinner Mon.-Thurs. 5pm-10pm, Fri.-Sat. 5pm-11pm, Sun. 5pm-9pm, $15-48) is a hip little restaurant in the historic Clipper Mill west of Hampden. They serve local meats and seafood and use fresh organic ingredients. The menu is based on what is seasonal and includes many regional dishes (think brined pork chops and oysters roasted in a wood-burning oven). The atmosphere is contemporary in design, and the space, a renovated 19th-century industrial mill, offers the warm ambience of exposed brick, wood, and soft lighting. On nice evenings, diners can also enjoy patio seating under market umbrellas and white lights. Reservations are a must on weekends and should be made weeks in advance if possible.

The **Corner Charcuterie Bar** (850 W. 36th St., 443/869-5075, www.cornercharcuteriebar.com, lunch Wed.-Fri. at 11 am, dinner daily at 4pm, brunch Sat.-Sun 11am-2:30pm, $9-19) is a treasure in Hampden. They offer Belgium-influenced fare with interesting dishes such as roasted bone marrow and ostrich tartare and a great selection of meats and cheeses. A chef's $20 meal option changes daily as does the discount cocktail of the day. They have a convenience charge on credit card sales.

It's hard to find a more local dining institution in Hampden than **Café Hon** (1002 W. 36th St., 410/243-1230, www.cafehon.com, Mon.-Thurs. 11am-9pm, Fri. 11am-10pm, Sat. 9am-10pm, Sun. 9am-8pm, $7-19), and it's hard to miss the two-story pink

Café Hon is a local institution in Hampden.

flamingo that stands over its front door. The café name is a tribute to the "hon" culture in Hampden (see Honfest in the events section of this chapter), and the café serves a mix of comfort food and seafood. The adjoining Hon Bar offers live music and oyster shucking. This purely Baltimore establishment even has a Baltimore, Maryland, dictionary (or Bawlmer, Murlin, if you will) on the website.

Accommodations

$100-200

If you want to be where the action is in Fell's Point, book a room at the **Admiral Fell Inn** (888 S. Broadway, 410/522-7380, www.admiralfell.com, $169-289). This historic European-style hotel includes seven buildings, some of which date back to the 1770s. Many stories surround the inn, as the building has served many purposes such as a ship chandlery, boardinghouse, theater, and YMCA. No two rooms are alike at the inn but each is decorated in modern furnishings with a cozy decor. Two specialty rooms are available, one with two levels and the other with a balcony overlooking the waterfront. The Tavern at the Admiral Fell Inn is open Wednesday-Saturday evenings to serve beer, wine, cocktails, and traditional spirits.

Travelers looking for a charming boutique hotel near bustling O'Donnell Street in Canton will be thrilled with the **Inn at 2920** (2920 Elliott St., 410/342-4450, www.theinnat2920.com, $175-215). This five-room inn is inside a rather regular-looking row house on Elliott Street. Look for the pale-green door on the corner. Once inside, the rooms are lovely, unique, and contemporary. They have exposed brick walls and modern furnishings. This hip little hotel is definitely something special, and you'll feel like a local stepping out onto the street. The water is within walking distance, but Fell's Point is a good 15-20 minutes by foot.

Budget-conscious travelers can have a great stay at the **Brookshire Suites** (120 E. Lombard St., 410/625-1300, www.brookshiresuites.com, $107-199) just a block away from the Inner Harbor on Lombard Street. The 11-story, 97-room hotel has a distinct exterior with a large black-and-white geometric pattern that can't be missed. The interior is contemporary with traditional-style rooms. The hotel caters to business travelers and offers a nice business center and laundry facilities, but its central location makes it a good choice for pleasure travel as well.

$200-300

The **Monaco Baltimore** (2 N. Charles St., 443/692-6170, www.monaco-baltimore.com, $209-309) is consistent with other Kimpton Hotels as a top-notch choice for accommodations. This warm and friendly hotel is housed in the restored B&O Railroad building on Charles Street a few blocks northwest of the Inner Harbor. The personal service and attention to detail they offer is hard to beat. The hotel has Tiffany stained glass windows, a marble staircase, and vaulted ceilings. The rooms are large and modern with high ceilings and a hint of funky styling that's unique to Kimpton. The staff is wonderful, and the location is convenient to many restaurants and attractions even though it's not right on the water. They offer bikes and bike route maps to guests and a hosted wine hour in the evenings. They have 24-hour valet parking with in-and-out services for $38. The hotel is pet friendly.

The ★ **Hyatt Regency Baltimore** (300 Light St., 410/528-1234, www.baltimore.hyatt.com, $239-439) offers one of the best locations in the Inner Harbor. Situated right across Light Street from Harborplace and connected to it by two skywalks, the hotel offers tremendous harbor views. The rooms are modern

Traveling with Fido

Baltimore is surprisingly pet friendly for such a large and industrial city. Many hotels throughout the city allow your best friend to accompany you in your room. Additional fees and rules may apply to your four-legged friend, so ask when you make a reservation. Some hotels that allow dogs include:

- **Admiral Fell Inn** (888 S. Broadway, 410/522-7380)
- **Biltmore Suites** (205 W. Madison St., 410/728-6550)
- **Brookshire Suites** (120 E. Lombard St., 410/625-1300)
- **Four Seasons Hotel Baltimore** (200 International Dr., 410/576-5800)
- **Hilton Baltimore Convention Center Hotel** (401 W. Pratt St., 443/573-8700)
- **Holiday Inn Express Baltimore—Downtown** (221 N. Gay St., 410/400-8045)
- **Holiday Inn Inner Harbor Hotel** (301 W. Lombard St., 410/685-3500)
- **Hotel Monaco** (2 N. Charles St., 443/692-6170)
- **Intercontinental Harbor Court Hotel** (550 Light St., 410/234-0550)
- **Pier 5 Hotel** (711 Eastern Ave., 410/539-2000)
- **Lord Baltimore Hotel** (20 W. Baltimore St., 410/539-8400)
- **Residence Inn Downtown Baltimore/Inner Harbor** (17 Light St., 410/962-1220)
- **Sheraton Inner Harbor Hotel** (300 S. Charles St., 410/962-8300)
- **Sheraton Baltimore North** (903 Dulaney Valley Rd., 410/321-7400)
- **Sleep Inn & Suites Downtown Inner Harbor** (301 Fallsway, 410/779-6166)

and comfortable with large bathrooms and contemporary furniture. The building's lit-up, glass-enclosed elevators seem to shoot through the lobby roof and along the outside of the hotel. They are beautiful to look at and afford incredible views to the people inside. The hotel staff is also extremely helpful and pleasant. Bistro 300 on the third floor serves breakfast, lunch, and dinner (and has a nice bar). There is a small gift shop on-site, a fitness room, and pool. Ask for a harbor-view room on an upper floor; the corner rooms offer spectacular floor-to-ceiling windows overlooking the water.

The ★ **Inn at Hendersons Wharf** (1000 Fell St., 410/522-7777, www.hendersonswharf.com, $197-325) is a lovely boutique hotel sitting directly on the water on the eastern side of Fell's Point. The hotel is located in a large brick building dating back to 1893, which it shares with condos and a conference center. The inn's 38 cozy rooms have exposed brick walls, colonial décor, feather beds, and 30-inch televisions with satellite service. There's a pretty interior courtyard. Rooms include a continental breakfast, access to a fitness center and pools, and high-speed Internet. Self-parking is available for $10 per night. The hotel is close to restaurants and shops in Fell's Point but far enough away to filter the noise. Ask for a harbor view.

The **Courtyard Marriott Baltimore Downtown/Inner Harbor** (1000 Aliceanna St., 443/923-4000, www.marriott.com, $249-304) has 195 rooms and 10 suites not far from the waterfront. The staff at this hotel is exceptionally friendly and helpful. They also offer great packages for family members of patients at Johns Hopkins Hospital, which include a discounted room rate, breakfast, and cab vouchers to and from the hospital. There is a small indoor swimming pool, a small fitness room, and an on-site restaurant and bar serving breakfast, lunch, and dinner. High-speed Internet is included. Ask for an upper-floor room on the harbor side of the hotel, where limited water views are available.

For a less expensive stay that is still convenient to the Inner Harbor, the **Days Inn Baltimore—Inner Harbor Hotel** (100 Hopkins Pl., 410/576-1000, www.daysinnerharbor.com, $199-229) is the ticket. Just a few blocks from the stadiums and Inner Harbor, the 250 rooms are clean and convenient. Although the rooms aren't large, this is a well-located hotel with an affordable price tag.

OVER $300

The **Inn at the Black Olive** (803 S. Caroline St., 443/681-6316, www.innattheblackolive.com, $289-439) is a boutique organic hotel offering 12 luxury guests suites along the waterfront on the border of Fell's Point and the harbor. All the suites are modern, with water views and spa bathrooms. Rooms include a basic organic breakfast. Other room amenities include balconies or sitting porches, king-size beds with organic mattresses, Sanijet pipeless hydrotherapy tubs, and high-speed Internet. All rooms are cleaned with natural chemical-free cleaners. There's an organic market and rooftop restaurant on-site called The Olive Room that serves Greek cuisine and has a large wine list. The Inn at the Black Olive is a LEED Platinum Inn.

A good choice on the waterfront in the Harbor East area of Baltimore between Fell's Point and the Inner Harbor is the **Baltimore Marriott Waterfront Hotel** (700 Aliceanna St., 410/385-3000, www.marriott.com, $269-489). This towering 31-story hotel is on the water's edge and offers stunning harbor views and great access to many of the best attractions. There are 733 modern rooms and 21 suites. Harbor-view rooms and city-view rooms are available.

Right near the Baltimore Marriott Waterfront Hotel is the **Four Seasons Hotel Baltimore** (200 International Dr., 410/576-5800, www.fourseasons.com, $509-2,500), which offers great views of the harbor and an elegant interior. There are 256 rooms and suites with views including the harbor, city, and marina. The rooms offer generous space, and the stunning Presidential Suite is more than 2,800 square feet. The corner suites offer stunning views. The service is on par with other Four Seasons hotels, which is to say much above average.

Information and Services

Helpful tourist information on Baltimore can be found on the **Baltimore Area Convention and Visitors Association** website at www.baltimore.org. The website has details on events and attractions throughout the city and answers many common questions. Special offers are also available through the website. The **Baltimore Area Visitor Center** (401 Light St., 877/225-8466, Apr.-Sept. daily 9am-6pm, reduced hours the rest of the year) in the Inner Harbor is a great place to begin any trip to Baltimore. The 8,000-square-foot center offers information on nearly everything the city has to offer.

The most widely read paper in the city is the ***Baltimore Sun*** (www.baltimoresun.com). It is also Maryland's largest daily newspaper and covers local and regional news. The Baltimore ***City Paper*** (www.citypaper.com) is a free alternative weekly paper that is distributed on Wednesday. It is known for having good coverage of clubs, concerts, restaurants, and theater. It also has political articles and covers subjects not featured in mainstream publications.

There are 31 hospitals in the metropolitan area of Baltimore. Top-ranking facilities include **Johns Hopkins Hospital** (1800 Orleans St., 410/955-5000, www.hopkinsmedicine.org) and the **University of Maryland Medical Center** (22 S. Greene St., 410/328-8667, www.umm.edu).

Getting There

AIR

The **Baltimore Washington International Thurgood Marshall Airport (BWI)** (410/859-7111, www.bwiairport.com) is just 10 miles south of Baltimore and a short 15-minute car ride from downtown Baltimore. This busy regional airport is a hub for Southwest Airlines and offers some of the best fares in the Washington DC/Baltimore area. Most other major airlines offer flight service to BWI as well. Parking is available at the airport by the hour or day, and there is a free cell phone lot for those who are picking up arriving passengers.

Car rentals are available at the airport from numerous national car rental companies, and courtesy shuttles run between the airport and major downtown hotels. The **SuperShuttle** (www.supershuttle.com, approximately $15 for a shared van) runs 24-hour service from the airport to locations throughout Baltimore and has a reservation counter on the lower level of the airport near baggage claims 1 and 10.

Cab service is also available from the airport, but this can be a costly option with fares running upward of $40 to downtown Baltimore.

Train service is available from the airport to downtown Baltimore through the Maryland Transit Administration (MTA) on their **Light Rail** (410/539-5000, www.mta.maryland.gov/light-rail, Mon.-Fri. 5am-11pm, Sat. 6am-11pm, Sun. 11am-7pm, $1.60). The BWI Marshall Light Rail station can be found outside the lower lever of the terminal near Concourse E.

CAR

Baltimore is a very accessible city. Strategically located right on I-95, it can be reached easily by car from both the north and south. The drive from major cities such as New York (3.5 hours, 188 miles), Philadelphia (2 hours, 100 miles), Washington DC (1 hour, 39 miles), and Richmond (2.75 hours, 152 miles) is a straight shot and takes between one and four hours. I-83 also runs into the city from the north.

TRAIN

Pennsylvania Station (1515 N. Charles St., 800/872-7245, www.amtrak.com) is centrally located on Charles Street near Mount Vernon and is less than two miles from the Inner Harbor. The stately 1911 building is nicely restored, and the station is one of the busiest in the country. Amtrak runs dozens of trains through Penn Station daily from all corners of the country. They offer ticket discounts for seniors, children, students, veterans, and conference groups.

A commuter rail service called **Maryland Area Rail Commuter (MARC)** (410/539-5000, www.mta.maryland.gov) operates trains on weekdays between Washington DC and Baltimore ($8 one way). This is another option for visitors traveling during the week.

BUS

Just south of downtown Baltimore in an industrial section of the city is the **Greyhound** bus station (2110 Haines St., 800/231-2222, www.greyhound.com). Bus service runs daily from multiple destinations. It is advisable to take a cab from the station to points around

Baltimore. Walking near the station is not advisable after dark.

A number of private bus lines provide service between cities in the mid-Atlantic and offer reasonable fares from cities such as Washington DC, Philadelphia, and New York City. An example is **Peter Pan Bus Lines** (800/343-9999, www.peterpanbus.com, $14 one-way from DC). Additional service can be found on www.gotobus.com.

Getting Around

Although walking is a viable option for getting to many of the sights in Baltimore, depending on where you are staying, it is often easiest (and safest at night) to move around the city by car. Public transportation does provide other alternatives; however, most public transportation is geared toward commuters and isn't the most convenient for visitors wishing to explore major attractions.

The exception to this is the **Charm City Circulator** (www.charmcitycirculator.com, year round Mon.-Thurs. 7am-8pm, Fri. 7am-midnight, Sat. 9am-midnight, Sun 9am-8pm). This free, eco-friendly shuttle service has a fleet of 30 Hybrid electric shuttles that serve four routes in Baltimore City. The Green Route offers transportation from City Hall to Fell's Point and to Johns Hopkins. The Purple Route serves locations from 33rd Street to Federal Hill. The Orange Route runs between Hollins Market and Harbor East and the Banner Route goes from the Inner Harbor to Fort McHenry. Shuttles stop every 10-15 minutes at each designated stop.

CAR

Downtown Baltimore is divided by two main streets. Baltimore Street runs east to west, and Charles Street runs north to south. All streets north of Baltimore Street (or above Baltimore Street if you're looking at a map) have the "north" designation (such as N. Highland Street). Likewise, those south (or below) Baltimore Street have a "south" designation. The same is true for the streets east and west of Charles Street (which is a one-way street running north downtown). Those streets to the east of Charles Street (or to the right) have "east" designations. Those to the west (left) have "west" designations.

When driving, it is very important to be aware that there are many one-way streets in Baltimore. Parking isn't too difficult in most parts of the city on weekends; however, garages right around the Inner Harbor can be expensive. Parking during the week is more of a challenge when commuters are in town and spaces are in short supply. There is on-street parking in many areas and pay lots are scattered throughout town. Be sure to read parking signs carefully, as many neighborhoods have resident-only parking and time restrictions.

Overall, driving in Baltimore is much as it is in other big cities. Drive with purpose and have a plan as to where you are headed. Sightseeing out the window in the middle of traffic can result in some less-than-friendly gestures from those in cars around you. When in doubt, or if you miss a turn, just drive around the block; it's difficult to get too lost if you keep an eye on the harbor.

BUS

Bus service provided by the **Maryland Transit Administration (MTA)** (410/539-5000, www.mtamaryland.com, $1.60) includes 73 routes in Baltimore. Forty-seven of these routes are local routes inside the city. Bus routes primarily serve commuters on weekdays and are more limited on weekends, but it pays to check out the latest schedule online.

RAIL

Two public rail systems serve Baltimore, although each only has one rail line. The first,

All Aboard the Water Taxi

Baltimore Water Taxi

For decades residents and visitors to Baltimore have enjoyed an alternative form of public transportation around the city. The **Baltimore Water Taxi** (410/563-3900, www.thewatertaxi.com) is a fun, easy way to travel between some of the best attractions, shopping areas, and restaurants in town. The famed blue-and-white boats can be seen zipping between 17 well-placed landings along the waterfront. The taxi service shuttles thousands of commuters and visitors alike on a daily basis, and local businesses rely on the service to bring their customers.

During the summer months, the taxi runs 10am-11pm Monday-Saturday and 10am-9pm Sunday. Hours are shorter during the remainder of the year. All-day adult passes are $14, and trip times range 10-20 minutes. Tickets can be purchased online with a credit card or on board with cash or a personal check. Landing areas are as follows:

- Landing 1: Aquarium
- Landing 2: Harborplace
- Landing 3: Science Center
- Landing 4: Rusty Scupper
- Landing 5: Pier Five
- Landing 7: Harbor East
- Landing 8: Maritime Park
- Landing 9: HarborView
- Landing 10: Locust Point
- Landing 11: Fell's Point
- Landing 14: Captain James Landing
- Landing 16: Canton Waterfront Park
- Landing 17: Fort McHenry

called **Light Rail** (410/539-5000, www.mtamaryland.com, Mon.-Fri. 5am-12am, Sat. 6am-12am, Sun. 11am-7pm, $1.70), runs from BWI Airport north to Hunt Valley Mall (in northern Baltimore County). This is only a good option if you are traveling between two specific points on the line, such as Camden Yards to Mount Vernon (there are no east/west stops). The second is the **Metro Subway** (410/539-5000, www.mtamaryland.com, Mon.-Fri. 5am-12am, Sat.-Sun. 6am-12am, $1.70) that runs from the suburbs northwest of town and into downtown and Johns Hopkins. The line is 15.5 miles, and has 14 stations. Trains run every 8-10 minutes during rush hour, every 11 minutes on weekday evenings, and every 15 minutes on weekends. Again, this line is geared toward commuters and isn't too helpful for visitors wishing to move around town between sights.

TAXI

Taxi service is available through three providers: **Yellow Cab** (410/685-1212), **Diamond** (410/947-3333), and **Royal** (410/327-0330). Hailing a cab on the street can be an impossible feat on busy nights in the city, so it's best to bring their phone numbers and try calling from your cell phone. Metered rates in Baltimore are $1.80 for the first one-eleventh of a mile or fraction thereof. Each additional one-eleventh of a mile is $0.20; $0.20 is also charged for each 30 seconds of wait time.

WATER TAXI

Water taxi service (410/563-3900, www.thewatertaxi.com) is available around the harbor between many of the popular sights. This is a great service for visitors. The little boats with the blue awnings that can be seen scooting around the harbor are the taxi boats. They move between 17 stops that include all the prime waterfront destinations (including Fell's Point, Canton, and Fort McHenry in the summer). The boat captains are often chatting and make excellent tour guides.

BIKE

Biking in Baltimore as a mode of transportation is becoming more popular. Many attractions have iron bike racks that look like bicycles stationed out front, so cyclists have a convenient place to lock up their bikes (yes, lock your bike). New bike lanes are being added around the city to encourage biking, although narrow roads and hills will always be a factor and riding in traffic can be risky when the streets are crowded.

Excursions

If you have extra time and want to venture outside of Baltimore for a half- or full-day excursion, Havre de Grace and Westminster are two very different, yet equally alluring towns to visit. Havre de Grace provides the attractions of a historic bayside community, while Westminster offers Civil War history and a wonderful farm museum.

HAVRE DE GRACE

Havre de Grace is a beautiful little town in Harford County that sits at the head of the Chesapeake Bay and the mouth of the mighty Susquehanna River. Its name in French means "Harbor of Beauty" or "Harbor of Grace."

The city was once seriously considered for the location of the nation's capital. Havre de Grace was incorporated in 1785 and has a population of around 13,000. Its seaside-like atmosphere makes it a popular tourist and outdoor recreation destination.

Havre de Grace is halfway between Baltimore and Philadelphia. It was, at one time, a popular stop for stagecoaches traveling between the two cities. Between 1912 and 1950, it was home to the Havre de Grace Racetrack, a popular horse-racing track.

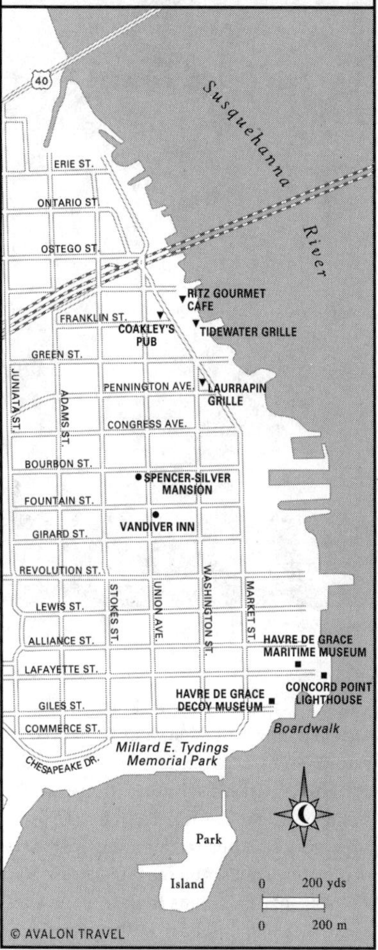

Famous horses such as Man o' War, his son War Admiral, Seabiscuit, and Challedon raced here during its heyday. For years, the Havre de Grace Handicap was one of the most highly regarded races in the northeast. The track was sold in 1951 to the owners of two other Maryland racetracks (Pimlico Race Course and Laurel Park Racecourse). The new owners closed the Havre de Grace course and moved the track's racing allotment dates to their own facilities.

Havre de Grace shelters well over 100 historic structures, and the town is designated a National Historic District. The town was first mapped in 1799, and the structures that remain today are of many different ages and architectural designs. Simple Victorian duplexes stand side by side with single-family homes and Queen Anne estates built by wealthy residents.

Sights

HAVRE DE GRACE MARITIME MUSEUM

The **Havre de Grace Maritime Museum** (100 Lafayette St., 410/939-4800, www.hdgmaritimemuseum.org, April 1-Oct.14 Wed.-Sat. 10am-5pm, Sun. 1pm-5pm, Oct. 15-Mar. 31 Sat. 10am-5pm, Sun. 1pm-5pm, $3) is a small window into the history of the upper Chesapeake Bay and lower Susquehanna River. Exhibits explore topics such as fishing, waterfowl hunting, lighthouses, navigation, the Native Americans who lived in the region, European settlers, and wooden boat building.

CONCORD POINT LIGHTHOUSE

The **Concord Point Lighthouse** (corner of Concord and Lafayette Sts., 410/939-3213, www.concordpointlighthouse.org, Apr.-Oct. Sat.-Sun. 1pm-5pm, free, donations appreciated) is a pretty little piece of history on the waterfront in Havre de Grace. The lighthouse was built in 1827 out of local granite and is one of the oldest lighthouses on the East Coast that has operated continuously. Now fully restored, it stands on a scenic stretch of the promenade. The climb up the 30-foot lighthouse tower is fairly short (as lighthouses go), so it's a fun activity to do with children (but they must be at least 42 inches tall). The lighthouse offers terrific views of the Susquehanna River and the Chesapeake Bay. There are a few informative exhibits at the Keeper's House (which used to be a bar) that give details on the lighthouse's first keeper, John O'Neil, and the history of the lighthouse. There is a gift shop.

HAVRE DE GRACE DECOY MUSEUM

The **Havre de Grace Decoy Museum** (215 Giles St., 410/939-3739, www.decoymuseum.com, Mon.-Sat. 10:30am-4:30pm, Sun. noon-4pm, $6) is more than a showcase for wooden birds. Decoys have been part of the culture on the Chesapeake Bay for centuries. Originally, they were not considered art, but were made purely to lure waterfowl within hunting range. Today decoys are an art form. Carvers create sophisticated reproductions of birds using century-old skills. This pretty little museum is home to one of the best collections of functional and decorative Chesapeake Bay decoys in existence. Visitors can learn the history of waterfowling on the upper Chesapeake Bay and also how decoys are made through exhibits, lectures, tours, and demonstrations. More than 1,200 decoys are on display. Annual festivals are held at the museum, and there is a nice little gift shop with decoys, books, and other waterfowl-related items.

the Concord Point Lighthouse

TYDINGS PARK

Tydings Park (350 Commerce St. at the southern end of Union Ave., 410/939-1800) is a 22-acre park on the waterfront in Havre de Grace. It is situated at the head of the Chesapeake Bay and is the site of several annual festivals and concerts. The park facilities include a fishing pier, boat ramp, picnic area, tennis courts, gazebos, and a playground. It is also the starting point of the half-mile **Havre de Grace Promenade,** a waterfront walkway that goes past the Maritime Museum and continues to the Concord Point Lighthouse. The park is also known as the **Millard E. Tydings Memorial Park.**

THE SUSQUEHANNA MUSEUM AT THE LOCK HOUSE

The Susquehanna Museum at the Lock House (817 Conesteo Street, 410-939-5780, www.thelockhousemuseum.org, mid-April-Oct. Fri.-Sun. 1pm-5pm, free) is a museum inside a historic house, which was built in 1840 and home to one of the lock tenders for the Susquehanna and Tidewater Canal (which ran 45 miles between Havre de Grace and Wrightsville, Pennsylvania). It also served as the office for the Toll Collector. The two-story brick building was almost twice the size of other lock houses on the Canal (there were 29 locks total). Exhibits in the museum recreate life along the canal and provide details on Havre de Grace's role in the growth of the country.

Recreation

There are several **boat launch sites** in Havre de Grace. The first two are at the mouth of the Susquehanna River. One is north of the train bridge at the intersection of Otsego and Union Streets (on Water Street at Jean Roberts Memorial Park). The second is just downstream, off of Franklin Street by the Tidewater Grille (this is just for cartop boats since there is no ramp). A third launch site is at Tydings Park off Commerce Street, on the south side of town. This site is right on the Chesapeake Bay. It is important to know that boating near the Aberdeen Proving Ground south of the city is strictly forbidden. In addition to getting a fine for trespassing, landing anywhere on the proving grounds can be very dangerous because there are live munitions. Obey all signage in the area and respect the buoy markers.

Three miles northwest of Havre de Grace is the beautiful **Susquehanna State Park** (410/557-7994, www.dnr.state.md.us, daily 9am-sunset, Nov.-Feb. weekends only, $4). The park offers boating ($12 launch fee), hiking, mountain biking, kayaking, fishing, a playground, and picnicking. There are also several historic buildings on-site such as a 200-year-old gristmill (visitors can tour its four floors), a stone mansion, a barn, a tollhouse, and a miller's house. All buildings are open on weekends between Memorial Day and Labor Day from 10am-4pm. A section of the former **Susquehanna and Tidewater Canal** can be seen in the park. This canal was built in 1836 and connected Havre de Grace with Wrightsville, Pennsylvania. Mule-drawn barges made this an important commercial route for more than 50 years. To reach the park, take I-95 to exit 89, and then proceed west on Route 155 to Route 161. Turn right on Route 161 and then right again on Rock Run Road.

Food

Cold beer, good pub food, and friendly service can be found at **Coakley's Pub** (406 St. John St., 410/939-8888, www.coakleyspub.com, Mon.-Sat 11am-10pm, Sun. 11am-9pm, $4-24) on St. John Street. This cozy spot offers quality fare with a Chesapeake Bay flair (try the crab pretzel). The food and service are consistent, and the atmosphere is casual and inviting.

The ★ **Laurrapin Grille** (209 N. Washington St., 410/939-4956, www.laurrapin.com, Mon.-Thurs. 4pm-10pm, Fri. 4pm-2am, Sat. 11am-2am, Sun. noon-6:30pm, $11-25) is a contemporary American restaurant that specializes in seasonally inspired food. They take fresh local ingredients and turn them into delicious and creative items that take advantage of the bounty of the surrounding area. The result is a wonderful menu with dinner entrées that include crab cakes, lamb, pasta, salmon, and steak. It is obvious that great care goes into developing each menu item, and the result is fresh and tasty. The atmosphere has a bit of a bar feel, but the back room is quieter.

The **Havre de Grace Ritz Gourmet Café** (421 St. John St., 410/939-5858, www.havredegraceritzgourmetcafe.com, Mon.-Sat. 11am-9pm, Sun. 11am-4pm, $9-14) makes superb sandwiches and panini. Kate's Kickin' Cajun Shrimp Panino, the New Yorker Deli Sandwich, and the prime rib tartine are just a few of the delectable choices. They also offer salads, seasonal selections, and breakfast on weekends.

A popular waterfront restaurant is the **Tidewater Grille** (300 Franklin St., 410/939-3313, www.thetidewatergrille.com, Mon.-Fri. 11am-10pm, Sat.-Sun. 9am-10pm, $8-44). They offer a traditional seafood menu with a great view of the Susquehanna and Chesapeake headwaters. Ask for a seat by the window or sit on the patio when it's nice out. Free docking is available for those coming by boat.

Accommodations

The elegant **Vandiver Inn** (301 S. Union Ave., 410/939-5200, www.vandiverinn.com, $145-165) offers 18 guest rooms in three beautifully restored Victorian homes. Eight are in the Vandiver Inn mansion (built in 1886), and an additional 10 are in the adjacent Kent & Murphy Guest Houses. All have private bathrooms. Each guest is treated to a lovely breakfast, free in-room wireless access, and in-room cable television. The inn is within blocks of the Chesapeake Bay and within the city of Havre de Grace. Many special events are held at the inn, so if you are looking for a quiet stay with little activity, ask about events during your stay when you make a reservation.

The only Victorian mansion built of the stone in Havre de Grace is the **Spencer Silver Mansion** (200 Union Ave., 410/939-1485, www.spencersilvermansion.com, $85-160). This nicely restored 1896 home offers four guest rooms and a lovely carriage house for rent. A full breakfast is served each morning until 10:30am. The mansion is a short walk to the Chesapeake Bay and is near the attractions in downtown Havre de Grace. It is also pet friendly.

Five miles south of Havre de Grace is the **Hilton Garden Inn Aberdeen** (1050 Beards Hill Rd., 410-/272-1777, www.hiltongardeninn3.hilton.com, $179-189) in Aberdeen, Maryland. This modern hotel offers a fitness center and indoor pool. All rooms have 32-inch HD flat-screen televisions, microwaves, refrigerators, and complimentary wireless Internet.

Camping

Camping is available at **Susquehanna State Park** (888/432-2267, www.dnr.state.md.us, Apr.-Oct., $22.49-51.49 plus $4 park fee and a nightly park facility fee $4.51-4.61). They have 69 sites (six have electric and six have camper cabins). There are two comfort stations with hot showers.

Information and Services

For additional information on Havre de Grace, stop by the **Havre de Grace Office of Tourism & Visitor Center** (450 Pennington Ave., 410/939-2100) or visit www.explorehavredegrace.com.

Getting There

Havre de Grace is approximately one hour by car (37 miles) north of Baltimore. It is off I-95, on the southern side of the M. E. Tydings Memorial Bridge. Exit onto Route 155 and follow that road past the Susquehanna Museum and into the historic district of Havre de Grace.

WESTMINSTER

Westminster is the seat of Carroll County and has a population of around 18,000. It was founded in 1764 and incorporated in 1838. This picturesque town surrounded by primarily farmland and rolling terrain saw a cavalry battle known as Corbit's Charge fought right on the downtown streets during the Civil War. It was also the first locale in the country to offer rural mail delivery.

Westminster is also the home of the late Whittaker Chambers's farm. He hid the "pumpkin papers," which were the key to a controversial case concerning espionage during the Cold War, in a hollowed-out gourd here. The papers resulted in the 1950 conviction of former State Department official Alger Hiss. This evidence confirmed Hiss's perjury in front of Congress when he denied being a Soviet spy.

Westminster is also known for its above-average number of tornadoes. No fewer than four major tornadoes have touched down in Westminster in its recorded history, resulting in varying degrees of destruction.

Today, Westminster is a lovely little city with many artists and art galleries. It is also home to **McDaniel College** (2 College Hill, 410/848-7000, www.mcdaniel.edu), a private liberal arts and sciences college founded in 1867 with just under 3,000 students.

Sights

DOWNTOWN WESTMINSTER

Downtown Westminster offers a lovely historic district along Main Street with many old buildings and stories to surround them. The area is friendly to pedestrians and shelters many independent shops, galleries, and restaurants. Large trees line the streets, and there is plenty of parking in two parking decks and outdoor lots.

Many buildings on Main Street in Westminster have a long history, but none as varied as **Odd Fellows Hall** (140 E. Main St.). This plain, three-story brick building was erected in 1858 for $9,000 by the Salem Lodge No. 60 of the Independent Order of Odd

Fellows. It was a central location for gatherings in Westminster.

Prior to the Civil War, the building was used by a local militia with Southern sympathies. Not long after the war, a comedian from Alabama performed at the hall and made jokes about President Grant and other officials in the government. As legend has it, the patrons did not appreciate the jokes and threw rocks at him. After being hit in the neck, the performer became upset and left the stage. The local sheriff offered him protection for the night, but the performer refused and went out back to saddle his horse. He was found dead behind the hall shortly after, having had his throat slit. Shortly after that day, and from then on, reports of people seeing a ghost behind the hall of a man engaged in monologue have been common. The building later became a town library, a saloon, a concert hall, and a newspaper office.

In 1912, the building was known as the Opera House, when the Odd Fellows created an opera room that became the first movie theater in town. In recent years it was home to the Opera House Printing Company, but at the time of writing, it was empty.

HISTORICAL SOCIETY OF CARROLL COUNTY

The **Historical Society of Carroll County** (210 E. Main St., 410/848-6494), on the east end of Westminster's downtown area, has exhibits on the heritage of Carroll County and the surrounding Piedmont area.

★ CARROLL COUNTY FARM MUSEUM

The **Carroll County Farm Museum** (500 S. Center St., 410/386-3880, www.ccgovernment.carr.org, Mon.-Sat. 9am-4:30pm, Sun. noon-4pm, adults $5, family $10) offers visitors a unique opportunity to see what rural life in the mid-19th century was like. Part of a 142-acre complex, the museum demonstrates how families had to be self-sufficient by producing everything they needed (food, household items, soap, yarn, etc.) right on their own land.

The museum features a three-story brick farmhouse and authentic farm buildings built in the 1850s, including a log barn, smokehouse, saddlery, broom shop, springhouse, and wagon shed. A guided tour conducted by costumed interpreters of the farmhouse's seven rooms is included with admission, as is a self-guided walking tour of the various exhibit buildings. The wagon shed houses the buggy that was used for the first rural mail delivery route. The route ran between Westminster and Uniontown. Although the route signaled the development of a sophisticated mail delivery system, many residents were not happy about it because they felt cut off from the rest of the community when they were no longer forced into taking regular trips into town to get news and socialize.

There are also public buildings on-site such as a firehouse, schoolhouse, and general store. Artifacts and antiques from the period (many of which were donated by local families) are also on display. There are many live animals at the museum such as sheep, geese, pigs, goats,

the Carroll County Farm Museum

and horses, which make this a great place to bring children. There is also a gift store.

ART GALLERIES

At the west end of the downtown area, the **Carroll Arts Center** (91 W. Main St., 410/848-7272, Mon., Wed., Fri., and Sat. 10am-4pm, Tues. and Thurs. 10am-7pm) houses two locally focused art galleries, the **Tevis Gallery** and the **Community Gallery.** It also has a 263-seat theater where it hosts concerts, plays, lectures, recitals, and films year-round. In addition, there are a handful of independent galleries along Main Street and Liberty Street.

The **Esther Prangley Rice Gallery** (410/857-2595), in Peterson Hall at McDaniel College, features work by students and local artists.

WALKING TOURS

Walking tours are popular in Westminster, and brochures with self-guided tours are available at the **Visitor Center** (210 E. Main St., 410/848-1388). One of the most popular is the Ghost Walk brochure that tells tales of local hauntings. The **Carroll County Public Library** (50 E. Main St., 410/386-4488) also offers guided one-hour ghost tours.

Shopping

Many national stores and chain restaurants can be found along Route 140, but the historic downtown area offers a mix of locally owned retail shops and restaurants. Westminster blends cultural experiences with the atmosphere of a small town.

The **Downtown Westminster Farmers Market** (Conaway Parking Lot, Railroad Avenue and Emerald Hill Lane) is held on Saturday mid-May through mid-November (8am-noon). It is a "producers-only" market and offers fresh produce, baked goods, flowers, and local honey.

Food

AMERICAN

A nice and cozy casual neighborhood restaurant is **Rafael's** (32 W. Main St., 410/840-1919, www.rafaelsrestaurant.com, Mon.-Thurs. 11am-9:30pm, Fri. 11am-10:30pm, Sat. noon-10:30pm, Sun. noon-9pm, breakfast Sat.-Sun. 8am-1pm, $7-19). They have good food and reasonable prices and are especially known for their hamburgers. They serve lunch and dinner daily and breakfast on weekends. The staff is friendly, and the food is consistent.

A popular local eatery with homebrewed beer is **Johansson's Dining House** (4 W. Main St., 410/876-0101, www.johanssonsdininghouse.com, Mon.-Thurs. 11am-10pm, Fri.-Sat. 11am-11pm, Sun. 10am-10pm, $8-31). This casual restaurant serves a varied menu (filet mignon, seafood, pizza, and sandwiches) and homemade desserts. The place has a lot of character, a good decor, and is in the heart of Westminster. The 1913 building opened as a restaurant in 1994.

IRISH

O'Lordans Irish Pub (14 Liberty St., 410/876-0000, www.olordansirishpub.com, Sun. and Tues.-Thurs. 11am-10pm, Fri.-Sat. 11am-11pm, $8-30) is a lively spot on Liberty Street. The pub has a traditional Irish pub feel with a fireplace, murals, dark wood, plank floors, and a stone facade. The bartenders are witty, and the food portions are ginormous and delicious. The pub offers a great happy hour menu and has developed a loyal fan base.

MEXICAN

Papa Joe's Mexican Restaurant (250 Englar Rd., 410/871-2505, www.papajoeswestminstermd.com, Mon.-Sat. 11am-10pm, $9-18) is the local favorite for Mexican food. They offer traditional Mexican dishes in a friendly, colorful atmosphere. The restaurant is family owned and operated, and they have fun specials such as a salsa bar night on Monday. The fajitas are a signature dish and come smothered in a wonderful cream sauce, which is a little different from traditional fajitas. Seating is limited, but there is outdoor seating when the weather is nice.

TEAROOM

The best tearoom in Westminster (okay, maybe it's the only tearoom in Westminster, but it's a good one) is **Gypsy's Tearoom** (111 Stoner Ave., 410/857-0058, www.gypsystearoom.com, Tues.-Sat. 10am-5pm, $9-30) in the oldest home in Westminster, which was built by town founder William Winchester. This English-style tearoom serves everything from tea with hors d'oeuvres to full-service dinners. They also offer event planning for special occasions. The tearoom is located in a rural setting near town. It also has a gift shop.

Accommodations

Accommodations right in Westminster are mainly limited to chain hotels such as the **Westminster Days Inn** (25 S. Cranberry Rd., 410/857-0500, www.daysinn.com, $79-89), and the **Best Western Westminster Catering and Conference Center** (451 WMC Dr., 410/857-1900, www.book.bestwestern.com, $113-117).

Eight miles southwest of town on the way to New Windsor is the **Yellow Turtle Inn Bed and Brunch** (111 S. Springdale Ave., New Windsor, 410/635-3000, www.yellowturtleinn.net, $120-199). This lovely bed-and-breakfast sits on three acres in the country and offers eight guest rooms with private bathrooms and two whirlpool suites.

Information and Services

Additional information on Westminster can be found at the **Carroll County Visitor Center** (210 E. Main St., 410/848-1388, www.carrollcountytourism.org, Mon.-Sat. 9am-5pm, Sun. 10am-2pm).

Getting There

Westminster is 35 miles northwest of Baltimore and 56 miles north of Washington DC. Route 140 runs through Westminster from east to west and Route 97 runs north to south.

Gypsy's Tearoom

Annapolis and Southern Maryland

Capital city Annapolis has been the crown jewel of Maryland throughout its rich history. The city is known as the sailing capital of the world, as the birthplace of American horse racing, and for having more 18th-century buildings than any other city in the United States. Annapolis has remained extremely well preserved as a colonial-era town despite its popularity with tourists and businesses. It is a fun place to visit, a great place to people-watch, and a fantastic place to eat seafood.

Southern Maryland offers a relaxed atmosphere compared to the bustle of Annapolis. The cities along the western shore of the Chesapeake Bay vary from sleepy seaside towns to active sailing communities. Crisscrossed with scenic roadways and state and national parks, this area makes for a lovely excursion.

PLANNING YOUR TIME

Annapolis and Southern Maryland can be explored in a long weekend or over several day trips from Baltimore. The distance between Annapolis and Point Lookout is approximately 82 miles (about two hours by car). Annapolis and Solomons Island are good choices for overnight stays or for boating on the Chesapeake Bay.

The closest airport to Annapolis is **Baltimore Washington International Thurgood Marshall Airport (BWI)** (410/859-7040, www.bwiairport.com), but parts of Southern Maryland are actually closer to **Ronald Reagan Washington National Airport (DCA)** (703/417-8000, www.metwashairports.com), just outside Washington DC in Arlington, Virginia (Point Lookout is 79 miles from DCA and 99 miles from BWI). Normally, the lowest airfares can be obtained by flying into BWI, so it pays to explore both options. Once you arrive in the region, it is best to explore by car. Parking is plentiful except for right in downtown Annapolis, but even there, most hotels have parking available and public garages can be found.

Previous: the docks at Sandy Point State Park; Maryland State House. **Above:** Annapolis Harbor.

Look for ★ to find recommended sights, activities, dining, and lodging.

Highlights

★ **Annapolis City Dock:** This public waterfront boasts beautiful scenery, impressive yachts, and many shops and restaurants (page 436).

★ **U.S. Naval Academy:** More than 60,000 men and women have graduated from this prestigious school and gone on to serve in the U.S. Navy and Marine Corps (page 436).

★ **Calvert Marine Museum:** This wonderful museum shares the whole history of the Chesapeake Bay, focusing on prehistoric times, the natural environment, and the bay's unique maritime heritage (page 450).

★ **Calvert Cliffs State Park:** More than just a beautiful sandy beach with stunning cliffs, this park offers superb fossil hunting (page 452).

★ **St. Mary's City's Outdoor Museum of History and Archaeology:** This living re-creation teaches visitors about life in Maryland's original capital city during colonial times (page 454).

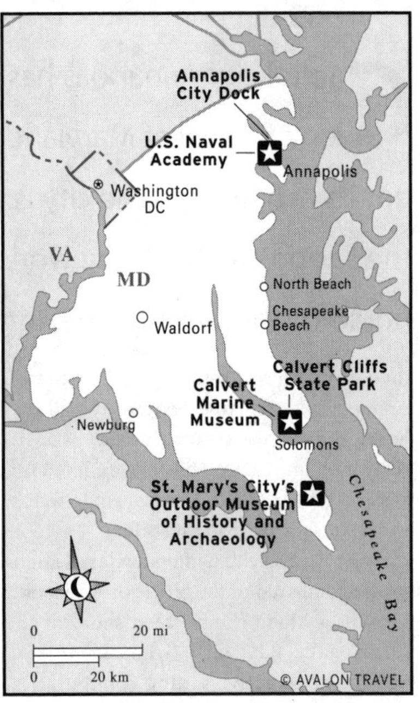

Annapolis and Southern Maryland

Annapolis

Maryland's capital city of Annapolis is a picturesque and historic seaport on the Chesapeake Bay. It is widely known as the "Sailing Capital of the World," due to its popularity as a sailing port for both resident and international vessels. Literally hundreds of sailboats cruise the surrounding waters year-round, with regular races being held several times a week during the summer.

In 1649, a settlement named Providence was founded on the northern shore of the Severn River by Puritans exiled from Virginia. The settlement was later moved to the southern shore and renamed several times before finally becoming Annapolis, a tribute to Princess Anne of Denmark and Norway, who was in line to be the queen of Great Britain. The city was incorporated in 1708. Annapolis prospered as a port and grew substantially during the 18th century. It even served as the temporary capital of the United States in 1783.

From its earliest days more than 300 years ago, Annapolis was known as a center for wealth, social activities, and a thriving cultural scene. It was also known for its cozy pubs and abundant seafood restaurants, which welcomed prosperous visitors from all over the globe. Annapolis was also the birthplace of American horse racing—several of the original stock of the American Thoroughbred line entered through its port, and people came from all over the colonies to watch and bet on horse races. George Washington is even said to have lost a few shillings at the local track.

Annapolis is a great place to visit and explore. It has a vibrant waterfront with many shops and restaurants, and is quaint and historical, yet welcomes an international crowd. The city was designed more like the capital cities in Europe with a baroque plan, rather than the grid layout customary to U.S. cities. Circles with radiating streets highlight specific buildings, such as St. Anne's Episcopal Church (one of the first churches in the city) and the State House. Numerous magnificent homes were built in the city's early days and hosted many of the founders of our country for lavish social events. Today Annapolis it is home to the U.S. Naval Academy and St. John's College.

The most popular neighborhood for visitors is the Historic Downtown area. This is where the scenic waterfront and City Dock are located, as well as charming boutiques, fabulous restaurants, and historic homes. Another popular tourist area is Eastport, just south of Historic Downtown. This area is home to "Restaurant Row" and offers sweeping Chesapeake Bay views and a fun-loving, slightly funky atmosphere.

SIGHTS

★ Annapolis City Dock

The **Annapolis City Dock** (Dock Street on the waterfront) is the heart of the downtown area. Annapolis boasts more 18th-century buildings than any other American city, and many of these charming structures line the dock area. Locally owned shops, boutiques, and souvenir stands beckoning shoppers off the busy streets and waterfront restaurants help fuel the energy of this hot spot. The public waterfront is where visitors can take in the beautiful scenery while getting a good look at many expensive yachts. The waterfront area is also known as **Ego Alley,** since a steady parade of high-end sailing and motor vessels can be seen going by on nearly every weekend and evening.

★ U.S. Naval Academy

The **U.S. Naval Academy** (121 Blake Rd., 410/293-1000, www.usna.edu) was founded in 1845 by the secretary of the navy. Since that time, more than 60,000 men and women have graduated from this prestigious school and gone on to serve in the U.S. Navy or the U.S. Marine Corps. The student body is referred

Annapolis

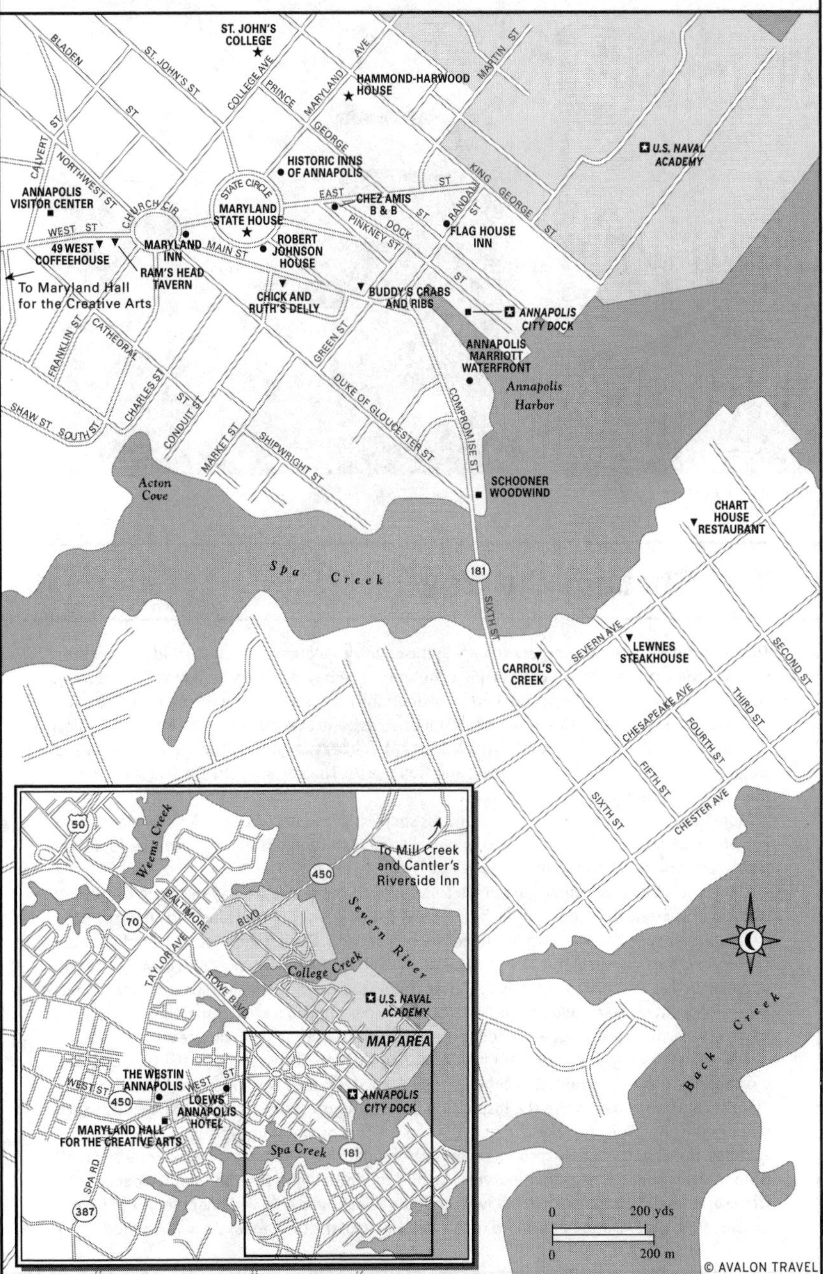
ST. JOHN'S COLLEGE
HAMMOND-HARWOOD HOUSE
U.S. NAVAL ACADEMY
HISTORIC INNS OF ANNAPOLIS
ANNAPOLIS VISITOR CENTER
CHEZ AMIS B & B
MARYLAND STATE HOUSE
FLAG HOUSE INN
49 WEST COFFEEHOUSE
MARYLAND INN
ROBERT JOHNSON HOUSE
RAM'S HEAD TAVERN
To Maryland Hall for the Creative Arts
CHICK AND RUTH'S DELLY
BUDDY'S CRABS AND RIBS
ANNAPOLIS CITY DOCK
ANNAPOLIS MARRIOTT WATERFRONT
Annapolis Harbor
Acton Cove
SCHOONER WOODWIND
CHART HOUSE RESTAURANT
Spa Creek
CARROL'S CREEK
LEWNES STEAKHOUSE
Back Creek
BLADEN
ST. JOHN'S ST
COLLEGE AVE
PRINCE GEORGE ST
MARYLAND AVE
MARTIN ST
KING GEORGE ST
CALVERT ST
NORTHWEST ST
CHURCH CIR
STATE CIRCLE
EAST ST
RANDALL ST
WEST ST
MAIN ST
PINKNEY ST
DOCK ST
FRANKLIN ST
CATHEDRAL ST
GREEN ST
CHARLES ST
CONDUIT ST
DUKE OF GLOUCESTER ST
COMPROMISE ST
SHAW ST
SOUTH ST
MARKET ST
SHIPWRIGHT ST
SIXTH ST
SEVERN AVE
SECOND ST
CHESAPEAKE AVE
THIRD ST
FOURTH ST
FIFTH ST
CHESTER AVE
181
50
Weems Creek
450
To Mill Creek and Cantler's Riverside Inn
BALTIMORE BLVD
70
Severn River
TAYLOR AVE
College Creek
ROWE BLVD
MAP AREA
THE WESTIN ANNAPOLIS
LOEWS ANNAPOLIS HOTEL
MARYLAND HALL FOR THE CREATIVE ARTS
SPA RD
387
0
200 yds
200 m

Annapolis City Dock

The Chesapeake Bay

The Chesapeake Bay is the largest estuary in the country. Its drainage basin includes more than 64,000 square miles with more than 150 tributaries. The bay is approximately 200 miles long, starting at the mouth of the Susquehanna River on the northern end and the Atlantic Ocean on the southern end. At its widest point it is 30 miles across, and at its narrowest point it is 2.8 miles.

The Chesapeake Bay is part of the **Intracoastal Waterway,** a 3,000-mile navigable inland water route that runs along the Atlantic and Gulf coasts. The bay links the Delaware River with the Albemarle Sound in North Carolina.

More than 300 species of fish and countless shellfish live in the Chesapeake Bay. Maryland is known for its abundant local seafood, especially the famed blue crab, which can be found on nearly every menu in the region.

Many shorebirds live all or part of their lives on the Chesapeake Bay or in the bordering wetlands, including bald eagles, great blue herons, ospreys, peregrine falcons, and piping plovers.

The Chesapeake Bay is a prominent feature in Maryland. During the second half of the 19th century and the first half of the 20th, the bay was a vital link between major cities in Maryland and Virginia, such as Baltimore and Norfolk, and was home to passenger steamships and packet boats (boats that kept regular schedules and were originally designed to transport mail, passengers, and freight). When road crossings were built in the late 20th century, making the steamboat industry obsolete, the bay became known for its seafood production, with a focus on the blue crab and oyster industries. By the mid-20th century, nearly 9,000 full-time watermen worked on the bay. Plentiful oyster harvests were the inspiration for Maryland's state boat, the **skipjack,** which remains the only type of working boat in the country that operates under sail.

Today, the Chesapeake Bay produces less seafood than it did in the last century due to runoff from many mainland areas, overharvesting, and the invasion of foreign marine species. The **Chesapeake Bay Foundation** (www.cbf.org), headquartered in Annapolis, is the largest conservation organization dedicated to the well-being of the Chesapeake Bay watershed.

to as the "Brigade of Midshipmen." The academy is directly northeast of downtown Annapolis at the confluence of the Severn River and the Chesapeake Bay. Guided walking tours of the more than 300-acre campus led by professional guides are offered to visitors through the **Armel-Leftwich Visitor Center** (52 King George St., 410/293-8687, www.usnabsd.com, Mar.-Dec. daily 9am-5pm, Jan. and Feb. Mon.-Fri. 9am-4pm, Sat.-Sun. 9am-5pm, $10.50). Tours are 1.25 hours and are offered throughout most of the day while the visitors center is open; they cannot be booked in advance. Tours provide a close-up look at the imposing marble buildings and monuments on campus, and cover topics such as history, architecture, traditions, and life as a midshipman.

Access to the Naval Academy grounds is limited. Government-issued photo identification is required for admission. Parking is available at the stadium on Rowe Boulevard inside the Noah Hillman Parking Garage (enter from Duke of Gloucester or Main Street). There are also parking meters around City Dock.

Maryland State House

The **Maryland State House** (100 State Circle, 410/260-6445, www.msa.maryland.gov, daily 9am-5pm, free, donations appreciated) is the oldest legislative house in the country that has been in continual use. It is also the oldest peacetime capitol. The State House was built in the 1770s, and the first Maryland legislature meeting was held here in 1779. The building is architecturally significant—its dome is the largest wooden dome constructed without nails in the United States.

During 1783 and 1784, when Annapolis served as the U.S. capital, the State House was home to the U.S. government. It was there that two significant events took place. The first was that George Washington resigned his commission before the Continental Congress on December 23, 1783, and the second was that the Treaty of Paris ending the Revolutionary War was ratified here on January 14, 1784. Self-guided tour information is available on the first floor of the State House.

St. John's College

St. John's College (60 College Ave.,

the Maryland State House

410/263-2371, www.sjca.edu) is the oldest college in town, despite the misconception that this distinction belongs to the U.S. Naval Academy. The school was founded in 1696 as the King William's School. It is the third-oldest college in the country behind Harvard and William & Mary. One block from the State House (across King George Street from the Naval Academy), the school sits on 32 scenic acres adorned with stately brick buildings, tree-lined paths, and sprawling lawn. It is also a National Historic Landmark with several 18th-century buildings.

St. John's College offers a liberal arts curriculum. Because of its location at the confluence of the Chesapeake Bay and the Severn River, the school offers strong sailing, crew, and rowing opportunities. Each April, St. John's College and the Naval Academy play each other in a highly anticipated croquet match on the front lawn of the St. John's campus. Both teams dress for the event, which has become a spirited spectacle.

St. John's College adopted the "Great Books" program of study in 1937. This mandatory four-year program requires students to read Western civilization's prominent authors in philosophy, theology, math, science, poetry, music, and literature. Classes are then discussion based. The school uses a series of manuals in place of textbooks, lectures, and exams. Grades are only released at the student's request and are based on papers and class participation.

Hammond-Harwood House

There are many historic homes in Annapolis. If you can only choose one to visit, the **Hammond-Harwood House** (19 Maryland Ave., 410/263-4683, www.hammondharwoodhouse.org, Apr.-Dec. Tues.-Sun. noon-5pm, Jan.-Mar. appointment only, $10) should be it. It is one of the most superb British colonial homes in the country and the most impressive in Annapolis. Designed in the Anglo-Palladian style (a variation of the classical Roman revival style), construction began on the house in 1774. It was completed sometime after 1776, but the exact year is unknown. The home is special because it offers perfectly preserved architecture and one of the best collections of furniture and decorative art from the 18th century in Maryland. It is a National Historic Landmark.

Fifty-minute walk-in tours begin at the top of each hour and provide insight into the history of the house, information on its architect and the people who lived in the home, and the opportunity to learn about the collections, such as a large collection of the works of Charles Willson Peale, a painter well known for his Revolutionary War period portraits. Visitors can also tour the garden at no extra cost. In-depth, two-hour architectural tours of the home are offered by appointment for $20.

St. Anne's Episcopal Church

St. Anne's Episcopal Church (1 Church Circle, 410/267-9333, www.stannes-annapolis.org, free) was the first church in Annapolis. The original structure was established in 1692 and completed in 1704 and was one of 30 original Anglican parishes in Maryland. Its bell was donated by Queen Anne. The original 65-foot-by-30-foot structure was razed in 1775 to make way for reconstruction of the second St. Anne's Episcopal Church on the same grounds. Building of the new church was delayed due to the Revolutionary War but was finally finished in 1792. The new church was larger and more structurally sound, but burned down on Valentine's Day in 1858 due to a furnace fire. The church that stands in Church Circle today was built in 1858 (although the steeple was finished in 1866). Its design incorporated part of the old tower. The clock in the church steeple actually belongs to the city due to a special agreement it made with the church when a city clock was needed. Visitors to St. Anne's can examine the church's Romanesque revival architecture with its original archways, pews, and stained glass windows. They can also visit the first cemetery in the city, which is located on the grounds. Four Sunday worship services are held weekly at 8am, 9:30am, 11:15am, and 5:30pm.

ENTERTAINMENT AND EVENTS

Nightlife

Annapolis harbors one of the best little venues in the mid-Atlantic for intimate concerts with big-name artists. **Rams Head on Stage** (33 West St., 410/268-4545, www.ramsheadonstage.com) is the performance venue at the popular **Rams Head Tavern** (www.ramsheadtavern.com), which has been a fixture in Annapolis for more than two decades. Rams Head on Stage is a reserved-seating venue with food and drink service during the shows. Nearly all shows at this venue are 21 and older. There are no bad seats in the house, and the bands play right in front of the tables. Samples of recent performances include the Smithereens, Cowboy Junkies, The English Beat, and Los Lobos.

The **49 West Coffeehouse, Winebar & Gallery** (49 West St., 410/626-9796, www.49westcoffeehouse.com) is a great place to kick back and enjoy coffee or a great martini (depending on the time of day) and listen to jazz. They host live music most nights and jazz for brunch on Sunday. The establishment is also an art gallery and features different artists monthly. They offer a neighborhood feel near the downtown area and serve breakfast, lunch, and dinner daily.

They'll Scare Ya Sober

Sometimes referred to as "a drinking town with a sailing problem," Annapolis has long known how to get its drink on. The city is filled with all kinds of history, including tales of hair-raising hauntings at local watering holes. **Annapolis Tours and Crawls** (443/534-0043, www.toursandcrawls.com, $18) offers a great two-hour haunted pub crawl through the downtown area. They take guests through some of the most haunted taverns, pubs, and bars while telling stories that are sure to give you goose bumps. Each stop is about 30 minutes and can be different each time. This drinking tour is a great way to learn the history of some of the best taverns in town, with an added twist. Tours meet at the top of Main Street and are for people 21 and over.

Performing Arts

The **Maryland Hall for the Creative Arts** (801 Chase St., 410/263-5544, www.marylandhall.org) is an active center for the performing arts. Resident companies include a symphony, opera, ballet, and chorale, offering performances throughout the year in the 800-seat theater.

Events

The **Maryland Renaissance Festival** (1821 Crownsville Rd., Crownsville, 410/266-7304, www.rennfest.com) is a long-standing tradition in Maryland. After passing through the entry gates to the festival, visitors become part of a wooded, 25-acre 16th-century English village named "Revel Grove." There are plenty of activities to keep the entire family busy, with shows on 10 major stages, a jousting arena, games, crafts, five pubs, and of course, tons of delicious food. The festival is open on Saturday, Sunday, and Labor Day Monday from the end of August through late October. The festival is held in Crownsville, eight miles northwest of Annapolis.

Many events are scheduled throughout the year in Annapolis, including several footraces such as the **Annapolis Ten Miler** (www.annapolisstriders.org), festivals, food celebrations, and art shows. For a list of events, visit www.downtownannapolis.org.

SHOPPING

There are many boutiques and locally owned shops in downtown Annapolis. Maryland Avenue, Main Street, and West Street are great places to start a shopping adventure. Some examples of the types of stores you can browse include jewelry stores, maritime stores, home furnishings shops, women's boutiques, antiques stores, glass shops, and fine-art galleries.

SPORTS AND RECREATION

Two-hour sailing cruises can be booked on two beautiful, 74-foot wooden schooners through **Schooner *Woodwind* Annapolis Sailing Cruises** (410/263-7837, www.schoonerwoodwind.com, mid-Apr.-late Oct. daily, $44). Cruises depart from the **Annapolis Waterfront Hotel** (across from the City Dock) and sail by the U.S. Naval Academy and into the Chesapeake Bay. Private cruises can also be booked.

Pirate Adventures on the Chesapeake (311 3rd St., 410/263-0002, www.chesapeakepirates.com, mid-Apr.-Memorial Day and Labor Day-Oct. Sat.-Sun., Memorial Day-Labor Day daily, sail times at 9:30am, 11am, 12:30pm, 2pm, 3:30pm, and 5pm, $22) is a children's adventure aboard a pirate ship. Kids quickly become part of a pirate tale with face painting, costumes, and a lot of imagination. Once aboard, they learn the rules of the ship, read treasure maps, and find a message in a bottle. They even engage in battle using water cannons. Cruises leave from the company's office in Annapolis. Face painting and dress-up begin 30 minutes prior to departure; sailing time is 75 minutes.

The **Baltimore & Annapolis Trail** (www.traillink.com/trail/baltimore-and-annapolis-trail.aspx) is a 13-mile paved rail trail that is part of the former route of the Baltimore & Annapolis Railroad. It opened in 1990 and runs from Boulters Way in Annapolis to Dorsey Road in Glen Burnie. The southern part of the trail is primarily residential and winds through pleasant suburban neighborhoods. The northern part of the trail is much more urban.

An extremely popular nearby park right on the Chesapeake Bay is **Sandy Point State Park** (1100 E. College Pkwy., 410/974-2149, www.dnr.state.md.us, daily Jan.-Oct. 7am-sunset, Nov.-Dec. 7am-5pm, boating 24 hours year-round, $7). This lovely 786-acre park, 10 miles northeast of Annapolis at the western terminus of the Chesapeake Bay Bridge, used to be the site of a ferry that shuttled people and cars between the mainland and the Eastern Shore prior to completion of the bridge. Today it offers a wide sandy beach, swimming area, bathhouse, boat landing, picnic areas, and stunning view of the Chesapeake Bay. It is also a great place for bird-watching. The park is off Route 50 at exit 32.

FOOD

American

The premier steak house in Annapolis is ★ **Lewnes Steakhouse** (401 4th St., 410/263-1617, www.lewnessteakhouse.com, Sun. 4pm-10pm, Mon.-Thurs. 4pm-10pm, Fri.-Sat. 4pm-10:30pm, $19-44). This independent restaurant opened in 1921 and is still owned by the same local family. They serve prime steak that is properly prepared to sear in the flavorful juice while browning the exterior. Their menu includes filet, prime rib, porterhouse, New York strip, rib eye, and some non-beef selections such as tuna steak and lobster. They also have an extensive, well-selected wine list. The food and wonderful staff are the lure of this restaurant, and the atmosphere is well suited for a romantic evening. This is a restaurant that really cares whether the guests are satisfied.

A local institution, the **Rams Head Tavern** (33 West St., 410/268-4545, www.ramsheadtavern.com, Sun. 10am-2am with brunch, Mon.-Sat. 11am-2am, $9-30) has been serving tasty pub food since 1989. This friendly, multiroom tavern (including the original space in the cozy downstairs) serves sandwiches, burgers, and pub favorites such as shepherd's pie, brats and mash, chicken stuffed with crab imperial, and shrimp and grits. They have a terrific brunch menu on Sunday with a wonderful variety of entrées that are beautifully presented. They also serve beer from the Fordham Brewing Company, which used to be on-site. The atmosphere is classically "pub" with warm, friendly service and convivial patrons. This can be a busy place on concert nights at the adjoining Rams Head on Stage.

Quarter-pound crab cakes with no filler,

seasoned to perfection, are the calling card of a local favorite named ★ **Chick & Ruth's Delly** (165 Main St., 410/269-6737, www.chickandruths.com, daily 6:30am-11:30pm, $6-33). Just a block from the State House, the sandwich shop was opened by Chick and Ruth Levitt in 1965, and it has been growing ever since. Specialty sandwiches named after politicians augment the traditional Jewish deli fare, along with seafood, pizza, wraps, burgers, and tasty ice-cream treats. This is a touch of New York with an Annapolis flair. They are open for breakfast, lunch, and dinner.

Vin 909 Winecafe (909 Bay Ridge Ave., 410/990-1846, www.vin909.com, $12-19) is a wine-tasting café. They offer more than 35 types of wine by the glass and an extensive selection of beer. The café is in what once was a private residence, a bit off the beaten path south of the historic area of Annapolis (across Spa Creek). Prices for wine and food are reasonable, and there is frequently a wait for a table. They specialize in pizza, panini, and plates to share. The ambience is cozy and modern with wooden floors and low lighting. There is an outdoor patio with seating when the weather is nice.

Crab Houses

If you like seafood, you can't visit Annapolis without eating local blue crabs. *The* place to go for the authentic crab house experience is ★ **Cantler's Riverside Inn** (458 Forest Beach Rd., 410/757-1311, www.cantlers.com, Sun.-Thurs. 11am-10pm, Fri.-Sat. 11am-11pm, $8-32), a short distance from the downtown area and accessible by both car and boat. It is situated on a cove right on the water in a mostly residential neighborhood and sells local steamed crabs by the dozen (in all sizes) as well as offering other fresh seafood like crab cakes, shrimp, and oysters. They also serve pizza and sandwiches for non-seafood eaters. This is not a fancy place; it is a place to relax, get messy picking crabs, and meet new friends. They have indoor seating, a covered deck, and outdoor picnic tables. This used to be where the locals went, but in recent years it has become a popular tourist restaurant also. They also have a large bar inside the dining room. Word of warning: Don't rub your eyes with Old Bay seasoning on your hands.

Another popular crab house right in the historic downtown area is **Buddy's Crabs and Ribs** (100 Main St., 410/626-1100, www.buddysonline.com, Mon.-Thurs.

Chick & Ruth's Delly

Feeling Crabby?

Cantler's Riverside Inn in Annapolis offers an authentic crab house experience.

Maryland is known for its blue crabs, and the full "crab" experience can be enjoyed at a number of traditional crab houses throughout the bay region. For those new to the authentic crab experience, be prepared that this is a casual event, but not necessarily a cheap one. Traditional crab houses will often have long tables spread with brown paper and equipped with wooden mallets, claw crackers, and picks. Cold beer can accompany the appetizer, main course, and dessert. Patrons bring a lot of time, good cheer, and their appetites. Eating crabs is a social and messy event, but it is also one of the best experiences on the Chesapeake Bay.

Where to crack a claw:

- **Abner's Crab House** (3748 Harbor Rd., Chesapeake Beach, 410/257-3689, www.abnerscrabhouse.com)
- **Bo Brooks Crab House** (2780 Lighthouse Point, Baltimore, 410/558-0202, www.bobrooks.com)
- **Cantler's Riverside Inn** (458 Forest Beach Rd., Annapolis, 410/757-1311, www.cantlers.com)
- **Captain James Crab House** (2127 Boston St., Baltimore, 410/327-8600, www.captainjameslanding.com)
- **Hamilton's Canton Dockside** (3301 Boston St., Baltimore, 410/276-8900, www.cantondockside.com)
- **Mike's Restaurant and Crab House** (3030 Riva Rd., Riva, 410/956-2784, www.mikescrabhouse.com)
- **Thursday's Steak and Crabhouse** (4851 Riverside Dr., Galesville, 410/867-7200)

11:30am-9:30pm, Fri. 11:30am-10pm, Sat. 11am-11pm, Sun. 9:30am-9pm, $11-39). This lively icon on Main Street is a family-owned restaurant and also the largest restaurant in Annapolis. They specialize in serving large groups and also give special pricing to kids. Steamed crabs are the entrée of choice at Buddy's, but the homemade crab cakes are also a front-runner. Buddy's has a wide menu for both the seafood lover and the non-seafood eater and offers three all-you-can-eat buffets. The first is their soup, salad, and pasta bar for $8.95 (offered Mon.-Fri. 11:30am-3pm), the second is their seafood dinner buffet for $22.95 (Fri. 4pm-9pm and Sat. 11am-9pm), and the third is their Sunday brunch for $14.95 (Sun. 9:30am-1:30pm).

Italian

If you're looking for good pizza in a family atmosphere and want to get away from the crowds of the downtown area, go to **Squisito Pizza and Pasta** (2625 Riva Rd., 410/266-1474, www.squisitopizzaandpasta.com, Sun.-Thurs. 11am-10pm, Fri.-Sat. 11am-11pm, $7-16). This casual restaurant serves delicious pizza, pasta, and sandwiches at very reasonable prices. They are a small franchised chain with a handful of locations (all in Maryland). Order at the main counter and then take a seat. A server will bring you your meal. This is a very casual restaurant that is popular with families with children.

Seafood

A great place for local seafood and waterfront dining is **Carrol's Creek** (410 Severn Ave., 410/263-8102, www.carrolscreek.com, Mon.-Thurs. 11:30am-9pm, Fri.-Sat. 11:30am-10pm, Sun. 10am-8:30pm, $7-34). A short walk from the historic area across the Spa Creek Bridge, the bright-red building is easy to spot along Restaurant Row in Eastport. The menu offers local seafood, fresh fish, steak, chicken, and vegetarian dishes. Their Southwestern scallops are to die for. They also have a large wine list. The restaurant is locally owned and run, and much of the staff has been there for decades. There is plenty of free parking. Reservations are recommended (ask for a seat by the windows).

The **Chart House Restaurant** (300 2nd St., 410/268-7166, www.chart-house.com, brunch Sun. 10am-2pm, dinner Mon.-Thurs. 4:30pm-9pm, Fri.-Sat. 4:30pm-10pm, Sun. 2pm-9pm, $20-43) offers fantastic waterfront views of the City Dock and is within walking distance of the historic district. The restaurant is a part of an upscale national chain and is housed in a nice historic building. The menu is heavily weighted toward seafood and steak, with fresh fish, crab, lobster, filet, and surf and turf. They also offer chicken and salads. The food and decor are above average, which is reflected in the prices, but the restaurant has a great location and the service is excellent. Reservations are recommended.

Another lovely waterfront restaurant is the **Severn Inn** (1993 Baltimore Annapolis Blvd., 410/349-4000, www.severninn.com, Sun. brunch buffet 10am-2pm, $36; lunch Mon.-Sat. 11:30am-2:30pm, dinner Mon.-Sat. 5pm-close, closed Mon. Jan.-Mar., $14-45), situated on the east side of the Naval Academy Bridge, overlooking Annapolis and the Severn River. They describe themselves as a "modern American seafood house" and serve local and nonlocal seafood and other dishes such as a wonderful filet mignon. They have a pleasant decor inside with white tablecloths and a comfortable, yet airy feel to the dining room as well as a large waterfront deck with pretty blue market umbrellas (open after April). Sunset is especially scenic, and if you're an oyster lover, grabbing a drink and a few oysters while watching the sun go down is a combination that's hard to beat.

ACCOMMODATIONS

$100-200

If you are looking for charming accommodations in a historic property, the **Historic Inns of Annapolis** (58 State Circle, 410/263-2641, www.historicinnsofannapolis.com, $120-270) offers three boutique hotels housed in 17th- and 18th- century buildings.

The **Maryland Inn** (16 Church Circle) has 44 guest rooms within view of the State House, Main Street, and the waterfront. The inn was built in the late 1700s and has hosted presidents, statesmen, and political dignitaries. The decor includes Victorian-era furnishings. It has a fitness center on-site, a restaurant, and a Starbucks. The **Governor Calvert House** (58 State Circle) is across the street from the Maryland State House and is one of the oldest buildings in Annapolis (built in 1695). It has 51 guest rooms, a colonial garden, meeting space, Internet, cable television, and views of the State House. Rooms are small, but this was originally a private home and was even the residence of two former Maryland governors. This property is where guests for all three historic properties check in. The **Robert Johnson House** (23 State Circle) is a smaller hotel with 29 guest rooms. This brick home was built in 1773 and has views of the Governor's Mansion and the State House. The house has Georgian-style architecture and is furnished with 19th-century furniture.

An alternative in this price range is the **Hampton Inn & Suites Annapolis** (124 Womack Dr., 410/571-0200, www.hamptoninn3.hilton.com, $109-134). The hotel is in a business park four miles from the historic area of Annapolis. The 117 rooms are comfortable and come with complimentary wireless Internet, a mini fridge, 37-inch television, and free breakfast. The hotel is pet friendly.

$200-300

For a comfy bed-and-breakfast stay, the lovely ★ **Chez Amis Bed and Breakfast** (85 East St., 410/263-6631, www.chezamis.com, $202-228) offers four beautiful rooms and wonderful service. Each room in this 1890s home has a private bathroom, a television, and free wireless Internet. A delicious three-course breakfast is served each day at 9am, and cookies and refreshments are available all day. The bed-and-breakfast is within walking distance to downtown Annapolis, but a complimentary shuttle is offered to restaurants. The owners live in the bottom floor of the home.

The **Flag House Inn** (26 Randall St., 410/280-2721, www.flaghouseinn.com,

Governor Calvert House

$189-350) is a wonderful bed-and-breakfast with off-street parking in historic Annapolis. Just a half block from the City Dock, this comfortable, friendly inn is a great home base for exploring Annapolis. They offer four guest rooms and a two-room suite with private bathrooms and a full hot breakfast each morning.

Over $300

Fabulous waterfront views can be found at the **Annapolis Waterfront Hotel** (80 Compromise St., 888/773-0786, www.annapoliswaterfront.com, $335-599). This Marriott hotel is the only waterfront hotel in Annapolis, and many of the rooms overlook the Chesapeake Bay and some have balconies (other rooms view Annapolis Harbor and the downtown area). The hotel is walking distance to historic attractions, shopping, restaurants, and the Naval Academy. Allergy-free rooms are available. The hotel offers standard amenities such as a fitness center and meeting facilities. Valet parking and Internet service are available for an additional fee. Their waterfront restaurant, **Pusser's Caribbean Grille,** is a popular dining spot for seafood and also offers great views. This premium location doesn't come cheap, but if you are after a room with a view, it delivers.

The **Westin Annapolis** (100 Westgate Circle, 410/972-4300, www.westinannapolis.com, $299-459) is an immaculate, top-notch hotel a short distance from all the action in downtown Annapolis. The 225 guest rooms are spacious and modern, and there's a lovely, well-stocked bar in the lobby. Free shuttle service is available to the downtown area, and there is parking on-site. There are an indoor pool and fitness center, and the hotel is pet friendly.

The **Loews Annapolis Hotel** (126 West St., 410/263-7777, www.loewshotels.com, $309-409) is a lovely hotel in downtown Annapolis within walking distance to many attractions (10 minutes to the City Dock). The bright, nautical decor is perfect for the hotel's location, and the 216 guest rooms are luxurious and large (there are also 18 suites). Parking is available on-site for an additional fee ($18 for self-parking and $22 for valet), and there is a complimentary local shuttle service operating throughout the historic district. There are a fitness room and spa (no pool) for hotel guests, and wireless Internet service is available in guest rooms for an additional fee. There is also a restaurant on-site.

INFORMATION AND SERVICES

For additional information on Annapolis, stop in the **Annapolis & Anne Arundel County Conference and Visitors Bureau** (26 West St., 410/280-0445, daily 9am-5pm) or visit www.visitannapolis.org.

GETTING THERE

Most people arrive in Annapolis by car. The city is a quick 45-minute drive east from Washington DC (32 miles) via U.S. 50 and about 30 minutes (26 miles) south of the Inner Harbor in Baltimore (via I-97).

Annapolis is 22 miles from **Baltimore Washington International Thurgood Marshall Airport (BWI)** (410/859-7040, www.bwiairport.com). Private shuttle service can be arranged from the airport to Annapolis through **Annapolis Airport Shuttle** (410/971-8100, www.annapolisairportshuttle.com) or by limousine through **Lighthouse Limousine** (410/798-8881, www.lighthouselimousines.com).

GETTING AROUND

Parking can be challenging in the downtown area but **The Circulator** (410/216-9436, www.parkannapolis.com, every 10 minutes Sun.-Thurs. 6:30am-midnight, Fri.-Sat. 6:30am-2:30am) is a great way to move around Annapolis. It is a trolley service that provides free transportation around the central business district and stops at four downtown parking garages. The four garages are **Gotts Court Garage** (25 Northwest St., 410/972-4726, first hour $2, $15 maximum), the **Noah Hillman Garage** (150 Gorman St.,

410/267-8914, \$2 an hour, \$20 maximum), the **Knighton Garage** (corner of Colonial Ave. and West St., 410/263-7170, \$1 first hour, \$10 maximum), and the **Park Place Garage** (5 Park Pl., \$1 an hour, \$10 maximum). Stops are located along the trolley's loop route from Westgate Circle to Memorial Circle and start at the Westin Annapolis Hotel at Park Place. Trolleys also stop at popular areas such as Church Circle and City Dock. If you aren't at a stop but want to get on the trolley, simply raise your hand when one drives by and it will pull over to pick you up.

There is also metered parking at City Dock near Spa Creek, and there is a parking lot at the Navy Marine Corps Memorial Stadium (off Rowe Blvd. on Taylor Avenue). Trolley rides from the stadium lot cost \$2 since it is not within the central business district.

Two free shuttle buses also run from the stadium to downtown. The **Navy Blue Shuttle** runs to the historic area and west Annapolis with stops at the Naval Academy Main Gate and Church Circle. It leaves the stadium parking lot every half hour Monday-Friday 9am-6pm, and Saturday and Sunday 10am-6pm. The **State House Shuttle** operates on a loop between the stadium and the State Legislative Buildings. It leaves the stadium every 15 minutes (every 5 minutes during rush hour) Monday-Friday 6:30am-8pm.

Southern Maryland

Southern Maryland contains a thousand miles of shoreline on the Chesapeake Bay and the Patuxent River. The region includes Calvert, Charles, and St. Mary's Counties and is a boater's playground, a bird-watcher's paradise, and a seafood lover's dream. Traditionally a rural agricultural area connected by steamboat routes, today Southern Maryland is traversed by scenic byways that connect charming towns and parks. The communities in the region have grown tremendously in recent decades and welcome tourists and those seeking outdoor recreation such as boating, fishing, crabbing, hiking, and biking.

CHESAPEAKE BEACH

Chesapeake Beach is on the mainland in Calvert County about 45 minutes south of Annapolis (29 miles). The town was founded in 1894 by the Chesapeake Bay Railway Company and was intended to be a vacation destination for Washingtonians. The town thrived as such during the early 1900s when visitors arrived by train. Today, long after the railroad days, visitors can still enjoy nice views of the Chesapeake Bay, beach access, and charter fishing.

Sights

A nice little museum that does a good job of presenting local history is the **Chesapeake Beach Railway Museum** (4155 Mears Ave., 410/257-3892, www.cbrm.org, hours vary by season, free). The small, three-room museum is housed in a restored train depot and provides information on the train that once ran between Chesapeake Beach and Washington DC. Artifacts, photos, maps, equipment, and postcards are on exhibit, and the volunteers are very friendly and helpful. The museum hosts many family events throughout the year.

If you're looking for summer fun and a break from the heat, bring the kids to the **Chesapeake Beach Water Park** (4079 Gordon Stinnett Blvd., 410/257-1404, www.chesapeakebeachwaterpark.com, daily mid-June-mid-Aug. Mon. 11am-6pm, Tues.-Sun. 11am-7pm, \$21). It features eight waterslides, pools, fountains, waterfalls, and giant floating sea creatures to climb on. There are even "adult" swim times.

Surfing enthusiasts will enjoy spending an hour or two at **Bruce "Snake" Gabrielson's Surf Art Gallery and Museum** (Route 261, three miles south of Chesapeake Beach,

240/464-3301, www.hbsnakesurf.com, open evenings by appointment on Mon., Wed., and Thurs., free). Maryland's only surfing museum opened in 2012 and showcases the personal treasures collected by its founder, surfing legend Bruce Gabrielson, over the course of 60 years. Featured items include antique surfboards, photographs, and posters signed by various surfing legends. It is a little off the beaten path in the offices of the National Surf Schools and Instructors Association.

Food

The two restaurants within the **Chesapeake Beach Hotel and Spa** (4165 Mears Ave., 410/257-5596, www.chesapeake-beachresortspa.com) are a couple of the best dining options in Chesapeake Beach. The **Rod 'N' Reel** (410/257-2735, daily 8am-2am, $10-33) serves breakfast, lunch, and dinner. They have a nice selection of sandwiches and seafood entrees and items from the land. They also have an extensive wine list. **Boardwalk Cafe** (Fri. 4pm-midnight, Sat. 11am-midnight, Sun. 11am-9pm, $8-25) is a casual restaurant on the resort boardwalk. They serve soup, salads, and casual seafood. It is a great spot to grab a drink and enjoy the scenery.

Another choice in Chesapeake Beach is the family-owned **Trader's Seafood Steak and Ale** (8132 Bayside Rd., 301/855-0766, www.traders-eagle.com, Sun. 7am-9pm, Mon.-Thurs. 8am-9pm, Fri.-Sat. 7am-10pm, $8-24), offering seafood, burgers, and other entrées for lunch and dinner and many traditional options for breakfast. The atmosphere is friendly and casual and they have a deck bar. They also have a breakfast buffet on Sunday (7am-1pm).

Accommodations and Camping

The **Chesapeake Beach Resort and Spa** (4165 Mears Ave., 410/257-5596, www.chesapeakebeachresortspa.com, $169-382) is a well-maintained property with 72 guest rooms. The hotel is on the Chesapeake Bay waterfront, and some rooms have balconies overlooking the water. A full-service spa is on-site, and there is also a marina. There are two waterfront restaurants at the hotel, a fitness room, sauna, game room, and an indoor swimming pool. Complimentary continental breakfast is served on weekdays. Fishing charters can be arranged through the hotel.

Breezy Point Beach and Campground (5300 Breezy Point Rd., 410/535-0259, www.co.cal.md.us, May-Oct., $50 per night) is a public beach and campground six miles south of Chesapeake Beach at **Breezy Point Beach** (410/535-0259, May-Oct. daily 6am-dusk, $10). The half-mile beach has a swimming area, bathhouse, picnic area, playground, and a 300-foot fishing pier. The camping available May-October includes water and sewage. Multiple-night minimums may be required on certain days. No pets are allowed on the beach or in the campground.

Information and Services

For additional information on Chesapeake Beach visit www.chesapeake-beach.md.us.

SOLOMONS ISLAND

Solomons Island sits at the southern tip of Calvert County at the confluence of the Chesapeake Bay and the Patuxent River. It is about a 1.5-hour drive southeast from Washington DC (61 miles), a 1.75-hour drive south of Baltimore (81 miles), and an 80-minute drive (58 miles) south from Annapolis. It is connected to St. Mary's County by the **Governor Thomas Johnson Bridge,** a 1.5-mile bridge over the Patuxent River on Route 4.

Solomons was first settled by tobacco farmers, but a surge in the oyster industry following the Civil War led it into the oyster processing and boatbuilding trades. The town quickly became a shipbuilding, ship repair, and seafood harvesting stronghold. In the 1880s, the local fishing fleet counted more than 500 boats, and many of them had been built right in Solomons. Among these were "bugeyes," which were large, decked-over sailing canoes, mostly built from shaped logs. The city soon became the dominant commercial center in Calvert County.

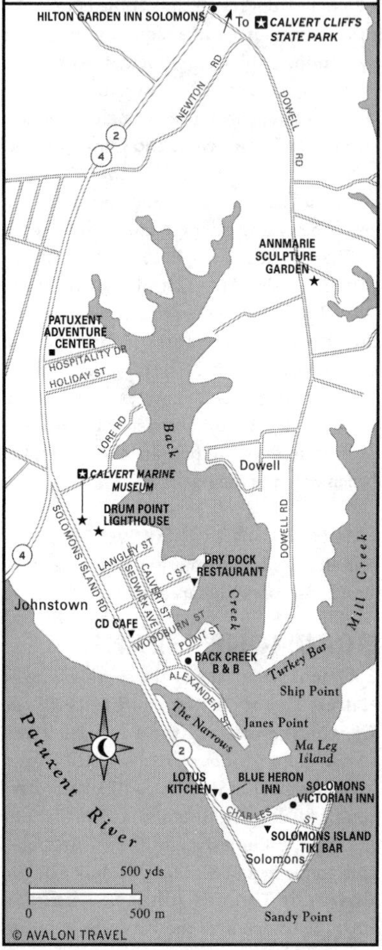

By the late 1920s, oyster harvests began to decline. This was followed by the Great Depression and the worst storm to ever hit the island (in 1933), which left the lower half of it under water. World War II brought better times when the island became a staging area for training troops readying for amphibious invasions.

Today, tourism, boating, and outdoor recreation play an important role in Solomons' economy. It houses countless marinas, boat suppliers, charter boat companies, a pilot station, and other types of water-related business such as kayaking outfitters. Many restaurants and inns serve the influx of tourists to this beautiful waterside town.

Sights

★ CALVERT MARINE MUSEUM

The **Calvert Marine Museum** (14200 Solomons Island Rd., 410/326-2042, www.calvertmarinemuseum.com, daily 10am-5pm, $9) does a wonderful job of sharing the story of the Chesapeake Bay, with exhibits on prehistoric times, the natural environment, and the bay's unique maritime heritage. There are three exhibit galleries totaling 29,000 square feet, including a discovery room with fossils, live animals (such as otters, fish, and rays), and a paleontology exhibit.

Behind the museum is a marsh walk that enables visitors to stroll over the salt marsh flats. Wildlife is abundant in the marsh, and you can expect to see signs of inhabitants such as raccoons, opossums, water snakes, crabs, herons, and ducks. This great natural exhibit is a living study of the local plant and animal life.

On the museum's waterfront is the iconic **Drum Point Lighthouse,** a "screwpile," cottage-style lighthouse that is one of only three that still stand out of an original 45 on the bay. The lighthouse is fully restored and houses early 20th-century furniture. Guided tours are available.

The museum's small-craft collection is housed in a 6,000-square-foot building that is open toward the boat basin. The collection has 19 boats in a range of sizes. Some boats are displayed on land, and others are in the water.

Those wishing to see an original seafood-packing house can visit the **Lore Oyster House** (May and Sept. weekends 1pm-4pm, June-Aug. daily 1pm-4pm, free). This restored National Historic Landmark is a little more than half a mile south of the museum campus on Solomons Island Road. It was built in 1934

SOUTHERN MARYLAND

Pirates of the Chesapeake

Although Blackbeard the pirate was best known for his ruthless handiwork in the Caribbean and his eventual beheading in Ocracoke, North Carolina, he often retreated to the Chesapeake Bay to repair his ship and prepare her for sea. He was not alone on the bay. The tobacco industry thrived along its shores for nearly 200 years (between roughly 1600 and 1800), bringing with it explorers from all parts of Europe as well as large populations of pirates.

Initially pirates settled in the southern part of the bay, but later they spread through most of the area. Although pirates often attacked colonial ships, the outlaws were tolerated by the colonies and in some ways helped them become independent from England. Pirates often sold goods to colonists that they could not purchase from England.

Despite their success, pirate life was very difficult, and most died young. Entire crews could be wiped out by disease, as living conditions were filthy on board their ships. Many also suffered fatal wounds during battle. Although some did go on to enjoy the riches they stole, this was the minority.

and now shares exhibits that explain oyster processing.

Sightseeing sailing cruises on the river leave from the museum dock weather permitting. They are one hour long and go through the inner harbor, underneath the Governor Thomas Johnson Bridge, and turn around at the Naval Recreation Center. The cost is $7. Trips can accommodate 40 passengers and leave the dock at 2pm Wednesday-Sunday (May-Oct.). On Saturday and Sunday in July and August additional 12:30pm and 3:10pm cruises are offered. Call 410/326-2042, ext. 41. Tickets can be purchased at the museum the day of the cruise.

The museum also has a woodworking shop and a reference library.

ANNMARIE SCULPTURE GARDEN AND ARTS CENTER

The **Annmarie Sculpture Garden and Arts Center** (13480 Dowell Rd., 410/326-4640, www.annmariegarden.org, sculpture garden daily 9am-5pm, arts building daily

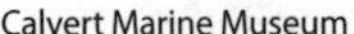

Calvert Marine Museum

10am-5pm, $5) features a lovely sculpture garden accessed by a quarter-mile walking path. The path goes through a wooded garden where sculptures both on loan and part of the center's permanent collection can be viewed. More than 30 sculptures are on loan from the Smithsonian Institution and National Gallery of Art. The Arts Building features a rotating exhibit space and a gift shop. The center offers many family activities throughout the year and also hosts annual festivals. This is a peaceful place to walk or bring the kids.

★ CALVERT CLIFFS STATE PARK

One of the prime recreation attractions in Calvert County is **Calvert Cliffs State Park** (10540 H. G. Trueman Rd., Lusby, 301/743-7613, www.dnr.state.md.us, daily sunrise to sunset, $5 per vehicle). This day-use park is about 7 miles north of Solomons Island, right on the Chesapeake Bay, and offers a sandy beach, playground, fishing, marshland, and 13 miles of hiking trails. The main attraction in this park, however, is fossil hunting along the beach. At the end of the Red Trail (1.8 miles from the parking lot), the open beach area gives rise to the dramatic Calvert Cliffs. More than 600 species of fossils have been identified in the cliff area, dating back 10 to 20 million years. The most common types of fossils found include oyster shells from the Miocene era and sharks teeth. Visitors can use sieves and shovels to look through the sand, but it is illegal to hunt fossils beneath the cliffs for safety reasons (dangerous landslides can occur). Swimming off the beach is allowed at your own risk, as there are no lifeguards on duty.

Sports and Recreation

Those wishing to rent a kayak or paddleboard (starting at $35 for three hours) or take a guided kayak tour ($75 per person), can do so from **Patuxent Adventure Center** (13860 C Solomons Island Rd., 410/394-2770, www.paxadventure.com). They also sell bikes and kayaks and other outdoor gear and accessories.

Nightlife

The **Solomons Island Tiki Bar** (85 Charles St., 410/326-4075, www.tikibarsolomons.com, mid-Apr.-mid-Oct.) is a local institution in Solomons. This well-known shack/tiki village near the harbor makes a killer mai tai and caters to pretty much anyone over 21 looking for a good time, good drink, and a fun island atmosphere. Visitors come by land and sea for this "adventure." Just be sure to decide ahead of time who is driving or sailing you home.

Food

Relaxed waterfront dining can be found at **The Dry Dock Restaurant** (C St., 410/326-4817, www.zahnisers.com, hours vary by season, $19-32). This harborfront restaurant specializes in steaks and seafood and prides itself on using as much local produce and sustainable seafood as possible. Large windows overlook the harbor, and there is outside deck seating in the warmer months. This is a small, intimate establishment that has been part of the marina for many years. There is an interesting collection of antique wooden decoys around the bar that were part of a private collection.

The ★ **CD Café** (14350 Solomons Island Rd., 410/326-3877, www.cdcafe.info, Sun. lunch 11am-3:30pm, dinner 5:30pm-9pm, Mon.-Sat. lunch 11:30am-3:30pm, dinner 5:30pm-9:30pm, $9-26) is a small, 11-table restaurant with a large menu of simply delicious food. They are open daily and serve lunch (pasta, burgers, salad) and dinner (seafood, steak, pasta, burgers). This is a popular restaurant, so expect to wait at prime times (there is a nice bar and waiting area), but the atmosphere is warm and inviting, the staff is genuinely helpful and friendly, and the food keeps residents and tourists coming back. Try the hummus, the cheesecake appetizer, and the salmon.

The **Lotus Kitchen** (14618 Solomons Island Rd., 410/326-8469, www.lotuskitchen-solomons.com, Wed.-Thurs. 9am-8pm, Fri. 9am-10pm, Sat. 9am-6pm, Sun. 9am-4pm, under $10) offers healthy food and a scenic view in a charming converted house right in town. The offering includes breakfast sandwiches, deli sandwiches, quiche, soup, meat and cheese boards, beer, wine, and coffee drinks. With menu items with names such as the Good Karma, the Garden Unicorn, and the Pot of Gold, half the fun is picking out your order. They are also known for their famous Kim's Key Lime Pie.

Accommodations

There is no shortage of wonderful bed-and-breakfasts in Solomons Island. The ★ **Back Creek Inn Bed and Breakfast** (210 Alexander Ln., 410/326-2022, www.backcreekinnbnb.com, $115-225) is a beautiful waterfront inn with seven clean and spacious guest rooms. They have two deepwater boat slips on their 70-foot pier (at mile marker 5 on Back Creek) and two bicycles for guest use. The inn is in a quiet part of town and can accommodate small business groups with indoor and outdoor meeting space. They also have free wireless Internet throughout the property. A full gourmet breakfast is served Monday-Saturday between 8:30am and 9:30am. Coffee, tea, juice, and coffee cake are available starting at 8am.

Another lovely waterfront bed-and-breakfast is the ★ **Blue Heron Inn** (14614 Solomons Island Rd., 410/326-2707, www.blueheronbandb.com, $179-249). The two suites have king-size beds, and the two guest rooms have queens. All rooms have private bathrooms and a water view (with either a private balcony or access to a common balcony). Wireless Internet and cable are included with all rooms.

Guests are treated to a gourmet breakfast each morning in a sunny breakfast room with access to the balcony (where breakfast can be served on nice days). A complimentary glass of wine is available each evening.

Solomons Victorian Inn (125 Charles St., 410/326-4811, www.solomonsvictorianinn.com, $135-250) offers great harbor views and a lush garden, and is within a short walk of shops and restaurants. At the southern tip of Solomons Island, on the western Chesapeake Bay shore, this gracious inn was built in 1906 and was the home of a renowned yacht builder. Several of the rooms are named after his boats. Six guest rooms and one carriage house with a separate entrance are available to rent, and each includes a private bathroom, television, wireless Internet, and a full breakfast. Most rooms have a harbor view.

A good option for hotel accommodations in Solomons Island is the **Hilton Garden**

Lotus Kitchen

Inn Solomons (13100 Dowell Rd., 410/326-0303, www.hiltongardeninn3.hilton.com, $159-195), which is a half mile from the downtown attractions. They have clean, comfortable rooms, a fitness center, indoor pool, seasonal outdoor pool, business center, and complimentary wireless Internet.

Information and Services

For additional information on Solomons Island, visit www.solomonsmaryland.com or stop by the **Solomons Island Visitor Center** (14175 Solomons Island Rd., 410/326-6027).

ST. MARY'S CITY

St. Mary's City is a small community an hour and 45 minutes south of Annapolis (73 miles) and two hours south of Baltimore (96 miles) in extreme Southern Maryland. It sits on the western shore of the Chesapeake Bay and the eastern shore of the St. Mary's River (a Potomac River tributary). Established in 1634, the area is the fourth-oldest permanent settlement in the country and is widely known as the "birthplace of religious tolerance."

St. Mary's City is in St. Mary's County, a beautiful rural area with abundant farmland and water access. St. Mary's County has many Amish and Mennonite communities, and motorists are warned to be alert for horse-drawn carriages along the highways. Amish farms dot the landscape and are recognizable by their windmills and the lack of power lines running along their properties.

St. Mary's was Maryland's capital for 60 years. Roman Catholics founded the city in their quest for religious freedom. When the state capital moved to Annapolis, St. Mary's went into deep decline and had dropped out of existence by 1720. In 1840, St. Mary's College was developed by Maryland legislature to celebrate the state's founding site. In 1966, the state of Maryland started the process of preserving the site and created the Historic St. Mary's City Commission. Today the city is still home to St. Mary's College and the outdoor museum of history and archaeology known as Historic St. Mary's City. Today, St. Mary's City is home to **St. Mary's College of Maryland** (Route 5, www.smcm.edu).

Sights

★ ST. MARY'S CITY'S OUTDOOR MUSEUM OF HISTORY AND ARCHAEOLOGY

Maryland's premier outdoor living-history museum, the **St. Mary's City's Outdoor Museum of History and Archaeology**

an Amish buggy near St. Mary's City

(18559 Hogaboom Ln., 240/895-4990, www.hsmcdigshistory.org, hours change by season, $10) is a re-creation of colonial St. Mary's City. The complex includes the *Dove* ship that first brought settlers to the area, an early tobacco plantation, the State House of 1676 (47418 Old State House Rd.), and a woodland Native American hamlet.

Although visitors should not expect the living museum to be on the same scale as Williamsburg, Virginia, the park is still a wonderful place to visit and has costumed interpreters, archaeological discoveries, a visitors center (18751 Hogaboom Ln.), outdoor living-history exhibits (where you can watch new buildings being erected in the town center, learn about Native American culture, and see the people and livestock at a tobacco plantation), reconstructed colonial buildings, the St. John's site museum, and a working 17th-century farm.

Visitors to St. Mary's City can participate in many hands-on activities and special events during the open season, such as a workshop on dinner preparation at the plantation and a hands-on pirate experience. Professional archaeologists are actively working to rediscover the city's past, and excavation sites can be seen throughout this National Historic Landmark.

POINT LOOKOUT

Point Lookout State Park (11175 Point Lookout Rd., Scotland, 301/872-5688, www.dnr.state.md.us, daily 6am-sunset, $7) encompasses 1,042 acres at the southern tip of St. Mary's County near Scotland, Maryland. The park is two hours (82 miles) south of Annapolis on a beautiful peninsula at the confluence of the Chesapeake Bay and the Potomac River. It is managed by the Maryland Department of Natural Resources.

Captain John Smith was the first to explore the peninsula in 1612, but the park is best known as the location of a prison camp during the Civil War. In the years leading up to the war, the area was a thriving summer resort thanks to its sandy beaches and stunning location. The coming of the war brought financial hardship, and the area was leased by the Union army as the site of a hospital facility, and then later the largest Confederate prison camp.

Conditions were horrible at the camp, which was primarily for enlisted men, and many of the prisoners froze to death during the winter months. Those who survived

Point Lookout State Park

were plagued by filth. It is said that more than 52,000 Confederate soldiers were held at the camp during the war, and between 3,000 and 8,000 died there. There are two monuments and an on-site museum that recall this part of the park's past.

Whether or not you believe in ghosts, the park boasts countless incidents of unexplained phenomena and firsthand encounters with "ghosts" of soldiers. The most haunted location is said to be the lighthouse, which is no longer in use.

Today the park is primarily known as a wonderful recreation spot. It has several boat launch locations ($12), canoe rentals, a camp store, fishing, hiking trails, picnic areas, a playground, beaches, swimming, and a nature center. The park is also pet friendly.

In addition to being surrounded by water, there is a large lake in the center of the park (Lake Conoy), which is a perfect spot for boating and fishing. A water trail guide for the park is available for purchase at the park headquarters.

Camping is offered in the park April-October on 143 wooded sites ($21.49). Twenty-six have full hookups ($38.49) and 33 provide electricity (33.49). There are also a half-dozen four-person camper cabins for rent ($50.49) on a nightly basis. Off-season camping is available with limited services. Call 888/432-2267 for reservations.

Maryland's Eastern Shore and Atlantic Beaches

Look for ★ to find recommended sights, activities, dining, and lodging.

Highlights

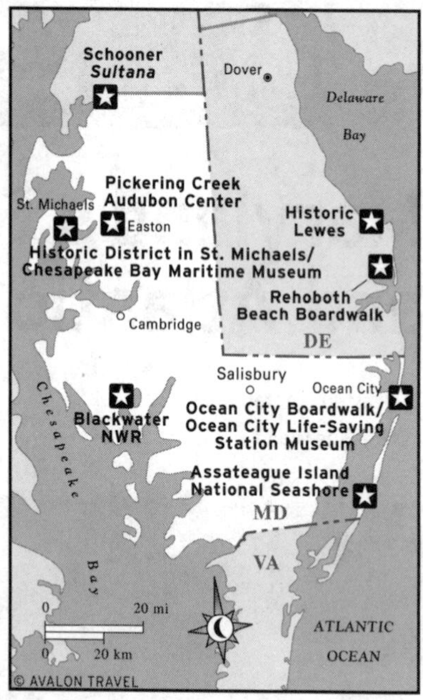

★ **Schooner *Sultana*:** This amazing replica of a British Royal Navy ship serves as an educational center and the site of the annual Chestertown Tea Party (page 462).

★ **Historic District in St. Michaels:** Beautiful churches, colonial homes, interesting shops, and great restaurants charm in this elegant downtown area (page 468).

★ **Chesapeake Bay Maritime Museum:** This wonderful museum in St. Michaels fills 18 acres with all things Chesapeake Bay (page 468).

★ **Pickering Creek Audubon Center:** This 400-acre farm in Easton includes forest, marsh, meadow, a freshwater pond, wetlands, and more than a mile of shoreline (page 473).

★ **Blackwater National Wildlife Refuge:** This beautiful waterfowl sanctuary features 27,000 acres of protected freshwater, brackish tidal wetlands, meadows, and forest (page 480).

★ **Assateague Island National Seashore:** These 37 miles of protected coastline are a haven for migrating birds and home to a herd of wild ponies (page 484).

★ **Ocean City Boardwalk:** Along three miles of wood-planked boardwalk sit dozens of hotels, motels, restaurants, shops, and amusement parks (page 487).

★ **Ocean City Life-Saving Station Museum:** Learn the history of rescues at sea along the Maryland coast (page 487).

★ **Rehoboth Beach Boardwalk:** This mile-long walkway offers stunning views of the Atlantic and enough activity and food to keep a family busy for days (page 499).

★ **Historic Lewes:** Victorian homes, upscale restaurants, and cozy inns are the trademark of this relaxing little coastal town (page 503).

Maryland is blessed with thousands of miles of shoreline along the Chesapeake Bay and Atlantic Ocean. One of the most scenic areas in the state, the Eastern Shore is made up of a series of bayside towns that retain the charm of yesteryear and are still partly supported by the local fishing industry.

Most travelers are welcomed to the Eastern Shore in the seafood haven of Kent Island after crossing the Chesapeake Bay Bridge. From there they head north to historic towns such as Chestertown and Rock Hall, or south to upscale St. Michaels or the quaint towns of Tilghman Island and Oxford. Easton and Cambridge offer their own special charm with bustling downtown areas and ample sports and recreation.

Maryland and Delaware share a thin strip of barrier island along the Atlantic coast, offering beachgoers many choices for a sun-filled vacation. On the very southern end, the Assateague Island National Seashore, which is shared with Virginia, is a quiet place to calm your spirits, view wildlife, and enjoy a long, pristine beach. Its northern neighbor is the bustling beachfront community of Ocean City. With its exciting boardwalk, active nightlife, and plentiful activities, Ocean City never sleeps. Three popular Delaware beaches, Bethany, Rehoboth, and Lewes, stretch to the north.

PLANNING YOUR TIME

The Eastern Shore of the Chesapeake Bay can be explored in a day or two, but many people choose to go there for extended relaxation and to spend a little downtime. Getting around by car is the best option, as public transportation is sparse. Route 301 is the major north/south route in the northern part of the Eastern Shore, while U.S. 50 is the major route in the middle and southern regions.

A good plan of action is to choose one or two towns to explore and spend a weekend enjoying them and learning about the Chesapeake Bay. The distance between Chestertown and Cambridge is about 52 miles, so the distances are not too cumbersome when traveling by car. Be aware,

Previous: Rehoboth Beach Boardwalk; Cambridge waterfront. **Above:** a sandpiper on Rehoboth Beach.

Maryland's Eastern Shore and Atlantic Beaches

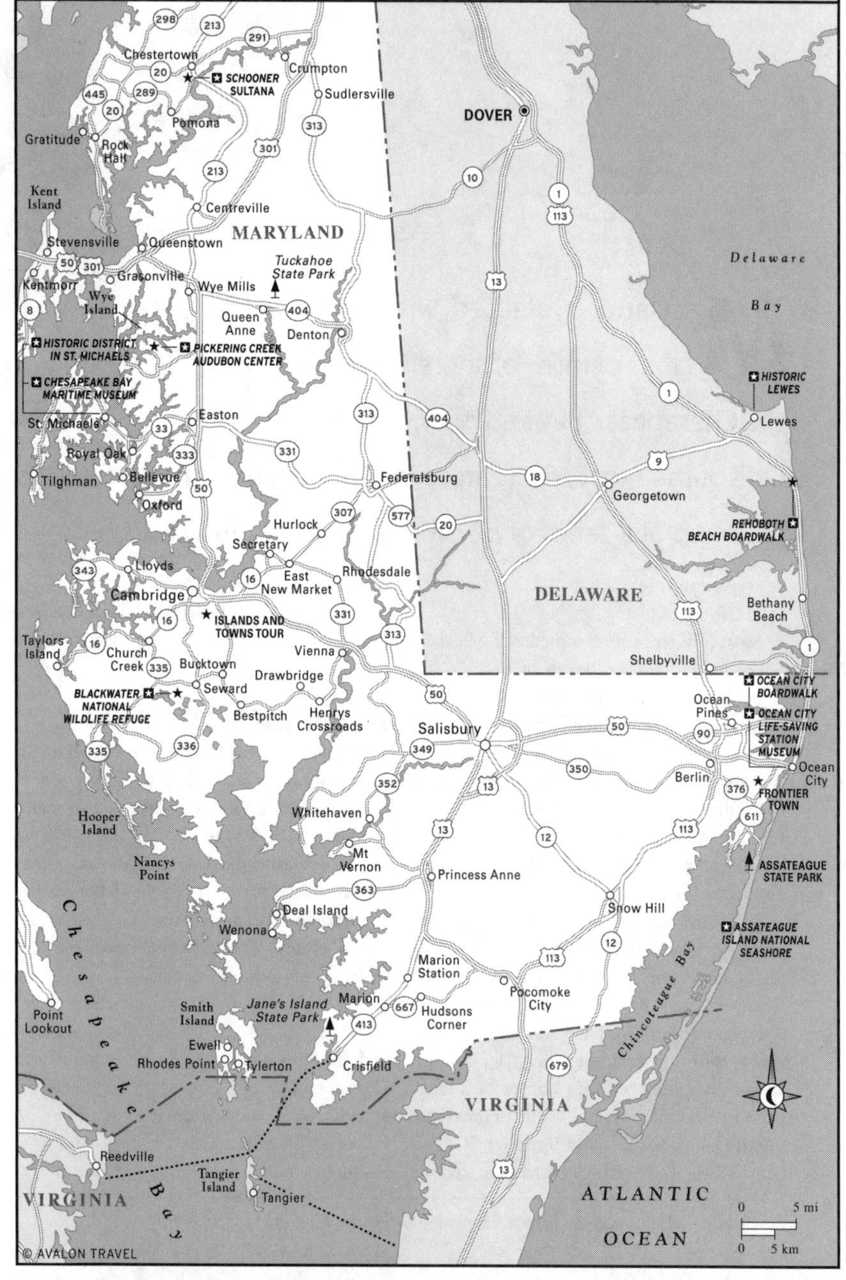

however, if you are traveling during the busy summer months, especially on a weekend, that traffic can back up on Route 50. Friday evening drives over the Bay Bridge (toll $4) can mean long wait times and bumper-to-bumper traffic.

The Atlantic beaches in Maryland and Delaware can be explored individually over a weekend, but they are often destinations that people spend a week at a time at over the summer months for a relaxing vacation. In the high season—generally, mid-June until Labor Day—many accommodations have minimum stays. The off-season is a great time to go if you don't have school constraints. Spring and fall offer cooler temperatures and fewer crowds at the beaches, and generally, prices for accommodations are reduced.

If you plan to just visit one of the beaches, keep in mind they all have unique characteristics. If you seek excitement, activity, and the bustling hubbub of a busy boardwalk, then Ocean City is a good choice. If you prefer the charm of a quaint, harborside historic town with close access to the beach, then Lewes, Delaware, may be a better option. If it's something in between that you are looking for, perhaps a more family-oriented beach scene with fewer hotels and more beach house rentals, then Bethany Beach is a good choice. Finally, if you seek the activity of a boardwalk, but a scaled-down version is more your style, then Rehoboth Beach may suit you.

Regardless of where you end up, you will find good seafood and many excellent choices for restaurants at all the beaches. Keep in mind, "Maryland is for Crabs," and delicious blue crab dishes are available in many places. This is *the* place to eat them.

The vast majority of visitors to the Maryland and Delaware beaches drive there. Once you arrive, it's difficult to get too lost as long as you know where the beach is. One main road, the Coastal Highway, runs along the coast; it goes by Route 528 in Maryland and Route 1 in Delaware.

The **Ocean City Municipal Airport** (12724 Airport Rd., Berlin, 410/213-2471) is three miles west of the downtown area of Ocean City and can accommodate general aviation and charter aircraft. Commercial air service is provided at the **Salisbury-Ocean City Wicomico Regional Airport** (5485 Airport Terminal Rd., Salisbury, 410/548-4827) five miles from downtown Salisbury on Maryland's Eastern Shore.

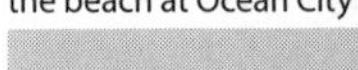

the beach at Ocean City

The Eastern Shore

The Eastern Shore holds a special place in many Marylanders' hearts. The wide peninsula between the Chesapeake Bay and the Atlantic Ocean contains endless miles of shoreline, beachfront resorts, nature preserves, and small seaside towns. Water is everywhere on the Eastern Shore and so are the culinary delights fished right from the bay. Amazing restaurants with million-dollar views, cozy inns, and plentiful outdoor activities welcome visitors nearly year-round.

KENT ISLAND AND KENT NARROWS

The Chesapeake Bay Bridge stretches from Sandy Point near Annapolis on the mainland to Kent Island. Kent Island is the largest island in the Chesapeake Bay and the gateway to the Eastern Shore. The island is bordered on the east by a narrow channel called the Kent Narrows.

Kent Island welcomes Bay Bridge drivers to a gathering of easily accessible waterfront restaurants. Visitors traveling Route 50 are immediately thrown into a seaside atmosphere, and the urge to stop and sample some of the local cuisine is hard to resist.

Food

The **Narrows Restaurant** (3023 Kent Narrows Way South, Grasonville, 410/827-8113, www.thenarrowsrestaurant.com, lunch Mon.-Sat. 11am-4pm, Sun. brunch 11am-2pm, dinner Mon.-Sat. 4pm-close, Sun. 11am-close, $10-36) is one of the most popular seafood restaurants on the island. It has a nice atmosphere and a great view. Patio seating is available.

Another local favorite is **Harris Crab House** (433 Kent Narrows Way, Grasonville, 410/827-9500, www.harriscrabhouse.com, daily lunch and dinner from 11am, $11-68). They have two levels of waterfront dining and outdoor seating. The views are great, and the seafood is plentiful. This is a casual place with a crab house atmosphere.

The **Fisherman's Inn & Crab Deck** (3116 Main St., 410/827-8807, www.fishermansinn.com, daily 11am-10pm, $19-40) serves great seafood and also has a seafood market.

CHESTERTOWN

Chestertown is a pretty waterfront colonial town with less than 5,000 residents. It is 40 minutes (29 miles) northeast of Kent Island on the Chester River, a tributary of the Chesapeake Bay. It is about 35 miles northeast of the Chesapeake Bay Bridge.

The town's history dates back to 1706, and it was known as one of Maryland's six "Royal Ports of Entry" (second only to Annapolis as a leading port). The town was a spot for the wealthy in its heyday, which is reflected in the numerous brick mansions and row houses that line the waterfront. The port is still a popular location for sailing ships and tourists. It is also home to **Washington College** (www.washcoll.edu), a private liberal arts college of which George Washington was a founding patron. The school was established in 1782, making it the tenth-oldest college in the country.

Sights

HISTORIC CHESTERTOWN

Chestertown is worth exploring on foot. The state's second-highest concentration of colonial homes (after Annapolis) can be found in Chestertown, and there is a scenic waterfront promenade.

★ SCHOONER *SULTANA*

The schooner ***Sultana*** (107 S. Cross St. on the waterfront, 410/778-5954, www.sultanaeducation.org) is a replica of a British Royal Navy ship that sailed during the 18th century and patrolled the North American coastline just before the Revolutionary War. The ship lives in the Chestertown Harbor and is used to

William Preston Lane Jr. Memorial Bay Bridge

Once upon a time, Marylanders had to depend on boats to cross the Chesapeake Bay. The first plan to connect the mainland to the Eastern Shore came in 1927 but was abandoned first until 1938 and then again until 1947. Finally, under the leadership of Governor William Preston Lane Jr. the State Roads Commission began building the "Bay Bridge" in 1949.

The original span of the bridge, which is used for eastbound traffic today, cost $45 million and became the longest continuous over-water steel structure in the world at 4.3 miles. It first opened to traffic on July 30, 1952. The bridge is part of U.S. Routes 50 and 301 and quickly became an important connection to the Baltimore/Washington DC area from the Eastern Shore and Ocean City, Maryland.

The second span, which currently carries westbound traffic, was started in 1969 at a cost of $148 million. This span opened in 1973. This architectural marvel has a vertical clearance of 186 feet, and the suspension bridge towers are 354 and 379 feet tall. The bridge starts on the mainland next to Sandy Point State Park and stretches to Kent Island. The bridge can accommodate 1,500 vehicles per lane per hour.

teach students about the Chesapeake Bay history and environment. Two-hour public sails are held on weekends from the end of April to the beginning of November ($30). Many events are offered throughout the season on the ship; a list is available on the website.

Events

The biggest annual event in Chestertown is the **Chestertown Tea Party** (www.chestertownteaparty.org), held at the end of May. In May 1774, five months after the famous Boston Tea Party when the British closed the port of Boston, residents of Chestertown resolved to prohibit the purchase, sale, or drinking of tea. Legend has it that they then held their own version of the Boston Tea Party staged on the schooner *Sultana* on the Chester River to show their colonial defiance. The annual festival celebrates this heritage through a reenactment of the tea party and a weekend of family events.

Aviation enthusiasts won't want to miss the annual **Potomac Antique Aero**

Squadron's Antique Fly-In (www.fly-ins.com, free but donations appreciated). This wonderful one-day antique aircraft show is held in June at the **Massey Aerodrome** (33541 Maryland Line Rd., Massey, www.masseyaero.org), approximately 17 miles northeast of Chestertown. It is sponsored by the Potomac Antique Air Squadron. More than 200 antique and rare aircrafts make up this impressive show. Visitors can see the airplanes up close, speak with the owners, and enjoy delicious food.

Shopping

A dozen or so art galleries, studios, and shops feature the work of local, regional, and international artists in the historic waterfront district of Chestertown.

From April to December a local farmers market is held on Saturday mornings in the heart of the downtown area between Spring Avenue and Cross Street. It features fresh bakery items, produce, plants, herbs, and local artwork.

Food

The most well-known eatery in town is the **Kitchen at the Imperial** (208 High St., 410/778-5000, www.imperialchestertown.com, Mon., Wed.-Sat. 11:30am-9pm, Sun. brunch 10am-3pm, dinner 3pm-9pm, $9-33). This wonderful restaurant was formerly located in Rock Hall but is now located in the Imperial Hotel, which first opened in 1903 and still offers three rooms for rent. The restaurant is open for lunch and dinner and offers a Bloody Mary brunch on Sunday. Their fresh menu varies seasonally but they usually have terrific local seafood dishes and meat from local farms.

Seafood, comfort food, and sophisticated choices can all be found at the **Lemon Leaf Café** (337 High St., 443/282-0004, www.thellcafe.com, Mon.-Wed. 11am-8pm, Thurs. 11am-9pm, Fri.-Sat. 7:30am-9pm, Sun. 7:30am-8pm, $7-30). This clean little gem has a signature dish of chicken and dumplings but also serves incredible authentic Maryland crab soup, great crab cakes, and a delicious lemon meringue pie. The friendly service really makes diners feel like part of the "family," and makes for a relaxed dining experience even though the restaurant is usually full.

Right next door to the Lemon Leaf Café, and accessible through the restaurant or off the street, is **JR's Past Time Pub** (337 High St., 443/282-0055, www.jrspub.net, daily 11am-1am, $7-30). This 60-year-old pub has the same owner as its popular neighbor. It has a unique vintage clock motif and is decorated with signs from businesses in Chestertown's past. They serve traditional pub fare and share some dishes with their sister restaurant. The food menu is printed on paper grocery bags and their drink menu on wine bags. The pub is popular with students from Washington College and also has a piano bar with live music on Sunday evenings.

If you're looking for a water view with your meal, the only game in town is **The Fish Whistle** (98 Cannon St., 410/778-3566, www.fishandwhistle.com, Mon.-Wed. 11am-8pm, Thurs. 11am-8:30pm, Fri.-Sat. 11am-9pm, Sun. 11am-7pm, late-night bar menu daily until

Tiki Bar Boat Stop

If you are exploring the Chesapeake Bay by boat and could use a taste of the islands and a party-hardy atmosphere, stop in **Jellyfish Joel's Tiki Bar** (22170 Great Oak Landing Rd., Chestertown, 410/778-5007, www.mearsgreatoaklanding.com, in-season Fri. starting 2pm and Sat.-Sun. starting 11am). This waterside bar sits on a peninsula by the beach on Fairlee Creek nine miles west of Chestertown and is a favorite boating stop. It offers a sandy beach, palm trees, and sunset beach parties every Friday during the summer. Boats can anchor or tie up on the floating docks. The bar is the main attraction, with cold beer and colder tropical drinks with names such as "Painkillers" and "Pain n'de Ass." They have live entertainment on the weekends and sell snacks and sandwiches.

11pm, $10-29). The location is excellent, right on the Chester River, and they serve a nice seafood menu with good daily specials. They have a large menu with bar food, sandwiches, and land and seafood entrées. Try the catfish fingers or the oyster potpie. Their slogan is, "It's all about the food," and they mean it.

Phenomenal oyster fritters are among the menu items at the **Blue Heron Café** (236 Cannon St., 410/778-0188, www.blueheroncafe.com, dinner Mon.-Sat. from 5pm, $16-30). This consistently good restaurant serves regional American cuisine such as crab cakes, filet, and lamb. The desserts are amazing. Reservations are a must on weekend nights.

A great place to grab a drink in the summer and watch the sun set is at **The Sandbar at Rolph's Wharf** (1008 Rolph's Wharf Rd., 410/778-6389, www.rolphswharf.com). This is a small outdoor bar that is primarily open on weekends. It offers wonderful views of the Chester River, cold beer, and snacks.

The **Chestertown Farmers Market** is held every Saturday (late March-late December) from 8am to noon at **Fountain Park** (220 High St.).

Accommodations

A pre-Revolutionary War landmark, the **White Swan Tavern** (231 High St., 410/778-2300, www.whiteswantavern.com, $150-280) is a cozy bed-and-breakfast in the historic district of Chestertown. The inn was built in 1733 and has been used for a number of purposes throughout its history, including a private home and a tavern. A special room in the inn houses many artifacts that were found when the building was restored in 1978. There are six guest rooms, one of which was the original one-room dwelling that housed shoemaker John Lovegrove prior to 1733. The rooms are large and comfortable, and the location of this inn couldn't be any better if you are looking to explore the downtown area and waterfront. A continental breakfast and afternoon tea are served to guests. The bed-and-breakfast can accommodate small weddings and conferences. Two additional apartments are available for long- or short-term stays near the inn.

A cute home away from home very convenient to Washington College (it's 100 yards from campus) and within a 15-minute walk to the riverfront is **Simply Bed and Bread** (208 Mount Vernon Ave., 410/778-4359, www.simplybedandbread.com, $129-149). They offer two allergy-friendly guest rooms in a 1947 Cape Cod-style home. One room has a queen bed, and the other has a

White Swan Tavern

king. Each clean, cozy room has ample space. The innkeepers do a great job of making guests feel welcome. A continental breakfast is served each morning, and guests are treated to welcome sweets upon arrival.

One mile outside of Chestertown is the lovely **Brampton Bed and Breakfast Inn** (25227 Chestertown Rd., 410/778-1860, www.bramptoninn.com, $180-380), a restored plantation house built in 1860. It now has 13 guest rooms, suites, and cottages available to visitors. All accommodations have private bathrooms, sitting areas, fireplaces, flat-screen televisions with DVD players (no cable), bathrobes, and bath amenities. The estate is well cared for with beautiful gardens and a large front porch. A full à la carte breakfast is served in the dining area daily between 8:30am and 10am, although guests may opt to have breakfast delivered to their rooms. One cottage on the property is pet friendly.

A few chain hotels are options near the historic district in Chestertown. The **Holiday Inn Express Hotel & Suites Chestertown** (150 Scheeler Rd., 410/778-0778, www.ihg.com, $95-122) has 81 guest rooms, complimentary breakfast, and free wireless Internet, and the adjacent **Comfort Suites** (160 Scheeler Rd., 410/810-0555, www.choicehotels.com, $110-120) has 53 guest rooms, complimentary continental breakfast, and an indoor pool.

Information and Services

For additional information on Chestertown visit www.chestertown.com or stop by the **Kent County Visitor Center** (corner of Rte. 213 and Cross St., www.townofchestertown.com, Mon.-Fri. 9am-5pm, Sat.-Sun. 10am-2pm).

ROCK HALL

Fourteen miles southwest of Chestertown is the small waterfront town of Rock Hall. Rock Hall sits directly on the Chesapeake Bay and has a population of less than 1,500 people. Sometimes referred to as the "Pearl of the Chesapeake," this quaint maritime town has a history of fishing and boating and during the colonial era was a stop for passenger boats and shipping boats transporting tobacco and seafood. Today Rock Hall still has a working harbor and a fleet of professional watermen.

Simply Bed and Bread

Sights

There are three small museums in Rock Hall. **The Rock Hall Museum** (at the Municipal Building on S. Main Street, www.rockhallmd.com, Sat.-Sun. 11am-3pm, free, donations appreciated) is a two-room facility a short walk from the town center housing artifacts from the town's history and focusing on the lifestyle, economy, and traditions of the community. **The Waterman's Museum** (in the Haven Harbour Marina, 20880 Rock Hall Ave., 410/778-6697, www.havenharbour.com, daily 10am-4pm, free) features a unique collection of vintage photographs taken during the watermen era, as well as boats and local carvings. The third museum, **Tolchester Beach Revisited** (Main St.

behind the Shoppes at Oyster Court, www.rockhallmd.com, Sat.-Sun. 11am-3pm), is a unique little place with artifacts and memorabilia from a former amusement park that was at a nearby steamboat landing. In its prime, it included 155 acres of amusement space and brought in as many as 20,000 visitors during a weekend by six steamships and one ferry. The park included a dance hall, bowling alley, bingo parlor, roller coaster, pony carts, a roller-skating rink, and numerous vendors. The park closed for good in 1962.

A warm and friendly local theater, **The Mainstay** (5753 Main St., 410/639-9133, www.mainstayrockhall.org) is a cultural and artistic center in Rock Hall. It occupies a building that was constructed more than a century ago. With just 120 seats, this is an intimate theater that offers more than 50 blues, folk, classical, and jazz concerts every year. They sell beer, wine, soft drinks, and home-baked treats during performances.

Food

The **Osprey Point Inn Restaurant** (20786 Rock Hall Ave., 410/639-2194, www.ospreypoint.com, dinner Wed.-Sun. starting at 5pm, Sunday brunch May-Sept. 10:30am-2pm, $18-25) features great water views from the Osprey Point Inn. The setting is comfortable and relaxing, and the young but highly skilled chef is truly passionate about his work. They have a fresh, seasonal menu with seafood and land-borne choices.

Another good choice in Rock Hall is **Uncle Charlie's Bistro** (834B High St., 410/778-3663, www.unclecharliesbistro.com, Mon.-Thurs. 11am-8pm, Fri. 11am-9pm, Sat., noon-9pm, $8-27). They offer American dishes, including seafood, salads, burgers, and sandwiches. The atmosphere and staff are very pleasant despite a not-so-impressive exterior.

Accommodations

The serene waterfront setting of the ★ **Inn at Huntingfield Creek** (4928 Eastern Neck Rd., 410/639-7779, www.huntingfield.com, $185-325) is hard to beat. Guests can literally swim, kayak, and bike right from the front door of this beautiful farm estate that was once a high-end hunting club and horse racing track. Four guest rooms in the manor house and four private cottages allow for a variety of accommodations (pets are allowed in the cottages). The estate is a blend of old-world charm and modern conveniences. It has lovely grounds, a view of the Chesapeake Bay, a saltwater pool, wireless Internet, and a library. Gourmet breakfasts are served daily in the gorgeous manor house.

The **Osprey Point Inn** (20786 Rock Hall Ave., 410/639-2194, www.ospreypoint.com, $180-280) offers luxurious accommodations in three settings. There are seven guest rooms in the main inn, three rooms in the farmhouse, and five rooms at the marina annex. Guests in all three locations can enjoy the amenities at the inn, including a pool and daily continental breakfast. A marina provides boat access, docks, and a bathhouse. There is also a lovely on-site restaurant that features delicious food in a waterfront setting (dinner Wed.-Sun. starting at 5pm, Sunday brunch May-Sept. 10:30am-2pm).

Information and Services

Additional information on Rock Hall can be found at www.rockhallmd.com or by stopping by the **Rock Hall Visitor's Center** (5585 Main St., 410/639-7611, www.rockhallmd.com, open daily).

ST. MICHAELS

The historic waterfront town of St. Michaels is approximately one hour (51 miles) from Annapolis (from Route 50, exit on Route 322 and follow the signs for Route 33 to St. Michaels). This charming vintage port is a popular tourist destination and features manicured colonial, federal, and Victorian homes, stunning churches, and a scenic shopping area with specialty stores, restaurants, exclusive inns, and bed-and-breakfasts. Seafood lovers can eat their fill of local crab, fish, and oysters, and those looking to go out on the water can take a cruise or launch a kayak.

St. Michaels was founded in the mid-1600s as a trading stop for the tobacco and trapper industries. The town's name came from the Christ Episcopal Church of St. Michael Archangel parish that was founded in 1677. The historic center of St. Michaels, known as St. Mary's Square (between Mulberry Street and E. Chestnut Street), was created in 1778 when a wealthy land agent from England purchased 20 acres and created 58 town lots. Many of the homes in St. Michaels that were built in the late 1700s and 1800s still stand today.

St. Michaels earned the nickname "the town that fooled the British" during the War of 1812, when residents protected their town from British gunfire using trickery as their defense. Warned of a nighttime attack from British barges positioned in their waters, the townspeople strung burning lanterns in the treetops above the town to fool the attackers into overshooting their targets. The plan worked, and only one house, still known today as the "cannonball house," was hit in the attack.

In the late 1800s and early 1900s, St. Michaels's economy was primarily supported by seafood processing and shipbuilding. Slowly, toward the end of the 20th century, the town became a popular tourist destination and a weekend getaway spot for Washingtonians and other regional residents.

Sights

★ HISTORIC DISTRICT IN ST. MICHAELS

The charming and historic downtown area of St. Michaels is a cornucopia of churches, colonial homes, shops, restaurants, and galleries. This elegant district was added to the National Register of Historic places in 1986 and is a destination for many tourists and area residents. The area includes a scenic harbor on the Miles River. South Talbot Street (Route 33) is the main artery through town, just a few blocks from the waterfront.

★ CHESAPEAKE BAY MARITIME MUSEUM

The **Chesapeake Bay Maritime Museum** (213 N. Talbot St., 410/745-2916, www.cbmm.org, daily May-Oct. 9am-5pm, Nov.-Apr. 10am-4pm, $15) is an 18-acre learning center for all things Chesapeake Bay. There are 10 exhibit buildings, a large display of traditional

Chesapeake Bay Maritime Museum

bay boats, and the Hooper Strait Lighthouse built in 1879.

The museum is a wealth of information on Chesapeake Bay history and the people who live there. Instead of relying on tour guides or reenactors to teach visitors about the bay, the Chesapeake Bay Maritime Museum employs real people of the Chesapeake who live and work on the bay and share their actual experiences. Examples include master decoy carvers, retired crab pickers, and ship captains. Visitors can also witness a boat restoration in progress in the museum's working boatyard or climb a lighthouse.

The museum offers scenic 45-minute cruises on the Miles River on a replica buyboat (May-Oct. Fri.-Mon. at noon, 1pm, 2pm, and 3pm). Buyboats were used to buy catches off watermen's boats and take them directly to market. Cruises depart from the lighthouse (tickets are sold in the Admissions Building, $10).

Both self-guided tours (by map) and guided tours are available with admission to view the museum's many exhibits, including art and maritime displays.

Recreation

St. Michaels is all about water. Those looking for an upscale sailing adventure can charter the *Selina II*, a vintage catboat, through **Sail Selina** (101 N. Harbor Rd., 410/726-9400, www.sailselina.com, May-Sept.). Passengers are limited to just six per two-hour outing and are offered a personal sailing experience/tour through the harbor and on the Miles River. Guests are invited to help sail the vessel or to just sit back and relax. The boat is docked at the Harbor Inn and Marina. Outings start at $65 per person.

Narrated cruises up the Miles River are also available through **Patriot Cruises** (410/745-3100, www.patriotcruises.com, early spring-late fall, $24.50). This two-level, 49-passenger cruising boat is climate-controlled and offers 60- to 70-minute tours. It leaves from 301 N. Talbot Street.

If you long to sail aboard an authentic skipjack, the **Skipjack *H. M. Krentz*** (800/979-3370, www.oystercatcher.com, Apr.-Oct. daily, $40) offers two-hour narrated cruises aboard a 70-foot working skipjack from the 1950s. Sailing cruises leave from the Chesapeake Bay Maritime Museum.

Kayaks ($30 per hour), stand-up paddleboards ($30 per hour), and bikes ($10 per hour) can be rented from **Shore Pedal & Paddle** (store: 500 S. Talbot St., dock: 125 Mulberry St., 410/745-2320, www.shorepedalandpaddle.com). They also offer guided two-hour kayak tours in St. Michaels Harbor on weekends and by appointment during the week. Bikes can also be rented from **TriCycle & Run** (929 S. Talbot St., 410/745-2836, www.tricycleand-run.com, Sun. 10am-2pm, Mon. 10am-5pm, Thurs.-Sat. 10am-5pm, $10 for 2 hours).

Shopping

Talbot Street is the place to start your shopping adventure in St. Michaels. For unique gifts, stop by **The Preppy Redneck** (310 S. Talbot St., 410/829-3635, www.thepreppyredneck.com), a fun gift shop; **NETime Designs** (404 S. Talbot St., 410/745-8001) for home decor, gifts, and jewelry; and **Ophiuroidea** (609 S. Talbot St., 410/745-8057) for coastal-inspired furnishings and gifts.

Food

AMERICAN

Good food with a romantic atmosphere and modern ambience can be found at **Theo's Steaks, Sides, and Spirits** (407 S. Talbot St., 410/745-2106, www.theossteakhouse.com, Wed.-Sun. for dinner at 4:30pm, $15-55) on Talbot Street. This popular eatery offers a small but diverse menu of pub fare and steaks, expertly prepared and presented.

Another good date-night spot is **208 Talbot** (208 N. Talbot St., 410/745-3838, www.208talbot.com, Wed.-Sun for dinner at 5pm, tavern menu $12-23, dining room menu $28-36). They offer delicious steak and seafood dishes such as pan-seared grouper, grilled ribeye, and seared sea scallops in the dining room and a casual menu with items

The Preppy Redneck gift shop

such as pizza, burgers, and shrimp and grits in their tavern. Reservations are recommended.

A good bet for casual American fare any day of the week is **Mike and Eric's Front Street Restaurant & Bar** (200 S. Talbot St., 410/745-8380, www.mikeandericsfrontstreet.com, Mon.-Sat. 11am-10pm, Sun. 9am-10pm, $13-27). They serve sandwiches, flatbread, and an eclectic selection of entrees that includes pasta, lamb, chicken potpie, salmon, and oysters.

ITALIAN

Theo's sister restaurant, **Ava's Pizzeria and Wine Bar** (409 S. Talbot St., 410/745-3081, www.avaspizzeria.com, daily 11:30am-9:30pm, $8-24) serves exceptional pizza, pasta, and sandwiches. They also have an extensive wine and beer menu. The atmosphere is fun and inviting with an outdoor patio, fireplaces, and even a waterfall. They do not take reservations, although they do have a call-ahead list. They are known for pizza, but the meatballs are out of this world.

MEXICAN

Feeling funky? Then try **Gina's Cafe** (601 Talbot St., 410/745-6400, Wed.-Mon. noon-10pm, $11-28). This tiny, 1,000-square-foot Southwestern eatery on the corner of Talbot Street and East Chew is barely large enough to be termed a restaurant, but they serve up interesting, south-of-the-border goodness with a nod to fresh seafood. They offer fish tacos, drinks, and house-made tortilla chips, in addition to a host of other unique favorites. This is the place to come when your taste buds need a break from the usual restaurant fare. People either love it for its uniqueness or dislike it for its quirkiness. Try the soft-shell tacos with crab and guacamole or the crab nachos.

SEAFOOD

A great view and a harbor atmosphere are the calling cards of the **Town Dock Restaurant** (125 Mulberry St., 410/745-5577, www.towndockrestaurant.com, Sun. 11am-8pm, Thurs. 4pm-9pm, Fri.-Sat. 11:30am-9pm, $15-30). This waterfront restaurant specializes in seafood, but also offers steak, ribs, and seasonal menu items. The atmosphere is casual, but it's best to come on a nice day so you can enjoy the harbor-side porch.

Another waterfront seafood house is the **St. Michaels Crab and Steakhouse** (305 Mulberry St., 410/745-3737, www.stmichaelscrabhouse.com, Thurs.-Mon. at 11am for lunch and dinner, $9-30). They offer a large menu of seafood favorites along with sandwiches, steak, pasta, and salad. All meals are made to order, and they pride themselves on being flexible in accommodating requests. The atmosphere is fun and lively. This is a good place to grab a drink and enjoy the local food and a good view.

ICE CREAM

Mouthwatering ice cream in a friendly atmosphere can be found at **Justine's Ice Cream Parlour** (106 N. Talbot St., 410/745-0404, www.justinesicecreams.com, Sun.-Thurs. 11am-8pm, Fri.-Sat. 11am-10pm, under $10) on North Talbot Street. They have been a staple in St. Michaels for more than 25 years. They serve ice cream, floats, shakes, and malts.

Accommodations

$100-200

There is no shortage of comfortable bed-and-breakfasts and inns in St. Michaels. The **Cherry Street Inn** (103 Cherry St., 410/745-6309, www.cherrystreetinn.com, $155-180) is one good option, with its convenient location, great breakfasts, and friendly, down-to-earth hosts. Just a short walk from the downtown area, this Victorian inn offers two suites with queen beds and private bathrooms. The inn was built in the 1880s by a steamboat captain and has been fully renovated.

$200-300

Bring your kayak or fishing rod to the **Point Breeze Bed and Breakfast** (704 Riverview Ter., 410/745-9563, www.pointbreezebandb.com, $205, minimum stays may be required). This lovely home has 400 feet of waterfront on the harbor, a pier, and complimentary kayaks, canoes, and bicycles for guest use. There are several guest rooms, all decorated with family heirlooms from five generations. Breakfast is included with each stay.

An additional nice bed-and-breakfast option is the **Snuggery Bed and Breakfast** (203 Cherry St., 410/745-2800, www.snuggery1665.com, $200-250), with two guest rooms in the oldest residence in St. Michaels.

OVER $300

Also located on Cherry Street is the ★ **Dr. Dodson House Bed and Breakfast** (200 Cherry St., 410/745-3691, www.drdodsonhouse.com, $290-385). This charming bed-and-breakfast is steps from Talbot Street and a stone's throw from the harbor. The inn was built in 1799 for use as a tavern and also served as the first post office in town. The home still has many of its original features, such as the fireplaces, woodwork, doors, and glass. It is considered to be one of the best-preserved examples of federal architecture in St. Michaels. The interior is modern but keeps with the character of its time. There are three guest rooms: two with queen beds and one with a king or two twins. All have fireplaces (either wood-burning or electric) and private bathrooms. There are large sofas on the first floor and a second-floor porch for guests to relax on. A wonderful breakfast is served each morning in the elegant dining area.

The lavish **Inn at Perry Cabin** (308 Watkins Ln., 410/745-2200, www.belmond.com/inn-at-perry-cabin-st-michaels/, $615-1,035) is a grand old resort and spa formerly owned by Sir Bernard and Lady Laura Ashley. It sits on the Miles River and has nice views of the water. The hotel was built around 1816 and is surrounded by antique gardens from the same period. Docking facilities (free for guest use), a fitness center, heated outdoor pool, and complimentary bicycles are part of the property amenities. There are 78 guest rooms and the resort is pet friendly. Ask for a room on an upper floor with a view of the water.

The **St. Michaels Harbour Inn Marina & Spa** (101 N. Harbor Rd., 410/745-9001, www.harbourinn.com, $279-729) is also located on the Miles River and offers 46 guest rooms and a full-service marina. This is a lovely property in a good location.

Information and Services

For additional information on St. Michaels, visit www.stmichaelsmd.org.

TILGHMAN ISLAND

Tilghman Island is one of the few remaining working watermen's villages in the mid-Atlantic. It provides an unvarnished look at life on the Chesapeake Bay. Tilghman Island is home to the last commercial sailing fleet in North America. The fleet is known as the Skipjacks in honor of the classic oyster boat (and Maryland's state boat), which visitors can see at **Dogwood Harbor,** on the east side of the island. Tilghman Island is in the middle Chesapeake Bay region and is separated from the Eastern Shore by Napps Narrows, but is easily accessed by driving over a drawbridge. Tilghman Island is three miles long and reachable via Route 33, 11 miles west of St. Michaels. It has a population of less than 800 people.

Sights

The **Phillips Wharf Environmental Center** (6129 Tilghman Island Rd., 410/886-9200, www.pwec.org, Apr.-mid-Oct. Thurs.-Mon. 10am-4pm, free, donations appreciated) is a wonderful place for children and adults to learn about creatures living in the Chesapeake Bay. The center gives visitors the opportunity to see, touch, and learn about the wildlife such as horseshoe crabs, turtles, and oysters.

The **Tilghman's Watermen's Museum** (6031 Tilghman Island Rd., 410/886-1025, www.tilghmanmuseum.org, Apr.-Dec. Sat.-Sun. 10am-3pm, free) features exhibits on the heritage of the local watermen. It houses a collection of artifacts, boat models, and artwork by local artists.

Recreation

Boat tours and charters are available on Tilghman Island through **Harrison House Charter Fishing** (21551 Chesapeake House Dr., 410/886-2121, www.chesapeakehouse.com, starting at $125). They have a charter fleet of 14 boats that can carry 6-40 passengers. They tout the "complete charter experience," regardless of the size of your party.

Lady Patty Classic Yacht Charters (6176 Tilghman Island Rd., 410/886-1127, www.ladypatty.com, $42) offers seasonal two-hour charters in the waters surrounding Tilghman Island. Beer, wine, and cocktail service is available on all charters. Private charters can be arranged.

Charters aboard the oldest working skipjack on the Chesapeake Bay can be arranged on the **Skipjack *Rebecca T. Ruark*** (410/829-3976, www.tilghmanisland.com, $30). This beautiful boat was built in 1886, and the wonderful captain helps make this a great two-hour sail. Sailing charters leave from **Dogwood Harbor** (21308 Phillips Rd.).

Several **Tilghman Island Water Trails** (410/770-8000, www.dnr2.maryland.gov/boating/Pages/eastern_north.aspx) are available for kayaking. The **East Tilghman Island Trail** is 10.2 miles and explores the eastern portion of the island, while the **Tilghman Island Trail** tours the entire island. Maps can be downloaded at the trail website. **Tilghman Island Marina** (6140 Mariners Ct., 410/886-2500, www.tilghmanmarina.com) rents kayaks and canoes.

Food

Two If By Sea Restaurant (5776 Tilghman Island Rd., 410/886-2447, www.twoifbysearestaurant.com, breakfast Mon., Tues., Thurs. 8am-11am, breakfast and lunch, Wed., Fri.-Sun. 8am-2pm, dinner Thurs. and Sun. 6pm-8:30pm, Fri. and Sat. 6pm-9pm, $15-24) is a cozy little restaurant serving breakfast, lunch, and dinner. They have wonderful traditional breakfasts, sandwiches, salads, fresh seafood, and homemade pastries. This is a delightful choice for a casual meal at a reasonable price.

The **Marker Five Restaurant** (6178 Tilghman Island Rd., 410/886-1122, www.markerfive.com, $11-27) offers a casual waterfront dining experience. They serve soup, sandwiches, local seafood, and other items such as barbecue and house-smoked ribs. They have an outdoor bar with more than 30 beers on tap.

If you're looking for a great view, laid-back atmosphere, and an interesting take on casual fare, grab a seat on the deck at the **Characters**

Bridge Restaurant (6136 Tilghman Island Rd., 410/886-1060, www.charactersbridgerestaurant.com, daily 11am-10pm, $8-29). The menu offers staples like local seafood, burgers, and steak, but also includes interesting dishes such as oyster pie and Cajun burgers. This is a great place to watch the boats on Knapps Narrows and the activity at the drawbridge.

Accommodations

For peace and serenity, stay a few nights at the ★ **Black Walnut Point Inn** (4417 Black Walnut Point Rd., Tilghman, 410/886-2452, www.blackwalnutpointinn.com, $150-350). This charming bed-and-breakfast is at the southern point of Tilghman Island and bounded by water on three sides. The main house is meticulously maintained and offers four rooms with private baths. Two nicely appointed cabins right on the Choptank River provide a larger, more private space, and one is wheelchair accessible. The innkeepers are extremely friendly and knowledgeable about the long history of the property. Full breakfast is served each morning in the dining room, and the beautiful grounds offer a swimming pool, hot tub, pier, bird-watching trails, and unrivaled views of the Chesapeake Bay.

The **Knapps Narrows Marina and Inn** (6176 Tilghman Island Rd., 410/886-2720, www.knappsnarrowsmarina.com, $120-260) is a wonderful little waterfront inn, restaurant, and tiki bar that offers 20 guest rooms and great views of the Chesapeake Bay. Each room has a private waterfront patio or balcony. The inn is three stories, and each room is nicely furnished but not overstuffed. The staff is truly accommodating and friendly. The inn is adjacent to the Knapps Narrows Bridge (the entrance to the island). There is an outdoor pool on-site.

The Lazy Jack Inn on Dogwood Harbor (5907 Tilghman Island Rd., 410/886-2215, www.lazyjackinn.com, $185-305) has two rooms and two suites with private bathrooms. This charming waterfront inn has watched over Dogwood Harbor for more than 150 years. It is within walking distance of several restaurants and activities in the harbor. Nicely restored, the current owners have owned and run the inn for more than 20 years. A full gourmet breakfast is included. This is a great place for a peaceful getaway with wonderful views.

Information and Services

For additional information on Tilghman Island, visit www.tilghmanisland.com.

EASTON

Easton is a wonderful small town on the Eastern Shore that was founded in 1710. It is an hour's drive (42 miles) southeast of Annapolis. Easton is the largest town in Talbot County, with a population of around 16,000. It offers residents and visitors a beautiful downtown area with colonial and Victorian architecture, casual and fine restaurants, shopping, antiques, and galleries, while also providing ample opportunities for recreation such as golf and water sports on the Chesapeake Bay..

Sights

ACADEMY ART MUSEUM

The **Academy Art Museum** (106 South St., 410/822-2787, www.academyartmuseum.org, Mon. and Fri.-Sun. 10am-4pm, Tues.-Thurs. 10am-8pm, $3) is a little museum near downtown Easton that has five studios. It is housed in a charming building was built in 1820 and was the location of the first chartered school in Easton. It is now a historic landmark. The museum offers both regional and national exhibits; hosts concerts, lectures, and educational programs; and offers performing arts education for adults and children. More than 70,000 visitors come to the museum each year. Past exhibits have included original works by Ansel Adams, Roy Lichtenstein, and N. C. Wyeth.

★ PICKERING CREEK AUDUBON CENTER

The **Pickering Creek Audubon Center** (11450 Audubon Ln., 410/822-4903, www.

Easton

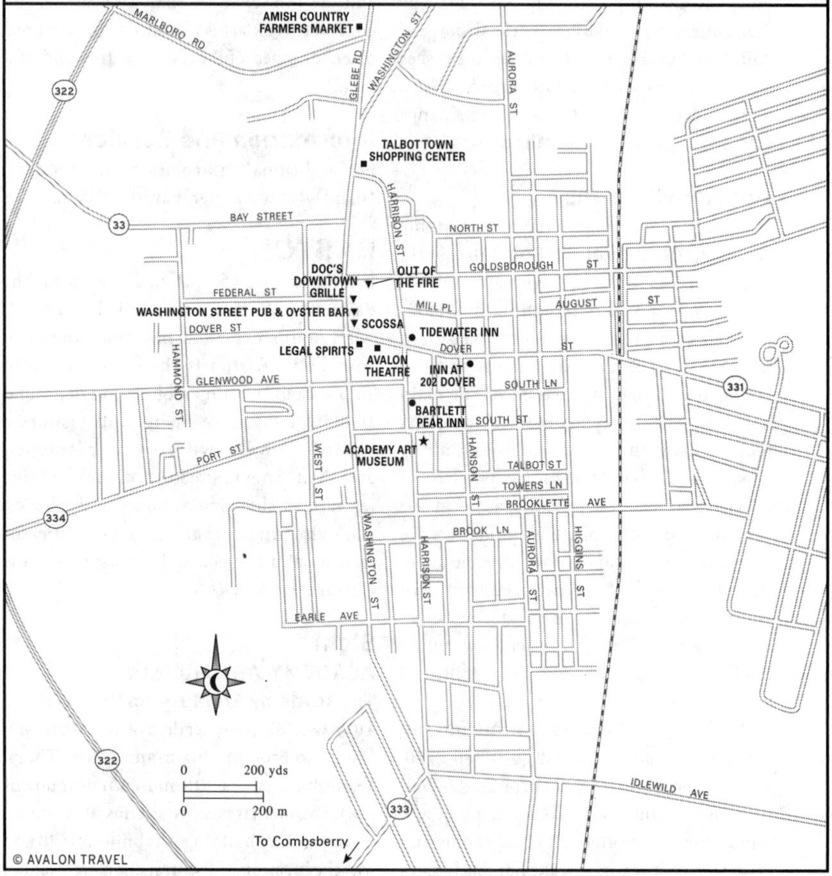

pickeringcreek.audubon.org, trails and viewing areas daily dawn-dusk, free) is a 400-acre working farm next to Pickering Creek in Talbot County. The property is a natural habitat of forest, marsh, meadow, a freshwater pond, wetlands, more than a mile of shoreline, and farmland. More than 3.5 miles of walking trails are available as well as gardens, a canoe and kayak launch, and 100 acres of hardwood forest. Trails and viewing areas are open to the public from dawn until dusk every day, and there is no admission fee. The center is great for bird-watching and features viewing platforms, a bluebird trail, and 90 acres of wetlands. Office hours at Pickering Creek are Monday-Friday 9am-4pm. The center is north of Easton: Take Route 662 north past the airport. Turn left on Sharp Road (west) and go right at the Y. Turn right (north) on Presquille Road and then right again on Audubon Lane.

THE AMISH COUNTRY FARMERS MARKET

The Amish Country Farmers Market (101 Marlboro Ave., 410/822-8989, www.amishcountryfarmersmarket.com, Thurs.

9am-6pm, Fri. 9am-7pm, Sat. 9am-3pm) is a tradition on the Eastern Shore. The market features numerous authentic Amish vendors from Pennsylvania selling a great variety of produce, dairy products, baked goods, meats, candy, furniture, and crafts. Many locals do their regular grocery shopping at the market, but it is a popular stop for tourists wishing to purchase fresh foods and handmade products.

Recreation and Entertainment

Easton is home to the popular **Hog Neck Golf Course** (10142 Old Cordova Rd., 410/822-6079, www.hogneck.com, $55). The facility offers an 18-hole championship course and a 9-hole executive course.

Visitors can catch a show at the **Avalon Theatre** (40 E. Dover St., 410/822-7299, www.avalontheatre.com). This cozy little theater has a full schedule of entertainment including theatrical performances, symphonies, bluegrass, jazz, comedians, and art festivals.

The largest annual event in Easton, and one of the best known on the Eastern Shore, is the **Waterfowl Festival** (www.waterfowlfestival.org, $15 for all three days). Taking place over three days in November, this event began in the early 1970s and now hosts 17,000 visitors, 300 of the best wildlife artists, craftspeople, and vendors, and 1,500 volunteers. This is a citywide event that closes several streets and prompts businesses to decorate their buildings with natural greens. The festival is a leader in promoting conservation of waterfowl and natural habitat.

Shopping

Downtown Easton is a shopper's delight, with many gift stores, antiques shops, crafts, clothing, and shops with collectibles. Two of the prime streets to include on your shopping journey are Harrison and Washington, although many lovely stores may be found on various side streets. The **Talbot Town Shopping Center** on North Washington Street offers national retail chains.

Food

Good Northern Italian food is served at **Scossa** (8 N. Washington St., 410/822-2202, www.scossarestaurant.com, lunch Thurs.-Sun. 11:30am-3pm, dinner Mon.-Thurs. 4pm-9pm, Sun. 4pm-8pm, Fri.-Sat. 4pm-10pm, $15-35) in the heart of the downtown

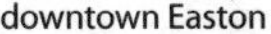
downtown Easton

area on North Washington Street. The owner/chef was born in northern Italy and has an impressive culinary résumé. The modern dining room is the perfect place to meet with friends, business associates, and family. The dinner menu is a step above traditional Italian with creative combinations, fresh ingredients, and daily specials that offer something new each visit. They also offer a prix fixe menu for $40. Lunch is a completely different experience and features wonderful salads and sandwiches. The bar area is very inviting and serves top-shelf wine and liquor. They have a large specialty drink menu. Sunday brunch is also served.

Another excellent choice for Italian food is **Out of the Fire** (22 Goldsborough St., 410/770-4777, www.outofthefire.com, lunch Tues.-Sat. 11:30am-2pm, dinner Tues.-Thurs. 5pm-9pm, Fri.-Sat. 5pm-10pm, $14-28) on Goldsborough Street. They serve gourmet pizza and other creative entrées made from high-quality ingredients procured from mostly local farmers and vendors (try the mussels). The wraps and sandwiches are delicious, and they offer organic and gluten-free choices. The atmosphere is very warm and relaxing with tile floors and soft lighting.

For a good pub-style meal in Easton, go to the **Washington Street Pub & Oyster Bar** (20 N. Washington St., 410/822-1112, www.washingtonstreetpub.com, Mon.-Thurs. 11am-2am, Fri.-Sat. 11am-2am, Sun. 11am-2am, $10-17). The trendy decor and lively atmosphere rival the food at this cozy pub and raw bar. They also have a good selection of beer on tap. Try the Chesapeake chicken sandwich (crab imperial and cheese on top of chicken); it is decadent to say the least.

The **Bartlett Pear Inn** (28 S. Harrison St., 410/770-3300, www.bartlettpearinn.com, Wed.-Sun. 5:30pm-10pm, $26-44) has a lovely upscale American bistro serving delicious entrées such as Alaskan halibut, New York strip steak, and curry-dusted sea scallops. They also offer a five-course tasting menu for $75 and a seven-course tasting menu for $95. The food is very flavorful, and the presentation is exquisite. The restaurant is part of a working inn with seven guest rooms.

Washington Street Pub & Oyster Bar

For a fun atmosphere or to watch your favorite sports event, dine at **Doc's Downtown Grille** (14 N. Washington St., 410/822-7700, daily 11am-2am, $11-30). They serve traditional pub food and delicious local seafood (crab cakes, shrimp po'boy, fried oysters, etc.). The restaurant is family owned and operated and their passion for their business is evident in the friendly service.

Accommodations

The ★ **Bartlett Pear Inn** (28 S. Harrison St., 410/770-3300, www.bartlettpearinn.com, $234-289) is a beautiful property on South Harrison Street in downtown Easton. This lovely inn dates back to the late 1700s and offers seven individually decorated guest rooms named for different types of pears. The handsome brick building with white covered porches is on a quiet street within walking distance to shopping and restaurants. The husband-and-wife owners are very gracious hosts, and they pay attention to the small details that make their guests feel welcome. The inn is pet friendly and can even accommodate large dogs. Ask for a room on the upper floor; this will provide the most quiet and privacy. There is an on-site restaurant that is open Wednesday-Sunday for dinner.

Luxurious accommodations can be found on Dover Street at the ★ **Inn at 202 Dover** (202 E. Dover St., 410/819-8007, www.innat202dover.com, $289-525). This grand, beautifully renovated home is truly a work of art. From the stately exterior of this historic 1874 mansion to the inviting common areas and the themed rooms and suites, every last detail is attended to. An example of this is the Safari Suite, which has an elephant vanity, exotic lamps, and themed details down to the bath soap. Each of the five rooms is furnished with antique and reproduction items, pillow-top mattresses, and comfortable linens. Air jet tubs, steam showers, high-speed Internet, and cable television are also standard. The upscale Peacock Restaurant serves delightful cuisine with Eastern Shore influence prepared by a Cordon Bleu-trained executive chef. They also have wonderful martinis.

The gracious **Tidewater Inn** (101 E. Dover St., 410/822-1300, www.tidewaterinn.com, $189-289) is the landmark lodging property in Easton. This elegant downtown hotel opened in 1949 and is known as a romantic getaway. The inn has 89 guest rooms with yesterday's charm and some modern conveniences such as wireless Internet and flat-screen televisions. The hotel does not have some of the amenities many travelers are used to such as a fitness room and on-site pool, although many of the rooms underwent renovations in early 2016. If you are looking for a comfortable manor house atmosphere with good service, this is a lovely choice. There is a good restaurant (the Hunter's Tavern) on-site and many more within walking distance.

Information and Services

For additional information on Easton, visit www.eastonmd.org or stop by the **Talbot County Visitors' Center** (11 S. Harrison St., 410/770-8000).

Bartlett Pear Inn

Getting There and Around

Most people arrive in Easton by car. There is a small public airport, the **Easton Airport** (29137 Newnam Rd., 410/770-8055, www.eastonairport.com), two miles north of Easton.

OXFORD

The small waterfront town of Oxford, 10 miles southwest of Easton, is a fun day-trip destination. Oxford was settled in the mid-1660s on just 30 acres and is one of the oldest towns in Maryland. It was selected shortly after its settlement to be one of only two ports of entry for the Maryland Province (the other was Anne Arundel, which later became Annapolis). What followed was a period of prominence for the little town, and it became known as an international shipping center and home to many thriving tobacco plantations. After the Revolutionary War, when British ships stopped visiting its waters for trade, the town declined. Today, Oxford has a population of less than 1,000 people, but it remains a scenic and inviting place.

Oxford-Bellevue Ferry

The **Oxford-Bellevue Ferry** (27456 Oxford Rd., 410/745-9023, www.oxfordbellevueferry.com, mid-Apr.-mid-Nov. daily, one-way/round-trip $12/20 car and driver, $6/9 motorcycle, $4/7 bike, $3/5 pedestrian) is one of the oldest privately run ferries in the country, dating back to 1683. It runs between Oxford and Bellevue, Maryland, across the Tred Avon River. The trip is less than a mile and takes approximately 10 minutes. The ferry accommodates cars, motorcycles, bikes, and pedestrians and has a capacity of nine vehicles. This is a popular connection for cyclists biking a circular route from St. Michaels.

Food and Accommodations

Overnight visitors to Oxford can enjoy a stay at the **Oxford Inn** (504 S. Morris St., 410/226-5220, www.oxfordinn.net, $50-190). This lovely bed-and-breakfast is on a charming street across from a small marina. The exterior of the building is white with a green roof, covered porches, and seven dormer windows. The seven guest rooms are quaintly decorated in a country style, and the inn has a wonderful European bistro, **Pope's Tavern** ($24-34), that offers elegant dinner space for 40 guests. They serve entrées such as chicken, crab cakes, beef tenderloin, and pasta. There is also a cozy teak bar with seating for 12. A note at

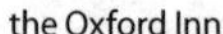
the Oxford Inn

the bottom of their menu states "unattended children will be given a double espresso and a puppy."

The ★ **Robert Morris Inn** (314 N. Morris St., 410/226-5111, www.robertmorrisinn.com, $145-240), near the ferry landing, is another wonderful choice for accommodations in Oxford. This historic building with a yellow exterior and large patio dates back to 1710 and was once the home of a prosperous merchant and famous financier of the American Revolution, Robert Morris. A close friend of George Washington's, Morris entertained Washington at his home on multiple occasions. In later years, author James Michener spent time at the inn while working on his novel *Chesapeake*. The rooms offer a choice of cozy period furniture and canopy beds or more modern furnishings.

The inn contains a great restaurant, **Salter's Tavern and Tap Room,** that serves breakfast ($4-12), lunch ($14-21), and dinner ($17-31). The ambience is warm and inviting with slate floors, redbrick walls, and timber beams. The casual menu is centered on the local seafood treasures found in the bay such as crab, oysters, and fresh fish, but also features land-based menu items such as burgers and salads. The restaurant is overseen by Mark Salter, a well-known British master chef.

Information and Services

For additional information on Oxford, visit www.oxfordmd.net.

CAMBRIDGE

Cambridge is 17 miles south of Easton off Route 50. It is the largest town in Dorchester County and one of the oldest colonial cities in Maryland, having been settled in 1684. It sits directly on the Choptank River (which was the setting for James Michener's book *Chesapeake*) near the Chesapeake Bay. The town was originally a trading center for tobacco.

In the late 19th century, Cambridge opened food processing businesses that canned foods such as oysters, tomatoes, and sweet potatoes. At its peak, the primary packing concern, Phillips Packing Company, employed 10,000 people. By the 1960s the decline in the canning industry had led to the closure of the company and left behind a struggling city that is still fighting to prosper.

Today Cambridge offers a pretty downtown area with historic 18th- and 19th-century

the Cambridge waterfront

homes and scenic waterfront parks and marinas.

Sights

HARRIET TUBMAN MUSEUM & EDUCATIONAL CENTER

The **Harriet Tubman Museum & Educational Center** (424 Race St., 410/228-0401, www.visitdorchester.org/harriet-tubman-museum-educational-center, Tues.-Fri. noon-3pm, Sat. noon-4pm, tours by appointment only, free) is a tribute to Harriet Ross Tubman (1822-1913), a freedom fighter and former slave who was known for leading many slaves to freedom through the Underground Railroad. This small museum is dedicated to telling stories of this heroine's life and features exhibits on her work helping dozens of slaves. Tubman was a Dorchester County native.

J. M. CLAYTON COMPANY

Pay a visit to the market at the world's oldest working crab house, **J. M. Clayton Company** (108 Commerce St., 410/228-1661, www.jmclayton.com, Mon.-Fri. 8am-5pm) on Commerce Street. This historic crab house is still operated by the same family that started it back in 1890. They even have an 80-year old canning machine. Their market is open daily where visitors can purchase local crabmeat and crab-related items.

RICHARDSON MARITIME MUSEUM

Visitors can learn about the lost tradition of wooden boatbuilding at the **Richardson Maritime Museum** (401 High St., 410/221-1871, www.richardsonmuseum.org, Sat. 10am-4pm, Sun. 1pm-4pm, $3). This historic brick building on the corner of High and Locust Streets housed a bank for almost a hundred years. One step into the museum takes visitors into the world of wooden sailing vessels and their role on the Chesapeake Bay. Boat models, building tools, and original artifacts are just some of the items on display. The rich wooden boat history includes everything from crabbing skiffs to dovetails to clipper ships and even schooners.

★ BLACKWATER NATIONAL WILDLIFE REFUGE

Blackwater National Wildlife Refuge (2145 Key Wallace Dr., 410/228-2677, www.friendsofblackwater.org, daily dawn-dusk, vehicles $3, pedestrians $1, cyclists $1) was established in 1933 as a sanctuary for waterfowl migrating along the **Atlantic Flyway** (a migration route along the Atlantic coast). The refuge 12 miles south of Cambridge encompasses 27,000 acres including freshwater, brackish tidal wetlands, meadows, and forest. It is open year-round.

More than 250 species of birds live in the refuge, and it is home to the largest breeding population of bald eagles on the East Coast north of Florida. The eagle population swells in the winter months, when many birds migrate here from northern areas. During the winter, the refuge is also home to more than 35,000 geese and 15,000 ducks. Fall (Sept.-Nov.) is the best time to see migrating waterfowl and songbirds.

A wide variety of mammals also live in the refuge. Delmarva fox squirrels, southern flying squirrels, voles, shrews, nutria, gray foxes, red foxes, river otters, mink, skunks, deer, and beavers all call the refuge home.

There is a wonderful visitors center on Key Wallace Drive (year-round Mon.-Fri. 8am-4pm, Sat.-Sun. 9am-5pm) with wildlife exhibits, nature books, birding guides, a butterfly garden, maps, restrooms, and a gift shop. The prime attraction in the refuge is the Wildlife Drive, a four-mile paved road where visitors can drive, bike, and walk through the refuge to view wildlife. There is also a great viewing platform over the marsh. In addition to the Wildlife Drive, the refuge has four land trails and three paddling trails. Visitors can also hunt, fish, and crab. Environmental education programs are also offered for young people.

Recreation and Events

One-hour **Historic High Street Walking Tours** (410/901-1000, $8) are offered by the West End Citizens Association. Reservations are not required but they are recommended. Tours meet at 11am on Saturday April-October at Long Wharf (High Street and Water Street).

One- or two-hour cruises on the skipjack ***Nathan of Dorchester*** (Long Wharf on High St., 410/228-7141, www.skipjack-nathan.org, most Saturdays May-Oct., two-hour sails $30, call for reservations) offer an authentic Chesapeake Bay experience. Tours go out on the Choptank River and teach the history of oystering.

There are two lovely parks in Cambridge that offer nice views of the Choptank River. **Great Marsh Park** (at the end of Somerset Ave. on the Choptank River, www.choosecambridge.com) has a boat launch, fishing pier, playground, and picnic tables. **Sailwinds Park East** (2 Rose Hill Pl., 410/228-1000, www.tourdorchester.org) is next to the Dorchester County visitors center. There is a playground, and the park is known as a good spot to fly kites.

Cambridge is the site of many endurance events including the **Ironman 70.3 Eagleman Triathlon** (www.ironman.com) in June, **Ironman Maryland** (www.ironman.com) in early October, and the **Six Pillars Century** bike ride (www.6pillarscentury.org) in early May.

Blackwater Paddle & Pedal (2524 Key Wallace Dr., 410/901-9255, www.blackwaterpaddleandpedal.com) offers guided three-hour bike tours and two-hour kayak tours. Bike tours depart from the Hyatt Regency, and kayak tours leave from the Hyatt Beach. They also offer rentals for bikes, kayaks, and paddleboards (call for pricing).

Food

★ **The High Spot** (305 High St., 410/228-7420, www.thehighspotgastropub.com, Mon.-Thurs. 11am-11pm, Fri.-Sat. 11am-midnight, Sun. 11am-10pm, $7-25) is a trendy gastropub serving lunch and dinner. Their food is innovative and tasty, and they have a great beer list and full bar. They also offer special events such as beer pairing dinners. This is a fun place to eat, with delicious food, a hip atmosphere, and cute little terrariums with cacti on the tables. The only drawback is that it is sometimes very loud inside, but that is due in part to its popularity.

An unexpected French treat in Cambridge is the ★ **Bistro Poplar** (535 Poplar St., 410/228-4884, www.bistropoplar.com, Thurs.-Sun. starting at 5pm, $24-30). They serve traditional French cuisine infused with local seafood flavors such as scallops and flounder. The restaurant is housed in a historic building constructed in 1895. The interior is unmistakably French with ornate floor tiles, dim lighting, a dark-framed bar, and red velvet cushions. The food is artfully presented by servers well versed in the menu. This is a special find in Cambridge and has won many awards.

The **Blue Point Provision Company** (100 Heron Blvd. at Rte. 50, 410/901-6410, www.chesapeakebay.hyatt.com, Wed.-Sun. 5pm-9pm, $20-45) at the Hyatt Regency is a waterfront restaurant with a great seafood menu and a wonderful deck overlooking the

The High Spot

Choptank River. The restaurant is at the far end of the resort, a short walk down the beach from the main complex. The interior is inviting with nautical touches and soaring ceilings, beautiful ceiling fans, parquet floors, and wooden furniture. There is also a large bar area. The menu offers goodies such as Maryland crab dip, Asian barbecued salmon, fried oysters, and the famous Drunkin' Dancin' Jumbo Shrimp. They also have fresh fish selections daily based on the local catch at area fish markets. For landlubbers, they offer steak and chicken.

For good beer and pub fare, stop in **RaR Brewing** (504 Poplar St., 443/225-5664, www.rarbrewing.com, Mon.-Thurs. 2pm-midnight, Fri. 2pm-2am, Sat.-Sun. noon-midnight, under $15). Located inside a former billiards hall, this friendly brewery is a local favorite. They serve a casual menu with pizza, crab dip, hummus, hot dogs, sandwiches, and more than a dozen delicious beers.

Good diner food at a reasonable price can be found at the **Cambridge Diner and Restaurant** (2924 Old Rte. 50, 410/228-8898, daily 6am-10pm, $10-15). They serve traditional comfort food in large portions.

Accommodations

At first glance, ★ **The Hyatt Regency Chesapeake Bay Golf Resort, Spa & Marina** (100 Heron Blvd. at Rte. 50, 410/901-1234, www.chesapeakebay.hyatt.com, $399-469 per night) seems a bit "glam" for the quiet town of Cambridge, but it does quite well in providing a self-contained oasis of luxury for both golfing and non-golfing visitors. One of the premier hotels on the Eastern Shore, it sits on 400 acres along the Choptank River and has beautiful views of the water and surrounding marsh. The resort offers elegant rooms and enough activities that visitors can easily park their car and never leave the compound during their stay. The resort is known for its golf course, the River Marsh Golf Club, but is also family friendly, with planned children's activities and many amenities (two pools, hot tub, mini golf, game room, fitness center, spa, water sports, etc.). It is also dog friendly on the first floor.

Guests can grab a drink or a bottle of wine and relax in one of the big rocking chairs that line the patio. The centerpiece is a large open fireplace where guests can toast marshmallows or gather for happy hour. There

The Hyatt Regency Chesapeake Bay Golf Resort, Spa & Marina

are several dining options at the hotel that are nice but not as exquisite as might be expected. Book a room with a view and/or balcony; it costs more but makes a big difference. Opening your curtains in the morning to look out at the water is worth the added expense. Rooms are clean and spacious, and the beds are comfortable. The staff does a good job of making guests feel welcome, and the hotel can also make arrangements for activities both on and off the property.

A wonderful waterfront bed-and-breakfast is the **Lodgecliffe on the Choptank Bed and Breakfast** (103 Choptank Ter., 866/273-3830, www.lodgecliffe.com, $180-200). This gorgeous mansion was built in 1898 and sits on a bluff with wonderful views of the lower Choptank River. The establishment was the first bed-and-breakfast in Dorchester County when it opened in 1986 and has remained a family business. There are four guest rooms, each with an individual personality. A glorious three-course breakfast is served each morning. This is a relaxing retreat with wonderful water views and matching service.

Another lovely inn in the historic area of Cambridge is the **Mill Street Inn** (114 Mill St., 410/901-9144, www.millstinn.com, $179-229). This beautiful Victorian-style home was built in 1894 and offers three individually decorated guest rooms. Each features high-quality linens and towels, specialty soaps, fresh flowers, cable television, DVD players, and free wireless Internet. It is a half block from the Choptank River and within walking distance to restaurants. The innkeepers, who are retired organic growers and bakers, pride themselves in serving delicious breakfasts, complete with locally grown produce and some unusual items from their yard such as figs and pecans.

Additional accommodations in Cambridge include large chain hotels such as the **Holiday Inn Express Cambridge** (2715 Ocean Gtwy., 877/859-5095, www.ihg.com, $117-135), which is clean, quiet, and well-located on Route 50. This hotel has 85 guest rooms, an indoor pool, wireless Internet, and a fitness room. Each room comes with a refrigerator. Another similar option is the **Comfort Inn and Suites** (2936 Ocean Gtwy., 410/901-0926, www.choice hotels.com, $190-210). This hotel is also on Route 50 and has 65 guest rooms. It also offers an indoor pool, fitness room, free breakfast, and free wireless Internet.

Information and Services

Additional information on Cambridge can be found at the **Visitors Center at Sailwinds Park East** (2 Rose Hill Pl., daily 8:30am-5pm) or online at www.visitdorchester.org/about-dorchester/visitor-center/.

Getting There

Most travelers arrive in Cambridge on U.S. Route 50. This east-west route runs from Ocean City, Maryland, to Sacramento, California. The road is known locally as the Ocean Gateway. The **Cambridge-Dorchester Airport** (5263 Bucktown Rd.) is southeast of Cambridge. It is a general aviation airport with one runway.

Assateague Island

Assateague Island sits opposite Ocean City across the Ocean City Inlet. It is considered part of both Virginia and Maryland. The inlet didn't always exist: It was formed during the Chesapeake-Potomac Hurricane in 1933, which created a nice inlet at the south end of Ocean City, and the Army Corps of Engineers decided to make it permanent.

In its southern reaches, Assateague Island borders Chincoteague Island. Both Assateague and Chincoteague are known for their resident herds of wild ponies and the famous **Wild Pony Swim** (www.chincoteaguechamber.com) that takes place each year in late July, when the herd is taken for a swim from Assateague Island across the channel to Chincoteague Island.

SIGHTS

★ Assateague Island National Seashore

Assateague Island National Seashore (www.nps.gov, year-round in Maryland, 24 hours, $5) was established in 1962. It is managed by three agencies: the National Park Service, U.S Fish & Wildlife Service, and the Maryland Department of Natural Resources. The island includes a beautiful 37-mile beach, dunes, wetlands, and marsh. The island is protected as a natural environment, and many opportunities exist for wildlife viewing. Assateague Island is a stopover for migrating shorebirds and provides important areas for feeding and resting. More than 320 bird species can be viewed here during the year, including the piping plovers, great egrets, and northern harriers.

Assateague Island is also known for its wild ponies. It is widely believed that the ponies originally came to the island years ago when a Spanish cargo ship loaded with horses sank off the coast and the ponies swam to shore. In 1997, a Spanish shipwreck was discovered off the island, which supports this theory.

Other mammals in Assateague include rodents as small as the meadow jumping mouse,

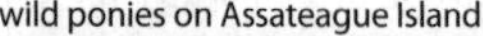

wild ponies on Assateague Island

along with red fox, river otters, and deer. Several species of whales feed off the island's shore, along with bottlenose dolphins.

There are two entrances to the national seashore. One is eight miles south of Ocean City at the end of Route 611. The second is at the southern end of the island at the end of Route 175, two miles from Chincoteague, Virginia. Visitors to Assateague Island mostly stay in Chincoteague or Ocean City since there are no hotel accommodations on the island, but camping is allowed and quite popular.

Park hours and fees are different in Virginia and Maryland and also vary by month in Virginia. Consult www.assateagueisland.com for specific information for the time of year and location you wish to visit.

The **Assateague Island Visitor Center** (Maryland District of Assateague Island, on the southern side of Route 611, 410/641-1441, Jan.-Feb. Thurs.-Mon. 9am-5pm, rest of the year daily 9am-5pm) offers a film on the wild ponies, brochures, aquariums, a touch tank, maps, and other exhibits.

Assateague Island Lighthouse

The red-and-white-striped **Assateague Island Lighthouse** (www.assateagueisland.com, 0.25 mile from Chincoteague Island and accessible from Chincoteague by car in approximately five minutes and from Maryland in an hour, 757/336-3696, Apr.-Nov. weekends 9am-3pm, free but donations encouraged) is on the Virginia side of Assateague Island. There is a trail that connects Chincoteague with Assateague Island that can be walked or accessed by bicycle. The original lighthouse was built in 1833 but was replaced by a taller, more powerful lighthouse in 1867. The lighthouse is still in operation and features twin rotating lights that sit 154 feet above sea level. The U.S. Coast Guard maintains the light as a working navigational aid, but the Chincoteague National Wildlife Refuge is responsible for the lighthouse preservation efforts. The top of the lighthouse can be visited by the public.

RECREATION

Due in part to its relative isolation, Assateague Island has one of the nicest beaches on the East Coast. Visitors can enjoy the area by kayaking, beach walking, swimming, fishing, biking, and bird-watching.

The **Maryland Coastal Bays Program** (www.mdcoastalbays.org/rentals) operates a kayak ($15 per hour), canoe ($22 per hour), paddleboard ($25 per hour), and bike rental ($6 per hour) stand at Assateague Island National Seashore (13002 Bayside Dr., Berlin, 410/726-3217, mid-Apr.-Memorial Day weekends 10am-4pm, Memorial Day-Labor Day daily 9am-6pm, Labor Day-mid-Oct. weekends only 10am-4pm). To find the stand, take the second right after the park tollbooth. A 3.5-mile paved bike path leads from Route 611 through the parks.

CAMPING

Camping is allowed on the Maryland side of the national seashore through the **National Park Service** (410/641-2120, $30). Oceanside and bayside campsites are available all year. Sites do not have hookups but can accommodate tents, trailers, and RVs. There are also horse sites ($50) and group tent sites ($50). Cold showers and chemical toilets are available on-site. Camping is also permitted in **Assateague State Park** (7307 Stephen Decatur Hwy., 410/641-2918, late Apr.-Oct., $30), also on the Maryland side of the island. There are 300 campsites here. Each site has a picnic table, fire ring, room for one car, and access to a bathhouse with warm showers. Backpackers and kayakers can also take advantage of backcountry camping. Camping information can be found at www.assateagueisland.com.

GETTING THERE

There are two entrances to Assateague Island National Seashore. One is eight miles south of Ocean City at the end of Route 611. From Ocean City, cross the bridge on Route 50 heading west. Turn left at the third traffic light onto Route 611. Follow the brown signs to the park. The second is at the southern end of the island at the end of Route 175, two miles from Chincoteague, Virginia. There are no hotel accommodations on the island; visitors to Assateague Island can stay in Chincoteague or Ocean City.

Ocean City

For many people, the quintessential summer vacation is a trip to the beach. Ocean City, the most popular destination in Worcester County, stretches for 10 miles along the Atlantic Ocean between Delaware and the Ocean City Inlet. It offers enough stimulation to keep kids of all ages entertained for days. The three-mile wooden boardwalk is packed with shopping, restaurants, games, and amusements and is open all year. Seemingly every inch of real estate is claimed along the strip, and more than 9,500 hotel rooms and 21,000 condominiums provide endless choices for accommodations.

Ocean City's history dates back to the 1500s, when Giovanni da Verrazano came through the area while surveying the East Coast in service of the King of France. By the 17th century, British colonists had settled the area, after moving north out of Virginia. Ocean City took off as a beach community in 1900 when the first boardwalk was built. Back then, the boardwalk was a seasonal amenity that was taken apart each winter, plank by plank, and stored until the following season.

Today, Ocean City is bustling, to say the least. It is a major East Coast destination for people who enjoy the beach, company, entertainment, and a lot of activity. Visitors can get a good taste for the town in a weekend, but many people stay for a week or more. Approximately eight million people visit Ocean City each year.

Ocean City is a family town but also a party town. Unlike its northern neighbor, Atlantic City, it lacks casinos and has limited development options and, as such, is able to keep the beach as its main focus. Although the city refers to itself as "The East Coast's Number One Family Resort," it is also a popular area for high school seniors letting off steam after graduation at what is traditionally known as

Ocean City Boardwalk

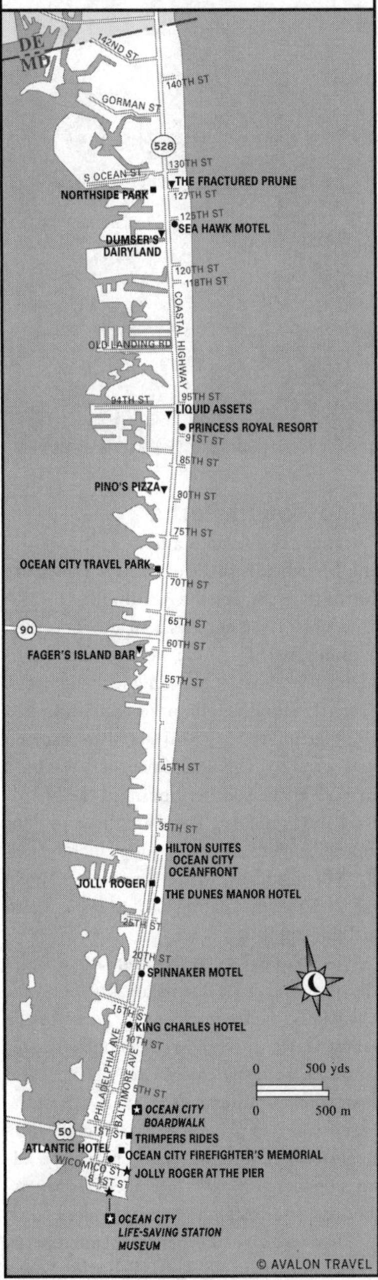

"Senior Week" or "Beach Week." Keep this in mind if you plan to visit in June. You will have a lot of young, unchaperoned company (the average number of graduating seniors visiting in June is 100,000). Some rental complexes even cater specifically to high school and college groups.

SIGHTS

★ Ocean City Boardwalk

The primary attraction in Ocean City is the three-mile-long boardwalk. It begins at the south end of the beach at the Ocean City Inlet. The boardwalk is lined with dozens of hotels, motels, condos, shops, restaurants, and entertainment venues. There is 24-hour activity on the boardwalk and many attractions and establishments orient visitors by their proximity to this popular landmark. During the summer season the boardwalk is very crowded, so if you like hearing the ocean, smelling french fries, and listening to the sounds of vacationers enjoying themselves, then this is the place to go.

Ocean City Beach

The beach in Ocean City is wide and sandy. Brightly colored umbrellas are lined up like soldiers in the sand in front of most hotels and are available for rent. Lifeguards are on duty throughout the season and go through a vigorous training program. The beach is swept every night so it remains in fairly clean condition. It is also patrolled regularly by the local police force. In peak season, the beach and water can get very crowded, so visitors should be prepared for a lot of company.

★ Ocean City Life-Saving Station Museum

The **Ocean City Life-Saving Station Museum** (813 S. Atlantic Ave., 410/289-4991, www.ocmuseum.org, May and Oct. daily 10am-4pm, June-Sep. daily 10am-6pm, Apr. and Nov. Wed.-Sun. 10am-4pm, Dec.-Mar. weekends 10am-4pm, $3) preserves the history of Ocean City and the U.S. Life-Saving Service (a predecessor of

Ocean City Life-Saving Station Museum

the coast guard that conducted marine rescues). Several fascinating historical exhibits, including one on rescue equipment used to save people who were shipwrecked, and aquariums housing local marine life are on display in a beautifully renovated historic building at the extreme southern end of the Ocean City Boardwalk. Visitors can learn about the history of the boardwalk and its lifeguards, how sailors were rescued at sea, and see examples of old-fashioned bathing suits. This well-maintained, one-of-a-kind museum offers an inexpensive learning experience, powerful exhibits, and great views of the beach. There is a gift store on-site and parking in the municipal lot next door.

Northside Park

Northside Park (125th-127th Sts. on the Bay, 410/250-0125, www.ococean.com) is a beautiful 58-acre park at the end of 125th Street. It has ball fields, a fishing lagoon, paths for walking or biking, a playground, a pier, a picnic shelter, an indoor gym, conference facilities, and a 21,000-square-foot sports arena. Regular events such as Sundaes in the Park (entertainment and make-your-own sundaes) are held regularly.

Amusement Parks

There are two famous amusement parks on the boardwalk in Ocean City. **Trimpers Rides** (S. 1st St. and the Boardwalk, 410/289-8617, www.trimpersrides.com, outdoor rides: summer starting in June, weekdays 3pm-midnight, weekends noon-midnight; indoor rides: year-round daily noon-midnight, unlimited rides during the day $26) is a historical icon in Ocean City. This amusement park was built in 1893 at the southern point of the boardwalk near the inlet. There are three outdoor amusement lots and a year-round indoor facility. A historic carousel, the Herschel-Spellman merry-go-round, dating back to 1902, is also at Trimpers Rides.

The **Jolly Roger at the Pier** (at the pier at the south end of the Boardwalk, 410/289-3031, www.jollyrogerpieroc.com) is home to the tallest Ferris wheel in town, a double-decker carousel, a coaster called Crazy Dance, and many other amusements. The view from the Ferris wheel is phenomenal. A second Jolly Roger Park is at 30th Street. There is no admission fee to the parks; the rides are "pay-as-you-go," and costs vary between rides.

There are several other amusement parks in Ocean City including the **Frontier Town**

Western Theme Park (Rte. 611, www.frontiertown.com, Apr.-Nov.), and **Baja Amusements** (12639 Ocean Gtwy./Rte. 50, www.bajaoc.com, June-Aug. 9am-midnight, shorter hours Apr.-May and Sept.).

Ocean City Firefighter's Memorial

The **Ocean City Firefighter's Memorial** (Boardwalk and N. Division St., www.ocvfc.com) is a six-foot-tall bronze statue of a firefighter that stands on a black granite base. The memorial honors "firefighters of the world, the Ocean City firefighters of the past, present, and future, as well as the 343 FDNY firefighters lost on 9/11." The memorial stands in a 2,500-square-foot plaza, surrounded by engraved brick pavers. A recovered piece of twisted steel from the World Trade Center also stands as a memorial to the firefighters who lost their lives on 9/11. A memorial event is held at the site each year on September 11.

ENTERTAINMENT

Nightlife

There's no shortage of nightlife in Ocean City. One of the premier hot spots is **Seacrets** (117 W. 49th St., 410/524-4900, www.seacrets.com), a Jamaican-themed entertainment complex featuring 14 bars and a dance club with nightly music (DJ and live). It is open all year and has an artificial beach and real palm trees. It is one place where people of different ages can mingle together. There is a dress code, so consult the website if you think your attire might be questionable.

The Purple Moose Saloon (on the Boardwalk between Talbot and Caroline Sts., 410/289-6953, www.purplemoose.com) is a nightclub on the boardwalk that offers nightly live rock and roll mid-May-August. It is one of the few places to walk into and have a drink on the boardwalk.

Fager's Island Bar (201 60th St. on the Bay, 410/524-5500, www.fagers.com) is a good place to have a drink on the bay. They offer nightly entertainment with dancing and DJs. Jazz and bluegrass music is featured early with pop and dance music taking over after 9pm. The establishment has a bit of a split personality. The restaurant side has an upscale feel to it, while the nightclub side caters to the younger dance crowd.

SPORTS AND RECREATION

Fishing

Ocean City is known as the "White Marlin Capital of the World." A large fishing tournament called the **White Marlin Open** (www.whitemarlinopen.com) is held there each year at the beginning of August. Anglers of all abilities will find plenty of places to cast a line, whether it be off a boat, pier, or in the surf. For starters, try the public fishing piers at **Inlet Park** (S. 2nd St.), the **Third Street Pier** (bayside), **Ninth Street Pier** (bayside), and **Northside Park** (125th Street, bayside). Fishing charter companies include **Fin Chaser Sportfishing Charters** (12806 Sunset Ave., 443/397-0315, www.finchasersportfishing.com, $800-2,550) and **Ocean City Girl** (302/448-4184, www.ocgirl.com, starting at $266).

Boating

There are several public boat ramps in Ocean City including ones at **Assateague State Park** (Rte. 611 at the Assateague Island Bridge), **Gum Point Road** (off Rte. 589), and **Ocean City Commercial Harbor** (Sunset Ave. in West Ocean City).

Kayaking, Paddleboarding, and Windsurfing

For some hands-on action on the water, rent a kayak or paddleboard from **48th Street Watersports** (4701 Coastal Hwy., 410/524-9150, www.48thstreetwatersports.com, starting at $15). This bayfront facility has a wonderful beach and is a great location to try out a number of water sports. Learn to sail, try out sailboarding—they have just about every type of water toy you can dream of. They will even deliver kayaks to your location and pick them up at no extra charge. Kayak rentals and tours are also available from **Ayers Creek**

Adventures (8628 Grey Fox Ln., Berlin, 443/513-0889, www.ayerscreekadventures.com, starting at $15) in nearby Berlin.

Boat Tours

Take a dolphin and nature excursion with **The Angler** (312 Talbot St. bayside, 410/289-7424, www.angleroc.net) aboard a 65-foot boat to explore the shores of Assateague Island and catch a glimpse of the resident ponies on land and dolphins at sea. Tours originate at the Ocean City Inlet. The Angler also offers deep-sea fishing ($65) and 45-minute scenic evening cruises.

Surfing

If surfing like a local is more your style, rent a board from **Chauncey's Surf Shop** (2908 Coastal Hwy., 410/289-7405, www.chaunceyssurfshop.com, $25). They also rent paddleboards.

Biking

Bike rentals are available from **Dandy Don's Bike Rentals** (1109 Atlantic Ave., 410/289-2289, www.dandydonsbikerentals.com, starting at $7). They rent beach cruisers, "Boardwalk Cars," banana bikes, and surreys. **Bike World** (6 Caroline St., 410/289-2587, www.bikeworldoc.com) also rents bikes and surreys near the boardwalk.

Miniature Golf

Ocean City boasts a wide selection of mini golf courses. Try one or two or a new one every day. **Old Pro Golf** (outdoor locations 23rd St. and 28th St., indoor locations 68th St. and 136th St., 410/524-2645, www.oldprogolf.com, $8.50) has four locations in Ocean City. The indoor golf course and arcades on 68th Street and 136th Street are open all year. **Lost Treasure Golf** (13903 Coastal Hwy., 410/250-5678, www.losttreasuregolf.com, open Mar.-Nov.) offers 18 holes dedicated to noted explorer Professor Duffer A. Hacker.

FOOD

American

Liquid Assets (9301 Coastal Hwy., 410/524-7037, www.la94.com, Sun.-Thurs. 11:30am-11pm, Fri.-Sat. 11:30am-midnight, $13-34) is a surprisingly trendy little restaurant hidden within a strip mall, inside a liquor store. Guests pick their wine right off the shelf with or without the help of the staff and pay a corking fee to drink it with dinner. The menu is wide-ranging, the food is delicious, and the presentation is appealing. This unusual little gem is geared toward adults and does not serve a children's menu. The bar area is rustic with oak barrels, and the bistro has couches and tables that are well spaced so you aren't sitting on top of your neighbor. There's normally a long wait for seating, but they do not take reservations.

Italian

For good pizza, try **Pino's Pizza** (8101 Coastal Hwy., 410/723-3278, open daily in summer season, hours vary by month, $8-37). This joint has terrific pizza with a zesty sauce and is open until 4am. They offer pick-up and delivery only—no dining in. They are very generous with their cheese (both mozzarella and white cheddar) and toppings, and the slices are delicious and filling. They have reliable, friendly service and often offer coupons on their website. Be aware when ordering the really large pizzas that sometimes the price of two smaller ones is much cheaper.

Seafood

★ **The Shark on the Harbor** (12924 Sunset Ave., 410/213-0924, www.ocshark.com, Sunday brunch 10:30am-3pm, lunch daily 11:30am-4:30pm, dinner daily 4:30pm-10pm, $12-35) offers an ever-changing menu of fresh seafood, dictated by what is available and fresh on that day. They serve lunch and dinner daily and have a happy hour and a kid's menu. The restaurant is on a commercial fishing harbor and is known for having great views of the harbor and Assateague Island. The owners describe the style of food offered as "globally influenced seasonal cuisine," which allows them to be creative in their daily menu offerings. Local seafood is prominently featured on the menu, and they also serve organic produce and natural dairy and meat products. Don't let the plain exterior fool you; the inside of this restaurant is hip and comfortable and has large windows. The large bar is the primary internal feature, with seating on three sides. The full menu can be ordered at the bar, at pub-style tables, or at regular dining tables. The clientele is good mix of vacationers and locals, and the owners are extremely friendly.

The **Captain's Galley Restaurant and Lounge** (12817 Harbor Rd., 410/213-2525, www.captainsgalleyoc.com, daily 11:30am-10pm, upstairs $6-14, downstairs $14-33) is on the waterfront in the harbor and offers free boat docking for customers. They specialize in seafood and are known for having some of the best crab cakes in Ocean City, which is a steep claim given the overwhelming competition. They also have a variety of steaks on the menu. The restaurant has two levels and two menus. The downstairs menu is a dinner menu (starting at 4:30pm), and the upstairs menu is casual (starting at 11:30am) with sandwiches, seafood baskets, steamed seafood, and individual sides. You can't mix menus, so choose which floor to dine on based on what you want to eat. Enjoy a great view of the harbor from the inside or dine outside on the large deck, which is a great place for digging into a pile of freshly steamed crabs. The interior is a bit dated, but the food and view compensate.

For great local crab cakes visit the **Crabcake Factory** (12000 Coastal Hwy., 410/250-4900, www.crabcakefactoryonline.com, Mon.-Thurs. 11am-9pm, Fri.-Sat. 9am-11pm, Sun. 9am-9pm). They specialize in local seafood, including their signature crab cakes, peel-and-eat shrimp, and crab pizza. They are also known for their breakfasts and Bloody Marys. Breakfast is served Friday-Sunday at the Ocean City location, and the second location in Fenwick Island (37314 Lighthouse Road, 302/988-5000) serves breakfast daily and has great views of the bay.

Doughnuts

The Fractured Prune (127th St. and Coastal Hwy., 410/250-4400, www.fracturedprune.com) is a well-known doughnut shop that was featured on the Food Network's *Unwrapped*.

The Shark on the Harbor

It is hidden in the North Bay Shopping Center near Ledo Pizza. The specialty is "hot-dipped, made to order" doughnuts, and they're home to the "create your own donut." Guests can select from 15 doughnut glazes and multiple toppings to create their dream doughnut. Standard Fractured Prune flavors include interesting names such as "Black Forest" and "Sand." This small shop turns out 840 yummy cake doughnuts each hour and has become an icon at the beach. The shop doesn't offer prune toppings; it was named after an iconic lady named Prunella, who lived in Ocean City in the early 1900s and traveled around competing against men in different sports. She was always on crutches from getting hurt, so the shop is named the Fractured Prune after her. There are five additional locations in West Ocean City (9636 Stephen Decatur Hwy.), on the boardwalk (Boardwalk and 14th Street), on 81st Street (81st and Coastal Hwy), at 28th Street (2808 Philadelphia Ave.) and 56th Street (5601 Coastal Hwy.).

Classic Beach Food

The beach and ice cream go hand in hand. **Dumser's Dairyland** (124th St. and Coastal Hwy., 410/250-5543, www.beach-net.com, Memorial Day-Labor Day daily 7am-11:30pm), which was established in 1939, offers beachgoers an ice-cream parlor and restaurant that is open late in the summer (hours are shorter in the off-season). They also have locations at 49th Street and Coastal Highway plus three stands on the boardwalk.

Another longtime favorite is **Thrasher's French Fries** (www.thrashersfrenchfries.com, under $5). They've been making french fries on the boardwalk since 1929. With three locations in Ocean City—at the Pier, 2nd Street and Boardwalk, and 8th Street and Boardwalk—the aroma of Thrasher's is one of the defining smells of the boardwalk.

Dolle's (500 S. Boardwalk at Wicomico St., 410/289-6000, www.dolles.com, daily 10am-6pm, Fri.-Sat. 10am-8pm) has been a staple on the boardwalk since 1910. They make mouthwatering saltwater taffy, fudge, popcorn, and other candy.

Fisher's Popcorn (200 S. Boardwalk, www.fisherspopcorn.com, 410/289-5638) is another Ocean City icon. This family-owned and operated business opened in 1937 and offers many flavors of mouthwatering popcorn. They are especially known for their caramel popcorn.

ACCOMMODATIONS

$100-200

A good value is the **Sea Hawk Motel** (12410 Coastal Hwy., 410/250-3191, www.seahawkmotel.com, $178-210). This older motel is a half block from the beach and offers 60 motel rooms and efficiencies with kitchens. Sleeping areas are separated from living areas. The rooms are spacious and clean, and there's an outdoor pool.

The **King Charles Hotel** (1209 N. Baltimore Ave., 410/289-6141, www.kingcharleshotel.com, $114-189) is a small hotel a block from the boardwalk. The 22 rooms are modest but competitively priced and clean. They are available with one queen bed or two double beds. There are small refrigerators and microwaves in the rooms. The hotel owners are very friendly and make it feel more like a bed-and-breakfast (minus the breakfast) than a hotel.

The **Atlantic Hotel** (oceanfront on the Boardwalk and Wicomico St., 410/289-9111, www.atlantichotelocmd.com, $160-250) was the first boardwalk hotel in Ocean City. It was built in 1875 and was considered one of the finest hotels on the East Coast. It burned down in a devastating fire in 1925 but was rebuilt the following year. Today, the hotel is still going strong and offers guests a central location on the boardwalk and a rooftop deck overlooking all the action and the ocean. They offer 100 rooms with one or two queen beds, and there are also two apartments for rent on a weekly basis. The rooms are small and cozy but clean. They feature dark wood furniture and small private bathrooms. There is an outdoor pool for guests. The staff is very friendly, and the location is ideal for those wanting to stay on the boardwalk.

$200-300

The ★ **Atlantic House Bed and Breakfast** (501 N. Baltimore Ave., 410/289-2333, www.atlantichouse.com, $200-250) is a diamond in the rough in a town packed with imposing hotels and motels. This little Victorian-style treasure built in the 1920s sits right on North Baltimore Street and is conspicuously different from the surrounding accommodations. The nine guest rooms (seven with private baths and two with semiprivate) are small since the home was originally a boardinghouse, but they are immaculate and tidy. Second-story room decor is mostly floral and wicker, while the third-floor rooms have paneling. The grounds are nicely maintained, and there is a wonderful front porch where guests can watch the bustle of activity on the busy street. The location is central to the Ocean City attractions, just one street back from the boardwalk. The innkeepers are extremely warm and helpful and are a great asset to the establishment. Breakfast is delicious and plentiful with egg dishes, meats, fruit, and waffles. Snacks are also offered each afternoon. This bed-and-breakfast gets a lot of repeat business.

The **Dunes Motel** (2700 Baltimore Ave., 410/289-4414, www.ocdunes.com, $269-309) is an older motel at the end of the boardwalk offering 49 oceanfront rooms and 62 poolside rooms. The decor is older, but the motel is a good value for budget-minded travelers and the rooms are clean. There's an outdoor pool and direct beach access. The motel's sister property, **The Dunes Manor Hotel** (2800 Baltimore Ave., 410/289-1100, www.dunes-manor.com, $449-469), is next door. It offers 174 rooms and an indoor pool that can be used by guests of both establishments.

The **Spinnaker Motel** (18th St. and Baltimore Ave., 410/289-5444, www.ocmotels.com, $242-346) offers 100 clean guest units within a short walk to the boardwalk (about a half block). Although not fancy, the rooms are reasonably priced and many have good views of the ocean. There is parking on-site, an outdoor pool, and free wireless Internet. This hotel is a good value for families on a budget.

Over $300

The **Hilton Suites Ocean City Oceanfront** (3200 N. Baltimore Ave., 410/289-6444, www.oceancityhilton.com, $579-659) is one of the nicest hotels in Ocean City. All 225 modern rooms are oversize, luxurious suites on the oceanfront and offer nicely sized balconies. Each suite has a kitchen. There are both an indoor pool and a lovely outdoor pool overlooking the ocean that has a swim-up bar. There is also a children's pool with a waterslide and a lazy river. The hotel is about five blocks from the boardwalk (10-minute walk). The hotel offers live music, movie nights, and children's activities. It is very family-oriented. Parking right at the hotel is limited, but there is additional parking across the street. This is a beautiful hotel with nice amenities, as it should be for the price.

The **Princess Royal Resort** (91st St. Oceanfront, www.princessroyale.com, $299-399) is an oceanfront hotel with 310 two-room suites and 30 condos. They offer pleasant rooms with kitchenettes, comfortable beds, and great views. Ask for a room with a good view; the staff will often do their best to accommodate the request. The hotel has a large indoor pool and scheduled activities such as movie night on the beach and live music by the outdoor bar. The furniture is a bit dated, but otherwise this is good choice for oceanfront accommodations. Their prime rib and seafood buffet is a tasty option for dinner.

Condos

There are many condos for rent in Ocean City. **Summer Beach Condominium** (410/289-0727, www.summerbeachoc.com) and **Holiday Real Estate** (800/638-2102, www.holidayoc.com) are management companies that offer weekly rentals.

the Princess Royal Resort

Camping

Frontier Town (Rte. 611 and Stephen Decatur Hwy., Berlin, 410/641-0880, www.frontiertown.com, Apr.-Nov., starting at $32) in nearby Berlin offers tent and RV facilities. They are open seasonally and only five minutes from Ocean City.

INFORMATION AND SERVICES

For additional information on Ocean City, visit www.ococean.com or stop by the **Ocean City Visitor Information Center** (12320 Ocean Gateway, 410/213-0552).

GETTING THERE

Ocean City is a 2.5-hour drive from Annapolis (109 miles). Most people arrive by car via Route 50 or Route 113 (the two primary routes to the area). **Greyhound** (12848 Ocean Gtwy., 410/289-9307, www.greyhound.com) bus service is also available to Ocean City.

GETTING AROUND

Route 528 is the only major road running north-south in Ocean City. It is called Philadelphia Avenue at the southern end and the Coastal Highway everywhere else. Streets running east-west in Ocean City are numbered beginning in the south, and run up to 146th before the Delaware border. Locations are normally explained by the terms "oceanside" (east of the Coastal Highway) or "bayside" (west of the Coastal Highway).

The **Boardwalk Tram** (410/289-5311, June-Aug. daily 11am-midnight, shorter hours spring and fall, $3 per ride or $6 unlimited daily pass) is a seasonal tram that runs the entire length of the boardwalk from the inlet to 27th Street. The tram stops at most locations along the boardwalk. It takes 30 minutes to ride the entire length of the boardwalk.

The Coastal Highway **Beach Bus** (410/723-2174, www.oceancitymd.gov, $3 all-day pass) is a municipal bus service that runs 24/7 along the Coastal Highway. Free parking is available at the two bus transit centers at South Division Street and at the West Ocean City Park and Ride.

Delaware Beaches

Just north of Ocean City, along the Coastal Highway, is the Delaware state line and some of the nicest beach resort areas in the mid-Atlantic. Three main areas—Bethany Beach, Rehoboth Beach, and Lewes—attract visitors year-round. They offer first-class restaurants, historic beach charm, and lovely accommodations in all price ranges. Although not as busy as their southern neighbor, they each offer their own attractions and have sights of historical interest.

GETTING THERE

DART First State and the Delaware Transit Corporation (www.dartfirststate.com) offers public bus transportation between Ocean City and the Delaware beaches. A parking lot ($8) is north of Rehoboth Avenue on Shuttle Road. With the price of parking, you receive four free unlimited-ride daily bus passes. Stops are located throughout the resort areas.

BETHANY BEACH

Bethany Beach is located in southeastern Delaware, 15 miles north of Ocean City, Maryland. It is part of a seven-mile stretch of beach referred to as the "Quiet Resorts," along with South Bethany Beach and Fenwick Island. Bethany Beach is small and much lower-key than nearby Ocean City and Rehoboth Beach. It is mostly residential, and there is a small shopping area at its heart.

Since 1976, visitors to Bethany Beach have been greeted by **Chief Little Owl,** a 24-foot totem pole that was donated to the town as part of a project by sculptor Peter Wolf Toth, who carved more than 50 wooden works of art in honor of famous Native Americans and gave one to every state. The current totem is actually the third version of the sculpture to stand in Bethany Beach. The first two were destroyed by decay. The current version was created in 2002 of red cedar and is expected to last 50-150 years.

downtown Bethany Beach

Sights

BETHANY BEACH

The beach at **Bethany Beach** is wide, sandy, and family-oriented. Although it would be a stretch to say it's empty during the season, it is mostly quiet at night and offers a relaxing atmosphere during the day. Visitors will need to pay to park (there are meters near the beach entrance on Garfield Street).

BETHANY BEACH BOARDWALK

The **Bethany Beach Boardwalk** is a pleasant family area with less fanfare than the boardwalk in nearby Ocean City. It is basically a nice walkway made of wooden planks. The boardwalk entrance is at the end of Garfield Street, and the boardwalk itself stretches between 2nd and Parkwood Streets. There is plenty to do and see with shops, restaurants, and free concerts at the bandstand on weekends during the summer.

BETHANY BEACH NATURE CENTER

The **Bethany Beach Nature Center** (807 Garfield Pkwy., Rte. 26, 302/537-7680, www.inlandbays.org, mid-June-Oct. Tues.-Fri. 10am-3pm, Sat. 10am-2pm, donations appreciated) offers interactive exhibits that enable visitors to explore the Inland Bays watershed and learn about local flora and fauna. It is housed in a beautiful cottage built around 1901. Nature trails on the 26-acre grounds take visitors through wetlands and forest. There is also a play area for children.

THE FENWICK ISLAND LIGHTHOUSE

The Fenwick Island Lighthouse (146th St. and Lighthouse Ave., http://fenwickislandlighthouse.org, end of May-June weekends 9am-noon, July-Aug. Fri.-Mon. 9am-noon, Sept. weekends 9am-noon, free) stands 87 feet above Fenwick Island. It was built in 1859 after an increase in shipwrecks near the Fenwick Shoals (a shallow area 6 miles offshore). The operational lighthouse tower is closed to visitors, but there is a small museum at its entrance that is run by the New Friends of the Fenwick Island Lighthouse. Visiting hours are Friday-Monday 10am-2pm during the summer. Admission is free but donations are appreciated.

DISCOVERSEA SHIPWRECK MUSEUM

The **DiscoverSea Shipwreck Museum** (708 Coastal Hwy., Fenwick Island, 302/539-9366, www.discoversea.com, June-Aug. daily 11am-8pm, free) is a dynamic museum that recovers and preserves the area's maritime history. Exhibits are centered on shipwreck artifacts dating back to the colonial era (gold, coins, cannons, personal items, even old rum). The museum is run by public donations and owner contributions. Exhibits change with the discovery and acquisition of new artifacts, but the average number of items on display is 10,000. Many additional items are rotated through exhibits around the world. Check the website for hours during the off-season.

Recreation and Entertainment

Delaware Seashore State Park (Rte. 1 between Bethany Beach and Dewey Beach, 302/227-2800, www.destateparks.com, daily 8am-sunset, $10) is to the north of Bethany Beach along the coast. The park of more than 2,800 acres covers a thin strip of land between the Atlantic and Rehoboth Bay. The primary attraction in the park is the beach itself—a six-mile-long beach lover's paradise—where visitors can swim and relax along the shore. There are modern bathhouses with showers and changing rooms, and lifeguards are on duty during the day in the summer. There are also snack vendors and beach equipment rentals such as chairs, rafts, and umbrellas. Fishing is popular in the park and can be done in the surf in designated locations or from the banks of the Indian River Inlet. There is also a special-access pier for the elderly or people with disabilities.

Just north of the inlet on the beach in Delaware Seashore State Park is a designated surfing and sailboarding area. The shallow bays are also good areas for sailboarding and sailing. A boat ramp for nonmotorized craft is also available.

Holt's Landing State Park (302/227-2800, www.destateparks.com, daily 8am-sunset, $10) is on the southern shore of the Indian River Bay (take Route 26 West from Bethany Beach and turn right on County Road 346 to the park entrance). Clamming, fishing, and crabbing are possible in the park, along with facilities such as a picnic pavilion, playground, horseshoe pit, and ball fields. Two great kayaking trails start in the park. The first is a 10-mile paddle to the **Assawoman Wildlife Area** (allow five hours), and the second is to Millsboro, which is just under 10 miles.

Mini golf is a staple at the beach, and **Captain Jack's Pirate Golf** (21 N. Pennsylvania Ave., 302/539-1122, www.captainjackspirategolf.com, seasonal daily 9am-11:30pm, $8.50) is the place to go in Bethany Beach. It has eye-catching features such as a large skeleton pirate and pirate's ship, rock and water features, and palm trees. The course is well maintained and a fun place for the entire family. There's a small gift shop on-site.

If you're visiting in early September, check out the one-day **Annual Bethany Beach Boardwalk Arts Festival** (Bethany Beach Boardwalk, 302/539-2100, www.bethany-beachartsfestival.com). More than 100 artists exhibit their work on the boardwalk and surrounding streets. Local and national artists partake in this anticipated event that draws more than 7,500 visitors. Admission is free.

Food

★ **Off The Hook** (769 Garfield Pkwy., 302/829-1424, www.offthehookbethany.com, Sun.-Thurs. 11:30am-9pm, Fri.-Sat. 11:30am-10pm, $8-27) offers excellent seafood in an off-the-beaten-path location. The seafood and the atmosphere are both fresh, with creative dishes and specials. They are known for the cioppino (a fish stew with shellfish, finfish, garlic confit, chorizo, and pesto in a tomato broth). The restaurant prides itself in supporting local farmers and anglers. They do not take reservations, so there can be a long wait time.

A local favorite is the **Cottage Café Restaurant** (33034 Coastal Hwy., 302/539-8710, www.cottagecafe.com, daily 11am-1am, $10-29). This is a good family restaurant serving local seafood. The staff is kind and patient,

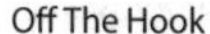

Off The Hook

and the menu is wide enough to satisfy most tastes. Menu selections include crab cakes, fried oysters, stuffed flounder, pot roast, pasta, and meat loaf. The food is not fancy, but it is consistent and reasonably priced.

For fresh crepes, visit **Sunshine Crepes** (100 Garfield Pkwy., 302/537-1765, summer daily 8am-2pm, under $10). This casual and affordable breakfast stop in downtown Bethany Beach by the boardwalk makes fresh savory and sweet crepes with a nice selection of fillings. You can even watch the kitchen staff at work. The atmosphere is not fancy, but the portions are large and the food is tasty. This is a nice alternative to regular bacon and eggs. If you like bananas, try the banana crepe. This is a wonderful local business offering something a little different coupled with friendly service.

Accommodations

Meris Gardens Bed & Breakfast (33309 Kent Ave., 302/752-4962, www.merisgardensbethany.com, $139-169) is a small, affordable bed-and-breakfast that used to be the Westward Pines Motel. They offer 14 comfortable rooms and are located in a quiet area of Bethany Beach. All rooms have private bathrooms and they are dog friendly ($20 charge). It is convenient to the beach (four blocks), and downtown Bethany Beach is within walking distance. Breakfast is included. This property offers simple, friendly accommodations with personal service.

The **Addy Sea** (99 Ocean View Pkwy., 302/539-3707, www.addysea.com, $175-375) is a renovated oceanfront Victorian home and guesthouse that is now an adults-only bed-and-breakfast. The home offers 13 guest rooms and is furnished with antiques, tin ceilings, and original woodwork. The rooms are comfortable, the staff is friendly, and the location is wonderful. The breakfasts are also plentiful with good choices. Book a room with an ocean view for the best experience. Not all rooms have private baths, and Room 12 is the only one with a television.

The **Sea Colony Resort** (Rte. 1, 888/500-4261, www.wyndhamvacationrentals.com) is a large and well-known condominium resort in Bethany Beach with 2,200 units. Condo rentals are available through a number of management companies. Amenities include tennis courts, a fitness center, a small shopping area, and pools. The beaches around Sea Colony are some of the busiest in Bethany Beach due to the large number of condos in the complex; however, the half-mile stretch of beach is for guests and visitors of the resort only, which does make it somewhat private. Units of different sizes are available for rent. Additional information can be obtained at www.resortquestdelaware.com.

Information and Services

For additional information on Bethany Beach, visit www.bethanybeachde.com or stop by the **Bethany-Fenwick area visitor information center** (daily Mon.-Fri. 9am-5pm, Sat. 9am-3pm) on the Coastal Highway between Fenwick Island State Park and Lewes Street.

REHOBOTH BEACH

Rehoboth Beach is 14 miles north of Bethany Beach. It is the happy medium among the Maryland and Delaware beaches. It is larger and more commercial than Bethany Beach, yet smaller and less commercial than Ocean City.

Rehoboth Beach was founded in 1873 as a Methodist Episcopal Church beach camp. Today, the town is known as "the Nation's Summer Capital," since so many visitors come from Washington DC each year. The town is also noted for its eclectic shops, wonderful eateries, artistic appeal, and the large number of gay-owned businesses. Downtown Rehoboth Beach is one square mile and has more than 200 shops, galleries, and spas, 40 hotels and bed-and-breakfasts, and more than 100 restaurants.

Just south of Rehoboth is **Dewey Beach,** which is known as a party town for young adults during the summer months. The two towns share a beautiful strand of sandy white

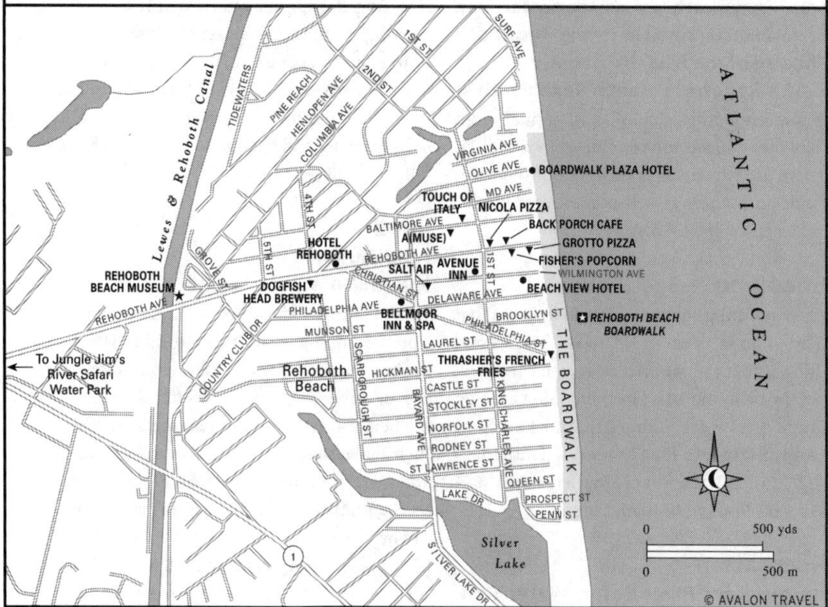

beach that continues to be the main attraction despite all the built-up distractions.

Dogs are not permitted to run loose on the beach in Rehoboth. They are prohibited from the beach and boardwalk 24 hours a day between May 1 and September 30, but they are allowed on the beach in Dewey prior to 9:30am and after 5:30pm (although they still must be leashed and have a Dewey Beach license). There is a strict leash law, and owners must pick up after their dogs.

Sights

★ REHOBOTH BEACH BOARDWALK

The easiest public access to the mile-long boardwalk in Rehoboth Beach is from Rehoboth Avenue. Less crowded than Ocean City, yet more lively than Bethany Beach, the boardwalk offers all the action you could want at the beach including terrific views of the ocean, french fries, T-shirt shops, games, candy stores, and entertainment. The boardwalk is wide and clean and stretches from Penn Street at the south end to Virginia Avenue at the north end. Parking is available on Rehoboth Avenue, and parking meters are enforced during the summer months 10am-midnight. The meters take quarters and credit cards. Change machines are available at the Bandstand on Rehoboth Avenue.

REHOBOTH BEACH MUSEUM

The **Rehoboth Beach Museum** (511 Rehoboth Ave., 302/227-7310, www.rehobothbeachmuseum.org, Labor Day-Memorial Day Mon.-Fri. 10am-4pm, Sat.-Sun. 11am-3pm, free but donations appreciated) is a small museum with displays portraying the history of Rehoboth Beach. Visitors can see vintage bathing suits, postcards, and classic boardwalk rides and games, and learn about the early beach hotels in town.

Entertainment and Events

The **Clear Space Theatre Company**

(www.clearspacetheatre.org) is a year-round professional theatrical company that presents musical and dramatic productions. Performances are held in the **Rehoboth Theatre of the Arts** (20 Baltimore Ave.).

The **Rehoboth Beach Jazz Festival** (www.rehobothjazz.com) is an annual event that takes place for four days in October. There are three stages throughout the town for performances as well as additional venues in local establishments.

Shopping

The first thing shoppers should know is that there is no sales tax in Delaware. The second thing is that every outlet store you can think of may be found in a large shopping area on Route 1 between Rehoboth and Lewes, at **Tanger Outlets** (36470 Seaside Outlet Dr., 302/226-9223, www.tangeroutlet.com, Mon.-Sat. 9am-9pm, Sun. 10am-7pm).

Recreation

Jungle Jim's River Safari Water Park (36944 Country Club Rd., 302/227-8444, www.funatjunglejims.com, daily in summer 10am-8pm, $38) is Delaware's largest water park and also offers go-karts, mini golf, batting cages, and bumper boats. **Funland at Rehoboth Beach** (6 Delaware Ave., 302/227-1921, www.funlandrehoboth.com, mid-June-mid-Aug. daily, games starting at 10am, rides starting at 1pm, park closes at 11pm, shorter hours on weekends in mid-late May and daily in early-mid-June) is a tradition on the boardwalk dating back to the early 1960s. It offers 19 rides and operates on a ticketed basis ($0.35 per ticket).

Food

AMERICAN

Salt Air (50 Wilmington Ave., 302/227-3744, www.saltairrestaurant.com, Sun., Wed. and Thurs. 5pm-9pm, Fri.-Sat. 5pm-10pm, $16-46) is a busy, upscale farm-to-fork restaurant with a good vibe. Patrons can watch the skilled kitchen at work and get a text message when their table is ready. The cuisine is American, and there are a lot of creative seafood dishes. Start with the crab deviled eggs; a plate of four can be a bite each for a small group. The menu is full of little surprises (but changes often) such as boardwalk fries, oven-roasted honey sriracha wings, and seafood stew. They also serve incredible salads, such as the kale caesar salad. The kids' menu is worth mentioning, because it strays from the usual chicken tenders to provide small portions of real

Rehoboth Beach Boardwalk

food, like filet mignon and grilled fish. This is a wonderful place for dinner and cocktails and their creativity includes a long list of delightful martinis.

a(MUSE.) (44 Baltimore Ave., 302/227-7107, www.amuse-rehoboth.com, Tues.-Sun. 5pm-9pm, Fri.-Sat. 5pm-10pm, small plates $5-18, main $22-31) is a one-of-a-kind restaurant that takes guests through a culinary amusement park of fresh, small plates made of local ingredients. If this doesn't sound like your cup of tea, they also offer full-size entrées that are just as delectable as the small plates. A sample of their menu includes potted chicken, yellow perch, north Atlantic halibut, and strip steak. Their menu changes according to what is available from mid-Atlantic farmers, fisherman, ranchers, and foragers. A five-course tasting menu is available for $69 and a seven-course tasting menu is available for $89.

The original **Dogfish Head Brewery** (320 Rehoboth Ave., 302/226-2739, www.dogfish.com, Sun.-Thurs. noon-11pm, Fri.-Sat. noon-1am, $6-26) is on the main strip of Rehoboth Avenue. They serve a nice variety of fish, burgers, sandwiches, and pizza along with many varieties of their delicious beer. Seasonal beers are always rotating with a few staples available all year. The Indian Brown Ale is a personal favorite, along with the salmon sandwich.

FRENCH

For several decades, the ★ **Back Porch Café** (59 Rehoboth Ave., 302/227-3674, www.backporchcafe.com, June-Sept. daily, May and Oct. weekends, lunch 11am-3pm, après-surf menu 3pm-5:30pm, dinner 6pm-10pm, $34-42) has delighted visitors with upscale creations from its award-winning chef and owner. The cuisine is unmistakably French, with many wonderful sauces, root veggies, and some entrées such as rabbit, but they also look to seasonal ingredients for inspiration. Start with the crab ravioli, a sure crowd-pleaser, and then choose carefully from the interesting array of main courses. If the wild king salmon is on the menu, it is one good choice; it is served with a savory butternut squash bisque. The interior is cozy with a bar and some outdoor seating. This restaurant is open for lunch, brunch, and dinner in the summer but is closed in the off-season. Reservations are encouraged. There is no kid's menu.

ITALIAN

Lupo Italian Kitchen (247 Rehoboth Ave., 302/226-2240, www.lupodimarerehoboth.com, Sun.-Thurs. 5pm-9pm, Fri.-Sat. 5pm-10pm, $10-29) is a beautiful little restaurant (formerly called Lupo di Mare) on the first floor of the Hotel Rehoboth on Rehoboth Avenue. It is light and airy inside and offers a menu of flatbread, salad, homemade pasta, and other delightful Italian choices. Their fried calamari is perhaps the best in the area. Their salads offer delicious combinations such as roasted beet and citrus with goat gouda, pickled shallot, beet chips, and candied pistachios. Entrees include lobster bucatini, crab and casarecce, and classics such as chicken parmesan and lasagna. They have shorter hours in the off-season and different off-season specials each night of the week (such as 25 percent off your check on Mondays).

Touch of Italy (19724 Coastal Hwy, 302/227-3900, www.touchofitaly.com, Sun.-Thurs. 10:30am-9pm, Fri.-Sat. 10:30am-10pm, $10-45) is a dine-in and carryout Italian deli focused on specialty meats, cheeses, and Italian pastries. They have a huge menu and all sandwiches are made to order.

It would be almost negligent to not mention the classic Rehoboth Beach pizza joint, **Nicola Pizza** (8 N. 1st St., 302/227-6211, www.nicolapizza.com, daily 11am-midnight, $5-27). This pizzeria has been a staple in town since 1971, and for many it is *the* beachy place to bring the family. The wood floors and booths are a reminder of the restaurant's long history. Wait times in the summer can easily be an hour or more. The most popular dish is the "Nic-o-Boli," which is their name for stromboli (they can sell up to 2,000 in one night). This is worth a try if you've never had one, although the regular pizza is also a good choice. There's a second location at 71 Rehoboth Avenue.

Another classic pizza place in Rehoboth is **Grotto Pizza** (36 Rehoboth Ave., 302/227-3278, www.grottopizza.com, Sun.-Thurs. 11am-10pm, Fri.-Sat. 11am-11pm, under $15). This well-recognized restaurant has been around since 1960 and has three locations in Rehoboth Beach. The other two locations are on the boardwalk at 15 Boardwalk and Baltimore Avenue and 17 Surf Avenue. They offer dine-in, carryout, and walk-up pizza.

SNACKS

Fisher's Popcorn (48 Rehoboth Ave., 302/227-2691, www.fishers-popcorn.com, daily Memorial Day-Labor Day, weekends year-round) is a staple on the Maryland and Delaware beaches. You can buy the addicting little morsels by the bucket (0.5-6.5 gallons). They are known for the caramel popcorn but offer several other flavors. Please note: It is easy to eat this until you feel sick. Stopping is hard to do. You've been warned.

Perhaps no beach trip is complete without at least one stop at **Thrasher's French Fries** (26 Rehoboth Ave., 302/227-7366, daily from 11am). This local icon serves up buckets of fresh boardwalk fries from the walk-up window on the boardwalk. Even die-hard ketchup lovers will want to try them with salt and vinegar.

A fun place to stop is **Kaisy's Delights** (70 Rehoboth Ave., 302/212-5360, www.kaisysdelights.com, Sun.-Thurs. 7:30am-5pm, Fri.-Sat. 7:30am-7pm, under $10) for an Austrian Kaisy (a treat made of sweet custardy dough with your choice of toppings such as ice cream or fruit sauce). Their delicious samples may lure you into a sweet Kaisy or even a breakfast Kaisy (they are available with eggs, sausage, and bacon). The coffee is also good. They're open all year.

Accommodations

The **Avenue Inn & Spa** (33 Wilmington Ave., 800/433-5870, www.avenueinn.com, $269-419) is an independently owned hotel one block from the beach. There are 60 guest rooms with many amenities such as full breakfast, complimentary wine and cheese, evening cookies, a day spa, indoor heated pool, fitness room, sauna, beach chairs, beach shuttle, and free parking.

The **Bellmoor Inn and Spa** (6 Christian St., 302/227-5800, www.thebellmoor.com, $379-639) is a comfortable inn about three blocks from the beach. They offer 22 guest rooms and suites. There are two pools on-site and an enclosed hot tub. Breakfast is served daily (with omelets on the weekends), and the staff is friendly and helpful.

The ★ **Boardwalk Plaza Hotel** (2 Olive Ave., 302/227-7169, www.boardwalkplaza.com, $324-679) is an elegant, Victorian-style oceanfront hotel right on the boardwalk. The hotel is furnished with antiques and antique-style furniture and offers oceanfront rooms with deluxe amenities. The hotel is friendly to children (and even offers special events for them such as craft time) but also has special amenities and areas for adults only (including a rooftop hot tub). The 84 guest rooms are comfortable, clean, and warmly decorated. The staff is friendly and goes out of its way to make visitors feel at home. There's also a restaurant on-site that offers water-view dining, a cozy bar, and a boardwalk patio.

A great choice for a clean, affordable, welcoming stay near the boardwalk is the **Beach View Hotel** (6 Wilmington Ave., 302/227-2999, www.beachviewmotel.com, $234-304). This small hotel offers ocean-view rooms with private balconies and poolside rooms with no balconies. Continental breakfast is included. This hotel is a good value in a convenient location.

Information and Services

For additional information on Rehoboth Beach, visit www.cityofrehoboth.com, www.rehobothboardwalk.com, and www.downtownrehoboth.com or stop by the **Rehoboth Beach-Dewey Beach Chamber**

of Commerce and Visitors Center (501 Rehoboth Ave., 302/227-2233, year-round Mon.-Fri. 9am-5pm, Sat.-Sun. 9am-1pm).

LEWES

Lewes is seven miles north of Rehoboth and can be summed up in one word: charming. This quaint little town near the beach is a relaxing alternative to the busier beaches along the Delaware and Maryland shore. Lewes is also known as the "first town in the first state," since it was the site of the first European settlement in Delaware, founded in 1631. The town has an upscale beach feel to it and draws visitors of many age groups who come to relax, drink wine, eat good food, and shop.

Sights

★ HISTORIC LEWES

The historic downtown area of Lewes is on the harbor, just a short distance from the Atlantic. Second Street is the main street in town and offers wonderful dining and shopping and a cozy, friendly feel. The downtown area is lovely all year round. It truly is one of the prettiest spots on the mid-Atlantic coast with its historic homes (some dating back to the 17th century), friendly atmosphere, and tidy, well-kept streets. Boutique stores and independently owned restaurants line the sidewalks, and the local residents are friendly and welcoming to tourists.

Shipcarpenter Square (www.shipcarpentersquare.com) is a community of delicately and accurately preserved and restored 18th- and 19th-century homes in the historic district. The homes in Shipcarpenter Square are mostly colonial farmhouses built in the late 1700s-late 1800s in other parts of Sussex County and moved to the site in the early 1980s. Other relocated buildings include three barns, a schoolhouse, an inn, a log home, a lifesaving station, a lighthouse, a market, and two Victorian houses.

The Shipcarpenter Square community stretches from 3rd and 4th Street on the east and west side to Burton Street and Park Streets on the north and south sides. Parking and walking access are provided to homeowners in this area. Pedestrians can enter a foot traffic-only area from Park Street and two areas on the north and south edges of the common greens that are located in the heart of the community.

harbor in Lewes

ZWAANENDAEL MUSEUM

The **Zwaanendael Museum** (102 Kings Hwy., 302/645-1148, http://history.delaware.gov, Apr.-Oct. Tues.-Sat. 10am-4:30pm, Sun. 1:30pm-4:30pm, Nov.-Mar. Wed.-Sat. 10am-4:30pm, free, donations appreciated) is an interesting-looking building (a replica of the Town Hall of Hoorn in the Netherlands) that features Dutch elements from the 17th century such as terra-cotta roof tiles, decorated shutters, a stepped facade gable, and stonework. The museum takes visitors through the history of Lewes as the state's first European settlement (by the Dutch) in 1631 and offers exhibits on the attack on Lewes by the British during the War of 1812, the Delaware coastline, and the Cape Henlopen Lighthouse. The museum also includes a maritime and military history of the town.

CAPE MAY-LEWES FERRY

The **Cape May-Lewes Ferry** (43 Cape Henlopen Dr., 800/643-3779, www.capemaylewesferry.com, Apr.-Sept. 8am-6pm, Oct.-Mar. 8:30am-4:30pm, car and driver one-way $27-45, extra passenger or pedestrian one-way $10) docks on Cape Henelopen Drive and makes daily 70-minute trips across Delaware Bay to Cape May, New Jersey. Auto and foot passengers are allowed on board, and there is no fee for bicycles. Ferry schedules vary throughout the season. Check the website for current departure times.

Shopping

The primary shopping district in historic Lewes is on 2nd Street, off Savannah Street. Upscale boutiques, houseware shops, and even a wonderful store for dogs line the manicured street. Ice-cream shops and other snack shops offer a nice break from sightseeing or shopping.

Sports and Recreation

Cape Henlopen State Park (15099 Cape Henlopen Dr., 302/645-8983, www.destateparks.com, daily 8am-sunset year-round, $10) covers five miles of shoreline at the mouth of Delaware Bay where it meets the Atlantic. It has a long military and shipping history. A storm in 1920 took out the lighthouse that used to guide ships through the bay, but breakwater barriers still provide a safe harbor during storms and rough water.

A military base was established at the cape in 1941, and bunkers were hidden among the dunes for protection. Observation towers built of cement, which are still standing, were also put in place along the shore to search for enemy ships. The park was created in 1964. Today the park provides many acres of seaside habitat. There's a nature center, hiking, fishing, swimming, a picnic pavilion, fishing pier, and camping in the park. The two swimming beaches are watched over by lifeguards in the summer.

There are several companies offering fishing supplies and charters in Lewes including **Katydid Charters** (Anglers Rd., 302/858-7783 or 302/645-8688, www.katydidsportfishing.com, starting at $375 for 10 people), **Angler's Fishing Center** (213 Anglers Rd., 302/644-4533, www.anglersfishingcenter.com, starting at $50), and **First Light Charters** (907 Pilottown Rd, 302/853-5717, www.firstlightcharters.net, starting at $275).

Sightseeing cruises are also available at the **Fisherman's Wharf** (107 Anglers Rd., 302/645-8862, www.fishlewes.com, $29-35). They offer two- and three-hour dolphin-watching cruises and a sunset cruise that leaves each evening during the summer at 6:30pm from the wharf docks. The trip goes down the canal and out to the ocean and then turns around near the ferry terminal.

Dogfish Head Brewery (302/745-2925, www.dogfish.com, $65) offers a "Pints and Paddles" tour May-October. This kayaking outing for beer enthusiasts is a unique out-and-back paddle on the Broadkill River in the McCabe Nature Preserve (a Nature Conservancy area), followed by a tour of the Dogfish Head Brewery (including samples for those over 21). Trips leave at noon on Wednesday, Friday, and Saturday from the

Beacon Motel parking lot (514 E. Savannah Rd.). A souvenir pint glass is included in the outing.

Golfers can enjoy a round at the **Marsh Island Golf Club** (21383 Camp Arrowhead, 302/945-4653, $55). This 18-hole course has a course rating of 65 and a slope rating of 96. It was designed by Herman John Schneider.

Food

The ★ **Agave Mexican Grill and Tequila Bar** (137 2nd St., 302/645-1232, www.agavemexicanrestaurant.net, Mon.-Sat. noon-9pm, Sun. 3pm-9pm, $7-24) is a funky, upscale, sought-after Mexican dining spot that Laura Bush even stopped in one evening unannounced to sample the authentic cuisine. All the food is delicious, but they do a particularly good job with their mole, shrimp and garlic guacamole, and fish tacos. For something a little different, try the apple and moon cheese guacamole. Brightly painted glasses adorn patrons' tables and hold three sizes of margaritas (they have more than 70 types of tequila). The atmosphere is great, the service is attentive and friendly, and the clientele is lively. The only downside to this fabulous little gem is the long wait times for a table (sometimes as much as two hours or more). Plan a late lunch or early dinner to get a jump on the competition. Another option is to put your name on the list and stroll around the town while you wait.

The Buttery (102 2nd St., 302/645-7755, www.butteryrestaurant.com, daily lunch and dinner and Sun. brunch, hours vary by season, $26-36) is a local favorite right on 2nd Street. This beautiful Victorian restaurant specializes in upscale seafood entrées and appealing food presentation. The service is professional yet personal, and they can even accommodate diet restrictions. The menu is not large, but everything is done top-notch. They also offer a casual pub menu in the evenings and a daily three course pre fixe menu from 5pm to 6:45pm for $33. There have a lovely year-round veranda and beautiful plantings around the house. Reservations are a must.

For good seafood in a lively pub atmosphere, dine at **Striper Bites** (107 Savannah Rd., 302/645-4657, www.striperbites.com, lunch and dinner daily from 11:30am, $10-28). They offer casual dining indoors or on a patio. The seafood choices are excellent, and the service is friendly and usually prompt. The decor is wood furnishings and things from the sea. This is a go-to place for many locals. They don't take reservations, and on a busy night it can be quite loud indoors, but for the most part it offers a pleasant dining experience and delicious food.

Crooked Hammock Brewery (36707 Crooked Hammock Way, 302/644-7837, www.crookedhammockbrewery.com, daily 11am-1am, $8-22) is a fun brewery that offers an energetic atmosphere and a large outdoor space. They have a good selection of craft beers and a menu of casual appetizers, salads, sandwiches, and main dishes such as chicken fried chicken, beef short rib, clam bake, and salmon.

The Buttery

Accommodations

INNS AND HOTELS

★ **The Inn at Canal Square** (122 Market St., 302/644-3377, www.theinnatcanalsquare.com, $245-625) is a pretty canal-front inn in the heart of Lewes. The inn has 22 rooms and three VIP suites and can accommodate short- or long-term stays. Most of the rooms have water views and balconies, and the suites offer two bedrooms, full kitchens, washers and dryers, fireplaces, screened porches, and decks. The grounds are adorned with lavish plantings, and fresh flowers are brought into the common areas weekly. Special packages such as golf package and a Dogfish Head Brewery package are available. Breakfast is included with your stay, and the friendly staff can assist with recommending the perfect restaurant for lunch and dinner. The inn is convenient to all the shops and dining options on 2nd Street, and it provides free parking and wireless Internet.

The **Hotel Blue** (110 Anglers Rd., 302/645-4880, www.hotelblue.info, $299-349) is a comfortable boutique hotel with some nice little touches such as mirrored televisions and glowing ice buckets. The lobby is inviting, and the 16 guest rooms are modern and spacious. Each room has a fireplace, private balcony, and pillow-top mattresses. There are also a beautiful rooftop pool and lounge area and a fitness room.

BED-AND-BREAKFASTS

There are several wonderful bed-and-breakfasts in Lewes near the historic district. Most have minimum night stays during the season, some do not allow small children, and some do not take credit cards, so be sure to ask about these things when you make your reservation if they are important to you.

The **Savannah Inn** (330 Savannah Rd., 302/645-0330, www.savannahinnlewes.com, $190-295) is a lovely turn-of-the-20th-century brick home that was remodeled and now offers six contemporary guest rooms with modern bathrooms. The owners are very personable and take pride in their establishment, which goes a long way in making guests feel welcome. The inn is very clean, and the decor is airy and inviting. It is an easy walk to the historic downtown area and the waterfront. The inn is a family-run business, from the reservations to the kitchen. There is an adorable yellow Labrador who lives here, but the owners are careful about not allowing him in guest areas.

The **John Penrose Virden House** (217 2nd St., 302/644-0217, www.virdenhouse.

The Inn at Canal Square

com, $175-245) is a charming green-colored 19th-century Victorian bed-and-breakfast centrally located on 2nd Street. The three guest rooms are well appointed with antiques and offer beach equipment such as towels and chairs. The hosts do a lovely job of making visitors feel welcome and greet guests with fresh fruit and flowers in their rooms. They also serve a scrumptious homemade breakfast to remember and hold a cocktail hour with snacks and beverages. Bicycles are also available for guests. They do not accept credit cards, only cash or checks.

The **Blue Water House** (407 E. Market St., 302/645-7832, www.lewes-beach.com, $200-235) is a bed-and-breakfast a short walk from the beach and geared toward sandy fun. It offers a slightly funky decor with bright colors. There are nine guest rooms, each with private bathrooms. The owner pays attention to every last detail and goes above and beyond to make guests feel welcome and to keep the house immaculate. Guests are offered many beach amenities such as towels, beach chairs, sunscreen, umbrellas, cold water, and bicycles. Children are welcome, and the house is equipped with games and books.

Information and Services

For additional information on Lewes, visit www.lewes.com or stop by the **Lewes Visitors Center** (120 Kings Hwy., 302/645-8073, www.leweschamber.com, Mon.-Fri. 10am-4pm).

Frederick and Western Maryland

Settled by German immigrants in 1745, Frederick was founded as a trading outpost and a crossroads for goods making their way to outlying settlements and farms. Today, the city's wonderful boutiques, antiques shops, and nearby Civil War attractions provide plenty of options for visitors to explore. Although the surrounding area has seen an explosion of suburban housing, the historic city center has maintained its colonial-era charm.

Beyond Frederick is Western Maryland, the "mountain side" of the state, where the biggest decision of the day can be whether to go fishing or hiking. Deep Creek Lake in Garrett County offers beautiful private homes, inns, restaurants, and parks providing year-round recreation.

Western Maryland also hosted several well-known Civil War battles, including the Battle of Antietam, and the Battle of Gettysburg was just over the Pennsylvania state line. Even just one day spent exploring these sites will give you a sense of the depth of history throughout this region. The historic town of Harpers Ferry, just over the West Virginia state line, is also included with this region. It was the location of abolitionist John Brown's 1859 raid on a national arsenal, an event that helped trigger the Civil War.

PLANNING YOUR TIME

How big a history buff you are will dictate how long it will take to explore Frederick and Western Maryland. Geographically, the area can be explored in 2-3 days, but the battlefields themselves can warrant a half day or even a full day of exploration for those with a keen interest in Civil War history. Major travel routes in the region include I-70 and I-68.

If your time is limited, select a couple of key towns to explore, such as Frederick, Gettysburg, or Harpers Ferry. Gettysburg is a must-see from a historical perspective; Harpers Ferry is both historic and an outdoor recreation haven; and Frederick offers a wonderful downtown and dining experience. All can be visited as day trips from Baltimore and Washington DC, although to thoroughly

Previous: Carroll Creek flows through downtown Frederick; Antietam. **Above:** St. Peter's Church in Harpers Ferry.

Look for ★ to find recommended sights, activities, dining, and lodging.

Highlights

★ **National Museum of Civil War Medicine:** Learn little-known facts about medical practices during the Civil War (page 512).

★ **Gettysburg National Military Park:** Commemorate the historic three-day Battle of Gettysburg that took place on July 1-3, 1863 (page 520).

★ **Harpers Ferry National Historical Park:** This well-preserved area at the confluence of the Shenandoah and Potomac Rivers includes more than 25 historic buildings and 3,700 acres of protected land (page 526).

★ **Antietam National Battlefield:** The Battle of Antietam was the bloodiest single-day confrontation in American history. The battlefield serves as a reminder of the 23,000 casualties suffered there (page 531).

★ **The Western Maryland Scenic Railroad:** This fun 32-mile excursion offers passengers a tour of the beautiful countryside between Cumberland and Frostburg (page 534).

★ **Thrasher Carriage Museum:** This little museum houses one of the country's best collections of horse-powered carriages (page 538).

★ **Spruce Forest Artisan Village:** A dozen cabins house working art studios where visitors can watch fine craftsmanship in progress (page 540).

★ **Savage River State Forest:** This 54,000-acre forest offers a wealth of outdoor recreation year-round (page 540).

★ **Deep Creek Lake State Park:** This beautiful park boasts one mile of shoreline and endless recreation (page 542).

Gettysburg National Military Park in Pennsylvania

explore Gettysburg an overnight trip is recommended unless you have a lot of energy.

The far western reaches of the state are best traveled by car and can be explored in a long weekend. Many people make the popular Deep Creek Lake area their destination for a longer vacation, which allows time to enjoy lake activities and visit the many parks along and near its shores. Those traveling in winter can enjoy skiing and other cold-weather activities but should be advised to check weather conditions prior to their trip. Driving through the mountains can offer challenges in inclement weather.

Harpers Ferry National Historical Park

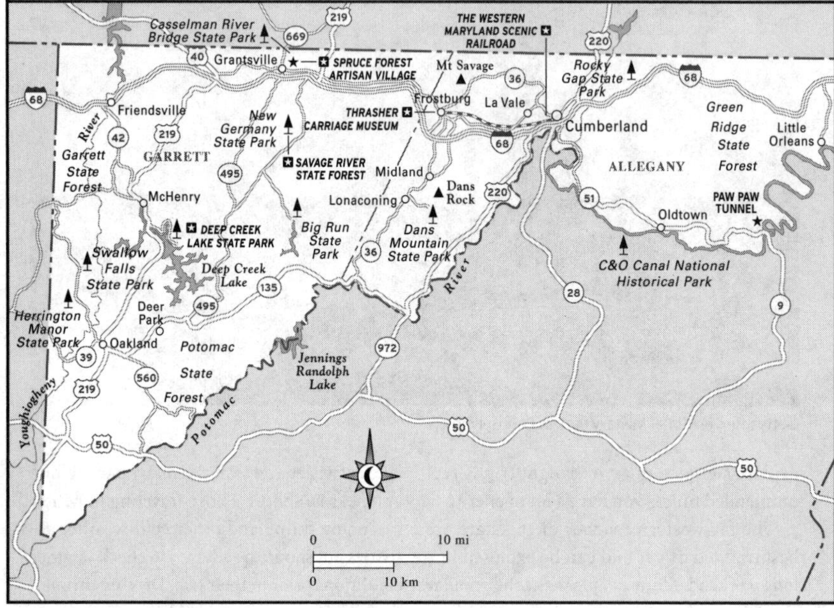

Frederick

The city of Frederick was founded by German settlers in 1745. It was an important crossroads during the Civil War, and several major battles, including those at Antietam and Gettysburg, were fought in the region. Frederick was spared from burning during the Civil War when a hefty ransom ($200,000) was paid by the townspeople to the Confederates. It served as a hospital town for those wounded in the battles fought around the region.

By the turn of the 20th century, Frederick had begun making its living off of canning, knitting, and tanning and utilizing the railroad to deliver its goods to Baltimore.

Today, downtown Frederick is a lovely collection of shops, galleries, restaurants, and antiques stores. It is less than an hour's drive from Washington DC and is a popular spot for a day trip of antiques hunting. There is a 40-block historic district, and the town is the hub of arts, culture, and commerce in Frederick County.

Many of Frederick's attractions and restaurants are near the center of town. Park your car on one of the side streets and make your way around on foot. The layout of the town is a simple grid, so it's hard to get lost. The central intersection is Market Street and Patrick Street.

SIGHTS

★ National Museum of Civil War Medicine

The **National Museum of Civil War Medicine** (48 E. Patrick St., 301/695-1864, www.civilwarmed.org, Mon.-Sat. 10am-5pm, Sun. 11am-5pm, $9.50) is tucked away on Patrick Street in the historic area of Frederick. This interesting little museum

the National Museum of Civil War Medicine

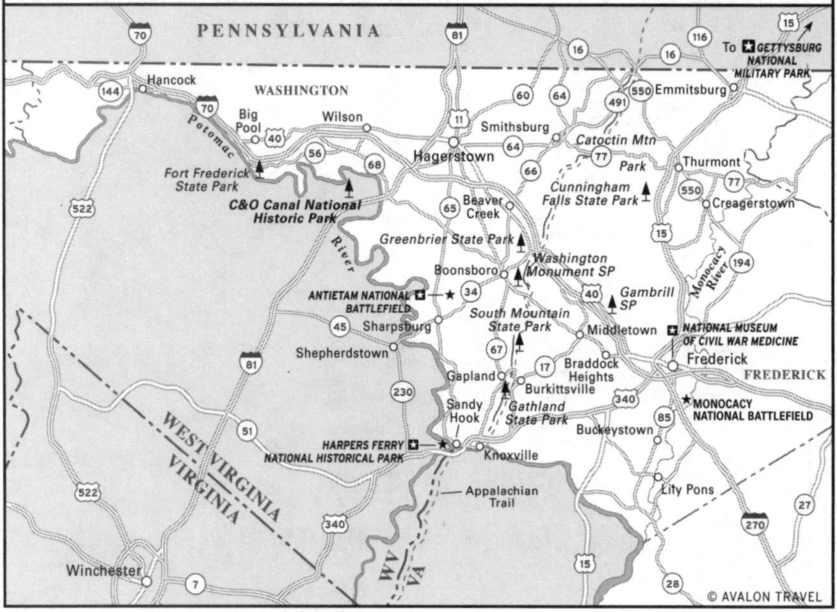

started as a private collection. Exhibits cover many little-known facts about medicine and disease during the war (such as two-thirds of the 620,000 soldiers who died during the war succumbed to disease, not wounds, and doctors at the time had no knowledge of antiseptic practices or germ theory). It even explains the process used to embalm dead soldiers on the battlefield so they could be transported home. In fact, the historic building that the museum is housed in served as an embalming station following the Battle of Antietam in 1862. Information on veterinary medicine during the war and the development of large-animal infirmaries is also featured, as the armies were dependent on horses and mules. There are also many original artifacts such as medical tools and even an operating table. The museum is not appropriate for small children, and kids under age 16 must be accompanied by an adult. Allow 1-2 hours to see the museum on the self-guided tour.

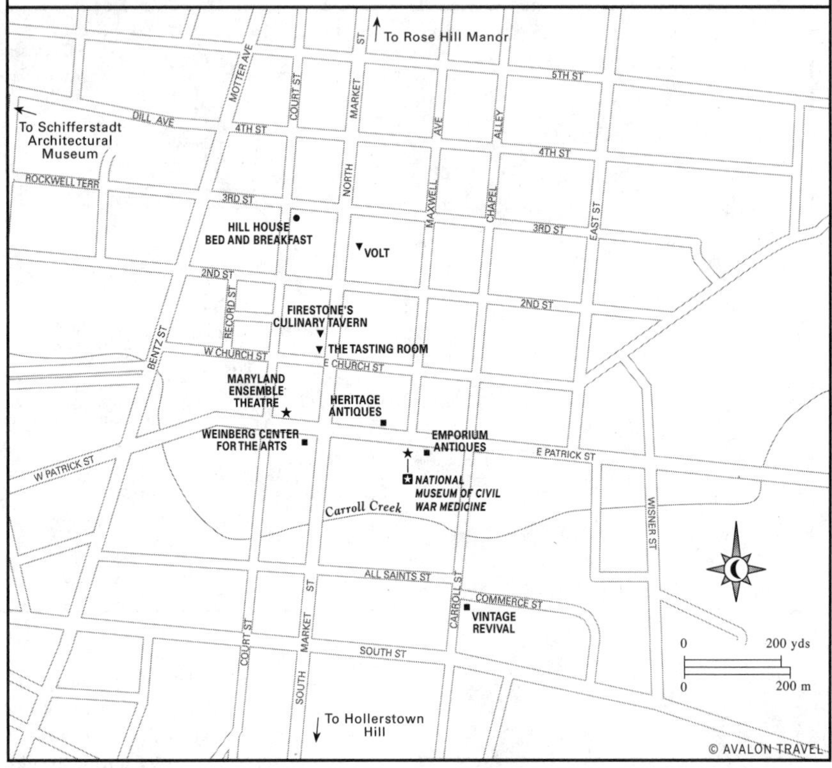

Schifferstadt Architectural Museum

The **Schifferstadt Architectural Museum** (1110 Rosemont Ave., 301/663-3885, www.frederickcountylandmarksfoundation.org, Apr.-early Dec. Sat.-Sun. 1pm-4pm, $5) is in one of the oldest homes in Frederick, dating back to 1758 and one of the best examples of early colonial German architecture in the nation. The simple stone home was built during the French and Indian War at a time when many settlers were forced to leave their farms due to raids. It is thought that Schifferstadt may have provided a safe refuge for entire families. The museum provides wonderful insight into the French and Indian War era and also shares information on early German settlers.

Monocacy National Battlefield

Southwest of the city is the **Monocacy National Battlefield** (5201 Urbana Pike, 301/662-3515, www.nps.gov/mono, daily sunrise-sunset, free), site of the "Battle That Saved Washington." The Civil War conflict that took place here in July 1864 is formally known as the **Battle of the Monocacy Junction,** so named since the fighting occurred on the banks of Monocacy River. It is often credited with saving the Federal capital because it was one of the last battles fought in Union territory as a Confederate army approached Washington DC and threatened to capture it.

Visitors should begin their exploration at the visitors center, which features interactive multimedia exhibits and maps of the

Schifferstadt Architectural Museum

battle. There is also a bookstore at the center. Information on driving and walking tours to five monuments located on the grounds can be picked up at the center.

ENTERTAINMENT

Theater

Two downtown theaters may be found on Patrick Street. The **Maryland Ensemble Theatre (MET)** (31 W. Patrick St., 301/694-4744, www.marylandensemble.org) is a 100-seat black box theater that puts on an eclectic schedule of thought-provoking plays. The **Weinberg Center for the Arts** (20 W. Patrick St., 301/600-2828, www.weinberg-center.org) is a historic performing arts venue with a full schedule of performances throughout the year including music, theater, dance, film, a speakers series, and other visual arts.

Brewery Tours

The **Flying Dog Brewery** (4607 Wedgewood Blvd., 301/694-7899, www.flyingdogbrewery.com, tours Fri. 3:30pm, 4:30pm, and 5:30pm, Sat. 12:30pm, 1:30pm, 2:30pm, 3:30pm, and 4:30pm, tasting room Thurs.-Fri. 3pm-8pm, Sat. noon-8pm, Sun. noon-6pm) is a great local brewery that produces terrific beer and offers one of the best brewery tours around. Tour leaders are humorous, informative, and present a good mix of interesting information and beer samples. This is a fun time for beer lovers. Tours are two hours and include five tastings and a souvenir glass. Tour participants must be 21 or older.

SHOPPING

Shopping is what brings many visitors to the historic district in Frederick. Many antiques shops line the streets, making the town a popular destination for treasure hunters. Some shops are even dog friendly, including **Emporium Antiques** (112 E. Patrick St., 301/662-7099, www.emporiumantiques.com), which offers more than 100 dealers and is known for vintage furnishings and home decor items; **Vintage Revival** (124 Carroll St., 301/624-4032), offering arts and crafts; and **Heritage Interiors** (39 E. Patrick St., 301/668-0299, www.heritageinfrederick.com), a consignment store carrying antique, traditional, and modern furniture. Art galleries and studios are also plentiful in Frederick as are home furnishings stores, clothing boutiques, and jewelry stores.

SPORTS AND RECREATION

A 15-minute drive north of Frederick on U.S. 15 will take you to **Cunningham Falls State Park** (Rte. 15, Thurmont, 301/271-7574, www.dnr2.maryland.gov, Apr.-Oct. daily 8am-sunset, Nov.-Mar. daily 10am-sunset, $5). This wonderful 5,000-acre park sits on Catoctin Mountain and offers swimming, hiking, a 43-acre lake, fishing, a boat launch ($5), canoeing, and a remarkable 78-foot waterfall. The park is made up of two primary areas. The Manor Area off U.S. 15 (three miles south of Thurmont) includes an aviary, camping, and the historic Catoctin Iron Furnace, where iron was made for more than 100 years. The second section, the William Houck Area, is three miles west of Thurmont on Route 77 and encompasses the lake, falls, and a camping area.

Adjacent to Cunningham Falls State Park is a unit of the National Park Service called **Catoctin Mountain Park** (6602 Foxville Road, Thurmont). The park has 25 miles of hiking trails, rental cabins, camping, and live demonstrations. The park is best known as the site of Camp David.

Northwest of Frederick is **Gambrill State Park** (8602 Gambrill Park Rd., 301/271-7574, www.dnr2.maryland.gov, Apr.-Oct. 8am-sunset, Nov.-Mar. 10am-sunset, $5). This beautiful park off Route 40 in the Catoctin Mountains in Frederick County is known for its 16 miles of trails suitable for hiking, mountain biking, and horseback riding. There are two primary areas in the park: Rock Run and High Knob, the latter with several stunning overlooks from its namesake 1,600-foot knob. The park offers camping, picnic areas, and a small fishing pond.

Frederick is home to the **Frederick Keys** minor league baseball team. This Class A affiliate of the Baltimore Orioles plays at **Harry Grove Stadium** (21 Stadium Dr., 301/662-0018, www.milb.com), which is a great family venue. Ticket prices are reasonable, and there's not a bad seat in the house. There are also many nice choices for food vendors.

FOOD

American

The **Firestone's Culinary Tavern** (105 N. Market St., 301/663-0330, www.firestones-restaurant.com, Tues.-Sat. 11am-1:30pm, Sun. 10am-1am, $10-44) is a fun place to meet friends or have a romantic dinner. The mix of wood, white tablecloths, and delicious gourmet menu items makes this a comfortable restaurant with an upscale feel. The dinner entrées include many steak and seafood choices such as pan-seared scallops, hanger steak, cowboy steak, and salmon. Their tavern menu offers pizza, sandwiches, and salad. Sunday brunch is lovely and includes traditional favorites such as eggs Benedict, as well as a great list of appetizers that can be combined into a meal.

★ **Volt** (228 N. Market St., 301/696-8658, www.voltrestaurant.com, brunch Sat.-Sun. 11:30am-2pm, dinner Tues.-Sun. 5:30pm-9:30pm, $80-150) may be in a league of its own for Frederick dining. This creative, upscale, American-style restaurant is perhaps the crown jewel of town. Executive chef Bryan Voltaggio (who was a contestant on Bravo's *Top Chef*) showcases his delicious creations in his hometown restaurant using fresh local ingredients. The menu changes frequently and includes seafood, pasta, meat, and game. The restaurant itself is a masterpiece, housed in a 19th-century brownstone mansion. The elegant yet contemporary dining room reflects the original Gilded Era building construction, while a glass-enclosed conservatory shows off the walled garden outside. There is also a chef's dining room.

The food at Volt is simply outstanding and very pricey. They offer a six-course tasting menu for $95 per person, with a $65 beverage pairing option. There is also a special seating at "Table 21" (a 21-course meal prepared and eaten right in the kitchen) for $150 per person. It is available Tues.-Thurs. at 7pm and Fri.-Sun. at 5:30pm and 8:30pm. It is not uncommon for the reservations for Table 21 to be booked weeks in advance, as there are only eight seats. Their dress code is business casual.

The Frederick Wine Trail

Travel historic roads around Frederick County to sample wine, tour vineyards, and enjoy many events.

- **Black Ankle Vineyards** (14463 Black Ankle Rd., Mount Airy, 301/829-3338, www.blackankle.com)
- **Elk Run Vineyards** (15113 Liberty Rd., Mount Airy, 410/775-2513, www.elkrun.com)
- **Linganore Winecellars** (13601 Glissans Mill Rd., Mount Airy, 301/831-5889, www.linganorewines.com)
- **Loew Vineyards** (14001 Liberty Rd., Mount Airy, 301/831-5464, www.loewvineyards.net)
- **Sugarloaf Mountain Vineyard** (18125 Comus Rd., Dickerson, 301/605-0130, www.smvwinery.com)

A popular modern American restaurant and wine bar is **The Tasting Room** (101 N. Market St., 240/379-7772, www.trrestaurant.com, Mon.-Thurs. 11am-10pm, Fri.-Sat. 11am-11pm, Sun. 11am-8pm, $30-50). This upscale establishment offers, as they say, a "cosmopolitan atmosphere" in the heart of downtown Frederick. The interior is nicely done with floor-to-ceiling windows that provide a view of the historic district. The food is consistently good, and the dishes are prepared with many local ingredients. Whether you have one of several delicious seafood selections, the rack of lamb, or a center cut of beef tenderloin, each is presented well and tastes equally remarkable. The service is highly professional, and the specialty drinks are imaginative. They also have a great wine list.

Scrumptious handcrafted sandwiches are the sought-after items at **a.k.a. Friscos** (4632 Wedgewood Blvd., 301/698-0018, www.akafriscos.com, Mon.-Thurs. 11am-7pm, Fri.-Sat. 11am-9pm, Sun. 11am-4pm, under $10). This lively, friendly place is a little hard to find (it's located in an industrial park), but it's still the best place in town for a sandwich. Try the "exploded" potatoes, a house special. Portions are generous, so arrive hungry.

Irish

The **Shamrock** (7701 Fitzgerald Rd., Thurmont, 301/271-2912, www.shamrockrestaurant.com, Mon.-Thurs. 11am-9pm, Fri.-Sat. 11am-10pm, Sun. noon-9pm, $8-26), in nearby Thurmont, is one of those places you pass by again and again (it's right next to U.S. 15) and think, "why is it always so crowded, even in the middle of the day?" This local landmark offers casual dining and a friendly atmosphere. They are known for their excellent fried shad roe, but also offer other traditional Irish fare. The restaurant is 15 miles north of Frederick and 15 miles south of Gettysburg, but is convenient if you're spending the afternoon at **Cunningham Falls State Park.**

ACCOMMODATIONS

$100-200

The **Fairfield Inn & Suites by Marriott** (5220 Westview Dr., 301/631-2000, www.marriott.com, $132-165) is a modern hotel with three floors and 105 guest rooms. The rooms are clean, the beds are comfortable, and a hot breakfast is included with your stay. They have a swimming pool and fitness center on-site as well as free wireless Internet. Ask for a room on one of the upper floors.

Hollerstown Hill (4 Clarke Pl., 301/228-3630, www.hollerstownhill.com, $129-149) is a quaint bed-and-breakfast with four cozy guest rooms. This late Victorian home was built around 1900. The house is amply decorated and showcases the owners' collectibles and antiques. It is located in a quiet neighborhood outside of the downtown area. Wireless Internet access is included.

Hill House Bed and Breakfast (12 W. 3rd St., 301/682-4111, www.hillhousefrederick.com, $145-195) is in a three-story Victorian town house in downtown Frederick. The location is perfect for easy access to shopping and restaurants (it is around the corner from Volt). The house was built in 1870 and offers four pleasant guest rooms. This is not a luxurious bed-and-breakfast, but if you are looking for convenience while visiting Frederick, the address is ideal.

$200-300

The perfect location for a relaxing weekend or romantic getaway is **Stone Manor Estate / The Inn at Stone Manor** (5820 Carroll Boyer Rd., Middletown, 301/371-0099, www.stonemanorcountryclub.com, $200-225). The inn is on a 100-acre estate eight miles from downtown Frederick in Middletown, Maryland. The manor house is a beautifully maintained 18th-century stone mansion with a sprawling stone terrace and manicured grounds. The house was built in three sections, the oldest dating to 1750. Each of the six guest suites is unique and individually appointed with appropriate period antiques. The innkeepers are well known for being warm, helpful, and making each guest feel welcome and comfortable. Since each suite is different, guests can select the specific amenities they want including a private porch, fireplace, whirlpool tub, or a separate sitting room. All suites have private, modern bathrooms, and your stay includes a hearty, homemade breakfast served with fresh fruit.

CAMPING

Camping is available in **Cunningham Falls State Park** (Rte. 15, Thurmont, 301/271-7574, www.dnr.state.md.us) from April through October in the William Houck Area (three miles west of Thurmont on Route 77) and Manor Area (off U.S. 15). They offer standard tent sites, campsites with electricity, camper cabins, 4-person cabins, and 6-person cabins. Reservations start at $21.49 per night plus reservation ($4.51-4.61) and daily use fees ($5). There are 180 sites total.

Camping is also available at **Gambrill State Park** (off Rte. 40 in the Catoctin Mountains in Frederick County, 301/293-4170, www.dnr.state.md.us) from June through August. They offer standard campsites, campsites with electricity, and camper cabins. Reservations start at $18.49 per night plus reservation ($4.51-4.61) and daily use fees ($5). There are 31 sites.

INFORMATION AND SERVICES

For additional information on Frederick, visit www.visitfrederick.org or stop by the **Frederick Visitor Center** (151 S. East St., 301/600-4047, daily 9am-5:30pm).

GETTING THERE

Most people travel to Frederick by car. Frederick is about an hour's drive northwest of Washington DC (49 miles) via I-270 and an hour's drive west of Baltimore (49 miles) via I-70. Bus service is available on **Greyhound** (100 East St. South, 301/663-3311, www.greyhound.com).

The **Frederick Municipal Airport (FDK)** is just east of the city. It is a general aviation airport with two runways.

Gettysburg, Pennsylvania

Gettysburg (10 miles from the Maryland state line) was the site of the famous Battle of Gettysburg. The town was founded in 1761 with a single tavern, but by 1860 it was home to 2,400 people and had a thriving community of tanneries, carriage manufacturing, shoemaking and other industries. The town was etched into American history in July 1863, when the Confederate Army of Northern Virginia (consisting of 75,000 men led by General Robert E. Lee) and the Union's Army of the Potomac (consisting of 95,000 men led by Major General George G. Meade) converged here for a bloody three-day battle.

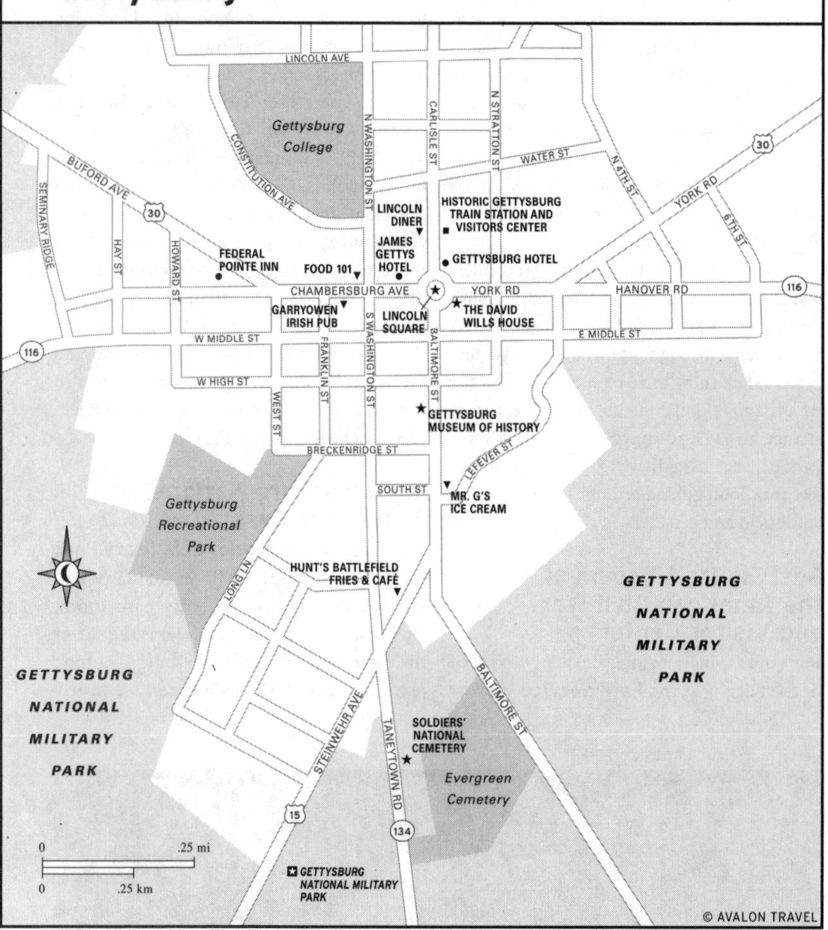

The Battle of Gettysburg is considered the great conflict of the Civil War. With 51,000 casualties, more men fought, died, and were wounded in this battle than in any other land engagement in American history. The battle also signaled a turning point in the war when the North's eventual victory became clear.

Several months after the battle, on November 19 of the same year, President Abraham Lincoln gave his famous Gettysburg Address here at the dedication ceremony of the Soldiers' National Cemetery, established as a final resting place for Union soldiers killed in the battle.

SIGHTS

When visiting Gettysburg, you feel the history all around. Since the town itself was part of the battlefield, many homes and businesses standing during the battle still bear the scars of bullet holes and other artillery fire, such as the famous **Jennie Wade House** (548 Baltimore St.), which was the site of the only civilian death during the Battle of Gettysburg (the house is now a museum and gift shop). **Lincoln Square** is a focal point of the town, where several primary roads come together at a traffic circle. Buildings here have a Lincoln Square street address, and there is a life-size statue of Lincoln next to a statue of a man dressed in modern-day clothing (so it looks as if Lincoln is talking to a tourist) in a prominent location in front of the David Wills House, where Lincoln slept the night before giving the Gettysburg Address.

The citizens of Gettysburg embrace their historical past and are eager to share it with visitors. Many historical tours and ghost tours are available throughout the town, and actors in period clothing are a common sight in the streets and establishments. By far the biggest attraction is Gettysburg National Military Park (the battlefield), which visitors can tour by car or foot, guided or unguided, to see the battlefield and cemetery.

Gettysburg Museum of the American Civil War and Visitor Center

The best place to begin your tour of Gettysburg is at the **Park Service Visitor Center** (1195 Baltimore Pike, www.nps.gov, Nov.-Mar. daily 8am-5pm, Apr.-Oct. daily 8am-6pm). Visitors can obtain information on the park and Gettysburg area in general at the visitors center, and can then take in the 22,000-square-foot **Gettysburg Museum of the American Civil War** (admission $12.50). This wonderfully detailed museum offers exhibits, Civil War relics, multimedia presentations, and interactive programs on Gettysburg. The museum covers the battle from start to finish and even provides details on the horrifying aftermath experienced by the town. Be sure to catch the film *A New Birth of Freedom,* narrated by actor Morgan Freeman. Outdoor ranger programs are also offered during the summer months, and lectures are held in the winter.

★ Gettysburg National Military Park

The **Gettysburg National Military Park** (1195 Baltimore Pike, 717/334-1124, www.nps.gov/gett, Apr.-Oct. daily 6am-10pm, Nov.-Mar. daily 6am-7pm, free) is the site of the three-day Battle of Gettysburg that took place July 1-3, 1863. Visitors can see nearly

Gettysburg National Military Park

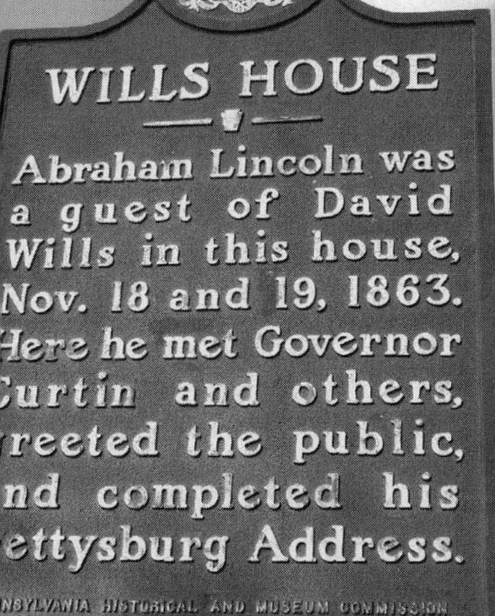

the David Wills House

1,400 monuments and historic markers on the 6,000-acre battlefield. Allow a minimum of four hours to explore the park. A self-guided auto tour (by map, no cost) and a self-guided audio tour (available for purchase at the visitors center bookstore, 717/334-2288) are great ways to tour the park. Field exhibits also help interpret significant sights throughout the battlefield.

Visitors are welcome to hike or bike through the park, and designated trails are marked for this purpose. Park brochures are available at the visitors center with trail maps. Biking is allowed on paved paths only.

For those wanting a more personal tour experience, licensed tour guides are available to drive you in your car as you explore the battlefield. Tours are about two hours in duration. Reservations are required at least three days in advance. Personal tour fees start at $65 and go up depending on the number of people in your group. Bus tours are available during peak summer months (two hours, $30). Reservations can be made ahead of time by calling 877/874-2478.

A unique way to see the park is on horseback. Tours are offered through **Hickory Hollow Farm** (717/334-0349, www.hickoryhollowfarm.com, $40) in groups of up to 10 riders. Tours last a minimum of two hours.

The **Gettysburg Heritage Center** (297 Steinwehr Ave., 717/334-6245) also offers iPad rentals containing a fully interactive Gettysburg battlefield tour app called **InSite Gettysburg.**

Soldiers' National Cemetery

The historic **Soldiers' National Cemetery** (97 Taneytown Rd., 717/334-1124, www.nps.gov, Apr.-Oct. daily 6am-10pm, Nov.-Mar. daily 6am-7pm, free) is a popular stop in Gettysburg. It is the burial site for thousands of Union soldiers who lost their lives here. The cemetery was dedicated when President Lincoln gave his famous Gettysburg Address on November 19, 1863. Graves marked by plain rectangular slabs of gray granite are arranged by state. Each marker extends nine inches above the lawn. Officers and enlisted men are buried next to each other in an effort to reinforce the egalitarian practices of the Union army. Additional war veterans have been buried here since the late 1880s. Visitors can park in a lot across Taneytown Road from the cemetery. A walking tour brochure is available at the visitors center (within walking distance to the cemetery).

David Wills House

The **David Wills House** (8 Lincoln Sq., 717/334-2499, www.nps.gov, May-Aug. 10am-5pm., reduced schedule rest of the year, $6.50) sits on the corner in Lincoln Square in downtown Gettysburg. The home weathered the famous battle in Gettysburg and soon after became the center of recovery efforts for the town. It is best known as the home where President Abraham Lincoln stayed the night before delivering the Gettysburg Address and the location where he finished writing the famous speech. The house is open to the public as a museum and contains exhibits on Gettysburg, the battle, and the creation of the Soldiers' National Cemetery. A life-size statue of Lincoln stands on the street just in front of the house.

Engraved bricks are fixed in the historic pathway in front of the house as a way for people to honor veterans, family, and friends. The bricks cost $150 each and become the property of the Borough of Gettysburg.

Gettysburg Lincoln Railroad Station

The **Gettysburg Lincoln Railroad Station** (35 Carlisle St., 717/334-6274, http://www.destinationgettysburg.com, Memorial Day-Labor Day daily 10am-5pm, shorter hours rest of year, free) was built in 1859 and was the western terminus of the Gettysburg Railroad line. It also served as a field hospital after the Battle of Gettysburg, processing some 15,000 wounded soldiers. During that time the station served as a symbol of hope, as it was the exit point for escaping the horror of the battle. President Lincoln arrived at the station on November 18, 1863, prior to delivering the Gettysburg Address. Visitors can see special exhibits throughout the year at this historic station, which is also available for event rentals. The station is listed in the National Register of Historic Places.

Gettysburg Museum of History

The **Gettysburg Museum of History** (219 Baltimore St., 717/337-2035, www.gettysburgmuseumofhistory.com, Sun. and Tues.-Wed. 11am-5pm, Thurs.-Sat. 11am-8pm, shorter hours in off-season, free, donations appreciated) is a great little museum stuffed full of interesting artifacts (4,000 of them). Easy to understand, easy to view, and covering history beyond the Civil War, this is a great gem of a museum right on Baltimore Street. Exhibits include artifacts from the Civil War, World War I, World War II, presidencies, and pop culture (including Elvis Presley's X-rays, books, and personal toiletries).

Lincoln Train Museum

Near the site of Lincoln's Gettysburg Address is the **Lincoln Train Museum** (425 Steinwehr Ave., 717/334-5678, www.lincolntrain.com, June-July daily 9am-9pm, shorter hours the rest of the year, $7.70). This museum offers a simulated interactive journey through American history with Abraham Lincoln. It also welcomes visitors aboard the full-size Lincoln Funeral Train Car. The museum also offers displays of working model trains.

Walking Tours

One of the most popular visitor activities in Gettysburg is taking a walking ghost tour. Several tour operators offer guided tours led by costumed interpreters/storytellers including **Gettysburg Ghost Tours** (47 Steinwehr Ave., 717/338-1818, www.gettysburgghosttours.com, starting at $9), **Sleepy Hollow of Gettysburg** (717/337-9322, www.sleepyhollowofgettysburg.com, starting at $8), and **Miss Betty's Ghosts** (443/789-9602, www.missbettysghostsingettysburg.com, $20).

Historical walking tours (not ghost related) are another great way to see the town. The **Gettysburg Convention and Visitors Bureau** (717/334-6274, www.destinationgettysburg.com) offers a free, self-guided walking tour that can be mailed out on request, downloaded from the website, and or downloaded as a free app. The tour helps visitors understand life in the town prior to the Civil War, as well as during and after the war.

Gettysburg Wine & Fruit Trail

Wine and food enthusiasts may enjoy the **Gettysburg Wine & Fruit Trail** (www.gettysburgwineandfruittrail.com). This agritourism trail showcases farms, orchards, vineyards, cafes, and accommodations in the South Mountain region of Pennsylvania. Information on the trail and each location featured can be found on the trail website.

ENTERTAINMENT AND EVENTS

Ten miles northwest of Gettysburg is the South Mountain Fairgrounds and the site of the annual **National Apple Harvest Festival** (Rte. 234 near Arendtsville, PA, www.appleharvest.com, $10). This annual event features more than 300 arts and crafts vendors and is held over the first two weekends in October. There is also live entertainment, food, hayrides, and other activities. If the weather is nice, the crowds can be large, so expect to be sitting in traffic on your way in.

Civil War buffs won't want to miss the annual **Gettysburg National Civil War Battle Reenactment** that is held in July in Gettysburg near the Gettysburg National Military Park. This three-day event includes three exciting battles, field demonstrations, live mortar fire demonstrations, and living history programs (www.gettysburgreenactment.com, $29 for one day, $49 for two days, and $69 for three days).

FOOD

American

The **Lincoln Diner** (32 Carlisle St., 717/334-3900, open 24 hours, under $10) is everything you'd expect from a small-town diner. The breakfast is all-American with eggs, pancakes, omelets, and french toast (okay, almost all American). The food is homemade (even the pies), dependable, and fresh, and they accommodate special orders. They somehow manage to cook eggs perfectly every time. Their milk shakes are a favorite also. If you're lucky, you'll witness the exchange of a few friendly insults between the regulars and waitstaff.

A "must" for cheesesteak lovers is ★ **Hunt's Battlefield Fries & Café** (61 Steinwehr Ave., 717/334-4787, daily 8am-8pm, under $10). This family-owned café is a true diamond in the rough. Walking in, you'd never expect to eat one of the best cheesesteaks of your life. Seat yourself, order a cheesesteak, and them amuse yourself by reading the vintage posters tacked on every wall. The friendly owners may come chat with you (they are longtime residents of the area). Be careful when ordering the fries, as a large bucket will feed a town. This restaurant is small, so expect a wait in peak tourist season or opt for takeout.

Another good option for outstanding casual fare is **Food 101** (101 Chambersburg St., 717/334-6080, www.food101gettysburg.com, Sun.-Thurs. 11am-8pm, Fri.-Sat. 11am-9pm, $7-16). They serve a little of everything, including pizza, salads, sandwiches, and entrees such as pasta, chicken, salmon, and steak. Their fried brussels sprouts are a winner, as is their mac and cheese.

Irish

Guinness and a Reuben. That's all you need to know about the **Garryowen Irish Pub** (126 Chambersburg St., 717/337-2719, www.garryowenirishpub.net, daily 11am-2am, $9-25). The most authentic Irish pub in town, Garryowen (aka "The GO") serves up great traditional Irish fare and equally impressive beer and whiskey selections. The prices are reasonable too. The staff and Irish owners are friendly, and the ambience is authentic and cozy. It's a great choice for celebrating St. Patrick's Day, but get there early! Beware if you order the fish-and-chips—the fish is bigger than your head.

Italian

Deliso Pizza (829 Biglerville Rd., 717/337-9500, under $15) is a wonderful casual Italian restaurant with great pizza. The homemade sauce and bread are worth the short drive just north of town. The atmosphere inside is very casual, but they offer pizza by the slice and takeout. Place your order at the counter and find a table if you're eating in. Their pastas and subs are good too. Entrées come with a fresh salad and bread.

Snacks

Curb your sweet tooth at **Mr. G's Ice Cream** (404 Baltimore St., 717/334-7600, under $5). They serve yummy homemade ice cream and also soft serve. There are many interesting flavors to choose from, and the building has a lot of character.

ACCOMMODATIONS

There are charming and historic hotels in Gettysburg that complement the historical nature of the town.

The **Gettysburg Hotel** (1 Lincoln Sq., 717/337-2000, www.hotelgettysburg.com, $234-294) is a charming historic property dating back to 1797. The hotel is a public landmark in Lincoln Square in downtown Gettysburg. It withstood the battle at Gettysburg and, nearly a century later, became the site of President Dwight D. Eisenhower's national operations center while he recovered from a heart attack suffered at his nearby farm. The hotel has undergone extensive renovations and currently offers 119 guest rooms and suites. It is also a popular choice for wedding receptions and offers a banquet room, fitness room, restaurant, pub, rooftop swimming pool, business center, and high-speed Internet. The rooms are comfortable and charming, but not extravagant. Parking is available in a public garage just behind the hotel. The hotel is centrally located within walking distance to the battlefield, museums, shops, and restaurants. Make your last stop before bedtime the bar at One Lincoln, just off the reception area. They offer a large variety of pints and have a friendly staff, and a quick drink will help make the beds a little more comfortable.

The **James Gettys Hotel** (27 Chambersburg St., 717/337-1334, www.jamesgettyshotel.com, $170-270) offers 12 guest suites in a historic downtown hotel. This glorified bed-and-breakfast has individually decorated rooms with a sitting room, kitchenette, and private bathroom. A continental breakfast basket is provided daily. Each suite has free wireless Internet. The interior is comfortable but a bit dated, and is decorated with European touches. The staff is friendly and helpful, and the hotel is within walking distance to many attractions. There is free parking, and no extra charge for the "ghosts" that may live there.

the Gettysburg Hotel

A beautiful and interesting hotel is the **Federal Pointe Inn** (75 Springs Ave., 717/334-7800, www.federalpointeinn.com, $180-200). This elegant boutique hotel is in a historic 1897 schoolhouse in downtown Gettysburg. It has 18 guest rooms and suites with modern amenities. The rooms are tasteful yet not overstuffed and have high ceilings and granite bathrooms. The innkeepers are professional and friendly.

GETTING THERE AND AROUND

Gettysburg is about 10 miles from the Pennsylvania-Maryland border off U.S. 15. It is a 45-minute drive (35 miles) north of Frederick. Most people arrive by car, but the **Gettysburg Regional Airport (GTY),** two miles west of Gettysburg, is a general aviation airport with one runway.

Harpers Ferry, West Virginia

Harpers Ferry is a beautiful historic town at the confluence of the Shenandoah and Potomac Rivers in West Virginia. It is well known as the location of **John Brown's Raid,** when in 1859, famous abolitionist John Brown led 20 men in a raid on a national arsenal. His plan was to use the weapons in the arsenal to start a slave uprising in the South. Five of the men in the raid were African Americans (three free African Americans, one freed slave, and one fugitive). At the time, it was illegal to assist a fugitive slave, which further compounded the severity of the raid. The raid resulted in a force of 86 marines coming to the town, led by Robert E. Lee. The raiders were captured but not without casualties.

Harpers Ferry is also known for its hard times during the Civil War, when the town changed hands eight times. It also was the site of the largest surrender of Federal troops during the war when, in 1862, General Stonewall Jackson captured a 12,500-soldier Union garrison.

Harpers Ferry is also the site of **Storer College,** one of the first integrated schools in the United States. It operated from 1865 to

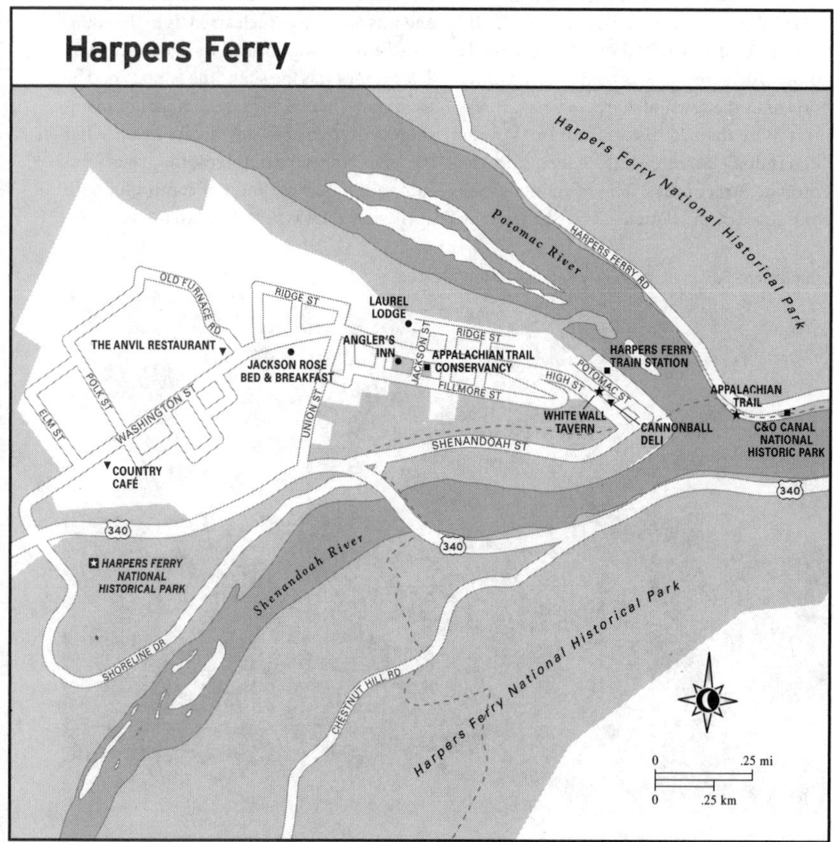

1955. The school's former campus is now part of Harpers Ferry National Historical Park.

Harpers Ferry is about a 1.5-hour drive from both Washington DC and Baltimore, Maryland. The town is known as an outdoor recreation destination and offers adventures in hiking, white-water rafting, tubing, canoeing and kayaking, mountain biking, and fishing.

Parking in the lower part of town is difficult. Strict parking restrictions were put in place to maintain the historic appearance of the town.

SIGHTS

★ Harpers Ferry National Historical Park

Harpers Ferry National Historical Park (304/535-6029, www.nps.gov/hafe, daily 9am-5pm, $10 by car, $5 on foot) is made up of 3,700 acres of parkland and the lower portion of the town of Harpers Ferry. It features more than 25 historic buildings in the Shenandoah Street, High Street, and the Potomac Street areas. The town sits at the confluence of the Potomac and Shenandoah Rivers (which makes it prone to flooding during high water).

The best way to begin exploration is to park at the **Visitors Center** (171 Shoreline Dr.), tour the center, pick up a map of the town, and then hop on a bus to the historic downtown area. It is possible to drive into the historic downtown area, but there is very limited parking since the Park Service does not allow street parking in an effort to preserve the original look of the town. There is a small parking lot at the **Harpers Ferry Train Station** on Potomac Street.

The park includes many 19th-century homes that were erected by the federal government for people working for the **Harpers Ferry National Armory.** The armory mass-produced military arms for the United States and was one of two such arsenals in the country (the other was located in Massachusetts). The armory was the site of the famous raid by abolitionist John Brown in 1859, part of an unsuccessful attempt to start a slave revolt. After the Civil War started in 1861, the armory became an important point of control for both armies since it was near the Mason-Dixon line.

John Brown's Fort in Harpers Ferry National Historical Park

Its strategic location resulted in much turmoil for Harpers Ferry, as the town changed hands numerous times during the war.

The armory site became the location of the **Harpers Ferry Train Station** in 1889 and remains as such today. **John Brown's Fort** (which was the armory's guardhouse) is the only surviving building from the Civil War. It was moved several times and now sits approximately 150 feet east of its original location (the original site is now covered by the railroad).

Victorian and federal-style homes in the town entertained well-known guests such as Woodrow Wilson, Mark Twain, and Alexander Graham Bell. General Stonewall Jackson also spent time in Harpers Ferry during the Civil War when he used the town as a command base.

There are many museums and historic landmarks in town, including a museum on **Meriwether Lewis,** who came to Harpers Ferry in 1803 to purchase weapons from the U.S. National Arsenal for his transcontinental expedition. Among the items he bought were 15 rifles, 15 powder horns, 30 bullet molds, knives, tomahawks, and repair tools. Another landmark is **White Hall Tavern** on Potomac Street. The tavern was owned by Frederick Roeder, the first civilian casualty of the Civil War in Harpers Ferry. The tavern was a drinking house for armory employees but was taken over by Northern forces after Roeder's death and used as a site for strategic planning. It was located on the south side of Potomac Street across from the original armory (now the train station).

Another historic building in the park is the **Stipes' Boarding House** (Shenandoah Street) where Cornelia Stipes took in visitors during the Civil War. Among others, she hosted military officers and one of the first war correspondents, James Taylor, who captured pieces of the war in his military sketches. Other buildings include a mill, blacksmith shop, dry goods store, and bookshop. Just outside the historic park area but still within the town of Harpers Ferry are shops and restaurants that are easily reached on foot.

The park is technically located in three states—West Virginia, Virginia, and Maryland—and is managed by the National Park Service. Harpers Ferry National Historical Park offers many opportunities for outdoor adventure including trail hiking, boating, biking, and guided ranger tours. Visitors can get a lovely view of the water gap where the Potomac and Shenandoah Rivers meet by hiking up to the spot visited by Thomas Jefferson on October 25, 1783, now called **Jefferson Rock.** From the lower part of town, make your way to High Street and the stone steps that lead up to St. Peter's Church. The steps continue past the church and turn into a steep 5-minute climb. The view is spectacular, and you will find out why Jefferson said it was "worth a voyage across the Atlantic." Much of the area is tree covered, and more than 170 bird species and 30 mammal species are found in the park.

Appalachian Trail Conservancy Headquarters and Visitors Center

Harpers Ferry is one of the few towns that the **Appalachian Trail (AT)** passes directly through. The **Appalachian Trail Conservancy Headquarters** (799 Washington St., 304/535-6331, www.appalachiantrail.org, daily 9am-5pm) is just a quarter of a mile off the trail. They offer maps, membership services, books, and other merchandise for sale. They can also answer all types of questions regarding the AT. The center is home to an enormous raised-relief map of the entire Appalachian Trail. It is one-of-a-kind and more than 10 feet long. Pictures of more than 15,000 Appalachian Trail thru-hikers and section-hikers who have passed through the town since 1979 are kept in photo albums in the headquarters building.

The **Harpers Ferry AT Visitor Center** is in the same building as the Appalachian

Following the Appalachian Trail

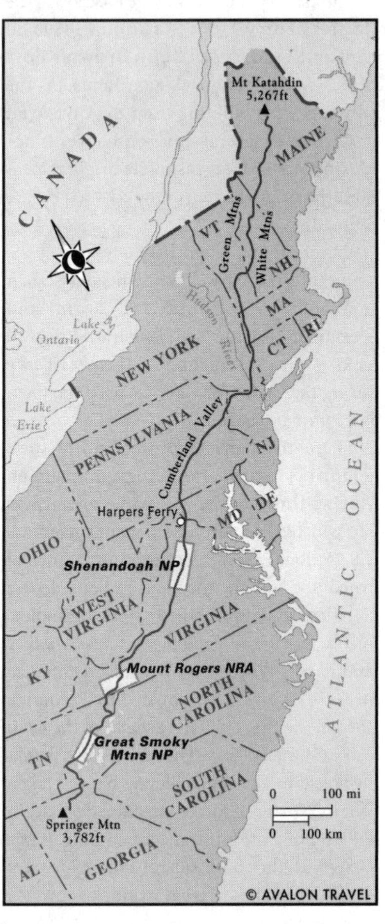

The Appalachian Trail passes through 14 states on the East Coast and is approximately 2,180 miles long. It is the longest continuously marked trail in the world. The trail's northern terminus is in Katahdin, Maine, and the southern terminus is at Springer Mountain in Georgia.

Each year, between 2 and 3 million people hike on the Appalachian Trail and more than 2,500 people attempt to hike the entire trail in one season. These people are called "thru-hikers." About 25 percent who start hiking with the intent of completing the trail in one season finish each year. For those who hike it end to end, it normally takes between five and seven months. Thru-hikers normally adopt a "trail name" or are given one by other hikers they meet along the way. The names are often funny or descriptive such as "Iron Toothpick," "Thunder Chicken," or "Mr. Optimist."

The Appalachian Trail was completed in 1937 and is part of the national park system, although it is managed by a combination of public and private entities. Although Harpers Ferry is home to the trail headquarters, only about four miles of the trail pass through West Virginia. Virginia claims the most miles along the trail at approximately 550.

There are literally hundreds of entrances to the Appalachian Trail, making it accessible to millions of people. Some people called "section-hikers" also hike the entire length of the trail, but do so in segments over several years. The total elevation gain on the Appalachian Trail equals the elevation gain of climbing Mt. Everest 16 times.

Additional information can be found on the Appalachian Trail Conservancy website at www.appalachiantrail.org.

Appalachian Trail Conservancy Headquarters and Visitor Center

Trail Conservancy headquarters and shares the same address, phone number, and hours. It offers great information on the town and is a starting point for many beautiful day hikes.

ENTERTAINMENT

For a great history lesson and a pleasant hour-long walk, join historian Rick Garland and his **Ghost Tours of Harpers Ferry** (304/725-8019, www.harpersferryghost.20m.com, $14). This is a wonderful and entertaining way to learn about the buildings in town and the stories behind them. The tour is family and dog friendly and sometimes draws a large crowd. Tours are given year-round and meet at the Piazza (front patio) of St. Peter's Catholic Church (100 Church Street).

SPORTS AND RECREATION

The **C&O Canal National Historical Park** (www.nps.gov/choh) is a great place to ride a mountain bike or hybrid bike just across the Potomac River from Harpers Ferry. Access to the park's towpath is from a walkway along the railroad bridge that crosses the Potomac River at the end of Shenandoah and Potomac Streets. Access to the **Appalachian Trail** is from the same footbridge and offers great hiking along the famous 2,180-mile trail.

If you're feeling adventurous, take a **Harpers Ferry Zip Line Canopy Tour** (408 Alstadts Hill Rd., 304/535-2663, www.harpersferryzipline.com, $99). A guide will take you high above the ground through the trees on seven zip lines ranging from 200 to 800 feet long. There are also ladders to climb and bridges to cross. Tours last three hours.

River Riders (800/326-7238, www.river-riders.com) offers white-water rafting trips on the Shenandoah and Potomac Rivers. Trips are 2-3 hours and available guided (Mar.-Nov., $79 includes picnic) or self-guided (Memorial Day-Labor Day, $54). River Riders also offers 1.5-to 2-hour flat-water tubing trips on the Shenandoah (May-Sept., $45), 1- to 3.5-hour white-water tubing trips on the Potomac River

(May-Sept., $44), full-day guided fishing trips (by boat) on the Shenandoah and Potomac Rivers (Apr.-Oct., $500 up to two people), and a "Potomac Play Pass" that allows you to canoe, kayak, stand-up paddleboard, and/or bike for 2-4 hours (Mar.-Nov., $29-39).

The **Harpers Ferry Adventure Center** (540/668-9007, www.harpersferryadventurecenter.com) is another outdoor outfitter in Harpers Ferry that offers guided white-water rafting on the Shenandoah and Potomac Rivers (Apr.-Aug., $72), flat-water tubing on the Shenandoah River (mid-April-Oct., all day $36), white-water tubing trips on the Potomac River (mid-April-Oct., $36), ropes courses, and zip line adventures.

Bike rentals are also available through **River & Trail Outfitters** (301/834-9950, www.rivertrail.com, $21 for a half day).

FOOD

A good place to grab a sandwich is the **Cannonball Deli** (148 High St., 304/535-1762, weekdays 10am-6pm, weekends 10am-8pm, under $10). They offer quick service, a pleasant staff, good food, and a nice patio. The menu has a variety of casual items such as sandwiches, gyros, and hot dogs. This is a popular stop with Appalachian Trail hikers.

If you're yearning for a mom-and-pop restaurant with a friendly atmosphere and good food, stop in the **Country Café** (1723 W. Washington St., 304/535-2327, www.country-cafe.com, Tues.-Sun. 7:30am-3pm, under $10). They serve breakfast and lunch in a cozy atmosphere and have been doing so since 1989.

The Anvil Restaurant (1290 W. Washington St., 304/535-2582, www.anvilrestaurant.com, Wed.-Sun. 11am-9pm, $7-28) is a lovely restaurant specializing in seafood with entrees such as fresh Maryland oysters, shrimp scampi, and their signature crab cakes, but they also offer sandwiches, chicken, pasta, and beef. This is a good choice for a relaxing lunch or dinner after a day outdoors. They have a beer, wine, and children's menu (not together).

ACCOMMODATIONS

An authentic experience in Harpers Ferry can be highlighted with a stay in a lovely historic inn or bed-and-breakfast.

The ★ **Laurel Lodge** (844 E. Ridge St., 304/535-2886, www.laurellodge.com, $165-195) is a charming bed-and-breakfast with a lot of character. It offers gorgeous views of the Potomac River and makes a great home base for exploring the area. There are four guest rooms (three with queen beds and one with two twins). Two have private en suite bathrooms, and the other two have private hall bathrooms. A delicious locally sourced breakfast is served each morning with a hot entrée. Little extras throughout the lodge make for an extra-comfortable stay such as locally made soap, plentiful board games, Civil War-era artifacts, and an overall tasteful décor.

The Jackson Rose Bed and Breakfast (1167 W. Washington St., 304/535-1528, www.thejacksonrose.com, $140-160) is known to have served as Stonewall Jackson's headquarters for a short time near the start of the Civil War. This beautiful bed-and-breakfast offers four nicely appointed guest rooms and welcoming innkeepers. They are also known for serving scrumptious breakfasts.

The Angler's Inn (867 W. Washington St., 304/535-1239, www.theanglersinn.com, $155-185) is another nice option in a good location on Washington Street. They offer four comfortable guest rooms with private bathrooms. Professional fishing guide services are available through the inn.

GETTING THERE

Harpers Ferry is 21 miles southwest of Frederick via U.S. Route 340 west. It is serviced by **Amtrak** (112 Potomac St., 800/872-7245, www.amtrak.com) and **Maryland Area Rail Commuter (MARC)** (410/539-5000, http://mta.maryland.gov, weekdays only). Both offer trains to the historic **Harpers Ferry Train Station** (Potomac and Shenandoah Sts.) that was originally built by the Baltimore and Ohio Railroad and dates back to 1889.

Western Maryland

Western Maryland is made up of a narrow strip of land that is sandwiched between Virginia, West Virginia and Pennsylvania. The area is rural, mountainous, and scenic. I-70 and, farther west, I-68 are the main travel routes through the region. I-68 ebbs and rolls just under the Pennsylvania border. Winter can come early in this part of the state due to its high elevation, and windy conditions often prevail. On average, the region receives about 200 inches of snow per year. Key towns to visit in Western Maryland are Sharpsburg, famous for Antietam National Battlefield; Cumberland, a historic railroad town; Frostburg, a small university town tucked in the mountains; Grantsville, originally founded as a small Amish and Mennonite settlement; and the popular vacation area of Deep Creek Lake.

SHARPSBURG

Sharpsburg is a small town about 70 miles northwest of Washington DC. It has a population of around 700 people and was founded circa 1740. It is best known as the location of the Battle of Antietam, the bloodiest single-day confrontation to ever take place on U.S. soil. Sharpsburg is the ending point on the 126-mile **Antietam Campaign Scenic Byway,** which begins in White's Ferry, Maryland. This byway follows the events of Robert E. Lee's army as they crossed the Potomac River into Maryland and then retreated back into West Virginia after the Battle of Antietam.

Sights

★ ANTIETAM NATIONAL BATTLEFIELD

The **Battle of Antietam** was the first Civil War battle held on Union ground. It was also the bloodiest battle to ever take place in a single day in U.S. history, with approximately 23,000 casualties (from both the North and the South). During the battle on September 17, 1862, the Union Army of the Potomac launched several assaults against the Confederates, who, for the first time, had invaded the North. Vicious counterattacks went back and forth between both armies in areas near Sharpsburg known as **Miller's Cornfield** and the **West Woods.** The day ended in a draw, but the Confederates were checked of any advancement into Northern territory. This tactical victory spurred Abraham Lincoln to issue the Emancipation Proclamation.

Antietam National Battlefield is a National Park Service unit that encompasses more than 3,200 acres in the foothills of the Appalachian Mountains. This park is a small treasure for historians and anyone wishing to visit a non-commercialized yet very relevant battlefield. Visitors should begin at the **Visitor Center** (5831 Dunker Church Rd., 301/432-5124, www.nps.gov/anti, daily 9am-5pm, three-day pass $5 per person and $10 per vehicle)

Antietam National Battlefield

Antietam and the Evolution of Photography

In the spring of 1861, thousands of young soldiers came to Washington DC to defend the capital. In their wake were many photographers, eager to capture camp scenes and confident young greenhorns wearing uniforms for the first time.

Photographer Alexander Gardner, who owned a studio in DC, was eager to increase his business and take advantage of the happenings around him. To that point, nobody had taken photographs on the battlefield as photography was still new, having originated in 1839. In September 1862, Gardner ventured to Antietam two times, once just two days after the battle, and the second time two weeks later when President Lincoln visited the battlefield. Gardner was the first to capture the horror of the battlefield before the dead were buried. This was merely a novelty at first, but ultimately transformed photography into an incredible medium for communication and signaled the true beginning of photojournalism.

to learn about that fated day in 1862 before heading out to the battlefield. The all-inclusive park entrance fee can also be paid there.

The visitors center offers exhibits on the battle and the Civil War, an observation room, ranger-led interpretive talks, and a museum store. A 26-minute orientation film narrated by James Earl Jones is shown every half hour.

The battlefield itself has an 8.5-mile paved road that visitors are welcome to drive, bike, or walk (a tour map can be downloaded from the park website or picked up at the visitors center). It is designed as a self-guided tour that takes approximately 1.5 hours. The route is well marked with informative signs and designated areas where you can get out of the car and tour on foot. Sights along the route include the famous Miller's Cornfield, where much of the early fighting took place; the West Woods, where 2,200 men were killed in under a half hour; and "Bloody Lane," a sunken road where 5,000 casualties occurred. A self-guided audio driving tour with 11 stops can be purchased at the Visitor Center museum shop. Private tours of the battlefield are also available through **R.C.M. History Tours** (301/491-0002, www.rcmhistorytours.com, starting at $62.50 for 2.5 hours), during which expert guides ride along with you in your car.

The battlefield features 96 monuments. Most are dedicated to Union forces since the former Confederacy was not able to pay for monuments after the war. The monuments were erected mostly by veterans of the battle to commemorate the sacrifices made by their fellow soldiers. Six generals fell during the Battle of Antietam, and each is honored at the spot where he was killed or mortally wounded by a mortuary cannon (a cannon barrel that is inverted inside a block of stone).

The battlefield park grounds are beautifully maintained and noncommercialized. It is easy to envision what happened during the battle since the site looks much the same as it did in 1862. The battlefield is open daily during daylight hours. During the summer months, frequent ranger talks are offered. A schedule is available daily in the visitors center. Allow a minimum of three hours for your visit.

ANTIETAM NATIONAL CEMETERY

A key attraction near the battlefield is the **Antietam National Cemetery** (E. Main Street, www.nps.gov, daily dawn-dusk, free). The site is maintained by Antietam National Battlefield and is part of the National Cemetery System.

After the Battle of Antietam, Sharpsburg became a sprawling hospital and burial ground. Soldiers who died during the fight were buried by the hundreds in shallow graves on property extending miles in all directions. After the end of the war, an effort was made to relocate the bodies to proper cemeteries, and the Antietam National Cemetery was formed. Due to a lack of funds from the South and hard feelings over the war in general, the cemetery became a Union cemetery and only contains the remains of Union soldiers from the Civil War (the remains of Confederate soldiers were moved to three other cemeteries in other towns). In later years the cemetery also became a site for graves of veterans and family from the Spanish-American War, World War I, World War II, and the Korean War. Like the battlefield, the cemetery is run by the National Park Service. It is 11 acres and contains more than 5,000 graves.

TOLSON'S CHAPEL

Tolson's Chapel (111 E. High St., www.tolsonschapel.org, tours available by appointment) is a historic African American church in downtown Sharpsburg. The small 1866 wooden church was a key spiritual and educational center for African Americans after the Civil War. The church no longer holds services, but local residents are working to preserve the building and its cemetery. The chapel is listed in the National Register of Historic Places. Tours can be scheduled by emailing tolsons.chapel@gmail.com.

Food

There aren't many choices for food in Sharpsburg, but **Captain Benders Tavern** (111 E. Main St., 301/432-5813, www.captainbenders.com, Mon. 4pm-midnight, Tues.-Thurs. 11am-midnight, Fri.-Sat. 11am-2am, Sun. noon-midnight, $9-29) offers a good selection of sandwiches, wraps, salads, and casual entrées. If you're up for the challenge, their "Monument Tower of Death," which includes three 8-ounce Black Angus burger patties with all the fixings (including cheese fries), is free if you eat it in 30 minutes. They also have a good bar and live music some nights. The tavern has been serving food since 1936 and is named after a C&O Canal boatman.

For a great scoop of ice cream, visit **Nutter's Ice Cream** (100 E. Main St., 301/432-5809, daily 1pm-9pm, under $5). They serve generous portions of delicious ice cream at a great price. The line can be out the door and they only take cash, but you won't be disappointed. Order a "lollipop"—it is the specialty.

Accommodations

The **Jacob Rohrbach Inn** (138 W. Main St., 301/432-5079, www.jacob-rohrbach-inn.com, $165-225) offers five beautiful guest rooms with private bathrooms. Guests are treated to a lovely multicourse breakfast, fresh-baked cookies, coffee, and beverages. The inn's garden provides many herbs, fruits, and flowers. The home was built in 1804 and is conveniently located in town near the battlefield. Gracious hosts add to the charm of this historic bed-and-breakfast.

Another choice is the **Inn at Antietam** (220 E. Main St., 301/432-6601, www.innatantietam.com, $135-195). This charming inn is next to the Antietam National Cemetery and offers five guest rooms. The rooms are comfortable but do not have televisions or Internet access. The inn serves a delightful breakfast and afternoon refreshments.

Captain Benders Tavern

the Inn at Antietam

Getting There

Sharpsburg is near the West Virginia border along Route 34. It is approximately 70 miles northwest of Washington DC and 22 miles west of Frederick.

CUMBERLAND

Cumberland is the largest city in Allegany County, with nearly 21,000 people. It was founded in 1787. Although it is the regional center for business, it is also one of the more economically challenged areas in the country based on per capita income.

Cumberland is going through a renaissance of sorts, with a focus on the revitalization of the downtown area with new stores, restaurants, and galleries. Downtown Cumberland is quaint and charming, with its trademark church steeples, pleasant cobblestoned pedestrian area on Baltimore Street, and extensive railway history. Outdoor enthusiasts will enjoy the Great Allegheny Passage trail and the C&O Canal trail and the sights at Canal Place.

Sights

CANAL PLACE

Canal Place (13 Canal St., 301/724-3655, www.canalplace.org) is a 58-acre park off Canal Street by the Western Maryland Railway Station. The park is home to the **Cumberland Visitor Center** (301/722-8226) for the **Chesapeake & Ohio Canal National Historical Park,** and marks the end of the C&O Canal Towpath. It also offers a picnic area, a replica of a canal boat, shops, and the jumping-off point to the Western Maryland Scenic Railroad. Exhibits at the visitors center explain how the canal was constructed and how cargo was transported on the canal, and also provide information on the locks and crew that kept the canal in operation.

The canal boat replica (called *The Cumberland*) is located in the Trestle Walk at Canal Place, a brick promenade that connects the train station and canal. Visitors can view the captain's cabin, the mule shed, and the hay house.

★ THE WESTERN MARYLAND SCENIC RAILROAD

Western Maryland is railroad country. Many historic railroad milestones occurred in the Cumberland area, including the use of the first iron rail made in the United States and the production of unique steam engines by the Cumberland & Pennsylvania Railroad. **The Western Maryland Scenic Railroad** (13 Canal St., 301/759-4400, www.wmsr.

The Chesapeake & Ohio Canal National Historical Park

The **Chesapeake & Ohio Canal National Historical Park** (301/722-8226, www.nps.gov/choh) is a 184.5-mile-long park covering 12,000 acres that runs parallel to the Potomac River. The park is a linear towpath (7-12 feet wide) along the old canal that extends from Cumberland, Maryland, to Georgetown in Washington DC.

The original canal was in operation between 1831 and 1924 and served many communities along the Potomac River by providing a transport system for coal, lumber, and agricultural products. The canal boats were pulled by mules that walked alongside the canal on the towpath. At one time there could be as many as 2,000 mules working on the canal (operating in six-hour shifts).

The 605-foot elevation change and many stream crossings along the canal were accommodated by 74 locks, more than 150 culverts, and 11 aqueducts. There is also a 3,118-foot tunnel—the Paw Paw Tunnel—that the canal went through.

Cumberland was not planned as the western terminus of the canal, but when the canal reached Cumberland, the project ran out of money. The end of the C&O Canal is marked in Cumberland and a statue of a mule stands nearby at the Chesapeake & Ohio Canal National Historical Park.

The park is a beautiful and popular multistate trail for biking, running, walking, and boating. It passes near several popular towns such as Harpers Ferry, West Virginia, and Sharpsburg, Maryland. Two reproduced canal boats (pulled by mules) offer historical rides in the park (301/739-4200, June-Aug. Fri.-Sun. 11am, 1:30pm, and 3pm, shorter hours rest of the year, $8).

Bike and boat rentals are available through two National Park Service partners at the downstream portion of the canal in Washington DC: **The Boathouse at Fletchers Cove** (milepost 3.2, 4940 Canal Rd. NW, Washington DC, 202/244-0461, www.fletcherscove.com, kayak $13 per hour, canoe $15 per hour, rowboat $15 per hour, bike $9 per hour) and **Thompson Boat Center** (milepost 0, 2900 Virginia Ave. NW, Washington DC, 202/333-9543, www.thompsonboatcenter.com, kayak $16.50 per hour, canoe $16.50 per hour, bike $10 per hour).

com, 11:30am departure, days vary by season, coach $40, lounge $65, first class $100) provides fun round-trip excursions from downtown Cumberland to nearby Frostburg on tracks that used to belong to the Western Maryland Railway. The trip is made by diesel locomotive and is 32 miles round-trip. The excursion takes 3.5 hours. There is a 1.5-hour stop in Frostburg where passengers can have lunch, sightsee, and watch the train rotate on a giant turntable to position itself for the return trip. This is an entertaining and educational ride through a scenic Appalachian landscape. The train even passes through the Narrows, a cut in the mountains that was considered at one time to be the gateway to the West. October is the busiest month, so make a reservation early. Dinner trips are also available (lounge $65, first class $125).

EMMANUEL PARISH OF THE EPISCOPAL CHURCH

The **Emmanuel Parish of the Episcopal Church** (16 Washington St., 301/777-3364, www.emmanuelparishofmd.org, free) is on the former site of Fort Cumberland, the place where George Washington started his military career. Earthwork tunnels built in 1755 from the original fort remain under the church and can be visited. The tunnels were created for several purposes: to keep perishable food fresh, to store gunpowder, and to provide British soldiers a safe route to reach their defenses during the French and Indian War. A hundred years later, the same tunnels were used by the Underground Railroad to harbor escaping slaves seeking safety. The gothic revival-style church was originally built in 1803, and the current structure was completed in 1851. It contains beautiful

Western Maryland Scenic Railroad

stained glass windows from three distinct periods. Services are still held regularly, and the public is welcome, as the church makes clear: "We extend a special welcome to those who are single, married, divorced, gay, filthy rich, dirt poor, yo no habla Ingles…those who are crying new-borns, skinny as a rail or could afford to lose a few pounds."

GORDON-ROBERTS HOUSE

The **Gordon-Roberts House** (218 Washington St., 301/777-8678, www.gordon-robertshouse.com, Wed.-Sat. 10am-4pm, guided tours on the hour, $7) is a three-story home offering visitors the chance to learn about life in Cumberland in the late 1800s. The second empire-style home is one of a handful in that style located in the historic district of Washington Street. The home is constructed from handmade bricks. It was owned by an upper-middle-class family and displays furnishings, textiles, art, toys, clothing, and other artifacts. The home is owned and run by the Allegany Historical Society.

Sports and Recreation

Two highly regarded trails meet in Cumberland: the **Chesapeake & Ohio Canal National Historical Park** and the **Great Allegheny Passage.** The Chesapeake & Ohio Canal National Historical Park runs 184.5 miles between Cumberland and Georgetown in Washington DC, and the Great Allegheny Passage runs 141 miles between Cumberland and Pittsburgh, Pennsylvania.

Rocky Gap State Park (12500 Pleasant Valley Rd., Flintstone, 301/722-1480, www.dnr2.maryland.gov, daily 7am- sunset, free) is seven miles northeast of Cumberland in

Great Allegheny Passage

Where the C&O Canal Towpath ends, the Great Allegheny Passage (GAP) begins. This 141-mile rail trail connects Cumberland with Pittsburgh, Pennsylvania, and is known as a great biking trail (although it is a multiuse trail and excellent for hiking also). Travelers can enjoy a fairly flat trail that meanders along rivers, through valleys, and through scenic small towns.

The Great Allegheny Passage is part of the Potomac Heritage National Scenic Trail, which is one of only eight scenic trails that is nationally designated. For additional information on the GAP, call 888/282-2453 or visit www.atatrail.org.

Allegany County. This picturesque 3,400-acre park is surrounded by mountains and has a beautiful 243-acre lake, Lake Habeeb, with white-sand beaches. The complex includes a snack bar, a ranger station, bathhouse, and a nature center. There are forested trails for hiking, mountain biking, and trail running, and the park is home to the **Rocky Gap Lodge and Golf Resort,** which features an 18-hole golf course.

Food

Ristorante Ottaviani (25 N. Centre St., 301/722-0052, www.ottavianis.com, Mon.-Sat. 5pm-10pm, Sun. 4pm-8pm, $13-38) offers top-notch Italian food in a romantic atmosphere (white tablecloths, dim lighting). This family-owned restaurant is a favorite in downtown Cumberland, despite its somewhat bland exterior. The menu is imaginative and contains recipes passed down for generations. The staff is extremely accommodating and goes out of its way on special occasions. The wine list is well planned and reasonably priced.

The **Baltimore Street Grill** (82 Baltimore St., 301/724-1711, Mon.-Sat. 11am-10pm, $11-30) is a great local place with lively conversation, friendly patrons (and staff), and good food. This is the "happening spot" in Cumberland, and in the summer the outdoor seating makes it even better. They have good pub food—think crab cakes, Cajun food, spicy wings, salads, and more.

The **M and M Bake Shop** (80 Baltimore St., 301/722-2660, Mon.-Sat. 5:30am-2pm) is an old-style bakery in downtown Cumberland. They sell all sorts of sweet delights, such as cookies, brownies, doughnuts, pies, and cakes, as well as bread. All items are made on-site.

For a good quick lunch and some local flair, stop by **Curtis Famous Weiners** (35 N. Liberty St., 301/759-9707, Mon.-Sat. 9am-9pm, under $10). This old-time hot dog shop has been a Cumberland fixture since the early 1900s. Generations of local families have memories of eating yummy hot dogs and fries and drinking root beer here. These are hands down the best hot dogs in town, and patrons have been known to drive several hours for them.

Accommodations

Several chain hotels have representation in Cumberland including the **Fairfield Inn & Suites Cumberland** (21 N. Wineow St., 301/722-0340, www.marriott.com, $156-179), which has 96 rooms in downtown Cumberland, and the **Ramada Cumberland Downtown** (100 S. George St., 301/724-8800, www.ramada.com, $92-99), which offers 130 rooms and is also downtown.

There are also a few good inns and resorts in the Cumberland area. The **Bruce House Inn** (201 Fayette St., 301/777-8181, www.brucehouseinn.com, $109-175) is one of the oldest homes in Cumberland, having been built in 1840. The house is a federal Italianate-style home with a brick exterior, high ceilings, and a pretty curved staircase. It sits on a hill with a view of the church steeples Cumberland is known for and welcomes guests with a simple but elegant charm. The inn has five guest rooms with private bathrooms. A full gourmet breakfast is served each morning, and wine and tea are offered each afternoon. The inn has modern amenities such as Internet access, but maintains an old-world charm.

The Inn on Decatur (108 Decatur St., 301/722-4887, www.theinnondecatur.net, $138) has two immaculate rooms, delicious full breakfast, and a wonderful innkeeper. This federal-style bed-and-breakfast (circa 1870) offers a relaxing atmosphere with modern amenities and a location just two blocks from the downtown pedestrian area. The knowledgeable host is also a tour operator and provides complimentary tours of Cumberland to her guests. There are no televisions in the rooms.

Rocky Gap Casino and Resort (16701 Lakeview Rd., Flintstone, 301/784-8400, www.rockygapcasino.com, $179-219) is on Lake Habeeb in **Rocky Gap State Park,** in nearby Flintstone. There are 220 guest rooms, a casino, an 18-hole golf course, a restaurant, and meeting facilities. The exterior and grounds of the lodge are lovely, and the location right in Rocky Gap State Park is hard to beat. The interior is pleasant but could use some updating. Rooms have a lake or golf course view, and there are many hiking and biking trails in the park. The lodge is a bit isolated, but extremely convenient to I-68. Drink prices at the lodge are very reasonable.

Information and Services

Additional information on Cumberland can be found at www.explorecumberland.com or by stopping by the visitors center in the **Western Maryland Railway Station** (13 Canal St., Rm. 100, 301/722-8226, daily 9am-5pm).

Getting There

Cumberland is best reached by car and is located off I-68. It is 90 miles west of Frederick (1.5-hour drive) and 138 miles from Washington DC.

FROSTBURG

Frostburg is eight miles west of Cumberland on I-68 and U.S. 40. It is a small city with a population of just under 8,000 and home to Frostburg State University. Frostburg has a small downtown area with local shops, pizza parlors, and other casual restaurants that are patronized mostly by students from the university.

Sights

★ THRASHER CARRIAGE MUSEUM

The **Thrasher Carriage Museum** (19 Depot St., 301/689-3380, www.thethrashercarriagemuseum.com, May and Sept. Fri.-Sun. 12:30pm-2:30pm, June-Aug. Thurs.-Sun. 12:30pm-2:30pm, Nov.-Dec. Sat.-Sun 12:30pm-2:30pm, closed Jan.-April, $2) is a fantastic little museum next to the railroad station on Depot Street (at the bottom of the big hill). The museum has one of the best collections of horse-powered carriages in the country (more than 50 vehicles) and features everything from milk carriages to funeral wagons. Visitors can learn from interpretive guides about carriages used for pleasure, work, and even sleighs in their renovated 19th-century warehouse. The museum offers a rare glimpse into the everyday lives of Victorian Americans and represents vehicles from all economic segments of the local community. It is a great site to visit when taking the Western Maryland Scenic Railroad.

OLD DEPOT

Across Depot Street from the carriage museum is the **Old Depot.** This historic station was built

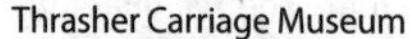

Thrasher Carriage Museum

in 1891 by the Cumberland & Pennsylvania Railroad Company, a local railway. It was originally a passenger and freight depot, but service subsided in 1942 when car travel became more popular. The station was renovated in 1989 and is now the turnaround point for the Western Maryland Scenic Railroad. A restaurant and shops are located in the depot, as is the large turntable used to turn around the steam engine for its return trip to Cumberland.

Food

The **Hen House Restaurant** (18072 National Pike, 301/689-5001, www.henhouserestaurant.com, Wed.-Fri. 5pm-9pm, Sat. noon-9pm, Sun. noon-7pm, $12-38) seven miles west of downtown Frostburg off Alternate Route 40 is known for seafood (especially crab), even though it is named after the staple of the first menu back in 1961, chicken. They are, in fact, the largest seafood restaurant in Maryland west of Frederick. The menu includes crab dip, crab cakes, blue crab ravioli, and other non-seafood items such as burgers and "damn fine chicken wings." The business has been owned and operated by the same family from the very beginning.

Good Italian food can be found just off Main Street in an old brick building. **Guiseppe's** (11 Bowery St., 301/689-2220, www.giuseppes.net, Sun. 4:30pm-9pm, Tues.-Thurs. 4:30pm-11pm, Fri.-Sat. 3pm-11pm, $11-33) serves traditional Italian dishes, a number of good house specials, and pizza. The ambience is warm and inviting, and they have a nice bar area.

Among the multiple choices for pizza in Frostburg, one place stands out. **Fat Boy's Pizza Shack** (116 E. Main St., 301/689-2727, Mon.-Sat. 11am-10pm, Sun. 11am-8pm, under $15), although unremarkable in ambience and decor, makes a great pizza. They also offer a nice pizza buffet for under $10.

Accommodations

The **Trail Inn Bed and Breakfast** (20 Depot St., 301/689-6466, www.trailinnatfrostburg.com, rooms $79-129, camping $15-25) offers basic accommodations in 12 rooms next to the Old Depot and near the Great Allegheny Passage. Queen rooms and bunk rooms are available. There is also a campground on-site. The Trail Inn is a pleasant, no-frills kind of place with reasonable prices. There is a café on-site. Downtown Frostburg is a steep hike up Depot Street (or five flights of stairs).

The ★ **Savage River Lodge** (1600 Mt. Aetna Rd., 301/689-3200, www.savageriverlodge.com, $235-280) is 10 miles from downtown Frostburg, or about a 30-minute drive.

Spruce Forest Artisan Village

Tucked into the 750-acre Savage River State Forest, the lodge is constructed of spruce and fir. Its 18 luxurious and private white pine cabins offer rustic but comfortable accommodations with upscale amenities. The beautiful lodge sits on 45 private acres and has a three-story multiuse area with 10,000 square feet of space. It also houses a library and meeting space. An on-site restaurant serves breakfast, lunch, and dinner. It has seating for 75 people and serves American cuisine. They provide a splendid, carefully selected wine list. There is a gift shop and ski shop at the lodge.

The guest cabins are stunning two-story log structures with beautifully appointed interiors. Each has a sleeping loft with a queen or king bed, a luxurious bathroom, a downstairs living area, a gas fireplace, and a kitchenette. Luxury yurts are also available for rent ($255-$280). The lodge is pet friendly.

Additional lodging in Frostburg includes the **Hampton Inn Frostburg** (11200 New Georges Creek Rd., 301/689-1998, www.hamptoninn3.hilton.com, $144-169) with 72 guest rooms and an indoor pool, and the **Days Inn Frostburg** (11100 New Georges Creek Rd., 301/689-2050, www.daysinn.com, $76-90), a pet-friendly hotel convenient to I-68.

Information and Services

For additional information on Frostburg visit www.frostburgcity.com.

GRANTSVILLE

Grantsville is a very small town in northern Garrett County with a population of less than 1,000. It is 14 miles west of Frostburg on U.S. 40. It was founded as a Mennonite and Amish settlement and was originally located in the middle of a tract of land owned by Daniel Grant (circa 1796).

Sights

★ SPRUCE FOREST ARTISAN VILLAGE

As you approach Grantsville from the east on U.S. 40, you will pass the **Spruce Forest Artisan Village** (177 Casselman Rd., 301/895-3332, www.spruceforest.org, hours vary by artisan, free). It is a half mile before Grantsville near the **Casselman Bridge** (a 354-foot-long stone arch bridge beside U.S. 40 that dates back to 1811). The artisan village was founded in 1957 and now has a dozen log and frame cabins. Many of the structures are historic and were relocated to the artisan village from other sites (some even date back to the Revolutionary War). The cabins house artist studios that sell items such as carvings, stained glass, handloom weaving products, baskets, teddy bears, and pottery. Visitors can stroll through the village and see the artists at work. This place is very cute and feels like a Bavarian village. It is worth a stop, especially when combined with a meal at the Penn Alps Restaurant.

★ SAVAGE RIVER STATE FOREST

The **Savage River State Forest** (127 Headquarters Ln., 301/895-5759, www.dnr2.maryland.gov, daily 24 hours, free day use) protects the watershed in Garrett County and encompasses more than 54,000 acres. The forest is part of the Appalachian Plateau, the western section of the Appalachian Mountains, and offers the 360-acre Savage River Reservoir, a boat launch, 100 miles of multiuse trails (hiking, biking, cross-country skiing, horseback riding, etc.), picnicking, and a shooting range ($5 permit required). Trail maps are available at the forest office.

There are 70 primitive campsites in the forest. Campers must register for their campsites within the first hour of occupancy at the Headquarters Office or at one of six self-registration sites. Pets are allowed in the forest but must be under control at all times.

There are two state parks within the boundaries of the Savage River State Forest. The 455-acre **New Germany State Park** (349 Headquarters Ln., 301/895-5453, www.dnr2.maryland.gov, daily 8am-sunset, free day use) is five miles from downtown Grantsville. It has a 13-acre lake with swimming and fishing and also offers 10 miles of multiuse trails for hiking, running, biking, and cross-country skiing. **Big Run State**

WESTERN MARYLAND

Park (10368 Savage River Rd., 301/895-5453, www.dnr2.maryland.gov, daily 8am-sunset, free day use), at the mouth of the Savage River Reservoir, also offers access to the reservoir for boating and other recreation as well as trails and picnic areas.

Food

The **Penn Alps Restaurant** (125 Casselman Rd., 301/895-5985, www.pennalps.com, Mon.-Thurs. 11am-7pm, Fri. 11am-8pm, Sat. 8am-8pm, Sun. 8am-6pm, $8-14) is next to the Spruce Forest Artisan Village, housed in the "last log hospitality house on the National Pike." It offers a variety of menu items, but is best known for its soup and salad bar and weekend buffet. They serve salads, sandwiches, and entrées with a German flair, such as roast pork and sauerkraut. There is a craft shop on-site that sells some items from the artisan village as well as from other local crafters. It is a great place to find one-of-a-kind gifts.

The **Casselman Inn** (113 E. Main St., 301/895-5055, www.thecasselman.com, Mon.-Thurs. 7am-8pm, Fri.-Sat. 7am-9pm, $8-14) has a charming restaurant serving breakfast, lunch, and dinner. The menu contains simple country food influenced by the Pennsylvania Dutch and the Amish. Sample dinner entrées include honey-dipped chicken, rib eye steak, and chopped sirloin. Homemade baked goods are prepared in the in-house bakery, and visitors are welcome to watch the bakers in action. There are two dining rooms: one in the original historic inn, and one in an addition that was built in the early 1970s. Both are cozy and comfortable.

Accommodations

The **Casselman Inn** (113 E. Main St., 301/895-5055, www.thecasselman.com, $195) is right on Alternate U.S. 40, the main road through Grantsville. Guests can be accommodated in the historic inn (which has one suite and two guest rooms, each with private bathrooms) or in the **Casselman Motor Inn** ($68-74), which is also on the property and offers 40 guest rooms.

The inn was built in the mid-1840s to serve travelers passing through the area. It is a pretty, three-story, federal-style brick home with a fireplace in each room. Many original features remain in the house today, including a stunning cherry railing on the third-floor staircase. A charming restaurant services both the inn and motel as well as visitors not lodging at the Casselman.

The **Comfort Inn** (2541 Chestnut Ridge

Casselman Inn

Rd., 301/895-5993, www.comfortinn.com, $114-139) is right off I-68. It has 96 standard, clean rooms and efficient service. Guests get a free hot breakfast with a room, and there is a fitness room and indoor pool at the hotel.

Camping

There are 70 primitive camping sites in the **Savage River State Forest** (127 Headquarters Ln., 301/895-5759, www.dnr2.maryland.gov, open all year, $10 per night). Guests can self-register for the sites at the Headquarters Office (127 Headquarters Ln.) or at one of six self-registration sites (a map is available on the website) within one hour of occupying the site. No more than six people are allowed at one site and no more than two tents or camping units (RVs, campers, etc.). No more than two vehicles are allowed at each site. Backpack camping is allowed throughout the forest. Backcountry campers must also self-register ($10 per night).

New Germany State Park (349 Headquarters Ln., 301/895-5453, www.dnr2.maryland.gov, Apr.-Oct., starting at $23.10 per night for tent sites, cabins $82-122 per night) features 63 sites total, including 11 cabins (2-8 people), as well as a bathhouse with restrooms and showers. Pets are permitted in nine sites.

Big Run State Park (10368 Savage River Rd., 301/895-5453, www.dnr2.maryland.gov, open all year) offers 29 primitive campsites ($10), two large group campsites ($56), and one pavilion for rent ($82). Each site has a picnic bench and fire ring. Leashed pets are permitted.

Information and Services

For additional information on Grantsville, visit www.visitgrantsville.com.

Getting There

Grantsville is best reached by car. It is off I-68 on U.S. 40.

DEEP CREEK LAKE

Deep Creek Lake forms the heart of Garrett County. It is 18 miles southwest of Grantsville (via Route 495) in the Appalachian Mountains and is 161 miles from Washington DC and 178 miles from Baltimore. Deep Creek Lake is a former logging and coal-mining area turned all-season vacation area, with mild summer temperatures and low humidity, and enough snowfall for winter sports.

Deep Creek Lake is a hydroelectric project that was constructed on Deep Creek in the 1920s. It was developed by the Youghiogheny Hydroelectric Company. The lake covers almost 4,000 acres and is the largest artificial lake in Maryland. In recent decades it has become *the* spot for vacation homes for many people from the busy Washington DC area.

Several small towns dot the shoreline of Deep Creek Lake, including **McHenry, Oakland,** and **Swanton.**

Sights

★ DEEP CREEK LAKE STATE PARK

Deep Creek Lake State Park (898 State Park Rd., Swanton, 301/387-5563, www.dnr2.maryland.gov, daily 8am-sunset, $5) sits along one mile of shoreline on beautiful Deep Creek Lake. It is 10 miles northeast of Oakland on the east side of the lake. It is also west of the Eastern Continental Divide and inside the Mississippi River watershed. The land was part of the historic Brant coal mine.

Wildlife is abundant in the park. Some of its residents include black bears, bobcats, white-tailed deer, wild turkeys, raccoon, skunks, red-tailed hawks, and great horned owls.

Public access is available for launching motorized and cartop boats (additional fees apply), beach swimming, fishing, canoeing, hiking, picnicking, and snowmobiling. There are trails in the park on Meadow Mountain that are open to hiking, mountain biking, horseback riding, wildlife viewing, hunting, snowmobiling, and snowshoeing. More than 100 campsites can also be reserved at the **Meadow Mountain Campground** spring through fall.

The park is home to the **Deep Creek Discovery Center** (898 State Park

Rd., Swanton, 301/387-7067, www.discoverycenterdcl.com, Memorial Day-Labor Day daily 10am-5pm, Labor Day-Memorial Day Fri.-Sun. 10am-4pm, included with park admission). The center is an interpretive resource for people of all ages and offers hands-on exhibits focusing on local flora and fauna and the area's historical heritage.

The Deep Creek Lake State Park headquarters is located at the intersection of Brant and State Park Roads.

WISP RESORT

Wisp Resort (296 Marsh Hill Rd., McHenry, 301/859-3159, www.wispresort.com, year-round) is a popular all-season recreation resort at the northern end of Deep Creek Lake. It is the only ski resort in Maryland (peak season lift tickets $29-59). They offer 34 slopes on 172 acres of terrain with an elevation of 3,115 feet. The vertical drop is 700 feet. There is night skiing on 90 percent of the slopes. Other winter activities include snowboarding, a terrain park, snowmobiling, and ice-skating.

Wisp also offers activities at all other times of the year. They have an 18-hole golf course and a partnership with a summer sports center that includes waterskiing, kayaking, wakeboarding, knee boarding, and tubing. The resort also has a canopy tour, a skate park, a paintball field, day camps, and disc golf. A mountain coaster is also available for kids of all ages. This hybrid coaster is a mix of a roller coaster and a mountain slide. It is 3,500 feet long and glides downhill for more than 350 vertical feet.

SWALLOW FALLS STATE PARK

Swallow Falls State Park (222 Herrington Ln., Oakland, 301/387-6938, www.dnr2.maryland.gov, Mar.-Oct. 8am-sunset, Nov.-Feb. 10am-sunset, $5) is a very popular recreation area a few miles west of Deep Creek Lake and nine miles northwest of Oakland. The Youghiogheny River passes along the border of the park through stunning rock gorges. The park has fantastic scenery and wonderful waterfalls, including **Muddy Creek Falls,** which is the highest waterfall in Maryland at 53 feet tall. A choice of pleasant, well-marked hiking trails can be found in the park, including a short, 1.5-mile hike that takes nature lovers past four waterfalls. Visitors can hike, mountain bike, and picnic in this gem of a park that features woods, rivers, and some of the most breathtaking scenery in Western Maryland. Camping is also available.

Sports and Recreation

Outdoor recreation is what Deep Creek Lake is all about. Bike, stand-up paddleboard, and kayak rentals are available from **High Mountain Sports** (21327 Garrett Hwy., Oakland, 301/387-4199, www.highmountainsports.com, kayaks $16 per hour, stand-up paddleboards $25 per hour, bikes $16 for two hours).

If the lake, area parks, and Wisp Resort don't satisfy your recreational itch, try participating in one of the many athletic events held in the area such as the **SavageMan Triathlon Festival** (www.savagemantriathlon.com) in September, or the **Garrett County Gran Fondo** (www.garrettcountygranfondo.org) bike ride, which comprises five rides of varying distances in June.

Those interested in horseback riding can take a trail ride at **Circle R Ranch** (4151 Sand Flat Rd., 301/387-6890, www.deepcreeklakestable.com, $25-50). They offer relaxing trail rides on well-cared-for and well-behaved horses. Trail rides are available for 30 minutes, 60 minutes, or 90 minutes. The minimum age is seven.

Food

MCHENRY

The **Mountain State Brewing Company** (6690 Sang Run Rd., McHenry, 301/387-3360, www.mountainstatebrewing.com, Mon.-Thurs. 11am-10pm, Fri.-Sat. 11am-11pm, Sun. 11am-10pm, $7-24) sits alone off Sang Run Road across from a cornfield. Don't let the drab exterior fool you—this is a fun place to eat with good food and even better brew. The rustic interior with wooden tables and chairs is the perfect setting for delicious homemade brick-oven pizza and craft-brewed beer. There are nice mountain views, and the patio is dog friendly.

DC's Bar and Restaurant (296 Marsh Hill Rd., McHenry, 800/462-9477, www.wispresort.com, breakfast daily 7am-11am, lunch daily 11am-4pm, dinner Mon.-Sat. 4pm-10pm, dinner entrées $10-28) in Wisp Resort offers a nice ambience with a cozy lodge decor and outstanding food. The menu has enough variety to please most tastes, and the food is fresh and well prepared. The breakfast menu has reasonably priced favorites such as pancakes, omelets, and eggs Benedict, and the dinner menu has salads, sandwiches, and entrées such as duck, prime rib, and pasta. The lunch menu is a modified version of the dinner menu with a focus on soups, salads, and sandwiches. Save room for dessert. They have three trays of goodies to show you, and they are as delicious as they look.

Canoe on the Run (2622 Deep Creek Dr., McHenry, 301/387-5933, Mon.-Fri. 8am-2:30pm, Sat.-Sun. 8am-3:30pm, under $10) serves breakfast, lunch, and espresso and coffee drinks. Breakfast is 8am-noon and includes sandwiches, cereal, breakfast burritos, and scones. Lunch is sandwich-oriented with wraps and original specialty sandwiches. Carryout is available.

No vacation spot is complete without a local ice-cream shop, and in Deep Creek the **Lakeside Creamery** (20282 Garrett Hwy., McHenry, 301/387-2580, www.lakesidecreamery.com, mid-Apr.-fall Sun.-Thurs. 11am-11pm, Fri.-Sat. 11am-midnight, under $10) fits the bill. This old-time ice-cream parlor makes more than 90 flavors of homemade ice cream and sherbet using milk from local dairy farmers. Arrive by car on Garrett Highway or by boat (it's about a mile south of the Route 219 bridge).

OAKLAND

The place for pizza at Deep Creek Lake is **Brenda's Pizzeria** (21311 Garrett Hwy., Oakland, 301/387-1007, www.brendaspizzeria.com, opens daily at 11am, $8-19). They are easy to find in a little shopping strip on Garrett Highway and dish out delicious and large pizzas. A great place for a group and also for kids, they offer a friendly atmosphere and tasty food made with fresh ingredients.

Good coffee and breakfast are served each morning downstairs from Brenda's Pizzeria at **Trader's Coffee House** (21311 Garrett Hwy., Oakland, 301/387-9246, www.traderscoffeehouse.com, opens daily at 7am, under $10) They have fresh baked goods and some interesting breakfast options such as a protein wrap with bananas, peanut butter, granola, and honey, as well as traditional breakfast sandwiches and waffles.

Waterfront dining can be found at the **Ace's Run Restaurant & Pub** at the **Will O' the Wisp Condominiums** (20160 Garrett Hwy., Oakland, 301/387-6688, www.acesrun.com, daily 11am-10pm, $9-27). They serve an American menu of burgers, salads, and entrées such as turkey pot pie, meat loaf, and steak. Large windows provide a view of the lake, and there is a dock for visitors coming by boat.

Accommodations

Carmel Cove Inn (105 Monastery Way, Swanton, 301/387-0067, www.carmelcoveinn.com, $175-195) in Swanton is a renovated monastery with 10 individually decorated guest rooms. This pretty little inn is lakeside on Deep Creek in a very pleasant, private setting. It is away from the main highway but close to restaurants and activities. Each guest room has a private bathroom, wireless Internet, and a flat-screen television with DirecTV and HBO. The inn provides fishing poles, canoes, inner tubes, paddleboats, mountain bikes, and snowshoes. There is also a tennis court on-site.

★ **The Lodges at Sunset Village** (23900 Garrett Hwy., McHenry, 301/387-2227, www.dclhotel.com, $229-379) provide a delightful stay in one of 20 individual log cabins for a reasonable price. The property is located close to skiing options and in the heart of the Deep Creek Lake area. There are five floor plans (for one and two levels) to choose from and all are nicely appointed with cozy yet modern log furnishings. Each cabin has free Wi-Fi, a flat-screen TV, a kitchenette, and a fireplace. Hot tub cabins are also available. The staff is very helpful and accommodating and the cabins are pet friendly.

Lake Star Lodge (2001 Deep Creek Dr., McHenry, 301/387-5596, www.lakestarlodge.com $149-299) offers 20 guest rooms and one three-bedroom suite on the north side of Deep Creek Lake in McHenry. The lodge is lakefront, and all rooms have a lake or mountain view. The lodge is near Wisp Resort and Deep Creek Lake State Park, so winter and summer activities are close at hand.

Wisp Resort (290 Marsh Hill Rd., McHenry, 301/859-3159, www.wispresort.com, $139-239) is a popular destination in the Deep Creek Lake area. It is a four-season resort with a ski area, mountain coaster (a hybrid mountain slide and roller coaster), summer adventure park, canopy tour, and golf course. The hotel offers traditional guest rooms close to the activities. Although the facility is a bit dated, it has nice amenities such as an indoor lap pool, fitness room (accessed at the far end of the pool), and a wonderful restaurant. The resort also operates a beach area at Deep Creek Lake State Park where it offers kayak rentals ($44 per day), canoe rentals ($64 per day), and paddleboard rentals ($59 per day). The staff is very friendly, and the lovely lobby is the perfect place to relax in front of the gas fireplace. The hotel is dog friendly.

The **Inn at Deep Creek Lake** (19638 Garrett Hwy., Oakland, 301/387-5534, www.innatdeepcreek.com, $194-274) has five types of spacious guest rooms with queen or king beds. The inn is right on Garrett Highway but sits back from the road for privacy. It is well maintained and has a warm and inviting decor. Rooms offer flat-screen televisions and free wireless Internet. Some rooms have fireplaces.

There are many private homes for rent in the Deep Creek Lake area. A good starting place to find the perfect rental is at www.deepcreek.com.

Camping

Camping is available in **Deep Creek Lake State Park** (898 State Park Rd., Swanton, 301/387-5563, www.dnr2.maryland.gov, spring-fall) at the **Meadow Mountain Campground.** There are 112 campsites and the complex includes heated restrooms with hot-water shower facilities. They offer primitive sites ($26.10), sites with electrical hookups ($32.10), an Adirondack-style shelter ($41.36 per night), two mini-camper cabins ($70.10 per night), and a yurt ($51.36 per night). Pets are allowed in designated sites.

Swallow Falls State Park (222 Herrington Ln., Oakland, 301/387-6938, www.dnr2.maryland.gov, mid-Apr.-mid-Dec., $21.49-32.49 per night) offers 65 wooded campsites and modern bathhouses with hot water. Each site has a fire ring, lantern post, and a picnic table. Three sites are available with electric, water, and sewer ($37.10) and there are several camper cabins ($55.10). Call 888/432-2267 for reservations. There is a two-night minimum on weekends and a three-night minimum on holiday weekends. Up to six people are allowed at one site.

Information and Services

Additional information on Deep Creek Lake can be found at www.deepcreek.com.

Getting There and Around

It is best to travel to Deep Creek Lake by car, as there is no public bus or train route to the area. Deep Creek Lake is on Route 219 (Garrett Highway). It is a three-hour drive from Baltimore and Washington DC; follow I-70 to I-68, and then take exit 14 onto Route 219 south. Follow Route 219 approximately 13 miles.

There is also no local public transportation system in the Deep Creek Lake area, so once you arrive, you will also need a car to get around.

Background

The Landscape

GEOGRAPHY

Together, Virginia and Maryland encompass more than 55,000 square miles and stretch from the Atlantic Ocean to the Appalachian Mountains.

Virginia and Maryland are divided into five geographic regions. The Atlantic coastal plain (also called the Tidewater), is the easternmost portion of both states, bounded on the west by Washington DC and Richmond. It includes salt marshes, coastal areas, the Eastern Shore, and the Atlantic beaches. The Piedmont is the low, rolling, fertile central region of both states and sits just west of the Atlantic coastal plain. It is the largest geographic region, extending from Richmond west to the Blue Ridge Mountains.

The Blue Ridge region is a narrow band that is mostly mountainous (over 1,000 feet). The highest peak in Virginia, Mount Rogers (5,729 feet), is in this region at the southernmost part of the state near the North Carolina border. West of the Blue Ridge is the Appalachian Ridge and Valley Region, which is a series of valleys divided by mountains. This region includes the Shenandoah Valley in Virginia, the Great Valley in Maryland, and a slice of the Allegheny Mountains. The far southwestern corner of Virginia and the westernmost reaches of Maryland are part of the Appalachian Plateau. This area is known for its forests, rivers, and streams. Maryland's highest peak, Backbone Mountain (3,360 feet) in Garrett County, is located in this region.

CLIMATE

Virginia and Maryland have what many residents feel is the perfect climate. There are four distinct seasons, and the weather is seldom extreme. Having said this, most of the region—eastern and central Virginia and Maryland—is considered subtropical, which is defined by hot, humid summers and mild, cool winters. The western portions of both states have a humid continental climate, which is defined by large seasonal temperature fluctuations with warm to hot summers and cold to severely cold winters.

The abundance of water to the east of both states, which includes the Atlantic Ocean, the Chesapeake Bay, and many large rivers and their tributaries, helps fuel the humidity commonly associated with the region. It's no surprise that the humidity is much higher in the coastal regions of both states, whereas the western mountain regions are typically 10 degrees cooler throughout the year and considerably less "sticky."

Springtime in Virginia and Maryland is fragrant and colorful. There are flowering fruit trees, blooming dogwoods, spring bulbs, and wildflowers throughout both states. Rivers swollen from melted winter snow rush by blankets of blooming bluebells, and azaleas explode throughout suburban neighborhoods. Temperatures in the spring can vary greatly, but overall offer comfortable warm days with chilly nights.

Summer brings ample sunshine with frequent afternoon thunderstorms. The humidity can be far more uncomfortable than the heat, but there are days, especially in August, where both seem unbearable and the air is so thick you'll think you can swim through it. The good news is, there are rarely washout days in the summer when it rains continuously, and when it does, it's a welcome break from the heat. The shore areas offer refuge during the summer as do the mountains, but

Previous: view of the Blue Ridge Mountains from Shenandoah National Park; a Civil War cannon at Manassas National Battlefield Park.

Tree Trivia

- Black walnuts give off a toxic chemical that inhibits other tree species from growing near them.
- The popular weeping willow is related to the black willow, but is native to Asia.
- Early settlers extracted the oil found in bitternut hickory nuts and used it as fuel for their oil lamps.
- Vessels in white oak wood are plugged with a substance that makes the wood watertight. This is why whiskey and wine barrels are made from the wood.
- The northern red oak is one of the most popular timber trees in the Atlantic region.

neither comes close to the comfort of modern air-conditioning.

Fall is brilliant in Virginia and Maryland. Temperatures are cool, the humidity recedes, and the landscape explodes from exhausted greens to vibrant reds and yellows. The autumn foliage is some of the best in the country, especially in the mountainous areas to the west. Peak foliage is normally in mid-October, but will vary year to year. The local news broadcasts usually keep tabs on the foliage and let people know the best days for leaf peeping. This spectacular natural display, coupled with crisp sunny days and chilly nights, make fall the best time to visit the region.

When the leaves finally fall and the pumpkins are ripe on the vine, winter is approaching. For most of Virginia and Maryland, winter temperatures usually set in sometime in December and don't thaw until early March. Even so, the area receives minimal snowfall, normally a handful of snow events each season. Although it is possible to get a large snowstorm, it does not happen every year. Likewise, temperatures can dip into the single digits, but that is not the norm. The thermometer normally rests somewhere between 25 and 40 degrees during the day in winter, but cold spells and also warm spells aren't unheard of. The exception to all of

Frederick County in Maryland

this is western Maryland, which can receive between 100 and 200 inches of snow annually and has temperatures on average of about 10 degrees cooler than the central and eastern parts of the state. Virginia's mountains can also see more snow than their neighbors in the Piedmont, but snow totals average about 25 inches a year.

ENVIRONMENTAL ISSUES

One of the biggest environmental issues in Virginia and Maryland is the health of the Chesapeake Bay. The bay faces many problems including nutrient and sediment pollution from agriculture, storm water runoff, wastewater treatment plants, and air pollution; contamination from chemicals; overharvesting; invasive species; and the effects of development on its shores and tributaries. All of these threats impact the health of the bay and its ability to maintain a viable aquatic ecosystem.

Excess nutrients are the primary pollutant in the Chesapeake Bay. They increase algae bloom growth, which blocks vital sunlight to aquatic grasses. These grasses are crucial to the bay's ecosystem since they provide food and habitat to aquatic animals, reduce erosion, and produce oxygen. In addition, when the algae die and decompose, it depletes the water of the oxygen that all aquatic animals need.

The issues facing the bay are not localized problems. The Chesapeake Bay's watershed covers 64,000 square miles through six states and DC. There are 17 million residents living in this area.

Mass media attention in recent years has led to a greater awareness of the issues facing the bay and its tributaries, but there is still a very long way to go before the problems are solved.

The **Chesapeake Bay Foundation** (www.cbf.org), headquartered in Annapolis, Maryland, is the largest conservation organization dedicated to the well-being of the Chesapeake Bay watershed. Its famous "Save the Bay" slogan defines the continued quest to protect and restore the bay's natural resources.

Another environmental issue that is common to both Virginia and Maryland is the need for healthy farming. Unsustainable farming practices have contributed to water and air pollution throughout both states and have also resulted in soil erosion, animal abuse, and poor human health. Organizations such as **Environment Virginia** (www.environmentvirginia.org) and **Environment Maryland** (www.environmentmaryland.org) are looking for ways to expand opportunities for sustainable farmers that grow food in ways that don't pollute the environment.

PLANTS

The state of Virginia published a book titled *Flora of Virginia*, which is the only existing guide to nearly 3,200 species of trees, grasses, shrubs, flowers, and cacti that currently grow in the state. This huge book (weighing nearly seven pounds) took 11 years and $1.7 million to put together. It is a testament to the wide variety of plant life that has taken root in this region over the centuries. Maryland shares much of the same flora as Virginia, although both have been cultivated since settlers first arrived.

Virginia and Maryland's central location on the East Coast allows them to boast both southern and northern flora. Visitors can see northern tree species such as spruce and fir in the western mountain areas and then drive east to visit cypress swamps in the coastal regions.

Trees

Forest covers roughly two-thirds of Virginia and one-third of Maryland. Much of the mountainous region in the western portion of both states is heavily forested and contains dozens of species of trees such as the eastern white pine (which can grow to 200 feet), Virginia pine, pond pine, eastern hemlock, and even red spruce. Forested areas can also

More Than Tasty Bivalves

Oyster lovers flock to the Chesapeake Bay region to feast on the famous eastern oyster. For more than 100 years, this delectable yet peculiar-looking creature flourished in the bay and was one of the most valuable commercial fishing commodities. However, in recent decades, overharvesting, disease, and pollution have severely reduced its numbers. This is more than just a bummer for oyster eaters; oysters are a vital piece of the Chesapeake Bay's ecosystem.

Oysters provide habitat for many aquatic animals. Their hard shells with many nooks and crannies act as much-needed reefs and are relied on by hundreds of underwater animals such as sponges, crabs, and fish. Oysters and their larvae are also an important food source for many aquatic residents and some shorebirds. In addition, oysters are filter feeders, which means they pump large amounts of water through their gills when they eat. This filters the water, removing chemical contaminants, nutrients, and sediments, which helps keep the water clean. One oyster can filter more than 50 gallons of water in a single day.

be found in the Piedmont and coastal regions of the states. In fact, the loblolly pine, which is the most important commercial timber tree in Virginia, grows near the coast in both states. Maryland is the northern reach of the loblolly pine's territory, and the same is true for the bald cypress.

Other common trees found throughout the region include the eastern red cedar, black willow, black walnut, bitternut hickory (swamp hickory), American beech, American elm, yellow poplar, sycamore, northern red oak, and white oak (which is the Maryland state tree).

Many ornamental trees are also native to the region such as holly, red maple, magnolia, and the flowering dogwood (which is both the state tree and the state flower of Virginia).

Plants, Shrubs, and Flowers

Because of the mild climate, there are many flowering shrubs and 85 species of ferns in Virginia and Maryland. Nothing announces the arrival of spring like the bright yellow blooms of the forsythia. This sprawling bush is a favorite of homeowners since it provides pretty blooms in the spring and a good screen in the summer. Several varieties of azaleas are native to the region, and in May residential neighborhoods are painted in their vibrant red, pink, purple, and white blooms. Rhododendrons are also native to the region, as are the butterfly bush (sometimes referred to as summer lilac) and the stunning hydrangea.

Spring and summer yield thousands of wildflowers across both states. Shenandoah National Park alone has 862 species, providing a breathtaking display from early spring through summer. Species include hepatica, violets, trillium, wild geraniums, mountain laurel, columbine, and wild sunflowers. In the coastal areas, wildflowers grow among marsh grasses and over sand dunes.

Although many native flowers grow quite well across both states, such as the woodland sunflower, hibiscus, lupine, lobelia, and phlox, some species are partial to either the eastern or western sides of the states since the geography is so varied between the two. At least two types of asters are found primarily in the mountain regions: the smooth blue aster and the New England aster. The American lily of the valley is also partial to the mountainous region. The coastal region has its own share of plant species that exclusively call the area home such as the New York aster and seaside goldenrod.

ANIMALS

Virginia and Maryland are full of wildlife, and their mild climate and varied geography allow for many types of animals to flourish.

large black bear at Shenandoah National Park

Since the mountainous areas are heavily forested and less populated, they are home to the most animals. Although most are shy, there are often sightings of foxes, skunks, raccoons, rabbits, chipmunks, squirrels, and white-tailed deer. In some of the park areas, the deer have become too friendly with humans and will literally walk right up to you. Under no circumstances should you feed the wildlife, no matter how cute and convincing they are. Other animals that live in the western regions include the coyote, bobcat, and black bear.

The central regions of both states (dominated by the large Piedmont region) provide shelter for many species of animals that have learned to coexist well with nearby human populations. Raccoons, opossums, squirrels, chipmunks, beaver, and more recently, coyotes, can be found throughout the region.

The coastal regions' wetlands, marshes, and rivers entice populations of lizards, muskrats, butterflies, and snakes. Animals from the Piedmont can also be found in coastal areas, but less forest means fewer places to hide from predators and the harsh summer sunshine.

There are three types of venomous snakes in Virginia and Maryland and 31 nonvenomous. The most common type of venomous snake, found across both states, is the northern copperhead, which has dark-colored cross bands shaped like an hourglass. Next comes the timber rattlesnake, which is found in all the mountainous regions of both states and in the southeastern corner of Virginia. It also has a patterned back with wavy cross bands. The eastern cottonmouth snake is only found in southeastern Virginia south of Newport News. It can be yellowish olive to black in color and has approximately 13 black cross bands that are wide at the sides and narrow at the backbone.

Birds

A huge variety of birds live in Virginia and Maryland, from migratory shorebirds to tiny songbirds—and even bald eagles. Virginia has 340 native bird species and Maryland 222, but these numbers are much greater if you include seasonal birds that do not actually nest in the states. In spring and early summer, the woods are alive with the happy calls of songbirds, but during winter, many migrate south. On the flip side, some northern birds, such as snow geese, come down from Canada because the winters are milder here.

Many hawks live throughout the region and the red-tailed variety can frequently be spotted (although they will surely see you before you see them). Another impressive and often seen bird is the turkey vulture, also known as a buzzard. They are huge and can have a wingspan up to six feet. Wild turkeys are also prevalent and look like they walked out of a children's Thanksgiving story. Game birds such as the grouse are residents of the area and sometimes startle hikers by launching themselves in the air when they see someone approach.

Migratory birds such as warblers frequent the mountain regions during the winter, and the Piedmont region offers sightings of bald eagles, pileated woodpeckers, great blue heron, cormorants, and bufflehead ducks. The coastal areas are prime for bird-watching. More than 40 types of ducks, geese, and swans alone have been documented in water-rich areas. This area is also home to osprey, oystercatchers, plovers, peregrine falcons, black skimmers, and dozens of other shorebirds.

great blue heron at Chincoteague

History

IN THE BEGINNING

It is believed that the first humans arrived in the Virginia and Maryland region approximately 18,000 years ago. They were hunter-gatherers most likely organized into seminomadic bands. As time went on, hunting tools became more efficient, and delicacies from the Chesapeake Bay such as oysters became an important food source. With new developments came the first Native American villages and the formation of social structures. Successive Native American cultures continued for thousands of years prior to the arrival of Europeans.

THE COLONIAL PERIOD

After many failed attempts at establishing a permanent settlement, in 1607 the first English settlers arrived at the mouth of the Chesapeake Bay in three ships and traveled 30 miles up the James River under the guidance of Captain John Smith. The settlers disembarked and promptly began to build a settlement at what later became Jamestown.

They found the coastal area inhabited by Algonquian natives (called the Powhatan Confederacy) who controlled land stretching from what is now North Carolina to the Potomac River. These native settlements included approximately 10,000 people who relied on hunting, fishing, and farming for survival. Another native group controlled what is now Maryland and the mountain regions of both states stretching west into the Allegheny Mountains.

The settlers were met with rich lands, many game animals, and initially friendly natives. Even so, they were not prepared for the physical labor and inevitable problems that came with starting a new settlement, and the colony nearly failed in the first few years. Around 1612, a colonist named John Rolfe brought in the first tobacco seeds, which he had gathered from an earlier voyage to Trinidad. The first tobacco crops were planted and were soon in high demand back in England. This provided an instant boost to the New World's economy.

Put mildly, life was very difficult for the early settlers. Disease, famine, and attacks from Native Americans wiped out much of the early population. Although the Native Americans were initially friendly, it didn't take long for their feelings to change when they realized the settlers intended to stay permanently. In just a couple of years, most of the Native American settlements had been seized, and it became unsafe for the settlers to venture past their settlement fences. A temporary truce resulted in 1614 from the marriage of the 13-year-old daughter of Chief Powhatan, named Pocahontas (who had earlier saved Captain John Smith's life when her father tried to kill him), to John Rolfe. The truce ended quickly with a surprise Powhatan attack that killed 400 settlers.

Meanwhile, in 1609, an Englishman named Henry Hudson arrived in the Delaware Bay. Working on behalf of the Dutch West India Company, Hudson was pleased with the wonderful conditions he found in the region. As a result, in 1631, a group of Dutch West India traders established a small whaling port and tobacco-growing center in what is now Lewes, Delaware. At the same time, Maryland's first European settler, William Claiborne, came to that region and established a fur-trading post on Kent Island.

In 1632, Charles I of England granted approximately 12 million acres north of the Potomac River and Virginia to Cecilius Calvert, second Baron Baltimore. The area was substantially larger than today's Maryland, and Maryland later lost some of the land to Pennsylvania. The first full settlement was established in 1634 on St. Clement's Island.

Maryland was established as a refuge for religious freedom for Catholics, although many Protestants moved there also. This caused religious feuds for years in the colony. At the same time, its economy relied on tobacco fueled by African slave labor and indentured servants. Farming, tobacco, and the abundance of land slowly brought prosperity to the early colonies.

As land along the coast filled up, pioneers began to move farther inland toward the mountains. New immigrants continued to arrive, including people from places such as Germany and Scotland.

In 1649 a settlement called Providence was founded on the north shore of the Severn River and was later moved to a more protected harbor on the south shore. It was then called Town at Proctor's, which changed to Town at the Severn, and later Anne Arundel's Towne. The city became very wealthy as a slave trade center. In 1694, the town became the capital of

Colonial Williamsburg

the royal colony and was renamed Annapolis for the future queen of Great Britain, Princess Anne of Denmark and Norway. Annapolis was incorporated in 1708 and flourished until the Revolutionary War.

By the early 1700s, many colonists in Virginia were enjoying generous fortunes earned through growing tobacco. The Church of England was the official church in Virginia, which differentiated it from Maryland and the New England colonies. But the church became a secondary interest since there was a short supply of clergy and houses of worship. In 1705, Virginia's capital was moved from Jamestown to nearby Williamsburg.

Virginia and Maryland were regions of large plantations and minimal urban development. Since much of the plantation labor was supplied by indentured servants, few women came to the area. This, combined with a high rate of disease, made for the slow growth of the local population.

By 1700, most Native Americans had been driven out of Virginia and Maryland. At the same time, the number of African slaves had grown rapidly in the region as the number of indentured servants declined. Throughout the first half the century, tensions between the colonies and their European motherland grew as England tried to squeeze as much money as possible out of the colonists through taxes while extending them far fewer rights than held by those living in the home country. One of the final straws came in 1763 with the passing of a law prohibiting westward expansion of the colonies, which angered many colonists. A passionate and heated speech delivered by Patrick Henry in Williamsburg in 1765 implied publicly that the colonies might be better off without King George III. Tension between England and the colonies continued to grow, and rebellious outbreaks such as the Boston Tea Party in 1773 began to grow more frequent. Maryland had its own tea party in Chestertown in 1774, when colonists burned the tea-carrying ship *Geddes* in the town's harbor.

In 1775 Henry delivered his famous speech at St. John's Church in Richmond where he was quoted as saying, "I know not what course others may take; but as for me, give me liberty or give me death."

THE REVOLUTIONARY WAR

Although no major Revolutionary War battles were fought in Maryland, it was the first colony to adopt a state constitution. Virginia became a primary center of war activity since it was the largest and most populated colony. Virginia experienced fighting from the earliest days of the war, although it managed to escape much of the destruction for the first three years. Virginia's capital was moved to a safer location at Richmond in 1780 after British ships sailed into the Hampton Roads area, and the capital has remained there ever since.

Major Virginia confrontations included the Battle of Great Bridge, where British authorities were removed from the colony, and the Yorktown Campaign. The Yorktown Campaign moved through Petersburg when British forces landed along the James River in 1781 in order to support Lord Cornwallis's army based in North Carolina. Twenty-five hundred British troops moved against Petersburg, and a clash with 1,200 militia occurred in what is now the neighborhood of Blanford.

The most well-known battle took place in Yorktown where 18,000 members of the Continental and French armies defeated British forces, causing their surrender in 1781. This battle was the final victory that secured America's independence.

EXPANSION

In 1788, Virginia became the 10th state in the new nation. One year later, Virginia-born George Washington became the first U.S. president. Many of the country's founding fathers came from Virginia, including Thomas Jefferson, James Madison, and George Mason. At the time, the state was home to 20 percent of the country's population and more than

30 percent of its commerce. A new law that enabled owners to free their slaves was also passed, and by 1790, there were more than 12,000 free African Americans in Virginia.

The city of Baltimore incorporated in 1797 and experienced rapid growth as a shipbuilding and industrial center. By 1800, its population outnumbered that of Boston, and the development of Maryland's resources became a priority. Virginia fell behind in this aspect of development, and the port in Hampton Roads paled in comparison to that in Baltimore.

Baltimore was spared seizure during the War of 1812, but suffered a 25-hour attack at Fort McHenry (during which Francis Scott Key wrote "The Star-Spangled Banner"). British troops went on to burn the young capital city of Washington DC.

After the war, steam locomotives and clipper ships were developed, greatly expanding trade possibilities. A series of canals was built, including the Chesapeake & Ohio Canal along the Potomac River, and railroads such as the Baltimore & Ohio Railroad were constructed. This greatly increased access between East Coast ports and land west of the Appalachians. By the mid-1800s, railroad lines ran through both Virginia and Maryland, bringing wealth and prosperity to many agricultural-based businesses, although it was not until after the Civil War that railroads connected all primary population centers in Virginia.

THE AMERICAN CIVIL WAR

Thomas Jefferson predicted a conflict regarding the issue of slavery. He felt that "God is just: that his justice cannot sleep forever" and a change in the current situation was very possible. Soon, calls for emancipation spread through the North, and scattered revolts against slavery gained momentum. In 1859, a raid on the federal arsenal in Harpers Ferry led by an American abolitionist named John Brown resulted in the death of 21 people—both free African Americans and whites—and the realization by the country that slavery opponents were willing to kill and die themselves for their cause.

In 1860, Abraham Lincoln was elected president and pledged to keep slavery out of the territories. In December that same year, South Carolina seceded from the Union and was followed shortly thereafter by Mississippi, Alabama, Georgia, Florida, Louisiana, and Texas.

Although technically still a slave state in

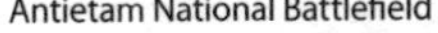
Antietam National Battlefield

1860, Maryland was one of the border states that stayed with the Union during the Civil War, but Maryland soldiers fought on both sides. Virginia, however, joined its southern neighbors and seceded from the nation in 1861, after which it became a prominent Confederate state.

Four years of bloody fighting took place on soil passionately defended less than a century before in the Revolutionary War. More than 600,000 Americans lost their lives in the war, more than those lost in both World Wars combined. Virginia suffered more casualties and witnessed more major battles than any other state. In just four years, the state was left in ruins. Some of the major battles fought in Virginia include the First and Second Battles of Bull Run (Manassas), Battle of the Ironclads, Seven Days' Battles, Battle of Fredericksburg, and Battle of Chancellorsville. Maryland also hosted several well-known battles, including the famous Battle of Antietam, the Battle of South Mountain, and the Battle of the Monocacy.

Richmond was burned on April 3, 1865. Six days later, General Robert E. Lee asked General Ulysses S. Grant for a meeting. Terms of the surrender were drafted and signed at Appomattox Court House, and the Confederate army turned over arms in a formal ceremony on April 12.

MODERN TIMES

The 1900s brought a diversification of industry to both Virginia and Maryland. Baltimore suffered a devastating fire in 1904, but recovered quickly. World War I gave a boost to Maryland by increasing the demand for industrial products, while Virginia benefited from enormous expansion to the Newport News shipyard. The Great Depression slowed growth in some markets, but overall, both Virginia and Maryland fared well through that difficult time.

By the middle of the 20th century, Virginia had evolved from a rural state into an urban one. World War II had again given a boost to the Hampton Roads area in support of the Norfolk Naval Base and shipyard. In contrast, as American industry diminished, Maryland turned to agriculture and U.S. government-related research and services.

RECENT HISTORY

In recent decades, the Washington DC area has experienced an economic and technological boom, resulting in an increase in population, housing, and jobs in both Northern Virginia and the capital region of Maryland. By the early 1990s, Virginia had a population of more than 6 million while Maryland had 4.7 million.

The early part of the new millennium was scarred for both states by the terrorist attacks on 9/11 and by the sniper shootings in the DC area in 2002 that left 10 people dead. A resilient community that was actually united by these events, Maryland and Virginia are today more closely bound as the two states face common issues such as rapid suburban development, economic downturns, and environmental preservation.

Government and Economy

VIRGINIA GOVERNMENT

Virginia is traditionally a conservative state. It is governed by the Constitution of Virginia, which was adopted in 1971 and is the seventh constitution. There are three branches of government in Virginia: the legislative, executive, and judicial branches. The executive branch has three elected officials: the governor, lieutenant governor, and attorney general, which are elected individually statewide to four-year terms.

Virginia's governor is the chief executive officer of the Commonwealth and the commander in chief of the state militia. Governors can serve multiple terms, but they must be nonconsecutive. The lieutenant governor is the president of the Senate of Virginia and first in the line of succession to the governor. A lieutenant governor can run for reelection. The attorney general is second in line of succession to the governor and the chief legal advisor to both the governor and the General Assembly. He or she is also the chief lawyer of the state and heads the Department of Law.

The legislative branch in Virginia is the General Assembly made up of 40 senators (serving four-year terms) and 100 delegates (serving two-year terms). The General Assembly claims to be the "oldest continuous law-making body in the New World" and traces its roots back to the House of Burgesses in Jamestown.

The Virginia judiciary is made up of the Supreme Court of Virginia and subordinate courts such as the Court of Appeals, the Circuit Courts, and the General District Courts. The judiciary is led by the chief justice of the Supreme Court, the Judicial Council, the Committee on District Courts, and Judicial Conferences.

Thomas Jefferson designed the State Capitol Building in Richmond, and Governor Patrick Henry laid the cornerstone in 1785.

MARYLAND GOVERNMENT

Maryland is traditionally a liberal state. Like Virginia, Maryland has a state constitution and three branches of government. Maryland is unique in the sense that it allows each of its counties to have significant autonomy.

There are five principal executive branch officers in Maryland: the governor, lieutenant governor, attorney general, comptroller, and treasurer. With the exception of the treasurer, all are elected statewide, with the governor and lieutenant governor running on one ticket. The treasurer is elected by both houses of the General Assembly on a joint ballot.

The legislative branch is a General Assembly made up of two houses with 47 senators and 141 delegates. Members of both houses are elected to four-year terms. Each house establishes its own rules of conduct and elects its own officers.

Maryland's judiciary branch consists of four courts. Two are trial courts (the District Court and Circuit Courts), and two are Appellate Courts (the Court of Special Appeals and the Court of Appeals). The Court of Appeals is the highest court.

VIRGINIA'S ECONOMY

Virginia is traditionally a wealthy state and typically has the most counties and independent cities in the top 100 wealthiest jurisdictions in the country. Perhaps the wealthiest southern state prior to the Civil War, Virginia recovered quickly from its Civil War scars and also weathered the Great Depression much better than the rest of the South. Much of the wealth is concentrated in the northern part of the state near Washington DC, where housing prices are sky-high. Loudoun and Fairfax Counties have two of the highest median household incomes out of all the counties in the nation. Virginia is one of 24 right-to-work states where union security agreements are prohibited.

Virginia's economy includes a balance of income from federal government-supported jobs, technology industries, military installations, and agriculture. The military plays a prominent role in the state's financial picture with facilities such as the Pentagon in Arlington, Marine Corps Base Quantico, and the privately owned Northrop Grumman shipyard in Newport News.

High-tech firms and government contractors have replaced dairy farms and now dominate Northern Virginia, which is home to seven Fortune 500 companies. Richmond has an additional nine, which puts it in the top six metro areas for bragging rights to the most Fortune 500 companies.

Although modern farming techniques have put many small farmers out of business and sent them to metropolitan areas in search of new careers, agriculture still plays a role in much of the state with crops such as tobacco, sweet potatoes, peanuts, tomatoes, apples, grains, hay, and soy. True to its roots, Virginia is still the fifth-largest tobacco producer in the country. Livestock is also a thriving commodity, and cattle fields can be seen along much of I-81 in the western part of the state. Despite the natural resources of the Chesapeake Bay, Virginia makes only a small portion of its revenue from the fishing industry.

The number of wineries is on the rise in Virginia with acres of vineyards in the Northern Neck, Charlottesville, and near the Blue Ridge Mountains. Predictions are that in decades to come, Virginia will rise through the ranks of the great wine-producing states.

MARYLAND'S ECONOMY

Maryland is a small but wealthy state whose economy has traditionally been heavily weighted toward manufacturing. Two Maryland counties, Howard and Montgomery, are consistently listed in the nation's top 10 richest counties.

In recent years, Maryland's economic activity has included a strong focus on the tertiary service sector, which is largely influenced by its proximity to Washington DC. Technical administration for the defense and aerospace industry and bioresearch laboratories is also key in its economy. In addition, many government agencies have satellite headquarters in Maryland for which they need staffing.

Transportation is another major revenue

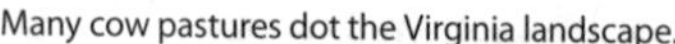

Many cow pastures dot the Virginia landscape.

maker for Maryland, thanks to the Port of Baltimore. The port is the second-largest automobile port in the country, but also accommodates a large variety of other goods including bulk commodities such as petroleum, sugar, iron ore, and fertilizers. These goods are distributed on land in trucks and by rail, further adding to the transportation influence.

A third major contributor to the state's economy is educational and medical research. Several key institutions are located in the state, the largest being Johns Hopkins University. Johns Hopkins is currently the largest single employer in the Baltimore area.

Maryland is also known for its food production thanks mostly to commercial fishing in the Chesapeake Bay and offshore in the Atlantic Ocean. Prime catches include blue crab, striped bass, menhaden, and oysters. Dairy farming in the Piedmont region also contributes to the economy.

People and Culture

PEOPLE AND CULTURE IN VIRGINIA

Traditionally, the people in Virginia were hardworking farmers, political pioneers, and sailors. The early colonists came mostly from rural England but were soon joined by French, Irish, German, and Scots-Irish who immigrated from abroad and also came to the Shenandoah Valley through Pennsylvania and Maryland. African Americans were a large part of early culture in Virginia; many initially arrived as indentured servants, followed by larger numbers through the African slave trade. Native American populations were devastated by European disease to the point that just a very small population survived to see modern times.

Today Virginia is largely diversified with 85 percent of its residents living in metropolitan areas. Northern Virginia especially is a highly transient area with residents from all over the globe. Many households speak a language other than English at home, and many fabulous restaurants serving authentic international cuisine can be found. Race relations are generally better in Virginia than in most southern states, although this is not apparent in every area.

African Americans make up the largest minority in Virginia, totaling nearly 20 percent. The African American population is heavily concentrated in the eastern portion of the state with the largest populations being in Richmond and Norfolk. Second is the Hispanic population, which comprises approximately 8 percent of the population (located primarily in Northern Virginia), followed by an Asian population of approximately 6 percent (also primarily in Northern Virginia).

Many parts of southern and western Virginia embrace the culture of the southern United States. It is there you can find authentic southern cuisine and Virginia-specific food such as Virginia ham (country ham produced in Virginia), Virginia barbecue (pork with a vinegar-based sauce, similar to North Carolina barbecue), marble cake, shoofly pie, Brunswick stew, and peanut soup.

The first colonists came to Virginia motivated primarily by material wealth rather than religious freedom. This is not to say that the colonists weren't religious; they just assumed religion and government went together and that the Anglican Church would be the designated church. There was some rivalry between Virginia and Catholic-established Maryland, although to attract settlers, the Anglicans of Virginia were flexible to newcomers. As such, they encouraged groups such as the Pennsylvania Dutch to move south into the Shenandoah Valley in part so they could alert eastern settlements of attacks by the French or

Native Americans coming from bases in the Ohio River Valley. To this day, the German Mennonite heritage is still evident west of the Blue Ridge.

Thomas Jefferson and James Madison led first Virginia and then the nation to end government involvement in religion. This spread tolerance of religious freedom throughout the state and resulted in a permanent acceptance throughout the Commonwealth of various forms of religion and the option to follow no religion at all.

It's almost impossible to summarize the attitudes of Virginians across the board because the state is so diverse. But in the smaller towns and rural areas, everyone waves, people ask strangers for directions, and you might get slipped a free piece of apple pie at a local diner for no apparent reason. Many areas in Virginia still offer a secure sense of community, although in some cities crime is unfortunately an issue.

PEOPLE AND CULTURE IN MARYLAND

Historically, Marylanders were fishers and farmers. Although southern and western Maryland are still mostly rural, the rest of the state is now primarily urban with dense populations, especially in Baltimore and near Washington DC. This makes for a unique blend of both southern and northern American culture and a melding of ideals from both regions.

Unlike Virginia, Maryland was founded as a place for Roman Catholics to escape religious persecution since the Catholic religion was repressed in England following the founding of the Anglican Church. The Catholic faith is still the most prevalent in Maryland, although it only makes up approximately 15 percent of the population.

During colonial times, groups of Quakers moved into Maryland from Pennsylvania, and in the mid-17th century a group of conservative Protestants called Puritans settled south of Baltimore. Although Puritans are not defined as such today, another conservative Protestant group, the Old Order Amish, is still strong in some areas of southern Maryland and the Eastern Shore. Their horse-drawn wagons can be seen on many roads throughout those areas.

Other religions quickly made their way into Maryland with the first Lutheran church being built around 1729 and the first Baptist church in 1742. Methodists came to the state as well, and a large Jewish population settled in Baltimore in the early part of the 1800s.

Today Maryland is widely accepting of religious diversity, and people from all faiths (and of no faith) can be found within its borders.

Maryland has always had a large African American population. During the time of slavery, Maryland had the largest population of free African Americans of the northeastern slave states. Today, African Americans make up 30 percent of Maryland's population.

Unfortunately, race relations have traditionally been strained in Maryland, and many neighborhoods are strictly delineated by race. Baltimore is the most diverse area of the state, while western Maryland (Garrett County) is the least.

THE ARTS

Virginia and Maryland offer numerous opportunities for residents and visitors to not only enjoy the arts but to become part of them. In fact, the arts are an important part of many people's lives in this region, whether they realize it or not. Access to top-rated performances, historic architecture, quality handicrafts, and literature is often taken for granted by the people who live here. A recent survey in Maryland, for instance, showed that 90 percent of the state's residents engaged in art in some form or another over the past year, whether by attending a musical performance, taking part in a festival, or visiting a museum or gallery. A stunning

84 percent said they create art in some form or another themselves. Another example is the **Virginians for the Arts** organization, which lists more than 4,500 state organizations and individual advocates for the arts in Virginia alone.

These states' long histories, diversified populations, proximity to the nation's capital, and relative tolerance for religious and social beliefs open the region to many traditional and forward-thinking expressions of art, which in turn, has created a thriving artistic community open to everyone who passes through the area.

Countless theatrical venues throughout the region, including world-renowned venues in Washington DC, invite the highest-quality performances to the doorstep of many local communities, and specialized venues provide access to cutting-edge artistic advances.

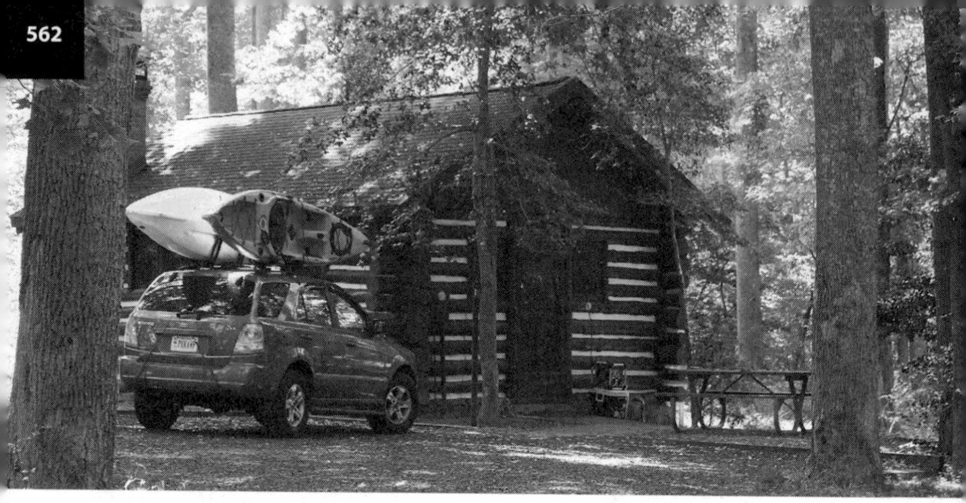

Essentials

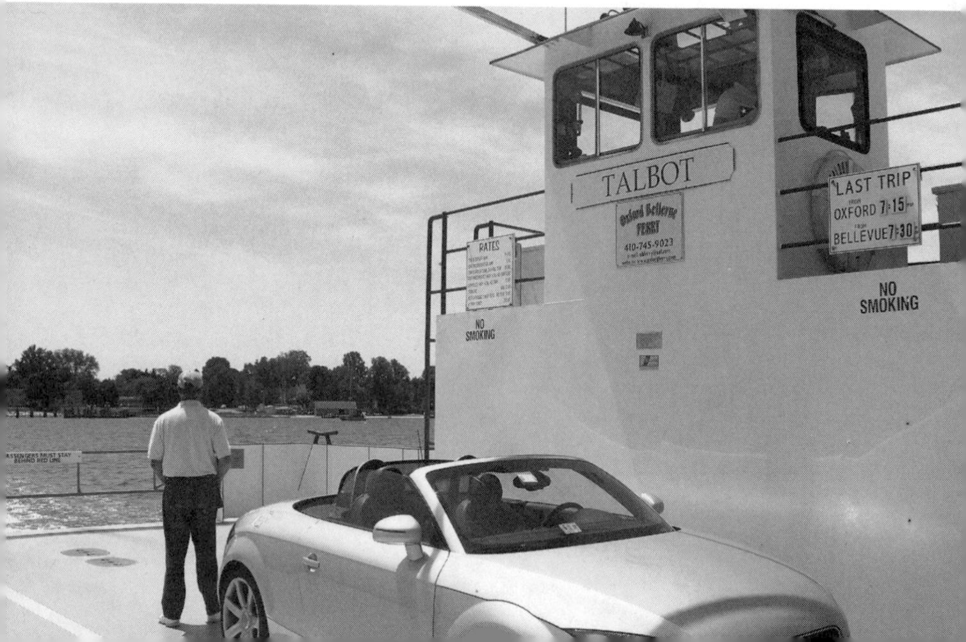
TALBOT
LAST TRIP
OXFORD 7:15
BELLEVUE 7:30
RATES
410-745-9023
NO SMOKING
NO SMOKING

Transportation

Due in part to their proximity to Washington DC, Virginia and Maryland are easily accessible from many parts of the United States and from other countries.

AIR

Most major airlines serve the three primary airports in Virginia and Maryland. The first is **Ronald Reagan Washington National Airport (DCA)** (703/417-8000, www.metwashairports.com), just outside Washington DC in Arlington, Virginia. It is a 15-minute drive from the airport to downtown Washington DC. The airport is serviced by the Blue and Yellow Metrorail lines. Taxi service is available at the arrivals curb outside the baggage claim area of each terminal. Rental cars are available on the first floor in parking garage A. A shuttle to the rental car counter is available outside each baggage claim area.

The second is **Washington Dulles International Airport (IAD)** (703/572-2700, www.metwashairports.com), 27 miles west of Washington DC in Dulles, Virginia. It is a 35-minute drive to downtown Washington DC from Dulles. Bus service between Dulles Airport and Metrorail at the Wiehle Avenue Station in Reston (Silver Line) is available through **Washington Flyer Coach Service** (888/927-4359, www.flydulles.com, $5 one way). Tickets can be purchased at the ticket counter in the Main Terminal at Arrivals Door #4 or at the Metrorail station at Wiehle Avenue. Buses depart approximately every 30 minutes. Passengers going from the Wiehle Avenue Metrorail station should follow signs for the Washington Flyer bus stop. Tickets can be purchased from the bus driver. At the time of publication, **Metrobus** (202/637-7000, www.wmata.com) operates an express bus (Route 5A) between Dulles Airport and the L'Enfant Plaza Metrorail station in Washington DC. Passengers can board the bus at the airport at the Ground Transportation Curb (on the Arrivals level) at curb location 2E. Metrobus has proposed the elimination of this route several times since the opening of the Metrorail Silver line, so check their website before relying on this route.

The third is **Baltimore Washington International Thurgood Marshall Airport (BWI)** (410/859-7040, www.bwiairport.com), 32 miles from Washington DC near Baltimore, Maryland. It is approximately 50 minutes by car from BWI to Washington DC and 15 minutes to downtown Baltimore. BWI is serviced on weekdays by MARC commuter trains at the BWI Marshall Rail Station. Free shuttles are available from the station to the airport terminal. Shuttle stops can be found on the lower-level terminal road. Metrobus service is available between BWI and the Greenbelt Metrorail station (Green Line) on the **BWI Express Metro.** Bus service is available seven days a week with buses running every 40 minutes.

The **Washington Dulles Taxi and Sedan** (703/554-3509, www.washingtondullestaxisedan.com) provides taxi and sedan service for passengers at all three airports. Shuttle service is also available from all three airports through **SuperShuttle** (800/258-3826, www.supershuttle.com).

The **BayRunner Shuttle** (www.bayrunnershuttle.com) provides daily, scheduled shuttle service between the Eastern Shore of Maryland and BWI and Western Maryland and BWI. Areas serviced on the Eastern Shore include Kent Island, Cambridge, Easton, and Ocean City. Areas serviced in Western

Previous: Westmoreland State Park; the Oxford-Bellevue Ferry

Maryland include Frederick, Cumberland, Frostburg, and Grantsville. Shuttle service is also available to the Baltimore Bus Terminal.

There are also major airports near Richmond, Norfolk, Newport News/Williamsburg, Charlottesville, and Roanoke in Virginia and near Salisbury and Hagerstown in Maryland.

Flying between locations in Virginia and Maryland is possible, but usually is cost-prohibitive and less convenient compared to other travel options.

CAR

Virginia and Maryland, like most regions of the United States, are easiest to explore by car. The two states together encompass a large amount of land. It can take six hours to drive from Washington DC to the southern end of Virginia and nearly four hours to drive from Western Maryland to the Eastern Shore. Thankfully, a large network of interstate highways provides access throughout the entire area, even in the more rural areas on the western sides of the states.

I-95 is the main north-south travel route along the East Coast and connects Baltimore, Washington DC, and Richmond. This highway is a toll road in Maryland. I-81 is the main north-south travel route in the western portions of the states and connects Roanoke, Harrisonburg, and Winchester in Virginia and cuts through a narrow portion of Maryland at Hagerstown before continuing into Pennsylvania.

In Virginia, I-66 is a primary east-west route in the northern part of the state, starting at the Washington DC border in Arlington and ending past Front Royal at I-81. I-66 has High Occupancy Vehicle (HOV) restrictions during rush hour on weekdays. The other primary east-west route is I-64, which connects Norfolk, Richmond, and Charlottesville, and ends near Staunton at I-81.

In Maryland, I-70 is the primary east-west route and links Baltimore to Frederick and runs out to Western Maryland before swinging north into Pennsylvania, at which point I-68 becomes the primary highway running east-west in the western corner of the state. I-270 is another primary route that runs north-south between Bethesda and Frederick. U.S. 50 is the major route through the Eastern Shore in Maryland. It starts in Ocean City, runs west to Salisbury, then turns north to Cambridge, across the Bay Bridge (where there is a toll), past Annapolis, and continues west into Washington DC. It then continues into Virginia as a minor route.

Washington DC is circled by I-495, also called the Beltway, which runs through both Virginia and Maryland as part of I-95. This massive highway has access points to many of the Virginia and Maryland suburbs and can have extreme rush hour traffic. Baltimore has a similar beltway, I-695, which is not part of I-95 but has a toll at Key Bridge.

Speed limits are posted throughout Virginia and Maryland. The maximum allowable speed limit in Virginia is 70 miles per hour, while in Maryland it is 65 miles per hour, although most roads in both states have speed limits posted much below their maximums. Keep in mind that state-maintained roads can have both a name and a route number.

In Virginia, all drivers are banned by law from text messaging, and drivers under the age of 18 are prohibited from using cell phones and text messaging. In Maryland, text messaging and handheld cell phone usage are banned for all drivers. Drivers under 18 are prohibited from all cell phone use. Seatbelt laws are enforced throughout both states.

The Washington area is not known for its efficiency at clearing snow off the roads in winter, but for the most part, state-maintained roads are plowed fairly quickly. The biggest hazard in both states is ice, specifically black ice, especially when above-freezing temperatures during the day melt ice and snow and then below-freezing temperatures at night cause a refreeze. Fog can sometimes be an issue when driving in the mountains, especially along Skyline Drive and in Western Maryland.

Both states' departments of transportation are good resources for maps, toll rates, webcams, road conditions, and details on HOV

driving in Shenandoah National Park

restrictions. Visit www.virginiadot.org and www.mdot.maryland.gov.

TRAIN

Amtrak (800/872-7245, www.amtrak.com) offers rail service to 20 stations in Virginia and eight stations in Maryland. There is also one station in Washington DC—Union Station. Although a train ticket can rival the cost of airfare, it can also be more convenient and more comfortable to travel by train.

Amtrak connects to the **Virginia Railway Express (VRE)** (703/684-1001, www.vre.org) in Virginia. VRE runs commuter train service between the Northern Virginia suburbs along the I-66 and I-95 corridors, to Alexandria, Crystal City, and Washington DC. They have 18 stations and 16 trains. Amtrak also connects to the **Maryland Area Rail Commuter (MARC)** (410/539-5000, www.mta.maryland.gov) train in Maryland. MARC operates on weekdays only and provides service to areas such as Harford County, Baltimore, Brunswick, Frederick, and Washington DC.

BUS

Many cities in Virginia and Maryland can be reached by **Greyhound** (800/231-2222, www.greyhound.com). Tickets are less expensive when purchased in advance and often discounts are available to students, seniors, and military personnel.

Local bus service is available in many cities, with the most extensive being the **Metrobus** (202/637-7000, www.wmata.com/bus) service in and around Washington DC and its suburbs. Metrobus has an incredible 11,500 bus stops on 325 routes throughout Washington DC, Virginia, and Maryland and is the sixth-busiest bus service provider in the nation. They have more than 1,500 buses.

Tourist-friendly bus systems exist in both Washington, DC with the **DC Circulator** (www.dccirculator.com, $1) and Baltimore with the **Charm City Circulator** (www.charmcitycirculator.com, free).

SUBWAY

Washington DC and the surrounding area has a clean, reliable, and generally safe subway system called **Metrorail** (202/637-7000, www.wmata.com/rail) that is run by the **Washington Metropolitan Area Transit Authority (WMATA).** The Metrorail system is commonly known as the Metro and provides service to more than 700,000 customers a day. The system is number two in the country in terms of ticket sales and serves more than 80 stations throughout DC, Virginia, and Maryland.

There are six color-coded rail lines: the Red, Orange, Blue, Yellow, Green, and Silver. The system layout is easy to understand, as most stations are named for the neighborhood they serve and getting from one station to another normally requires no more than a single transfer. Metrorail stations are marked with large "M" signs at the entrance that have colored stripes around them to show which line they serve. A complete list of fares and a map of each train line can be found on the website. Metrorail opens at 5am on weekdays and 7am on weekends. It closes at midnight Sunday-Thursday and 3am Friday and Saturday. Bicycles are permitted during non-peak hours.

WATER

If you're lucky enough to cruise into Virginia or Maryland on a private boat, you'll have options for docking in marinas along the Chesapeake Bay, the Intracoastal Waterway, and the Potomac River. Most towns on the water offer marina slips, but making plans ahead of time is advised, especially during the prime summer months and in popular areas such as Annapolis.

Recreation

If you can dream it, you can do it in Virginia and Maryland. Well, almost anyway. People in this region are crazy about getting outside, and with the mountains and seashore just a few hours apart, the opportunities are endless.

HIKING

Thousands of hiking trails are available throughout Virginia and Maryland, including a large portion of the **Appalachian Trail.** The best part is, you only need a good pair of trail shoes or hiking boots and you're on your way. **Shenandoah National Park** alone has more than 500 miles of trails, but other favorites include the C&O Canal Towpath, the Washington & Old Dominion Trail, and the Virginia Creeper Trail.

The **Potomac Appalachian Trail Club** (www.potomacappalachian.org) is a wonderful resource for hikers throughout the area and offers maps, books, and trip information.

BIKING

Whether you like to road bike, mountain bike, or just toddle along on a cruiser enjoying the scenery, Virginia and Maryland are the places to do it. From the flat Eastern Shore to the challenging mountains of the Shenandoah and Western Maryland, there are endless choices for getting out and pedaling.

For those who are competitive, the racing scene is thriving in the region, and road races are held most weekends April through October. Mountain bike races are also very popular and run even later in the year.

Road Cycling

Many organized rides take place in Virginia and Maryland, including the famous **Seagull Century** (www.seagullcentury.org), held each October on the Eastern Shore of Maryland. Wide, flat roads with little traffic make the Eastern Shore a favorite place to bike almost any time of the year. The terrain is nearly pancake flat, although there is often a headwind. **Bike Virginia** (www.bikevirginia.org) is a six-day bike tour that goes through a different part of Virginia each year in June. Riders can choose from a variety of distances to pedal each day.

More challenging rides include the fierce **Mountains of Misery** (www.mountainsofmisery.com) ride in southern Virginia and the **Garrett County Gran Fondo** (www.garrettcountygranfondo.org) in Western Maryland.

Not all roads are conducive to road cycling, given the extreme traffic conditions in many urban areas. Be wise about choosing a biking route; accidents do happen, and usually the bike is on the worse end of it.

Mountain Biking

Mountain biking is big in the mid-Atlantic, and Virginia and Maryland are no exception. Charlottesville, Virginia, was even rated the eighth-best dream town in the country for mountain bikers by *Mountain Bike* magazine. Mountain bike trails can be found near the cities, in the rural areas, and throughout the mountains. Fat-tire races are also held throughout the year. **Mountain Biking Virginia** (www.mountainbikevirginia.com) and **Singletracks** (www.singletracks.com) are good resources for mountain biking in the region.

CANOEING AND KAYAKING

Canoeing is one of the most popular ways to enjoy the multitude of rivers, creeks, and lakes throughout Virginia and Maryland. Dozens of outfitters and liveries rent canoes and many offer guided trips.

Flat-water kayaking has become extremely popular in Virginia and Maryland over the last decade. This part of the country may have lagged behind other water-influenced regions in the adoption of this sport, but it has fully caught on. Kayak tours and instruction are now available on many eastern rivers, lakes, the Chesapeake Bay, and at the beaches.

White-water kayaking is a much more specialized sport enjoyed throughout the region on rivers such as the Potomac and James. A training center for racing is located on the Potomac River. Additional information can be obtained from the **Potomac Whitewater Racing Center** (www.potomacwhitewater.org).

BOATING AND SAILING

Saltwater, lakes, marinas, dock-and-dine restaurants—Virginia and Maryland have them all. The Chesapeake Bay alone has 11,684 miles of shoreline, which is more than the West Coast of the United States. Every town on the bay has a marina and access can also be gained from public boat ramps in many locations. Many visitors even arrive from other regions by water. Take a look at the boats in Annapolis Harbor and where they're from; there's a good reason Annapolis is called the "Sailing Capital of the World." It's a sailor's dream.

Commercial and recreational powerboats must be registered in Virginia or Maryland if that is where they are primarily used.

FISHING

Fishing is a favorite activity in Virginia and Maryland. There are more than 2,800 miles of trout waters in the Blue Ridge alone. Whether you prefer fishing in a quiet lake, fly-fishing in a mountain stream, surf fishing, or taking a deep-sea fishing charter, you can do it all in this region. Most state parks offer fishing, and some areas are stocked through breeding programs.

Some favorite fishing spots in Virginia include Smith Mountain Lake (striped bass), the South Fork of the Shenandoah River (redbreast sunfish), the New River (yellow perch), the Chesapeake Bay (bluefish, flounder, and drum), and off the shore of Virginia Beach (marlin, sea bass, and sailfish). Favorite spots in Maryland include Sandy Point State Park (striper, white perch, and rockfish), Deep Creek Lake (bass), Point Lookout State Park (rockfish, bluefish, and hardhead), and Assateague Island (surf fishing for stripers).

Licenses are required in both states and Washington DC. Virginia fishing licenses can be purchased online from the **Virginia Department of Game and Inland Fisheries** (www.dgif.virginia.gov/fishing/regulations/licenses.asp). Both "freshwater" licenses (resident $23, nonresident $47) and "freshwater and saltwater" licenses (resident $40, nonresident $71) are available. If you wish to fish in designated trout-stocked waters, an additional trout license (resident $23, nonresident $47) is required. Licenses are good for one year from the date of purchase.

Maryland fishing licenses can be purchased online from the **Department of Natural Resources** (www.dnr.state.md.us/service/license.asp) or by calling 855/855-3906. Nontidal licenses are $20.50 for residents and $30.50 for nonresidents. Chesapeake Bay and coastal sport-fishing licenses are $15 for residents and $22.50 for nonresidents. Licenses are valid from January 1 to December 31 of the same year.

Fishing licenses in Washington DC can be purchased from the **District Department of the Environment** (www.green.dc.gov). Licenses are $10 for residents and $13 for nonresidents and are valid from January 1 to December 31 of the same calendar year.

CRABBING AND CLAMMING

Getting dirty in the mud and risking losing a finger are free in Virginia and Maryland if you are doing so to crab or clam for personal use only. Public access to beaches and marsh areas is prevalent in both states, but keep in mind that limits and regulations apply. Current Virginia regulations can be found at http://mrc.virginia.gov/regulations/recfish&crabrules.shtm and those for Maryland at http://dnr.maryland.gov/service/fishing_license.asp.

GOLF

Hundreds of public golf courses are located in Virginia and Maryland. A listing of courses in Virginia can be found at www.virginiagolf.com, and a listing of Maryland courses can be found at www.golfmaryland.com.

ROCK CLIMBING

Two great rock-climbing areas are located near Washington DC. **Great Falls Park** in Virginia has more than 200 climbing routes, and **Carderock** in Maryland has more than 100. There are also several dozen climbing areas along the Blue Ridge Mountains.

WINTER SPORTS

It's no surprise that winter sporting opportunities are concentrated in the western regions of Virginia and Maryland. A handful of ski resorts such as **Massanutten Resort** (near Harrisonburg in Virginia) and **Wisp Resort** in the Deep Creek Lake area of Maryland are open during the winter months. The **Liberty Mountain Snowflex Center** in Lynchburg, Virginia, offers year-round skiing on fabricated snow.

Cross-country skiing and snowmobiling are available on a limited basis when the weather cooperates on designated trails. Ice-skating and hockey, however, are available throughout both states in indoor and seasonal outdoor facilities.

Travel Tips

FOREIGN TRAVELERS

Visitors from other countries must present a valid passport and visa issued by a U.S. consular official unless they are a citizen of a country eligible for the Visa Waiver Program (such as Canada) in order to enter the United States. A foreign national entering the country by air that is a citizen of a country eligible for the Visa Waiver Program must present an approved Electronic System for Travel Authorization and a valid passport. A list of exceptions can be found on the Department of Homeland Security website at www.cbp.gov.

ACCESS FOR TRAVELERS WITH DISABILITIES

Accessibility is in the eye of the beholder. Despite the Americans with Disabilities Act, it is unfortunate that universal access in public places is still not a reality in most parts of the country. Virginia and Maryland are no exceptions. Although many restaurants, theaters, hotels, and museums offer ramps or elevators, some smaller, privately owned establishments (such as bed-and-breakfasts) do not always provide these necessities. Many historic properties are also not up to ADA standards because they are prevented from updating by law or by architecture. It is best to call ahead and verify the type of access that is available.

Accessible Virginia (www.accessiblevirginia.org) is a great resource for information on access throughout Virginia. A list of state and public lands in Maryland that offer accessible amenities can be found on Maryland's Department of Natural Resources website at www.dnr.state.md.us/publiclands/accessforall.asp.

SENIOR TRAVELERS

Numerous hotels, venues, and attractions offer discounts to seniors; all you have to do is ask when making your reservations or purchasing your tickets. The **American Association of Retired Persons (AARP)** (www.aarp.org) is the largest organization in the nation for seniors. They offer discounts to their members on hotels, tours, rental cars, airfare, and many other services. Membership in AARP is just $16 a year, so it's worth joining.

GAY AND LESBIAN TRAVELERS

Virginia as a whole tends to be on the conservative side, but especially so south of the Washington DC suburbs. Some of the more densely populated areas such as Richmond, Charlottesville, Norfolk, and Virginia Beach have LGBT-friendly communities and businesses, but these are rarer in rural areas. Washington DC, Baltimore, and Rehoboth Beach have large LGBT populations and readily accept same-sex couples and families. Most other parts of Maryland welcome business from everyone, so unless you need specialized accommodations, travel shouldn't be a concern. The **Gay and Lesbian Travel Center** (www.gayjourney.com) is a great resource for travel.

TRAVELING WITH CHILDREN

Although most places don't make specific accommodations for children, in general, most tourist attractions throughout Virginia and Maryland are family friendly (except for obvious exceptions where noted). Some cities such as Baltimore and Charlottesville offer museums devoted specifically to children, but many other sights have a children's component to them. For a list of kid-oriented attractions in Virginia, visit the "Cool Places for Kids" section of the Virginia is for Lovers website at www.virginia.org/coolplacesforkids.

TRAVELING WITH PETS

In recent years more and more pet-friendly establishments have been popping up in the Virginia and Maryland region. Many higher-end hotels (such as the Kimpton hotel chain) allow four-legged family members, and some establishments even host doggie happy hours. It's not uncommon for attractions, stores, historical sites, campgrounds, outdoor shopping

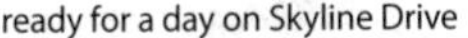

ready for a day on Skyline Drive

malls, parks, beaches, and even the patios at some restaurants to welcome dogs with open arms. It is always best to call ahead before assuming an establishment is pet friendly. Service and guide dogs are welcome nearly everywhere with their human companions.

TIPPING

A 15-20 percent tip is standard throughout Virginia and Maryland on restaurant bills. Other service providers, such as taxi drivers and hairstylists, typically receive 10-15 percent. Bellhops and airport personnel normally receive $1-2 per bag.

Information and Services

TOURIST INFORMATION

For information on tourism in Virginia, visit the **Virginia is for Lovers site** (www.virginia.org) or the official **Virginia state site** (www.virginia.gov/visit). For information on tourism in Maryland, visit the **Maryland Office of Tourism site** (www.visitmaryland.org). For information on tourism in Washington DC, visit the official **DC tourism site** (www.washington.org).

COMMUNICATIONS AND MEDIA

Cell Phone Coverage

Cell phone coverage is generally available in most parts of Virginia and Maryland. As with any state, there are scattered pockets of spotty coverage even near large cities, but overall, coverage is reliable. As a rule, the more rural the region you are traveling through (such as Central and Southern Virginia and Western Maryland), the less coverage is available, but for the most part, the major highways have fairly consistent coverage. Once you leave the major highways, coverage can be a concern. Large parks, such as Shenandoah National Park, do not have reliable coverage, especially once you leave the main roads (like Skyline Drive). Any time you head into the backcountry, be sure to bring supplies in case of an emergency instead of relying on your cell phone.

Internet Access

Internet access is readily available in hotels throughout Virginia and Maryland and is very commonly included with the price of a room, or else as an add-on. A few cities even offer wireless Internet access throughout their downtown areas, such as Roanoke and Charlottesville (on the pedestrian mall). A list of free Wi-Fi hotspots in both states can be found at www.openwifispots.com.

Media

Major city newspapers and magazines are available throughout Virginia and Maryland. The most widely circulated daily newspaper in the Washington DC area (including Northern Virginia and the Capital Region of Maryland) is the ***Washington Post*** (www.washingtonpost.com). The paper features world news and local news and places an emphasis on national politics. The ***Washington Times*** (www.washingtontimes.com) is another daily newspaper that is widely circulated. Weekly and specialty newspapers include the ***Washington City Paper*** (www.washingtoncitypaper.com), an alternative weekly newspaper, and the ***Washington Informer*** (www.washingtoninformer.com), a weekly newspaper serving the DC area's African American population.

The most widely read paper in Baltimore is the ***Baltimore Sun*** (www.baltimoresun.com). It is Maryland's largest daily newspaper and covers local and regional news. The Baltimore ***City Paper*** (www.citypaper.com) is a free alternative weekly paper that is distributed on Wednesdays. It is known for having good coverage of clubs, concerts, restaurants, and theater. It also has political articles and covers subjects not featured in mainstream publications.

Many smaller cities offer daily local papers. They are typically found in convenience stores, grocery stores, and on newsstands.

Health and Safety

For emergencies anywhere in Virginia and Maryland, dial 911 from any telephone at no charge. From a cell phone, the state police can be reached by pressing #77. Generally speaking, hospitals in both states are very good, and excellent in the larger cities. Emergency room treatment is always costlier than a scheduled appointment, but emergency care facilities can also be found in most areas to treat minor conditions.

LYME DISEASE

Virginia and Maryland are in prime tick area, so **Lyme disease,** which is transmitted through the bites of deer ticks, is a risk. Use insect repellent, and check yourself thoroughly after spending time in the woods or walking through tall grass. If you are bitten, or find a red circular rash (similar to a bull's-eye), consult a physician. Lyme disease can be life-threatening if it goes untreated.

INSECTS

Mosquitoes are common throughout Virginia and Maryland and aside from being annoying can carry diseases. Damp, low areas can harbor large populations of these little vampires, so use insect repellent and steer clear of stagnant water. **Bees, wasps, yellow jackets,** and **hornets** are all permanent residents of the region and are particularly active (and aggressive) in the fall.

Female **black widow spiders** are also found in the region and can be identified by a small red hourglass shape on their black abdomens. They live in dark places such as rotting logs and under patio furniture. Symptoms of their bite include severe abdominal pain and should be treated. The males are harmless. The **brown recluse spider,** contrary to common belief, is not native to this region. They can on occasion be found here, but only as a transplant.

ANIMALS

There are three types of **venomous snakes** in Virginia and Maryland. The most common is the northern copperhead. This snake can be found across both states and has dark-colored cross bands shaped like an hourglass. The second type is the timber rattlesnake, which is found in all the mountainous regions of both states and in the southeastern corner of Virginia. It also has a patterned back with wavy cross bands. The eastern cottonmouth snake is only found in southeastern Virginia (south of Newport News). It can be yellowish olive to black in color and has approximately 13 black cross bands that are wide at the sides and narrow at the backbone.

Swimming in the Atlantic Ocean or the Chesapeake Bay could put you in contact with stinging **jellyfish** or **sea nettles** (especially in the Chesapeake Bay). **Sharks** are also found occasionally in both bodies of water and have even been spotted in the Potomac River near Point Lookout.

PLANTS

Poison ivy, poison oak, and **poison sumac** are all native to the region and should be avoided even if you have never had a prior allergic reaction (you can develop one anytime). As the saying goes, "Leaves of three, let it be." Local mushrooms and berries can also be poisonous, so don't eat them unless you are 100 percent sure of their identification.

WEATHER

In addition to the obvious presence or prediction of a tornado, tropical storm, hurricane, or snowstorm (all of which are possible but rare in the region), be aware that **lightning** is a greater danger on exposed ridges, in fields, on golf courses, on the beach, or anywhere near water. Thunderstorms can pop up quickly, especially during the summer months, so check the weather before venturing out and be prepared with a plan B. Hypothermia can also be an issue. Being wet, tired, and cold is a dangerous combination. Symptoms include slurred speech, uncontrollable shivering, and loss of coordination.

CRIME

As in many states, downtown areas of larger cities such as Richmond, Baltimore, parts of Washington DC (including neighboring Prince George's County), and Norfolk can be unsafe, especially at night. Ask hotel staff about the safety of the area you're staying in, lock your doors, take a cab instead of walking, and don't leave valuables in your car.

Resources

Suggested Reading

HISTORY

General History

Barbour, Philip, and Thad Tate, eds. *The Complete Works of Captain John Smith, 1580-1631.* Chapel Hill: University of North Carolina Press, 1986. Three volumes of Captain John Smith's work.

Dabney, Virginius. *Richmond: Story of a City.* Charlottesville: University Press of Virginia, 1990. Tells the story of Virginia's state capital.

Doak, Robin. *Voices from Colonial America: Maryland 1634-1776.* Washington DC: National Geographic, 2007. First-person accounts, historical maps, and illustrations tell Maryland's history.

Jefferson, Thomas. *Notes on the State of Virginia.* Chapel Hill: University of North Carolina Press, 1996. This classic shows Jefferson's personality and discusses life in the 18th century.

Kelly, C. Brian. *Best Little Stories from Virginia.* Nashville, TN: Cumberland House Publishing, 2003. A collection of more than 100 stories since Jamestown's founding.

McWilliams, Jane W. *Annapolis, City on the Severn.* Baltimore: The Johns Hopkins University Press, 2011. The story of Annapolis.

Civil War History

Catton, Bruce. *America Goes to War: The Civil War and Its Meaning in American Culture.* Middletown, CT: Wesleyan University Press, 1992. An interesting study on the Civil War.

McPherson, James. *Battle Cry of Freedom: The Civil War Era.* New York: Ballantine Books, 1988. Perhaps the best single-volume history of the war.

SCIENCE AND NATURE

Duda, Mark Damian. *Virginia Wildlife Viewing Guide.* Helena, MT: Falcon Press, 1994. Provides information on 80 of Virginia's best wildlife-viewing areas.

Fergus, Charles. *Wildlife of Virginia and Maryland and Washington, D.C.* Mechanicsburg, PA: Stackpole Books, 2003. Provides details on the animals in the diverse habitats throughout Virginia and Maryland.

Frye, Keith. *Roadside Geology of Virginia.* Missoula, MT: Mountain Press, 2003. Provides general information on the state's geology.

Gupton, Oscar. *Wildflowers of the Shenandoah Valley and Blue Ridge Mountains.* Charlottesville: University of Virginia Press, 2002. A unique guide dedicated to wildflowers.

RECREATION

General Outdoor

Carrol, Steven, and Mark Miller. *Wild Virginia.* Helena, MT: Falcon Press, 2002. A guide to wilderness and special-management areas throughout Virginia with a focus on the western and southern areas.

High, Mike. *The C&O Canal Companion.* Baltimore: Johns Hopkins University Press, 1997. A well-written guide to the C&O Canal National Historical Park.

Hiking

Adkins, Leonard. *Explorer's Guide 50 Hikes in Maryland.* Woodstock, VT: The Countryman Press, 2007. A good resource for hiking in Maryland.

Adkins, Leonard. *50 Hikes in Northern Virginia.* Woodstock, VT: The Countryman Press, 2000. A good resource for hiking in Northern Virginia.

Blackinton, Theresa Dowell. *Moon Take a Hike Washington DC: 80 Hikes within Two Hours of the City.* 2nd edition. Berkeley, CA: Avalon Travel, 2013. A terrific resource for hiking the Washington DC area including hikes in metropolitan DC, the Shenandoah, Western Maryland, Eastern Maryland, and Virginia's Piedmont and Coastal Plains.

Burnham, Bill, and Mary Burnham. *Hiking Virginia.* 3rd Edition. Guilford, CT: Falcon Guides, 2013. A lively and award-winning guide to hiking in Virginia.

de Hart, Allen. *The Trails of Virginia: Hiking the Old Dominion.* Chapel Hill: University of North Carolina Press, 1995. A very comprehensive resource for hiking in Virginia.

Bicycling

Adams, Scott. *Mountain Bike America: Virginia.* Guilford, CT: Globe Pequot, 2000. Scott Adams is one of the best guidebook writers for mountain biking, and this is a great and informative read.

Adams, Scott, and Martin Fernandez. *Mountain Biking the Washington, D.C./Baltimore Area.* 4th Edition. Guilford, CT: Falcon Guides, 2003. A great guide to mountain biking around Washington DC and Baltimore.

Eltringham, Scott, and Jim Wade. *Scott & Jim's Favorite Bike Rides.* Arlington, VA: S&J Cycling, 2007. A fun guide to biking in Northern Virginia and central Maryland.

Homerosky, Jim. *Road Biking Virginia.* Guilford, CT: Falcon Guides, 2002. Wonderful resource for road bikers in Virginia.

Fishing

Beasley, Beau. *Fly Fishing Virginia: A No Nonsense Guide to Top Waters.* Tucson, AZ: No Nonsense Fly Fishing Guidebooks, 2007. An award-winning guide to fly-fishing spots in Virginia.

Gooch, Bob. *Virginia Fishing Guide.* 2nd Edition. Charlottesville: University Press of Virginia, 2011. A wonderful guide to fishing in Virginia.

Moore, Steve. *Maryland Trout Fishing: The Stocked and Wild Rivers, Streams, Lakes and Ponds.* Calibrated Consulting, 2011. An informative guide to trout fishing in Maryland.

Kayaking

Gaaserud, Michaela Riva. *AMC's Best Sea Kayaking in the Mid-Atlantic*. Boston: Appalachian Mountain Club Books, 2016. A great resource for coastal kayaking in Virginia and Maryland.

Rock Climbing

Horst, Eric, and Stewart M. Green. *Rock Climbing Virginia, West Virginia, and Maryland*. Helena, MT: Falcon Press, 2013. Detailed information on climbs in Shenandoah National Park, Great Falls, and Carderock.

Internet Resources

STATE RESOURCES

www.virginia.com
General travel information within Virginia.

www.virginia.gov
The official Commonwealth of Virginia website.

www.virginia.org
The official visitors website for the Commonwealth of Virginia.

www.maryland.gov
The official Maryland website.

www.visitmaryland.org
The official tourism website for Maryland.

WASHINGTON DC

www.washington.org
www.visitingdc.com
Visitor information on Washington DC.

www.si.edu
Information on the Smithsonian Institution.

www.wmata.com
Information on Metrorail and Metrobus service.

HISTORY

www.vahistorical.org
The Virginia Historical Society's comprehensive website.

www.mdhs.org
Information on historical Maryland.

www.dchistory.org
The interesting and helpful website of the Historical Society of Washington DC.

www.civilwar-va.com
A great resource for planning a Civil War-related trip.

RECREATION

www.nps.gov
The National Park Service website, a comprehensive guide to national parks throughout the country.

www.dcr.virginia.gov
Information on the Virginia Department of Conservation and Recreation.

www.dnr.maryland.gov
Information on the Maryland Department of Natural Resources.

www.hikingupward.com
Contains a wonderful interactive map of Virginia hikes.

www.baydreaming.com
Offers an excellent list of marinas and boating facilities in the Chesapeake Bay area.

www.thebayguide.com
A guide to boating in the Chesapeake Bay area.

www.findyourchesapeake.com
The Chesapeake Bay Gateways Network website provides information on public access parks around the bay.

LOCAL RESOURCES

www.hometownfreepress.com
A guide to local newspapers.

www.mtnlaurel.com
A nice resource for life in Virginia's Blue Ridge.

www.chesapeakeboating.net
Chesapeake Bay Magazine is full of interesting articles on the bay area.

www.baydreaming.com
A guide to Chesapeake Bay events.

Index

A

B

C

D

E

F

G

H

I

J

K

L

M

N

O

P

QR

S

T

U

V

W

XYZ

List of Maps

Photo Credits

Title Page: Thomas Jefferson Memorial © Songquan Deng | Dreamstime.com; page 6: lobster buoys in Reedville © Michaela Riva Gaaserud; page 7: shop sign in Colonial Williamsburg © Michaela Riva Gaaserud; page 8 (top left) © Michaela Riva Gaaserud, (top right) © Zrfphoto | Dreamstime.com, (bottom) © Daniel Thornberg | Dreamstime.com; page 9 © all © Michaela Riva Gaaserud; page 10 © Diane Penland, National Air and Space Museum, Smithsonian Institution; page 11 (top) © Michaela Riva Gaaserud (bottom right) © Drew McMullen, (bottom left) © Michaela Riva Gaaserud; page 13 © Michaela Riva Gaaserud; page 14 (top) © Michaela Riva Gaaserud, (bottom) © Katie Smith | Dreamstime.com; pages 15-17 © Michaela Riva Gaaserud; page 18 © Americanspirit | Dreamstime.com; page 19 © Charlottep68 | Dreamstime.com; pages 20-22 © Michaela Riva Gaaserud; page 23 © Steveheap | Dreamstime.com; page 25 (top) © Sandra Manske | Dreamstime.com, (bottom) © Michaela Riva Gaaserud; pages 27-31 © Michaela Riva Gaaserud; page 33 © Avmedved | Dreamstime.com; page 35 © Edwin Verin | Dreamstime.com; page 38 © Indy2320 | Dreamstime.com; pages 39-41 © Michaela Riva Gaaserud; page 42 © Eric Long, National Air and Space Museum, Smithsonian Institution; page 45 © Sborisov | Dreamstime.com; page 46 © Michaela Riva Gaaserud; page 49 © Joseph Gough | Dreamstime.com; page 50 © Nick Cannella | Dreamstime.com; pages 53-56 © Michaela Riva Gaaserud; page 59 © Demerzel21 | Dreamstime.com; pages 61-82 © Michaela Riva Gaaserud; page 89 (top) © Michaela Riva Gaaserud, (bottom) © Alexandre Fagundes De Fagundes | Dreamstime.com; pages 91-97 © Michaela Riva Gaaserud; page 105 © Americanspirit | Dreamstime.com; pages 120-135 © Michaela Riva Gaaserud; page 138 © Peter Gaaserud; pages 140-159 © Michaela Riva Gaaserud; page 161 © Adam Parent | Dreamstime.com; pages 165-173 © Michaela Riva Gaaserud; page 182 © Kclarksphotography | Dreamstime.com; pages 183-204 © Michaela Riva Gaaserud; page 206 *Neptune* sculpture by Paul DiPasquale © 2005, photo © M.P. Prucha; page 208 © Michaela Riva Gaaserud; page 213 courtesy of the Cavalier Hotel; pages 218-226 © Michaela Riva Gaaserud; page 228 (top) © Howiewu | Dreamstime.com, (bottom) © Cmrenda | Dreamstime.com; page 229 © Zrfphoto | Dreamstime.com; pages 236-237 © Michaela Riva Gaaserud; page 238 © Jon Bilous | Dreamstime.com; pages 240-251 © Michaela Riva Gaaserud; page 260 (top) © Michaela Riva Gaaserud, (bottom) © John Keith | Dreamstime.com; pages 261-272 © Michaela Riva Gaaserud; page 291 © Joseph Sohm/123rf.com; pages 295-300 © Michaela Riva Gaaserud; page 302 © Brenda Kean | Dreamstime.com; page 303 © Jill Lang | Dreamstime.com; page 307 courtesy of Primland; page 308 © Michaela Riva Gaaserud; page 310 © Konstantin Lobastov | Dreamstime.com; page 311 © Larry Metayer | Dreamstime.com; pages 315-337; page 342 (top) © Luckydoor | Dreamstime.com, (bottom) © Zrfphoto | Dreamstime.com; page 343 © Avmedved | Dreamstime.com; page 348 © Nicolas Raymond | Dreamstime.com; pages 349-351 © Michaela Riva Gaaserud; page 354 © Avmedved | Dreamstime.com; page 358 © Suparat Wongthongdee | Dreamstime.com; page 359 © Michaela Riva Gaaserud; page 364 © Cvandyke | Dreamstime.com; pages 366-423 © Michaela Riva Gaaserud; page 426 © La Wanda Wilson | Dreamstime.com; pages 429-431 © Michaela Riva Gaaserud; page 432 (top) © Michaela Riva Gaaserud, (bottom) © Dave Newman | Dreamstime.com; page 433 © Vladimir Ivanov | Dreamstime.com; pages 438-457 © Michaela Riva Gaaserud; page 459 © Robert Crow | Dreamstime.com; pages 461-482 © Michaela Riva Gaaserud; page 484 © Zrfphoto | Dreamstime.com; pages 486-506 © Michaela Riva Gaaserud; page 508 (top) © Cvandyke | Dreamstime.com, (bottom) © Daniel Thornberg | Dreamstime.com; page 509 © Jruffa | Dreamstime.com; page 511 (top) © Jon Bilous | Dreamstime.com, (bottom) © Cvandyke | Dreamstime.com; pages 513-515 © Michaela Riva Gaaserud; page 520 © Bambi L. Dingman | Dreamstime.com; page 524 © Michaela Riva Gaaserud; page 526 © Jon Bilous | Dreamstime.com; page 529 © Michaela Riva Gaaserud; page 531 © Susanne Riva; page 533 © Michaela Riva Gaaserud; page 534 © Susanne Riva; pages 536-541 © Michaela Riva Gaaserud; page 546 (top) © Jon Bilous | Dreamstime.com, (bottom) © Mark Vandyke | Dreamstime.com; page 548 © Steven Roncin | Dreamstime.com; pages 551-552 © Howard Nevitt, Jr. | Dreamstime.com; pages 553-569 © Michaela Riva Gaaserud

Also Available

MAP SYMBOLS

Expressway
Primary Road
Secondary Road
Unpaved Road
Trail
Ferry
Railroad
Pedestrian Walkway
Stairs

Highlight
City/Town
State Capital
National Capital
Point of Interest
Accommodation
Restaurant/Bar
Other Location
Campground

Airfield
Airport
Mountain
Unique Natural Feature
Waterfall
Park
Trailhead
Skiing Area

Golf Course
Parking Area
Archaeological Site
Church
Gas Station
Glacier
Mangrove
Reef
Swamp

CONVERSION TABLES

°C = (°F - 32) / 1.8
°F = (°C x 1.8) + 32
1 inch = 2.54 centimeters (cm)
1 foot = 0.304 meters (m)
1 yard = 0.914 meters
1 mile = 1.6093 kilometers (km)
1 km = 0.6214 miles
1 fathom = 1.8288 m
1 chain = 20.1168 m
1 furlong = 201.168 m
1 acre = 0.4047 hectares
1 sq km = 100 hectares
1 sq mile = 2.59 square km
1 ounce = 28.35 grams
1 pound = 0.4536 kilograms
1 short ton = 0.90718 metric ton
1 short ton = 2,000 pounds
1 long ton = 1.016 metric tons
1 long ton = 2,240 pounds
1 metric ton = 1,000 kilograms
1 quart = 0.94635 liters
1 US gallon = 3.7854 liters
1 Imperial gallon = 4.5459 liters
1 nautical mile = 1.852 km

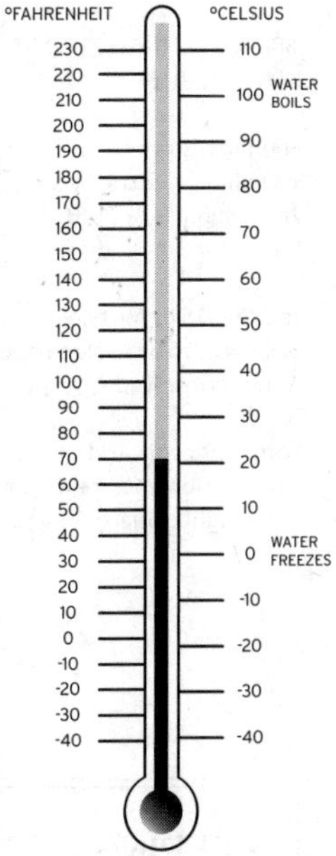

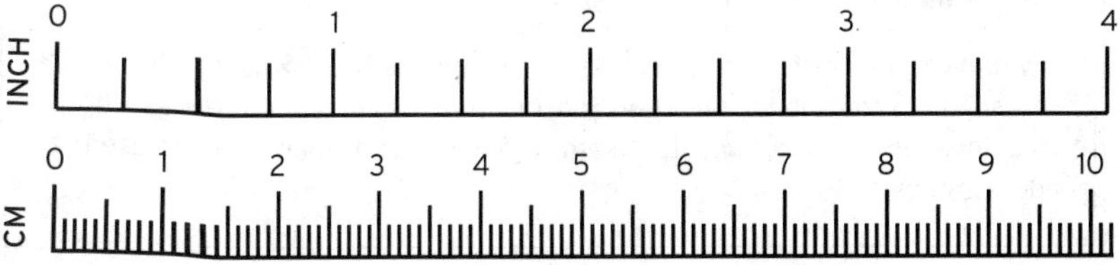

MOON VIRGINIA & MARYLAND
Avalon Travel
An imprint of Perseus Books
A Hachette Book Group company
1700 Fourth Street
Berkeley, CA 94710, USA
www.moon.com

Editor: Rachel Feldman
Series Manager: Kathryn Ettinger
Copy Editor: Brett Keener
Graphics Coordinator: Elizabeth Jang
Production Coordinator: Elizabeth Jang
Cover Design: Faceout Studios, Charles Brock
Interior Design: Domini Dragoone
Moon Logo: Tim McGrath
Map Editor: Mike Morgenfeld
Cartographers: Austin Ehrhardt and Mike Morgenfeld
Indexer: Rachel Kuhn

ISBN-13: 978-1-63121-395-3
ISSN: 2332-0168

Printing History
1st Edition — 2014
2nd Edition — April 2017
5 4 3 2 1

Front cover photo: aerial view of Maryland's Chesapeake Bay © Cameron Davidson/Getty Images

Back cover photo: Colonial Williamsburg © Bon4ire | Dreamstime.com

Printed in Canada by Friesens

All recommendations, including those for sights, activities, hotels, restaurants, and shops, are based on each author's individual judgment. We do not accept payment for inclusion in our travel guides, and our authors don't accept free goods or services in exchange for positive coverage.

Although every effort was made to ensure that the information was correct at the time of going to press, the author and publisher do not assume and hereby disclaim any liability to any party for any loss or damage caused by errors, omissions, or any potential travel disruption due to labor or financial difficulty, whether such errors or omissions result from negligence, accident, or any other cause.

KEEPING CURRENT

If you have a favorite gem you'd like to see included in the next edition, or see anything that needs updating, clarification, or correction, please drop us a line. Send your comments via email to feedback@moon.com, or use the address above.